LIBRARY OF THE HISTORY OF IDEAS

VOLUME X

Renaissance Essays

II

LIBRARY OF THE HISTORY OF IDEAS

ISSN 1050–1053

Series Editor: JOHN W. YOLTON

RENAISSANCE ESSAYS

II

Edited by

WILLIAM J. CONNELL

UNIVERSITY OF ROCHESTER PRESS

This collection first published 1993

University of Rochester Press
200 Administration Building, University of Rochester
Rochester, New York 14627, USA
and at PO Box 9, Woodbridge, Suffolk IP12 3DF, UK

ISBN 1 878822 23 3 hardback
ISBN 1 878822 28 4 paperback

Library of Congress Cataloging-in-Publication Data
(Revised for vol. 2)

Renaissance essays.
  (Library of the history of ideas, 1050–1053 ; v. 9–10)
  Originally published: New York : Harper & Row, 1968.
  Vol. 2 edited by William J. Connell.
  Includes bibliographical references.
  1. Renaissance. I. Kristeller, Paul Oskar, 1905– . II. Wiener,
Philip P. (Philip Paul), b. 1905. III. Connell, William J. IV. Series.
CB361.R385 1992   940.2'1   92–41703
ISBN 1–878822–18–7 (v. 1)
ISBN 1–878822–19–5 (v. 1 : pbk.)
ISBN 1–878822–23–3 (v. 2)
ISBN 1–878822–28–4 (v. 2 : pbk.)

British Library Cataloguing-in-Publication Data
Renaissance Essays. – Vol.2. – (Library of the
History of Ideas, ISSN 1050–1053; Vol.10)
  I. Connell, William J. II. Series
  190
  ISBN 1–878822–23–3
  ISBN 1–878822–28–4 pbk

This publication is printed on acid-free paper

Printed in the United States of America

TABLE OF CONTENTS

ACKNOWLEDGEMENTS

The articles in this volume first appeared in the *Journal of the History of Ideas* as indicated below, by volume, year and page numbers.

Black, Robert, "Ancients and Moderns in the Renaissance: Rhetoric and History in Accolti's *Dialogue on the Preeminence of Men of His Own Time*," 43 (1982) 3–32.

Colish, Marcia L., "The Idea of Liberty in Machiavelli," 32 (1971) 323–350.

Drake, Stillman, "Renaissance Music and Experimental Science," 31 (1970) 483–500.

Fleisher, Martin, "Trust and Deceit in Machiavelli's Comedies," 27 (1966) 365–380.

Giustiniani, Vito R., "Homo, Humanus, and the Meanings of 'Humanism,' " 46 (1985) 167–195.

Gravelle, Sarah Stever, "The Latin-Vernacular Question and Humanist Theory of Language and Culture," 49 (1988) 367–386.

Hariman, Robert, "Composing Modernity in Machiavelli's *Prince*," 50 (1989) 3–29.

Headley, John M., "On the Rearming of Heaven: The Machiavellism of Tommaso Campanella," 49 (1988) 387–404.

Kelley, Donald R., "*Historia Integra*: François Baudouin and His Conception of History," 25 (1964) 35–57.

Monfasani, John, "Was Lorenzo Valla an Ordinary Language Philosopher?" 50 (1989) 309–323.

Phillips, Mark, "The Disenchanted Witness: Participation and Alienation in Florentine Historiography," 44 (1983) 191–206.

Schiffman, Zachary S., "Montaigne and the Rise of Skepticism in Early Modern Europe: A Reappraisal," 45 (1984) 499–516.

Schmitt, Charles B., "Perennial Philosophy: From Agostino Steuco to Leibniz," 27 (1966) 505–532.

Seigel, Jerrold E., "Ideals of Eloquence and Silence in Petrarch," 26 (1965) 147–174.

Siraisi, Nancy G., "Girolamo Cardano and the Art of Medical Narrative," 52 (1991) 581–602.

Waswo, Richard, "Motives of Misreading," 50 (1989) 324–332.

Westfall, Carroll W., "Painting and the Liberal Arts: Alberti's View," 30 (1969) 487–506.

INTRODUCTION

By William J. Connell

Almost twenty-five years ago a collection of essays on Renaissance topics from the *Journal of the History of Ideas*, edited by Paul O. Kristeller and Philip P. Wiener, was published in a Harper Torchbook edition that quickly established itself as a successful seminar text and as an important source of ideas for scholars.[1] When the Library of the History of Ideas and the University of Rochester Press recently agreed to republish that first collection, it was decided that to attempt to update the original essays, or to eliminate some of them and to add others more recent, would only diminish the historical integrity of a volume that continues to age gracefully in the absence of such tampering. Instead, in order to illustrate the many further developments that have taken place in Renaissance scholarship, and to make available to a larger readership some of the best work on the Renaissance that has been done in the intervening years, the Library of the History of Ideas has decided to publish this fresh gathering of seventeen important essays on Renaissance themes.

In numerous respects the present collection of Renaissance essays illustrates the consequences, both intended and unintended, of the revolution in European and North American Renaissance scholarship that has been effected in the post-war period through the efforts of Paul Kristeller.[2] In the first volume of *Renaissance Essays*, many of the contributions were still largely in agreement with the once predominant Burckhardtian interpretation of the Renaissance, grounded in a Renaissance "discovery of the individual," which, it was claimed, led to the formulation of a new "philosophy of man," generally identified with Renaissance humanism. Against the background of the ebullient

---

[1] *Renaissance Essays*, eds. Paul O. Kristeller and Philip P. Wiener (New York, 1968), now reprinted as Library of the History of Ideas, vol. IX (Rochester, 1992).

[2] The first synthetic statement of this revisionist program appeared in Paul O. Kristeller, "Humanism and Scholasticism in the Italian Renaissance," *Byzantion*, 17 (1944–45), 346–374, reprinted in his *Studies in Renaissance Thought and Letters*, I (Rome, 1956): 553–583. For a recent restatement, see his essay, "Humanism," in the *Cambridge History of Renaissance Philosophy*, eds. Charles B. Schmitt, Quentin Skinner, Eckhard Kessler, and Jill Kraye (Cambridge, 1988), 113–137. For one of the many tributes to his work, see Maryanne C. Horowitz, "Paul O. Kristeller's Impact on Renaissance Studies," *JHI*, 39 (1978), 677–683.

Renaissance literature of the 1940s and 50s, Kristeller undertook a vigorous campaign to bring the study of Renaissance humanism *e caelo in terram*. For Kristeller, the humanism of the Renaissance was not a philosophy; rather it represented a phase in the rhetorical tradition of Western culture.[3] According to Kristeller, the contribution of the humanists was circumscribed within the disciplines of the *studia humanitatis*, or the liberal arts, comprising grammar, rhetoric, poetry, history and moral philosophy. How a word that originally stood for a specific kind of educational pursuit came to acquire the imposing array of connotations which "humanism" now possesses is the subject of the important essay by Vito R. Giustiniani included in this collection.[4] In Kristeller's view, the many disputes between humanists and scholastics during the Renaissance deserved to be seen not as mortal disputes between philosophical schools, but rather as academic quarrels between the followers of two different disciplines, rhetoric and philosophy, which never seriously challenged one another's right to exist. Stripped of its philosophical pretensions, Kristeller's humanism became a humanism of words, grammar, texts.

The impact of the spreading acceptance of what might legitimately be called the "Kristeller paradigm" was twofold. First, and more noticeable in the present volume, it has led to a broader and deeper examination of the rhetorical culture of the Renaissance. Second, however, Kristeller has largely liberated the study of Renaissance philosophy from a neo-Burckhardtian search for sources of "individualism" for which he found little support in the texts of such writers as Ficino and Pico. The impact of the Kristeller challenge on the study of philosophy is registered in a characteristic way in Charles B. Schmitt's classic essay, here republished, on the idea of perennial philosophy in the thought of Agostino Steuco, a sixteenth-century neo-Platonist.[5] Schmitt tells us that reading Steuco he discovers "a Renaissance somewhat different from the one described in the conventional histories. Where is the emphasis on man's originality, individualism, power to discover and change the

---

[3]   Paul O. Kristeller, *The Classics and Renaissance Thought*, Martin Classical Lectures, 15 (Cambridge, Mass., 1955), p. 11.

[4]   See also Augusto Campana, "The Origin of the Word 'Humanist,' " *Journal of the Warburg and Courtauld Institutes*, 9 (1946), 60–73.

[5]   Schmitt's essay has also been reprinted in his *Studies in Renaissance Philosophy and Science* (London, 1981). On Steuco, see also Mariano Crociata, *Umanesimo e teologia in Agostino Steuco. Neoplatonismo e teologia della creazione nel 'De perenni philosophia'* (Rome, 1987); and R. K. Delph, "Italian Humanism in the Early Reformation: Agostino Steuco (1497–1548)," Ph.D. diss., University of Michigan, 1987. On the Platonic tradition, see James Hankins, *Plato in the Italian Renaissance*, 2 vols., 2nd impression (Leiden, 1991).

world of which we so often read? Where is the sharp break with tradition which the Renaissance is supposed to be? In Steuco we find none of these things." Although Schmitt does not think that Steuco was an especially forceful or original philosopher, he shows that he was an historically important syncretist in the tradition of Ficino and Pico. In Schmitt's essay, as in Kristeller's own work on Ficino, a philosopher's writings are not studied in order to discover an underlying philosophy of the Renaissance, but, more modestly, to reconstruct a particular moment in the historical tradition of Platonism.

However it has been in his encouragement of study of the grammatical and philological concerns of the humanists, of their educational methods, and the ways in which these were institutionalized, that Kristeller has had his widest and most controversial impact, as many of the essays in this volume attest. Changing and contested relationships among the various academic disciplines are the subject of essays by Carroll W. Westfall, who discusses Leon Battista Alberti's attempt to include painting among the liberal arts,[6] and by Donald R. Kelley, who explains how history came into its own as a *scientia* in the hands of French humanists of the later sixteenth century who transformed history into a "methodical" discipline capable of absorbing and organizing all branches of human knowledge. Stillman Drake's article on the relationship between music and the rise of experimental science shows how music, which had been included in the medieval quadrivium as a mathematical science, played a new and important role in the sixteenth-century development of modern scientific experimentation.[7]

A sense of the possibilities and the limitations of humanist rhetoric emerges from Jerrold E. Seigel's essay on the role of private rhetorical study in the writings of Petrarch.[8] According to Seigel, although

[6] Some of the material in this essay later appeared in Carroll Westfall, *In This Most Perfect Paradise: Alberti, Nicholas V, and the Invention of Conscious Urban Planning in Rome, 1447–55* (University Park, 1974). On the theme treated here, see Paul O. Kristeller, "The Modern System of the Arts," *JHI*, XII (1951), 496–527, XIII (1952), 17–46, reprinted in his *Renaissance Thought and the Arts*, expanded edition (Princeton, 1990), 163–227. On Alberti, see the translation by David Marsh of Alberti's *Dinner-Pieces*, (Binghamton, 1987); and Roberto Cardini, *Mosaici. Il "nemico" dell'Alberti* (Rome, 1990).

[7] For a full discussion of this theme, see now Ann E. Moyer, *Musica Scientia: Musical Scholarship in the Italian Renaissance* (Ithaca, 1992).

[8] A subsequent version of this essay appeared in Jerrold E. Seigel, *Rhetoric and Philosophy in Renaissance Humanism* (Princeton, 1968), 31–62. More recently on Petrarch's humanism, see Paul O. Kristeller, "Petrarcas Stellung in der Geschichte der Gelehrsamkeit," in *Italien und die Romania in Humanismus und Renaissance. Festschrift für Erich Loos zum 70. Geburtstag*, eds. K. W. Hempfer and E. Staub (Wiesbaden, 1983), 102–21.

Petrarch believed that when philosophy was pursued apart from rhetoric it became barren as a discipline, he did not think that rhetorical pursuits could ever adequately replace philosophical speculation on eternal truths. Seigel argues that Petrarch, in his promotion of rhetoric, was trying neither to encroach on the terrain of the Scholastics, nor to win them over to the liberal arts, but rather to defend liberal studies against the excessive claims of the Schoolmen. Thus, in Petrarch's writings, it is possible to trace his troubled search to achieve both eloquence and philosophical wisdom. And Seigel concludes that, for Petrarch, the private, meditative recourse to rhetoric became a way of managing the conflicting claims of this twofold search.

A skeptical approach to the rhetoric of humanists is taken by Robert Black in his essay on Benedetto Accolti's *Dialogue on the Preeminence of Men of His Own Time*. Black maintains that comparisons between the present generation and earlier ones were commonplace in the Latin literary tradition, and that individual authors showed surprisingly little concern to portray either the past or the present in a consistently more favorable light. Although other scholars have often focused on such comparisons between "ancients" and "moderns" when trying to judge an author's historical understanding of the relation between his own and previous ages, Black argues that these comparisons, particularly when used in a professional context, as was apparently the case when Accolti composed his *Dialogue*, have a formulaic quality that renders them of little evidentiary value in determining a writer's historical outlook.[9]

Zachary S. Schiffman's article on Michel de Montaigne explores the educational methods of the humanists in his discussion of one Renaissance intellectual who, as a child, was schooled according to humanist practices.[10] Against the view that Montaigne's skepticism was due to the revival of Sextus Empiricus, Schiffman argues that as a result of the essayist's extensive experience with humanist commonplaces and with discourse *in utramque partem* – the making of arguments on both sides of a case – he became convinced that it was impossible to "establish verisimilitude in human affairs," since, for any given question, there

---

[9] Compare Hans Baron's 1959 essay, "The *Querelle* of the Ancients and Moderns as a Problem for Renaissance Scholarship," *JHI*, 20 (1959), 3–22, reprinted in *Renaissance Essays*, eds. Kristeller and Wiener, 95–114, and revised in Hans Baron, *In Search of Florentine Civic Humanism*, 2 vols. (Princeton, 1988), II:72–100, with a response to Black on 94–95 n. 25. A revised version of the material published in Black's essay appears in his *Benedetto Accolti and the Florentine Renaissance* (Cambridge, 1985), 184–223, 286–298.

[10] Most of this essay has now reappeared in Zachary S. Schiffman, *On the Threshold of Modernity: Relativism in the French Renaissance* (Baltimore, 1991).

were "too many contradictory answers." Early modern skepticism was born of the failures of the humanist educational program.[11]

Throughout his writings Kristeller has consistently sought to distinguish rhetoric from philosophy; however in the works of certain Renaissance humanists there seems to be something more ambitious going on. By focusing on what the humanists wrote about rhetoric and language, a significant group of scholars has come to the conclusion that, in the writings of certain humanists, most notably of Lorenzo Valla, it is possible to discern something akin to a Renaissance philosophy of language.[12] The exchange between John Monfasani and Richard Waswo matches a scholar who argues that Valla, in accordance with the Scholastic understanding of language, "subordinated logic and language to an objective reality," against one who maintains that Valla arrived at the idea that "language does not reveal or reflect reality" but rather constitutes it.[13] Sarah Stever Gravelle's essay shows how, not just in Valla's writings, but also in the writings of other humanists who were engaged in comparative philological studies in Latin and the vernacular, there can be found a sophisticated historical understanding of the relationship between language and culture.[14]

In recent decades scholars have also been exploring the role of the narrator in Renaissance texts. This has become one of the more fascinating and successful means by which the "individual" of Burckhardt's

[11] For a related and enlightening approach to Montaigne, see Victoria Kahn, *Rhetoric, Prudence, and Skepticism in the Renaissance*, (Ithaca, 1985), 115–151. On the educational practices of the humanists, see Anthony Grafton and Lisa Jardine, *From Humanism to the Humanities* (Cambridge, Mass., 1986); Paul F. Grendler, *Schooling in Renaissance Italy: Literacy and Learning, 1300–1600* (Baltimore, 1991); and the review essay by Robert Black, "Italian Renaissance Education: Changing Perspectives and Continuing Controversies," *JHI*, 52 (1991), 315–334.

[12] Still basic to discussions of Valla are the treatments of Donald R. Kelley, *Foundations of Modern Historical Scholarship: Language, Law and History in the French Renaissance* (New York, 1970), 17–50; and Salvatore I. Camporeale, *Lorenzo Valla. Umanesimo e teologia* (Florence, 1972).

[13] For an appraisal of the Monfasani – Waswo exchange which gives credit to both authors, see now Ian Maclean, *Interpretation and Meaning in the Renaissance: The Case of Law* (Cambridge, 1992). For a brief and lucid account of Valla's critique of Scholasticism, see the forthcoming essay of Salvatore I. Camporeale, "Renaissance Humanism and the Origins of Humanist Theology."

[14] For Gravelle on Valla, see her essay, "Lorenzo Valla's Comparison of Latin and Greek and the Humanist Background," *Bibliothèque d'Humanisme et Renaissance*, 44 (1982), 269–289; and also her response to John Monfasani: "A New Theory of Truth," *JHI*, 50 (1989), 333–336.

Renaissance has been restored to the scholarly stage.[15] Mark Phillips's study of single episodes in the chronicles or histories of five Florentine citizens (Dino Compagni, Alamanno Acciaioli, Giovanni Cavalcanti, Alamanno Rinuccini, and Francesco Guicciardini) argues that, in each of these cases, history-writing became a way for the writer to distance himself from the failure of the moral community to which he belonged. Nancy G. Siraisi offers a new approach to the venerable theme of "*historia* as diagnosis" in her essay on the interplay of autobiography, the classical tradition in medicine, contemporary professional practice, and efforts toward self-promotion in the composition of Girolamo Cardano's medical case histories.

A good share of the finest English-language scholarship on the Renaissance in the last three decades has been concentrated in the field of political thought, with studies of Niccolò Machiavelli proliferating at an especially swift rate.[16] The essay by Marcia L. Colish demonstrates, through careful examination of Machiavelli's use of the word *libertà*, how the Florentine secretary's understanding of liberty differed from that of the ancients and from that of his humanist predecessors, while she also shows that Machiavelli restored to the concept of liberty the twin affirmation of both the legal rights of the individual and the good of the community that had been present in the Roman conception of *libertas*. Martin Fleisher's essay, on "Trust and Deceit in Machiavelli's Comedies," anticipates the themes of a number of recent studies which have emphasized the anthropological vision that is displayed in a relatively consistent fashion throughout Machiavelli's theoretical, historical and literary works.[17] The essay by Robert Hariman offers an innovative account of Machiavelli's "composition" of modernity through his use of rhetoric in a revolutionary, performative manner in *The Prince*.[18] And

[15] Most of this literature is now indebted to the neo-Hegelian view of the self expressed in Stephen Greenblatt, *Renaissance Self-Fashioning: From More to Shakespeare* (Chicago, 1983).

[16] For indications of recent directions in the history of Renaissance political thought, see the review by Donald R. Kelley of Quentin Skinner's *Foundations of Modern Political Thought*, JHI, 40 (1979), 663–687, reprinted in *Essays on Political Philosophy*, ed. Patrick Riley, (Rochester, 1992), 80–91; and J. G. A. Pocock, "Between Gog and Magog: The Republican Thesis and the *Ideologia Americana*," JHI, 48 (1987), 325–346.

[17] Mark Hulliung, *Citizen Machiavelli* (Princeton, 1983); Hanna Fenichel Pitkin, *Fortune is a Woman: Gender and Politics in the Thought of Niccolò Machiavelli* (Berkeley, 1984); Wayne A. Rebhorn, *Foxes and Lions: Machiavelli's Confidence Men* (Ithaca, 1988); Sebastian de Grazia, *Machiavelli in Hell* (Princeton, 1989); and John Najemy's forthcoming study of the Machiavelli – Vettori correspondence.

[18] Compare Michael McCanles, *The Discourse of 'Il Principe'* (Malibu, 1983).

John M. Headley's study of the uneasy relationship between religion and the state in the writings of Tommaso Campanella shows how one very important dissident thinker of Counter-Reformation Italy selectively absorbed and transmitted the teaching of Machiavelli.

Consideration of the essays comprised in this volume leads naturally to speculation concerning the direction of future studies in the field of Renaissance thought. There is still a great deal more to be learned about Renaissance science, and about the cultural context for Renaissance interest in astrology and magic. The Aristotelian tradition remains a rich and promising field for Renaissance research. There remains, however, the question of how to approach humanism.[19] During a panel discussion devoted to Renaissance humanism at a recent historical convention, one prominent historian of Renaissance humanism issued a call to study the anthropology implicit in humanism; a few minutes later, a second prominent historian called on scholars to adopt an anthropologist's approach to the humanists themselves. Although the kinds of monograph envisioned by the two historians could hardly be more different – the first involving extensive investigation of the moral thought of the humanists, the second the study of the their behavior as ritual – both historians seemed to be agreeing, by implication if not explicitly, that it was in the moral, social, and political arenas that Renaissance humanism had it most important historical impact.[20]

Let us return to the paradigm for research in the field of Renaissance humanism offered by Paul Kristeller. Although he has consistently tried to separate humanism, as a fundamentally rhetorical phenomenon, from philosophy, Kristeller has often acknowledged that rhetorical approaches may have philosophical implications, particularly in the areas of moral and political philosophy.[21] He has been somewhat reluctant to explore those implications in his own historical studies; however, as many of the contributions to this volume make clear, the rhetorical interpretation of humanism has now been advanced in such a way as to

[19] The very helpful collection, *Renaissance Humanism: Foundations, Forms and Legacy*, ed. Albert Rabil, Jr., 3 vols. (Philadelphia, 1988), gives a good idea of the study of humanism as it now stands.

[20] See the recent collections of interpretive essays by Hans Baron, *In Search of Florentine Civic Humanism*; and Riccardo Fubini, *Umanesimo e secolarizzazione da Petrarca a Valla* (Rome, 1990).

[21] For his most extensive discussion of the matter, emphasizing the genres and themes of the moral literature of the Renaissance, see Paul O. Kristeller, "The Moral Thought of Renaissance Humanism," an essay of 1961 reprinted in his *Renaissance Thought and the Arts*, 20–68.

enrich our understanding of most branches of the intellectual life of the Renaissance.[22]

One aspect of Renaissance philosophy that has perhaps been poorly accommodated in the scholarship of past decades has been the problem of its relation to the great philosophical systems of the early modern period. An earlier generation attempted to synthesize a general Renaissance philosophy from the scattered, and often wildly divergent statements of the Renaissance humanists. A subsequent search for genuinely "systematic" philosophies in the period before Descartes and Hobbes has instead turned up a few interesting philosophers, none of them overhelmingly original, most of them clustered about the historical traditions of Aristotelianism and Platonism. It now seems clear that to request highly original systematic philosophies of the Renaissance is to ask of it more than it can offer.[23] All the same, if we acknowledge that there was much that was philosophically novel in the moral and political thought of the Renaissance, it becomes easier for us to see how the revolutionary philosophies of the early modern period may well have been attempts to construct epistemologically satisfactory systems that accomodated rhetorical, moral, and political paradigms established during the Renaissance. And the careful exploration of such an underlying role for Renaissance thought in the philosophy of the early modern period is a historical project that has barely yet begun.

As was the case with its forerunner, the contributions to *Renaissance Essays II* have been arranged in an order which is not always strictly chronological or topical, although some effort has been made to effect intelligent juxtapositions and to provide a feeling of directed movement. Minor corrections, mostly of typographical errors, have been made to the essays of Colish, Giustiniani, Hariman, Headley, Phillips, Schiffman, Seigel, Siraisi, Waswo and Westfall. The responsibility for

---

[22] See especially Charles Trinkaus, *In Our Image and Likeness: Humanity and Divinity in Italian Humanist Thought*, 2 vols. (London, 1970); and his *The Scope of Renaissance Humanism* (Ann Arbor, 1983); with the essays by Donald Weinstein, "In Whose Image and Likeness? Interpretations of Renaissance Humanism," *JHI*, 33 (1972), 165–176; and William J. Bouwsma, "Renaissance and Reformation: An Essay on Their Affinities and Connections," reprinted in his *A Usable Past: Essays in European Cultural History* (Berkeley, 1990), 225–246. Other important interpretations include Nancy S. Struever, *The Language of History in the Renaissance* (Princeton, 1970); Kahn, *Rhetoric, Prudence, and Skepticism*; and Brian Vickers, *In Defence of Rhetoric* (Oxford, 1987).

[23] On this problem, see the concluding chapter of the excellent survey by Brian P. Copenhaver and Charles B. Schmitt, *Renaissance Philosophy* (Oxford, 1992), pp. 329–357.

selecting these particular essays from among the sixty or so excellent articles on Renaissance subjects that have been published in the *JHI* since the mid 1960s has been mine. The contributors deserve thanks for their many pleasant communications regarding various matters. I should especially like to thank Donald R. Kelley, John W. Yolton, and Robert Easton of the University of Rochester Press for their invitation to edit this volume, Paul O. Kristeller for his interest and encouragement, and Salvatore I. Camporeale, James Hankins and Thomas F. Mayer for a number of suggestions regarding the project.

Villa I Tatti
Florence
December 1, 1992

I

IDEALS OF ELOQUENCE AND SILENCE IN PETRARCH

By Jerrold E. Seigel

Fundamental to the program of Renaissance humanism was the desire to combine wisdom with eloquence, to join together philosophy and rhetoric. Around the humanists' pious hope for the union of a true knowledge of things with literary skill clustered the most characteristic features of their cultural program: the demand for a kind of intellectual activity which would find fulfillment in virtuous action; the attack on scholasticism; the revival of ancient literature itself. Recent students of humanism have brought us closer to an understanding of the importance of this basic aim of humanist thought.[1] Yet the meaning of the slogan and the place it occupied in the development of humanism are still not fully understood. A careful consideration of humanist demands for the union of eloquence and wisdom reveals that the desire to join these things together affected humanist culture in pervasive and sometimes unsuspected ways. The present paper is an attempt to define and analyze the relationship between oratory and philosophy as it appears in the thought of the first and most influential humanist, Petrarch.

1. The vision of the combination of rhetoric with philosophy was an essential element in Petrarch's views of both true eloquence and true philosophy. His discussions of each make quite plain his conviction that neither was complete without the other. Indeed, the relationship between them is in some of Petrarch's writings made to appear so close that the two activities almost merge into one.

The indispensability of wisdom for true eloquence and the true orator is most clearly spelled out in a chapter of the *De remediis utriusque fortunae,* titled "De eloquentia." Here Petrarch stated his agreement with two great masters of Latin oratory, Cato and Cicero, that neither true eloquence nor the true orator could be found apart from virtue and wisdom. Cato had defined the orator as "a good man skilled in speaking," and Cicero had said that eloquence was nothing more than wisdom speaking copiously. Mere skill in speech by itself could produce only foolish talk. "If therefore you are seeking the

---

[1] See most recently, Hannah H. Gray, "Renaissance Humanism: the Pursuit of Eloquence," *JHI,* XXIV (1963). Fundamental to the present study, however, are also: Paul O. Kristeller, "Humanism and Scholasticism in the Italian Renaissance," *Byzantion,* XVII (1944), and now available both in Kristeller's *Studies in Renaissance Thought and Letters* (Rome, 1956) and his paperback *Renaissance Thought* (New York, 1961); also Kristeller's "Il Petrarca, l'umanesimo e la scolastica," *Lettere Italiane,* VII (1955); Richard McKeon, "Renaissance and Method in Philosophy," *Studies in the History of Ideas,* III (New York, 1935), 37–114; Ciro Trabalza, *La Critica Letteraria* (Milan, 1915), ch. 1.

title of orator and the true honor of eloquence, give your attention first of all to virtue and wisdom." [2]

From this passage one receives the impression that Petrarch regarded wisdom and virtue as independent of eloquence, and having no need to rely on it. But precisely the opposite conclusion is conveyed by many of Petrarch's treatments of moral philosophy. In his eyes the exemplars of true moral philosophy were especially Cicero and Augustine. In *On His Own Ignorance* he described their work.

The true moral philosophers and useful teachers of the virtues are those whose first and last intention is to make the hearer and reader good, those who do not merely teach what virtue and vice are, and hammer into our ears the brilliant name of the one and the grim name of the other, but sow into our hearts love of the best and eager desire for it, and at the same time hatred of the worst and how to flee it.[3]

Clearly Petrarch's true moral philosopher required eloquence quite as much as his true orator needed wisdom. His task was precisely the *docere* and *movere* of classical rhetoric. The humanist's criticism of Aristotle as a moral philosopher (perhaps he meant only the Aristotle represented in medieval Latin translations) was that he failed to move. "His lesson lacks the words that sting and set afire and urge toward love of virtue and hatred of vice, or, at any rate, does not have enough of such power." [4]

These statements about the need for eloquence in moral philosophy reveal an important feature of Petrarch's concern for rhetoric, and one which has often been misunderstood. For him the ideal of eloquence was not fulfilled primarily by speech which achieved harmony and beauty—perfection of form in an aesthetic sense. Eloquent language was marked by its ability to communicate with and persuade its listeners. Eloquence was persuasive power. To be sure Petrarch appreciated the sheer beauty of Cicero's speech; he tells us that it attracted him from his earliest youth, before he was able to understand its meaning.[5] But even this aesthetic pleasure is close to emotional effect. Most typically, Petrarch praised eloquence for its power. Thus Horace was able to move his readers (in a way Aristotle could not) despite the roughness of his style.[6] Cicero was the prince of Latin eloquence: "He held the hearts of men in his hands; he ruled his listeners as a king." [7] What Petrarch sought in eloquence was

[2] *De remediis utriusque fortunae* I, ix; (Rotterdam, 1649), 31–32.

[3] *On His Own Ignorance and That of Many Others*, tr. Hans Nachod in *The Renaissance Philosophy of Man*, ed. E. Cassirer, P. O. Kristeller, J. H. Randall, Jr. (Chicago, 1948), 105.   [4] *Ibid.*, 103.

[5] *Senilium rerum libri*, XV, 1, in *Opera* (Basel, 1554), II, 1046; Fracassetti numbers this letter XVI, 1—cf. *Lettere Senili . . . volgarizzate . . . da* G. Fracassetti (Florence, 1869–70).   [6] *On His Own Ignorance*, 103–4.

[7] *Rerum memorandarum libri*, ed. G. Billanovich (Florence, 1945), II, 17, 6.

the force it could exercise for moral suasion, to make philosophy active and help men to be good.

How much eloquence can accomplish in the shaping of human life is known both from reading in many authors and from the experience of everyday life. How great is the number of those we recognize in our own day, to whom even examples [of virtue] were of no help, who have been aroused and turned suddenly from a most wicked manner of life to a perfectly ordered one simply by the sound of others' voices! [8]

Only when it is recognized that for Petrarch eloquence meant this kind of power is it possible to see how much alike oratory and true moral philosophy were in his eyes.

Petrarch's primary source for this view was the Roman who had demonstrated the greatest concern with the problem of relating rhetoric to philosophy, Cicero. The humanist's devotion to the great orator is well-known. Without ever saying so expressly, Petrarch seems to have pictured his own rôle as that of an eloquent teacher of philosophical maxims after the model of Cicero, "adapting it to the needs of his century." [9] Like St. Jerome, Petrarch feared lest his love of the Roman orator be excessive.[10] Sometimes the facts of Petrarch's biography are difficult to determine, so closely does his own account of them follow some passage in Cicero.[11] Yet Petrarch seems never to have called himself an orator. The title he favored, of course, and with which he often coupled that of moral philosopher, was that of poet. In the *Letter to Posterity* he said that his mind was especially adept at poetry and moral philosophy, adding that with the passage of time he had neglected the first of these activities.[12] An official Venetian document relating to Petrarch's proposal to leave his library to the Republic of San Marco referred to him as "a moral philosopher and a poet," titles which Petrarch may well have suggested himself.[13]

For Petrarch, however, just as for Cicero, poetry was also closely related to rhetoric. Poetry was a branch of the tree of eloquence, and

[8] *Familiarium rerum libri*, ed. V. Rossi, *Le Familiari* (Florence, 1933–42), I, 9, 6; cf. Cicero, *De Inventione* I, ii, 3.

[9] Pierre de Nolhac, *Pétrarque et l'humanisme* (Paris, 1907), I, 215. Much of the literature on Petrarch contains some reference to the humanist's reliance on Cicero, but de Nolhac's discussion is among the most useful. G. Billanovich's "Petrarca e Cicerone," *Misc. Giovanni Mercati* (Vatican City, 1946), IV, 88–106, is less helpful. On Cicero himself in this connection the most complete treatment is A. Michel, *Rhétorique et Philosophie chez Cicéron* (Paris, 1960).   [10] *Fam.* XXI, 10.

[11] Umberto Bosco, *Francesco Petrarca* (Bari, 1961), 113ff. Petrarch took inspiration of this sort from other classical figures too.

[12] *Posteritati*, in Francesco Petrarca, *Prose*, ed. G. Martellotti, P. G. Ricci, E. Carrara, E. Bianchi (Milan and Naples, 1955), 6.

[13] See *Petrarch's Testament*, ed. T. E. Mommsen (Ithaca, 1957), 45–6 and note.

Virgil was an exemplar of verse eloquence just as Cicero was of prose.[14] This coupling of poetry and rhetoric had been common in earlier writers. It came to Petrarch from Cicero, and from a medieval tradition which drew especially on Horace, and which attributed to rhetoric and poetry the same aims and methods.[15] Petrarch's own work was described in these terms by his closest followers. Referring to his proficiency in both verse and prose, Coluccio Salutati said that Petrarch was "the one man . . . in whom eloquence demonstrated all its powers." [16] Moreover, the change Petrarch described in his own intellectual development, from poetry in his early years to moral philosophy later on, paralleled similar changes Petrarch observed in the careers both of Cicero and of Augustine, but in which the first stage was not poetry but rhetoric. Petrarch sometimes described Cicero's career as a movement from rhetoric to philosophy.[17] He was aware that Augustine's intellectual development began with the study and teaching of rhetoric, and he sometimes spoke of the great Father's movement to philosophy, helped by the reading of Cicero's lost treatise *Hortensius*.[18]

The evolution Petrarch described as his own was probably modeled on the similar development of Cicero and Augustine. Indeed, Petrarch's comments on the change in his activities have a somewhat artificial and imitative ring. It is true that Petrarch spoke plainly in the years of his maturity of having given up the study of poetry and classical literature in favor of moral philosophy and the sacred authors. In the *Invective Against a Certain Physician*, written in 1352 and 1353, he said he had given up the poets. "Now I study to make myself a better man, if I can." [19] And in a letter written a few years afterwards he added, "Once I read the things which delighted, now I read those which can benefit me." Petrarch's orators had become Ambrose, Augustine, Jerome, and Gregory; his philosopher, Paul; his poet, David.[20] But the humanist's movement from pagan eloquence to Christian philosophy is not so clear as this passage would make it seem. In the same place Petrarch admitted that he had not wholly abandoned the classics. It was only that he was careful to distinguish

---

[14] *Fam.* VI, 4, 12; *Rer. mem.* II, 17, 7.

[15] Cicero, *De oratore* I, xv, 70; on the tradition of Horace, C. S. Baldwin, *Ancient Rhetoric and Poetic* (New York, 1924), 224ff., esp. 246. Ernst Robert Curtius attributes the transfer of rhetoric to Roman poetry to Ovid, *European Literature and the Latin Middle Ages*, tr. W. R. Trask (New York, 1953), 66. On Petrarch's conception of poetry in this sense see especially Francesco Tateo, *"Retorica" e "Poetica" fra Medioevo e Rinascimento* (Bari, 1960), 221-9.

[16] *Epistolario di Coluccio Salutati*, ed. F. Novati (Rome, 1891–1911), I, 183.

[17] *Fam.* IV, 15, 7; *Rer. mem.* I, 15, 2 (where Cicero's study of philosophy in his youth is also mentioned).   [18] *On His Own Ignorance*, 116.

[19] *Invective contra medicum*, ed. P. G. Ricci (Rome, 1950), 74.

[20] *Fam.* XXII, 10, 5–7.

between the things which might be admired for their style, and those which were to be preferred for their content. Ten or more years later, in the treatise *On His Own Ignorance*, Petrarch said, "I still read the works of poets and philosophers, particularly those of Cicero," while carefully rejecting whatever parts of them were suspect from a Christian point of view.[21] We may be permitted to doubt that Petrarch's earlier statement about having given up the poets really described the whole of his literary activity. He made it both to suggest his putting aside childish things for the concerns of maturity, and in imitation of Cicero and Augustine. Given the close connection between eloquence and moral philosophy noted above, a movement in Petrarch's terms from rhetoric and poetry to ethics would not have been at all difficult, for Petrarch's pursuit of eloquence wos contemporaneous with his activity as a moral philosopher.

Petrarch developed the same theme of turning from the pursuits of youth to those of maturity in his attacks on the dialectic philosophers of his day. In this connection the plea to put aside childish things appears often in his work, first in a series of letters written in the years just after 1350, then in the *Invective Against a Certain Physician* of 1352 and 1353. In the letters Petrarch's criticism appears to be directed only against dialecticians themselves, especially those of the British Isles, for whom the solution of sophisms and argument for its own sake had replaced any concern for finding truth through philosophic speculation.[22] In directing this criticism against British philosophers, Petrarch showed a certain understanding of some of the regional differences among scholastics.[23] But in the *Invective*, which followed these letters by only a little more than a year, the poet censured the same fault in medieval philosophic culture in general, as represented by the physicians. The physician against whom Petrarch wrote seems to have undertaken the defense of the dialectician attacked in the earlier letters,[24] and the humanist reproached him with the same mistaking of dialectical proficiency, which should be a way to truth, for a goal in itself.[25] Petrarch may sometimes have felt that a devotion to poetry and eloquence should be restrained in a similar fashion, but he never turned the force of his bitter invective against these studies or against those who practiced them.[26] Decidedly he favored a moral philosophy which reflected the influence of rhetoric but not that of dialectic.

Petrarch's long dispute with physicians was itself concerned with

---

[21] *On His Own Ignorance*, 78. [22] *Fam.* I, 7; I, 10; I, 11; I, 12.

[23] Cf. P. Duhem, "La Dialectique d'Oxford et la Scolastique Italienne," *Bulletin Italien*, XII (1912), pt. III, pp. 110–20.

[24] *Inv. contra medicum*, ed. Ricci, 46. [25] *Ibid.*, 51–3.

[26] In fact he justified the continued study of the poets in old age when Boccaccio contemplated giving them up. See *Sen.* I, 4.

the defense of eloquence to a much larger degree than is usually realized. Carried on in the *Invective* already mentioned, and in a series
of later letters, this polemic made up a good part of Petrarch's defense of what was coming to be humanistic culture. Better known
than Petrarch's championing of eloquence is his defense of poetry,
especially as set out in Book III of the *Invective*.[27] But the cause of
rhetoric is taken up no less vigorously than that of poetry in the
treatise. The physicians' attempt to make rhetoric subservient to
medicine was to Petrarch's mind "an unheard-of sacrilege." "I ask
you, O lord of philosophy and the arts, with what mind would Cicero
have discussed rhetoric in so many books and with so much zeal, had
he known that it would become the slave of such a talent [as
yours]?" Indeed, the place of rhetoric was the crucial point at issue
between Petrarch and his opponent.

Not to tarry in details, I come to the crux of our dispute. Even if you
make all of the arts, however noble and ingenious, the servants of your low
and mercenary craft, by the fact of their being useful or necessary to your
end (and I know not by what right this should be permitted to you),
rhetoric will never thus be made your servant; for it is not only of no use
toward the end to which you would turn it, but is even of great harm. . . .[28]

Petrarch continued that physicians ought to cure their sick patients
in silence, not make long-winded speeches to them. Arousing or calm-
ing emotions was the work of the orator, not of the doctor.

The penchant of physicians for meddling with eloquence had been
a sore point with Petrarch from the beginning of his dispute with
them, and in his later letters the position of rhetoric was the central
point at issue. The controversy from which the *Invective* emerged
arose from a letter Petrarch wrote to Clement VI when the Pontiff
was ill, urging him to beware of the crowd of physicians that surrounded him, and to choose one "outstanding not for his eloquence
but for his knowledge and faith." [29] Here, as in the passage just cited
from Book III of the *Invective*, Petrarch's tone seems almost dispar-
aging toward eloquence. Referring to the letter in Book I of the treatise, he said he had warned the pope against any doctor who was
"interested not in knowledge, but in empty eloquence (*inanis eloquentie*)." [30] But it was not eloquence itself against which Petrarch
cautioned; it was the way physicians approached it. This is clear from
the later letters. Petrarch's position seems clearest from a late letter
to a physician called William of Ravenna. The tone was friendlier
than in the letter and *Invective* of the 50's, and the argument clearer.

---

[27] This defense was itself directed towards other studies than poetry. Cf. the discussion of F. Tateo cited above in note 15.   [28] *Inv. med.*, 29f., 40–41, 77–8.
     [29] *Fam.* V, 19, 5.   [30] *Inv. med.*, ed. Ricci, 29.

No one will call in a physician who seeks eloquence, but one who seeks health. To this end drugs are useful, not words (*herbis non verbis*); medicinal scents, not rhetorical colors; the arguments of physics, not those of rhetoric. It is the care of the body which is entrusted to you; to care for souls and move them should be left to true philosophers and orators.[31]

The coupling of "true philosophers and orators" shows Petrarch's real attitude. It had not been Petrarch's purpose to depreciate oratory or to say that eloquence was "empty." Only the rhetoric of the physicians was *inanis*. Physicians ought not to meddle with rhetoric, not because rhetoric itself was unworthy, but on the contrary because eloquence was associated with true philosophy, not with the juvenile dialectic of the physicians and the schools.

It is worth noting how far Petrarch is in this passage from illustrating the commonplace view of the humanists as apostles of literary culture to the barbarians. Instead he appears as the defender of an embattled intellectual territory. Remembering that the culture of physicians represented the highest level of Aristotelian learning in Italian universities in the fourteenth century, and that Petrarch found these men too devoted to dialectic, one might look for a suggestion from him that they temper their abstract speculation with some literary and rhetorical culture. Instead he seems anxious to shield rhetoric from them. The same impression is gained from the *Invective*.

You advise me to change my way of life until now, and become a doctor, not a very great thing, and wholly impossible. I advise you never to turn your attention to rhetoric, so that you finally begin to be a doctor. . . .[32]

Or, as Petrarch prefaced this remark, "You tell me to violate the boundaries of others, I warn you to return within your own."

It is often said that the humanists objected to the scholastics' neglect of literary subjects, but this was not always true. Here Petrarch censured precisely the breadth of their interests. As he said in an early passage (which gives a good idea of the tone of the *Invective*): "You want to speak on every subject, forgetful of your profession, which is, if you don't know, to contemplate urine and other things that modesty forbids me to name."[33] Indeed Petrarch seems at times to want to deprive the physicians of the right to any higher learning at all, even in dialectic. In a letter already referred to he suggested that dialectic was of no use to the practice of medicine; in another he said that a physician had admitted to him that medical theory, while it delighted the mind, had no connection with medical practice; in a third place he asserted that his whole dispute was with the high theoretical art of the physicians, not the humble and prac-

---

[31] *Sen.* III, 8; *Opera* (Basel, 1554), II, 861. Cf. *Sen.* XII, 2.
[32] *Inv. med.*, ed. Ricci, 80. [33] *Ibid.*, 34.

tical surgeons. The latter were mere mechanics, but they were concerned with curing, not disputing.[34]

Scholars have always realized that when Petrarch attacked physicians he had in mind the Aristotelians who populated the medical faculties of his day. What has not been clearly enough understood is that Petrarch's most persistent complaint against them was not their concern with the inhumane details of natural philosophy, but their attempt to intrude upon the study of rhetoric. What this attempt involved is not clear from Petrarch's statements, but we can be sure that from his point of view it entailed a reduction of the dignity and importance of rhetoric. This was the usual tendency of the scholastic organization of the arts under the headship of dialectic philosophy, in which rhetoric was assigned a much lower place than the Romans had given it.[35] Petrarch's complaint was not that the scholastics ignored oratory, but that they approached it in a way which made it subordinate to their own pursuits.

The humanist's position appears in sharper relief in connection with the scholastic attitude toward moral philosophy. It is often said that the humanists objected to the failure of scholastic philosophy to concern itself with ethics. But as with rhetoric, Petrarch's statements about ethics in the *Invective* suggest quite a different situation. It appears that in the humanist's eyes the schoolmen were trying to encroach upon moral philosophy as well as upon rhetoric. The physician against whom Petrarch wrote his polemic had claimed that the teaching of medicine was related to that of ethics. The humanist replied that "Medicine has nothing in common with ethics, and much that is contrary to it." [36] Interest in moral philosophy was in fact rather widespread in late XIIIth- and XIVth-century scholasticism,[37] and quite evident in Italy. Dante heard lectures at the Dominican school of Santa Maria Novella in Florence from a Thomist with a wide interest in ethical problems.[38] At roughly the time of Petrarch's disputes with the physicians, a doctor of medicine, Francesco da Conegliano, was lecturing on Ethics in the *Studio* in Florence.[39] Thus

---

[34] *Sen.* III, 8; *Sen.* V, 5 (= V, 4 in Fracassetti's numbering); *Sen.* XII, 2.

[35] Cf. Maurice de Wulf, *History of Medieval Philosophy*, tr. from the 6th French edition by E. C. Messenger (London, 1952), I, 54.   [36] *Inv. med.*, 76.

[37] Cf. Georges de Lagarde, *La Naissance de L'Esprit Laïque au Déclin du Moyen Age*, II: *Secteur Social de la Scolastique* (Louvain and Paris, 1958).

[38] M. Grabmann, "Die Italienische Thomistenschule des XIII und beginnenden XIV. Jh., 5: Remigio de' Girolami," *Mittelalterliches Geistesleben* (Munich, 1926), I, 361–69.

[39] Francesco da Conegliano is mentioned in the documents of the *Studio* as a teacher of philosophy and medicine on October 17, 1364, and in February 1365 (1364, *stile fiorentino*). On April 20, 1366 he is described as *artis Medicine dottorem*, reading philosophy, and on festivals ethics as well, *in quantum sibi placeat*.

Petrarch's pursuit of moral philosophy, like his study of rhetoric, was not unique; moral philosophy, too, had to be defended against the claims of scholastic philosophers to deal in their way with it. This is the meaning of his insistence that "to care for souls and move them should be left to true philosophers and orators."

Petrarch's prescription for true moral philosophy in these writings is clear enough: join wisdom closely enough to rhetoric to make it effective in men's lives. This was the moral philosophy he found in Cicero, but which his scholastic opponents did not practice. Led by certain statements in Cicero, the humanist even tried sometimes to claim that this was Aristotle's attitude toward ethics too, so that the whole of Antiquity was lined up on his side against the barbaric schoolmen. In the treatise *On His Own Ignorance* he described his opponents thus: "From Aristotle's ways they swerve, taking eloquence to be an obstacle and a disgrace to philosophy, while he considered it a mighty adornment and tried to combine it with philosophy, 'prevailed upon,' it is asserted, 'by the fame of the orator Isocrates.'"[40] Like Cicero, however, whom he quoted in this passage, Petrarch was not altogether certain about Aristotle's regard for eloquence. He denied in the same treatise that Aristotle's moral writings actually achieved the power of eloquent speech.[41] In an earlier work he had perhaps resolved this contradiction, saying that it was the Latin Aristotle which showed such weakness. The translations had been made by men of little talent, who, unable to be as eloquent as Aristotle, had tried to make the philosopher as barbarous as themselves.[42]

Petrarch revealed a similar attitude toward the learning of his day in connection with another important intellectual pursuit of XIVth-century Italy, law. Writing in 1356 to a friend who had begun the study of law, Petrarch recalled the great tradition of legal study in Antiquity, when lawyers and orators were the same people, and he expressed the hope that his friend would pursue his career with

---

This is the first reference to the teaching of moral philosophy in the published documents of the Florentine *Studio*. At this time Francesco's salary was raised from 90 florins to 100, apparently to compensate him for his added duties. The salary was reduced again to 90 florins the following October, on the grounds that the ordinances of the commune forbade such increases. The directors of the *Studio* made it clear, however, that they did not wish Francesco to curtail his reading of ethics. The documents are printed in A. Gherardi, *Statuti della Università e Studio Fiorentino . . .* (Florence, 1881), 304, 315, 319, 321.

[40] *On His Own Ignorance*, 53–4; cf. Cicero, *Tusc. Disp.* I, iv, 7, and *De oratore* III, xxxv, 141.

[41] *On His Own Ignorance*, 103. While Cicero usually praised Aristotle for his eloquence and recommended the study of Peripatetic philosophy to the aspiring orator, he had Antonius in *De oratore* suggest at one point that in reality Aristotle "despised" rhetoric. *De or.* II, xxxviii, 160.   [42] *Rer. mem.* II, 31, 8.

their example in mind. Among the Latins Petrarch had particular praise for Cicero and the two interlocutors of *De oratore*, Crassus and Antonius. What is of special interest about this letter is Petrarch's description of how legal studies had declined in his own day. This had occurred because the study of law had become separated from that of oratory.

Just as the first step [in the decline of legal studies] was from the manifold learning and heavenly citadel of eloquence to the single subject of equity and civic knowledge, so assuredly the second step was from that to a loquacious ignorance. . . . [43]

Like philosophy, law could only decline when it became independent of rhetoric. In their revival of Antiquity, the humanists often referred to the central place occupied by oratory in ancient culture. It was as rhetoricians that they most often appeared to their scholastic opponents, and it was the pursuit of eloquence which best tied together their various interests and activities.[44]

But the ancient rhetorical tradition on which the humanists drew so heavily was by no means circumscribed by an uncritical celebration of eloquence. Cicero was harsh toward the "Greekling" philosophers of his day, but he recognized that the greatest thinkers of ancient Greece had often been suspicious of the oratory of professional rhetoricians, and in creating his image of the ideal orator he took account of their criticisms. Petrarch too was aware that the power of eloquence could be harmful if used unwisely, as the chapter "De eloquentia" in the *De remediis* makes clear. Moreover, in some of the humanist's other writings one finds an attitude toward the cultivation of eloquence which was not merely cautious, but suspicious and even hostile. The unquestioning devotion to rhetoric found in Petrarch's dispute with the physicians marks these letters and treatises as polemic, and cautions us to regard them more as an affirmation of the poet's place in the intellectual controversies of his time than as a complete expression of his own cultural ideal. In some of his other writings we find a more complex and far richer understanding of the culture of classical rhetoric.

2. The life of the orator was always a public life; his speech sought to move an audience and win its praise. Despite this, there is no immediate reason why the ideals of eloquent speech must be foreign to the inner, private life of individuals. Nor did Petrarch usually find them to be so. The humanist sought eloquent writers even as the companions and inspiration of his most intimate meditations. He required the power of their speech to give an impetus to his

---

[43] *Fam.* XX, 4, 23.

[44] For a general statement of this view of humanism, see the article of Hannah H. Gray, cited in note 1, above.

mind.[45] Thus the contrast between Petrarch's moods of praise for eloquence and his realizations of its inadequacy may not be explained merely by the "public" or "private" character of some of the writings in which the differing attitudes appear. Nonetheless, the distinction between the needs of the inner man and the life of his exterior companion is an important element in the formulation of Petrarch's contrasting attitudes toward eloquence. As Petrarch had Augustine remind him in the *Secret*:

What does it matter that your listeners perhaps have approved the things you say, if those things are condemned by yourself as judge? Even though the approval of one's listeners appears to be a fruit of eloquence which ought not to be spurned, if the inner approval of the orator is missing, how little pleasure the noise of the crowd can offer![46]

Or, as Petrarch wrote in the *De vita solitaria,*

The doctor who helps a sick man by his advice is not necessarily a well man himself; often he dies of the same sickness which he has cured in many others. I do not reject speech that is carefully elaborated and artfully composed to be of help to the many, and I approve of a useful work, whoever is its author. But truly this is for us a school of life, not of rhetoric, nor should we seek the empty glory of the tongue, but the lasting quiet of the mind.[47]

These two passages come from the two works in which Petrarch's doubts about the pursuit of eloquence are most prominent. Significantly, the *Secret* and the *Life of Solitude* are not only Petrarch's most personal writings; they are also the ones which most clearly reflect his devotion to St. Augustine. For although some of Petrarch's criticism of rhetoric may be traced to other sources, in part to Cicero himself, it is in Augustine that we must seek its deepest roots. Augustine began his intellectual career as a teacher of rhetoric, and his *De doctrina christiana* passed along much of ancient rhetorical doctrine to the tradition of Christian learning and preaching. But his conversion led him to a concern for truth as against mere display which turned him against the sophistic of the IVth century, and toward a recreation of the reformed rhetoric of Plato's *Phaedrus*. This is the rhetoric of the *De doctrina christiana*. For Augustine, spiritual progress could be represented by a movement from speech to silence, from outer appearance to inner truth.[48] Petrarch spoke sometimes in the same terms. "Truly then, unless our purpose is to seem [learned] rather

---

[45] E.g., *Fam.* I, 9, 11.

[46] *De secreto conflictu curarum mearum*, ed. E. Carrara, in the above cited volume, Petrarca, *Prose*, 72. (Cited hereafter as *Secret*.)

[47] *De vita solitaria*, ed. G. Martellotti, in Petrarca, *Prose*, 324.

[48] See J. A. Mazzeo, "St. Augustine's Rhetoric of Silence," *JHI*, XXIII (1962).

than to be so, the applause of the foolish crowd will not please us so much as truth in silence." [49] *Veritas in silentio* may be taken as the motto of Petrarch's Augustinian criticism of rhetoric. Part of the humanist poet's objection to city life was its noise. The rubric of one of his letters reads: "Even those who follow the public life may live innocently and piously, and from that clatter they may aspire to the silence of a higher life." [50]

Silence has many meanings in Petrarch's work, but often it is associated with a suspicion of speech. Augustine in Petrarch's *Secret* criticizes the humanist for his pursuit of words. Nothing seemed to demonstrate better the emptiness of his life. Not only did this concern turn Petrarch from the cares of his inner life, the pursuit of eloquence was itself a hopeless and useless quest. Speech was far too small a thing to encompass man's experience.

How many things there are in nature for which no names exist! How many others which, even though names can be found for them, you know that until they are actually experienced human eloquence cannot succeed in expressing their dignity with words. How often I have heard you yourself [Augustine was speaking] complain, how often I have seen you silent and indignant that neither your tongue nor your pen sufficed to express things which were so clearly and easily conceived by your mind! What is this eloquence of speech therefore, so small and weak, that neither embraces all nor holds that which it has embraced? [51]

The notion of the inadequacy of human speech, its inability to serve man's spiritual needs, reappears in other places in Petrarch's work. But the suggestion Petrarch makes here—that eloquence cannot encompass wisdom—is denied in some of Petrarch's other writings. The clearest expression of the opposite view comes in a passage to which we have already referred, the discussion of Aristotle's eloquence in the *Rerum memorandarum*. Here, it will be remembered, the humanist attacked the scholastics who did not believe in Aristotle's eloquence.

They say that he, in the way of one who would understand the highest things, held all eloquence in contempt, as if there were no place in the high reaches of knowledge for splendor of language. On the contrary, however, sublime knowledge is worthy of a high style, and how very true is Cicero's statement: "When you speak," he said, "of great things, the matter itself

---

[49] *Fam.* I, 8, 20. On the general question of Petrarch's relation to St. Augustine, see P. P. Gerosa, "L'Umanesimo Agostiniano del Petrarca," *Didaskaleion* (N.S.), III (1925), fasc. 2, 63–113; fasc. 3, 13–29; IV (1926), fasc. 1, 107–37; V (1927), fasc. 1, 69–127; VII (1929), fasc. 1, 125–48. Gerosa's view of the distinction between Christian and pagan psychology as these attitudes appear in Petrarch's writings seems to me exaggerated. See below, 165f.

[50] *Fam.* III, 12.   [51] *Secret,* 74.

takes hold of the language. Thus the more elevated is the subject of a speech, the more splendid is its style." [52]

The contradiction presented by these two passages is of great importance for Petrarch's humanistic ideal of culture. In the first instance knowledge of the highest things is regarded as contrasting with the pursuit of eloquence; in the second such knowledge is said to aid in the production of eloquent speech. In the *Secret* Petrarch denied the intellectual premise on which the Ciceronian notion of Aristotle's eloquence affirmed in the *Rerum memorandarum* was based. It is interesting to note how Petrarch's relationship to the scholastics changes from the *Rerum* to the *Secret*. In the one treatise it was a scholastic opinion that "there is no place in the high reaches of knowledge for splendor of language." In the other it is an Augustinian opinion, and Petrarch would make it his own. The conclusion to be drawn from this is not that Petrarch regarded Augustine as a scholastic. It is instead that the contrast between Petrarch the humanist and the scholastics on the philosophical capability of eloquent speech is nearly identical with a conflict within Petrarch himself between what he presents as Ciceronian and Augustinian views of the relation between eloquence and wisdom. The Augustine of the *Secret* is a man who is sceptical about the possibility of combining these things. He warns Petrarch that to give attention to expression will interfere with the attainment of proper knowledge, with philosophy.

That the claims of rhetoric had to be made in full consciousness of the demands of philosophy appears from a letter of 1350–51 entitled "De studio eloquentie." [53] It begins: "The care of the soul requires the philosopher, the learning of the tongue is proper to the orator. Neither should be neglected by us. . . ." Petrarch went on to distinguish the fruits of the pursuit of eloquence from those of the love of wisdom.

What will be the result of your immersing yourself totally in the Ciceronian fount, that none of the writings either of Latins or Greeks pass you by? You will surely be able to speak ornately, clearly, sweetly, high-soundingly; but you will not yet be able to speak weightily, strictly, wisely, and, what is most important, consistently. Since unless first all our desires accord one with another, which I know can befall only the man of wisdom, just as we have divergent cares, so necessarily will our speech and our character diverge. The well-disposed mind is capable of unmoved serenity, is always placid and tranquil; it knows what it desires, and what it has once desired it does not cease to will. Therefore, even though the ornaments of the art of oratory do not aid it, it elicits from itself magnificent and weighty speech, which is surely self-consistent.[54]

[52] *Rer. mem.* II, 31, 8; cf. Cicero, *De finibus* III, v, 19.
[53] *Fam.* I, 9.   [54] *Fam.* I, 9, 3.

The last part of this seems to call to mind the passage from the *Rerum memorandarum* about Aristotle's eloquence: "When you speak of great things, the matter itself takes hold of the language." But in fact this is a quite different adaptation of the idea. Whereas there Petrarch had affirmed the relevance of eloquence to higher philosophic learning with the intention of showing the Philosopher's concern for eloquence, here the same *locus communis* is made to indicate that the independent pursuit of eloquence was nearly superfluous to the man of wisdom.

To be sure, Petrarch went on to make a place for rhetoric by the side of philosophy, and indeed to describe the effect of eloquence (as we have seen above) in terms which made it nearly identical with that of moral philosophy.[55] There is much that is ambiguous in this letter; the provinces of rhetoric and philosophy are by no means clearly separated in it. But whereas the moving of men's minds is sometimes ascribed by Petrarch to moral philosophy and sometimes to rhetoric, the characteristics of the philosophic mind indicated in the passage just quoted seem to be those which the humanist associates only with philosophy, and never with rhetoric. The chief of these characteristics is *consistency*. It is this which only the study of philosophy can bring, and which Petrarch finds to be the most important fruit of such study. In the treatise *On His Own Ignorance* Petrarch affirmed that "Philosophers must not be judged from isolated words but from their uninterrupted coherence and consistency."[56]

The ideal of consistency and the attempt to achieve it appear many times in Petrarch's work. In a sense it was for him the highest ideal, both in philosophy and in life. It was essential to the spiritual state at which he was aiming in the *Secret*. Augustine attributed Petrarch's failure to arrive at his goal to his inability to give a consistent direction to his quest. The malady which had taken possession of Petrarch was that of letting his mind be deceived by worldly phantasies, a crowd of diverse impressions and experiences which pushed him first in one direction, then in another. The mind, weakened by its entrance into a body, "invaded by these phantasy impressions and oppressed by many differing preoccupations ceaselessly at war among themselves, cannot determine to which of these to turn first, which to cultivate, which to suppress, or which to repel. . . . You are turned about with a marvelous inconstancy, partly here and partly there, and never anywhere wholly and completely."[57] In the *De vita solitaria* Petrarch censured those who wavered continually among various ends, and he made consistency one of the chief purposes of the search for wisdom in solitude. "To wish always for a single and well-defined thing is a sign of wisdom. Inconstancy of purpose is the best argument for a person's foolishness." In the words of Seneca, no wind

---

[55] Cf. above, at note 8.   [56] *On His Own Ignorance*, 87.   [57] *Secret*, 66–8.

is favorable for the man who knows not what port to seek.[58]

Since Petrarch was so much aware of the importance of consist-ency, and thought it so close to wisdom, it is striking to be reminded that his own writings are full of inconsistencies. Augustine's descrip-tion of Petrarch's mind in the *Secret* provides some warning of this, but it is still worthwhile to examine these contradictions a bit more closely. The most important are found in the maxims of moral phi-losophy which Petrarch chose to repeat in his various writings. A re-cent study of Petrarch's ethics, based largely on the *De remediis utriusque fortunae*, has found the humanist's statements to be a chaos of contradictions.[59] Following as he did now one ancient source, now another, Petrarch several times reversed himself on the question whether fortune, of which he often spoke, actually existed or not. Moreover, on a whole range of issues identifiable from the *De finibus* and other of Cicero's writings as debated by Stoics and Peripatetics, the humanist expressed by turns the view first of one side, then of the other. This is true on such central questions as whether moral philos-ophy sought the extermination of passions or the mere tempering of them, whether prosperity of fortune was a real good or only an ap-parent one, and whether conversely adversity was a true evil or only seemingly harmful.

Where ought one to look for some explanation of these contrasting statements? Klaus Heitmann's suggestion that in the end Petrarch did not feel the contradictions as such, and that he accepted the vary-ing statements in the Augustinian spirit that "all things which are true are true from God," [60] is not sufficient. It does not take account of the yearning for consistency which animates so many of Petrarch's writings. Occasionally we can do away with a particular contradiction by attributing one of the humanist's statements to the requirements of polemic, but this will aid us very little. We find, however, that Petrarch himself offers some other leads to help us.

One of these is that human inconsistency follows from man's con-dition in this life. Man loves life, but fears to recognize that its end is death. To desire to live and not to die is the same as to wish to move and to stand still at the same time. This is man's inconsistency. Or, since as Cicero said this thing we call our life is but death, we both love and hate death above all things; from this come man's vacillations and his constant repetition of the comic poet's phrase, *volo nolo, nolo volo*.[61]

---

[58] *De vita solitaria*, 384–6. For similar themes in Petrarch's verse, see U. Bosco, *Francesco Petrarca*, 62–67 and *passim*.

[59] Klaus Heitmann, *Fortuna und Virtus, Eine Studie zu Petrarcas Lebensweisheit* (Cologne, 1958). See especially the conclusion and the tabular view of contradictory maxims, 251.   [60] *Ibid.*, 256.   [61] *Fam.* X, 5, 17–18.

This passage, interesting as it is, does not really furnish us with a map to guide us among the actual inconsistencies of Petrarch's statements, particularly the contrasting assertions of Stoic and Peripatetic doctrines. A more satisfying explanation leads us back along the path of Petrarch's concern with rhetoric. The primary observation is a simple one: the humanist's seesaw allegiance to Peripateticism and Stoicism recalls Cicero's various attempts to argue persuasively for these and other philosophic schools in such treatises as the *De finibus, De officiis,* and *Tusculan Disputations.* Since Petrarch often shared Cicero's ideal of moral philosophy, the Roman orator's ability to support both Peripatetic and Stoic teachings helps us to understand the Italian humanist's.

But Petrarch himself offers some further explanations, closely related to this one. One is that rhetorical procedures themselves are a source of the inconsistency which plagued his life. He finds the rhetorical principle of imitation to be often at the base of men's failure to follow a consistent direction. To imitate models may be a useful council for developing one's style, but it does great harm to those who make it a method for virtuous living.

How could it be possible that the tenor of life remain constant for those who take as their guide not virtue, not their own judgment, not the counsels of friends, but give themselves over to emulation, to the ineptness of others and the madness of the foolish? Those who give up their own nature, reject their ancestral customs, and admire only that which is foreign and adventitious—these must needs change their goal every time they find something which to admire. There will be no limit to their changes, because there is no limit to imitation.[62]

Despite the elements of other concerns easily discernible in this passage (Petrarch was about to censure those Italians who uncritically accepted foreign ways—he does not say in what things), the point is clearly made that imitation of models may be the source of the kind of inconstancy Petrarch lamented in the *Secret.* The models may have something admirable in them, but as they differ among themselves, a life built on imitation of them cannot achieve the desired consistency. Imitation of models, even exemplars of virtues, is not the same as a constant striving for virtue itself.

This passage is striking because much of Petrarch's notion of moral philosophy—like that of the rhetorical tradition and humanism in general—was based on such imitation. It was because imitation of great men was thought worthwhile that the study of history seemed an important ethical study for Cicero and the humanists. In the letter "De studio eloquentie," Petrarch praised the imitation of examples of virtue as a part of the care of the soul, perhaps giving to examples a higher value than speech itself.[63] Moreover, many of his major writ-

[62] *De vita solitaria,* 388.   [63] *Fam.* I, 9, 5.

ings were concerned with presenting to the reader models to be imitated. This is true of the *De viris illustribus,* on which Petrarch worked throughout his life, of parts of the *Rerum memorandarum* and of the *De remediis utriusque fortunae,* and even of some sections of the *De vita solitaria* itself. Thus the passage just cited appears as a kind of condemnation of much of Petrarch's own work. The imitation of models, which the humanist often encouraged, was here censured as leading men not to virtue, but towards an ever-increasing accumulation of human weakness and vice.

Petrarch seems in other places to criticize his own writings on moral philosophy. In the *De vita solitaria* Petrarch spoke disparagingly of those "who go around the cities, harangue the crowds, speak much of vices and virtues." It was to them that he addressed the reminder that "This is for us a school of life, not of rhetoric." [64] But of whom is Petrarch speaking here if not of himself? To be sure he did not literally travel about haranguing the crowd, but his purpose as a moral philosopher was precisely to address men in eloquent language about virtue and vice. When the physician against whom he wrote the *Invective* referred to the humanist's writings as homilies, Petrarch did not object. He only pointed out that this was a *genre* "which is known to have pleased the most holy and most learned men." [65] In the *Secret,* however, he had Augustine reproach him: "If you had studied for yourself and not for others, and if you had turned the reading of so many books into a rule for your own life, instead of toward the windy approval of the crowd and empty show, you wouldn't now say such silly and stupid things." [66]

Petrarch seems thus to criticize his own work in moral philosophy in two ways, first because it was based on imitation of examples and not on the direct pursuit of virtue, and secondly because it was addressed to an audience—the crowd—rather than to his own inner needs. These two criticisms were closely connected. For just as Petrarch identified wisdom with consistency, so did he find its source in fleeing from the crowd. In the *Secret* Augustine told Petrarch that the impetus for his own spiritual progress was given by this phrase in Cicero: "[The crowd] is not able to see anything with the mind; it judges all things according to the testimony of its eyes. It is the task of a higher spirit to recall his mind from his senses, and to remove his thoughts from the common practice." [67]

Just as the imitation which Petrarch saw as leading to inconstancy was an adaptation of the rhetorical principle of imitation, so the man most tied to the crowd was in Petrarch's view the orator. In the *De vita solitaria* Petrarch was convinced that all true philosophers of all times would flee the city and seek solitude.[68] In fact Petrarch

---

[64] *De vita solitaria,* 324.   [65] *Inv. med.,* 75.   [66] *Secret,* 32.

[67] *Secret,* 67. Cf. *Tusc. Disp.* I, xvi, 37–8. Petrarch also quotes this sentence from Cicero in the *De vita solitaria,* 353.   [68] *De vita solitaria,* 424–6.

runs down the list of human occupations, including those of emperors and captains of armies, and finds in all of them the desire for solitude and freedom from the crowded city. Only one group was constitutionally opposed to the flight from town: orators.

It is a peculiar characteristic of orators that they take pleasure in large cities and in the press of the crowd, in proportion to the greatness of their own talents. They curse solitude, and hate and oppose silence where decisions are to be made (*silentium iudiciorum*).[69]

Petrarch referred specifically to Cicero in this passage, and to his belief (best expressed at the beginning of *De oratore*) that while other activities might find excellence in the flight from everyday life and common sense, rhetoric could seek its glory only among these things.[70]

The implications here are striking in view of Petrarch's many statements of the close kinship of orators and moral philosophers. If orators are stuck in the city and tied to the crowd, while the beginning of wisdom is the withdrawal from the commonplace thoughts of most men, then the opposition between rhetoric and philosophy must be complete. Petrarch does not stop short of this conclusion.

Both the diversity of their ways of life and the wholly opposed ends for which they have worked make me believe that philosophers have always thought differently from orators. For the latter's efforts are directed toward gaining the applause of the crowd, while the former strive—if their declarations are not false—to know themselves, to return the soul to itself, and to despise empty glory.[71]

Philosophy must seek consistency and proper self-knowledge by a withdrawal from the foolish fancies of the multitude; rhetoric, tied to the city, cannot participate in the philosophic flight. It can never escape from the fantasies and turbulence of the world.

All this adds up to the most surprising contradiction in all of Petrarch's writing, that between the close coupling of moral philosophy with oratory in the treatise *On His Own Ignorance* and the various stages of the polemic against the physicians, and the wholly divergent conclusions of the *Secret* and the *Life of Solitude* that rhetoric and philosophy are not only differing but opposing pursuits. Petrarch's realization that the ideal of the harmony of oratory and philosophy could not be consistently maintained when the contrasting ends of the two activities and the ways of life imposed by them are set against each other would seem to constitute an open declaration that the humanist ideal of a union of eloquence with wisdom was unattainable, a contradiction in terms. True philosophy could be such only in removing itself as far as possible from the concerns of oratory.

---

[69] *Ibid.*, 534.   [70] Cf. *De oratore*, I, iii, 12.   [71] *De vita solitaria*, 540.

Yet despite the openness of this admission, and the stream of criticism of rhetoric which runs through much of Petrarch's writing, the humanist never abandoned the pursuit of eloquence or the attempt to combine it with wisdom. Perhaps an understanding of how this could be so may help us to account for some of the humanist's other contradictions.

3. To begin with we must examine more closely the moral philosophy of solitude and silence from which the pursuit of eloquence was excluded. In what does the attainment of true wisdom and virtue consist? The answer Petrarch gives to this is clear. Man has achieved true self-knowledge and has thus set out on the path to virtue when he has attained to an engrossing and moving meditation on his own death. It is this to which Augustine spurs Petrarch in the *Secret*. The Saint's first words to the humanist are a reproach ending, "Do you not remember that you are mortal?" He adds that he abhors no human characteristic more than "that you pretend not to recognize the danger which confronts you." [72] This recalls the letter quoted above in which Petrarch found the springs of human inconsistency precisely in man's refusal to come to terms with his own mortality.[73] This theme of the *Secret* appears in other places in Petrarch's writings. In the *Invective Against a Certain Physician* he concluded that "true philosophy is that which some have said to be nothing other than thinking upon death." [74] *Cogitatio mortis:* this is true moral philosophy in a higher, Augustinian sense.

For Petrarch this was a firmly Christian conception of moral philosophy, but we must be careful not to regard the contrast between it and the rhetorical moral philosophy he described elsewhere as one between Christianity and paganism.[75] Petrarch himself understood that this description of philosophy had a pagan origin, and he was careful in the *Secret* to have Augustine remind him of the Father's dependence on Platonic philosophy and on Cicero.[76] The goal which Petrarch set for himself in the *Secret* was not to replace a pagan consciousness with a Christian one. It was to achieve a more

[72] *Secret*, 28; cf. *De vita solitaria*, 356.   [73] Cf. above, at note 61.

[74] *Inv. med.*, 54. Cf. *Tusc. Disp.* I, xxx, 74.

[75] The attempt of Aurelia Bobbio, "Seneca e la formazione spirituale e culturale del Petrarca," *La Bibliofilia* XLIII (1941), 224–91, to suggest that Petrarch's writings contain a movement toward a specifically Christian concept of virtue is stimulating as well as pious, but it is not convincing. The author is forced to admit that Petrarch never made an open statement of the contrast between Stoic and Christian ideas of virtue. What we find in Petrarch is not a "critica sordina al sistema stoico" from a Christian point of view, but an open declaration that Stoic Philosophy is inadequate from the viewpoint of a total—but not specifically Christian—description of human nature. See below.   [76] E.g., *Secret*, 66.

profound and effective *cogitatio mortis* than he had previously known. This is the goal to which man should direct himself amid the distracting phantasies of life.

When Augustine told Petrarch that a man's first step in rising to a higher state must be a meditation on death, the humanist replied that he had often practiced such meditation, but that "so far it has been in vain." The Father's response is well known: Petrarch had not focused all the power of his mind on his meditation. He had not willed it enough. Petrarch is slow to accept this, but Augustine insists on it. In fact we discover that the question of man's power to will his own happiness, to achieve a virtuous life by an undiluted desire for it, is the central issue of the *Secret*. "Nor are my hopes for you so weak," the Saint says, "that I do not think you will see for yourself (if you put your mind to it) that no one falls into misery except by his own will. For on this question our whole dispute is founded." [77]

Thus the higher kind of moral philosophy is revealed as an intensely personal, individual pursuit. It is the inner man who must attain it by the working of his own will. Petrarch has Augustine describe his own conversion as working upon him finally after much perplexity.

I pulled my hair, I hit my head, I bent my fingers, and finally hugging my knees with my hands I filled heaven and the atmosphere with the most bitter sighs, and my tears softened the earth around me. And yet with all that I remained what I had been before—when finally a profound meditation forced before my eyes a vision of all my unhappiness. And thus, from the moment when I willed totally, so I was immediately able, and with wonderful and most happy rapidity to transform myself into another Augustine, the events of whose history, if I am not mistaken, you know from my *Confessions*.[78]

Such an attainment of wisdom must occur within oneself. It is not immediately obvious, however, that reading or listening to eloquent moralists might not help to prepare one for such an experience, and in fact Petrarch seems to imply that it could. He often referred to the importance of Cicero to Augustine in this regard, especially of Cicero's lost treatise *Hortensius*.[79] But just as there was no sign of Cicero at what Petrarch conceived to be the crucial moment in Augustine's spiritual development, so was the orator unable to provide the humanist with the spiritual force which he found lacking in himself. In the *Secret*, when Augustine recommends to Petrarch the reading of Seneca and Cicero, particularly the *Tusculan Disputations*, the following exchange takes place.

[77] *Secret*, 36–8. It should be noted that Petrarch would have found this notion in Cicero as well as in Augustine. Cf. *Tusc. Disp.* IV, xxxi, 65, and IV, xxxviii, 83.
[78] *Secret*, 40.   [79] E.g., *On His Own Ignorance*, 105; *Fam.* II, 9, etc.

P: You know that I have read all those writings, and not negligently.

A: And didn't they help you at all?

P: On the contrary, while I was reading them they helped a great deal. But as soon as the book was out of my hands, all of my assent vanished.[80]

The speech of the prince of eloquence was powerful, but not powerful enough to do the permanent work of moral philosophy. If Petrarch was to achieve the sort of meditation which had transformed Augustine, it would have to be by some other means.

Indeed, the feeling that eloquence does not have the power which Petrarch elsewhere attributed to it is present in the *De vita solitaria* as well as in the *Secret*. There, in only one place did Petrarch come near to questioning the ideal of the solitary life. Following Cicero, he agreed that there was no activity "happier, more worthy of man, or more like to God than to save and help as many other people as possible. He who can do this and doesn't seems to me to reject that noble duty of man, and therefore to lose his human nature and the name of humanity."[81] Here we see how close Petrarch could come to the ideals of active life which would dominate later humanism, and how much these ideals would owe to the cult of oratory. For the kind of helping one's fellows which Petrarch had in mind here was nothing other than the activity of speaking eloquently about virtue and vice, to which in the end the humanist replied (as we have already twice observed) that "this is a school of life, not of rhetoric." He made another response to them as well: that their work does not really help at all.

There are many who claim to exercise activities which are useful to the community and more worthy than any solitude. I know it; but how many, I ask you, have we seen who do what they had promised? Perhaps there are some, perhaps there are many; show me a single one and I shall be quiet.[82]

Thus the rhetorical ideal of an activity ennobled by its usefulness to men is denied with a strong dose of scepticism about the much vaunted power of eloquence. The power which Cicero seemed to lack in the *Secret* is missing in other orators as well.

As a reminder of how complete the contradiction between this attitude and Petrarch's pro-rhetorical mood is, let us recall this passage quoted earlier in our discussion:

How much eloquence can accomplish in the shaping of human life is known both from reading in many authors and from the experience of everyday life. How great is the number of those we recognize in our own day, to whom even examples [of virtue] were of no help, who have been aroused and turned suddenly from a most wicked manner of life to a perfectly ordered one simply by the sound of others' voices![83]

[80] *Secret*, 122.

[81] *De vita solitaria*, 322.

[82] *Ibid.*

[83] Cf. p. 149 above (*Fam.* I, 9, 6).

The moral philosophy of the *Secret* and the *De vita solitaria* seems to render the rhetoric of the statement such as this both superfluous and powerless. And yet, as we shall now see, the divergence between the two Petrarchan moods we have been examining has a rationale, even a kind of necessity, in Petrarch's mind. In a sense, Petrarch's contradictions spring from a deeper consistency.

The statements that eloquence is powerless to help man toward true virtue, is trapped in the crowded city and forever distant from wisdom, find a kind of compliment in some of Petrarch's utterances about philosophy. If rhetoric aims too low to satisfy man's highest needs, the wisdom which is the goal of the *Secret* and the *De vita solitaria* is sometimes described as superhuman, above man's nature. In one passage of the *Secret*, Augustine pictures to Petrarch the fully rational man, who lives in total conformity to the reason which separates him from the beasts.

He will be conscious of his own mortality, so that he has it before his eyes every day; he will regulate his life according to this vision, and scorning mortal things will aspire to that life where, still more intensely rational, he will cease to be mortal. Then finally will he have true and useful knowledge of the definition of man.[84]

Augustine further tells Petrarch that for him to arrive at some of the goals he must set himself "it would be necessary for you to divest yourself of your humanity and become a god"[85] Petrarch's feeling that the aim of the Augustinian counsels of the *Secret* is not human but divine is clarified by a passage in one of his letters.

You will act differently as a philosopher than you do as a man. No one is so given to wisdom that he does not, when he returns to the common human state, condescend also to public ways of acting.[86]

The notion that philosophy raises man to a superhuman state was a common one in ancient philosophy. It should be enough to recall the conclusion of Aristotle's *Ethics*.[87] Petrarch echoes this idea, and seems to include the philosophy defined as the "true and useful" knowledge of man's mortality in it. In the *Secret* the poet excuses himself to Augustine for not directing his path more resolutely toward higher things by a reference to "the necessity of human nature."[88] This is the human state which makes man as man a different being from man as philosopher. The whole movement of the *Secret* is between Petrarch's yearning to give himself to a superior wisdom and his repeated discovery that he is unable to.

---

[84] *Secret*, 52–4.   [85] *Ibid.*, 92.

[86] *Fam.* XXI, 13, 1. alterum ut philosophus facis, alterum ut homo; nemo tam sapientie deditus, qui non quandoque as humanitatem redeat comunem et publicis moribus condescendat.

[87] *Eth.Nic.*X, &, 1177b, 26–32.   [88] *Secret*, 90.

This sense of always striving for something beyond his human nature is at the very center of Petrarch's personality, and it has often been remarked. It is the famous *dissidio*, the internal psychological conflict between the poet's human nature and his divine vision.[89] While Petrarch yearned intensely for a higher plane of existence, he never refused to admit that he was destined to remain on a lower, fully human one. Thus, while the ideal of full rationality, or wisdom, or philosophy, as it variously appears, represents for Petrarch man's highest aspirations, it carries with it an unattainability which makes it not fully suited to man's earthly state. It is from this point that rhetoric retains, after all, its value for Petrarch. For the orator, though he does not participate in the philosophic flight from man's common life towards true virtue, at least remains amid man's everyday cares, working imperfectly but with some gain to remind man of the call to virtue. If it be admitted that man's lot is to remain at the level of humanity, that his strivings to rise above it cannot succeed, then virtue for him must be defined in a fashion which accepts this fate. Conceived thus, the path to virtue is the way of the orator, not that of the philosopher.[90]

This valuation of rhetoric is in harmony with Petrarch's view that virtue is not of a single kind only, but exists in a hierarchy of degrees or stages. This division was neo-Platonic in origin, and Petrarch knew of it from Macrobius' comment on the part of Cicero's *Republic* known to the Middle Ages as "The Dream of Scipio." As Petrarch himself recounted,

According to this division, the political virtues hold the lowest grade; these may be attained by men who are occupied with everyday affairs—not all such men, but only those whose activities aim at virtue itself, and at the public good. . . . The "purgative virtues" occupy the next grade up, which doubtless adorn those who flee the city in search of leisure and true philosophy. These uproot from the soul the passions which the first sort of virtues had tempered. The third grade upwards is that of the virtues called those of the purified soul, whose task is to make the soul forget entirely about the passions which the political virtues had softened and the purgative virtues put to flight. These are the virtues of the perfect, who exist in I know not what place—but if there were any such, they would love solitude. . . . The fourth and highest place is given to the exemplary virtues, which are above men, and, as they say, exist only in the mind of God.[91]

---

[89] On the *dissidio* see Bosco, *op. cit.*, 83–100, and Gerosa, *op. cit.*, Part One.

[90] This conclusion will be seen to bear an interesting similarity to the discussion of Petrarch by Eugene F. Rice, Jr., *The Renaissance Idea of Wisdom* (Cambridge, 1958), 30–36. Rice's treatment of Petrarch is most interesting, and it is admirably concise, but at the cost of taking the *De remediis* to represent nearly the whole of Petrarch's thought about wisdom, and of never considering the central problem of the relation of wisdom to eloquence.

[91] *De vita solitaria*, 342.

Following this order, the flight to solitude of the *De vita solitaria*, while perhaps directed toward the third grade of virtue, was immediately concerned with the second. In fact, while he specifically restricts to God only the fourth stage of virtue, Petrarch seems to regard the third one as out of reach as well (the "perfect" exist in some place beyond his knowledge), so that only the first and second have any relevance to man as Petrarch knew him. But if we ask what Petrarch thought his own state to be, the answer must be that he thought himself only in the first stage, since the humanist never supposed himself capable of fully quieting the passions of his soul.

In other terms, Petrarch regarded the attempt to eradicate or exterminate man's passions as Stoic, and the more modest proposal that man's passions be tempered as Peripatetic. For himself, he did not find it possible to rise above Peripatetic virtue. [92] In the *Secret* Petrarch's present spiritual state is by no means described as wholly depraved; at one point the poet had the Saint compliment him on his sobriety and temperance. When Petrarch asserted that he did not think himself guilty of the vice of anger (a belief which appears elsewhere in Petrarch's writings, and which must strike the reader of the invectives as strange), Augustine replied that on this point "I shall allow that you limit yourself to the attenuation offered by the Peripatetics." In general, however, the Saint's plea was for Petrarch to rise above this level. As the poet remarked early in the dialogue: "You recall me to the teaching of the Stoics, far removed from popular opinion, and nearer to truth than to custom." [93]

Thus there seems to be a rough equivalence in Petrarch's mind between the division which separated the first two grades of Plotinian virtue, and that which distinguished Peripatetic and Stoic concepts of virtue. The first or Peripatetic grade was associated by Petrarch with common practice or life in the city (two notions which have the same value in this context), and in each case this was the level to which he found himself able to attain. The second or Stoic grade sought tranquillity of soul, a state which Petrarch yearned to achieve, but always admitted remained beyond his reach. Petrarch was led to acknowledge in this way the superiority of Stoicism and to admit that in comparison with it Peripateticism represented only an incomplete devotion to virtue. But Petrarch stopped well short of accepting Stoic doctrine. His failure to embrace fully what he considered to be "true philosophy" stemmed from what he recognized as the limitations of human nature. Man could not achieve the serenity, perfection, and consistency which the Stoics envisioned. Stoic teaching was acceptable to human reason, but it was not capable of reach-

[92] See Heitmann, *Fortuna und Virtus*, 256–7.
[93] *Secret*, 96, 98, 34.

ing the man of sense.[94] Thus it was not sufficient by itself. Peripateticism might be less consistent and less praiseworthy, but at least it was realistic and might be effective. It did not describe the highest virtue which rational man could conceive for himself, but it did describe a kind of virtue which everyday man could experience in himself and hope to see in others.

In other terms, Petrarch's 'Peripatetic virtue' may be regarded as a love of virtue, but not of virtue *only*. It is a love of virtue in the midst of a life of distractions from it, to which man also finds himself attracted. Petrarch's statements to this effect reflect the Peripatetic doctrine that virtue is the chief good, but that there are other goods as well, goods of the body, and of external circumstance. At the same time Petrarch was drawn to the Stoic ideal of a love of virtue only, which he (like Cicero) recognized as more noble and more consistent, but of which in the end he was not capable. This is only another expression of the *dissidio,* but now we see that it is Petrarch's recognition of man's total nature which is responsible for the "chaos of contradictions" found in the humanist's writings on moral philosophy. The contradictions are necessary to man as Petrarch regards him because man is both a Stoic and a Peripatetic, a being of reason and of sense, drawn to the love of virtue alone yet unable to devote himself fully to it. Moral philosophy must speak to both sides of human nature.

For the same reasons, "true moral philosophy" changed from time to time in Petrarch's eyes from an activity inspired by rhetoric to one wholly at odds with it. Even though Petrarch seems nowhere to have quoted Cicero's direct statements of the harmony between Peripateticism and oratory,[95] he must have felt the connection. The virtue he thought the Peripatetics urged, like the first grade of Plotinian virtue it resembled, was a kind of excellence man could achieve while living among his fellows and accepting the burdens of everyday life. This, as Petrarch observed in the *De vita solitaria,* was the career to which the orator, more than any other man, was characteristically committed. The terms in which Petrarch refused his final allegiance to Stoicism, when confronting it with Peripateticism, were the same as those in which he asserted the irrelevance of "philosophy" to man's condition. "No one is so given to wisdom that he does not, when he returns to the common human state, condescend also to public ways

---

[94] *Fam.* XXIII, 12, 11, quoted by Heitmann, 256–7. Ad summam sic me invenio, ut sepe ratio stoica, sensus *mihi* perypateticus semper sit.

[95] *De oratore* III, xix, 71; *De finibus,* V, iv, 10; IV, iii, 6. In general the discussion in Book IV of *De finibus* and the criticisms of Stoic moral philosophy made there give a clear indication of Cicero's understanding of the harmony of Peripatetic doctrine with everyday life and with the tasks of the orator.

of acting." [96] Clearly, the man who speaks to this "human state" is the orator. If it is the task of moral philosophy to urge men to virtue, then for most of man's life, the rôle of "true moral philosopher" will be filled by him.

Because the various orders of contradictions in Petrarch's works reflect what was for the humanist a basic aspect of human nature, we should not expect it to be possible to organize the conflicting statements according to any chronological pattern. There is in Petrarch's writings no consistent development from one attitude to the other. If we examine the succession of some of the writings we have been considering here, we discover a seesaw allegiance to the divergent ideals of moral philosophy we have encountered and a final admission that this inconstancy could not be overcome.

The first of his major works to be begun was the *De viris illustribus,* on which Petrarch first worked between 1338 and 1343.[97] This work had as a chief purpose to encourage the imitation of virtuous examples, a procedure which would be criticized later in the *De vita solitaria.* In 1342 and 1343 Petrarch produced the first version of the *Secret,* with its Augustinianism or Stoicism, and its statement that Cicero's eloquence did not have the lasting effect necessary to move Petrarch to virtue. Immediately afterwards, from 1343 to 1345, Petrarch was at work on the *Rerum memorandarum,* a book whose organization was based on Cicero's *De inventione,* which contained a general celebration of everyday life and common speech, and like the *De viris* embodied the notion of moral philosophy as the imitation of virtuous examples.[98] This work was never completed, but soon after he stopped work on it, Petrarch began in 1346 to write the *De vita solitaria,* the most anti-rhetorical of all his writings, in which the ideals of rhetoric and philosophy were plainly said to be at odds, and in which imitation as a principle of ethics was sharply criticized. Petrarch continued to work on this book for the next ten years. During that period he wrote the letter "De studio eloquentie," in which both groups of his ideas seem to appear: the insistence that only philosophy leads man to the high goal of consistency, and the affirmation that eloquent speech can move man to the path of a virtuous life. In the years immediately following the writing of this letter (1352–3),

---

[96] Cf. above, note 86.

[97] On the dates of Petrarch's Latin writings, see the critical notes in Petrarca, *Prose, op. cit.,* 1161–79, and the literature cited there; also the helpful list given by Bosco, *Petrarca,* 293–302. For the dates of the letters, see the invaluable manual of E. H. Wilkins, *The Prose Letters of Petrarch,* rev. ed. (New York, 1951), and the literature cited for each letter.

[98] See the Introduction to this treatise by G. Billanovich in his edition of it (Florence, 1943), esp. part X of the Introduction.

Petrarch wrote the books making up the *Invective Against a Certain Physician,* where the defense of rhetoric is a leading motif, but in which the definition of philosophy as a *cognitio mortis* also appears. From 1351 to 1353 Petrarch worked on a second version of the *De viris* (more Christian than the first, but no less inspired by the ideal of imitation). From 1354 to 1360 Petrarch was at work on the treatise called *On the Remedies for Both Kinds of Fortune (De remediis utriusque fortunae).* This treatise, Petrarch's most extensive writing on moral philosophy, is largely Stoic in conception and tone, but it contains both Peripatetic and Stoic maxims, as Klaus Heitmann has pointed out. Moreover, it contains what we may regard as an additional justification for the internal contradictions which characterize Petrarch's writings on ethics. This explanation takes the form of an exposition of Heraclitus, whose view of the world as continually in motion and characterized by the struggle of opposites was famous in Antiquity. The importance of Heraclitus for the *De remediis* has been pointed out by Marcel Françon.[99] With a multitude of examples Petrarch developed the notion that the struggle of opposing forces was a universal law of existence. It characterized all of human life, not only man's relations to other creatures and other men, but even to himself.

Let those who are called *physici* inquire with what contrary humors the body boils and is disturbed. But let each man ask only himself about the diverse and adverse influences by which the soul struggles with itself, and let each one respond how it is partly carried hither, partly thither by such varying and reversible impulses of the mind: never whole, never one, differing with itself, pulling itself to pieces.[100]

The similarity of this to the description of his own mind which Petrarch placed in the mouth of Augustine in the *Secret* some years earlier is close. Here, however, Petrarch has introduced the notion not only as a personal one, but as a description of all reality, of which man is only a part, and Petrarch an example.

Thus Petrarch provides us himself with a further buttressing of the conclusion of Umberto Bosco that the poet was *senza storia,*[101] without a history, if by "history" is meant any development in a consistent direction. There is a different kind of consistency in Petrarch, but it is the constant affirmation of his humanity, with all its inescapable contradictions. A recent suggestion that students seek to discover a clear chronological development in Petrarch's thought must be rejected. Hans Baron's warning against believing that the contradictory opinions pointed out by Klaus Heitmann "actually coexisted

[99] Marcel Françon, "Petrarch, Disciple of Heraclitus," *Speculum* XI (1936), 265–71.

[100] *De remediis,* quoted by Françon, 267.   [101] Bosco, 7.

in Petrarch's mind" [102] is uncalled for. Our analysis of the source of these contradictions in Petrarch's thought and his own affirmation of their existence demonstrate not only that they did coexist, but also that Petrarch thought their coexistence to be a necessary aspect of his moral philosophy, and an inescapable condition of his mind.

But the shifting attitudes we have identified here do not appear in Petrarch simply as the product of his own personality. The problem of accounting for the many contradictory statements in Petrarch's writings is, as Rodolfo de Mattei has pointed out in another context, "not referable to a type of man, but to a type of culture." [103] The fundamental importance of the tradition of classical rhetoric to Petrarch's cultural ideal has been pointed out before, but the complex and pervasive concern which the humanist—influenced by Cicero and Augustine—demonstrated for the problem of relating the cultivation of eloquence to the pursuit of wisdom has not. In this context Petrarch's final recognition that philosophic consistency remained beyond his grasp has a special meaning. He could never give himself fully to the life of solitude and silence he so often praised. His discussions of virtue and vice—looked at in an over-all view—reveal imperfections which Petrarch criticized from the point of view of Augustinian or Stoic philosophy, but which he associated with the inescapable conditions of ordinary human life. In the best possible sense, his was the moral philosophy of an orator.

Princeton University.

[102] Hans Baron, "The Evolution of Petrarch's Thought: Reflections on the State of Petrarch Studies," *BHR*, XXIV (1962), 12.

[103] Rodolfo de Mattei, *Il Sentimento Politico del Petrarca* (Florence, 1944), 19.

II

HOMO, HUMANUS, AND THE MEANINGS OF 'HUMANISM'

BY VITO R. GIUSTINIANI

'Humanism' is one of those terms the French call *faux amis*. Although it occurs in all modern languages in very similar forms, its meaning changes not only from continental European languages to English, as in most English borrowings from Latin or French,[1] but also from Italian and German to French. Even in the same language the meaning of 'humanism' can fluctuate. It could hardly be otherwise. 'Humanism' comes from *hūmanus* which comes from *hŏmo*. Although modern linguists may question whether Latin *ŏ* can change into *ū*, both terms have been regarded as related to one another since antiquity, which is what matters here.[2] Human nature is complex and contains conflicting tendencies, and cannot be defined completely or from a single point of view. A person consists not only of body and soul but the soul too, as Dante put it, has *"principalmente tre potenze"*[3]; or according to Plato, it is divided into three parts: the rational soul, the emotional soul, the appetitive soul.[4] In other words, very different faculties and powers are mingled in human nature: intelligence, passions, instincts. People have a natural desire for knowledge, as Aristotle affirms[5] and Cicero repeats,[6] but people also despise learning and prefer to have "a good time." They can be compassionate and self-denying, but also violent and ruthless. Lexically, all these aspects of our nature are entitled to be called 'human' and to reappear in the term which can be coined by adding to *humanus* the suffix *'ismus'* which, to make matters even worse, is again equivocal. Thus the meaning of 'humanism' has so many shades that to analyze all of them is hardly feasible.

[1] E.g., actual, appropriation, doctrine, emergence, emphasis, eventual, evidence, fabric, factory, philosophy, reclamation, &c. Such a list can be enlarged as one pleases.

[2] There is no other evidence of an *ŏ* changing into *ū* in Latin phonology. But cf. A. Walde-J. B. Hofmann, *Lateinisches etymologisches Wörterbuch*, vol. 1 (Heidelberg, 1938), 663: "daß *humanus* zu *homo* gehört, war dem lateinischen Sprachgefühl stets bewußt und sollte nicht bezweifelt werden".

[3] *Convivio* 3.2.1

[4] *Respublica* 439D; *Timaeus* 69E-70DE: *tò logistikón, thumós, tò epithumetikón*. Cf. V. R. Giustiniani, "Il Filelfo, l'interpretazione allegorica di Virgilio e la tripartizione platonica dell'anima" in *Umanesimo e Rinascimento*. Studi offerti a P. O. Kristeller (Firenze, 1980), 33-44.

[5] *Metaphysica* 980a22: "All men naturally desire knowledge"; Greek passages will be quoted from the translation given by the Loeb Classical Library.

[6] *De finibus* 5.18.48: "Tantus est igitur innatus in nobis cognitionis amor et scientiae, ut nemo dubitare possit, quin ad eas res hominum natura nullo emolumento invitata rapiatur."

1. Etymology of the Term 'Humanism' and of its Components

The common meaning of *humanus* as 'whatever is characteristic of human beings, proper to man' (which survives in modern derivative borrowings or 'loan translations' of the term and also in one notion of 'humanism') should not monopolize our inquiry. In Classical Latin *humanus* had also two more specific meanings, namely 'benevolent' and 'learned'. Whereas *humanus* as 'benevolent' is still current today, *humanus* as 'learned', though perhaps prevailing in classical times,[7] was lost in Middle Latin[8] and is no longer perceived in such words as English *human(e)*, French *humain*, Italian *umano* (direct derivatives) or German *menschlich*, Russian *čelovečeskij, čelovečnyj* (loan translations). In no modern language does a 'humane' person signify a 'learned' person. Nor can any famous scientist be nowadays addressed as a 'very humane person' though '*humanissime vir*' is the usual Latin way to address scholars.[9] It has been assumed that this meaning, as attested by Cicero, goes back to Isocrates[10] or perhaps to Aristippus,[11] the Cyrenaic philosopher whose works are lost to us, but were known to Cicero. No matter whether Cicero draws on Isocrates or on Aristippus or on neither; for him, speech is the essential hallmark of man.[12] It indicates the real difference between

[7] In the new *Oxford Latin Dictionary* (1968-82), s.v. 'learned' comes at the fifth place; 'kindly, considerate, merciful, indulgent' comes at the sixth. The *Thesaurus* too mentions 'eruditus, doctus, urbanus, politus' under II.B.IV.b; 'comis, mitis etc.' under II.B.IV.g.

[8] Although it cannot be ruled out that such a meaning possibly occurs even in Medieval Latin texts, I was not able to find any evidence of *humanus* as 'learned' either in Ducanges's or Niermeyer's or Blaise's Middle or Church Latin dictionaries. Nor does it occur in Dante's Latin writings, cf. E. K. Rand, E. H. Wilkins, A. C. White, *Dantis Alagherii operum Latinorum concordantiae* (Oxford, 1912).

[9] Of course, expressions like 'humane literature' and 'humane studies' are not unknown in English, cf. *Oxford English Dictionary*, s.v. 'humane' § 3; cf. also e.g. H. M. Jones, *American Humanism. Its Meaning for World Survival* (New York, 1957), 91-92 (World Perspectives 14). But here 'humane' clearly reflects the Latin use. Anyway it sounds rather as 'refined, polite' than as simply 'learned, erudite'.

[10] XV *De permutatione* 253-257; 294; III *Ad Nicoclem* 5-9: "It is the power of speech that distinguishes man from brute, Greek from barbarian, because speech has developed civilization". Cf. B. Snell, "Die Entdeckung der Menschlichkeit" (1947), in *Die Entdeckung des Geistes* (4th ed. Göttingen, 1975), 231-243; 317-319, with further references. Snell's assumptions triggered some criticism, cf. K. Büchner, "Humanum und humanitas in der römischen Welt" (1951), in *Studien zur römischen Literatur*, vol. 5 (Wiesbaden, 1965), 47-65 (p. 48n). (Books and articles are quoted after their last print, but also with the year of their first publication).

[11] Diogenes Laertius, *Vitae philosophorum*, 2.70: "It is better [Aristippus] said, to be a beggar than to be uneducated: the one needs money, the other needs to be humanized." Cf. Snell, above, note 10. It seems that Aristippus equates *anthropismós* with 'education', but cf. below, note 76.

[12] *De oratore* 1.8.31-33: "Hoc enim uno praestamus vel maxime feris, quod colloquimur inter nos et quod exprimere dicendo sensa possumus"; *De inventione* 1.4.5: "Ac mihi quidem videntur homines ... hac re maxime bestiis praestare quod loqui possunt." Cf. H. M. Hubbel, *The influence of Isocrates on Cicero, Dionysius and Aristeides.* Diss. Yale 1913.

man and animal and assures the progress of civilization. Speech is human *par excellence,* and has a continuous impact on state and society[13]; the *litterae* (by metonymy 'writings') are the depository and the vehicle of speech, or the foundation of learning. Therefore they are called *humanae* (otherwise *litterae* would signify 'correspondence letter' or simply 'alphabet'). In other words, in antiquity *humanus* defined human nature downwards towards the animal,[14] both in character and more specifically in mind, while in the Middle Ages it rather mattered to define human nature upwards, towards God. Anyway, whether rooted in a Greek premise or not,[15] 'learned' is a substantial component of Classical Latin and not of Middle Latin *humanus* and its modern derivatives. This is the first statement to be made when examining the various meanings of 'humanism'.

As for *-is-mos,* this is a Greek suffix, resulting from the combination of the nominal suffix *-mos* with the verbal suffix *-iz-*[16]: *-mos* marks the *nomina actionis* and corresponds to Latin *-mentum* or *-io* (*-tio*); *is-mos* originally marked the *nomina actionis* derived from *-izo* verbs. It was particularly frequent in the Hellenistic-Roman epoch, when through the Latin Bible translations (*Itala* and *Vulgata*) it found its way into Christian Latin (*baptismus* < *baptizo* 'immersio'; *catechismus, exorcismus*). It occurs in Romance languages from their very beginnings, either in learned form (Fr.-*isme;* It., Sp. *-ismo*)[17] or in vernacular form (It. *cristianesmo/cristianesimo; battésimo; Fr. baptême*). Today it is no less frequent in English,[18] German, and Russian.

Its functions extended more and more beyond the original area of *nomina actionis* to the following uses: (1) to form collective nouns, e.g. English *mechanism* 'set of mechanical parts'; *organism* 'all organs of a body'; *vocalism* 'vowel system of a language' etc.; cf. also Italian *ruotismo* 'gear', Milanese *sbragalismo* 'din, uproar, many noises mixed together'

[13] *De oratore* 1.8.31: "Quid enim est tam admirabile . . . quam populi motus . . . unius oratione converti?"

[14] Cf. G. Paparelli, *Feritas, humanitas, divinitas* (Firenze-Messina, 1960), esp. Chap. 4.

[15] Greek adjectives related to 'man' (*anthrópeios, anthropikós, anthrópinos*) do not mean 'learned'; cf. V. R. Giustiniani, "Umanesimo: la parola e la cosa", in *Studia humanitatis.* Festschrift E. Grassi (Munich, 1973), 23-30 (p. 29n). Cf. also S. Prete, '*Humanus*' *nella letteratura arcaica latina* (Milan, 1948) (Collezione filologica diretta da G. B. Pighi, B/8).

[16] Cf. P. Chantraine, *La formation des noms en grec ancien* (Paris, 1933), 138, 147; E. Schwyzer. *Griechische Grammatik,* Vol. 1 (Munich, 1959), 491 (Handbuch der Altertumswissenschaft 2/1/1); F. Blass-A. Debrunner, *Grammatik des neutestam. Griechisch* (Göttingen, 1943), 52; cf. also W. Rüegg, *Cicero und der Humanismus* (Zürich, 1946), 1-6.

[17] Cf. C. Nyrop, *Grammaire historique de la langue française,* Vol. 3, 4th ed., rpt. (Genève, 1979), 161; G. Rohlfs, *Historische Grammatik der italienischen Sprache,* Vol. 3 (Bern, 1954), § 1123.

[18] Cf. H. Marchand, *The Categories and Types of Present-day English Word Formation,* 2nd ed. (Munich, 1969), 306-307.

and also such collectives as *rheumatism,* etc.; (2) to form nouns denoting not a status or result, but a trend or way of behaving, e.g. *favoritism, nepotism,* 'trends to favor someone, to protect one's relatives,' etc.; (3) denoting a trend on a practical level is not far from denoting an ideology or philosophy on a theoretical level, the essence of an issue.[19] Thus the boundless field of political, religious, and social denominations was opened to adopt the old suffix of baptism and applied to more and more terms like *socialism, communism, materialism, Catholicism, Protestantism* (adj. + *ism*), or *fascism, falangism, racism* (noun + *ism*), or *Kantism, Marxism, Stalinism, Hitlerism,* etc. (proper name + *ism*). Perhaps such terms as *Latinism, Gallicism,* can also be referred to this category by synecdoche or *pars pro toto.*

In such new terms the suffix *-ism* is neither the mark of a *nomen actionis* nor does it form a collective noun or denote a trend, for it denotes a way of thinking and of acting. Of course, all these classes of nouns, the close and static ones like *baptism,* and the open, developing ones like *socialism* are not water-tight compartments, they transform into one another in ways worth further study. I have simply pointed out here the possibilities and functions this suffix has. It seems to be a very creative one in every language.

Together with *-ismos* another Greek suffix, *-is-tes* or *-ista,* also a union of verbal *-iz-* with nominal *-tes*[20] (the latter parallel to Latin *-tor*) had filtered into Christian Latin where it was to play an important role in forming new *nomina actoris: baptista* 'immersor'; *evangelista; exorcista; psalmista,* etc. This suffix proved from the very beginning to be almost as creative as *-ismos.* In modern languages, especially in English, it denotes most professions (industrialist, optometrist, *et al.*). *Nomen actoris* and *nomen actionis* were fated to join forces and to form symmetrical *-ista / -ismus* pairs semantically linked to an *-izo* verb: *baptizo / baptismus / baptista; exorcizo / exorcismus / exorcista,* etc. However, this method of word formation never proved in either ancient or modern times to be as regular and, as it were, automatic as others are. Very soon *-izo / -ismus- / ista* began to develop independently from one another. Many nouns of the one class lack their corresponding nouns in the other, e.g. *evangelizo / evangelista,* but, at least in Latin, no *evangelismus; artist,* but no *artizo* or *artism; violinist; organism; vocalism* (*organizo, organist, vocalist* mean something else). Sometimes both terms exist separately, e.g. *Latinism / Latinist; mechanism / mechanist.* Sometimes too the *-ista* noun prompted the creation of the corresponding *-ismus* noun, which then usually denotes

---

- [19] Compare Heidegger's statement below, note 37.
  [20] Cf. Chantraine, *op. cit.,* 320; Nyrop, *op. cit.,* 164, 166; Rohlfs, *op. cit.,* § 1126; Marchand, *op. cit.,* 308-310. Cf. also G. Billanovich, "Auctorista, humanista, orator" in *Studi in onore di A. Schiaffini* (=Rivista di cultura classica e medievale 7, 1-3), 1965, 143-163 (p. 143-146).

an activity common to many people, e.g. *lobbyist / lobbyism; journalist / journalism.*[21] This is the way *humanist* fathered *humanism,* and this is the second principle to be noted when examining the different meanings of 'humanism'. Humanist in its turn reflects *humanus* in the Classical Latin meaning of 'learned'. This meaning is unfortunately not familiar today to most people writing about humanism. Confusion inevitably arises with the other sense of humanism reflecting the more common meaning of 'generally pertaining to man' and continuously growing in the effort to understand 'humanism' in a single way.

2. *Humanism from 'humanist' as the study of classical antiquity*

During the 15th century 'humanista' was at the Italian universities or *studi* the teacher of those subjects which right then had recovered their ancient name of *humanae litterae,*[22] which denoted the resurgent classical culture, today called 'classical heritage', with no particular emphasis on all the values entailed by the Latin term *humanus* in its broadest sense. *Humanae litterae* were what classical culture had been, viz. learning, but learning for learning's sake, *otium,* remaining within the limits of human knowledge, aimed at neither transcendence nor practical purposes. Only occasionally the 'humanista' taught philosophy also, and then only moral philosophy.[23] His teaching did not include the Bible for two reasons: it was *litterae divinae,* i.e. revelation and not learning, and it did not pertain to the classical heritage. Nor did the 'humanista' teach law or medicine. Thus *humanae litterae* were tantamount to what is now called literature, more precisely profane literature and grammar, as the 'legista' taught civil law, and the 'canonista' taught canon law. The term developed from the first term of *humanae litterae* as later *literate, man of letters* or *homme de lettres,* developed from the second term. The domain of the 'humanista' was Latin and Greek, since in the fifteenth-century view there was no other kind of grammar or of literature considered worth studying at universities.

The Italian or Latin term *humanista* quite soon found its way into

---

[21] Compare also It. *ciclista > ciclismo; protagonista > protagonismo,* a term recently coined by the *Giornale* (1979) to denote those judges who in Italy at present indulge in self-importance, somehow playing in trials the part of protagonists on the stage. (Asterisks are used in linguistics to mark a reconstructed word lacking verifiable evidence).

[22] Cf. the basic study by P. O. Kristeller, "Humanism and scholasticism in the Italian Renaissance" (1945), in *Renaissance Thought,* Vol. 1 (New York, 1951), 92-119 (p. 111) (Harper Torchbooks); A. Campana, "The Origin of the Word 'Humanist' " in *Journal of the Warburg and Courtauld Institutes,* 3 (1946), 60-73; H. Rüdiger, "Die Ausdrücke humanista, studia humanitatis, humanistisch", in *Geschichte der Textüberlieferung,* Vol. 1 (Zürich, 1961), 525-526; cf. Billanovich and Rüegg, *op. cit.*

[23] Kristeller, *op. cit.,* 109.

the German speaking world[24] where *Humanist,* while keeping its specific Italian meaning, later gave birth to further derivatives, such as *humanistisch* for those schools which later were to be called *humanistische Gymnasien,* with Latin and Greek as the main subjects of teaching (1784).[25] Finally *Humanismus* was introduced to denote 'classical education' in general (1808)[26] and still later for the epoch and the achievements of the Italian humanists of the fifteenth century (1841).[27] This is to say that 'humanism' for 'classical learning' appeared first in Germany, where it was once and for all sanctioned in this meaning by Georg Voigt (1859).[28] Still later, its use was extended to a second rebirth of classical studies in Germany, with a strong emphasis on Greece at the expense of Rome, during the time of Winckelmann, Goethe, Schiller, and others

[24] *Epistolae obscurorum virorum,* hrsgg. von A. Bömer 1.7, Vol. 2 (Heidelberg, 1924), 17: Magister Petrus Hafenmusius magistro Ortvino Gratio ". . . . et isti humanistae nunc vexant me cum suo novo Latino, et annihilant illos veteres libros, Alexandrum, Remigium, Ioannem de Garlandia, Cornutum, Composita verborum, Epistolare magistri Pauli Niavis. . ."

[25] *Humanistische Schulen* occurs in Fr. Nicolai, *Beschreibung einer Reise durch Deutschland und die Schweiz,* Vol. 4 (Berlin-Stettin, 1784), 677; *humanistische Studien* occurs in Fr. Gedicke, *Gesammelte Schulschriften,* vol. 1. Berlin 1789, 24. Cf. H. Schulz, *Deutsches Fremdwörterbuch,* vol. 1. Straßburg 1913, 274. Rüdiger, cit., 526 quotes *humanistische Commissionen* (concerning classical studies) from a letter of Winckelmann (Nov. 27th, 1765), in: *Briefe,* hrsgg. von W. Rehm, vol. 3. Berlin 1956, 139.

[26] Fr. I. Niethammer, *Der Streit des Humanismus und Philanthropismus in der Theorie des Erziehungsunterrichts unserer Zeit* (Jena, 1808); Niethammer, a Bavarian teacher, was a friend of Hegel. *Humanismus* appears also in *Brockhaus Konversationslexicon,* Vol. 4, 1815, 835, as a "pädagogisches System, das alle Bildung auf die Erlernung der alten Sprachen baut". Later on the term was used by F. W. Klumpp, *Die gelehrten Schulen nach den Grundsätzen des wahren Humanismus und den Anforderungen der Zeit* (2 vols., Stuttgart, 1829-30). Klumpp's assumptions were countered by an anonymous writer (actually H. Ch. W. Sigwart) with the pamphlet *Bemerkungen zu Herrn Prof. Klumpps Schrift* . . . . (Tübingen, 1829). A further reply (by G. Schwab) was printed in *Blätter für literarische Unterhaltung* (Leipzig, 1830).

[27] K. Hagen, *Deutschlands literarische und religiöse Verhältnisse im Reformationszeitalter* (3 vols., Erlangen, 1841), e.g., Vol. I, 58, 59, 79, 132; Vol. II, 3.

[28] G. Voigt, *Die Wiederbelebung des classischen Alterthums, oder das erste Jahrhundert des Humanismus* (1859), 3rd ed. (1893) besorgt von M. Lehnerd, 2 vols. Berlin 1960 (reprint). Research concerning the history of the German term is plentyful, cf. K. Brandi, "Das Werden der Renaissance" (1908), in: *Ausgewählte Aufsätze.* Oldenburg-Berlin 1938, 279-304 (p. 304 note by W. Brecht); E. Heyfelder, "Die Ausdrücke 'Renaissance' und 'Humanismus' ", in: *Deutsche Literaturzeitung* 34 (Sept. 1913), cols. 2245-2250; E. König, " 'Studia humanitatis' und verwandte Ausdrücke bei den deutschen Frühhumanisten", in: *Festschrift J. Schlecht.* München-Freising 1917, 202-207. Cf. also Billanovich, Campana, Rüdiger, Rüegg, Snell cit. In the German discussion the term was better and better defined e.g. by K. Burdach, *Reformation, Renaissance, Humanismus* (1914, 2nd ed. 1926, Darmstadt 1978 (reprint); R. Wolkan, "Über den Ursprung des Humanismus", in: *Zeitschrift für die österreichischen Gymnasien* 67 (1916), 241-268; R. Newald, "Humanitas, Humanismus, Humanität" (1947), in: *Probleme und Gestalten des deutschen Humanismus.* Berlin 1963, 1-66. Cf. also H. Oppermann (ed.), *Humanismus.* Darmstadt 1970 (Wege der Forschung 17); C. Vasoli (ed.), *Umanesimo e Rinascimento* (Palermo, 1969), (Storia della critica 7).

(German *Neuhumanismus*).[29] During the Weimar Republik a third Humanismus was looming on the German academic horizon,[30] but it was soon stunted by Hitler's seizure of power and the ensuing World War II.

From Germany this specific meaning of 'humanism' spread all over Europe. Italy in particular hastened to espouse this term she especially needed, as soon as Voigt's masterwork was translated.[31] *Umanesimo* became the current term for the country's literary production in Latin during the fifteenth century, today a favorite and fruitful field of research. Attempts to catch its spirit and character followed one another, until Eugenio Garin penetratingly defined it as a confrontation of the present with the past, the ascertainment that the ancient world is bygone and not to be judged by modern standards.[32] In England the term 'humanism' had already been thriving during previous times in theological and philosophical use.[33] As 'study of the Greek and Roman classics' it seems to have been introduced into English in the wake of German pedagogical discussions about *humanistische Gymnasien* and classical education by the beginning of the nineteenth century (1836).[34] No wonder that this second meaning never prevailed and the others reappeared soon, as will be shown below. In America Paul O. Kristeller, the very distinguished scholar on the Italian Renaissance, defines 'humanism' more specifically as the fifteenth-century continuation and development of the medieval grammatical and rhetorical heritage improved by a better acquaintance with classical style and literature.[35]

---

[29] Cf. H. Rüdiger, *Wesen und Wandlungen des Humanismus* (Hamburg, 1937), Chap. 7 "J. J. Winckelmann"; Chap. 8 "W. von Humboldt und der Neuhumanismus".

[30] W. Jaeger, *Antike und Humanismus* (Leipzig, 1925).

[31] G. Voigt, *Il risorgimento dell'antichità classica, ovvero il primo secolo dell'umanismo*, trad. di D. Valbusa, 2 vols. Firenze 1888-89.

[32] E. Garin, *L'umanesimo italiano* (Bari, 1952), Introd. § 6 "Umanesimo e antichità classica".

[33] E.g. for 'belief in the mere humanity of Christ', 'devotion to human interests', 'religion of humanity'; cf. *Oxford English Dictionary*, s.v.

[34] In a book review published in the *Edinburgh Review* 62 (Jan. 1836), 421n, W. Hamilton translated the title of Klumpp's work (see above, note 26) as *Learned schools according to the principles of genuine humanism* . . . . This is probably the first time 'humanism' appeared in English as a literary term; cf. *Oxford English Dictionary*, s.v. Hamilton's book review was later reprinted in his *Discussions on Philosophy and Literature* (New York, 1858), (270). Forty years later J. A. Symonds, *Renaissance in Italy*, Vol. 2: "Revival of Learning" (London, 1877), 71n., still observed: "The word humanism has a German sound and is in fact modern".

[35] Kristeller, *op. cit.*, 100: "The humanists continued the medieval tradition in these fields, as represented, for example, by the *ars dictaminis* and the *ars arrengandi*, but they gave it a new direction toward classical standards and classical studies, possibly under the impact of influences received from France after the middle of the thirteenth century"; cf. also 95: "By humanism we mean merely the general tendency of the age to attach the greatest importance to classical studies, and to consider classical antiquity as the

In France, however, *humanisme* expanded its meaning to include concern for literary tradition in general and the study of the great authors of the past, no matter in which epoch and which authors are meant, whether those of Greece and Rome, or those of the most different cultures and origins. In particular the French like to include in their notion of humanism their medieval Latin literature as evidence of the continuity of the Roman heritage in France during the Middle Ages, or rather of the literary superiority the Carolingian Renaissance bestowed upon France so that she became for some time a sort of *fille ainée* of European culture also.[36] But the French use of *humanisme* can include also Byzantine, Arab, Persian, Indian, and Chinese authors, as shown in the programs of the Association Guillaume Budé, the deserving sponsor of classical culture in France and Europe, which provides editions of medieval and oriental authors in addition to its excellent editions of Greek and Latin classics.

Is such an extension of the term advisable? Probably not, and for many reasons. First, *humanus* was reinstated in its classical Latin meaning of 'learned' only during the *Quattrocento,* the Italian fifteenth century, in the course of that renewal of Latin grammar and vocabulary which the *humanistae* undertook in deliberate opposition to the Middle Ages, when *humanus* was rather regarded as opposite to *divinus* and hardly meant 'erudite'; second, if there is no doubt that in Roman times *humanus* meant 'erudite' and was applied to literature, it obviously did not include the oriental heritage, much less medieval literature yet to come; third, and last but not least, modern research is more and more split up into specific branches and more and more specific terms are needed to cope with new particular fields. If a term like 'humanism' has been generally accepted and is widely used to denote an historically and culturally defined subject like the culture of the Italian Quattrocento, there is no point in making out of it an all-purpose word.

3. *Humanism as a Philosophy of Homo*

At the same time that humanism was coined from humanist, i.e. from *humanus* as 'learned' to denote a literary trend, another humanism was coined directly from *humanus* as 'generally pertaining to man' to denote a philosophy of man, the same way as *socialism* developed from social,

---

common standard and model by which to guide all cultural activities." This meaning, however current among scholars specializing in humanities (e.g. M. P. Gilmore, *The World of Humanism 1453-1517* [New York, 1952] is in America far less popular than the other one, which will be examined further below.

[36] E.g. *Quelques aspects de l'humanisme médiéval* (Paris, 1943); P. Renucci, *L'aventure de l'humanisme européen au Moyen-Age* (Paris, 1953); cf. also F. Robert, *L'humanisme. Essai de définition* (Paris, 1946); cf. esp. A. Buck, "Gab es einen mittelalterlichen Humanismus?" (1963), in *Die humanistische Tradition in der Romania* (Bad Homburg, 1968), 36-56.

communist from *common,* etc.[37] If literary humanism can be more or less exactly defined, whether referred to the Italian *Quattrocento* or to some other period, it is all the more difficult to define philosophical humanism. The term was doomed to assume as many different shapes as the points of view from which *homo* can be considered, either as man really is with all his shortcomings or as the ideal of perfection he is assumed to reach potentially.

'Humanism' as a philosophical term seems to have appeared first in France in the second half of the eighteenth century, about the same time as it appeared in Germany in its other meaning.[38] Later on, this use of *Humanismus* appeared in Germany too. About 1840 it occurs in some writings of Arnold Ruge (1802-80); he also used *human* instead of *menschlich*[39] and in some quotations of Karl Marx which however were discovered only in 1932 and cannot have contributed to the German fortunes of the term.[40] The whole philosophy of Ludwig Feuerbach (1804-

---

[37] Cf. M. Heidegger, "Brief über den Humanismus" (an J. Beaufret, Autumn 1946), in *Gesamtausgabe,* Vol. 9 (Frankfurt, 1976), 313-364, 345): "Das *humanum* deutet im Wort auf die *humanitas,* das Wesen des Menschen. Der *-ismus* deutet darauf, daß das Wesen des Menschen als wesentlich genommen sein möchte". In other words, Heidegger understands humanism as a trend towards a complete realization of man's being, but in a particular way, as will be explained below. Heidegger's *Brief* is also available in French: *Lettre sur l'humanisme.* Texte allemand traduit et présenté par R. Munier (Paris, 1964).

[38] One of the earliest examples occurs in the French review *Ephémérides du citoyen, ou Bibliothèque raisonnée des sciences morales et politiques* 16/1 (1765) 247: L'amour général de l'humanité ... vertu qui n'a point de nom parmi nous et que nous oserions appeler 'humanisme', puisqu'enfin il est temps de créer un mot pour une chose si belle et nécessaire;. Cf. F. Brunot, *Histoire de la langue française,* Vol. 6 (Paris, 1966), 119. 'Humanisme' occurs also in Proudhon's writings as 'culte, déification de l'humanité' and in Renan's "L'avenir de la science" (1848-49; publ. 1890), in *Oeuvres complètes,* Vol. 3 (Paris, 1949), 809: "Ma conviction intime est que la religion de l'avenir sera le pur humanisme". Cf. W. von Wartburg, *Französisches etymologisches Wörterbuch,* Vol. 4 (Basel, 1951), 509.

[39] Cf. A. Ruge's review of W. Heinse's works in *Hallische Jahrbücher,* 3rd Year (31.8.1840), col. 1671: "Seine Weltlichkeit, seine Aufgeklärtheit, seinen Humanismus (und alle zusammen werden ihm Namen eines Begriffes) findet nun der Genius in der eleganten Parrhesie, womit er im griechischen Costume seines Herzens Lust und Empfindung darstellt." Cf. also Ruge's review of E. M. Arndt's *Erinnerungen aus dem äußeren Leben,* ibid. (8.10.1840), col. 1936: "Es sind schon früher Schritte genug in Preußen geschehen, um den Grad des Humanismus, die definitive und totale Verwirklichung des Christenthums, die bis jetzt in Europa bloß eine hohle Redensart war, in Amerika aber bewährte Existenz für sich hat, auch bei uns ins Leben zu rufem." Cf. furthermore, A. Ruge, *Der Patriotismus* (1844), edited by P. Wende (Frankfurt a.M., 1968), (Sammlung Insel), esp. 47, 85; A. Ruge, *Die Loge des Humanismus* (Leipzig, 1851); K. Fischer (=Frank), "A. Ruge und der Humanismus", in *Wigands Epigonen* 4 (1847); M. Heß, *Die letzten Philosophen* (1847), edited by A. Cornu und W. Mönke (Berlin, 1961), esp. 390-391, with references to M. Stirner, *Der Einzige und sein Eigenthum* (1844). Ruge's dates: 1802-1880.

[40] E.g., "Die heilige Familie" (1844-45), in *Die Frühschriften,* edited by S. Landshut (Stuttgart, 1971), (209), 317-338 (p. 326): "Wie aber Feuerbach auf theoretischem Gebiete,

72), who was at first like the young Marx a Hegelian of the left wing, with his emphasis on the humane and reduction of the devine to the humane, was termed "humanism' or 'humanistic realism'. Not much later *umanismo* appeared as philosophical term in Italy too, well before it was reserved for the *Quattrocentro*.[41] But it is in the wake of Marxist ideology that humanism was to become next to what can be called a consistent, though utopian and simplistic philosophy. In the Marxist view, humanism is human fulfillment and perfection, tantamount to happiness, the natural aspiration of all who are thwarted from achieving it by economic need and workers' exploitation, the inherent evils of all societies from their beginnings. By removing these obstacles, communism claims to achieve mankind's moral advancement,[42] but this is not possible without a thorough revolution both in society and in the individual, enhancing and pursuing the truly humane.[43] Thus humanism can be considered the last goal and stage of communism, the realization of ultimate moral progress. It is not clear how Marxism can explain all the high creative performances in history due to those who have suffered much economic want and exploitation (it suffices to think of Dante and

---

stellte der französische und englische Kommunismus auf praktischem Gebiete den mit dem Humanismus zusammenfallenden Materialismus dar." A few more quotations in "National-ökonomie und Philosophie" (1844), *ibid.*, 225-316, esp. 281.

[41] Extensive research on this subject has yet to be done. I can only avail myself of some notes I took at random, e.g., G. Ferrari, *La federazione repubblicana* (Londra [actually Capolago], 1851) Chap. 9: "Accusando il formalismo, in Alemagna si prende il nome di umanisti ed in Francia quello di socialisti"; F. DeSanctis, "Zola e l'Assommoir" (1879), in *Saggi critici*, Vol 3 (Bari, 1963), 277-299 (p. 287): "L'umanesimo apparve fin dal tempo che nella commedia di Terenzio un attore diceva: homo sum, humani nihil a me alienum puto" cf. below, note 50). Although familiar with German culture and presumably also with Voigt's *Wiederbelebung*, DeSanctis does not use 'humanism' in the literary sense. G. Curti, *Umanismo e realismo* (Lugano, 1857) opposes 'umanismo' (literary education at high schools) to 'realismo (education based on technics, as in the German Realschulen).

[42] Cf. *Filosofskaja Enciklopedija*, Vol. I (Moskow, 1960), 414, s.v. 'Socialistiĉeskij gumanizm': "Marxism is the only scientific way to understand man, the prerequisites for his actual liberation and the perspectives of development he has, because Marxism understands man both in his concreteness and within his historical context. It defines man's existence as the result of social conditions. The practical solutions of all contradictions inherent in the individual and in society, as well as the contradictions between liberty and individual development is made possible by society in its whole. Society grants the full well-being and the free, perfect development of all its members (cf. V. I. Lenin, *Works*, Russian ed., Vol. 6, 37)". The article goes on extolling the achievements made in the USSR in favor of the working class. On socialist humanism cf. E. Fromm (ed.), *Socialist Humanism. An International Symposium* (Garden City, 1966) G.S. Sher (ed.), *Marxist Humanism and Praxis* (Buffalo, 1978)—twelve papers contributed by Yougoslav writers, but not from the orthodox Yougoslav stance.

[43] Lenin, *ibid.*, 70: "To this purpose masses must change. This is possible only in the frame of a concrete movement, namely through a revolution. The whole old husk must be thrown away, so that a new society can arise."

Cervantes) and the low creative output in those societies in which, as in the present Western world, economic want and exploitation have been reduced.

Although in Germany since Voigt's days *Humanismus* kept being used principally as a literary and historical term and the scattered attempts made by some Hegelians to establish under this name a new moral philosophy did not materialize and were soon forgotten, humanism staged in German philosophy a resounding come-back with Martin Heidegger's (1889-1976) *Letter on Humanism.*[44] It remains on the field of pure speculative theory. To the question his French follower J. Beaufret had asked him: "comment redonner un sense au mot humanisme," Heidegger answers first by enunciating his own definition of man. Basically man 'is' insofar as he 'exists', namely *sistit-ex,* emerges into 'being' (*das Sein,* absolute being, different from *das Seiende,* a distinction difficult to render in English), outside of which he originally dwells. This happens when man steps out of nature. Man actualizes himself when he is *geworfen* (thrown) into the *Lichtung* (clearing) of 'being' and starts upholding its truth, becomes its *Hirt* (shepherd). Man and 'being' need one another: there is no man without 'being' and no 'being' without man.

Heidegger's thought as condensed here may appear difficult and absurd, but it can be more easily understood in the light of Heidegger's next affirmation that "die Sprache ist das Haus des Seins" ('being' dwells in the home of language), inasmuch as language gives the individual the possibility of thinking, thinking transcends the individual and enables him to assimilate the wealth of concepts, reactions, desires, and feelings which make the man and are independent of the individual. Language gives man his individuality (an intuition going back to Isocrates and Cicero, as indicated above), once he is admitted to it. Thus Heidegger thinks *anfänglich* (rethinks) the concept of *exsistentia* and transforms its traditional use to the point that he refuses to call his philosophy 'existentialism'. *Sisto* means originally 'to cause to stand'[45] and has had many derivatives: *adsisto, consisto, insisto, persisto, resisto,* and others. Maybe Heidegger resorted to *ex-sisto* because it sounds familiar, but it does not make Heidegger's concepts familiar to the reader. More than an 'existing' in the modern sense Heidegger intends to express the continual emergence or escape from our natural status into the truth of 'being'. 'Existing' from nature (going out, jumping out) and entering into 'being' safeguards one's own 'truth' as individual in a world of one's own, but as ingredient or substantial constituent of 'being'. Heidegger's humanism differs from

[44] See above, note 37.
[45] *Sisto* is a reduplicative form of *sto,* Gr. *si-stemi* > *hístemi* (compare *gen-* > *gi-gno; si* > *siso* > *sero,* Gr. *sí-semi* > *hiemi*). Such forms are especially frequent in Greek. The *Oxford Latin Dictionary,* s.v., adduces at the third place 'to come into being, emerge, arise.'

Marx's and from other philosophies of man, insofar as these consider man in himself, albeit conditioned by society or other factors. For Heidegger on the contrary, every humanism which conceives man other than belonging to 'being' makes him non-human: only that humanism is true, which sees man as a function of 'being'. This is independent of man, who keeps its truth. Thus Heidegger's final conclusion is that it is not correct to speak about humanism in general, a term which philosophically lacks all meaning and is something like a "lucus a non lucendo".[46]

Parallel to the German elaboration of a philosophical humanism, another one took place in the Anglo-Saxon world, especially in America, where it fanned out in very different directions.[47] To begin with the last in time but the most outspoken and popular one, its program was formulated after a long period of gestation in the *Humanist Manifesto* of 1933, signed by 34 leading personalities of American culture of that time, including John Dewey (1859-1952).[48] An attempt to sum up and to develop systematically the ideas there summarily expressed was made in 1949 by Corliss Lamont (born 1902).[49] The *Humanist Manifesto* (somewhat reminiscent in its title of Marx's *Kommunistisches Manifest* of 1848) is an effort to replace traditional religious beliefs by stalwart confidence in our capability to achieve moral perfection and happiness along the lines and within the limits of our earthly nature. The 15 articles of the *Manifesto* are a blend of old tenets of 18th-century Enlightenment and worship of reason, of utilitarianism à la Bentham, of positivism and Darwinism, of 19th-century absolute faith in the power of science and so on, not without a considerable touch of American pragmatism. For the *Manifesto* "the universe is self-existing and not created" (§ 1); "religion consists of those actions, purposes, and experiences which are humanly significant. Nothing human is alien to the religious. It includes labor, art, science, philosophy, love, friendship, recreation—all that is in its degree expressive and intelligently satisfying human living" (§ 7). A person's relation to society is no less vaguely outlined: "the humanist finds his religious emotions expressed in a heightened sense of personal

[46] Heidegger, op. cit., 345: Das Wesen des Menschen ist für die Wahrheit des Seins wesentlich, so zwar, daß es demzufolge gerade nicht auf den Menschen, lediglich als solchen, ankommt. Wir denken so einen 'Humanismus' seltsamer Art. Das Wort ergibt einen Titel, der ein "lucus a non lucendo" ist." Cf. J. Jaeger, *Heidegger und die Sprache* (Berne-München, 1971).

[47] W. H. Werkmeister, *A History of Philosophical Ideas in America* (New York, 1949), 579-583; W. G. Muelder, L. Sears, A. V. Schlabach, *The Development of American Philosophy,* 2nd. ed. (Cambridge, Mass. 1960).

[48] First appeared in *The New Humanist* 6/3 (1953). *The New Humanist* was published in Chicago from 1928 to 1938. The *Manifesto* was reprinted in O. L. Reiser, *Humanism and New World Ideals* (Yellow Springs, Ohio, 1933), and in C. Lamont, *The Philosophy of Humanism* (1949, New York, 1965) as appendix. The 6th edition of Lamont's book (1982) reflects the polemics stirred in the USA by the Humanist Movement and contains a second *Humanist Manifesto* (first published in *The Humanist,* 1973).

[49] See above, note 48. Our references are made to the 1965 edition.

life and in a co-operative effort to promote social well-being" (§ 9); and "the goal of humanism is a free and universal society in which people voluntarily and intelligently co-operate for the common good" (§ 14).

The all-out negation of everything supernatural and transcendental makes this *Manifesto* opposed to what Revelation preaches. Its emphasis on the individual and not on society, the acceptance of people as they are, voluntarily striving by self-perfectibility towards the establishment of a better society to be achieved without revolution, opposed it to Marxism. Compared with traditional faiths, it lacks the appeal exerted by the hope in a superior justice and in a better future life. Compared with Marxism, it lacks every theoretical consistency: such terms as 'intelligent', 'intelligently satisfying', 'humanly relevant' do not stand a thorough philosophical examination any better than Terence's famous maxim "homo sum, humani nil a me alienum puto"[50] or Richard Wagner's 'Rein-Menschliches', and are insufficient to define ideals and the way to pursue them. Although avowedly atheistic, the *Manifesto* seems to accept traditional religions insofar as "they reconstitute their institutions, ritualistic forms, ecclesiastical methods and communal activities as rapidly as experience allows, in order to function effectively in the modern world" (§ 13). On the whole, the humanist *Manifesto* claims to be rather a new brand of faith than a philosophy of man. It ranges along the lines of American religious movements. Its church, if such a word can be used here, is the American Humanist Association[51] with its branch in Britain (British Humanist Association). The comfortable approach to the *Manifesto*'s ideas, the possibility of everybody making the most of them, the permissiveness to which they eventually may lead, explain the popularity of the American Humanist Association and the meaning 'humanism' has acquired as simply opposed to the transcendental.

A further development of such ideas is the 'scientific humanism' which essentially rests on the theory of evolution: "scientific humanism" is rooted in the assurance that there is an understandable regularity behind

[50] Terentius, *Heautontimoroumenos* verse 77. About the real meaning of this verse, translated in the Loeb edition as "I am a man, I hold that what affects another man affects me"; cf. Prete (see above, note 15) 41. See also above, note 41.

[51] According to the *Encyclopedia of Associations,* 16th ed. (1982), 1114: "the American Humanist Association, based in Amherst, N.Y., has 10 regional and 35 local chapters. It believes that humanism presupposes humans' sole dependence on natural and social resources and acknowledges no supernatural natural power . . . Morality is based on the knowledge that humans are interdependent, and, therefore, responsible to one another." Remarkable was this Association's criticism of Pope Paul VI's encyclica *Humanae vitae* condemning the use of contraceptives. Many other associations in the USA call themselves 'humanist' and have similar programs (see *ibid.*). Humanist clubs spread everywhere, e.g. there is a 'Humanist Institute' in Toronto, Ont., which offers to visitors "a personal acquaintance service." It is significant that Christian Voice, another association, based in Pasadena, Calif., campaigns against 'pornographers, homosexuals, humanists.' In Munich, Germany, a 'Humanistische Union' also operates on the level of human problems.

the pattern of events, and that there is therefore sound hope of the ultimate achievement of a synthesis of knowledge to be reached by multiplying and co-ordinating our efforts and seeking the broad and long view of the processes in nature and society."[52] In the same way as all species evolved materially and biologically through countless generations, man evolved also spiritually and keeps evolving towards a higher realization of his being (one is tempted to use an Aristotelian term: *entelécheia*).

Although the *Manifesto*'s humanism is the most representative and by far the prevailing one in America, the term indicates also other currents of thought. In the Twenties and Thirties a score of American intellectuals termed themselves 'new humanists', apparently with no direct reference to the above mentioned German *Neuhumanisten* of Winckelmann's time.[53] This movement was headed by Paul Elmer More (1864-1937) and Irving Babbitt (1865-1933). Babbitt's ideal, as formulated in 1930,[54] three years before the *Manifesto* was published, is a perfect balance of all powers and trends present and acting in human nature and human behavior; "the virtue that results from a right cultivation of one's humanity, in other words, from moderate and decorous living, is poise,"[55] and "humanists . . . are those who, in any age, aim at proportionateness through a cultivation of the law of measure."[56] That is, of course, a more precise and consistent definition than the acceptance of "all that is humanly significant" aimed at by the *Manifesto*. If man reaches a perfect balance of all his powers, he discovers and practices also what he has in common with all other men, and this is the truly human in the human being, the very point in which everyone recognizes his true humanity and to which all energies should converge.[57] This point cannot be attained without an effort of self-restraint and self-control. Although no less based on the purely human than the theories of the *Manifesto*, Babbitt's ideas are on

[52] O. L. Reiser, *A Philosophy of World Unification: Scientific Humanism as an Ideology of Cultural Integration* (Girard, Kansas, 1946), 7; cf. also L. Stoddard, *Scientific Humanism* (N.Y.-London 1926; O. L. Reiser, *The Promise of Scientific Humanism* (New York, 1940), and above all J. Huxley (ed.), *The Humanist Frame* (New York, 1961).

[53] On this movement, which has some indirect affinity with the 'historical' humanism, cf. L. J. A. Mercier, *Le mouvement humaniste aux Etats-Unis* (Paris, 1928); C. H. Grattan, *The Critique of Humanism* (1930); (Port Washington, 1968) reprint; J. D. Hoeveler, Jr., *The New Humanism. A Critique of Modern America 1900-1940* (Charlotteville, 1977).

[54] I. Babbitt, "Humanism. An Essay at Definition," in N. Foerster (ed.), *Humanism and America* (New York, 1930), 25-51. Partially reprinted in Muelder & Others (see above, note 47), 535-544.

[55] *Ibid.*, 29.

[56] *Ibid.*, 30.

[57] This view seems to provide an adequate answer to the objection made by A. Tilgher, "I. Babbitt e P. E. More o l'umanesimo americano," in *Filosofi e moralisti del Novecento.* Roma 1932, 104-111 (p. 109): "Ma da dove è venuto all'uomo questo principio superiore, che deve ridurre in soggezione quello inferiore? In fondo, I. Babbitt non si propone nemmeno la domanda."

the practical level not very far from traditional moral tenets, which Babbitt does not at all reject. In the final instance he means that people, in order to unfold the truly human in them, must overcome the less worthwhile trends of the self and keep at bay passions and instincts, which upset our internal balance and disturb our contacts with other people. Consequently Babbitt sharply criticizes the "naturalistic" concept of humanism, as later formulated by the *Manifesto*, for leading to permissiveness,[58] since it will "affirm life rather than deny it and seek to elicit the possibilities of life, not flee from it" (§ 15).

Babbitt's humanism, his concern with people as individuals with their nature and life as worthy in themselves, are as American as the *Manifesto*'s and like the *Manifesto*'s bare of any theoretical overlay à la Marx or à la Heidegger. Babbitt's thought is only better founded as a system and vested in terms reminiscent of ancient philosophy. Compared with the *Manifesto*, it is difficult to say to what extent both really differ in their innermost contents. Lamont sternly rejects Babbitt's ideas[59] but, in spite of the different interpretation he gives of the "intelligently human" of the *Manifesto*, nothing prevents considering Babbitt's self-control also as "intelligently human". Babbitt's balance of all human powers rests on the pre-Socratic aphorism "nothing too much" (*meden agan*) and above all it goes back to that "energy of the soul" Aristotle stresses in the *Nicomachean Ethics*.[60] But since Babbitt aims at what is *allgemein menschlich*, he upholds it with plenty of examples he collects also from other civilizations of all epochs, from Confucius to B. Croce (Babbitt's bent for quotations and references, especially during his classes, was the talk of Harvard).

Also primarily concerned with man's actual being is a third Anglo-Saxon philosopher, whose work goes further back in time: F. C. S. Schiller (1864-1937). Born in England, Schiller lived in America and was the first one to use 'humanism' in English with a specific philosophical sense.[61] He defined his humanism in the following way: "Humanism is merely

---

[58] Babbitt, cit. 32: "The reason for the radical clash between the humanist and the pure naturalistic philosopher is that the humanist requires a centre to which he may refer the manifold of experience." Cf. also I. Babbitt, *Rousseau and Romanticism* (1919). Austin-London 1977, 104 (reprint).

[59] Lamont, *op. cit.,* 21: "(Babbitt's educational program) turned the obvious need of human self control in the sphere of ethics into a prissy and puritanical morality of decorum".

[60] Babbit, cit., 41: "Though Aristotle, after the Greek fashion, gives the primacy not to will but mind, the power of which I have been speaking is surely related to his 'energy of the soul' ". Babbitt apparently refers to the *Nicomachean Ethics,* 1098a14: "If then the function of man is the active exercise of the soul's faculties *(psuchês enérgeia)* in conformity with rational principle, or at all events not in dissociation from rational principle . . . from these premises it follows that the Good of man is the active exercise of his soul's faculties in conformity with excellence or virtue. . . ."

[61] F. C. S. Schiller, *Humanism* (London, 1903); *Studies in Humanism* (London, 1907).

the perception that the philosophic problem concerns human beings striving to comprehend a world of human experience by the resources of human minds. . . . It demands . . . that man's complete satisfaction shall be the conclusion philosophy must aim at, that philosophy shall not cut itself loose from the real problems of life by making initial abstractions which are false and would not be admirable, even if they were true."[62] This definition already heralded the trends which were to be particular to the later currents of American humanism and is a far cry from the blurred use of 'humanism' in English philosophy during the second half of the nineteenth century, perhaps under the crossed influences of German and French sources (Ruge, Proudhon, Renan).[63]

Like Babbitt, F. C. S. Schiller also starts from the beginnings of Greek thought. He attempts to reconstruct fully the philosophy of Protagoras, the pre-Socratic thinker criticized by Socrates in Plato's *Theaetètus*. According to Plato's account (which however in Schiller's view does not give an adequate idea of Protagoras's philosophy), Protagoras's main principle, the basis of his whole reasoning, is that "man is the measure of all things." This principle serves as Schiller's motto and the starting point of his humanism.[64] But this motto leads Schiller, unlike the *Manifesto*'s subscribers and Babbitt, who were rather concerned with moral issues, to focus on the problem of cognition. He deals primarily with epistemology, in order to go over to logic and metaphysics. Every individual conceives truth in his own way and all conceptions of truth are equally true. This does not mean of course that all of them are valid in the same measure: they are better or worse, their value and not their absolute truth is to be checked by experience. Thus Schiller's humanism, while starting once again from his pragmatist vision of man, is more of a theoretical system than the *Manifesto*'s or even Babbitt's. Actually it enjoyed a broad popularity both in America and in Europe among professional philosophers. In Italy it was introduced in the wake of American pragmatism which found followers like G. Papini[65] and others before World War I.

Many more attempts to establish a philosophy of man were made also outside the Anglo-Saxon world, which cannot be reviewed here in

---

[62] *Idem,* "Definition of Pragmatism and Humanism", in *Studies, op. cit.,* 12-13.

[63] For these earlier meanings of 'humanism', see above, note 33.

[64] F. C. S. Schiller, "From Plato to Protagoras", in *Studies, op. cit.,* 22-70; "Protagoras the Humanist", *ibid.,* 302-325; "A Dialogue Concerning Gods and Priests", *ibid.,* 326-348.

[65] G. Papini, "F. C. S. Schiller" (1906), in *Tutte le opere,* vol. 2: *Filosofia e letteratura* (Milano, 1961), 811-816; M. T. Viretto Gillio Ros, "L'umanismo di F. C. S. Schiller" in R. Istituto di Studi Filosofici, Sezione di Torino: *Filosofi contemporanei* (Milano 1943), 161-222. On Schiller's philosophy in general, cf. R. Abel, *Humanistic Pragmatism. The Philosophy of F.C.S. Schiller* (New York, 1966).

full, such as Jacques Maritain's Christian humanism,[66] the biological and racist humanism of the Third Reich with all its inhuman absurdities, or Sartre's existential humanism,[67] somehow reminiscent of Guicciardini's 'particulare' (one's own good).

4. *Humanitas, paideia, humanism in historical perspective*

If it cannot be our aim to deal with all recent and earlier attempts to probe the multifarious complexities of human nature, our brief and scanty notes can nonetheless help answer the question which is our primary concern. As seen above, confusion arises first between a concept of humanism reflecting the common (ancient and modern) use of *humanus,* and the German and Italian concept of humanism reflecting the specific, now obsolete Roman use of *humanus* as 'learned'. Modern humanisms reflect the current meaning of *humanus,* but they are once again as different from one another almost as each one of them is different from the 'learned' humanism. To lump all humanisms together is clearly incorrect, but is it possible to look for a deeper connection between the different sorts of humanism, as the use of the common term suggests.

Perhaps it will be useful to recall at this point a statement made by Heidegger: "every humanism either takes for granted a metaphysics, or expresses one".[68] The point is that for Heidegger 'historical' humanism, namely Renaissance humanism, or, rather, Italian *umanesimo,* as it will henceforth be termed here to avoid circumlocutions and repetitions, is also a philosophy of man, as Marxist, Christian, existential humanism (Sartre's style) or even Anglo-Saxon or American humanism are (which latter Heidegger, not surprisingly for a German philosopher, completely ignores).[69] This philosophy is for him the resurgence of Greek humanism, used here *ante terminum* to denote the Greek ideal of man, "the goal of excellence, the means of achieving it, and (a very important matter) the approbation it is to receive..., which are all determined by human judgment. The whole outlook is anthropocentric: man is the measure of

---

[66] J. Maritain, *Humanisme intégral* (1936), new ed. (Paris 1947). English translation: *True Humanism* (Westport, 1941). On Petrarca and Erasmus as forerunners of Christian humanism, cf. P. P. Gerosa, *L'umanesimo cristiano del Petrarca.* (Torino, 1966); H. de Lubac, *Exégèse médiévale,* vol. 4 (Paris, 1964), 427-474.

[67] J. P. Sartre, *L'existentialisme est un humanisme* (Paris 1946).

[68] Heidegger, *op. cit.,* 321: "Jeder Humanismus gründet entweder in einer Metaphysik oder macht sich selbst zum Grund einer solchen."

[69] Attempts have been made in Italy to distinguish between *umanesimo* (Italian revival of classical antiquity), and *umanismo* (philosophy of man), cf.e.g. M.Jannizzotto, *Saggio sulla filosofia di Coluccio Salutati* (Padova, 1959), 30. As seen above, *-ismus* has given birth in Italian to two allotropes: *-ismo* (inlearned words) and *-és(i)mo* (in vernacular words). But a distinction between *umanesimo* and *umanismo* would be arbitrary and artificial, since it cannot be extended to other cases, e.g. *cristianesimo* vs. *cristianismo.* Actually it has not been accepted.

all things" [70] (the same aspect of Greek thought pointed out by F.C.S. Schiller with a different purpose).

Still, these theories about persons never developed into a metaphysics during the great ages of Greek civilization: the absolute idea of human personality is not Greek. No Greek philosopher ever dealt seriously with it. Absolute standards and values rest for the Greeks with the gods and not with mortals.[71] Consequently Heidegger can refer only to the form in which this ideal of man was defined and codified in the Hellenistic period, namely to the *paideía,* a system of education rather different from that of the classical epoch, with a strong emphasis on literary and philosophical teaching.[72] In other words, *paideía* is for Heidegger the philosophical humanism of Greece, not intrinsically different from modern humanisms, except that it is based on the meaning of 'humanus' as 'learned' and not on the common meaning of 'humanus.' Heidegger points out that this humanism was introduced into Roman culture after the Romans came in touch with the Greeks during their conquest of Greek speaking countries. In his view the same humanism revived later in the Italian *umanesimo* and in the German *Neuhumanismus* of the 18th century, mentioned here only for Heidegger's sake and not for its impact on European culture, since it was limited and cannot be compared with that of the Italian *umanesimo.* Heidegger goes further and maintains that every 'historical' humanism cannot be anything else than a resurgence of Greek *paideía.*[73] His view is rooted in the general German view of antiquity. This interpretation may be true for the German *Neuhumanismus,* which, again not surprisingly for a German philosopher, Heidegger highly overrates: but it does not fit ancient Roman humanism or Italian *umanesimo.*

As for *Neuhumanismus,* Heidegger is misled by the Latin translation of *paideia* with *humanitas,* a term which easily suggest a connection with humanism. To be sure, this translation is endorsed by a famous passage of Gellius, who equates *humanitas* with *paideía.*[74] But beyond this equa-

---

[70] M.Hadas, *Humanism. The Greek Ideal and its Survival* (New York, 1960), 13.

[71] Cf.Snell (see above, note 10), 231: "Das ist ungriechisch und vollends unplatonisch. Nie hat ein Grieche im Ernst von der Idee des Menschen gesprochen ... Norm und Wert liegen noch für Platon durchaus im Göttlichen und nicht im Menschlichen".

[72] Cf.H.L.Marrou, *Histoire de l'éducation dans l'antiquité.* Paris 1948, Chap. 2/1: "La civilisation de la paideia". Of course, Jaeger's *Paideia* remains fundamental, but it is less specific for our purposes.

[73] Heidegger, *op. cit.,* 320: "Zum historisch verstandenen Humanismus gehört deshalb ein *studium humanitatis,* das in einer bestimmten Weise auf das Altertum zurückweist und so jeweils auch zu einer Belebung des Griechentums wird."

[74] A.Gellius, *Noctes Atticae,* 13.17: "Qui verba Latina fecerunt quique his probe usi sunt, *humanitatem* non id esse voluerunt quod vulgus existimat quodque a Graecis *philanthropía* dicitur et significat 'dexteritatem quandam benivolentiamque erga omnis homines promiscuam': sed 'humanitatem' appellaverunt id propemodum quod Graeci *paideian* vocant, nos 'eruditionem institutionemque in bonas artes' dicimus.

tion, Gellius more properly translates *paideía* with 'eruditio institutioque in bonas artes'. The whole passage must be correctly assessed by the modern reader: since *humanus* means *also* 'learned', *humanitas* means *also* 'learning', but it includes other values (character, *virtus* etc.), while *paideía* focuses mainly on culture. These values are much more important than Heidegger seems to admit.[75] *Humanitas* does not have any corresponding term in Greek.[76] If it is used as *paideía,* it is a synecdoche or *totum pro parte*.[77] If Varro and Cicero made *paideía* coincide with *hu-*

---

[75] Heidegger, *op. cit.,* 320: "Der *homo humanus* ist hier der Römer, der die römische *virtus* erhöht und sie veredelt durch die 'Einverleibung' der von den Griechen übernommenen *paideía*".

[76] Cf.Snell (above, note 10), 237: "Es gibt im Griechischen kein Wort, das 'höheres Menschentum' und 'Menschlichkeit' zugleich bezeichnete". The discussion about Roman 'humanitas,' especially in Germany, has been going on for a long time and is now so vast that it is impossible to report on it in a footnote. It has been from the very first invalidated by the obsessive German conviction that all important values of the ancient world are Greek and not Roman. Consequently 'humanitas' has been equated to a variety of Greek concepts, none of which entirely corresponds to 'humanitas,' e.g. as already seen *paideía* (learning), *philanthropía* (benovolence) and even *anthropismós,* a *hápax legómenon* ascribed to Aristippus (see above, note 11), but probably reflecting Roman concepts (Diogenes Laertius lived later than Cicero). As already seen, in this discussion a certain confusion between 'humanitas' and 'humanism' came about often, which is even less admissible: 'humanitas' is a quality, a virtue, perhaps a goal, 'humanism' is a trend. But for Goethe, *Dichtung und Wahrheit* 3.13 (Jubiläums-Ausgabe vol.24, 143) 'Humanismus' is 'humaneness': "Unter den Sachwaltern als den Jüngern, sodann unter den Richtern als den Ältern, verbreitete sich der Humanismus, und alles wetteiferte, auch in rechtlichen Verhältnissen höchst menschlich zu sein." Only in recent times concepts cleared up and now the genuine Roman value of 'humanitas' begins to be recognized. Among recent contributions to the discussion, other than Snell's and Büchner's (see above. note 10), cf.F.Klingner, "Humanität und humanitas" (1947), in: *Römische Geisteswelt,* 5th ed. (Stuttgart, 1979), 707-746; F.Beckmann, *Humanitas* (Münster, 1952); H.Haffter, "Römische humanitas" (1954), in H. Oppermann (ed.), *Römische Wertbegriffe* (Darmstadt, 1974), (Wege der Forschung 14), 468-482; W.Schmid, review of Haffter's article, *ibid.,* 483-502.

[77] Another synecdoche is the use of *humanitas* in French and English not only as 'learning', but as 'learning in the form it had in antiquity', when education was restricted to literature and philosophy. The *umanisti* borrowed the term *humanitas* from Cicero and passed it to modern European languages. *Humanitas* and *Humanities* extended in turn their semantic area to include all literatures (in the same way that French *humanisme* too extended its semantic area) together with history, philosophy, and connected subjects (German *Geisteswissenschaften*). Today in discussions about educational programs, 'humanities' face science and technology. In Italy 'humanities' are called *materie letterarie. Umanità,* probably in the wake of the Jesuits' *ratio studiorum* denoted still by the middle of the past century two high school grades between *grammatica* and *retorica,* roughly corresponding to the pupils' 14th and 15th years of age (the later *ginnasio superiore*). In Germany *studia humaniora* denoted generally 'classical learning.' *Humanität* has in Germany a history of its own, only partially related to the discussion about Roman *humanitas.* It goes back to Herder's *Briefe zur Beförderung der Humanität* (1792). Cf.Newald (see above, note 76), Klingner *(ibid.),* and more recently R.Schwarz, *Humanismus und Humanität in der modernen Welt* (Stuttgart-Berlin, 1965), (Urban Bücher 89).

manitas,[78] the reason is that in the different Greek and Roman conception of man, both *humanitas* and *paideía* represent the high stage of perfection to be aimed at.

But our concern is rather with Italian *umanesimo* than with ancient Rome. The *umanisti* too made every effort to set up a theory of education comparable to *paideía* or to Greek education in general.[79] Like the Hellenistic Greeks they indulged in theories about education. They also eagerly translated Isocrates's and Plutarch's paedagogical writings and shared Plotinus's assumption that man has to model himself in the way a sculptor smooths and shapes his work.[80] So they set up a new school system with new teaching methods, which were successful enough to last until the French Revolution and the Romantic epoch: their replacement by German philosophical methods has since been widely regretted.[81] Only from this point of view, can Italian *umanesimo* be compared with the later German *Neuhumanismus:* but its educational theories are complementary to its main performance, which was the disclosure of classical antiquity. They were rather the result of the work of the *umanisti* and had mostly practical purposes, often not identical with those of their models, while for the *Neuhumanisten* Hellenistic *paideía* was the climax of all aspirations, Germans and Greeks being in their view the only two peoples of "Dichter und Denker."

Whether ancient Roman and Italian humanism really correspond to the ideal of Greek *paideia* as Heidegger understands it, remains to be seen. Furthermore it remains to be seen whether the educational ideal of the *umanisti* can be considered that metaphysics of man which Heidegger assumes to be the basis of every humanism. To be sure, a given educational system results in a theory of what man ought to be. But neither the Greek ideal of the *kalòs kagathós,* nor the Roman ideal of

---

[78] Cicero. *Pro Murena* 29.61: "audacius paulo de studiis humanitatis disputabo"; *Pro Archia* 1.2: "artes quae ad humanitatem pertinent"; 2.3 "de studiis humanitatis ac litterarum"; 3.4 "artibus quibus aetas puerilis ad humanitatem informari solet." For the later Latin use of the term cf.R.Rieks, *Homo, humanus, humanitas, Zur Humanität in der lateinischen Literatur des 1.Jhrhs.* (München, 1967).

[79] Paul O. Kristeller, "The Philosophy of Man in the Italian Renaissance" (1946), in *Renaissance Thought* &c. (see above, note 22), 120-139 (p. 124): "Even more important was the emphasis on man which was inherent in the cultural and educational program of the Renaissance humanists." On the *umanisti's* paedagogy, cf. among the more recent works: E.Garin, *L'educazione in Europa 1400-1600.* Bari 1957; *Il pensiero pedagogico dell' umanesimo* (Firenze, 1958), (I classici della pedagogia italiana 2); G.Müller, *Bildung und Erziehung im Humanismus der italienischen Renaissance. Grundlagen, Motive, Quellen* (Wiesbaden, 1969), with F.R.Hausmann's review in *Studi Medievali* 3/11 (1970), 300-307.

[80] Plotinus, *Enneades* 1.6.9. . . . to make it pure and beautiful.

[81] Cf.V.R.Giustiniani, *Neulateinische Dichtung in Italien 1850-1950* (Tübingen, 1979), 9-12 (Beihefte zur Zeitschrift für romanische Philologie, 173).

humanitas, be it the sum of all human powers and qualities, or only learning, give an answer about man's existence and the great questions it poses.

The Italian *umanisti* tried their hardest to establish a philosophy of man of their own: it suffices to mention Salutati, Fazio, Manetti, Valla, Pico. But the *umanesimo* was from the very beginning something else than a new philosophy of man. The umanisti "were neither good nor bad philosophers, but were no philosophers at all."[82] In the ancient authors they discovered and deliberately followed, they did not find any model suitable for their conceptions and for further development. Their efforts in this direction do not go beyond inherited beliefs and commonplaces. Their writings about human nature are filled with quotations from the classics and from the Church Fathers,[83] even when they try to emphasize man's excellence and superiority. The great speculative performances of their age, if any, lay outside of the specific activity of the *umanisti.* Ficino and Pico, who however had enjoyed a thorough humanistic education, cannot be considered *umanisti* in the strict sense of the word.[84] The university teaching of philosophy continued to rest on its mediaeval foundations.[85] The contribution of the *umanisti* to the philosophy of their epoch was either marginal—in providing and translating Greek philosophical texts until then unknown in Western Europe, or in the grammatical and philological interpretation of single Greek terms and

[82] Paul O.Kristeller, "Human." *op. cit.,* 100; *ibid.,* 99: "The other interpretation of Italian humanism . . . considers humanism as the philosophy of the Renaissance which arose in opposition of scholasticism. . . . Yet this interpretation of humanism as a new philosophy fails to account for a number of obvious facts"; "The Philosophy of Man," *op. cit.,* 124: "If I am not mistaken, the new term 'humanism' reflects the modern and false conception that Renaissance humanism was a basically new philosophical movement." (See also above, note 35). Garin's (see above, note 32) and even Kristeller's later appraisal of humanistic philosophy is more favorable. For a general account of the different opinions, cf.Garin, *op cit.,* ch.1 of the Introduction: "Umanesimo e filosofia".

[83] Kristeller, "Philosophy of Man," *op cit.,* 125. See also below, note 104.

[84] Kristeller, *ibid.,* 126-127.

[85] Kristeller, *ibid.,* 134. Secular Aristotelian views were so deeply rooted at the Italian universities and so cherished by the students, that these even refused the innovative interpretation of Aristotle brought by Aegidius Columna or Thomas Aquinas. Cf.A.Rinuccini, *Lettere e orazioni,* ed. by V.R. Giustiniani (Firenze, 1953), (Testi umanistici inediti o rari 9), 137 (Letter to Dominicus of Flanders, Dec. 18, 1473): "fuerant autem ad magistratum nostrum non semel tantum, imo saepius a scholaribus litterae perlatae, qui querebantur lectiones tuas non iuxta communem philosophantium opinionem, sed ex beati Thomae aut Aegidii sententia procedere; hunc autem (Giovanni Bianchi, a Venetian Carmelite) esse fatebantur, qui secundum commentatoris doctrinam lectiones esset, idque complures expetere inscripta nomina declarabant." A.Rinuccini was *Ufficiale dello Studio* in Florence and in charge of hiring new professors. Cf.also: I.Barale-Hennemann, *Aspekte der aristotelischen Tradition in der Kultur der Toskana des 15.Jhrhs.* Diss.Freiburg 1971 (Pisa, 1974).

passages,[86] as the *entelécheia* polemics shows[87] and uncounted references in their epistles indicate—or indirect, in bestowing upon their pupils and philosophers to be a solid knowledge of Latin and Greek.

The dissimilarity of Italian *umanesimo* and other humanisms, ancient and modern, has been either hinted at[88] or clearly set out by many competent scholars. F. C. S. Schiller, e.g., honestly tries to justify the use of the same word for two concepts which have little or nothing in common by proposing "to convert to the use of philosophical terminology a word which has long been famed in history and literature, and to denominate 'humanism' the attitude of thought which [Schiller] knows to be habitual in W. James and himself." [89] A comparison between *umanesimo* and modern humanisms becomes more difficult, the more the philosophical content of modern humanisms remains vague. As Paul O. Kristeller puts it, "in our contemporary discussion, the term 'humanism' has become one of those slogans which through their very vagueness carry an almost universal and irresistible appeal. Every person interested in 'human values' or in 'human welfare' is nowadays called a 'humanist' . . . The humanism of the Renaissance was something quite different from that of the present day."[90]

---

[86] Kristeller, "Philosophy of Man," *op. cit.,* 135: "Pomponazzi . . . was indebted to the humanists for his knowledge of the Greek commentators of Aristotle and of non-Aristotelian ancient thought, especially Stoicism." F.Filelfo, e.g., often refers in his letters to Plato's tripartite division of the soul and to other doctrines of Platonic or Aristotelian philosophy, but he seems to be not clearly aware of the difference between both systems. See above note V.R.Giustiniani, "Philosophisches und Philologisches in den lateinischen Briefen F.Filelfos (1398-1481)" in *Der Brief im Zeitalter der Renaissance.* (Mitteilungen der Kommission für Humanismusforschung der Deutschen Forschungsgemeinschaft IX, Weinheim, 1983), 100-117.

[87] Cf. on this subject G.Cammelli, *G.Argiropulo* (Firenze, 1941), 176-178n.

[88] Cf.e.g.Burdach (above, note 28), 91f: "Es haftet daran (am *Humanismus*) ein doppelter Begriff. Zunächst die Vorstellung und das Gebot einer geistigen Bildung, die als ihren Inhalt und ihr Ziel das Menschliche sucht, wir dürfen sagen, das Ideal des Menschen. Anderseits verknüpft sich damit, in einem spezielleren Sinne, eine bestimmte, geschichtlich bedingte Richtung des Studiums, welche dieses Ideal des Menschen auf einem einzigen, fest umgrenzten Wege zu finden und sich anzueignen glaubt: durch Vertiefung in eine längst vergangene Epoche menschlicher Kultur, in das griechisch-römische Altertum" (no less than Heidegger in 1946, Burdach in 1914 ignores every attempt to understand humanism as a philosophy of man in the Anglo-American way. Humanism is for him only a 'Bildungsideal'). Cf. also Oppermann, *Humanismus* (above, note 28), Preface, ix: "Angesichts der Vieldeutigkeit, die dem Wort Humanismus anhaftet, ist es nötig, klarzustellen, welcher Sinn dieses Wortes in den Aufsätzen dieses Bandes gilt oder wenigstens dominiert. Humanismus wird hier verstanden als Bildungsbegriff, als Bildungsideal und als der diesem Bildungsideal zugehörige Bildungsweg". Babbitt, cit., 30, and Lamont, cit., 19 make also a list of the different historical and philosophical meanings of humanism.

[89] F.C.S. Schiller, *Humanism* (see above, note 61), Preface xv-xvi.

[90] Kristeller, "Philosophy of Man", *op. cit.,* 120.

5. Two intuitions of the umanisti: virtus as leading power, history as evolution

What Heidegger does not say, is that the metaphysics or philosophy he sees is inherent in every humanism but this can either be expressed in philosophical terms or be a latent attitude of spirit, a mental background and an unconscious guideline behind an epoch's cultural achievements, or, to put it in German, the *Zeitgeist* of an epoch. This distinction is essential to pose correctly the question of *umanesimo* and humanisms, since the philosophy of the *umanesimo* is concealed in the mentality and activity of its epoch. It must be gleaned from the various elements we know of that period: this is the only way to assess whether or how much the *umanesimo* or rather its *Zeitgeist* corresponds to modern formulations of humanism. The age of the *umanisti* teems with artists, scientists, explorers, merchants, politicians, *condottieri,* churchmen, spurred altogether in their activity by the same spirit which spurred the *umanisti* in their studies. This spirit is very different from that of the Middle Ages and also of antiquity and can be pieced together only from the cultural, political, historical bequest of the Italian fifteenth century: works of art, treatises on mathematics (e.g. on perspective), even on double book-keeping *(partita doppia),* handbooks of geography and of commerce *(pratiche della mercatura).* In their works of erudition, of grammar, of history, in their pedagogy, even in their polemics, the *umanisti* voice this spirit far better than in their attempts at a philosophy of man or than the professional philosophers of this epoch do. It is a truism to state that modern humanists do not have to the spirit of our age the same relation the *umanisti* had to theirs. Modern humanist thinking is isolated and marginal in the vast flow of modern culture. These philosophers do not have any counterpart like Cosimo dei Medici, Francesco Sforza, Leonardo, Luca Pacioli, Paolo Toscanelli or Amerigo Vespucci and Giovanni da Verazzano.[91]

The key to the secret of human nature and human personality was for the *umanisti* the concept of *virtus.*[92] They reinstated this term in its ancient Roman meaning of 'innermost energy' by cutting down all Chris-

---

[91] A valuable attempt to give a global interpretation of Humanism and Renaissance in Italy has been made by L.M. Batkin, *Die Historische Gesamtheit der Italienischen Renaissance* (Dresden, 1979), (Fundus Bücher 66-68). On the difference between the two concepts, which goes back to Voigt and Burckhardt, cf.E.Garin, "Umanesimo e Rinascimento", in: *Questioni e correnti di storia letteraria,* vol.3 (Milano, 1949), 358.

[92] On the *umanisti's* rediscovery of Roman *virtus,* cf.V.R.Giustiniani, "Plutarch und die humanistische Ethik", in: *Beiträge zur Humanismusforschung* 5 (1979), 45-62; on Roman *virtus* in general, cf. W.Eisenhut, *Virtus Romana. Ihre Stellung im römischen Wertsystem* (München, 1973), (Studia et testimonia antiqua 13); L.Curtius, "Virtus und constantia" (1944-64) in Oppermann (see above, note 76), 370-375; K. Büchner, "Altrömische und horazische virtus," (1939-62), *ibid.,* 376-401.

tian accretions which had distorted it past recognition during the Middle
Ages. *Virtus* is shown at work, through its effects, on the vast screen of
history: history is presented as the result of individual achievements, of
single men's performances, of courage and determination on the one
hand, or failures on the other hand. This goes far beyond the elaboration
of a theory of man or the establishment of an educational program. The
great Bible of this philosophy of action is Plutarch's biographical work,
the *Vitae parallelae,* translated from Greek into Latin by various *umanisti*
during about fifty years and printed in 1470.[93] This translation, soon
followed by translations into Italian and other modern languages, became
a best seller, was repeatedly reprinted, and it is no exaggeration to say
that it had on Italian (and European) culture an impact similar to that
of Plato's works in Latin by M. Ficino, published about 1484.[94] The
effects of *virtus* on history were best brought out by Plutarch's literary
skills and enhanced by his method of comparing two different personalities, a Greek and a Roman, acting under similar circumstances: almost
all his 48 *Vitae* concern men of action: even Demosthenes and Cicero
have been chosen more for the part they had in the political life of Athens
and Rome than for their rhetorical talents.

One point which should not be forgotten: in Plutarch's own translation
of Roman *virtus* by the Greek *areté* and its subsequent retranslation into
Latin by *virtus,* both philological mishaps, but accepted without objection
since antiquity, the *umanisti* found the best support for their restoration
and popularization of the ancient Roman concept, which returned to
Latin with the prestige of Greek philosophy, in their opinion personified
by Plutarch, who was rather a gifted essayist or reporter. What could
appear as a modest lexical performance was to have, like the similar
restoration of *humanus* in its meaning as 'learned,' an importance far
beyond the limits of philology. Plutarch's *Vitae* stirred the interest in
biography, which became a favorite literary genre. It corresponded not
only to the new interest in personal achievements, but also to the reading
needs of a new social class, the bourgeoisie, delighting in narrations which
may be considered the forerunners of the modern historical novel. Plutarch himself had traced the lines of this development, aimed at portraying characters through a phrase or a jest, which can be more revealing
than victory in battles where thousands fall.[95]

---

[93] Hain +13125, IGI 7920, Goff P-830. Cf.also V.R. Giustiniani, "Sulle traduzioni
latine delle Vite di Plutarco nel Quattrocento", in *Rinascimento* 12 (1961), 1-59.

[94] Hain +13062, IGI 6860, Goff P-771.

[95] Plutarch, *Alexander* 664-665; *Phocion* 744, echoed by Rinuccini (see above, note
85), 163: "Cum tamen alicuius vitam et mores non tam seriae gravesque res gestae, sed
leviora etiam facta, verba quoque et ioci melius persaepe ante legentium oculos ponant
. . .". Cf.F.Leo, *Die griechisch-römische Biographie nach ihrer literarischen Form* (1901);
reprint (Hildesheim, 1965), 147: "*Historía* schildert die *práxeis* von Völkern und Männern,
bíos schildert das êthos eines Mannes". Cf. also A.J. Gossage, "Plutarch," in: T.A. Dorey

This human philosophy of the *umanisti* cannot yet be considered a sort of anthropocentrism as modern and ancient humanisms are. It is not necessarily opposed to transcendence. Nor were the leanings of the epoch opposed to it. Three centuries later Manzoni saw in Napoleon an example of *virtus* (which Plutarch and the *umanisti* certainly would have liked) [96] but also a mightier evidence of God's creative power. Through Alberti and Machiavelli *virtus* was to become a cornerstone of Italian mentality until our days. It was clearly a merit of the *umanisti* to have forged it out of Roman values. The man who stands and succeeds against destiny is a typical Roman conception, opposite to the Greek submission to the *moira* (fate) and unknown to the Greek *paideia*, to which Heidegger tries to relate every 'historical' humanism. But it does not contradict either the Christian doctrine of free will, and in fact it did not prevent the *umanisti* and their contemporaries from remaining faithful to the religious tradition and the Church, all the more since the Church itself with Nicholas V and Pius II had accepted *umanesimo* and protected the *umanisti*.

The awareness the *umanisti* had acquired of man's power to control events led soon to another, even deeper and more important, though once again unelaborated conception of history. Until the fifteenth century history had been a loose succession of events, similar to the change of weather, ruled by powers man was not able to recognize (whether the pagan fate or God's inscrutable will, or simply chance) since they lay outside of him and beyond his reach. The principle of imitation of the great models of the past which the *umanisti* established as the supreme rule of literary work was their main achievement and merit, not so much from the point of view of stylistic elegance, but for the very impact it was to have on Western ways of thinking. Since this principle recognized that the present form of being, the appearance of a thing as perceived by us in a given moment, is not the only possible one, that past forms can be recreated along lines which can be retraced, and that what is gone can be reborn *(renasci)*. This provided a point of reference from which the course of events could be observed and understood in a human dimension. This was another way to see things. It would end up in a new category of thought: evolution, the hallmark and dynamics of Western civilization, unknown to all other great civilizations of the past. [97]

6. *Italian umanesimo as a whole.*

At this point the question reappears whether those links between

---

(ed.), *Latin Biography*. N.Y. 1967, 45-77 (59); A. Wardman, *Plutarch's Lives* (Berkeley and Los Angeles, 1974), 7-8.

[96] A.Manzoni, *Il cinque maggio*, vv. 32-36: "Nui / chiniam la fronte al Massimo / Fattor che volle in lui / del creator suo spirito / più vasta orma stampar".

[97] Cf. on this subject my article, cited above, note 15.

umanesimo and modern humanisms, which on a strictly theoretical level cannot be found, can be discovered in the global attitude of spirit, in the *Zeitgeist* of the *Quattrocento.* Although itself not a philosophy of man, Italian *umanesimo* unquestionably entails many cues or hints at philosophical issues of great momentum. But strangely enough these cues received from modern humanists less attention than, e.g., that kind of anthropocentrism which, right or wrong, can be perceived in the term 'humanism' itself. Thus the more the essential suggestions of Italian *umanesimo* are hidden in the spirit of the epoch, the easier it has been for everybody to shape this spirit as one pleased, to make of it the most for one's own purposes, and to bring one's own conceptions back to it, in an attempt to ennoble one's own views with a reference to the acknowledged great achievements of the Renaissance.

Lamont, while striving with his ideas "to go in philosophic scope and significance far beyond Renaissance humanism," includes in his own humanism what he thinks were its most enduring values, namely "first and foremost a revolt against the otherworldliness of mediaeval Christianity, a turning away from preoccupation with personal immortality to make the best of life in this world. Renaissance writers like Rabelais and Erasmus gave eloquent voice to this new joy of living and to the sheer exuberance of existence. For the Renaissance the ideal human being was no longer the ascetic monk, but a new type—the universal man—the many-sided personality delighting in every kind of this-earthly achievements. The great Italian artists, Leonardo da Vinci and Michelangelo, typified this ideal." [98] This is the more or less traditional way of considering the Renaissance and the *umanesimo* which was its first stage. It may have inspired some beautiful lyrics of Carducci,[99] but is hardly supported by facts. To be sure, the human type changes together with the *Zeitgeist:* Lamont however could have better referred to L. B. Alberti and Castiglione and to that ideal of human perfection they aim at in their writings, than to Renaissance writers and Michelangelo.

Actually, Michelangelo, instead of making "the best of life in this world" is, like Petrarca, constantly haunted by the idea of death, which in Renaissance literature and art is much more present than Lamont imagines: it suffices to think of Collenuccio's *Canzone alla morte* or of the *Giudizio Universale,* which does not precisely celebrate the joy of living. Such avowals as Lorenzo's "chi vuol esser lieto sia, / di doman non c'è certezza" or Poliziano's "non si rinnovella / l'età, come fa l'erba" [100] seem to hint less at the joy of living than at the worry about

---

[98] Lamont, *op. cit.,* 19-20.

[99] E.g., *Ad Alessandro D'Ancona, Alle fonti del Clitumno* &c. Carducci sees the spirit of the Middle Ages in such movements as the *flagellanti,* which was no less an aberration than modern ones, like the recent collective suicides in Guyana.

[100] Lorenzo dei Medici, *Trionfo di Bacco e Arianna;* A.Poliziano, *Ben venga maggio,* both reminiscent of Horace's *carpe diem.*

inescapable death. Moreover both poets are clearly reminiscent of *topoi* from Horace and composed their verses for popular feasts, which are no special hallmark of their epoch. But even if these verses would evidence a new joy of living, a new "affluence of love and time", they do not prove that spending time in love and fun was the current way of life in that time. Giannozzo Manetti, e.g., "treasured time very highly and never wasted an hour in spite of all the preoccupations he had for the republic or for himself. He used to say that of the time which we have spent in this life we must give an account moment for moment, basing himself on the text of the Gospel" [101]—an attitude of spirit which better fits Domenico Cavalca's sermons[102] than Lamont's vision of the Renaissance.[103] Nor is it necessary here to remember how the *umanisti* were concerned about faith and otherworldliness. Manetti himself learned Hebrew to better understand the Bible and discuss its truth with Jewish scholars. Most umanisti translated Greek Church Fathers too along with Greek classics.[104]

Nor is it true that the Middle Ages were oriented only towards the other world. The *gai saber* played at Provençal courts a part similar to that of vernacular poetry at Italian Renaissance courts. Tournaments and pageants were in the Middle Ages no less frequent and magnificent than during the Renaissance. St. Francis liked to be called "the juggler of the Lord." The bourgeoisie of the mediaeval Italian city-states did not thrive on trade and did not embellish their towns with splendid walls and gates only out of otherworldliness. The first Italian private palaces were also built during the Middle Ages. Frederick II delivered in 1230 with the Constitutiones Melfitanae a clear model of this-worldly legislation, granting the Church no special privileges.

Babbitt too, perhaps with some deeper insight into the character of the Italian Renaissance, tried to tie it to his own brand of humanism. The *umanisti* were "not content with opposing a somewhat external imitation of the Ciceronian and Virgilian elegance to the scholastic carelessness of form. They actually caught a glimpse of the fine proportionateness of the ancients at their best. They were thus encouraged to aim at a harmonious development of their faculties in this world rather than at an otherworldly felicity. Each faculty, they held, should be cultivated in due measure without one-sidedness or overemphasis, whether that of the ascetic or that of the specialist. 'Nothing too much' is indeed the

---

[101] Vespasiano da Bisticci, "Giannozzo Manetti" in *Vite,* ed. by A.Greco, vol. 1 (Firenze, 1970), 491. The Gospel text referred to is probably Mt 5.26 or Lc 12.59; cf. also Dante, *Purg.* 3.78: "Ché perder tempo a chi più sa più spiace," and other passages as listed by H.Gmelin, *Kommentar zur Göttlichen Komödie,* vol. 2 (Stuttgart, 1955), 73.

[102] Cf.R.Quinones, *The Renaissance Discovery of Time* (Cambridge, Mass. 1972), 10.

[103] Cf. also Batkin (see above, note 91), 175-177.

[104] Cf.C.L. Stinger, *Humanism and Church Fathers. A.Traversari (1386-1439) and Christian antiquity in the Italian Renaissance* (Albany, 1977).

central maxim of all genuine humanists, ancient and modern." [105] Like
Lamont, Babbitt fails to refer more precisely to Alberti and Castiglione,
where he would have found the best confirmation of his theory. He
ascribes to the *umanisti* qualities whose models he found also in China
and in India and seems unaware that his ideal of restraint and moderation
could be easily expressed in Christian terms by the four cardinal virtues:
fortitude, justice, prudence, and temperance, which in Dante's *Divine
Comedy*, i.e. along the lines of orthodoxy, grant the great spirits of
paganism admission to *limbo* and *nobile castello*,[106] since they are not
eligible for Paradise, reserved to those who have been reborn "ex aqua
et spiritu sancto." [107]

In other words, both Lamont and Babbitt do not focus on the central
issues of Italian *umanesimo*. Lamont completely rejects the study of
ancient authors,[108] recommended by Babbitt as the cornerstone of education. Since the *Zeitgeist* of that epoch, like every *Zeitgeist*, eludes a
precise theoretical formulation, they refer to it for the part they prefer
and consider it simply as an effort to find in man himself the vindication
of his being. Marxists do more or less the same, and acknowledge Italian
umanesimo (together with other humanisms, which they discover in
China from the 8th to the 12th century, in Armenia and Georgia [USSR],
from the 10th to the 12th century, in Russia during the 15th and 16th
centuries) as a stage of what they call 'pre-Marxist humanism,' to be
further developed by Copernicus, Galilei, and Saint-Simon.[109] On the
other hand, Maritain rejects Italian *umanesimo* as a form of anthropocentrism for the same reason others praise it, since anthropocentrism is
inadequate to provide a full understanding of human personality.

Humanism as an ideal of Greek *paideia,* humanism as a revival of
ancient culture, humanism according to Ruge, Marx, Schiller, Babbitt,
the *Humanist Manifesto,* and to Heidegger: humanism as discovery of
man's *virtus,* as a new vision of history and establishment of new ways
of thinking: all these humanisms show how differently human beings can
be and actually have been understood from one time to another, from
one cultural area to another, from one language to another. It has been
said that our epoch undergoes a sort of reversal of what happened when
the Tower of Babel was being built and "non audivit unusquisquam
vocem proximi sui." [110] Nowadays a common vocabulary is being worked
out in all languages to express the new values which continuously appear

[105] Babbitt, *op. cit.,* 26.

[106] *Inf.* 4.31 ff.; 106.

[107] John 3.5.

[108] Lamont, *op. cit.,* 22.

[109] *Filosofskaja Enciklopedija* (see above, note 42), 412-414. The source of this article
seems to be N.I. Konrad, "Ob epohe vozroždenija" in *Literatura epohi vozroždenija i
problemy vsemirnoj literatury* (Moskva, 1967), 7-45.

[110] Genesis 11:7.

and the way the old ones are understood. The same terms occur in almost the same shape everywhere. But *humanism, humanisme, Humanismus, umanesimo* or *umanismo, gumanism*, are doomed to be a perpetual *signum contradictionis*. God's curse still rests on a term which should define the very essence of God's most perfect creature.

University of Freiburg im Breisgau.

III

PERENNIAL PHILOSOPHY:
FROM AGOSTINO STEUCO TO LEIBNIZ

BY CHARLES B. SCHMITT

I. Introduction

Of the philosophical phrases which have come into popular use during the XXth century, perhaps none is more curious than "perennial philosophy" or, in its more common Latin form, *philosophia perennis*. Although there is no agreement on the precise meaning of the phrase, it is usually taken to indicate that some sort of continuous theme runs throughout the history of philosophy, that certain enduring and lasting truths are recognizable in the philosophical writings of all historical periods. *Philosophia perennis* is a philosophy which endures; its truth is considered to persist from generation to generation, long after ephemeral philosophical fads and fashions come and go. Particularly during the past seventy years has "perennial philosophy" become a popular term, and numerous books and articles have discussed its meaning in detail.[1] What precisely *"philosophia perennis"* means is not easy to determine, and the task of determining it is made more difficult by the fact that a great many philosophers of various persuasions have, as it were, appropriated the conception and so bent it that their own philosophy turns out to be perennial philosophy. It has been adopted *inter alia* by adherents of Thomistic Scholasticism,[2] Scholasticism in general,[3] Platonism,[4] mysticism,[5] positivism,[6] naturalism,[7] Catholic philosophy,[8] Western

---

[1] We cannot here go into these recent discussions, which we hope to treat in some detail in a subsequent study. For some indications see James Collins, *Three Paths in Philosophy* (Chicago, 1962), 255-79, "The Problem of a Perennial Philosophy."

[2] Jacques Maritain, An *Introduction to Philosophy*, trans. E.I. Watkin (New York, 1937) 100, for example. The Thomists have most pertinaciously clung to the opinion that their philosophy is perennial. A veritable flood of references to other writers could be cited.

[3] Erwin J. Auweiler, "Quaracchi: 1877-1927," *New Scholasticism*, I (1927), 105.

[4] Paolo Rotta, "Platone e la filosofia perenne," *Rivista di filosofia neo-scolastica*, XVII (1925), 8-22.

[5] Aldous Huxley, *The Perennial Philosophy* (New York, 1944).

[6] Roberto Ardigò, "La perennità del positivismo," *Rivista di filosofia e scienze affini*, VII (1905), 1-9. [7] Cornelius Krusé in the Foreword to John Herman Randall, Jr., *How Philosophy Uses Its Past* (New York, 1963), xii.

[8] Otto Willmann, *Aus der Werkstatt der Philosophia perennis* (Freiburg i. Br.,1912), esp. 44-54. What Willmann calls *katholische Philosophie* is a sort of Idealism, rooted in the Neoplatonic tradition and accepting the religious tenets of Catholicism. See also his *Geschichte des Idealismus* (Braunschweig, 1894-97).

philosophy,[9] and world-wide philosophy, Eastern and Western.[10] This is but a partial list! I have not yet seen scepticism referred to as *philosophia perennis*, but I expect to any day. Seeing the diversity of meanings given the term, it may be worthwhile to inquire into the origin and early history of the notion of perennial philosophy, in order to learn just what its initial signification was.

It has often been thought that the concept of perennial philosophy originated with Leibniz, who uses the term in a frequently quoted letter to Remond, dated August 26, 1714.[11] But careful research reveals that *"philosophia perennis"* was used much earlier than Leibniz; indeed, it was the title of a treatise published in 1540 by the Italian Augustinian, Agostino Steuco (1497–1548).[12] Although Steuco was perhaps the first to employ this phrase—and was certainly the first to give it a fixed, systematic meaning—he drew upon an already well developed philosophical tradition. Drawing upon this tradition he formulated his own synthesis of philosophy, religion, and history, which he labelled *"philosophia perennis."*

We shall discuss the sources upon which Steuco drew, analyze the use he made of them in his formulation, and trace the influence which his notion of perennial philosophy had on thinkers up to the time of Leibniz. Doing this, we hope to be able (1) to indicate the philosophical tradition from which "perennial philosophy" grew, (2) to place Steuco in his proper historical context, (3) to indicate what success Steuco had in the eyes of those who came after him and (4) to set the stage for a more extensive consideration of the *fortuna* of Steuco's happy phrase in more recent times.

If we wish to find the sources of the notion of perennial philosophy

[9] Maurice de Wulf, "Cardinal Mercier, Philosopher," *The New Scholasticism*, I (1927), 1–14, esp. 14.

[10] S. Radhakrishnan (ed.), *History of Philosophy, Eastern and Western* (London, 1952), II, 439–48, esp. 447.

[11] "La vérité est plus répandue qu'on ne pense, mais elle est très souvent fardée, et très souvent aussi enveloppée et même affoiblie, mutilée, corrompue par des additions qui la gâtent ou la rendent moins utile. En faisant remarquer ces traces de la vérité dans les anciens, ou (pour parler plus généralement) dans les antérieurs, on tireroit l'or de la boue, le diamant de sa mine, et la lumière des ténèbres; et ce seroit en effect perennis quaedam Philosophia." C. J. Gerhardt (ed.), *Die philosophischen Schriften von Gottfried Wilhelm Leibniz* (Berlin, 1875–90), III, 624–25.

[12] Most reference works now attribute the origin of the concept to Steuco. Aldous Huxley, *op. cit.*, vii, however, still attributed the origin of the concept to Leibniz. Others give Steuco credit but do not realize that his conception of perennial philosophy is somewhat different from XXth-century notions. Ernst Hoffman, for example, tries to place Steuco in the general tradition of Thomistic schólasticism. See his *Platonismus und christliche Philosophie* (Zurich-Stuttgart, 1960), 337–52 and the review of this book by Paul Oskar Kristeller, *Journal of the History of Philosophy*, I (1963), 99–102, esp. 100.

we must go back beyond Leibniz and Steuco. Although the latter seems to have been the first to make significant use of the term, the type of philosophy which he denominated "perennial" has a long history. As we shall see more fully below, when Steuco wrote his *De perenni philosophia,* he meant to indicate by this title a philosophy which has more right to be called "enduring" or "lasting" than any other. Before analyzing Steuco's own attitude toward philosophy and theology, we shall indicate briefly the tradition upon which he built his perennial philosophy.

Probably the most direct intellectual predecessors of Steuco were Marsilio Ficino (1433–99) and Giovanni Pico della Mirandola (1463–94). These two men, important in popularizing non-Aristotelian philosophical traditions during the Renaissance, drew their doctrines from a wide variety of sources and formulated philosophical systems which stood in contrast to traditional Aristotelian Scholasticism. But although the two are usually considered to be of the same broad cultural tradition and did in fact hold many philosophical doctrines in common, we must not overlook the very real differences between their teachings. Some understanding of the philosophy of each is necessary for a proper evaluation of Steuco's own philosophy. We shall concern ourselves principally with their opinions regarding the relation of philosophical to religious truth and with the sources from which they derived these opinions.

II. Marsilio Ficino

As founder of the Platonic Academy of Florence and translator of Plato, Plotinus, and other Neo-platonic philosophers, Marsilio Ficino occupies an important position in the development of early modern philosophy.[13] Since Ficino was a conscious reviver of Platonism and entitled his major systematic work *Theologia Platonica,* it may seem pointless to raise the question of his philosophical orientation. But merely to read him off as a Platonist would much oversimplify matters. Besides absorbing a healthy amount of Aristotelian Scholasticism, Ficino also drew significantly, in one way or another, from a number of other philosophers, including Lucretius, Plotinus, Jamblichus, Augustine, Proclus, Pseudo-Dionysius, Psellus, Pletho, and a variety of pseudonymous and mystical writings, including the Hermetic *corpus,* the *Chaldaic Oracles,* and the pseudo-Orphic writings.[14] Ficino can be called a Platonist only with reservations.

---

[13] On Ficino see particularly P. O. Kristeller, *Il pensiero filosofico di Marsilio Ficino* (Florence, 1953); *idem, Studies in Renaissance Thought and Letters* (Rome, 1956); Raymond Marcel, *Marsile Ficin* (Paris: 1958); Giuseppe Saitta, *Marsilio Ficino e la filosofia dell'umanesimo,* 3rd. ed. (Bologna, 1954).

[14] See especially P. O. Kristeller, "The Scholastic Background of Marsilio Ficino," *Studies. . . ,* 35–97.

One of the central themes of Ficino's philosophy is that there is a unity to the world which is far more deeply real than the apparent diversity of things. This notion, although found in Plato's own writings, was spelled out with much greater precision as Neoplatonism developed systematically, in late ancient times. Ficino speaks of unity in several ways. In the *Commentary on the Symposium,* love is the binding force which orders and unites the universe.[15] In the *Platonic Theology* the soul plays the rôle of the *vinculum universi:* Ficino conceived the universe in such a way as to give the soul a central position as connecting link between the upper and lower worlds.[16] This metaphysical unity of the world seems to have a counterpart in the historical development of philosophy and theology, which are called "sisters" in one of Ficino's characteristic letters.[17] There is a fountain of truth from which two parallel streams run their historical course; the one is philosophy, the other is theology. True philosophy is Platonism and true theology is Christianity. These two varieties of truth are ultimately joined, for Ficino accepted at face value the story of Plato's having come into contact with the Pentateuch, several times quoting Numenius' characterization of Plato as a "Greek-speaking Moses." [18]

Although the Scriptures form the basis of true religion and the writings of Plato the basis of true philosophy, according to Ficino there had already been in even more ancient times a long development of philosophical truth. This is found principally in the *prisca theologia* (or *prisca philosophia* or *philosophia priscorum*), a long religio-philosophical tradition, held by Ficino to date back to Moses:

In those things which pertain to theology the six great theologians of former times concur. Of whom the first is said to have been Zoroaster, head of the *magi;* the second is Hermes Trismegistus, originator of the priests of Egypt. Orpheus succeeded Hermes. Aglaophemus was initiated to the sacred things of Orpheus. Pythagoras succeeded Aglaophemus in theology. To Pythagoras succeeded Plato, who in his writings encompassed those men's universal wisdom, added to it, and elucidated it.[19]

[15] *Opera* (Basel, 1576), 1320–63. All further references to Ficino's writings will be to this edition unless otherwise noted. For the *Symposium* commentary see also the modern edition, *Marsile Ficin: Commentaire sur le Banquet de Platon,* ed. Raymond Marcel (Paris, 1956).

[16] *Opera,* 119–21. For the evolution of Ficino's position on this important doctrine see Kristeller, *Il pensiero . . ,* 86–123.   [17] *Opera,* 853–54.

[18] See particularly the letter entitled "Concordia Mosis et Platonis," *Opera,* 866–67. Numenius' quotation is preserved by Eusebius (*Praep. evan.,* II, 10, 14) and Clement of Alexandria (*Strom.,* I, 22, 150).

[19] *Opera,* 386; similar statements are found frequently in Ficino's writings. Cf. 156, 268, 854, 871, 1537, 1836. See Kristeller, *Il pensiero. . . ,* 16–20; *idem, Studies. . . ,* 36–37; Bohdan Kieszkowski, *Studi sul platonismo del Rinascimento in*

Ficino emphasizes that the philosophy of the ancients (*prisci*) is nothing other than a "learned religion (*docta religio*)"; [20] and he seems to have identified the whole tradition with a *pia quaedam philosophia*, which was consummated in Plato,[21] emphasizing, for example, that "Plato was imbued with the divine mysteries of Hermes Trismegistus." [22]

The notion of the constancy of the philosophical tradition from the ancient theologians to Plato and the Neoplatonists plays an important rôle in Ficino's own philosophy, but it certainly was not original with him. Even in ancient times Plutarch had called "the venerable theologians the oldest of the philosophers (οἵ τε πάλαι θεολόγοι, πρεσβύτατοι φιλοσόφων ὄντες)." [23] A high regard for these traditions was also maintained by a number of other late ancient thinkers such as Jamblichus [24] and Diogenes Laertius,[25] and even by Christians such as Augustine [26] or Lactantius.[27] Proclus seems to have been eminently favorable toward the tradition of the *prisca theologia*, being reported as once going so far as to single out the *Chaldaic Oracles* and the *Timaeus* as the two most valuable books written up to that time.[28] Michael Psellus (1018–78), a Byzantine Platonist, later admired and translated by Ficino,[29] also provided a major impetus to the tradition of the *prisci*. He not only emphasized the compatibility of the tradition of the *prisca theologia* with Christianity, but also utilized the Hermetic and Orphic writings along with those of the Neoplatonists to explicate the Scriptures.[30] It was, however, Georgius Gemistus

---

Italia (Florence, 1936), 113–27. There is some basis for this in the writings of Plato. Pythagorean and Orphic doctrine are evident in the *Phaedo*. Hermes is cited at *Phaedrus* 263E and *Protagoras* 322C. For Zoroaster see the probably spurious dialogue *Alcibiades* I, 122A.

[20] *Opera*, 853–54. Cf. Kieszkowski, *op. cit.*, 82–88; Ivan Pusino, "Ficinos und Picos religiös-philosophische Anschauungen," *Zeitschrift für Kirchengeschichte*, XLIV (1925), 504–43; Eugenio Garin, *L'umanesimo italiano*, 2nd. ed., (Bari, 1958), 105–12.

[21] *Opera*, 871.   [22] *Ibid.*, 854.

[23] *De animae procreatione in Timaeo*. 33, 103A-B. A standard Latin translation of this passage reads as follows: Prisci porro theologi qui erant philosophorum vetustissimi. . . . *Plutarchi Scripta Moralia*, ed. Frederick Dübner, (Paris, 1841), 1260. See also his *De Iside et Osiride*, 10, where he discusses the Egyptian influence on Greek wisdom.

[24] *De mysteriis*, I, 1–2.   [25] *Vitae*, I, prologue.

[26] *De civ. Dei*, VIII, 1–13; Cf. Clement of Alexandria, *Stromata*, I, XV, 69–70, 71.   [27] Esp. *Div. inst.*, I, 6 and IV, 6.

[28] Marinus, *Vita Procli*, XXXVIII; Cf. Proclus, *The Elements of Theology*, ed. E. R. Dodds, (Oxford, 1933), xxii–xxiii.

[29] Christos Zervos, *Un philosophe néoplatonicien du XIᵉ siècle: Michel Psellos* (Paris, 1919), esp. 141–43, 326–51.   [30] *Ibid.*, 189–91.

Pletho who probably had the greatest direct influence on Ficino's own conception of the *prisca theologia.* Although there are still a number of unsolved problems regarding Pletho's general philosophical and theological orientation,[31] his emphasis on the continuity of the tradition of the *prisca theologia* seems beyond dispute.[32] Pletho, a foremost defender of Plato and Platonism, finds one of the most conclusive arguments for the preeminence of Platonic philosophy to lie in the fact that Plato himself was heir to a long tradition of truth, that of Zoroaster and the Pythagoreans.

Pletho's attitude toward philosophy apparently had an important influence on Ficino's own outlook. His attribution of the *Chaldaic Oracles* to Zoroaster was accepted by Ficino and became part of the tradition.[33] Besides Pletho, many other sources known and admired by Ficino—Augustine,[34] Jamblichus, Proclus,[35] Psellus—emphasized that philosophical and theological truth was preserved within the Platonic-Neoplatonic tradition, broadly considered.

As we saw above in Ficino's codification of this scheme, the pre-Platonic philosophers or theologians who contributed in a significant way to the "true philosophy" of Plato were five: Zoroaster, Hermes Trismegistus, Orpheus, Aglaophemus, and Pythagoras. All of these, with the exception of Aglaophemus,[36] had an ancient tradition behind them which became more prominent during the Renaissance.[37] From

[31] Some of the problems are pointed out in Kristeller's review of François Masai, *Pléthon et le platonisme de Mistra* (Paris, 1956) in *Journal of Philosophy*, LVI (1959), 510–12.

[32] Milton V. Anastos, "Pletho's Calendar and Liturgy," *Dumbarton Oaks Papers*, IV (1948), esp. 279–303; Kieszkowski, *op. cit.*, 34–36.

[33] Pletho seems to have been the first to make this attribution specific, although there are at least hints that Zoroaster is to be identified with the author of the *Oracles* as early as the Ist century of the Christian era. See Anastos, *op. cit.*, 287–88; Joseph Bidez and Franz Cumont, *Les mages hellénisés* (Paris, 1938), 158–63.

[34] Kristeller, *Studies. . .* , 368–72.

[35] See H. D. Saffrey, "Notes platoniciennes de Marsile Ficin dans un manuscrit de Proclus (Cod. Riccardianus 70)," *Bibliothèque d'Humanisme et Renaissance*, XXI (1959), 161–84, esp. 168.

[36] Aglaophemus is a very obscure figure about whom we know practically nothing. He is the supposed Orphic teacher of Pythagoras (thus connecting Pythagoras and ultimately Plato with the Orphic tradition). References to him in ancient writers are very meager. See the article by E. Wellmann in Pauly-Wissowa, *Real-Encyclopädie*, I (1894), col. 824 and Jamblichus, *De vita Pythagorica*, 146; and C. A. Lobeck, *Aglaophamus* (Berlin, 1829).

[37] On the *fortuna* of these traditions during the Renaissance see Karl H. Dannenfeldt, "The Pseudo-Zoroastrian Oracles in the Renaissance," *Studies in the Renaissance*, IV (1957), 7–30; *idem*, "Hermetica philosophica" and "Oracula Chaldaica," in *Catalogus translationum et commentariorum*, ed. P. O. Kristeller, I (Washington, 1960), 137–51, 157–64; Kieszkowski, *op. cit.*, 113–27; D. P. Walker, "Orpheus the

Ficino the influence spread in many directions: to Giovanni Pico,
Francesco Giorgio, Steuco, Patrizi, Champier and many others. For
Ficino—as for many other of the more liberal-minded thinkers of the
Renaissance [38]—the tradition of the *prisca theologia* was one to be
studied carefully, for in it were embedded many particles of truth.
Some found that the ancient theology was an aid to them in understanding Christian Scripture; [39] others found in the partial agreement
of the Christian with the non-Christian tradition the basis of a principle of toleration and the beginnings of a perennial philosophy. It
is with this latter aspect that we are here particularly concerned. The
prisci theologi, it was held, developed the kernel of truth which, inchoate in them, blossomed forth as a unified and comprehensive philosophical system in *noster Plato*. So important for Ficino is the
philosophy of Plato and the tradition which it sums up that "all
those who desire to taste of the most delicious waters of wisdom must
drink from that perennial fountain (*hunc . . . perennem fontem*)." [40]

III. Giovanni Pico

With Giovanni Pico [41] we find a somewhat more ambitious at-

Theologian and Renaissance Platonists," *Journal of the Warburg and Courtauld
Institutes*, XVI (1953), 100–20; *idem*, "*The prisca theologia* in France," *Journal of
the Warburg and Courtauld Institutes*, XVII (1954), 204–59; *idem, Spiritual and
Demonic Magic from Ficino to Campanella* (London, 1958); Edgar Wind, *Pagan
Mysteries in the Renaissance* (New Haven, 1958); Kristeller, *Studies. . .* , 221–57;
idem, "Lodovico Lazzarelli e Giovanni da Correggio, due ermetici del Quattrocento
e il manoscritto II.D.I.4 della Biblioteca Comunale degli Ardenti di Viterbo," *Biblio-
teca degli Ardenti della città di Viterbo: Studi e ricerche nel 150° della fondazione*
(Viterbo, 1961), 13–37; *idem*, "Giovanni Pico della Mirandola and His Sources," in
L'opera e il pensiero di Giovanni Pico della Mirandola (Mirandola, 1965), I, 35–133;
Frances Yates, *Giordano Bruno and the Hermetic Tradition* (Chicago, 1964). For
these traditions in ancient times see, among others, W. K. C. Guthrie, *Orpheus and
Greek Religion* (London, 1935); Bidez and Cumont, *op. cit.* (on Zoroaster); A. J.
Festugière, *La révélation d'Hermès Trismégiste* (Paris, 1945–54).

[38] On this see the interesting observations of D. P. Walker, "Orpheus. . . ," 119–
20 and "The Prisca Theologia. . . ," 252–59.

[39] As Giovanni Pico, for example, in his *Heptaplus*, or Johann Reuchlin. On the
latter see Lewis W. Spitz, *The Religious Renaissance of the German Humanists*
(Cambridge, Mass., 1963), 61–80.

[40] Ficino, *Opera*, 1945.

[41] Of the large literature on Pico the following should particularly be mentioned:
Eugenio Garin, *Giovanni Pico della Mirandola: vita e dottrina* (Florence, 1937);
idem, La cultura filosofica del Rinascimento italiano (Florence, 1961); *idem, Gio-
vanni Pico della Mirandola* (s.l., 1963); Kristeller, "Giovanni Pico. . ."; Anagnine,
G. Pico della Mirandola: sincretismo religioso-filosofico, 1463–1494 (Bari, 1937);
E. Cassirer, "Giovanni Pico della Mirandola: A Study in the History of Renaissance
Ideas," this *Journal* III (1942), 123–44, 319–46.

tempt to utilize the philosophies and theologies of the past in the formulation of a single system of philosophical truth. For Pico the emergence of truth was not confined to a particular philosophical, theological, or scientific tradition, but all traditions had something to contribute. We find therefore that Pico, not content with the teachings of a single tradition nor even of several, drew in his own writings upon an enormous range of sources.[42] Ficino had emphasized the Christian and Platonic traditions as twin sources of truth, but Pico went much further. In his famous *Conclusiones* we see the range of his sources.[43] In Ficino there was a strong tendency to try to bring various philosophical traditions into accord, but where insoluble disagreement was found other traditions had to bend to the authority of Platonism. Pico seems to have held all philosophers in equal esteem, guided only by the truth which he found in their writings.[44] The conflict between Pico's attitude and Ficino's becomes apparent in their discussion regarding the argument of Platonic and Aristotelian metaphysics. Pico argued that Aristotle agreed with Plato that Being and Unity are coextensive. Ficino later rejected this interpretation, holding with the Neoplatonists the position that the One is above Being, a position which emphasizes the differences between the doctrine of Plato and that of Aristotle.[45]

This is not to say that Pico accepted everything uncritically into his system, for he did not. This is most obvious in respect to astrology, which he rejected quite vehemently: another point upon which he disagreed with Ficino.[46] He seems, however, to have been indebted to Ficino for his knowledge of and enthusiasm for the *prisca theologia*. In his *Conclusiones* he devoted separate sections to the teachings of Hermes, the *Chaldaic Oracles*, and the *Hymns* of Orpheus;[47] more

[42] See P. O. Kristeller, "Giovanni Pico. . . ." For the range of sources accessible to Pico see Pearl Kibre, *The Library of Pico della Mirandola* (New York, 1936).

[43] *Ioannis Pici . . . Opera . . .* (Basel, 1601), 42–76; cf. Cassirer, *op. cit.*, 123–31; Garin, *Giovanni Pico . . .* (1937), 73–88.

[44] This is most evident in the controversy with Ermolao Barbaro regarding philosophical style. The most convenient edition of the letters is Eugenio Garin (ed.), *Prosatori latini del Quattrocento* (Milan, 1952), 804–23, 844–63. Cf. Quirinus Breen, "Giovanni Pico della Mirandola on the Conflict of Philosophy and Rhetoric," this *Journal*, XIII (1952), 384–426.

[45] Pico's *De ente et uno* in *De hominis dignitate, Heptaplus, De ente et uno,* ed. E. Garin (Florence, 1942), 386–441 and Ficino's commentary on the *Parmenides* in *Opera*, 1157–64, esp. 1164; cf. Raymond Klibansky, "Plato's Parmenides in the Middle Ages and the Renaissance," *Mediaeval and Renaissance Studies*, I, esp. 312–25; Kristeller, *Il pensiero. . .* , 36–38; Garin, *Giovanni Pico. . . .* (1937), 75–82.

[46] See the *Disputationes adversus astrologiam divinatricem,* ed. E. Garin, (Florence, 1946–52); on the disagreement of Ficino and Pico see Garin, *Giovanni Pico . . .* (1937), 173–74.   [47] *Opera*, 54, 69–70, 71–72.

over, he speaks of the same tradition several times in the *Oratio*.[48]
It is in this latter work—the one for which Pico had gained a wide
popular fame—that Giovanni Pico expressed clearly just how his
position differs from Ficino's. Not content with the teachings of
Hermes, the Chaldeans, Pythagoras, and the Hebrew mystics, Pico
proposed other theses to defend, including the harmony between
Plato and Aristotle.[49] It is precisely here that he went beyond Ficino's
notion of twin unbroken traditions of philosophical and theological
truth. Truth, instead of residing in two traditions only, resides in
many. Ficino's *prisci theologi* have no special access to truth, but
aspects of it are to be found in Averroes, the *Koran*, the Cabala, the
writings of the medieval schoolmen, and in many other places as
well.[50] In Pico we have one of the high points of the syncretistic or
eclectic tendency, which was to become even more popular and far-
reaching in the XVIth century.

IV. Other Syncretistic Thinkers

After the death of Pico and Ficino, the tradition which we have
been discussing was extended to an ever-widening circle. We may
single out for particular mention the Frenchman, Symphorien Champier (c. 1472–c. 1539), and the Italian, Francesco Giorgio (1460–
1540). In these men was kept alive the strong syncretistic and harmonizing tendency which we found in Ficino and Pico. Champier,[51]
a physician from Lyon, published several important books in the
general tradition of Ficinian Neoplatonism. Particularly significant
are his *De quaduplici vita* (1507) and *De triplici disciplina* (1508),
both of which make considerable use of the *prisca theologia* tradition.
One section of the latter work, which has the heading: "On the invention and the origin of Orphic and Platonic theology and why the
Orphic teachings are mixed with ours," [52] clearly indicates the tenor

[48] *De hominis dignitate*. . . , 144, 150, 160–62.   [49] *Ibid.*, 144.

[50] See Kristeller, "Giovanni Pico. . . ," 30–31, who also suggests that Pico's attempt to bring many traditions into concord may be just an extension of Ficino's
more limited scheme.

[51] See P. Allut, *Étude biographique et bibliographique sur Symphorien Champier*
(Lyon, 1859) and James B. Wadsworth, *Lyons 1473–1503: The Beginnings of Cos-
mopolitanism* (Cambridge, Mass., 1962), esp. 73–97. According to D. P. Walker
(*Spiritual and Demonic Magic*. . . , 167, and "The Prisca theologia in France," 204–
07), Champier was the earliest and most important representative of Ficinian Neoplatonism and of the *prisca theologia* in France. Jacques Lefèvre d'Étaples, however,
edited Ficino's translations of Hermes' *Pimander* in 1494. See Kristeller (ed.), *Sup-
plementum Ficinianum* (Florence, 1937), I, pp. LVII, 97.

[52] *Symphoriani Champerii* . . . *De triplici disciplina* (Lyon, 1508), fol. C$_v$v. See
also his *Le livre de vraye amour*, ed. J. B. Wadsworth (The Hague, 1962), 51–52
and the Introduction, 11–35.

of the man's thought. Francesco Giorgio (or Zorzi), a minorite from Venice, was the author of the extensive compilation, *De harmonia mundi totius cantica tria* (Venice, 1525),[53] which stands squarely in the syncretistic tendency of the Renaissance. Here, indeed, is one of the high points of the whole tradition. The structure of the work itself and the very titles of its divisions—songs and tones—indicate to us a striving for an internal harmony, meant to reflect the concord which the author found in the universe. Giorgio makes much of the basic agreement of the *prisci theologi* with Christian theologians, indicating that the seeming "dissonances" which we find in different philosophies and religions really disappear when we look more closely.[54]

Mention should also be made of the attempt of Cardinal Nicholas of Cusa (1401–64) to promote a conciliation among the various religious traditions. Although in a somewhat different context and having a somewhat different aim than the attempts of Ficino, Pico, and their followers, it does have certain similarities. Nicholas himself was much more actively involved in the XVth-century ecumenical activities of the Church than were Pico and Ficino. The work which most interests us here is his *De pace fidei* (1453), a dialogue among representatives of various lands and adherents to various religions.[55] The ecumenical tone of the work was rooted in the conviction that there is a basic concord among the religions which will bring them ultimately to a perpetual peace.[56] This, coupled with Cusanus' well-known teaching of the "coincidence of opposites," [57] provided a solid metaphysical and religious basis for a philosophy of tolerance, a point which gives the German cardinal a close connection not only with Ficino and Pico, but with Steuco and a number of later thinkers as well.

---

[53] The work was reprinted in Paris in 1544. The author has not been studied very carefully but see Cesare Vasoli, "Francesco Giorgio Veneto, testi scelti," in *Testi umanistici sull'ermetismo* (*Archivio di Filosofia*, 1955), 78–104 and D. P. Walker, *Spiritual and Demonic Magic. . .* , 112–19.

[54] *Francisci Georgii . . . De harmonia mundi totius cantica tria . . .* (Venice, 1525), esp. "Tonus secundus cantici primi: Qua consonantia rerum principia et eorum descriptores conveniant," fols. XXV^v–XXXVIII^v. Mention should also be made of Girolamo Seripando, the important theologian at Trent, whose writings form a direct link between Ficino and Steuco. In many ways Seripando is a direct precursor of Steuco's notion of *philosophia perennis*. See Herbert Jedin, *Girolamo Seripando: sein Leben und Denken im Geisteskampf des 16. Jahrhunderts* (Würzburg, 1937), I, 62–68, 79.

[55] Nicolai de Cusa, *Opera omnia* vol. VII, eds. R. Klibansky and H. Bascour, (Hamburg, 1959). See Edmond Vansteenberghe, *Le cardinal Nicholas de Cues (1401–1464)*, (Paris, 1920), 400–08, and Cesare Vasoli, "L'ecumenismo di Niccolò da Cusa," in *Cusano e Galileo* (*Archivio di Filosofia*, 1964), 9–51.

[56] *Opera*, VII, 3–4, 62–63. [57] *De docta ignorantia*, *Opera*, I.

V. Agostino Steuco

Let us now turn to a consideration of Agostino Steuco,[58] in whom we find one of the staunchest defenders of the tradition of *prisca theologia*. In him we find also perhaps the most sustained effort to develop the theme of harmony, of consonance, of universal agreement into a coherent philosophical system, and this he did most notably and fully in his *De perenni philosophia* (1540). As we shall see, the program of Cusanus, Ficino, and Pico, with its roots in Plutarch, Neoplatonism, the Fathers and other ancient writers on religion, comes to full realization in Steuco. Moreover, we shall find that although Steuco did indeed desire to incorporate all traditions in his synthesis, he was not entirely uncritical, for he did cast by the wayside certain doctrines which would not fit into his concordistic scheme.

Before we analyze Steuco's perennial philosophy and its career or "fortune," let us first say a few words about his life and general intellectual orientation. Agostino Steuco was born in the Umbrian hilltown of Gubbio either in 1497 or early in 1498.[59] He entered the Augustinian convent in that city in 1512 or 1513, and remained there until 1517. Most of the period from 1518 to 1525 was spent in study at the University of Bologna. There he became particularly proficient in languages, learning some Aramaic, Syriac, Arabic, and Ethiopic, in addition to Greek and Hebrew. Thereafter, he was librarian of the famous collection of Cardinal Domenico Grimani in Venice for several years (1525–29), before sojourns at Reggio in Emilia (1529–33) and Gubbio (1533–34) to perform the duties assigned him by his religious superiors. He finally came to Rome in 1534, was named bishop of Kisamos in Crete in 1538, and became librarian of the Vatican Library in the same year. He went to Trent for the Council in 1546 and returned to Bologna early in 1548, where he died a few months later.

Steuco was principally a theologian and Biblical scholar. The bulk of his writings reflect these interests, although he did write on other subjects as well.[60] In many ways he represents, as D. P. Walker

---

[58] The most detailed treatment of Steuco is Theodor Freudenberger, *Augustinus Steuchus aus Gubbio, Augustinerchorherr und päpstlicher Bibliothekar (1497–1548) und sein literarisches Lebenswerk* (Münster, 1935). See also Otto Willmann, *Geschichte des Idealismus*, III, 170–77; Hermann Ebert, "Augustinus Steuchus und seine Philosophia perennis. Ein kritischer Beitrag zur Geschichte der Philosophie," *Philosophisches Jahrbuch*, XLII (1929), 342–56, 510–26; XLIII (1930), 92–100; Eugenio Garin, *La filosofia* (Milan, 1947), II, 86–88; Giuseppe Saitta, *Il pensiero italiano nell' Umanesimo e nel Rinascimento*, 2nd. ed. (Florence, 1961), II, 79–82. In general we shall use the following edition of Steuco's works: *Augustini Steuchi Eugubini . . . Opera omnia . . .* (Venice, 1591), 3 vols.

[59] For this, as for most of the factual information regarding Steuco's life, I rely on Freudenberger, *op. cit.*, 20–139.

[60] For a listing of the editions of Steuco's works see Freudenberger, *op. cit.*, 367–94.

has noted, the liberal wing of XVIth-century Catholic theology and scriptural study.[61] Works like the *Cosmopoeia* (1535) and *De perenni philosophia* (1540), which attempt to make many varieties of pagan philosophy and theology compatible with the orthodox tradition, amply indicate a liberal outlook. About this we shall speak in detail below. On the other hand, he shows definitely conservative tendencies in other works. He wrote a treatise against Valla's famous proof of the forgery of the Donation of Constantine; [62] and, even though he was extremely receptive to the doctrines of the *prisca theologia*, he was as staunch as any rock-ribbed conservative in his rejection of the teachings of Calvin and, particularly, of Luther.[63] In fact, he found the various pagan and non-Christian traditions of religion much more acceptable than the teachings of the reformers. Whereas Stoic philosophy, for instance, is considered to be in many ways acceptable,[64] Lutheranism is a "plague," which cannot be other than "the contempt of piety, the ruin and downfall or opposition to religion." [65]

Steuco's most famous work is the *De perenni philosophia*, dedicated to his friend and protector Paul III and printed four times before the end of the XVIth century.[66] Although highly regarded by a number of scholars in the two centuries after its publication, it was gradually forgotten until Willmann "rediscovered" it at the end of the XIXth century.[67] In the XVIIth century the book was highly praised: Kasper von Barth (1587–1658) calls it a "golden book" [68] and

[61] See above note 38. On Scriptural studies in general during the period see John Warwick Montgomery, "Sixtus of Siena and Roman Catholic Biblical Scholarship in the Reformation Period," *Archiv für Reformationsgeschichte*, LIV (1963), 215–34.

[62] *Contra Laurentium Vallam, de falsa donatione Constantini, libri II* (1546), in *Opera*, III, fols. 209ᵛ–241ʳ. See Freudenberger, *op. cit.*, 306–47.

[63] See especially his *Pro religione adversus Lutheranos* (1530), in *Opera*, III, part ii, fols. 1ʳ–24ᵛ; Freudenberger, *op. cit.*, 265–300; Friedrich Lauchert, *Die italienischen literarischen Gegner Luthers* (Freiburg i.Br., 1912), 315–28.

[64] See Julien-Eymard d'Angers, "Epictète et Sénèque d'après le *De perenni philosophia* d'Augustin Steuco (1496–1549)," *Revue des sciences religieuses*, XXXV (1961), 1–31.

[65] *Opera*, III, part ii, fol. 1ᵛ. Luther's whole attitude toward reason and philosophy and their rôle in religion was almost diametrically opposed to Steuco's. For a recent and balanced study see B. A. Gerrish, *Grace and Reason: A Study in the Theology of Luther* (Oxford, 1962). esp. 1–56.

[66] The first edition was Lyon, 1540. It was reprinted separately at Basel in 1542 and in the editions of the *Opera* of Paris, 1577–78 and Venice, 1590–91. See Freudenberger, *op. cit.*, 380–82.

[67] Willmann's treatment of Steuco (*Geschichte des Idealismus*, 170–177) remains one of the most sympathetic.

[68] *Adversariorum commentariorum libri LX* . . . (Frankfurt, 1624), 313.

Daniel Georg Morhof (1639–1691) refers to it as an "opus admirabile." [69] The work itself is long and complex, one of the more prepos-
sessing examples of Renaissance erudition and learning, although at
times it tends to be rambling and repetitive. In our brief analysis here
we can barely scratch its surface. Consequently, we shall delimit our
focus somewhat, and concentrate on a discussion of what Steuco
means by perennial philosophy; also, other themes will help us to
understand this main one.

At the very beginning of the *De perenni philosophia,* when Steuco
gives his reason for writing the work, his strong eclectic, concordistic
bent becomes apparent. It is generally recognized, he says, that there
is "one principle of all things, of which there has always been one and
the same knowledge among all peoples." [70] This agreement of all peoples is one of the key themes which runs through Steuco's work. One
might almost say *the* key theme: this is, in fact, what perennial philosophy is. The enduring quality of this philosophy consists in the
supposition that there is always a single *sapientia* knowable by all. [71]

We are, however, acquainted with the history of philosophy, of
religion, of theology, and such a universal agreement is not at all obvious. Were not the difficulties of such a position apparent also to
Steuco, as they must be to all who endeavor to show the unity of
many seemingly disparate elements? A question comes immediately
to mind. What was Steuco's view of history? How did he interpret
the process and development of man's thought so that he could argue that there is a constant irreducible core of agreement? As Garin
has so aptly observed, "Steuco is lacking certainly in any concept of
progress." [72] It is the *continuity* of history that is to be emphasized,
according to Steuco. There are changes to be sure, but these are minor
when compared to the elements of continuity. Steuco speaks of "progress," but this usually means merely a "moving forward" or "advance"
of time. [73] In fact, if anything, Steuco has a tendency to go back to
the Greek notion that there has been a steady degradation in history.
Knowledge, for example, passes through three stages. In the first stage
it is perfect, having been handed down to man by God. It soon becomes dissipated and scattered. Finally, it seems to us to be like a
mere story or dream. That which was known clearly in the earliest
centuries soon becomes either completely forgotten or obscure and

---

[69] *Polyhistor,* 3rd ed., (Lübeck, 1732), II, 526.

[70] *De per. phil.,* I, 1; fol. 1ʳ. I shall give the book and chapter number of this
work, followed by the folio number of volume III of the 1590–91 edition of the
Opera.

[71] "... unam necessario semper fuisse sapientiam ... sicque in unam omnia
spectare veritatem." *Ibid.;* fol. 2ᵛ.   [72] *L'umanesimo italiano,* 152.

[73] As at *De per. phil.,* I, 2; fol. 2ᵛ (see the following note) and VI, 1; fol. 83ᵛ.

uncertain, like a story or myth.[74] Truth and wisdom, it seems, have been parcelled out in a single bundle and have been transmitted to the later generations from Adam,[75] diminishing perhaps somewhat in the process. The thread of truth runs through history, preserved most fully, as we shall see, in the tradition of the *prisca theologia*.

Here we are at the height of the Renaissance! But it is a Renaissance somewhat different than the one described in the conventional histories. Where is the emphasis on man's originality, individualism, power to discover and change the world of which we so often read? Where is the sharp break with tradition which the Renaissance is supposed to be? In Steuco we find none of these things. History flows like time, it knows not "dark ages" and "revivals." There is but a single truth that pervades all historical periods. It is perhaps not equally well-known in all periods, but it is accessible to those who search for it. True theology, for example, is nothing other than the revealed truth which has been known to mankind from the earliest times.[76] As we shall see, this view of history serves almost as a prerequisite for his over-all interpretation of the *philosophia perennis*.

What was Steuco's view of philosophy in general? Into which tradition does he fit? What were his favorite sources? The answer to these questions should be partially apparent from what we have already said. We shall find him (like Cusanus, Ficino, and Pico) more sympathetic to Plato than to Aristotle; and, what is perhaps more significant, he was very much influenced by the whole Neoplatonic movement with all that it sums up. We shall find him sharing the "open" attitude of the Renaissance Platonists, in opposition to the "closed" attitude of the Aristotelians.[77] As we have already said, he adhered to Platonic monism.[78] Not only does Steuco lean more toward

---

[74] "Igitur, ut a sapientia inchoemus superiorem rationem strictius repetentes, dicimus sapientiam sive veritatem venientem ad homines vel offerentem se de coelo tribus gradibus esse progressam. In primis hominibus uberiorem, largam, et tradente Deo perfectam; postea crescentibus annis dissipatam, disiectam eversam magnisque temporum atque homnium iniuriis affectam ad posteros tamquam fabulam et somnium vilem laceramque pervenisse . . . notissima priscis saeculis, posteris aut penitus ignorata aut ita obscura et incerta, ut tantum non pro fabulis habita fuerit." *De per. phil.*, I, 2; fol. 2ᵛ.

[75] This is clear in *De per. phil.*, I, 1; fol. 1ʳ.   [76] *Ibid.*, X, 23; fol. 201ᵛ.

[77] By this we mean that he shared with the Platonists an interest in a wide range of philosophical and religious traditions. The Aristotelians of the same period —although there are significant exceptions—were content, for the most part, to focus their attention on the writings of Aristotle and the Aristotelians. By my distinction, I mean that the Platonists were usually more receptive to new and different ideas that were the Aristotelians. As we can see from Steuco and others of Platonic learnings this, cannot always be considered to be a virtue.

[78] See above.

Plato than toward Aristotle, but he is even somewhat critical of Aristotle on a number of specific issues. I think that we can make two general statements regarding Steuco's view of philosophy. First, Platonic philosophy is to be preferred to Aristotelian; secondly, Plato and the tradition which he represents is in basic agreement with Christianity. Although Aristotle is not to be despised—and this separates Steuco from a number of Renaissance humanists and Platonists —it must be noted that it is in the study of Plato and his predecessors and followers that we come to a clearer notion of God:

> But in the range of talents, greater is Plato than Aristotle, who delighted more in the study of lower things and those things known by the senses and left the study of the hidden things, surpassing human abilities, the mysteries of the ancients, and the secrets of God to Plato and others. . . .[79]

This is a point of view shared with several other Renaissance defenders of Platonism.

For Steuco it is *divinus Plato* [80] who is in general agreement with Christian theology and through whom religious and philosophical truth flows. Furthermore, Steuco is very definite in stating precisely what rôle philosophy plays in the religious life of the individual. Philosophy is an adjunct to religion, an aid to its practice, and leads to a knowledge of God. In echoing the position of Simplicius, he argues, "This is the end of philosophizing: piety, namely, and divine love." [81] Philosophy here has the same quasi-religious import that it had in Plato and the ancient Neoplatonists; the end of philosophy is knowledge of God and union with Him. For Steuco, as for the Neoplatonists in general, there is no real distinction between philosophy and religion. Although they may be distinguished in theory, both lead in the same direction, both have the same end. The syncretistic, harmonizing tendency which Neoplatonism fostered had no real problem in alleviating philosophical doubts, for it teaches a unity which goes beyond all difference. Acceptance of the Plotinian One precludes scepticism regarding philosophy and the traditional faith-reason problem has no meaning in the context of Neoplatonism. Moreover, Jamblichus' argument that knowledge of God is somehow innate and lies beyond all criticism exerted a notable influence on Steuco; [82] and,

---

[79] *De per. phil.*, IV, 1; fol. 59ʳ.

[80] He uses this term in *De per. phil.*, III, 10; fol. 52ᵛ, in quoting from Syrianus.

[81] "In philosophandi finis: pietas scilicet amorque divinus. Hoc dicit Simplicius non Christianus, Aristotelicae philosophiae interpres. . . . Eiusmodi nostrae quoque philosophiae finis." *De per. phil.*, X, 9; fol. 193ᵛ. This whole chapter is of interest for the present discussion.

[82] *Jamblichi De mysteriis liber*, ed. Gustavus Parthey (Berlin, 1857), I, 3; 7–10. See Ueberweg-Heinze, *Grundriss der Geschichte der Philosophie*, 12th ed. (Basel, 1960), 614–15.

indeed, it is at the very heart of the whole tradition giving eminence to the *prisca theologia*. Therefore, Steuco can say that "the aim of philosophy is the knowledge of God, and, as it were, the actual beholding of Him." Moreover, "the true and perfect philosophy" is the one which above all others demonstrates God and most clearly reduces all causes and principles to the single source which is God.[83] The end of philosophy is piety and the contemplation of God; when a philosophy reaches this proper end, we have Christian Philosophy.[84]

We are now in a better position to understand Steuco's conception of perennial philosophy. It turns out to be little more than *prisca theologia* in slightly novel dress. Plato, Plutarch, Plotinus, Jamblichus, Proclus, Psellus, Pletho, Cusanus, Ficino, Pico, Champier, and Giorgio are Steuco's predecessors. The word *priscus,* probably best translated as "venerable," is one which recurs often in Steuco. He speaks of *priscis saeculis,*[85] in former centuries, *prisci philosophi,*[86] *prisca philosophia,*[87] and *prisci*[88] alone, referring to "the venerable philosophers and theologians." None of this is accidental. Truth flows from a single fountain, as it were, but is manifested in various forms. Moreover, the revelation of truth dates back to the most ancient times, to the *prisca saecula,* and we can find truth in the writings deriving from this period. The wisdom of earliest times is then transmitted to the later centuries,[89] truth and wisdom being as old as man himself. Philosophy itself is not something new, but is *vetustissima.*[90] Wisdom and philosophy did not begin with the Greeks, Steuco insists; it is far more ancient than Thales and the earliest Greek philosophers. It was in truth from the barbarians that philosophy came to Greece.

[83] "Sic omnis vitae philosophiaeque finis est, ut videas Deum sive nunc sive in posterum. Nunc in tota philosophia non est alius scopus quam Dei scientia et quasi contuitus; hunc omnis vel promittit vel cupit ostentare philosophia . . . id etiam sit ex his perspicuum, quoniam dicitur philosophiae finis Dei contemplatio, eam denique veram perfectamque probari philosophiam, quae supra caeteras omnes ostendit Deum clariusque principia causasque omnes ad hunc suum revocat fontem." *De per. phil.* X, 9; fol. 193ʳ. This has certain similarities to Ficino's formulation. See Kristeller, *Il pensiero. . .* , 346–49, 237–43, 259–60.

[84] Steuco uses the phrase *philosophia Christiana* several times. See *De per. phil.,* VI, 11; fol. 94ᵛ; X, 6; fol. 190ᵛ.

[85] *Ibid.,* I, 1; fol. 2ᵛ; IX, 1; fol. 164ᵛ; X, 23; fol. 201ᵛ.   [86] *Ibid.,* II, 19; fol. 43ʳ; III, 3; fol. 46ʳ; III, 4; fol. 47ʳ; IV, 1; fol. 59ʳ.   [87] *Ibid.,* III, 7; fol. 49ᵛ; and *prisca theologia,* X, 22, fol. 200ʳ; X, 26; fol. 202ᵛ.   [88] *Ibid.,* I, 4; fol. 4ʳ; II, 1; fol. 28ʳ; II, 2; fol. 29ᵛ; IX, 24; fol. 180ᵛ; X, 20; fol. 199ᵛ; etc.

[89] "Haec [scientia] partim nota a prima hominum origine per omnes aetates devoluta est ad posteros." *Ibid.,* I, 1; fol. 1ʳ.

[90] *Ibid.,* I, 27; fol. 24ᵛ. Typical is his statement regarding the divine nature of souls: "Igitur convenere omnes omnisque vetus ac nova philosophia sacra et profana animos esse e genere divino, divina natura et incorporea." *Ibid.,* IX, 24; fol. 181ʳ.

That is not to say that the Greeks accepted everything which they found in the philosophy of the barbarians, but they did accept those things which are true, as they rejected the superstitions.[91] Steuco more or less follows the scheme of transmission of knowledge which Ficino had offered, placing particular emphasis on Hermes Trismegistus as the *priscus, par excellence.* In one place he seems to give Hermes an importance equal to that of Moses in transmitting the truth about a single God.[92] Elsewhere he argues that when Platonic philosophy reaches an understanding of mystery it comes from Hermes.[93] Indeed, the Augustinian canon goes so far as to call Hermes the *fons Graecae philosophiae.*[94]

These are key themes which run through the *De perenni philosophia.* The emphasis seems to be on showing that there is really nothing new in the world of philosophy, that certain truths were known already to the most ancient thinkers, and that these have been transmitted from generation to generation throughout history. Here we have the fusion of philosophical and theological knowledge characteristic of Neoplatonic thinkers. Religion is something natural to man and gives man access to the truth. Steuco's debt to Ficino on this point is most evident. It is religion which separates man from brute animals, a religion largely identifiable with philosophy.[95] Moreover, this religio-philosophy is something natural to man as man. It is a *vera philosophia,* the "true philosophy" to which Steuco devotes a good deal of attention in his work.[96] This "true philosophy" is a philosophy which leads to piety and the contemplation of God. It is "true religion and philosophy . . . which always teaches us and implores us to be subject to God." Moreover, they who endeavor to follow God and His commandments are "true philosophers" and live the most praiseworthy life.[97] The "true philosophy," which is in agreement with true religion, arouses in us the desire to become similar to

[91] "A barbaris enim, ut idem perhibet ad Graecos venit philosophia. . . . Ut autem a barbaris meliorem quandam sapientiam Graeci hauserunt; in omni autem professione sunt adulterina et vera. Sic superstitiones erant repudiandae, sola melior scientia recepta." *Ibid.,* V, 3; fol. 76ᵛ. Very similar statements are to be found at I, 1; fol. 2ʳ and II, 2; fol. 30ʳ. See Plutarch, *De Iside et Osiride,* 10, for an ancient statement of the same position.

[92] *Ibid.,* IV, 1; fol. 59ʳ.

[93] "Hunc locum haud dubie sumpsit ex Mercurio Trismegisto, a quo tota ferme Platonica philosophia, ubi mysteria attingit, defluxit." *Ibid.,* V, 9; fol. 81ʳ.

[94] *Ibid.,* I, 10; fol. 8ʳ. Hermes is praised highly elsewhere also. See *inter alia,* I, 1; fol. 2ᵛ; I, 25; fol. 25ʳ; II, 17; fol. 42ʳ; III, 2; fol. 46ʳ.

[95] *Ibid.,* X, 1; fol. 188; cf. Garin, *L'umanesimo italiano,* 151–52. On Ficino's view of religion see Kristeller, *Il pensiero. . . ,* 342–49.

[96] Esp. X, 3–6; fols. 189ᵛ–191ʳ.   [97] *Ibid.,* X, 5; fol. 190ʳ.

God, for God is the "clear and true goal," the model we strive to emulate. "True philosophy" has always been defined in this way and always will be so defined. There can be no "true philosophy" without
God, for it flows from Him, who is the *magnus dux et declarator
sapientiae*.[98]

For Steuco the term "perennial philosophy" indicates the real
historical continuity of "true philosophy." Surprisingly enough,
Steuco does not use the phrase *philosophia perennis* very often. Although his work bears the title from which the phrase originated,
he uses the words "perennial philosophy" much less often than do
most self-respecting contemporary manuals of scholastic philosophy.
Perennial philosophy is, in brief, that philosophy which exists "even
from the beginning of the human species." [99] As Steuco argues at the
very outset of his work, there is a single truth, a single wisdom, which
has always existed. This *sapientia* is attainable either through a study
of the historical tradition in which it is embedded or through a direct
application of our intellectual abilities to philosophical contemplation.
This unity of knowledge can be called either "the universal agreement" or "perennial philosophy." [100]

These are perhaps the only two passages in which Steuco employs
the term which he chose to use for the title of his book. Although
they do not indicate clearly what "perennial philosophy" means, they
do give us, taken in conjunction with some of his correlative notions
like "true philosophy," "Christian Philosophy," and *prisca philosophia*, a pretty good understanding of his meaning. It is a philosophy
or quasi-theology in which God is accessible to us through the use of
reason. It is a philosophy heavily influenced by late ancient Neoplatonic ideas, as well as those of the Renaissance thinkers who revived
them. The *philosophia perennis* has an epistemology in which God is
knowable by human reason; it is a religious philosophy which induces
piety and a desire for the contemplation of God. Steuco looked upon
his philosophy as "Christian Philosophy," in the same way as Justin
looked upon his as Christian. But, unfortunately, we have no standard
by which to judge which of these is more Christian, or by which to
compare these as to Christian content with the philosophy of Thomas

[98] *Ibid.*, X, 3; fol. 189ᵛ. See also X, 6; fols. 190ᵛ–191ʳ, which argues that "true
Christian philosophy (*Christiana vera philosophia*)" is in basic argeement with
Jamblichus' definition of "true wisdom (*vera sapientia*)."

[99] ". . . ut dixi, perennis haec fuit usque ab exordio generis humani philosophia. . . ." *Ibid.*, X, 1; fol. 188ᵛ.

[100] "Huius operis autem duplex erat ratio, ut quoniam ostensum est unam necessario semper fuisse sapientiam, sive successione proditam, sive coniecturis et iudiciis
exceptam utranque revocare et conferre cum vera; propterea conformationes aut de
perenni philosophia sunt appellatae." *Ibid.*, I, 1; fol. 2ᵛ.

Aquinas or of Etienne Gilson.[101] Certainly, Steuco's philosophy has as much claim to be called Christian as any other, for it is a philosophy which is fully absorbed into Christianity. It is a philosophy in which the religious aspects are nearly indistinguishable from the non-religious. We must leave it for others to judge whether Steuco's philosophy is truly a "Christian philosophy." What is certain is that it has every right to be called "perennial." Steuco claims to have found a common chord which has sounded throughout the history of philosophy; and, according to him, the Christian philosophical tradition, particularly that of his own day, was in complete agreement with this.[102]

The weakness of a syncretism such as Steuco's is evident. Even the medieval theologians who labored to bring Aristotle into accord with Christianity had their share of difficulty, and theirs was a more modest attempt. Their ultimate success was at the expense of transforming certain central Aristotelian doctrines into a sort of Neoplatonism. Again, Giovanni Pico's attempt to bring Aristotle and Plato into agreement resulted in his making havoc of Plotinus.[103] Steuco's task was even more difficult, for he tried to make nearly everyone agree. With the enormousness of this task in view, we can perhaps forgive him for a few rough edges and misinterpretations. Steuco was not quite up to the job which he set himself. He in some ways lacked the critical abilities which would have allowed him to see that some of the positions which he tried to reconcile were, and always will remain, at odds. On the other hand, had he possessed these abilities it is doubtful whether he would have undertaken his project in the first place. Still, in fairness to him, we cannot agree with certain modern critics who argue that he was quite without critical ability.[104] If he accepted spurious works as genuine, he was in the good com-

---

[101] The controversy over what is the nature of Christian philosophy and, indeed, whether there is such a thing as Christian philosophy is one that still rages. Of the large literature on the subject see especially the following: Etienne Gilson, *A Gilson Reader* (New York, 1957), 169–221; Maurice Nédoncelle, *Is There a Christian Philosophy?* trans. I. Trethowan (New York, 1960), with further references; Cornelia de Vogel, "'Ego sum qui sum' et sa signification pour une philosophie chrétienne," *Revue des sciences religieuses*, XXXV (1961), 337–55; Fernand van Steenberghen, "La philosophie en chrétienté," *Revue philosophique de Louvain*, LXI (1963), 561–82.

[102] "Non aliud est hodierna philosophia quam divinae probitatis, iustitiae, bonitatis imitatio. Ecce una omnium religio, mens omnibus una, unus vitae finis, una eademque philosophia Deum imitari, voluptates ex hac imitatione nascentes solas prosequendas, solas veras, synceras." *De per phil.*, X, 18; fol. 198ʳ.

[103] See Klibansky, *op. cit.*

[104] Esp. Freudenberger, *op. cit.*, 122, 298–300, 363–65, and Ebert, *op. cit.*, 96.

pany of most of his predecessors and contemporaries. To rebuke him for not having the same ability as XXth-century philologists to distinguish the genuine from the spurious seems to be somewhat harsh. He did in truth have some reservations about the philosophies he was trying to bring into accord. He did not hesitate to criticize even his favorite sources. He upon occasion disagrees with Plato, Jamblichus, and other highly esteemed predecessors.[105] It is also noteworthy that Steuco very seldom mentions Ficino and Pico by name in the *De perenni philosophia*. In fact, the only reference to them which I have found is one in which he criticizes their interpretation of Proclus.[106] Yet his debt to them is most obvious; and our major thesis has been that Steuco represented a continuation of certain aspects of philosophy strongly emphasized by Ficino and Pico. This merely indicates more clearly that Steuco was not *kritiklos*—at least no more so than his XVth-century predecessors—but that he fell prey to some of the intellectual shortcomings of his age. The limitations of his program are apparent and the inconsistencies of his thought are obvious to the modern critic.

His chief shortcoming was to place too much confidence in the authority of the *prisca theologia*. These writings, to which he attributed such an important rôle, were all later proven to be forgeries dating from hardly before the advent of the Christian era. In the case of the Hermetic writings, in which Steuco had such great confidence, their spurious nature was recognized for the first time only by Isaac Casaubon in 1614; and, even after that date, they were not entirely without influence.[107] The conception of the *prisca theologia* is certainly a respectable one and those who supported it could not really know beforehand that it would turn out to be a *cul de sac*. Indeed, the approach used by Steuco and the others is not wholly different from certain contemporary attempts to find elements of experience common to all peoples at all times.

VI. Reactions to Steuco

While Steuco's work did not exactly fall "deadborn from the press," it by no means elicited the interest which discussions of perennial philosophy have elicited in our own time. It did gain some attention in the centuries after its publication and did inspire several works on the same theme; on the whole, however, it attracted rela-

---

[105] For Plato see *De per. phil.*, fols. 149ᵛ, 150ʳ, 185ᵛ and for Jamblichus, fols. 94ᵛ, 157ʳ. Steuco also wrote a work, no longer extant, *Liber contra theologiam Platonicorum*. See Freudenberger, *op. cit.*, 63–65, 73–74, 393.

[106] *De per. phil.*, II, 18; fol. 42ᵛ.

[107] Frances Yates, *op. cit.*, esp. 398–431.

tively little notice. In general, those who took an interest in Steuco and admired his work were, as we might expect, of the same general philosophical orientation as Steuco himself. He was much more admired among the nonscholastic theologians and philosophers than among scholastics. Steuco and his conception of "perennial philosophy" were consistently identified with the tradition of Augustine, Cusanus, Ficino, and Pico. One has to wait until the XXth century to find the term applied to other philosophical traditions. Leaving aside the question of later interpretation, let us focus on the reactions to Steuco's work before Leibniz.

First of all we should note that, whatever the scholastic reaction to *De perenni philosophia*, it was never placed on the Index. On the other hand, Steuco's *Cosmopoeia*,[108] a commentary on Genesis which expresses many of the same ideas as the *De perenni philosophia*, was condemned in 1583 and again in 1596.[109] Although the *De perenni philosophia* did not incur official condemnation it was criticized, sometimes quite harshly. Among the most outspoken of the critics of Steuco's position were the Jesuits, Benito Pereira (1535–1610) [110] and Denis Petau or Petavius, (1583–1652).[111] Both of these men found Steuco to be almost completely on the wrong track, as far as his theology was concerned. In addition to stating that Steuco defended specific positions which are "not only false, but even most absurd and completely inconsistent with Christian teaching." [112] Pereira opposed Steuco's contention that the ancient philosophical and religious traditions are in general agreement with the teachings of Moses. In a way not too different from Tertullian or Bonaventure, Pereira argued that the Hebreo-Christian tradition differed radically from the *prisca theologia* so dear to Steuco's heart.[113] Fifty years later Petau

---

[108] In *Opera* I, fols. 1–77. See Freudenberger, *op. cit.*, 201–19. For the importance and influence of this work see also Otto Zoeckler, *Geschichte der Beziehungen zwischen Theologie und Naturwissenschaft mit besonderer Ruecksicht auf Schoepfungsgeschichte* (Guetersloh, 1877–79), I, 634–39.

[109] Heinrich Reusch, *Die Indices Librorum Prohibitorum des Sechzehnten Jahrhunderts* (Tübingen, 1886), 389, 540; *idem, Der Index der verbotenen Bücher* (Bonn, 1883), I, 570; and Freudenberger, *op. cit.*, 228–29.

[110] For Pereira see De Backer-Sommervogel, *Bibliothèque des écrivains de la compagnie de Jésus* (Liège-Lyon, 1869–76), II, cols. 1861–66; III, cols. 2405–06.

[111] For Petau see P. Galtier, "Denys Petau," *Dict. de theol. cath.*, XII (1933), cols. 1313–37; J. C. Vital Chatellain, *Le père Denis Petau d'Orléans, Jésuite: sa vie et ses oeuvres* (Paris, 1884); De Backer-Sommervogel, *op. cit.*, II, cols. 1891–1909; III, cols. 2414–15.

[112] *Benedicti Pererii . . . Commentariorum et disputationum in Genesim, tomi quatuor* (Cologne, 1601), 17b. See Freudenberger, *op. cit.*, 229. The first edition of this work appeared in 1589.

[113] Pereira, *op. cit.*, 8a.

repeated Pereira's attack in nearly the same terms. He found not only that Steuco's errors were not tolerable in a Christian, but that his whole emphasis on the agreement of the Platonists with .Christianity was out of place in a theologian.[114]

The attempt to promote a general concord between Christianity and the other ancient traditions was vehemently rejected also by Giambattista Crispo of Gallipoli. In his *De ethnicis caute legendis* (1594), a work approved by a number of theologians, including Francisco Suarez,[115] Steuco's *philosophia perennis* was severely attacked. According to Crispo, Steuco had not been cautious enough in his reading of the Platonists and had absorbed some errors from them.[116] Again, he criticizes "that celebrated writer on perennial philosophy (*celebrem illum de perenni philosophia scriptorem*)" for comparing Moses to Plato: "Steuco's odious comparison (*odiosa Eugubini comparatio*)," Crispo calls it.[117] This criticism of Steuco was evidently supported by Suarez, as well as by Pereira and Petau. How different, it must be observed, has been the attitude of their Jesuit successors toward *philosophia perennis* after its having been appropriated as the *mot juste* of Thomistic scholasticism.[118]

[114] *Dionysii Petavii . . . Theologicorum dogmatum tomus tertius* (Paris, 1644), 94. For a discussion of Petau's opinion that the ancient philosophers had no knowledge of the true God and were basically in error see J. C. Vital Chatellain, *op. cit.,* 386 and also Richard Simon, *Critique de la bibliothèque* (Paris, 1730), II, 25 and Morhof, *op. cit.,* III, p. 526.

[115] The approval for the publication of Crispo's book in which Suarez' name is included is found in *Ioannis Baptistae Crispi De ethnicis caute legendis disputationum libri* XXIII . . . (Rome, 1594), fol. a4ᵛ. I have been unable to learn much about Crispo. Some information is to be found in Nicolò Toppi, *Biblioteca napoletana . . .* (Naples, 1678), 132, 339 and Camillo Minieri Riccio, *Memorie storiche degli scrittori nati nel regno di Napoli* (Naples, 1844), 113, 394. It was already noted by J. G. Schelhorn, *Amoenitates literariae* (Frankfurt, Leipzig, 1726–31), V, 265, that he criticized Ficino and Steuco for attempting to reconcile the Scriptures with gentile philosophy.   [116] *op. cit.,* 36.

[117] *Ibid.,* 39; cf. *De per. phil.,* I, 5; fol. 5ʳ; II, 11; fol. 30ʳ. Steuco also speaks of *philosophia Mosaica* (VII, 11; fol. 126ʳ). For general information on this tradition see Danton B. Sailor, "Moses and Atomism," this *Journal,* XXV (1964), 1–16, treating some of the same thinkers covered here.

[118] In a recent statement we read, "We approve and recommend the admissibility and desirability of a variety of methods and approaches to achieving the basic insights and commitments proper to the Philosophia Perennis. . . . Without violating this admirable pluralism in approach, care should be exercised in staffing departments to select teachers who are philosophically committed to the basic insights of the Philosophia Perennis. . . . While affirming that every living philosophy must be constantly open to philosophical insights from any source, the philosophy departments of Jesuit colleges and universities are committed to the following positions as basic to the Philosophia Perennis and normative for unity." "Statement of Positions," *Jesuit Educational Quarterly,* XXV (1963), 9–10. *Philosophia perennis* is

Other critics of Steuco and his work include Gerardus Johannes Vossius (1577–1649), Richard Simon (1638–1712), and Johannes Matthaeus Gesner (1691–1761). Vossius, the important classical philologist and Protestant theologian active in the Netherlands, openly attacked Steuco for holding that the ancient gentile religions were in general agreement with Christianity. He charges Steuco with twisting Plato's words to make them agree with Christian teaching. Vossius can see no connection between the teachings of the *prisci theologi* and Christianity, and concludes that no one who knows Plato well could agree with Steuco's interpretation.[119] Simon, the brilliant French scriptural scholar, criticized Steuco for depending excessively on the *prisci theologi* and also for misinterpreting them.[120] Gesner, the learned German philologist, found Steuco, along with Psellus and Ficino, to have erroneously held that religious truths may be known without actual access to the Scriptures. He maintained that the Augustinian canon had claimed that many things which are known by revelation alone were taught by the pagan writers and philosophers (*gentiles scriptores et philosophos*).[121]

With few exceptions, all of these criticisms amount to the same thing. They revolve around what must be considered a perennial problem for the Christian philosopher: to what extent are the Christian Scriptures unique, teaching truths which are to be found nowhere else; and to what extent are they the most perfect expression of truths which have been known throughout history to men of all philosophies, all religions, all ethnic backgrounds? Steuco, as we have said, tended toward a liberal position in which many truths are held to be accessible to man's reason unaided by revelation. Most of those who criticized him were of a more conservative persuasion.

Among those favorable to Steuco we find syncretists of all varieties. The syncretistic tendency of the XVIth century was very strong and a number of works appeared which attempted to make two or more of the ancient traditions agree on basic issues.[122] Steuco stands

---

consistently capitalized and is not italicized. There is a single criticism of Steuco in *Roberti Bellarmini . . . De controversiis Christianae fidei* (Venice, 1721), IV, 15a (the treatise *De gratia primi hominis*, ch. 8). The Jesuit, Antonio Possevino, however, praised Steuco several times. See his *Bibliotheca selecta* (Cologne, 1607), 17, 33, 38, 56 and *Apparatus sacer* (Venice, 1606), I, 147–48.

[119] *Gerardi Joannis Vossii et clarorum virorum ad eum epistolae . . .* (London, 1690), 112b–113a, a letter to Abraham Van der Meer, dated Nov. 19, 1627. Further references to Steuco and his work are in *De theologia gentili et physiologia Christiana*, in Vossius' *Opera* (Amsterdam, 1700), V, 3b, 4b, 15a.

[120] Richard Simon, *op. cit.*, II, 18–30. See Freudenberger, *op. cit.*, 147, 152, 219.

[121] *Primae lineae isagoges in eruditionem universalem nominatim philologiam, historiam, et philosophiam . . .* (Leipzig, 1774), II, 285.

[122] Of such works we might mention the following: *Sebastiani Foxii Morzilli . . .*

squarely in this tradition. He, like Bessarion, Cusanus, Ficino, Pico, Giorgio, Champier, and others, is often cited by the syncretistic branch of XVIth-century philosophy.

Hardly before the ink was dry on the *De perenni philosophia* it was noted by Guillaume Postel (1510–81), whose enormous range of interests surpassed even Steuco's. Postel cited Steuco and the *De perenni philosophia* as early as 1543 in his *De rationibus Spiritus Sancti.*[123] A year later he published an avowedly syncretistic work, more worthy of Giorgio perhaps than of anyone else in the tradition, the *De orbis terrae concordia.*[124] Steuco's work was also noticed early by Julius Caesar Scaliger (1484–1558), who had highest praise for its author, calling him "a divine man and easily a prince of true literature." [125] The admiration which the elder Scaliger had for Steuco and his work is clearly told by Joseph Scaliger in his *Life* of his father.[126] The Platonic bent of Steuco's perennial philosophy was duly noted by the Frenchman Jacques Charpentier (1524–74), author of a long work comparing Plato and Aristotle. Charpentier, who was looking for material in support of his own view that Platonism and Christianity are reconcilable, cited evidence from Steuco that such an end can be accomplished.[127]

De naturae philosophia seu de Platonis et Aristotelis consensione libri V (Paris, 1560); Gabriel Buratellus, *Praecipuarum controversiarum Aristotelis et Platonis conciliatio* (Venice, 1573); *Iacobi Mazonii . . . De triplici hominum vita, activa nempe, contemplativa, et religiosa methodi tres . . .* (Cesena, 1577); *Iacobi Mazonii . . . In universam Platonis et Aristotelis philosophiam praeludia sive de comparatione Platonis et Aristotelis* (Venice, 1597); Francesco de' Vieri, *Vere conclusioni di Platone conformi alla dottrina cristiana et a quella d'Aristotile* (Florence, 1590); *Pauli Beni . . . In Platonis Timaeum sive in naturalem omnem atque divinam Platonis et Aristotelis philosophiam decades tres* (Rome, 1594).

[123] (Paris, 1543), fol. 33ᵛ. See William J. Bouwsma, *Concordia Mundi: The Career and Thought of Guillaume Postel (1510–1581),* (Cambridge, Mass., 1957), 59, 194. Another early reader of Steuco, who used his work as a source of Platonic doctrine was Marcantonio Maioragio. See his *Reprehensionum contra Marium Nizolium . . . Libri duo* (Milan, 1549), 197 and Quirinus Breen, "The *Antiparadoxon* of Marcantonius Majoragius," *Studies in the Renaissance,* V (1958), 37–48, esp. 45.

[124] (Basel, 1544). On his syncretistic tendency see Bouwsma, *op. cit.,* 99–137, 194–96.

[125] *Iulii Caesaris Scaligeri epistolae et orationes* (Hanover, 1612), 48–49. This is from the prefatory letter to his translation, *Libri de plantis falso Aristoteli attributi* (1556). See Freudenberger, *op. cit.,* 123.

[126] William Bates (ed.), *Vitae selectorum aliquot virorum . . .* (London, 1681), 413. See Schelhorn, *op. cit.,* V, 266, and Freudenberger, *op. cit.,* 123.

[127] Iacobus Carpentarius, *Platonis cum Aristotele in universa philosophia comparatio* (Paris, 1573), I, 234, 272. For a summary of Charpentier's own view see his preface, I, fol. D_{III}.

One of the most enthusiastic early followers of Steuco's philosophy was Paul Scalichius (1534–1574),[128] a philosopher and theologian from Zagreb. Scalichius, who studied at Bologna and Rome, was sympathetic toward the writings of Giovanni Pico in particular and to the tradition of the *prisca theologia* in general.[129] He admired Steuco and the *De perenni philosophia* so much that he apparently appropriated large sections of it for use in his own treatise *De iustitia aeterna seu de vera promissione gradatio* and gave only nominal credit to Steuco.[130]

The spirit of Ficino, Pico, and Steuco is almost evident in a work of the Italian Muzio Pansa (c. 1560–1640), which was completed in 1601.[131] Pansa, known also for having written the first book on the Vatican Library, perhaps carries the tradition of *philosophia perennis* to its apogee, as the title of his work, *Tract on The Kissing or Consensus of Ethnic and Christian Philosophy,* indicates. His dependence on Steuco is obvious from the opening words of his Preface: "Wisdom and piety. . . , born from the same sources and always seeking one goal, are seen to be joined to one another in such a way that they cannot be separated." [132] We need not go into detail here on just how close the resemblance is between Pansa's work and Steuco's. Of the immediate predecessors by whom Pansa had been especially influenced, he cites by name in his Preface, Cusanus, Bessarion, Pletho, and Steuco.[133] A comparison of Pansa with Steuco discloses that many passages have been taken nearly word for word from the latter, although, like Scalichius, he rarely cites him.[134] Pansa's work is essentially an early XVIIth-century reiteration of the principles of perennial philosophy.

[128] Gerta Krabbel, *Paul Skalich: ein Lebensbild aus dem 16. Jahrhundert* (Münster, 1916) and Ioannes Georgius Schelhorn, "De vita et scriptis Pauli Scalichii commentatio," *Bibliotheca historico-philologico-theologica,* VII (1723–24), 1027–51.

[129] Krabbel, op. cit., 8, 119–20, 185–88, 191–92; Schelhorn, "De vita. . . ," 1044, 1049.

[130] Krabbel, op. cit., 186–90; Schelhorn, "De vita. . . ," 1049–50; Freudenberger, op. cit., 123. There is a rare copy of Scalichius' *Opera* (Basel, 1559) in the Universitätsbibliothek, Basel.

[131] *De osculo seu consensu ethnicae et Christianae philosophiae tractatus. Unde Chaldaeorum, Aegyptiorum, Persarum, Arabum, Graecorum, et Latinorum mysteria tanquam ab Hebraeis desumpta fidei nostrae consona de Deo deducuntur* (Marburg, 1605). The dedicatory letter is dated 1601 (fol.):(4v). On Pansa see Michaud, *Biographie universelle,* new ed., (Paris, s.d.), XXXII, 76–77; Toppi, op. cit., 217–18, 365; Leonardo Nicodemo, *Addizioni copiose . . . alla biblioteca . . . del dottor Toppi* (Naples, 1683), 177; Minieri Riccio, op. cit., 253.

[132] *De osculo. . . ,* fol.):(5r.

[133] *Ibid.,* fol.):(7v. See Morhof, op. cit., III, 526 and *Iacobi Bruckeri . . . Historia critica philosophiae . . .* (Leipzig, 1766–67), IV, 753–54.

[134] *De osculo. . . ,* 88 for a rare specific reference to Steuco.

Steuco and his work were known throughout the XVIIth and early XVIIIth century. Interestingly, those favorably disposed toward his notion of perennial philosophy during this period seem to have been predominantly Protestant. Moreover, greater attention seems to have been given him in England than elsewhere. We shall not go into detail regarding those who drew upon Steuco's teaching during this period, but we shall mention a few who cited him. Besides the general historians of learning such as Morhof (1639–91) who discuss him, he was known to Theophilus Gale (1628–78),[135] Edward Stillingfleet (1635–99),[136] and Johann Lorenz von Mosheim (c. 1694–1755).[137] There was an attempt among the philosophers and theologians of this period, as there has been in all other periods, to demonstrate that the differences which divide the various theological and philosophical systems are not as great as they sometimes appear. In fact, the period from about 1580 to about 1750 in many ways represents the high point of this movement, in spite of what the textbooks say about the tendency to separate philosophy and theology after Descartes. The question of the relation between different religions and philosophies is one which occupied the attention of numerous thinkers during the period, including Jacopo Mazzoni, Francesco de' Vieri, Ralph Cudworth, Tobias Pfanner, Pierre Daniel Huet, Herbert of Cherbury, and Daniel Clasenius.[138]

Finally, one who stands very much in this tradition and all that it sums up is Gottfried Wilhelm Leibniz (1646–1716). Although it is more fashionable today to see Leibniz as a "precursor of modern logic and mathematics" or as a brilliant metaphysician, his affinity to the tradition of perennial philosophy as envisioned by Steuco is most clear. Leibniz's whole philosophy of harmony is very similar to that expressed by Steuco and the others we have discussed, although in Leibniz the metaphysical foundations of such a *Harmonistik* are much more carefully worked out, recalling in some ways Cusanus' attempt to give a metaphysical basis to a "philosophy of concord." Leibniz perhaps understood better than any of his contemporaries the importance of properly evaluating the history of philosophy and the importance of being able to pick out what is valuable from all systems

---

[135] *The Court of the Gentiles*, 2nd ed. (London-Oxford, 1672–77), I, fol. *2ʳ, pp. 5–7, 35–61 *passim;* II, 227, 358, 362.

[136] *Origines sacrae*, 8th ed., in *Works*, II (London, 1709), part ii, 37.

[137] "Dissertatio in qua solvitur haec quaestio: num philosophorum a vera religione aversorum aliquis mundum a Deo ex nihilo creatum esse docuerit?" in *Radulphi Cudworthi . . . Systema intellectuale huius universi . . .* (Jena, 1733), 957–1000, esp. 959–60.

[138] This list is merely indicative and is by no means complete. For further indications see Brucker, *op. cit.,* IV, 750–75.

and all periods of history.[139] In a sense, Leibniz is the most eminent defender of the tradition called by Steuco *philosophia perennis*. Moreover, Leibniz's attempts to bring about religious unity [140]—in a century not reputed for its ecumenical spirit—hark back to Cusanus, as well as to Ficino and Pico.

Leibniz is not the originator of the notion of perennial philosophy. Far from it! He was but the heir to a long and prolific tradition of concordism. Leibniz himself already knew Steuco's work by 1687, when he mentioned it in a letter to Simon Foucher (1644–96).[141] Although Leibniz felt that Steuco's work gave a good summary of the points in which the pagan religions agree with Christianity, he found du Plessis-Mornay's *De la vérité de la religion chrétienne* superior to it.[142] Leibniz knew Steuco well, however, and traces of his influence can be found throughout Leibniz's writings.[143]

VII. Conclusion

From all of these things, we can draw several general conclusions, I think. Our investigation has focused upon what is admittedly an undercurrent in early modern philosophy and one which does not fit in very well with many generalizations which we read concerning the Enlightenment, atheism, the rise of "modern science," and the secularization of philosophy during the XVIth, XVIIth, and XVIIIth centuries. Nevertheless, the tradition of perennial philosophy does rep-

[139] His famous remark "That the opinions of the theologians and of the so-called scholastic philosophers are not to be wholly despised," (*Discourse on Metaphysics*, XI), indicates this as does his preface to Nizolio's *De veris principiis*, where he astutely evaluates his predecessors.

[140] On this see particularly Jean Baruzi, *Leibniz et l'organisation religieuse de la terre* (Paris, 1907). The article by J. H. Crehan, "Leibniz and the Polemics of Reunion," *Thought*, X (1935), 16–29, is an expression more of fevered polemic than of sound scholarship.

[141] "J'ai vu Augustinus Steuchus Jugubinus [!] de perenni philosophia, mais son dessein est principalement d'accommoder les anciens au christianisme (ce qui est en effect très beau), plustost que de mettre les pensées de philosophie dans leur jour." C. J. Gerhardt ed., I, 395. Leibniz has also been connected to Steuco but without any real evidence being cited by Nedoncelle, *op. cit.*, 75.

[142] "Augustinus Steuchus fit un enchaînement assez joli de toutes ces choses dans son livre *De perenni philosophia*. Mais l'ouvrage de M. du Plessis Mornay de la vérité de la Religion Chrétienne le surpassa de beaucoup." Cf. G. Leibniz, *Opera omnia. . .*, ed. Dutens (Geneva, 1768), VI, p. 244. Du Plessis-Mornay's work was first printed in 1581 at Antwerp and many times thereafter, both in French and in Latin and English (by Sir Philip Sidney) translation. See Raoul Patry, *Philippe du Plessis-Mornay, un huguenot homme d'état (1549–1623)*, (Paris, 1963), 293–300.

[143] He is also cited in the preface to the *Theodicy* (Erdmann ed., 488a) and in Gottfried Wilhelm Leibniz, *Sämtliche Schriften und Briefe*, Prussian Acad. ed., II ser., vol. I (1926), 176; VI ser., vol. I (1930), 532.

resent one strand of early modern thought, an element which seems to me to be underestimated and imperfectly understood. Not only has there been lack of understanding of the whole tradition leading up to Steuco's *De perenni philosophia* and of the whole tradition streaming from it, the very notion of *philosophia perennis* has been consistently applied to traditions with which it has little or no historical connection.

From this study, I think that we can safely present the following significant, if modest, conclusions. First of all, Leibniz was not the originator of the notion of *philosophia perennis*. Secondly, it is not a concept which grew up in the scholastic tradition and it does not seem to have any particular affinity to the philosophy and theology of Thomas Aquinas. Thirdly, it does not seem to have been appropriated by scholastic philosophy until the dawning of the XXth century. Fourthly, the conception of perennial philosophy is an outgrowth of the Neoplatonic interest in the *prisca theologia* and of the attempt to produce harmony from discord, unity from multiplicity. Fifthly, Agostino Steuco probably originated the term *philosophia perennis* and certainly gave to it a definite meaning, which seems to have become less precise as it became more widely used. Steuco's meaning, strongly tied to Ficino's notion that truth derived from the "perennial fountain" of Platonism, exerted a limited but noticeable influence on philosophers and theologians of the XVIth, XVIIth, and XVIIIth centuries, ultimately finding a place in the writings of Leibniz, the most eminent concordist of them all.

Finally—although, on this point I cannot be as insistent as on the others—the evidence seems to indicate that Leibniz was the first to speak of *philosophia perennis* without specifically referring to Steuco as the author of the notion. In his letter to Remond, which has often been cited as the first use of the term, Leibniz does not specifically mention Steuco. From this time onward the connection of "perennial philosophy" with the theologian from Gubbio was often lost. At some later point in its history the term was appropriated by the Scholastics and others, gaining something in emotive value, but losing its precise philosophical meaning in the process. These are some of the questions which remain to be treated elsewhere.[144]

Fordham University.

[144] This paper was read to the Columbia University Seminar on the Renaissance on December 15, 1964 and to the U.C.L.A. Philosophy Colloquium on October 22, 1965. I am indebted to Professors P. O. Kristeller, Edward Mahoney, and Robert Mulvaney for a number of helpful suggestions in connection with its preparation.

IV

WAS LORENZO VALLA AN
ORDINARY LANGUAGE PHILOSOPHER?

By John Monfasani

Someday a brave soul will write a book on the pathologies of scholarship. One chapter surely will have the title "The Winds of Fashion." It will discuss how scholars suddenly discover in texts ideas which happen to be fashionable today. Such discoveries are essentially humorous. Either they are wrong and therefore ridiculous, or they are right and therefore the joke is on us as we catch up to the past. Another clue we can call the *redivivus* argument, found when a past author and a contemporary author are quoted together to show how they are really saying the same thing and, sometimes—lo and behold!—in the same words. Mistranslation is, of course, typical, though not peculiar to the malady. More characteristic is the generous quotation of modern authorities to tell us what we are supposed to find in a historical text. Similarly, a heavy dose of the latest social scientific, literary, linguistic, or philosophical theories to explain what is under, between, around, and behind the lines of a text is *prima facie* evidence for suspecting that a piece of writing has more to do with present vogue than past fact.

In varying degrees all these symptoms appear in the current effort to make out of the Renaissance humanist Lorenzo Valla (1407-57) an ordinary language philosopher in the mode of the "later Wittgenstein."[1] The latest and most explicit attempt to interpret Valla as a "later Wittgenstein" *ante litteram* is to be found in the writings of Richard Waswo.[2] However, Waswo identifies as preceding him in the effort Salvatore Camporeale's *Lorenzo Valla: Umanesimo e teologia* published in 1972 (Florence) and Hanna-Barbara Gerl's *Rhetorik als Philosophie: Lorenzo Valla* published in 1974 (Munich).

In the main, this seems to me to be a correct view of the scholarly tradition. But certain observations are in order. For one, as we shall see below, Sarah Stever Gravelle should be added to the list. For another, neither Camporeale nor Gerl ever mention Wittgenstein in their books. Furthermore, while Camporeale analyzes very sympathetically Valla's theory of linguistic *consuetudo* as the basis of Valla's attack on scholastic philosophy, nowhere in his book does he interpret Valla as holding the position which Waswo and Gerl attribute to Valla, namely, "that language does not reveal or reflect reality but constitutes

I wish to thank Alan Perreiah, Frederick Purnell, Jr., Mirko Tavoni, and Brian Vickers for commenting on an early draft of this paper.

[1] The views of Ludwig Wittgenstein (1889-1951) are in no way at issue in this paper. But it is relevant to note that one of his best known and most distinguished students denied that Wittgenstein was an ordinary language philosopher even in his later writings; see N. Malcolm, "Wittgenstein, Ludwig Josef Johann," *The Encyclopedia of Philosophy*, VIII, 337a.

[2] First in "The 'Ordinary Language Philosophy' of Lorenzo Valla," *Bibliothèque d'Humanisme et Renaissance*, 41 (1979), 255-71; and then in *Language and Meaning in the Renaissance* (Princeton, 1987), 88-112, especially 98.

it."[3] However, in a recent article, Camporeale does associate Valla with Wittgenstein,[4] and seems to affirm the Gerl-Waswo thesis of Valla's constitutive view of language.[5] Also, Camporeale's book is a very different sort of work than Gerl's and Waswo's. Camporeale explores a wide spectrum of Valla's writings, while Gerl and, much more so, Waswo examine a relatively narrow band of Vallan texts from a rather single-minded ideological perspective. Camporeale handles ably the critically important manuscript traditions of Valla's writings, whereas Gerl ignores this material[6] and Waswo shows himself noticeably inept the few times he deals with it.[7] Lastly, neither Gerl nor Waswo are up to Camporeale's competence in Latin.[8]

[3] Waswo, *Language and Meaning*, 219.

[4] Lorenzo Valla, "*Repastinatio, liber primus*: retorica e linguaggio," O. Besomi and M. Regoliosi (eds.), *Lorenzo Valla e l'umanesimo italiano: Atti del convegno internazionale di studi umanistici (Parma, 18-19 ottobre 1984)* (Padua, 1986), 217-39; he places a quotation from Wittgenstein at the head of the article (217); he states (233): "Dunque, tutta l'argomentazione del Valla, nel capitolo ora indicato come per l'intero *liber primus* della *Repastinatio* (e altrove) è fondata sulla *consuetudo loquendi*; e questa, a mio avviso . . . non è qualcosa diverso da ciò che il Wittgenstein delle *Ricerche filosofiche* e del *Libro blu e Libro marrone* chiama 'la grammatica della parola.' "

[5] Waswo's article of 1979 is conspicuous by its absence from Camporeale's discussion of the same problems and texts in his own article of 1986. Nor does Camporeale see fit to cite Gerl as agreeing with him anywhere in the article; cf., in contrast (228-29, n. 12) his warm praise of Donald Kelley, whose work on Valla he did not know at the time of his earlier book. Yet, some of Camporeale's ideas in the article are identical with those of Gerl and Waswo, for instance (219): "E sono le realtà espresse e contenute nel linguaggio che costituiscono l'oggetto, la verità, cui il pensiero tende di fatto e a cui è soltanto capace di tendere."

[6] Her book is a study of Valla's *De vero bono* and *Dialectica*; but though she cites (26, n. 31) an early article of G. Zippel on the different recensions of the *Dialectica* and (81, n. 2, and 100, n. 3) an article of M. Lorch de Panizza on the recensions of the *De vero bono*, she seems not to have seen any version of these texts other than that of the 1540 *Opera omnia*.

[7] Waswo's absurd paleographical note on a reading in his article "The 'Ordinary Language Philosophy' " (266, note *) has already been adequately exposed by M. Szymański, "Philosophy and Language," *Bibliothèque d'Humanisme et Renaissance*, 44 (1982), 151. In his book Waswo deals with the manuscript tradition of the *Dialectica* only twice and he gives his own reading (109-10, n. 34) of a brief passage from one of the manuscripts of the *Dialectica* (Bibl. Apostolica Vaticana, Ottob. lat. 2075) and creates a new error (at p. 124.23 in G. Zippel's critical edition, *Laurentii Valle Repastinatio dialectice et philosophie* [2 vols.; Padua, 1982]), reporting *quia* where Zippel has *quam*. I verified by direct inspection that Zippel is correct. Again, not understanding that editors of critical editions of Renaissance Latin texts are expected to punctuate for sense and not try to duplicate the punctuation of the manuscripts or early editions, he criticizes (106, note) Zippel for departing from the punctuation of the Basel *Opera* and the final "manuscript" [*sic*] version. He also apparently thinks that the manuscripts of a text are all punctuated alike. Otherwise how else can he claim in the same note to know the punctuation of the final recension after having consulted only one manuscript?

Waswo seems not to appreciate the superiority of a proper critical edition over a sixteenth-century edition of a text that had already gone through several printings. Even though he had Zippel's edition of the *Dialectica* available when he came to write *Language and Meaning*, Waswo prefers to quote the Basel, 1540 edition of Valla's *Opera omnia*,

If, however, on the scholarly level, the evolution of this particular scholarly tradition has been for the worse, in terms of clarity and precision of presentation Waswo far exceeds his immediate predecessor, Gerl. Gerl wished to demonstrate Valla's philosophy of "ordinary sense" (*Gemeinsinn*) as concretized in ordinary language (*Gemeinsprache*): "Gemeinsinn ist Gemeinsprache" (195).[9] Typical of the book's style and sentiment is this initial programmatic passage about the creative power of language:

These two factors, the words by which poets and the people name things and thus create them in their objective (that is to say, human) form, along with the utilization of these words at particular historical instances by orators, are of necessity sequentially ordered for the formation and maintenance of human

---

as he had in his earlier article and thus creates further confusion. For instance, at 123.25-26 in Zippel, Waswo gives the false reading of the 1540 *Opera*: "res est vox sive vocabulum omnium vocabulorum *significatu suo* complectens [*my emphasis*]," which he renders: " 'thing' is a word or term embracing in its meaning all terms." But from Zippel's apparatus it would seem that the reading *significatu suo* in the 1540 *Opera* replaced the preferable *significata suo* of the *editio princeps*. The manuscripts give the even better *significationes suas* or *significationes sua*. The correct reading (against Zippel, in this instance) is *significationes sua*, so that the sentence should read: " 'thing' is an utterance or a word which embraces *in its signification* the significations of all words." In short Valla is not saying that *res* embraces all other words but that its meaning embraces the meaning of all other words.

[8] Gerl's book is full of translations of Valla which I have not worked through methodically, but as a random sample see the two passages from her book which I quote and comment on below. In each case she translates a line from Valla, and in each case her translation is wrong. Waswo, both in his article and his book, translates only two passages from Valla's *Dialectica* (corresponding to 18.22-20.14 and 123.3-124.16 in Zippel's critical edition) and one passage from the *Antidotum in Facium* (see notes 13 and 14 below) and so badly botched them that M. Szymański had to correct the more absurd renderings in a later issue of *Bibliothèque d'Humanisme et Renaissance* (see the previous note). In the same issue Waswo wrote a response (377-78), where he accepted the corrections, although in his subsequent book he fails to acknowledge the debt. But Szymański corrected only the most blatant of Waswo's errors. For instance, after explaining that *voces* are *imagines significationum* and in the form of letters are properly called *vocabula*, Valla concludes that what we say are words; even our descriptions of words are still words: "And whatever we say, it is this [i.e., *vocabulum*], even 'substance' itself, 'quality,' and 'action,' and 'thing' itself" ("Atque hoc est quicquid loquimur: etiam ipsum 'substantia,' 'qualitas,' 'actio' atque adeo ipsum 'res' "; Zippel, 123.15-17). Waswo makes nonsense out of Valla's conclusion (*Meaning and Language*, 105): "Hence 'this' is whatever we say; it is in fact substance, quality, action; and therefore it is a 'thing,' " as if Valla had reached the trivial conclusion that the word "this" is a thing.

[9] I am trying to capture what Gerl herself views as the central perspective of her book, and therefore I omit anything she has to say specifically about Valla's *De vero bono*, a subject which occupies much of her book but which is not germane to this article. On her discussion of language (65): "Die Sprache—und das ist für Valla immer die Volkssprache, Umgangssprache oder Sprachgewohnheit—tritt gerade in den schärfsten Gegensatz zur Abstraktion, denn die Abstraktion (nach der Interpretation des Realismus) glaubt *über* den Dingen zu stehen. . . . Die Sprache bei Valla dagegen tritt nur im Zusammenhang mit den Dingen auf, und zwar im Sinne einer notwendigen Bewältigung der Dinge für den Menschen."

affairs, and together they make for *eloquentia*. *Eloquentia*, namely, rhetoric in this comprehensive sense, is the keyword for Valla. By it he understands what he calls the "godly" activity of men in as much as it establishes a reality for men which the previous philosophical separation of *res* and *verbum* had taken away. . . .

In this sense Valla can even understand wisdom as the fruit of Word: "The true wisdom is born through the Word" [*translating* "Non est verbigena nisi vera sophia"]. This notion holds the key for Valla's whole *oeuvre*, i.e., for his view of the godly character of the Word. This is also the issue that concerns this book on "Rhetoric as Philosophy." [10]

Without commenting on the quality of her exposition, I think it still fair to point out that she mistranslates the sentence which she claims encapsulates Valla's vision (as it stands, it should read "there is no making of words without true wisdom"). Worse, she is not quoting Valla, but—though she apparently does not realize it—the *Doctrinale* of the thirteenth-century grammarian Alexandre de Villedieu. [11] Worse still, in the very text Gerl quotes, Valla was actually attacking this sentence as nonsense. So, even if we grant what she says is true, it is true of Alexandre de Villedieu, not of Valla.

Towards the end of the book, she summarizes some of her conclusions in a section entitled, "The Word as the Meaning of the Thing in its Human Aspect":

The threefold coincidence of Thing, Word, and Understanding entails the following conclusion. *Res* does not exist for men apart from *verbum* whether the latter means a particular *res* or its general idea. Things are available to men as men only in so far as we recognize them, i.e., give them names. The notion of a fixed, real world in which we are born is false. Language itself is, indeed, already the expression of the alienation between the objective world and man. Therefore, we do not assimilate our words to things. Nor can language in general be a mirror, a silhouette of "reality," for it is precisely the distance to this reality. Rather the first reality of man to be formed is essentially a creation of the word, which transforms the undetermined and unknown into the determined and known, and thereby selects out of an infinity of possibilities one which it

[10] *Ibid.*, 16-17.

[11] The quotation comes from the *Emendationes quorundam locorum ex Alexandro ad Alfonsum primum Aragonum regem*, first printed in 1503 and reprinted in Lorenzo Valla, *Opera omnia. Con una premessa di Eugenio Garin* (Turin, 1962), II. The authenticity of the *Emendationes* is denied by L. Cesarini Martinelli, "Note sulla polemica Poggio-Valla e sulla fortuna delle *Elegantiae*," *Interpres*, 3 (1980), 48ff., and defended (properly, I believe) by P. Casciano, "Ancora sull'*Ars grammatica* di Lorenzo Valla," *Scrittura, biblioteche e stampa a Roma nel Quattrocento. Atti del 2° Seminario, 6-8 maggio 1982* (Littera Antiqua, 3), eds. M. Miglio, P. Farenga, and A. Modigliani (Vatican City, 1983), 57-70. In any event the structure of the work is that of a commentary, i.e., Valla quotes a lemma and then follows it with some sort of clarification, correction, and/or exemplification. The words quoted by Gerl (*Opera*, II, 93) form one of the lemmata from Alexandre: "Non est verbigena nisi Christus, vera sophia" (D. Reichling [ed.], *Das Doctrinale des Alexander de Villa-Dei: Kritish-exegetische Ausgabe*, Monumenta Germaniae paedagogica, 12 [Berlin, 1893], 542). Though the printed text omits "nisi Christus," it is clear from Valla's comments (beginning "Non est Christus ex verbo, sed ex patre eternaliter, ex matre temporaliter. Ipse est verbum.") that the identity of Christ with *verbigena* was the crucial issue.

identifies as reality. Hence one must assign a transcendent role to the word. To be sure, the world itself is not a creation of the word. But the *human* world is such a creation [of the word], not in that it is, as much as possible, a true copy of things or a superficial description of an object that has been determined once and for all, but in that it interprets things in regards to men: "So everything comes forth just as it happens in men" [*translating* "ut quaeque res nascitur sicut in hominibus fit"].[12]

Again, since Waswo explicitly appropriates her ideas, my purpose in quoting Gerl at length is to document her approach to Valla. However, it should be pointed out that she seriously distorts Valla's meaning in the quotation which ends the passage. She wants Valla to be understood in this quotation as denying an external, objective reality in so far as it has relevance for humans. A reading of the Latin will show that her interpretation is bizarre. Perhaps not by coincidence, in his 1979 article Waswo, too, made a hash of these very same words. Mikolaj Szymański took pains to correct Waswo's translation in a later article.[13] In his book of 1987, Waswo acknowledges that the passage will not bear the interpretation Gerl laid upon it, and silently corrects his earlier rendering, still without getting it quite right—despite having available to him Szymański's correction, which he does not mention.[14] The words in question come from Valla's *Antidotum in Facium* and form part of one of Valla's best known *dicta*. The passage runs (I italicize the words Gerl quoted): "Et certe nihil iniquius est quam ad generalia semper et impropria confugere et hanc verborum inopiam pati malle quam suum, *ut queq̃ue res nascitur, sicut in hominibus fit*, attribuere nomen et ingeniosum inventum proprie appellationis honore fraudare."[15] The proper sense of this is: "And certainly nothing is more wicked than always to find refuge in abstract and improper words, and to prefer enduring this penury of words than *to assign something its own name when it is born, as is done in the case of new-born human beings*, and to defraud an ingenuous invention of the honor of its own proper name." Before one brandishes about the words of Valla, it helps to understand what they mean.

In a sense, Waswo is a gloss on Gerl. Both in his earlier article on Valla and in his book, he quotes her extensively and asserts that his goal is to confirm

[12] *Rhetoric als Philosophie*, 224-25.

[13] See Waswo, "The 'Ordinary Language Philosophy' of Lorenzo Valla," 260-61: "for anything is born just as it is created in relation to men"; and Szymański, "Philosophy and Language," 150, who translates correctly: "allot to each thing its name when it is born as is done with men."

[14] *Language and Meaning*, 99: "when it is born, just as is done among men." Waswo spoils Szymański's correction by substituting "among" for "with," thereby making Valla's meaning unclear unless one reads the Latin and knows that Valla meant that we should give names to new-born things just the way we give names to new-born babies. In view of his attitude towards Zippel's critical edition of the *Dialectica*, it is not surprising that Waswo does not quote M. Regoliosi's critical edition of the *Antidotum in Facium* (Padua, 1981), but the *Opera* of 1540.

[15] Valla, *Antidotum in Facium*, I:14.22 (ed. Regoliosi, 106). On this passage see M. Tavoni *Latino, grammatica, volgare: Storia di una questione umanistica* (Padua, 1984), 159-65.

her "principal thesis."[16] What he adds are references to Wittgenstein,[17] whom Gerl does not cite,[18] a greater lucidity in laying out the "principal thesis," and correction of some of Gerl's more extravagant proofs.[19] Unlike Gerl, who argues her case by quoting snippets, Waswo bases his interpretation primarily on the translation and analysis of two long passages of Valla's *Dialectica* (ed. Zippel, 18.22-20.14 and 123.3-124.17).[20] In the first passage the key for the "principal thesis" lies in these lines, as translated by Waswo: "But since there is falsehood in ourselves, why is there not also truth? Certainly when we affirm anything to be false or true, it is referred to the mind of the speaker, because it is in his mind that truth or falsehood reside. For false bread, false wine, and false prophet are, we affirm, by no means, bread, wine, prophet; and true bread, true wine, true prophet are nothing other than bread, wine, or prophet. Thus truth and falsehood are in ourselves, that is, in our mind."[21] In the second passage, the "principal thesis" primarily draws comfort from Valla's assertion that "it makes no difference whether we say, what is wood, what is stone, what iron, what man, or what does wood, stone, iron, man signify." Shortly after Waswo concludes:

As Gerl says, "Being and meaning, the thing and the word, are in the world of human beings not to be separated." What the thing is is what the word means. This equation is Valla's most profound critique of all the assumptions about the relation of word/object/meaning contained in the traditional process of signification or representation. It denies both the correspondence theory of truth and the referential theory of meaning, which is no longer to be sought in

[16] *Language and Meaning*, 102: "The fullest account of this view is presented by Gerl, whose principal thesis my analysis has sought to confirm."

[17] *Ibid.*, 24 and n. 20; 98; and 103-4, n. 28. See also "The 'Ordinary Language Philosophy' of Lorenzo Valla," 255, 260, and 264.

[18] I do not know if Gerl's ideas derive from a reading of Wittgenstein; her enthusiasm for *Gemeinsprache* and the constitutive powers of language could stem from a variety of sources.

[19] See *Language and Meaning*, 100, n. 23; 105, n. 30; and 108.

[20] *Ibid.*, 95-96, 105-6; see n. 8 above.

[21] Waswo translated the text in the 1540 *Opera*, which is that of the second recension. I take my text from Zippel's edition (19.17-20.10) and italicize the additions and changes of the third recensions. For the purposes of later reference, I also give more of the text at the start and end than is reproduced in Waswo's translation: "'Verum' sive 'veritas' est proprie scientia sive notitia cuiuscunque rei, et quasi lux animi, que ad sensus quoque se porrigit. Hanc lucem esse volo ipsius animi, quasi oculorum vim videndi et visum, non exteriorem quandam velut solarem: quanquam ut sol oculis colores corporum, ita Deus menti rerum qualitates ostendit et exhibet. Hoc nonnihil diverse protulit Plato in libris *De re publica* cum ait veritatem esse velut solem, scientiam notitiamque, velut sincerum aspectum. Sed cum in nobis falsitas sit, cur non sit et veritas? Certe cum quid verum falsumque esse affirmamus, id ad animum loquentis refertur, quod in eo veritas sit aut falsitas. Nam falsus panis et falsum vinum et falsus propheta nequaquam est panis, vinum, propheta; et verus panis, verum vinum, verus propheta non aliud est quam panis, vinum, propheta, ut nos *sentimus* [opinamur *recen. secund.*]. Itaque in nobis, idest in animo nostro est veritas et falsitas: *sed fons veritatis nostre in Deo sicut nostre lucis in sole. Falsitatis vero in obstructione divini fontis, sicut obscuritatis in subductione solis, ut proprie Deus sit veritas sicut sol lux, quod Plato modo sentiebat.*"

objects but rather in the words that name and categorize them. That is, language and the people who use it do not "represent" a reality but constitute one.[22]

This is the "principal thesis."

Waswo makes some surprising concessions concerning it. As he points out, some of the other texts Gerl adduces in support are beside the point.[23] So we are left with these passages, which because of their inherent "difficulty and inconsistency" yield the Gerl-Waswo interpretation only after considerable analysis. In short, Valla was unclear in his own mind as to what he was doing and only revealed the truth in rather opaque fashion in two passages of a work which contemporaries and later Renaissance readers could not properly decipher. Yet Valla is supposed to stand at the head of a Renaissance tradition, which Waswo sums up as follows in speaking about Erasmus: "The whole humanist focus on language as a sociohistorical product implied what Valla sporadically inferred from it: that semantics is epistemology, that language does not reveal or reflect reality but constitutes it."[24]

This interpretation of Valla and subsequent Renaissance figures is less than persuasive for several reasons. Even if Valla was confused in what he meant and inarticulate in saying it (novel charges, to say the least) and even if this interpretation is correct (which I shall dispute shortly), one may justifiably be suspicious of an argument for Valla's radical philosophy of language that adduces from a large book whose subject matter was logic, language, and philosophy only these two unclear passages and a third one to be quoted later. Indeed, nothing in support can be found in Valla's other philosophical writings, namely, the *De vero falsoque bono*, which he kept revising late into his career, and the *De libero arbitrio*, nor, as far as I can tell, in any other of Valla's voluminous writings.[25] If Valla was an early-day ordinary language philosopher, he kept his secret well.

In point of fact Gerl and Waswo have misinterpreted Valla on every critical point, misunderstanding not only what Valla had to say about truth and meaning but also what his attitude was towards ordinary language.

To start with "truth," when Valla said that truth and falsity are in us, he was not denying "the correspondence theory of truth."[26] Quite the contrary, he was affirming it. What he was denying was that "true" was a transcendental term. Not the objects themselves, but our judgments about them are true or false. In short, he fully agreed with the traditional scholastic *adaequatio* theory of truth, in which truth resides in the adequation of our judgment to the thing itself.

Waswo's attempt to escape this fact is a *tour-de-force* of logical sleight of hand. The sequence of his argument runs: conception resolves itself into name,

---

[22] *Language and Meaning*, 109-10.

[23] See n. 19 above.

[24] *Language and Meaning*, 219.

[25] An interesting test case is Valla's *Sermo de mysterio Eucharistiae* (*Opera*, II, 63-72), which would have been an ideal place to talk about the constitutive powers of language ("This my body etc."); but nothing like that is to be found in the oration.

[26] See also Gerl, *Rhetorik als Philosophie*, 218-19, where she argues that Valla transcended the traditional *adaequatio intellectus ad rem* theory of scholasticism.

name into language; language becomes knowledge; this form of knowledge is a "direct denial of Platonic truth that exists outside ourselves . . . it is 'we' [who establish truth] and not God"; which all means that "the crucial connection between measurement and truth lies in the operation of language itself."[27]

There are at least six things wrong with this argument. The first is that it literally puts words in Valla's mouth. Valla spoke of truth and error being in us, in our *animus*, in our thinking.[28] In Waswo's analysis, truth and falsity reside in our language. But since his thesis is that Valla considered language as constitutive, and not merely expressive, of thought, this jump was necessary for him. Ironically, in the passage under discussion Valla clearly distinguishes between thought and language: "ideoque oratio potest esse falsa, animo non errante, cum quis aliter loquitur ac sentit."[29]

Second, if Waswo's argument has any validity, it applies to the scholastic *adaequatio* theory of truth as much as it does to Valla's *Dialectica* (i.e., conception = name = knowledge).[30] Waswo and Gerl should give credit where credit is due. Indeed, it is strange to see both of them praising Valla's view that language and the meaning of words are human conventions as some sort of historic discovery when this is exactly the opinion of Aristotle and of such standard scholastic logical authorities as Peter of Spain and Paul of Venice.[31]

Third, Plato did not posit an external truth. What he posited in the *Republic*, in the *Theaetetus*, and in the *Sophist* was an external reality, to which our opinions must conform if they are to be true.[32] But this is also Valla's view. So in one stroke Waswo was able to distort the views of two thinkers.

Fourth, far from condemning Plato, Valla twice in the *Dialectica* voiced approval of Plato's use of the sun as a metaphor for how truth is revealed.[33]

Fifth, Valla quite forcibly posited God as the external source of truth. Indeed, though the references are brief, they strongly suggest that Valla held a theory of truth that depended on divine illumination. The most explicit statement to this effect is an addition Valla made in the final recension of the *Dialectica*, a passage which Waswo chose to ignore. Having already explained that truth is a *lux animi* and that God reveals the qualities of things to the human mind, Valla then concludes in the new passage that "the source of our truth is in God, as the source of our light is in the sun. The source of falsity, however, is the obstruction of the divine source as the source of darkness is in the withdrawal

[27] *Language and Meaning*, 101.

[28] See note 21 above.

[29] *Dialectica*, ed. Zippel 20.11-12.

[30] The classic discussion of this notion is Thomas Aquinas, *De veritate*, quaest. 1, art. 2.

[31] Aristotle, *Int.*, 16a20 (tr. H. Cooke in the Loeb Classical Library series): "A noun is a sound having meaning established by convention alone"; Peter of Spain, *Tractatus*, ed. L. M. De Rijk (Assen, 1972), 2: "Vox significativa ad placitum est illa que ad voluntatem instituentis aliquid representat, ut 'homo'"; and 3: "Oratio est vox significativa ad placitum"; and Paulus Venetus, *Logica Parva*, tr. A. Perreiah (Munich, 1984), 121-22: "A term which signifies by convention [*ad placitum*] is one which is not representative of the same for everyone: e.g., the term 'man' (*homo*) in speech or in script which among us signifies men and among certain other nations signifies nothing."

[32] *Rep.* 6.507-7.517; *Soph.* 240D-241E; *Theat.* 187 ff., esp. 195C-D.

[33] See note 21 above.

of the sun. For God is properly truth as the sun is properly light, which is what Plato meant [in the *Republic*]."[34] Valla seems to be saying that God continually illuminates our mind, since he states that when we err, it is because the divine "source" has been obstructed in some way. What is unequivocally clear is that for Valla truth is *ontologically* grounded in God as the *fons veritatis*. Objective truth exists. God is its guarantor.

Sixth, we have Waswo's systemic fallacy, i.e., that somehow Valla reached Waswo's conclusions and passed them on to posterity without actually stating them. In this instance, Waswo's words are: "Valla's unstated transition thus compels his readers to work out for themselves that the crucial connection . . ." (101).

Intimately related to Valla's supposed denial of the correspondence theory of truth is Valla's supposed denial of the referential theory of meaning. The decisive text for this interpretation is quite brief, namely, the assertion that to ask what a thing is is equivalent to asking what its name signifies (*Dialectica*, ed. Zippel, 124.8-11: "Quapropter nihil interest utrum dicamus: 'quid est lignum?,' an 'quid est lapis?,' 'quid ferrum?,' 'quid homo?,' an 'quid significat lignum, ferrum, lapis, homo?' "). On this slender reed Waswo rests his belief that Valla denied the referential theory of meaning. Unfortunately, the reed does not exist; it is a mirage created by an ideologically inspired misreading of the text.

All Valla was saying in these lines is that our definition of a thing (as Valla explained in the *Dialectica*, the definition is the answer to the question *quid est*[35]), is equivalent to the meaning of the name we assign to the thing (the answer to the question *quid significat* [*nomen*]). Valla is talking about the relationship between mental concepts, logical terms, not the relationship between language and reality, not between what a thing is and its name, but between its name and its definition. It is not a statement about how language constitutes reality, but merely about logical relationships. If we are to put words in Valla's mouth, it seems patent to me that he is not saying that *sermo et res convertuntur*, as has been suggested,[36] but rather that *diffinitio rei et significatio vocis convertuntur*. Logical categories, not reality and words, are convertible. Of course, if our definition of a thing corresponds to what that thing is in fact, then, in Waswo's words, it would be true to say "what the thing is is what the word means." But to acknowledge this correspondence would be to affirm the referential theory of meaning.

Valla subordinated logic and language to an objective reality. This is espe-

---

[34] *Ibid.* For a survey of the theory of divine illumination see J. Owens, "Faith, Ideas, Illumination, and Experience," N. Kretzmann, A. Kenny, and J. Pinborg (eds.), *The Cambridge History of Later Medieval Philosophy* (Cambridge, 1982), 440-59; and J. Rohmer, "La Théorie de l'abstraction dans l'école franciscaine d'Alexandre de Hales à Jean Peckam," *Archives d'histoire doctrinale et littéraire du moyen âge*, 3 (1928), 105-84.

[35] *Dialectica*, ed. Zippel, 163.19ff.

[36] The words are Camporeale's, "Valla, retorica et linguaggio," 238 and 239; see also G. Di Napoli, *Lorenzo Valla: Filosofia e religione nell'umanesimo italiano* (Rome, 1971), 85: "res et vocabulum convertuntur." See Gerl, *Rhetorik als Philosophie*, 220-25. For Waswo see note 39 below.

cially clear in the case of *res*, the only term Valla would accept as a transcendental and which he defined as "an utterance [*vox*] signifying the meaning and sense of all other utterances."[37] Nonetheless, he made sure that the reader understood that this universal term, as a word, as a part of language, is still no more than a sign (*signum vel nota*) of something else, namely, an objective *res*, external to the words of the speaker: "Itaque 'res' significat rem; hoc significatur, illud huius est signum vel nota; illud non vox, hoc vox est. . . ."[38] To avert the force of this statement, Waswo suggests that Valla was joking when he made it.[39]

Even odder is Waswo's interpretation of a text which Valla added in the third recension of the *Dialectica*, and which therefore played no role in the later influence of the *Dialectica*:

Denique significatio est vocis que sub predicamentum venit, quia "predicamentum" idem est quod vox universaliter significans. Res significata sub predicamentum non venit, ut significatio vocis "homo" sub predicamento est; ipse autem homo qui significatur, sub tecto est aut sub celo, non sub predicamento, nec aliud est cum dicis "homo est animal," quam hac appellatione "homo" subauditur "animal" sive subintelligitur significatio animalis.[40]

According to Waswo, Valla was denying here "the referential theory of meaning, which is no longer to be sought in objects, but rather in the words that name and categorize them."[41] Waswo realized that this interpretation blatantly contradicts Valla's own words (if there is a *res significata*, then by definition the sign refers back to the *res*, the object, for the truth of its signification). So he argues that Valla's language was not adequate to his thought, that his new conception required "a different process than that of 'signifying' to describe the new constitutive role of language."[42]

A more reasonable interpretation would be that Valla knew exactly what he wanted to say, and said it. In the passage, Valla illustrated the difference between the ontological order of objects and the logical order of terms. He did so by examining what is meant by the phrase "coming under a category." His point is simply that objects do not "come under a category," only meanings (*significationes*) do; real objects, such as men, may come under a roof, the sky, etc., but not under a category because to come under a category is to be part of the

---

[37] *Dialectica*, 124.14-16: "est vox significans omnium aliarum vocum intellectum sive sensum." Cf. also 123.25-25: "res est vox sive vocabulum omnium vocabulorum significationes sua complectens" (see the end of note 7 above for *sua*).

[38] *Ibid.*, 123.23-24. Whether he knew it or not, Valla was taking sides in a medieval debate on whether words are signs primarily of things or of concepts; see A. Maurer, "William of Ockham on Language and Reality," *Sprache und Erkenntnis im Mittelalter: Akten des VI. internationalen Kongresses für mittelalterliche Philosophie* (2 vols.; Berlin, 1981), II, 795-802.

[39] Waswo, *Language and Meaning*, 108: "if we can write, *res significat rem*, is the statement, *illud non vox, hoc vox est* to be taken as a simple statement of fact, a paradox (even a joke?), or a genuine contradiction?" Having assumed that Valla identified things and words, Waswo then goes on to wonder how he could contradict himself by continuing to talk of the sign and signified.

[40] *Dialectica*, 124.17-25.

[41] *Language and Meaning*, 109.

[42] *Ibid.*, 110.

logical order. Terms form part of the logical order, and therefore come *sub predicamento*. All this is hardly revolutionary, since it was standard scholastic doctrine that logic was a science not of extramental objects but of second intentions of the mind.[43] Implicitly, Valla was denying an identity between the ontological and logical orders. However, except for extreme realists such as the followers of Raymond Lull, scholastic philosophers agreed with Valla in this distinction.

But all this is beside the point if we turn to Sarah Stever Gravelle's 1982 article which used a different set of texts to prove "Valla's theory of linguistic determination of thought."[44] Interestingly enough, Gravelle's argument is more persuasive than Gerl's and Waswo's because she changed the language under discussion, focusing on Valla's approach to Greek rather than Latin. She cites three apparently clear instances where Valla's discussion of Greek demonstrates his "theory of linguistic determination of thought." First, she states that Valla

devotes several paragraphs to show that *ens* is a meaningless abstraction unless said of God. By avoiding its use Latin authors are more concrete than Greeks. But the Greeks may be forgiven because they do not have a word equivalent to *res* and therefore cannot know that *ens* is nothing more than *ea res quae est*. Valla says of *res*: "I think it is better than that word of the Greeks which is usually translated *negotium*."[45]

Thus, according to Gravelle, Valla said that the Greeks created the false abstraction *ens* (in Greek, *to on*) because they had no word comparable to the Latin *res*. This will come as news to anyone who knows Greek. Valla knew Greek, and a few lines down from the sentence Gravelle quoted, Valla very clearly explained his position: "This may be the reason perhaps why Aristotle often preferred to use *to on* rather than *pragma*. If he had observed the nature and force of the words, he would have used *pragma* rather than *to on*."[46] In short, the failing was Aristotle's. The Greek language had a perfectly good word, *pragma*, to express the most universal of categories. Aristotle did not properly observe "the nature and force of words." Not "linguistic determination" but an error in judgment led Aristotle to treat "being" (*to on*) rather than "thing" (*pragma*) as the fundamental category of reality.

As Gravelle points out, Valla further noted that different Latin indefinite pronouns, such as *ullus* ("anyone"), *aliquis* ("someone"), and *quidam* ("a

---

[43] See I. M. Bocheński, *A History of Formal Logic*, tr. I. Thomas (Notre Dame, 1961), 154-56; and C. Knudsen, "Intentions and Impositions," *The Cambridge History of Later Medieval Philosophy*, 479-95.

[44] S. Stever Gravelle, "Lorenzo Valla's Comparison of Latin and Greek and the Humanist Background," *Bibliothèque d'Humanisme et Renaissance*, 44 (1982), 286; and cf. 284.

[45] *Ibid.*, 283-84.

[46] *Dialectica*, 18.1-4: "Quo factum est fortasse ut Aristoteles sepius voluerit uti '*to on*' quam '*pragma*,' qui si vocum animadvertisset naturam ac vim, '*pragma*' potius quam '*to on*' usus fuisset."

certain one"), are rendered in Greek by a single form (the enclytic *tis*).[47] But Gravelle misunderstands the point Valla was making.[48] Though Valla was more than happy to demonstrate the lexical penury of Greek in comparison to Latin on the matter of indefinite pronouns, his quarrel was really not with the Greek language. He was not arguing that Greek could not express certain meanings. He knew perfectly well that the indefinite Greek pronoun *tis* can mean "someone," "anyone," or "a certain one" depending on how it is used in the context.[49] Rather, Valla was attacking the Latin translators and logicians who allow this "defect" of forms in Greek to control their Latin. They err, Valla argued, in pretending that *tis* can be translated indifferently as *aliquis* or *quidam*, or that *aliquis* and *quidam* can be treated as equivalent in all propositions.[50] Different meanings in the Greek demand different indefinite pronouns in the Latin.

When we come to Gravelle's last instance, Valla's discussion of the Greek interrogative pronoun (the non-enclytic *tis*), she would seem to have struck gold. Valla does seem to speak here of how the limitations of the Greek language determined Greek thought. But a close reading will show that he actually rejected this possibility. Unlike Latin, which has the form *quis* for the interrogative pronoun and the form *qui* for the interrogative adjective, Greek uses the non-enclytic *tis* for both functions (*tis* = who; *tis anthropos* = what man). Valla argued that this limitation led Porphyry (and, by implication, Aristotle) to ask

[47] *Ibid.*, 194.1-8: "Item quo Greci carent 'ullus' et quod ab eo profluxit 'nonnullus,' quo item illi carent, et neutrum 'nonnihil.' Quorum nullo fere alio dialectici nostri utuntur nisi uno 'aliquis,' non putantes illud distare a 'quidam,' quia Greci non distinguunt pro duobus his nostris unum tantum habentes, immo pro tribus. Nam '*tis*' pro his duobus et pro quis usurpatur." And *ibid.*, 196.13-21: "Neque vero solum lingue Grece defectus in causa est cur a nonnullis in parum intelligenda hac differentia sit erratum, sed quod aliquando nihil ea differunt aut nihil videntur differre quale est si dicas: 'reperies historicos omnes aliquibus' sive 'quibusdam in locis mentitos.' Preterea quod nonnunquam reperiunt (et si rarissime) 'aliquis' pro 'quidam,' sed non tamen 'quidam' pro 'aliquis.' Quorum differentia magis ex negatione apparebit" (see n. 50 below).

[48] I note here some inaccurate statements she also made about another humanist, George of Trebizond. Contrary to her opinion, George did not believe that (276) "the uglier a philosopher's speech, the better his philosophy. The more indifferent one is to the vain show of words, the more successful he is as a thinker"; nor (*ibid.*) did he defend "the medieval versions of Aristotle as better than any the moderns were likely to produce"; nor did he ever say (277) that "Albert the Great wrote as smoothly as any ancient Greek." George never asserted (278) "that Greek philosophy cannot be translated into Latin"; and it is a half-truth to contend that (277) he "recommends the old translations which are as accurate as ugly." What he argued was that even with all their flaws the literal medieval translations of Aristotle distorted the text less than the new free versions of Theodore Gaza. Finally, when she avers (281) that "Trebizond expresses his fears about modern translations and predicts the coming of a time when each individual will see fit to make not only his own translations but his own interpretation," it helps to know that George was speaking exclusively about the Bible and not texts in general.

[49] E. g., see E. Schwyzer and A. Debrunner, *Griechische Grammatik* (2nd ed.; Munich, 1959), II, 214-15; and W. W. Goodwin and C. B. Gulick, *Greek Grammar* (Boston, 1958), 217-18.

[50] See his discussion of the difference between *aliquis* and *quidam* when put in the negative; *Dialectica*, 205.1ff.

improperly in respect to definition "what sort of animal (*poion zoon*) is man" instead of "which animal (*ti zoon*) is man."[51] Valla was both unfair and inaccurate in his criticism,[52] but that is not the issue at hand. What is important for us is that Valla then criticized Boethius for "Greekicizing" by translating Porphyry's phrase as *quale animal* instead of *quod animal,* and elsewhere, speaking in his own person, by asking "quale vocabulum est homo" instead of "quod vocabulum est homo."[53] According to Valla, Priscian similarly "Greekicized" when he wrote: " 'Arma' que pars orationis? Nomen. Quale nomen?" instead of "Quod nomen?."[54] But Valla's criticism of Boethius and Priscian only makes sense if he accused them of translating Greek words instead of Greek meaning, i.e., that in certain contexts the Greek adjective *poios* is to be translated as *qui* and not *qualis.* In these contexts, *poios* means "what" or "which" and not "what sort of."[55] He says precisely this in a passage unique to the third recension of the *Dialectica:*

Here an observation forces itself upon us concerning the Greek language, which is otherwise very rich, yet in this respect in some way defective. For since there are three things, as the rhetoricians tell us,[56] which enter into an inquiry: "whether it is," "what is it," and "of what sort is it," they [*the Greeks*] employ the last of these for what is "which is". . . .[57]

[51] *Dialectica,* 163.24-164.6: "Quapropter Boetius cum de multis viris, tum de sua lingua male meritus est, cuius proprietatem non animadvertens ad grecissandum nos inducit, qui ita Porphyrium transfert: 'Diffiniunt autem et eam hoc modo: differentia est que de pluribus et differentibus specie, in eo quod quale sit predicatur. "Rationale" enim et "mortale" de homine predicatur in eo quod, quid [*sic*]. "Quid est enim 'homo'?" interrogatis nobis, conveniens est dicere "animal." "Quale" autem inquisiti, "quoniam rationale et mortale," convenienter assignabimus.' " The quotation of Porphyry's *Isagoge* is a senseless jumble at "in eo quod, quid," which I have marked with a *sic.* Whether the error is Valla's or a scribe's, it was caught (as Zippel's apparatus shows) by an editor of one of the sixteenth-century printings. The correct reading of Boethius's version of Porphyry according to A. Busse, ed., *Porphyrii Isagoge et in Aristotelis Categorias Commentarium* (Berlin, 1887), 37.8-9, is: "in eo quod quale quidam est homo dicitur, sed non in eo quod quid est."

[52] For the confusion in Valla's quotation of Porphyry see the previous note. Valla implies that both Aristotle and Porphyry believed the definition of a thing could be given in response to the interrogative *quale* ("of what sort"), even though both make it abundantly clear that the proper interrogative is *quid* ("what"). His criticism of Boethius for using *qualis* instead of *qui* is unfair because the interrogative adjective *qualis* ("what kind of?") can be answered by naming a sub-group of the substantive *qualis* modifies. Valla is more unjust to Porphyry and Priscian since the questions he quotes from them are answered by adjectives: "Quid est homo? Animal. Quale animal? Rationale et mortale." " 'Arma' que pars orationis? Nomen. Quale nomen? Appellativum."

[53] *Dialectica,* 164.6-10, quoting Boethius's commentary on the *Categories* of Aristotle.

[54] *Ibid.,* 164.10.13.

[55] See H. D. Liddell, R. Scott, and H. S. Jones, *A Greek-English Lexicon* (Oxford, 1940), 1431b7ff., for instances of *poios* meaning "what, which?"

[56] Zippel does not annotate this reference; but see Quintilian, *Inst. orat.* III:5.6; Cicero, *Orat.* 45; *Part. orat.* 62; and *De orat.* II:104, 114, 132.

[57] *Dialectica,* 168.22-27: "Hoc nobis in loco illud se offert animadvertendum de lingua Greca alioqui uberrima, tamen manca quodammodo in hac parte. Etenim cum tria sint,

So the main issue concerning the non-enclytic *tis* is not whether Greek has the needed meaning, but whether Latin authors forsake that meaning and pervert Latin when they slavishly follow Greek forms. Nonetheless, Valla did recognize that his criticism may have something to do with philosophical and not merely linguistic differences. After all, if he so chose, a classical Greek author could express "what animal" by *ti zoon* instead of *poion zoon*.[58] Consequently, despite the fun he was having exposing the failings of Greek in comparison to Latin, Valla was also challenging the philosophic judgment of his opponents. Valla admitted as much in the paragraph following his quotation of Porphyry. He said:

You have noticed that the very nature of speech teaches us that we should ask "which animal," not "what sort of animal." In this matter, even if above I made excuses for the Greeks when they put questions in the form "of what sort" because they do not have, as we do, separate forms for "what" and "which," nonetheless, I do not allow this excuse everywhere. I do not think Aristotle or others rightly put questions when they ask "of what sort is fire?," "of what sort is air?," "of what sort is stone?."[59]

Finally, there is the issue of ordinary language. *Pace* Gerl and Waswo, ordinary language was not an absolute *philosophical* standard for Valla. To be sure, Valla frequently appealed to linguistic *consuetudo* in criticizing philosophical opinions. Indeed, he would even descend to blatant sophisms if they allowed him to take the side of linguistic *consuetudo* against Aristotle.[60] But the fact is that he openly disregarded it or even corrected it when it contradicted what he felt to be the truth. For instance, in discussing truth, he mocked the notion of "true bread," "true wine," and so forth, though that is ordinary language.[61] In the first recension of the *Dialectica*, after noting the fallacy of some common expressions, he states: "It is one thing to speak according to truth, another to speak according to popular custom, common to almost every kind of men."[62] Elsewhere, in the second and third recensions, he avers that ordinary speech speaks nonsense when it asks "what is beyond the heavens" or "what was before

---

ut a rhetoribus traditur, que in disquisitionem veniant: 'an sit,' 'quid sit,' 'quale sit,' horum ultimum usurpant pro eo quod est 'quod sit'. . . ."

[58] See Goodwin and Gulick, *Greek Grammar*, 217, num. 1011.

[59] *Dialectica*, 165.13-19: "Animadvertisti ut ipsa sermonis natura nos docet interrogandum 'quod animal,' non 'quale animal'? In quo etsi [et si *Zippel*] Grecos excusavi superius interrogantes per 'quale', quia 'quid' non habent ut nos distinctum, tamen non ubique admitto excusationem, nec recte puto querere Aristotelem aliosque, cum querunt 'qualis est ignis?,' 'qualis est aer?,' 'qualis est lapis?.' "

[60] In *Dialectica*, 148-49, he defended against Aristotle the popular *consuetudo* of calling a jar empty when it is merely filled with air. To do so, he first confused relative qualities (e.g., soft, hard) with potentially absolute qualities (e.g., full, empty); and, second, he asserted that air is nothing though a few lines earlier he had said that skins and sails can be filled with air and though in Bk. I, ch. 11, he accepted air as one of the four elements.

[61] See n. 21 above.

[62] *Dialectica*, 386.26-28: "Sed aliud est loqui ad legem ipsam veritatis, aliud ad consuetudinem popularem et pene omni generi hominum communem." I owe this reference to M. Tavoni, *Latino, grammatica, volgare* (see above, n. 15), 144-45.

time" since there cannot be heavens beyond the heavens or a time before time; the best he can say in defense of this *consuetudo sermonis humani* is to argue that it has "some sense" (*nonnihil rationis*) because of theological reasons, which "we somehow divine and suspect."[63] And, as Mirko Tavoni points out, Valla's well-known use of the Ciceronian comparison between the goldsmith's scale and common man's balance is directed *against* the truth of ordinary usage.[64]

The second point to be made concerns what Valla considered to be linguistic *consuetudo*. As Tavoni proves beyond a doubt,[65] the only truly authoritative *consuetudo* for Valla was the literary practice of the best authors, not ordinary language in the modern sense.[66] Valla's linguistic standard was thoroughly and self-consciously belletristic. It is well known that Valla scorned the vulgar language of his day. What Tavoni has brilliantly shown is that Valla thought the vulgar language of the Romans to be not much different from the *Volgare* he himself heard everyday in Rome: "Itaque non modo quondam loquebantur, verum etiam nunc vulgo Latine Romani loquuntur."[67] Classical ordinary language as well as Renaissance ordinary language were no models or sources of truth for Valla.

All this, of course, is not to deny the importance of linguistic analysis in Valla's recasting of philosophy. But that linguistic analysis seems to me to have been primarily inspired by the discipline of grammar in the broad sense, with linguistic *consuetudo* being only one, albeit perhaps the most important, of several grammatical principles upon which he based his "new" philosophy. For instance, etymology was important in Valla's philosophical thinking, e.g., of *virtus* (85.15b), *logos* (70.22ff), or *ratio* (71.6ff). Also important was a certain form of grammatical analysis, exemplified by his insistence that *quid* is resolvable into *quae res* (124.13) or *ens* into *ea res que est* (12.9-10). A thorough investigation of Valla's grammatical and linguistic conceptions probably must await a critical edition of his *Elegantiae*. But in any event, such a methodical investigation rather than the mere grinding of ideological axes should be the goal of scholars interested in Valla's understanding of language.

State University of New York at Albany.

---

[63] *Ibid.*, 331.9ff.

[64] See the end of note 62 above.

[65] *Latino, grammatic, volgare*, 144-47; cf. also his "Lorenzo Valla e il Volgare," *Lorenzo Valla e l'Umanesimo italiano*, 199-216, 212-13.

[66] An exception must be made for neologisms naming objects and institutions unknown in antiquity. In such cases, Valla asserted, correct Latin should accept the current vernacular terms; see O. Besomi, "Dai *Gesta Ferdinandis Regis Aragonum* del Valla al *De Orthographia* del Tortelli," *Italia medioevale e umanistica*, 9 (1966), 75-121; and Tavoni, *Latino, grammatica, volgare*, 159-65. See p. 427 above.

[67] *Latino, grammatica, volgare*, 150-65. The Latin sentence is from Valla's *Apologus II* against Poggio; see *ibid.*, 263, § 25.

V

MOTIVES OF MISREADING

BY RICHARD WASWO

John Monfasani's attack on the Gerl-Waswo (problematically, -Camporeale) thesis about Lorenzo Valla's linguistically critical philosophy presents itself as reassuring the neo-Latin scholarly world that no serious attention need be paid to a couple of interlopers. They get the texts ludicrously wrong because they're ignorant of the language and the discipline, and are motivated only by fashion and ideological axe-grinding—not by any respectably disinterested and methodical investigation of "past fact." This assertion of motive, and its contrast to a proper motive, is of course not stated, but is unmistakably implied in both the opening paragraph and the final sentence of his article. It's quite nicely implied—civilly avoiding the *ad hominem*—in a tone of bluff geniality and brisk amusement. The tone well and strategically conveys his particular sense of offended expertise. Outrage, the perhaps more frequent expression of this sense, would be too strong a response to these pygmy adversaries, would necessarily grant them some power. Humor is more dismissive. Still, if they're so inept, why do they even need dismissing? Well, because they threaten to add up, as bacteria can make an epidemic: the image is Monfasani's, pleasantly postulating "pathologies" of scholarship, of which my own work is a prime "symptom"[1]

This metaphor of disease is interesting: strategically, it supplies the importance necessary to justify the attack. And like most metaphors, it is rich in implications that are double-edged, simultaneously characterizing both its targets and its inventor. I and my associates in error are sick; a healthy diagnostician is required to prevent the infection from spreading, to protect—whom, exactly? The excessiveness of the metaphor is patent enough: for scholarly purposes it would seem sufficient merely to prove that we're wrong, as indeed Monfasani labors to do. Why must we also be sick? Here the metaphor reveals what the tone attempts to mask: anxiety. The writer is made very ill at ease (dis-eased) by the thesis that Valla was not merely reproducing the dualistic linguistic philosophy of Plato and the scholastics, but was challenging it, criticizing it. To reensconce Valla in the world view he inherited is the entire aim of Monfasani's (highly reductive, as we shall see) treatment of my argument.

The main symptom of the malady, like the whole metaphor, also reveals the assumptions of the diagnostician. This symptom is the use of contemporary theories "to explain what is under, between, around, and behind the lines of a text." I, therefore, am the sickest of the bunch because I do this most explicitly. (Indeed I do, and I defend the procedure at the beginning of the book, which Monfasani ignores.) The crowning indication of my being the farthest gone in disease is my actual mention of Wittgenstein—an acute state not yet reached in the books of Gerl and Camporeale. But the latter, alas, shows signs of succumbing to the infection by himself actually quoting Wittgenstein in a recent

---

[Citations of the preceding article by John Monfasani have been adjusted to reflect the pagination of the present volume.]

[1] Richard Waswo, *Language and Meaning in the Renaissance* (Princeton, 1987); hereafter *LM*.

article, and, even worse, appearing to endorse Gerl and Waswo's view that Valla occasionally arrived at a constitutive notion of language that was opposed to tradition.[2]

There are two large problems here that need unpacking: the first (and most important) concerns what a text is and how we are to read it. The second is simply the bizarre identification of seeing a relation between contemporary and Renaissance thinking as a disease. What makes it especially bizarre is that Monfasani neither explains nor contests it. The mere fact of my having drawn parallels between Valla and Wittgenstein is observed (n. 17) and is regarded from the outset as the ultimate pathology. But none of these parallels *(LM,* 1034), which compare the subject, aim, situation, and strategy of the two philosophers, is ever discussed, let alone contested. Presumably this is because none depends on the two main disputed passages from the *Dialectica* that, removed from the context of my argument, Monfasani later focuses on. That Camporeale exhibits similar parallels Monfasani also observes, and then must do his best to prevent this appearing as consensus or support for me, so that I can enter the isolation ward alone. So Monfasani must insist (n. 5) that Camporeale never actually quotes my earlier article. So what? That we are making very similar points is not at all surprising, since my own reading of Valla was partially inspired by Camporeale's first book, as I noted in my own, and as Monfasani himself admits (p. 86). But still, Father Camporeale is to be extricated from the (always undiscussed) contagion of Wittgenstein because "neither Gerl nor Waswo are [*sic*] up to Camporeale's competence in Latin" (p. 87). Now in my case, this is certainly true. I am not a professional Latinist; I need all the help I can get from the experts, and I have solicited it. I have made (and will doubtless continue to make) blunders—though not so many as Monfasani thinks—in translation. I have admitted them in print? I do the best I can, and it is sometimes not good enough. It does not follow from this that I am terminally ill; nor does it invalidate the comparisons that both Camporeale and I have made between Valla and Wittgenstein. But it indeed separates me from him: he is an expert, and a fine one, in the field. So rather than substantiating what the metaphor implies about our mutual infection with Wittgenstein, Monfasani drops Camporeale and the subject in the second paragraph, having already evaded the issue (in n. 1) by refusing to discuss Wittgenstein. If this great thinker is a rampant virus that has contaminated even an expert, we really ought to hear why. Since we don't, we're left with just the metaphorical innuendo, which condemns without a hearing, and a consequent suspicion of the writer whose rhetoric employs it.

But the most important problem is the assumption about the nature of a text, which emerges from Monfasani's obvious contempt for the effort to explain what lies "under, between, around, and behind" its lines. This handsome list of prepositions is designed to imply that we trendy sicides look everywhere but

---

[2] Salvatore I. Camporeale, "Lorenzo Valla, 'Repastinatio, liber primus': Retorica e linguaggio," *Lorenzo Valla e l'umanesimo italiano,* ed. Ottavio Besomi and Mariangela Regoliosi (Padua, 1986), 217-39. Hereafter cited as "RL."

[3] Monfasani recurs to this at length (ns. 7 and 8), faulting me for not repeating the acknowledgment to Szymanski in the book. Once was enough, given the tone of his reproaches.

at the text itself. This latter, as the article goes on to deal with it, turns out to be just the words on the page—well, of course, those words as seen by the experts who know their MS variants and how they really aren't any different from the same words used by earlier philosophers. I am pointing out that Monfasani's polemically implied characterization of a text (as something nice, simple, straightforward, something quite clearly there in order to be danced around and distorted by the invalids) is falsified in his own practice. The characterization makes possible the whole tone of his reproaches, the bluff heartiness, the no-nonsense, plain-as-the-nose-on-your-face attitude that is designed to make the invalids ridiculous. The falsification emerges from the necessary effort to read the text, for which some context is required. Monfasani perforce supplies one, a far too narrow one. No text can read itself. No text that has syntactical coherence greater than that of, say, a telephone directory, declares its own meaning. What is "under, between, around, and behind" it are whatever contexts we as readers bring to its interpretation. Those prepositions can also describe tensions that are internal to a text (especially one that makes a serious effort at thinking); they're where the action is. I've just been demonstrating how much such action there is even in Monfasani's text. This particular action is a perfect illustration: his article assumes as a mode of insult an impossibility—a text that has no need of prepositional scrutiny—which is belied by his informing us of the scholastic meanings that are really "behind" Valla's words. To the rhetoric of metaphorical innuendo is added the structure of selfcontradiction.

One final assumption provides a corollary to the implicit (and false) one of the plain, self-declaring text. This is the explicit (and equally false) statement that when scholars like me discover adumbrations of contemporary ideas in past thinkers, "either they are wrong... or they are right" (p. 86). Isn't that neat? There's no middle ground, no grey area, no possibility of ambiguity, of shading, of nuance, of emphasis—indeed, of anything that we might recognize as any form of either past thinking or its present study. I know of no body of thinking nor of any scholarly account of one that is "either wrong or fight." At no level of serious work—above that of the freshman essay, and often not even there—are "right" or "wrong" attributable in this blanket and rudimentary fashion. Any argument about the meaning, diffusion, and consequences of ideas will inevitably provoke agreement here and disagreement there, will have strengths and weaknesses, will present, to the different viewpoints of different critics, an inevitable (and seldom the same) *mixture* of "right" and "wrong." But not to Monfasani, whose "either/or" view of the interpretation of a text postulates a far simpler (and non-existent) world of discourse where he can find comfort in the detection of fictitious "errors" and delight in the diagnosis of fictitious diseases.

The first such error Monfasani detects (90; ns. 13, 14) concerns the phrase, "ut quaeque res nascitur, sicut in hominibus fit." My translation of this, corrected from the article to the book (as he notes), is "when [such an object] is born, as is done among men." This accords perfectly with Monfasani's own, deliberately labored and literal version (90). But I still haven't got it "fight," he says, because I substituted "among" for the suggested "with." Now, this makes here absolutely no difference. The ablative case covers a multitude of

English prepositions: "to" or "by" would work here just about as well. I preferred "among," since what seems to me the sense is that of a well-established custom in a community. "Among" is conventional in this sense, and avoids the remote but possible sense of instrumentality in "with." The meaning—that newly invented objects should get named as new-born men do—is uncontested in any case. This is not an error; it's a choice among a plurality of perfectly possible candidates. By itself, this point is trivial; that Monfasani makes very heavy weather of it is symptomatic. Less trivial is the very different reading of the phrase that I myself, under what I regarded as just correction, rejected. This reading has since been offered by an expert. Maristella de Panizza Lorch, herself an editor of Valla's *De vero falsoque bono*, does not translate the phrase, but paraphrases and quotes it as follows: "In fact the object, the *res*, comes to light (and life) the moment the *word*, the man-made word, is born: 'Quaeque res nascitur sicut in hominibus fit.' "[4] Now, when the experts disagree to this extent, it surely makes no sense at all to regard the matter as an "either/or" question of "right" or "wrong." Brandishing such accusations is staggeringly irrelevant to whatever real argument might be possible about a seminal Renaissance thinker.

Just about all such argument is foreclosed by what Monfasani imagines to be "error." In an earlier note (8) I am alleged to make hash of this sentence (I cite the Basel text, precisely because Zippel's punctuation *already* decides the interpretation—of which more soon): "Atque hoc est quicquid loquimur: etiam ipsum substantia, qualitas, actio: atque adeo ipsum res." My version: "Hence, 'this' is whatever we say; it is in fact substance, quality, action; and therefore it is a 'thing.' " Monfasani's version: "And whatever we say, it is this [i.e., *vocabulum*], even 'substance' itself, 'quality,' and 'action,' and 'thing' itself." Monfasani has Valla making the point that "even our descriptions of words are still words"—a nice point that in no way contradicts my whole treatment of Valla. I have him, however, making the point (which Monfasani claims is "nonsense") that "the word 'this' is a thing." Indeed I do: I have him drawing a conclusion from his earlier observation in the passage that *written* words are "images" of spoken ones (*vocum imagines*), which they are. As such, they are objects; they can be pointed to, cut out and pasted in albums, or eaten. The observation threatens, as does the whole passage, the neat and venerable dichotomy of *res/verba*. This interpretation is not erroneous nonsense; it is possible; it is even interesting. So is Monfasani's. Valla's language, in either its fifteenth-century MS or sixteenth-century printed forms, is not (it should be needless to say) self-evident. But Monfasani treats it, and ridicules me, as if it were.

One of the main reasons it is not self-evident is that it is unpunctuated by any modern forms of pointing that indicate a metalanguage—the italics or quotation marks that signal a discussion of the word and not the thing it names. To decide where to point requires a prior determination of meaning. So far am I from "not understanding that editors . . . of Renaissance Latin texts are expected to punctuate for sense" (n. 7), that I insist on asking: *whose* sense? And I insist on giving readers the actual texts in which Valla was read by posterity. Zippel's critical edition of the *Dialectica* is a fine and helpful thing;

---

[4] *A Defense of Life: Lorenzo Valla's Theory of Pleasure* (Munich, 1985), 10.

but the interpretations that it determines by its punctuation are not by any means the only possible ones.[5]

Monfasani, however, continually imagines that only his own interpretations are possible. Having rapped my knuckles for not following the authority of Zippel, he proceeds to contradict it himself (n. 7). Of the four extant choices for one phrase, "it seems to" Monfasani "that the correct reading ... is certainly" x; and he picks a variant that Zippel did not. The point concerns whether *res* includes all terms or the meanings of all terms in itself. Only the latter is "correct," according to Monfasani. And indeed, Valla says just this at the end of the disputed passage *(LM,* 106). My point is that he is also saying the former: i.e. that the word "res" can mean all words, in this context written words taken as objects. The very existence of four variants of the phrase suggests a problem, a crux, something not entirely figured out either by Valla or a few generations of scribes and printers. Such problems do not have "correct" solutions. Again and as usual Monfasani is postulating certainty where none is to be had.

And it is just this desire that determines Monfasani's misreadings of Valla and non-readings of me. For the initial reductions he practices on my argument amount to not reading it. He quotes my summary (derived from Gerl) of the "thesis" that Valla held a constitutive view of the relation between language, meaning, and the world (p. 92). He then remarks that I make "some surprising concessions concerning it." Now these concessions could surprise only the "either/or" habit of mind. They are: 1) I dispute some of Gerl's evidence; 2) I stress throughout the "difficulty and inconsistency" of Valla's effort to change the conceptual semantic framework of his day; 3) 1 subject the passages I quote to "considerable analysis." From 1), Monfasani makes the claim that all "we are left with" as evidence for the thesis are the two disputed passages from the *Dialectica*. He thus chooses not to read the first half-dozen pages of the chapter, which present Valla's *practice* as textual interpreter and grammarian in the *Donation* and the *Elegantiae* as being by itself an implicit version of the "thesis." The emphasis and close reading of 2) and 3) are, for Monfasani, merely further excuses for blunt ridicule. From them, he draws this inference: "In short, Valla was unclear in his own mind as to what he was doing..." It's his inference, since I never say any such thing. I can only talk about texts, about their tensions and gaps and problems; I never presume to know what was in Valla's mind. Monfasani paraphrases me into absurdity which he can then triumphantly detect: "Even if Valla was confused in what he meant and inarticulate in saying it (novel charges, to say the least)...." Novel indeed, and never charged by me. My charge is that these texts of Valla exhibit the energy, fascination, variety of register and tone, ambiguity, and inconsistency that are part of a radical effort to rethink how language works. Monfasani sees no such effort, does not read the context of my argument about it, reduces the evidence to two passages, and reduces my careful analyses of those passages to absurd statements about Valla's interior convictions. All of these reduce the issue to that rudimentary (and mythical) level where Monfasani can find, as he concludes, "that Valla knew

---

[5] In the same note, Monfasani does manage to convict me of two real errors, which I happily acknowledge: I agree that in the MS passage "quia" should be "quam." The issue here is the deciphering of an abbreviation—on which matter I, erroneously, followed the advice of an expert. 1 should also have said "this" MS version instead of "the."

exactly what he wanted to say, and said it." And Monfasani knows just what Valla wanted to say by reducing *him* to merely repeating the received linguistic ideas of scholasticism.

And if this is all Valla ever did, then his whole career and the notorious controversies and invectives that filled it become incomprehensible, as does his subsequent reputation. Valla was perceived by his contemporaries and successors (I document how in the case of Vives) as assaulting most previous common wisdom about language. We have therefore *prima facie* reason to suspect Monfasani's reconfinement of him to that wisdom. Monfasani's sneers at me for finding in Valla what later readers could not "decipher" (ignoring my constant attempt to explain why), are highly ironic in the light of what Monfasani finds. How could Poggio possibly have been so outraged by Valla's radical historicizing of grammar (and the consequent criticisms of his own Latin) as to put out a contract for his assassination? How could the literal-minded late scholastic of Monfasani's portrayal ever offend anyone? If Valla was this harmless, then his prominent enemies can only be regarded as pathological in the extreme. "Pathologies" seem a logical necessity in Monfasani's "either/or" discursive world. Fortunately, only he need inhabit it, since its picture of Valla cannot possibly account for the simultaneous and equally intense *mixture* of reprobation and reverence with which he, like other great and innovarive philosophers, was actually regarded.

Now for those two passages to which, in this weird world of Monfasani's, my argument has been reduced. They are indeed important passages, about which Monfasani makes a very damaging admission—given that he so confidently knows "exactly" what they say. Such confidence sorts ill with his earlier remark that out of a big book I adduced "only these two unclear passages" (p. 92). Unclear indeed; that's just why I, and other scholars, have found them worth puzzling over. They're unclear because they're attempting to say something different, to redefine the venerable vocabulary of discourse, to alter the received understanding of what and how words mean. Their .unclarity resides mainly in their transitions, in the gaps between the primary terms and processes ("truth," "concept," "word," "thing") they are discussing. Though the exact relations between these terms—the precise alteration of their received understanding—are indeed disputable, the attempt to alter them is patent. But Monfasani is blind to this attempt even in Valla's most obvious metaphor.

This metaphor, in the first disputed passage, is of truth as the light of the mind (n. 21; *LM*, 95-96). How Valla develops it is the key to his denial both of the correspondence theory of truth and the referential theory of meaning. That he denies these is my "thesis." The fake precision of Monfasani's enumeration of the "six things wrong with it" is amusing: the six points are neither logically separate nor parallel (pp. 93-4); the first five all concern the location of truth; the sixth is a mystifying refusal to perceive that unsignaled transitions are important. The question of meaning as reference follows in respect to the second disputed passage.

On truth: Valla insists that "this light belongs to the mind itself... it is not a light that comes from outside, such as the sun. Yet, as the sun displays the colors of bodies to the eyes, so God exhibits the qualities of things to the mind. Plato elaborated this somewhat differently in the *Republic*, when he said that truth is like the sun...." The distinction Valla is here making, so obvious that I did not stress the point in my analysis, is that between a power (specifically the faculty of sight) and the enabling medium in which it operates. Light, for the eyes, and God, for the mind (presumably in his role as Creator) is that medium. Neither the sun nor God is what that power discerns—i.e. truth. *That* light belongs to the mind; it is a property of conception, and conceptions of the world are what ordinary words ("bread," "wine," "prophet") give us. Truth belongs to our mind, is in us—not in Plato's postulated conformity nor in the scholastic *adaequatio* of concept to object; for there are no objects here. There are words, language as the way in which the mind works to discern truth. Of course Plato postulated an external reality (like the sun, in the *Republic),* and one that we could not by definition nakedly gaze at, as that which we must know if we are to know truth. Valla does not; his metaphor and his quiet irony regarding Plato's opinion both depend on the difference between the medium and the object of perception (sight or concept); he makes Plato's sun the former, not the latter. The sun and God are what make it possible for us to see; what we see may be truth (or falsehood); and how we do so is by using words.

Of course Valla elsewhere refers to God as the "source of truth"—in just this carefully restricted sense. He is not, however, its location, nor its guarantor— any more than the light of the sun, without which, or in the obstruction of which, we cannot see, can guarantee that what we see is true. That light comes from outside; but the light that is truth is cast by the human mind, and is cast through, by means of, and in language.

Two corollaries: 1) that Valla observes that truth may exist differently in "mind or mouth" does not separate thought from language, but merely conscious deception of others (lying) from unconscious deception of ourselves (mistaking). False "speech" and true "thought" (or vice-versa) are not here being separated theoretically; they are merely describing a psychological intention in a particular case—"when someone speaks otherwise than he feels." 2) Of course the association between the sound and the meaning of words was regarded as arbitrary and conventional by Aristotelian scholastics; this is not what Gerl and I are praising Valla for. We are praising him for the effort to see as cognitive and constitutive the association between word and object. This association, for both realists and nominalists, was ontological: sound/meaning was arbitrary, but meaning/object was not. The semantic determiner for them was reference to an external, pre-constituted object world; the semantic determiner for Valla (as for Wittgenstein) is the use of the word in the language.

This brings us to the second passage (*LM,* 105-6). Monfasani finds the "decisive text" here the conflation of the two questions, "what is x?" and "what does x signify?" And he decides (94) that "all" that's being conflated here is a "name" and a "definition"—not, as I argue, a thing and its name. It has only to do with "logical relationships," says Monfasani, not with the relation of language to reality. Now, if this were the case, if "all" Valla were saying is that the "definition... is the meaning of the name," then he is asserting a relationship that is not logical, but tautological; he is saying something that is not worth saying. But he's not; he is not talking here about "definition" at all (which he treats fully later on, as Monfasani notes). Valla is taking the question, "what is x?" in its ordinary use and is *criticizing* that use, claiming that this question, which ordinarily assumes a previously constituted object in the world as its answer, is really the same as the question, "what does the word x mean?" He is collapsing ontology into semantics, insisting that to state the meaning of words is precisely what we know about reality. The latter is not constituted in advance but in language. Valla illustrates the point at the end of the passage, with respect to the word "res," which is, for him, the only "transcendental" term because *neither* question ("what is a thing?" "what does 'thing' mean?") can apply to it, for it is the word signifying the meaning of all other words. And this is discovered by asking the question, "what *word* is 'thing?.'" Thus by finding the one term that can mean anything and everything, we find that its meaning cannot be determined by any (of its infinitely possible) referents in the world. Likewise, the meaning of "wood" or "stone" does not reside in the objects thus named, but in the use of the word so to name them.

This conflation of questions about being into questions about meaning is indeed the crucial point, and Valla makes it more than once.[6] Monfasani insists on missing it because it contradicts all the assumptions of the traditional vocabulary of "signifying"—which indeed Valla continues to use. But he has still radically modified its use. For Monfasani, however, this vocabulary is unmodifiable: "if there is a *res significata,* then by definition the sign refers back to the *res,* the object, for the truth of its signification" (95). By whose definition? Not by Valla's: Valla makes the matter as clear as he can in the last recension of the passage, cited from a MS *(LM,* 109-10). It is sufficiently clear that even Monfasani can't miss it; he can only misread it. He paraphrases it thus: Valla's "point is simply [*sic*] that objects do not 'come under a category,' only meanings *(significationes)* do." Just so. Objects—"res significatae"—are *not* meanings; they're in the world, under roofs or skies, not under categories. Valla is wittily insisting, as he states, that "meaning belongs to words" *(significatio est vocis),* i.e., to language as that which operates a system of categories. Meaning does not belong to the "res significata." Valla is not merely denying correspondence between logical and ontological orders, like some scholastics; he is denying that reference is meaning; he is asserting as plainly as possible that "significatio" is *not* the "res significata." This is the revolution that Monfasani refuses—merely because the experts already know, "by definition," that the "res significata" confers meaning on the sign. Valla is saying, on the contrary, that the things words may signify are not their meanings, that meaning is a property of language itself. He is proposing—not without difficulty—a *re*definition of what "signifying" means.

This redefinition has not been refused or overlooked by worthier Latinists than I. Camporeale (who's written three books on Valla) concludes that his entire critical project against Aristotelian scholasticism "is to deontologize language." For Valla, he writes, "the entire reality of the 'thing signified,' is identified with and subsists, for us, in the 'meanings of words.'" Truth is therefore "only and exclusively a property of mind and in the last analysis a property of discourse." He finds Valla's original contribution to philosophy the

[6] Camporeale, "RL," 235, conveniently lists other passages.

principle that "there is no *res* without *sermo*" ("RL," 218-19, 223, 227).[7] Another scholar quotes and discusses this crucial passage on the conflation of "being" and "meaning" questions. He finds at issue precisely "the relation between language and reality," and finds that Valla resolves this into "the relation between distinct linguistic signs."[8] All of these descriptions acknowledge that Valla was mounting a radical attack on the ontologically-bound semantics of traditional "signifying."

And he was doing so from the primary standpoint of "consuetudo loquendi,"—i.e., by examining the ordinary use of language as determining how we know the world. Neither Gerl nor I claim this, as Monfasani finally alleges (99), as Valla's "absolute" standard. Only Monfasani wants things to be "absolute." Valla invokes (as does Wittgenstein) as many varieties of register and usage as may suggest the multiple functions of language: he appeals constantly to "common" usage, to that of the "vulgar," of the "learned," of "great men"—in all cases as opposed to that of philosophers.[9] And he also, as we have seen, *criticizes* ordinary usage when that usage postulates a prior ontology exempt from linguistic mediation. In all these ways he was attempting in the fifteenth century what Wittgenstein was attempting in the twentieth: to change the paradigm, to alter the received conceptual framework in which language was assumed to have meaning.

That Monfasani refuses to perceive this has disabling consequences for the study of the history of ideas. I too would welcome "methodical investigation" of Valla's dense and difficult texts—but all depends on the method chosen. If, like Monfasani's, it assumes the transparency of isolated texts, imagines cozy concord among experts, ignores all those prepositional dimensions of interpretation, and assimilates any residual unclarity to the already known—then it will get us precisely nowhere. For Monfasani will not admit that one can use an inherited vocabulary *differently*. But all we have are inherited vocabularies. If the great thinkers that modify them are not—"by definition"—allowed to do so, then ideas can have no history; they can only get perpetually repeated. If we cannot recognize an attempt to shift a paradigm—and it seems to be as hard to recognize as to perform—we prevent ourselves from ever knowing how ways of thinking can change at all.

University of Geneva.

---

[7] He also, of all experts the one who has longest pondered the first book of the *Dialectica*, claims not yet to understand it fully ("RL" 228). And Monfasani sneers at me for stressing its difficulty.

[8] Eckhard Kessler (ed. and tr.), Valla, *De libero arbitrio* (Munich, 1987), 32.

[9] Camporeale ("RL," 230-31) limits himself to thirteen examples but gives references to forty more.

VI

THE LATIN-VERNACULAR QUESTION AND HUMANIST THEORY OF LANGUAGE AND CULTURE

By Sarah Stever Gravelle

This study seeks to deepen our understanding of the Quattrocento humanists' contribution to philosophy of language. This contribution has been generally recognized but needs more proofs and demonstrations from sources other than Valla.[1] Several other humanists shared his understanding that linguistic difference is a cause of the differences in the character and mind of cultures. Like Valla, these humanists used a comparative study of language to establish the connection of language, culture, and mentality.

Two comparative studies were very fruitful for humanist language theory. One was that of Latin and Greek, the other that of the vernacular and Latin.[2] This latter study led to reflection on linguistic change within cultures and its significance for the intellectual history of an age.

---

[1] For Valla see Salvatore Camporeale, *Lorenzo Valla: Umanesimo e teologia* (Florence, 1972); Hanna-Barbara Gerl, *Rhetorik als Philosophie: Lorenzo Valla* (Munich, 1974); Charles Trinkaus, *In Our Image and Likeness: Humanity and Divinity in Italian Humanist Thought* (Chicago, 1970), I, 103-71; Lisa Jardine, "Lorenzo Valla and the Origins of Humanist Dialectic" *Journal of the History of Philosophy*, 15 (1977), 143-64. For the question of philosophy of language in the Renaissance see Nancy Struever, *The Language of History in the Renaissance: Rhetoric and Historical Consciousness in Florentine Humanism* (Princeton, 1966); Jerrold Seigel, *Rhetoric and Philosophy in Renaissance Humanism: The Union of Eloquence and Wisdom, Petrarch to Valla* (Princeton, 1966). Thomas Greene, *The Light from Troy: Imitation and Discovery in Renaissance Poetry* (New Haven, 1982); Richard Waswo, *Language and Meaning in the Renaissance* (Princeton, 1987).

[2] Sarah Stever Gravelle, "Lorenzo Valla's Comparison of Latin and Greek and the Humanist Background," *Bibliothèque d'Humanisme et Renaissance*, 44 (1982), 269-89. The literature on the *Volgare*-Latin question is extensive. For the fifteenth century, see Cecil Grayson's many scholarly studies: *A Renaissance Controversy: Latin or Italian* (Oxford, 1960); "Lorenzo, Machiavelli and the Italian Language," *Italian Renaissance Studies* (London, 1970), 410-33; "Dante and the Renaissance," *Italian Studies Presented to E. R. Vincent* (Cambridge, 1962), 57-75. See also Robert Hall, Jr., *The Italian Questione della Lingua: An Interpretative Essay* (Chapel Hill, 1942); Ettore Bonora, *Critica e letteratura nel Cinquecento* (Turin, 1964); "Questione della lingua," in *Dizionario critico della letteratura italiana*, II (Turin, 1973), 432-41; Maurizio Vitale, *La questione della lingua* (Palermo, 1978); U. Holmes, "The Vulgar-Latin Question and the Origin of the Romance Tongues," *Studies in Philology*, 25 (1928), 51-61; R. Fubini, "La coscienza del latino negli umanisti: An latina lingua Romanorum esset peculiare idioma," *Studi Medievali*, s. 3, 2, no. 2 (1961), 505-50; Waswo, *Language and Meaning*, 134-207. On the relation of fifteenth- and sixteenth-century discussions see Carlo Dionisotti, *Gli umanisti e il volgare fra quattro e cinquecento* (Florence, 1968). See also Karl Otto Apel, *Die Idee der Sprache in der Tradition des Humanismus von Dante bis Vico* (Bonn, 1963).

The discussion of humanist attitudes to the *Volgare* has been obscured by past misinterpretations. Several years ago P. O. Kristeller summarized the mistaken "general view" of the question: "The rise of the vernacular against Latin is pictured as a fight of the lay spirit against Church authority, of democracy against the forces of feudalism and absolutism, of patriotism against foreign or international influences, or of the open-minded plain citizen against the narrow professional interests of Academic cliques."

To refute this "familiar view" Kristeller makes the following points: First, clerical or religious interest was not identical with Latin, as the extensive religious literature in the *Volgare* demonstrates. Second, the vernacular often was promoted at feudal and monarchical courts, whereas Latin was cultivated in free republics. Third, the heritage of ancient Rome was seen not as foreign but as part of a national heritage. Finally, Latin was not incomprehensible to plain citizens but was often more readily understood than other Italian dialects.[3]

Since Kristeller's article, Hans Baron's *Crisis of the Early Italian Renaissance* was published. Although generally and rightly praised for his correlation of ideas and the social and political world of the early Renaissance, Baron has perhaps perpetuated some aspects of this flawed general view of the humanist attitude to the *Volgare*. He considers the Latin-vernacular debate as an episode in the story of civic humanism. He believes the frequent humanist preference for Latin reflects "humanist prejudice" or "classicist bias." According to Baron, the favorable treatment of the vernacular depended on the victory of civic humanism over "radical" and "militant classicism."[4]

For the most part, fifteenth-century humanists were not divided into two rival antagonistic camps, for and against the vernacular. Moreover, their reservations about Italian were founded on a theory of language, not on bias or prejudice. It is important to remember that even in the sixteenth century the equality of Latin and Italian was understood to be potential not actual. This positive attitude to Italian as the potential equal of Latin was made possible by the knowledge gained from humanist study of classical languages.

Most fifteenth-century humanists chose to write in Latin because of their conviction of its superiority to the vernacular for prose composition.

---

[3] Paul Oskar Kristeller, "The Origin and Development of the Language of Italian Prose," *Renaissance Thought*, II (New York, 1965), 122, reprinted from his *Studies in Renaissance Thought and Letters* (Rome, 1956). There is a more recent reprint in his *Renaissance Thought and the Arts* (Princeton, 1980). See also his "Latin and Vernacular in Fourteenth- and Fifteenth-Century Italy," *Journal of the Rocky Mountain Medieval and Renaissance Association*, 6 (1985), 105-26.

[4] Hans Baron, *The Crisis of the Early Italian Renaissance* (Princeton, 1966), 333 and 346; 295 and 285. See also "classicistic prejudice," 288. See my comments, below, 17-19.

This conviction was based on their misgivings about certain features of the vernacular admitted even by its advocates. Leon Battista Alberti, Cristoforo Landino, and Lorenzo de' Medici acknowledged flaws in the vernacular but believed these flaws came not from inherent inferiority but from historical neglect. Their opinion derived from the humanist study of the historical nature of language, not from the opposition of the partisans of the *Volgare* to the classicism of humanism.[5]

The *Volgare* was judged inferior to Latin on two counts: vocabulary and grammar. First, its vocabulary was thought to be meager compared to the *copia* of Latin. The defense of the vernacular had to reckon with the charge that it could only express thought in a crude and clumsy way. These discussions of vocabulary contributed to a theory that linked the growth of language and intellectual capacities.

The second count against the vernacular was that it was ungrammatical, an idea inherited from earlier philology and shared by at least one humanist. According to this idea, the modern languages were disordered and ungrammatical; the ancient, regular and grammatical. Before the *Volgare* could be treated on an equal footing with Latin, the humanists had to come to a better understanding of grammar. And pursuing this inquiry into the nature of grammar, some humanists would link grammar and the structure of thought.

Although there are a few similarities, fifteenth-century comparisons are different from earlier ones, as Dante's and Boccaccio's ideas about the relative merits of the two languages show. Both see the greater use and currency of the vernacular as an asset, as do later humanists. Indeed, for Dante the vernacular is more noble than Latin because of its greater use. Both Dante and Boccaccio believe its defect to be want of grammar, art, and regularity.

Dante justifies his use of the vernacular in the *Convivio* by saying that the work in Latin would be as useless as gold and pearls buried in the ground.[6] In his *Life of Dante* Boccaccio praises Dante's decision to write the *Divine Comedy* in the *Volgare* for the benefit of his fellow citizens, who had been abandoned by the learned. To write for them in Latin would be like giving a newborn a crust of bread to swallow. Boccaccio says that Dante considered but rejected a Latin version, of which three lines are cited.[7]

Still, Dante's choice of the vernacular is not altogether praiseworthy to Boccaccio. The *Comedy* is likened to a peacock. The peacock's distinctive features are flesh that will not rot, gorgeous form and "foul feet

---

[5] See below, 14-17.

[6] *Convivio*, ed. G. Ceriello (Milan, 1952), 1, 9, 27-65.

[7] *Trattatello in Laude di Dante* in Giovanni Boccaccio, *Opere in versi*, ed. Pier Giorgio Ricci, *La letteratura italiana: Storia e testi* (Milan, 1965), 636-37; *Life of Dante*, tr. P. H. Wicksteed, *The Early Lives of Dante* (London, 1904), 93.

and noiseless tread." Where one expects Boccaccio to liken the content of the *Comedy* to the flesh and its form to the feathers, one is surprised to find the vernacular form compared to the "foul feet and noiseless tread!"[8] Moreover, Boccaccio says in his *Commentary on Dante* that the *Comedy* would have been "much more full of art and more sublime in Latin because Latin speech has much more of art and dignity than the maternal speech."[9]

Dante and Boccaccio are both sure that Latin is richer than the *Volgare*, and therefore many more things can be conceived in Latin. Latin is then a superior language:

> Thus speech which is ordained to make manifest the thoughts of men is good when it does this, and that kind of speech which does this most successfully is best. Wherefore, inasmuch as Latin makes manifest many things conceived in the mind which the vulgar tongue cannot (as those know who have command of both kinds of speech), the goodness of the former language is greater than that of the latter.[10]

Poverty of language is a flaw also frequently imputed to the vernacular in the fifteenth century. However, because of a better understanding of the historical nature of language, the humanists began to argue that the *Volgare* could become sufficiently copious. Moreover, from the discussions of *copia* comes a theory of culture: as language grows through certain stages, so do the intellectual powers of a civilization.

Valla calls *copia* "a faculty and a power."[11] *Copia* is an important idea in humanist philosophy of language, a concept used to demonstrate the nexus of language and thought. Besides this epistemological motive, *copia* is used in theory of culture.

Many humanists share an idea of the history of language and culture which is as follows: Languages develop through stages. In the primitive inchoate stage, few words are used to mean many things. The next stage is maturity in which the use of language becomes self-conscious. There is reflection about language itself, which produces grammars and lexicons. The last phase is decline in which the better conventions of the previous age are abandoned. This last stage is to be censured for perversely ignoring or willfully debasing good conventions. The unconsciousness of the primitive age and the oblivion of the decadent produce similar linguistic habits; the former, in its ignorance, is excused; the latter, condemned.[12]

---

[8] *Trattatello*, 647-49: "sozzi piedi e tacita andatura." Wicksteed, 107-9.

[9] *Comento a Dante*, ed. Guerri (Bari, 1918), I, 115, cit. Grayson, "Dante and the Renaissance," 63: "molto più artificioso e più sublime percioche molto più d'arte e di gravità ha nel parlar latino che nel materno."

[10] *Convivio*, 1, 5, 80, tr. W. W. Jackson, *Dante's Convivio* (Oxford, 1909), 44.

[11] *Elegantiarum libri sex* in *Opera Omnia* (Basel, 1540; repr. Turin, 1962), I, 144: "Copia facultas potestasque est."

[12] *Eleg.*, 151.

This idea that a flourishing age has copious usage and a primitive age, a scanty and arbitrary one, explains one aspect of early humanism. Many early humanists wrote lexicons which they thought would restore to speech the capacity to make fine distinctions. Examples are Barzizza's *Vocabularium*, a lost treatise by Andrea Biglia, Pier Candido Decembrio's *Grammaticon*, Mafeo Vegio's *De Significatione Verborum*, and Antonio da Rho's *Imitationes Latinae Linguae.*[13] Of course, the most brilliant example is Valla's *Elegances*.

Although not as discursive as the *Elegances*, many of these works do spell out a theory of *copia* and culture. One of the earliest instances of the theory is found in the *Scriptores Illustres Latinae Linguae* by the Paduan Sicco Polenton. Although not completed until 1433, most of the work was done in the 1420s, which makes it contemporaneous with the lexicons.

In this lengthy history of Latin letters, Polenton divides the past into stages. He says there was a long inchoate state in the history of Latin which precluded speculative thought. Definitions were then explicated by written traditions and especially by Cicero, who "explained obscure things by definition" and "distinguished words that were uncertain."[14] After the classical and post-classical eras, the decline began with the barbarians who were foreign "as in language, so in customs (*uti lingua, ita moribus.*)"[15]

Another early humanist lexicon is the *Grammaticon* of Pier Candido Decembrio. In the prologue he argues the necessity of a rich stock of words for conceptualization. He compares ancient and modern usage and says that, whereas in ancient times there were many words, each with distinct meanings, in modern usage a few words have been invested with many meanings. The result is ambiguity and cramped imagination. Poverty of vocabulary reflects on conceptualization. The authors conceive the purpose of their lexicons to be to furnish words not merely for the

[13] Barzizza, *Vocabularium* (Venice, 1523); Biglia's lost work is numbered among his other writings by Fazio, *Bartholomaei Facii De Viris Illustribus Liber*, ed. L. Mehus (Florence, 1745), 40. Mafeo Vegio's *De Significatione Verborum* is in his *Opera* (Lodi, 1613). The manuscript of Antonio da Rho's *Imitationes* is incomplete, although it can be partially reconstructed from Valla's *Annotationum in Antonium Raudensem Libellus, Opera Omnia*, I, 390-438. For Decembrio see below, n. 16. On these works see A. Corbellini, "Appunti sull'umanesimo in Lombardia," *Bollettino della Società Pavese di Storia Patria*, 16 (1916), 109-63; E. Garin, "La cultura milanese nella prima metà del secolo XV," *Storia di Milano* (Milan, 1955), VI, 545-608.

[14] *Scriptores Illustres*, ed. B. Ullman (Rome, 1928), 448: "Res namque involutas diffiniendo explicavit, ius laudavit civile, quae vero ambigua erant verba distinxit." Leonardo Bruni's discussion of Cicero in his *Vita Ciceronis*, to which Polenton makes reference (452) is similar: Hans Baron, *Leonardo Bruni Aretino: Humanistisch-Philosophische Schriften* (Leipzig, 1928), 114-15.

[15] *Scriptores Illustres*, 509.

decoration of prose but for thought itself. Again, the epistemological interests of early humanism are clear in these works:

> Those who diligently pursue the study of eloquence do not so much aim at license in writing or the noise of empty speech but rather they imitate the sense and propriety of words, in which there is such power that whatever we conceive in the mind we can elegantly express and clearly articulate and easily fashion. . . . Certainly many clamor in longish writings with inelegant and doubtful order of speech. Whatever [Cicero] proposes to say, everywhere speaking with studied diction, he so clearly fashions, so openly arranges, so elegantly explains that you will easily understand that, what is all spelled out at great length by others, by Cicero is explained nicely and briefly. Therefore, whereas in Cicero many different words mean the same thing, among us one word has to serve for many different things. He maintains that a richness of words can convey the same thought, whereas we say that the plurality of thoughts are contained in the words alone.[16]

Pier Candido's less famous but important brother Angelo shares the idea of *copia* (as well as the occasional obscurity of prose). The idea of *copia* figures in the comparison of Latin and the *Volgare*, which is directly addressed in his *De Politia Litteraria*.[17] This work arose from the conversations at the court of Leonello d'Este at Ferrara in the 1440s. In the dialogue Leonello is the interlocutor who maintains the superiority of Latin to the vernacular.[18] His position is approved by the guiding light of the circle, Guarino Veronese. Guarino's argument for the superiority of Latin to Italian is based on *copia*, as is his idea of the superiority of

---

[16] Pier Candido Decembrio, *Grammaticon*, Florence, Biblioteca Laurenziana, Cod. Ashb. 913, ff. 39-40: "Qui eloquentiae studio diligentius occupantur non tam scribendi lasciviam et inanis dicendi sonos consectari solent quam verborum sensus ac proprietatem imitari quibus tanta vis inest ut quae animo concepimus eleganter exponere dilucide exorare faciliter imprimere possimus. . . . Nempe cum multi longioribus scripti ineleganti suspensaque disserendi ratione auribus obstreperent, hic quae dicere praeposuit passim et eruditis vocabulis edisserens, sic clare imprimit, sic aperte conglutinat, sic eleganter exponit, ut facile intelligas quae ab aliis longe oratione nimis limpide dissertata sunt ab hoc commode brevibus verbis explicari. Igitur quae apud ipsum variis distincta vocabulis idem significant, haec unico apud nos plura edicere videntur. Is verborum ubertatem eandem sententiam innuere affirmat. Nos sententiarum pluralitatem solis verbis dicimus contineri."

[17] On this work see Werner Gundersheimer, *Ferrara: The Style of a Renaissance Despotism* (Princeton, 1973), 104-20; Michael Baxandall, "A Dialogue on Art from the Court of Leonello d'Este," *Journal of the Warburg and Courtauld Institutes*, 26 (1963), 304-25; E. Garin, "Motivi della cultura filosofica ferrarese nel rinascimento," *La cultura filosofica del rinascimento italiano* (Florence, 1961), 402-31; A. Della Guardia, *La 'Politia litteraria' di Angelo Decembrio e l'umanesimo a Ferrara nella prima metà del sec. XV* (Modena, 1910); R. Sabbadini, *Storia e critica di testi latini* (Padua, 1971); Mario Di Cesare, *Vida's Christiad and Vergilian Epic*, (New York, 1964), 51-59.

[18] For a discussion of whether this is an accurate representation of Leonello's opinions, see G. Fatini, "Dante presso gli Estensi," *Giornale Dantesco*, 17 (1909), 126-44. See also Gundersheimer, 113-14.

Greek to Latin. Both arguments contain a sophisticated idea of the interdependence of form and content. Just as the Greek intellectual heritage is richer than Latin because of the very nature of the language, which dictates what can be thought, so are Latin traditions richer than Italian.

Angelo has Guarino liken Italian and the modern languages to the primitive stage of Latin, all marked by poverty of words. And the condition of language determines culture. In the primitive state there may be poetry but no reflection on language or theory:

> In the barbarian fashion, diverse forms are used for singular signs which they intend to express the meaning of diverse things. And this manner of writing or rather painting in primal signs continued until definition in the Roman fashion. Thus, in earlier days you find no reflection existed on the grammatical art, still less on the oratorical or poetic.[19]

This philological theory of culture had already been expounded by Guarino in a letter written earlier in his career. His thinking about the history of Latin is based on ancient thought but has a certain perspective gained by historical distance. Guarino numbers four phases of Latin. The first was the primitive tongue, "scattered, uncultivated almost to the point of speechlessness, and confused."[20] Meaning had not yet been fixed by convention and authority. In this primordial tongue priests and priestesses gave religion and prophecy to the Romans. The second stage was represented in the *Twelve Tablets*, archaic but literate, the language of laws and kings. The third stage followed: "That third speech succeeded, now beautiful, now mature, and now harmonious, which I would call truly Roman, that is vigorous. In this speech flourished too many poets, orators, and historians to number here."[21] The barbarian invasions brought the last stage. Thus Guarino designates the stages of language: the speech of myth and prophecy, then of laws and kings, then of arts and science, then of decline.

Guarino's thinking clearly influenced Angelo Decembrio's criticism of Italian. The arguments against the *Volgare* in *De Politia* should not be discounted merely because they are not prescient of the future victory of the modern language over the ancient. They are evidence of humanist

[19] *De Politia litteraria* (Basel, 1562), 7, 81, f. 146: "... barbarorum more uti pro singulis characteribus multiformibus rerum figuris singulas quasque intelligi velint rerum diversarum significationes, in quo scribendi seu pingendi ritu excepta primorum characterum ad Romanum morem expositionem, ut in superioribus diebus habuistis nulla grammaticae artis nedum oratoriae vel poesis extat consideratio."

[20] *Epistolario di Guarino Veronese*, ed. R. Sabbadini (Venice, 1915-19), 2, 505: "[lingua] disseminata, inculta quidem velut infans, incondita."

[21] *Epistolario*, 2, 506: "Successit tertia iam formosa iam adulta iam concinna, quam recte romanam, id est robustam, appellaverim. In ea tot effloruere poetae, oratores, historici quos enumerare longa mora est."

philosophy of language. Decembrio has Leonello say that vernacular translations of Latin works cannot but fail because of the imperfect capacity of the *Volgare* to render complicated and intricate thought: "The translators will gain as the wages of their labor the accusation of wiser men that they have put good Latin authors into poor *Volgare* . . . that they commit many errors in the places that are more difficult to understand."[22] Leonello says that, although he has no serious objections to princely patronage of vernacular translations of Latin works, the better course is to promote the study of the originals:

If works of this kind, and especially histories, are to be done because of the whims of certain Princes, we have no serious objections. But since classical works are being put into the vernacular, I do wonder about the Prince and his people, as both seem to lack training in literature. To be content with translation is like being content with earthenware and coarse cloth rather than pearls and things of great value.[23]

The pearls suggest the swine; Leonello's argument, however, is not elitist. He deplores the lack of training in the populace; he does not want them excluded from literate culture. Instead, his (or Angelo's) argument is based on a theory of the equipollence of language and thought. To revive ancient thought, ancient form must be revived. Only with the revival of true latinity can the lessons of Rome be fully grasped. Decembrio's vision of culture insists that Latin must become the natural and familiar mode of organizing experience for that experience to rival the ancients'. His negative attitude to the *Volgare* should not be taken out of context. He argues that the revival of antiquity cannot be accomplished through a piecemeal acquaintance with the sources through digests and translations.[24] Both the vernacular and vulgar Latin carry with them the baggage of monkish and medieval learning.[25]

The dialogue about *copia* continues into the second half of the fifteenth century. Vernacular literature is rather weakly defended in the earlier discussions and more vigorously in the later. However, the continuity should be stressed; the discussions of the second half of the century do not signify departure from earlier ideas, but refinement. By the 1440s

[22] *De Politia*, 1, 6, f. 10: "sed eiusmodi tandem laboris sui mercedem interpretes accepturi, nempe a sapientioribus accusentur, ex latinis bonis vulgares non bonos reddidisse . . . multaque a se delicta committi locis intellectu difficilioribus."

[23] *De Politia*, 1, 6, f. 10, tr. R. E. Wanner in Gundersheimer, 113.

[24] *De Politia*, 1, 7, f. 11v. Humanist thought on the relation of form and content is at issue here. For the wider study of that important question see John W. O'Malley, "Content and Rhetorical Forms in Sixteenth-Century Treatises on Preaching." *Renaissance Eloquence: Studies in the Theory and Practice of Renaissance Rhetoric*, ed. James J. Murphy (Berkeley, 1983), 238-52 and his *Praise and Blame in Renaissance Rome* (Durham, N.C., 1979).

[25] *De Politia*, 5, 64, f. 115; 3, 27, f. 57. See Mario Di Cesare, 54-56, for a discussion of Chapter 64 where Dante is unfavorably compared to Vergil.

one prejudice against the *Volgare* has already been removed and so does not figure in Leonello's criticism. The philological studies of the humanists led them to think mistaken the idea inherited from earlier language theory that the vernacular languages are ungrammatical.

The humanist debates about grammar are the foundations of a new theory of language and culture. This is perhaps most clearly understood by contrast with some prehumanist ideas of grammar and language. The question of grammatical inferiority is different from the question concerning *copia*. The first considers vocabulary, the second the structure of language. Again it is instructive to compare humanist and prehumanist ideas, as before in the question of *copia*. In Dante's words, Latin is "perpetual and incorruptible" because grammatical.[26] Grammar is an art that was devised to arrest change and variety. In *De Vulgari Eloquentia* he says that change motivated "the inventors of the art of grammar, which is nothing else but a kind of unchangeable identity of speech in different times and places."[27]

Dante believes the vulgar tongue to be governed by mutable usage, to which Latin is impervious because established by art and grammar. Art and grammar give it regularity, and this regularity makes it more beautiful than the vernacular:

> Therefore that language is the most beautiful in which the parts correspond most perfectly as they should, and they do so in Latin more than in the vulgar tongue, because custom regulates the latter, art the former; wherefore it is granted that Latin is the more beautiful, the more excellent, and the more noble.[28]

Copia and regularity make Latin as superior to Italian as wheat to rye.[29]

Dante's idea is relevant here for two reasons. The first pertains to the question of the two languages, the second to a wider issue of language and reality. The immutability of ancient languages, an ahistorical idea, is described in the first pages of *De Vulgari Eloquentia*. There he discusses the origin of speech in Eden. He says that language is only necessary to man; neither God nor the angels have need of it. They communicate their ineffable meanings without the clumsiness of speech. Their glorious thoughts are exchanged silently, mind to mind. Only man has need of words: "Nor does it happen that one man can enter into the mind of

---

[26] *Convivio*, 1, 5, 8: "lo latino è perpetuo e non corruttibile."

[27] *V. E.*, 1, 9, 8, ed. Pio Rajna (Milan, 1907), 10-11, tr. A. G. Ferrers Howell, *Dante's Treatise "De Vulgari Eloquentia"* (London, 1860), 21-22. This passage has engendered much controversy; see G. Vinay, "Ricerche sul *De Vulgari Eloquentia*," *Giornale Storico della Letteratura Italiana*, 136 (1959), 236-58; C. Grayson, " '*Nobilior est vulgaris*': Latin and Vernacular in Dante's Thought," *Centenary Essays on Dante* (Oxford, 1965), 54-77.

[28] *Convivio*, 1, 5, 101, tr. Jackson, 44-45.

[29] *Convivio*, 1, 10, 1.

another by spiritual insight, like an angel, because the human spirit is hindered by the grossness and opacity of its mortal body."[30]

Dante then conjectures about who spoke the first word and in what speech. He says that the biblical story says Eve spoke the first word but then dismisses the idea that the first recorded speech was made by a woman as contrary to common sense and reason. Adam spoke first; he was moved to utter certain words rendered distinct by Him who has distinguished greater things.[31]

Dante says that the first language was Hebrew. Divinely instituted, the connection of word and thing was not arbitrary but established by God, as was the grammar: "We assert that a certain form of speech was created by God together with the first soul. And I say, 'a form,' both in respect of the names of things and of the grammatical construction of these names, and of the utterance of this grammatical construction."[32] The unity of language and reality was destroyed at Babel, although Hebrew survived so that Christ "might use not the language of confusion but of grace."[33]

To measure the originality of humanist philosophy of language, Valla's comments about language, Adam, and Babel should be compared with the passage from *De Vulgari Eloquentia*. To Valla all meaning is created by man and history, not God and nature:

Indeed, even if utterances are produced naturally, their meanings come from the institutions of men. Still, even these utterances men contrive by will as they impose names on perceived things. . . . Unless perhaps we prefer to give credit for this to God who divided the languages of men at the Tower of Babel. However, Adam too adapted words to things, and afterwards everywhere men devised other words. Wherefore noun, verb, and the other parts of speech per se are so many sounds but have multiple meanings through the institutions of men.[34]

Valla's idea of meaning owes much to earlier philology. By the time of the *Repastinatio*, humanists had begun to work out a theory of philological determinism. They recognized that each language has its distinct grammar and vocabulary which provide the way to structure and perceive

---

[30] *V. E.*, 1, 3, 2-3, tr. Howell, 6.

[31] *V. E.*, 1, 4, 1-5.

[32] *V. E.*, 1, 6, 4-5, tr. Howell, 12.

[33] *V. E.*, 1, 6, 5, tr. Howell, 13.

[34] *Repastinatio Dialecticae et Philosophiae Libri III*, Cod. Urb. lat. 1207, ff. 84r.-v.: "Verum licet naturaliter proferantur voces earumque significationes sint ex institutione hominum, tamen et ipsas voces iidem arbitratu suo excogitarunt, perceptis rebus nomina imponentes . . . nisi hoc ad Deum referre volumus qui linguas hominum ad turrim Babel divisit. Quanquam et Adam aptavit rebus nomina, et postea passim caetera vocabula confinxerunt. Quocirca nomen, verbum, et reliquae orationis partes per se tantum soni sunt, sed muliplicem habent ex institutione hominum significantiam." See now the Thesaurus Mundi edition by Gianni Zippel (Padua, 1982), 433-34.

reality. One language does not perfectly and accurately express reality, as Dante's Hebrew.

An idea akin to Dante's of the identity of grammar and Latin persisted in the Quattrocento, when it was rejected by most humanists. In the famous debate about the vernacular in ancient Rome, Bruni takes a position reminiscent of Dante's. This debate took place in 1435 in the antechamber of Eugenius IV among Bruni, Antonio Loschi, Flavio Biondo, Cencio dei Rustici, Andrea Fiocco, and Poggio. The issue was whether there was a vernacular in ancient Rome. Bruni maintained that bakers and gladiators could not have mastered grammar and Latin. Loschi agreed; the others did not. Later other humanists, Guarino, Valla, and Filelfo, heard of the debate and wrote against Bruni.

Salvatore Camporeale, among others, has discussed this debate, which is important in the story of humanist thought about grammar and the rival claims of authority and common usage as determinants of language.[35] The debate is one instance of the confrontation of two different concepts of rhetoric. The first concept is that of Antonio Loschi: rhetoric is a formal art, higher than ordinary discourse. He says: "Eloquence is a higher thing [than the conventions of daily speech] and more removed from vulgar speech and, even if it often concerns uncertainties and common things, still it is contained in its own peculiar and certain principles."[36]

The second concept of rhetoric emphasizes the semantic and linguistic science of speech. The opponents of Loschi and Bruni argue that meaning arises from the historical and mutable conventions of ordinary usage, although they all admit the importance of literate authority in establishing usage. Thus the creative force in language is general cultural conventions.

A good example of how these philological debates produced theory of culture comes from Poggio's writings. Although he got somewhat tangled in the debate with Valla on usage and authority, still, there is a coherent strain of thought about culture in his writings. Biondo reports that at the debate most of the participants agreed with Poggio's arguments against Bruni. Poggio said that he was reluctant to believe that the splendid age of antiquity did not confer a common tongue on all. The Romans understood literary Latin (which Bruni had denied) by the

---

[35] Camporeale, 180-92. Bruni's letter is in *Epistolarum Libri VIII*, ed. L. Mehus (Florence, 1741), II, 62-68. All the studies cited above, n. 3 consider this debate. The letter is now translated in G. Griffiths, J. Hankins, and D. Thompson, *The Humanism of Leonardo Bruni: Selected Texts* (Binghamton, N.Y., 1987).

[36] *Inquisitio super Undecim Orationes Ciceronis* (Venice, 1477), f. 154: "Sed altior res est eloquentia et a vulgari sermone remotior, quae licet plaerumque in ambiguis communibusque versetur, ea tamen proprio quodam ac certo instituto continetur." On Loschi see G. Da Schio, *Sulla vita e sugli scritti di Antonio Loschi* (Padua, 1958).

beneficium of the age, even without formal schooling. Latin literature is not the artificial language of a professional caste.[37]

Later in life, Poggio was still using these philological terms towards an analysis of the ills of the culture of his day. Writing to Andrea Alamanni, Poggio reproves Alamanno Rinuccini for suggesting a foreign teacher of eloquence be brought to Florence to reverse the decline from the days of Salutati, Bruni, Rossi, Niccoli, and Marsuppini. He says the decline is not from lack of teachers but from the atrophy of Florentine culture. The "precepts" of eloquence are found not in the disquisitions of pedagogues and grammarians but in "common use." Poggio reminds Alamanni that: "Richness, eloquence, elegance, beauty of speech, and excellence of speaking cannot be taught by doctrine and precepts."[38] Crassus, Anthony, Caesar, and the Gracchi did not learn their eloquence from teachers but from the usages of their social world; and so did the early Florentines. This is more than nostalgia; it is a vision of culture. The excellence of schools and teachers is a product, not the cause, of the intellectual powers of a civilization.

Flavio Biondo's contribution to the debate is very interesting. Biondo begins his *Historiarum ab Inclinatione Romanii Imperii Decades* shortly after this debate. In that history the fate of letters is tied to that of culture. Biondo's writings are good examples of the interdependence of philological and historical thought in the Renaissance. He records linguistic as well as historical change with concrete documentation, both in his history and in the letter he writes in the debate. As evidence that the illiterate spoke Latin in ancient Rome, Biondo cites some Latin words still used by peasants in remote and backward places. On his travels he noticed that the Latin words for knives, hoes, and farm animals survive in mountainous regions.

In his letter he tries to sort out the different roles of grammar, art, and usage. He decides that grammar is not prior to but is the observation of usage; without any grammatical instruction, people speak sensibly. This is because there is something in *"the nature of language"* itself, that establishes sense in discourse:

I have no doubt that the multitude never know tense, mood, number, and case from art, and, although they sometimes make mistakes, still, I observe them say much correctly and coherently. Everywhere, among all the Italians, even those who speak with the most corrupt vulgarity, we see something instilled by the nature of language so that no one is so rustic, crude, and dull that, if he

---

[37] B. Nogara, *Scritti inediti e rari di Flavio Biondo* (Rome, 1927), 118.

[38] *Epistolae*, ed. T. Tonelli (repr. Turin, 1964), III, 13; III, 184: "nulla doctrina aut praeceptis ubertatem facundiam elegantiam ornatum orationis neque dicendi praestantiam tradi posse . . . usus frequens qui omnium magistrorum praecepta superaret."

can speak at all, he will not know in speech to vary somehow tense, case, mood, and number according to the exigencies of time and sense in narration.[39]

This passage intimates a linguistic theory of perception that anticipates Valla's. Bruni's position is that one must first learn the logic of a "difficult" language like Latin before one can use it. Biondo replies that language itself contains the logic that establishes sense in discourse.

The difference between the two positions is illuminated by reference to a thirteenth-century grammarian who understands grammar as Dante. The grammarian says that all languages have similar grammars because the similarities of things (res) impose a common logic on all languages: "All languages are one grammar ... because the nature of things, the ways of being and understanding are similar among all, and consequently similar are the ways of signifying, structuring, and speaking from which grammar is derived." Many humanists looked rather to the differences in languages to explain differences in the perception of things, which is sometimes the basis of their argument for the priority of rhetoric to philosophy. On the other hand the thirteenth-century grammarian, demeaning his study as Renaissance grammarians generally did not, says: "Therefore, not the grammarian but the philosopher discovered grammar as he considered carefully the peculiar natures of things, from which the appropriate ways of being of various realities are known."[40]

---

[39] Nogara, 127-28: "Stationibus, ut video, erumpet, impetumque faciet quispiam et cornuta urgebit quaestione verborum ne desinentias et tempora ac modos nominumque inflexionem et numeros servasse an penitus confundisse multitudines credam. . . . Tempora vero modos numerosque et casus ab arte illas nequaquam nosse non dubito, quas tamen alicubi errante multa recte et ordine video proferre; quamquam omnibus ubique apud Italos corruptissima etiam vulgaritate loquentibus idiomatis natura insitum videmus, ut nemo tam rusticus, nemo tam rudis, tamque ingenio hebes sit, qui modo loqui possit, quin aliqua ex parte tempora casus modosque et numeros noverit dicendo variare, prout narrandae rei tempus ratioque videbuntur postulare."

[40] Cited by A. Marigo ed. and tr., V. E. (Florence, 1938), 72, n. 59: "Omnia ydiomata sunt una gramatica ... quia natura rerum et modi essendi et intelligendi similes sunt apud omnes, et per consequens similes modi significandi et construendi et loquendi a quibus accipitur gramatica." The passage comes from an anonymous treatise De modis significandi cited by Charles Thurot, Extraits de divers manuscrits latins pour servir à l'histoire des doctrines grammaticales au moyen âge (Paris, 1863), 125. See the discussion of the passage and the modistae conception of language by Ronald G. Witt, Hercules at the Crossroads: The Life, Works, and Thought of Coluccio Salutati (Durham, N. C., 1983), 260. See also G. L. Bursill-Hall, Speculative Grammars of the Middle Ages (The Hague, 1971). The thirteenth-century grammarians's statement, "Non ergo gramaticus sed philosophus proprias naturas rerum diligenter considerans ex quibus modi essendi appropriati diversis rebus cognoscuntur, gramaticam invenit," resembles the following dialogue cited by W. Keith Percival:

A. An anima pertinet ad considerationem grammatici?
B. Non.

This debate about grammar, besides producing ideas about knowledge and culture, enabled the *Volgare* finally to be treated on a par with Latin. In his letter Guarino concludes that all languages, ancient and modern— Hebrew, Greek, Latin, and Italian—are governed by everyday usage (*consuetudine*) not the reasonings of grammarians (*grammaticorum rationibus.*)[41]

Francesco Filelfo also contributed evidence on the side of the opponents of Bruni. He declares the importance of comparative philology in understanding the nature of language. Filelfo writes of Bruni: "He cites *suppellex* and some other nouns which, he says, could never have been declined through its cases by the illiterate. He says the same thing of verbs. [Poggio makes the same mistake.] If Leonardo and Poggio had really grasped Greek literature and the vulgar tongue, they would never have fallen into so great an error."[42] Their errors stem from an imperfect understanding of language, the knowledge of which is gained by comparative study.

This argument that Bruni would have understood language and Latin better had he studied the vernacular shows how far the humanists have progressed from the idea that grammar is exclusively an attribute of ancient languages. Valla too makes the argument that an understanding of Latin can be deduced from observation of the vernaculars in his debate with Poggio about usage and authority. In arguing the priority of *usus* to *ratio*, he asks: "Who demands reason of French, Spanish, German, Florentine, Neapolitan, Venetian, and the rest and is not content with usage?"[43]

Armed with the knowledge of humanist philology, the defense of the *Volgare* began. Cecil Grayson has shown how much Alberti's treatment of Italian owes to his Latin studies. From Latin he borrowed words to

---

A. Quare?

B. Quia grammatica nomina rerum tractat, non res ipsas, nisi quatenus significantur nominibus. Itaque grammaticus neque substantiam animae, neque vires eius, neque operationes, neque organa tractat, sed de nomine animae pronuntiat, unde derivetur, et quae significata habeat.

The dialogue was written by a Westphalian humanist, Alexander Hegius, "more traditional" than some of his Italian colleagues, as Percival points out in his "Grammar and Rhetoric in the Renaissance," *Renaissance Eloquence*, 309.

[41] *Epistolario*, II, 509.

[42] *Epistolae* (Venice, 1502), f. 261v.: "Adducitque in medium supellex et alia nonnulla nomina quae dicit declinari ab illitteratis nullo pacto per suos casus potuisse. Idemque facit de verbis. Si et Leonardus et Poggius graecam litteraturam, vulgaremque linguam tenuissent, nunquam in tantum cecidissent erroris."

[43] *Apologus: Secundus Actus*, ed. Camporeale, 528: "Quis de lingua gallica, hispana, germanica, florentina, neapolitana, veneta et item de reliquis rationem exigit et non ipso usu contentus est?" See Camporeale's comments on the text, 189.

increase the *copia* of Italian.[44] W. Keith Percival has said of Alberti's *Regole della lingua fiorentina*: "The first Italian grammar was therefore in the nature of a theoretical demonstration that it was possible to write a grammar for the vernacular." It had to adhere closely to the Latin model to be judged a successful vindication.[45]

Alberti got the model for his Italian grammar from his rhetorical studies: was Italian to imitate the usage of Dante, Petrarch, and Boccaccio or the reason of Latin speech? Alberti chose the latter course. He saw his work as a step towards realizing the potential equality of Italian to Latin. In *Della Famiglia* he says: "Our own tongue will have no less power [than Latin] as soon as learned men decide to refine and polish it by zealous and arduous labors."[46]

The *Regole* date from 1450; the defenders of the *Volgare* of the latter half of the century also use the ideas formulated in the first half. Thus, *copia* figures in Poliziano's claims for Italian, which, however, do not extend to equality to Latin. In the prefatory letter to the *Raccolta Aragonese* of 1476, he says: "Let no one scorn this Tuscan language as plain and meager; if its riches and ornaments are well and justly appraised, this language will be judged not poor, not rough, but copious and highly polished."[47]

Copia and comparative philology are also used by Cristoforo Landino in his discussion of the *Volgare* in the *Commentary on the Commedia* of 1481. He says that Dante was the first to make elegant the coarse vernacular by imitating the art of Latin speech. Petrarch further ennobled it. Landino's discussion of Petrarch's poetry reminds him of Pindar, of whom he says, "There was no one who better succeeded at forming words combined from others. But this is so much part of the Greek language, that neither Latin nor Tuscan can do it. But, by God, let it be said without envy...."

---

[44] "L. B. Alberti and the Beginnings of Italian Grammar," *Proceedings of the British Academy*, 49 (1963), 219-311. See also his "Appunti sulla lingua dell'Alberti," *Lingua Nostra*, 16 (1955), 105-10; and G. Ghinassi, "Leon Battista Alberti fra latinismo e toscanismo: La revisione dei *Libri della Famiglia*," *Lingua Nostra*, 22 (1967), 1-7. See also M. Baxandall, *Giotto and the Orators* (Oxford, 1971), 49-50, where he shows that the choices Alberti made in translation were "sophisticated and self-conscious."

[45] "Grammatical Tradition and the Rise of the Vernaculars," *Current Trends in Linguistics*, ed. Thomas Sebeok, *Historiography of Linguistics*, 13 (The Hague, 1975), 231-75, 248. See also his "Renaissance Grammar: Rebellion or Evolution?" in *Interrogativi dell'umanesimo II: Atti del X Convegno internazionale del Centro di studi umanistici "Angelo Poliziano,"* ed. Giovannangiola Tarugi (Florence, 1976), 73-90.

[46] *I Primi tre libri della famiglia*, ed. F. C. Pellegrini and R. Spongano (Florence, 1946), 233, tr. Renée N. Watkins, *The Family in Renaissance Florence* (Columbia, S. C. 1969), 153.

[47] D. Thompson and A. Nagel, *The Three Crowns of Florence: Humanist Assessments of Dante, Petrarca, and Boccaccio* (New York, 1972), 105. See I. Maier, *Ange Politien, La Formation d'un poète-humaniste (1469-1480)*, (Geneva, 1966), 226.

Angelo Decembrio argued for the greater *copia* of Greek as compared to Latin based on the readiness with which new compound words were formed. In *De Politia* he said that Latin developed by imitation of Greek richness. Landino now argues that Tuscan will come to rival Latin but only by close imitation of Latin and by transferring Latin words into Tuscan speech:

But, in turning back to our language, I assert that, as in the older centuries first the Greek language and then the Latin, through a great many writers who polished it across the years, turned from poor and coarse to finely finished, so too with our tongue. Already now by virtue of the writers I have mentioned it has become abundant and elegant, and every day, if studies are not lacking, it will improve all the more. But let there be no one who thinks himself not only an eloquent but even a tolerable writer, if he have not first a true and perfect understanding of Latin letters. For no one doubts that all discourse is composed of words and thoughts: the words are always inept without the oratorical precepts and the thoughts are frivolous without varied learning. But neither theoretical art, nor any other doctrine, can be known without either the Greek or Latin language; thus the Latin at least is necessary. . . . Everyone understands how the Latin tongue became abundant by deriving many words from the Greek; thus it is necessary that ours will become even richer than it is if every day we transfer into it more new words taken from the Romans and make them commonplace among our own.[48]

One last Quattrocento comment on the vernacular is Lorenzo de' Medici's, which, like Landino's, is the fruit of earlier philological studies. Lorenzo was the recipient of the letter Filelfo wrote on the 1435 debate about the vernacular in ancient Rome. In his *Commentary on his Sonnets* Lorenzo says there are four prerequisites of excellence in language. The first is *copia:*

What is truly praiseworthy in a language is its fullness and abundance and its being apt for expressing well the mental sense and concept. Thus the Greek language is judged more perfect than the Latin and the Latin better than the Hebrew, for the one expresses better than the other the mind of the speaker or writer.[49]

The second prerequisite is sweetness and harmony. He understands that this is a matter of opinion. Humanist philology included the rec-

---

[48] *Proemio, Comento . . . sopra la Comedia di Danthe Alighieri (1481),* tr. Thompson and Nagel, 128-29. See M. Santoro, "C. Landino e il volgare," *Giornale Storico della Letteratura Italiana,* 131 (1954), 501-47; P. Giannantonio, *C. Landino e il volgare,* (Naples, 1971); R. Cardini, *La critica del Landino* (Florence, 1970). In the *Prolusione* to his lectures on Petrarch in the Florentine Studio, Landino insists the knowledge of Latin is necessary to vernacular eloquence. See Landino, *Scritti critici e teorici* ed. R. Cardini (Rome, 1974), I, 37ff.

[49] E. Bigi, *Scritti scelti di Lorenzo de' Medici,* tr. Thompson and Nagel (Turin, 1965), 143.

ognition that euphony comes from familiarity; a foreign language always sounds dissonant in comparison to one's own.[50] The third prerequisite is an important literary tradition, his acknowledgment of the role of authority in usage. The fourth prerequisite is wide currency, which depends not on the inherent qualities of the language but on fortune and history.

Then, evaluating his own tongue, Lorenzo says: "Yet we shall conclude that men have been lacking to exercise the language rather than that the language has not been sufficient to the men and material."[51] With Alberti and Landino, he treats the *Volgare* as a potential rival of Latin, not inherently flawed but historically immature. This assessment, based on the categories and reasonings of the fifteenth century, would persist in the sixteenth century. As Kristeller has pointed out, as late as 1540 the Florentine Academy expresses its purpose of making scientific thought possible in Italian. He reminds us: "The progress of the vernacular at the expense of Latin was hence much slower than it is usually presented."[52]

Hans Baron has a somewhat different interpretation of the Italian-Latin question.[53] Baron sees Bruni as the first spokesman of the positive attitude to the vernacular based on the statement in his *Life of Dante* of 1436: "Each language has its own perfection, its own sound, and its own polished and learned diction" (*scientifice parlare*). Baron says that this statement reverses Bruni's earlier argument that the *Volgare* is inferior to Latin and the shift is proof of the humanist's passage from radical classicism to civic humanism.[54]

It may be that Bruni's position in *The Life of Dante* is not inconsistent with the earlier one or even much changed. He says in the later work that certain abstract concepts "can only be said poorly in the vulgar tongue." Bruni is here not so much taking sides in polemics as speculating on the linguistic habits of an age. Thus, he says that Dante chose to write in the vernacular, a language fit more for poetry than prose, because of his proclivity and that of his age to poetic expression: "His century was given to rhymed speaking; the men of his age understood nothing

---

[50] *Apologus: Secundus Actus*, 526: "Cui non aliena lingua difficilis absona atque adeo barbara?"

[51] Thompson and Nagel, 146.

[52] Kristeller, 137-40.

[53] *Crisis*, 285-346.

[54] *Crisis*, 345-46 and 290. Bruni's position is called vacillating by V. Rossi, "Dante nel Trecento e nel Quattrocento," *Scritti di critica letteraria: Saggi e discorsi su Dante* (Florence, 1930), 237-38. See also David Marsh, *The Quattrocento Dialogue* (Cambridge, Mass., 1980), 24-37; E. H. Gombrich, "From the Revival of Letters to the Reform of the Arts: Niccolò Niccoli and Filippo Brunelleschi," in *The Heritage of Apelles: Studies in the Art of the Renaissance* (Ithaca, 1976), 93-110; D. Quint, "Humanism and Modernity: A Reconsideration of Bruni's Dialogues," *Renaissance Quarterly*, 38 (1985), 423-46.

of speaking in prose."[55] This is one of the first instances of the juxta-position of poetic and prosaic ages. Bruni's characterization of a century as an age of poetry to explain the propensities of an individual's mind reminds us of Vico. The historical significance of the passage is lost if we see the Latin-Italian debate as a struggle between two antagonistic camps rather than as one part of the humanist investigation into the connection of language, mind, and culture.

Eugenio Garin has questioned Baron's interpretation of the genesis of Quattrocento ideas in the prehumanist traditions represented by men like Cino Rinuccini. In Cino's *Invective against Certain Slanderers of Dante, Petrarch, and Boccaccio* Baron sees signs of the rise of civic humanism and the defense of the vernacular. Garin argues the invective is instead a defense of the old learning and an attack on new ideas. As he points out, very little attention is given to the *Volgare* or to Dante, Petrarch, and Boccaccio. Much of the treatise is devoted to the defense of scholastic logic, of which Rinuccini makes Dante and even Petrarch champions.[56]

This invective is not a prelude to the favorable treatment of the vernacular in the Quattrocento, which owes little to prehumanist *Volgare* traditions and a great deal to classical and humanistic studies. Recognition of the historical nature of language was a key to the defense of Italian. But Cino ridicules discussion of the history of language and culture, such questions as: "whether before the time of Nino there was history" and "which grammar is better, that of the time of the comic poet Terence or of the heroic Virgil."[57]

Cino also mocks the discussion of diphthongs and "the great fuss" made about comparisons of Virgil and Homer.[58] These were topics considered in the comparison of Latin and Greek, which sharpened humanist understanding of *copia*. Alberti, Lorenzo, and Landino took such concerns seriously and were not content, as Cino, to admit the poverty of vernacular vocabulary and then say that therefore to versify in Italian is a greater feat than in Latin. This is a rather weak defense.

The gulf between humanism and Cino's thought is apparent in one

[55] Thompson and Nagel, 69-71.

[56] *Crisis*, 273; E. Garin, "Dante nel Rinascimento," *Rinascimento*, 7 (1967), tr. Thompson and Nagel, ix-xxiv, xxiv.

[57] *Invettiva contro a cierti caluniatori di Dante e di messer Francesco Petrarca e di messer Giovanni Boccaccio*, ed. A. Wesselofsky, *Il Paradiso degli Alberti: Ritrovi e ragionamenti del 1389* in the series *Scelta di curiosità letterarie* (Bologna, 1867), 86 (2), 309: "se dinanzi al tempo di Nino si trovano istorie o no"; 306: "qual gramatica sia migliore, o quella del tempo del comico Terrenzio o dell' eroico Virgilio." On this invective see R. G. Witt, *Hercules at the Crossroads: The Life, Works, and Thought of Coluccio Salutati*, 269-70. On the date of the invective see Giuliano Tanturli, "Cino Rinuccini e la scuola in Santa Maria in Campo," *Studi medievali*, 3rd ser., 17 (1976), 625-74. See also George Holmes, *The Florentine Enlightenment, 1400-1450* (New York, 1969), 1-6.

[58] Wesselofsky, 310.

other matter. Cino stands by the old learning against the new: "They dismiss logic as a sophistical science, very long and not very useful, and do not take care to know whether terms are to be understood by signification, or species, or word; accordingly the term 'man' can mean Peter or animate sensible substance, or human species, or else a bisyllabic word."[59]

Cino also attacks the historical and semantic concept of rhetoric; to him rhetoric is still a formal art:

They plot how large was the number of first-rate orators, maintaining that rhetoric is nothing and that man has it naturally, not knowing what the fourfold exordium is, the latent insinuation, the brief, lucid narration. . . . Nor again do they care what an accepted enthymeme is, or a demonstrative syllogism, or the parts of logic which are very useful in disputations and philosophic proofs.[60]

As he does in Bruni's case, so Baron suggests that the precedent for the statements of another humanist, Giannozzo Manetti, about the *Volgare* are found in Cino and other prehumanists. In his *Life of Dante* of the 1440s, Manetti says that Dante did for Italian what Homer and Virgil did for Greek and Latin. A closer and more obvious source would be the discussions of *copia* and authority among humanist philologists.[61]

Both Manetti's and Alberti's positive attitudes to the vernacular are ascribed to espousal of civic humanism by Baron. Thus Alberti saw things in Florence to "shake his classicistic prejudice."[62] We have seen that the humanist reservations about the vernacular were not founded on prejudice but theory, theory to which the defense of the vernacular owed much. The humanists engaged in classical studies were not his rivals but his colleagues.

Cecil Grayson has objected to another part of Baron's argument. He says that it is not clear that the criticism of Alberti's *Theogenio*—that he violated the majesty of Latin thought and profaned treasures reserved for the educated few—was made by humanists, as Baron assumes.[63] Alberti says of similar critics in *Della Famiglia*: "How pleased I would be indeed if my vociferous critics were capable of earning praise as well as of condemning others. . . . These critics' own knowledge of the ancient

[59] Wesselofsky, 307: "Di loica dicono ch'ell 'e iscienza sofistica e molto lunga e non molto utile e per questo non curano di sapere se 'l termine si piglia per lo suo significato o pella spezie o pello nome; verbi grazia, questo termine uomo puo significare Piero, sustanza animata, sensibile, e puo significare la spezie umana e uno nome bisilibo."

[60] Wesselofsky, 307, tr. Thompson and Nagel, xxv.

[61] *Crisis*, 352.

[62] *Crisis*, 348.

[63] *Opere volgari*, ed. A. Bonucci (Florence, 1839-49), III, 160; *Crisis*, 349. See the comments of Grayson, "Humanism of Alberti," *Italian Studies*, 12 (1957), 48.

tongue meanwhile extends only to keeping silent in it."[64] This seems rather to exonerate than inculpate the humanists.

For the most part, the humanists were not afraid of casting pearls before swine or sullying treasures reserved for the elite. I am not aware of humanist rhetoricians arguing that knowledge is not to be profaned by exposure to the masses. Pico della Mirandola comes to mind; but his exclusive and esoteric idea of learning is not characteristic of the rhetorical tradition and, in fact, is expressed while belittling that very tradition.[65] I have argued that humanists' discussions of modern versus ancient Latin are, for the most part, free of elitism and antiquarianism.[66] Their comparisons of Latin and Italian show the same critical historical perspective. These discussions are important contributions of humanism to linguistic philosophy.

Recent scholarship has vindicated humanist rhetoric against the old charge of emptiness. Scholarly studies have shown that humanist rhetoricians researched the connection between language and thought and language and culture. The evidence has mostly come from Valla. This study has looked at some dialogues and debates among his contemporaries which show that the principles of his philology were shared by other humanists. With varying success they sought not only to claim but also to prove that language determines culture and thought. In doing so, they established the beginnings of comparative philology and theory of culture. Comparison with prehumanist thought shows how much the humanists owed to the recovery of ancient rhetoric. Still, they had a wider perspective gained by the passage of time and the diversification of languages. Thus, humanist thought goes beyond ancient towards a new philological science of history and culture.

University of Detroit.

---

[64] *I primi tre libri della famiglia*, 233, tr. Watkins, 153.

[65] In his letter to Ermolao Barbaro of June, 1485 in Quirinus Breen, *Christianity and Humanism* (Grand Rapids, Mi., 1968), 15-26.

[66] "Humanist Attitudes to Convention and Innovation in the Fifteenth Century," *Journal of Medieval and Renaissance Studies*, 2, no. 2 (1981), 193-209.

VII

PAINTING AND THE LIBERAL ARTS: ALBERTI'S VIEW

By Carroll W. Westfall

A general ambiguity has accompanied the interpretation of painting as a liberal art during the *quattrocento*. The reason for this is twofold. In the first place, the fundamental article by Professor Rensselaer W. Lee[1] on the humanist theory of painting concentrates on the sixteenth and seventeenth centuries; the substantive contributions of Alberti are relegated to footnotes used to show sources for later ideas. Furthermore, Lee interpreted *quattrocento* painting as a period of preparation for the self-assured realism of the later centuries and *quattrocento* humanism as a period deprived of a handy and reliable Latin translation of Aristotle's *Poetics*; without the *Poetics,* it was impossible to elaborate on Horace's doctrine, *ut pictura poesis.*[2] Additionally, achievements in studies of the Renaissance since 1940 have made Lee's interpretation of humanism in need of supplementation and modification.

The second reason for the ambiguity arises from the nature of the first treatise to advance a humanist theory of painting, Leon Battista Alberti's *della pittura.* It was the first to treat perspective systematically as a method artists could use; therefore, it has been studied strictly for that contribution to Renaissance art. Other ideas in the treatise were obviously derived from principles of rhetorical composition; therefore, its relationship to humanists' conceptions of rhetoric has been another fruitful subject of study, but again separate from other ideas in the treatise. Lacking is a study of the relationships between *quattrocento* humanism, the theory of perspective, and the principles of rhetorical composition. Alberti wrote as a humanist, not as an art theorist; it is therefore essential to interpret his theory of art in its proper place in humanist thought from about 1400 to 1435. In that way, it will be possible to gain a clearer understanding of his intentions for painting and of the relationship he envisaged between painting and other liberal arts.

The first, Latin version of *della pittura* appeared in 1435; it was followed in the next year by Alberti's own Italian translation.[3] Its

[1]*"Ut Pictura Poesis:* The Humanist Theory of Painting," *Art Bulletin*, XXII (1940), 197–269. The essay has now been issued independently as a paperback.

[2]*Ibid.*, esp. 199–202.

[3]New researches by Cecil Grayson and reported by Samuel Y. Edgerton, Jr., "Alberti's Perspective: A New Discovery and a New Evaluation," *Art Bulletin,* XLVIII

structure in itself reveals the treatise's close relationship to humanist thought in that it deals with the theoretical basis, the practical means, the purpose, and the rewards of a particular activity. In typical humanist, or at least in typical Albertian, fashion, he outlines the scope of the work in the preface which in this case he addresses to Brunelleschi. Alberti states that Book I is "all mathematics, concerning the roots in nature which are the source of this delightful and most noble art." There, after a brief outline of the aims and scope of painting which he develops at greater length later, he introduces the first complete discussion of theoretical (or artificial) perspective. The chapter heading in the Latin edition had called this the "Rudiments." In Bk. II, which the Latin called "Painting," he amplifies his ideas about the purpose of practicing painting. This Book "puts the art in the hands of the artist, distinguishing its parts and demonstrating all." Here he ignores perspective and encourages the use of shop techniques and devices, especially of the artist's memory and experience and of a device he calls a *velo sottilissimo*. Composition, color, and the subject matter of painting are discussed, and the object of painting is said to be the production of an *istoria*. In Book III, in Latin, the "Painter," Alberti elaborates on what he means by an *istoria*; here he stresses the purpose of a painting. In the Preface he had told Brunelleschi that the last book "introduces the artist to the means and the end, the ability and the desire of acquiring perfect knowledge in painting."

It has not been sufficiently stressed that Book I with its discussion of perspective is quite distinctly separated from the next two books. Alberti had taken an apologetic tone while explaining perspective.

Some will say here of what use to the painter is such an investigation [of the geometry of planes developed with theoretical perspective]? I think every painter, if he wishes to be a great master, ought to understand clearly the proportions and combinations of the surfaces which only a very few know . . . . I beg studious painters not to be embarrassed by what I say here. It is never wrong to learn something useful to know from anyone.[4] . . . . [All that I have written is] such that, either because of the newness of the material or because of the brevity of the commentary, perhaps not much will be understood by

(1966), 367–78, (368, n.5), indicate that the Italian edition is much more than a simple translation. A critical edition of both texts is greatly desired. Except for one or two technical points, this study has avoided those problems which depend too heavily on the nonexistent critical text. Used here are the edition of Luigi Mallè (*Raccolta di fonti per la storia dell'arte,* vol. 7, Florence, 1950), cited as A/M for Alberti/Mallè, and *On Painting,* translated by John Spencer, revised ed. (New Haven and London, 1966), cited as A/S for Alberti/Spencer. Spencer's translation is cited only because Mallè's is so inaccessible; his translations have not been depended upon. I wish to express my appreciation to Professor P. O. Kristeller for assistance on many of the translations from Alberti's Italian.

[4] A/M, 64–65; A/S, 51.

the reader. . . . Up to this point I have said things useful but brief and, I believe, not completely obscure . . . . He who does not understand this at the first glance will scarcely learn it no matter how much effort he applies.[5]

And finally, the concluding passage of Book I:

I hope the reader will agree that the best artist can only be one who has learned to understand the outline of the plane and all its qualities. On the contrary, never will he be a good artist who has not been most diligent in knowing what we have said up to now. Necessary things were these intersections and surfaces. There follows to write of the painter in a manner as to be able to follow with his hand what his intelligence has comprehended.

The best painter must and will understand the theory; other painters have the second book to fall back on. Alberti had tried to convince the reader that he was not speaking as mathematicians who "with their singular intelligence measure the forms of things separated from all material." He wished to speak as painters who deal with the object as it is to be seen.[6] But this is a pose which he abandoned, as the last words of Book I, just quoted, indicate. He begins his instruction in Book II after a long string of introductory remarks: "Painting is divided into three parts; these divisions we have taken from nature,"[7] which leads into the first direct and forthright assertion about how to paint. Only now does Alberti begin to deal with practical issues. He explains how to look at forms in nature and then describes the *velo sottilissimo* or intersection. "This veil I place between the eye and the thing seen, so the visual pyramid penetrates through the thinness of the veil. Using this veil can be of no little commodity."[8] By mentioning the visual pyramid it is clear that the veil is based on perspective theory, but the veil itself, not theoretical perspective, is the device the artist actually uses in painting. The principles of painting based on the theory of perspective is one subject and is treated in Book I; the rest of the treatise, the process of painting, deals with quite another subject.[9]

In the treatise as a whole Alberti is more concerned about the practice of painting than about the principles of painting because painting

[5]A/M, 74; A/S, 58.

[6]A/M, 55; A/S, 43.

[7]A/M, 81; A/S, 67.

[8]A/M, 83; A/S, 68–69. This veil is often considered Alberti's invention. See for example Richard Krautheimer with Trude Krautheimer–Hess, *Lorenzo Ghiberti* (Princeton, 1956), 229, n.1.

[9]S. Edgerton, *op. cit.*, 370, says: "The whole of Book I in Alberti's treatise on painting is an exegesis on optics with the technical, conceptual, and dull vocabulary of scientific Latin wonderfully synonymized in homely and thoroughly visualizable expressions which could be grasped by painters . . . ." The statement is a bit exaggerated in both extremes. It is important to separate the creation of a space on a panel with perspective

has a quite practical, humanist goal. His description of the function of a painter is quite explicit:

to describe with lines and to tint with color on whatever panel or wall is given him similar observed planes of any body so that at a certain distance and in a certain position from the center they appear in relief and seem to have mass. The aim of painting: to give pleasure, good will, and praise to the painter more than riches. When painters follow this [aim] their painting will hold the eyes and the soul of the observer.[10]

The extent to which the painter can hold the "eyes and the soul of the observer" measures his effectiveness. The purpose of painting is to produce a vivid representation, not merely to reveal a perspective construction or its facsimile. As Alberti said several times, *la istoria è somma opera del pittore*,[11] and in Book II, "Painting is most useful to that piety which joins us to the gods and keeps our souls full of religion."[12]

The *istoria* which you would be able to praise and to admire will be one that with its pleasantness will appear as decoration and grace and will hold with delight and the movement of the soul whatever learned or unlearned person looks at it.[13]

---

from the filling in of that space with figures, as Edgerton himself points out. But little more than the space as defined by architectural elements would be drawn exactly. The unfortunate face of the Madonna in Masaccio's fresco in Santa Maria Novella is an excellent example of what happens when the artist does not "fudge" (Edgerton's word). Except for the space-defining architecture, the rest of that fresco was executed free-hand. See the remarks by H. W. Janson, "Ground Plan and Elevation in Masaccio's *Trinity* Fresco," *Essays in the History of Art Presented to Rudolf Wittkower* (London, 1967), 83–88, esp. 87. Alberti often advocates the use of two tools for drawing, the veil and memory, the one to allow for observations for later use and the other for making up figures later on; see A/M, 88–89, 94, 109–110; A/S, 73, 78, 94–95.

[10] A/M, 103; A/S, 89. Book III.

[11] A/M, 85, 87, 111; A/S, 70, 72, 95.

[12] A/M, 76; A/S, 63. Anthony Blunt, *Artistic Theory in Italy, 1450–1600* (corrected ed., Oxford, 1962), 11–12, is virtually alone in stressing a sort of aesthetic, detached purpose for the painting. Giulio Carlo Argan, "The Architecture of Brunelleschi and the Origins of Perspective Theory in the Fifteenth Century," *Journal of the Warburg and Courtauld Institutes,* IX (1946), 96–121; Spencer, in his introduction to the translation of *della pittura, op. cit.,* 23ff, and Edgerton, *op. cit.,* stress the central position of the *istoria* in the treatise. The means of making an effective *istoria* based on the rules of rhetoric has been outlined by Spencer, *"Ut rhetorica pictura,* A Study in Quattrocento Theory of Painting," *Journal of the Warburg and Courtauld Institutes,* XX (1957), 26–44.

[13] A/M, 91; A/S, 75. Contrast Horace, *Ars poetica,* 99–103, a passage singled out by Michael Baxandall to show Alberti's originality and dependence in "Bartolomaeus Facius on Painting: A Fifteenth-Century Manuscript of the *de viris illustribus," Journal of the Warburg and Courtauld Institutes,* XXVII (1964), 90–107, esp. 98. Alberti implies that for holding the attention of the viewer a more important consideration than

When discussing how to make an *istoria* Alberti says nothing about perspective; instead, he emphasizes the role of experience and of shop techniques and advises the artist to solicit the opinions of friends and of the man on the street. But so far the painter has only been making the *istoria,* that is, painting or composing it. "Every praise" of the *istoria,* however, derives not from its composition but from its invention.[14] Alberti took this term from the vocabulary of rhetoric and meant by it the selection and development of the subject of the *istoria.*[15] Poets and orators, who "have many embellishments in common with painters and have a broad knowledge of many things," provide subjects for *istorie.* Alberti names two examples, the Calumny of Apelles told by Lucian, and the story of the three sisters known from Hesiod."[16] After recounting each subject he explains their allegorical interpretations. Using the subject matter well, "the painter will surely acquire much praise and renown in his painting . . . . Thus we who are more eager to learn than to acquire wealth will learn from our poets more and more things useful to painting."[17]

The relationship between poets and painters is a recurrent theme in Alberti's writings. In an important passage in *della pittura* he says:

I should like youths who first come to painting to do as those who are taught to write. We teach the latter first separately, showing all the forms of the letters which the ancients called elements. Then we teach the syllables, next we teach how to put together all the words. Our pupils ought to follow this rule in painting. First of all they should learn how to draw the outlines of the planes well. Here they could be exercised in the elements of painting . . .

and in general, the passage continues, in those methods which might be called draftsmanship, but not in perspective.[18]

Neither poetry nor theoretical perspective are necessarily within the competence of the artist; they would, however, be understood by

----

beauty is familiarity; see A/M, 107–109; A/S, 92–94. Baxandall, "Guarino, Pisanello, and Manuel Chrysoloras," the same *Journal,* XXVIII (1965), 183–204; pp. 200–201, points out that Alberti's ideas about effectiveness and what is desired in the *isoria* closely parallel the ideas of Guarino as worked out in Ferrara.

[14] A/M, 104; A/S, 90.

[15] "Invention" here as in Cicero and Quintilian means only the choice of the material to be presented, not the composition and not the "idea." R. W. Lee, *op. cit.,* 264, Appendix 2, discusses the three rhetorical terms *inventio, dispositio,* and *elocutio.* See also André Chastel, *Art et humanisme à Florence au temps de Laurent le Magnifique* (2d ed., Paris, 1961), 97–98.

[16] A/M, 104–105; A/S, 90–91. See also Kenneth Clark, "Leon Battista Alberti on Painting," *Proceedings of the British Academy,* XXX (1944), 283–302; reprinted Oxford, 1946; the reprint, p. 11.

[17] A/M, 105; A/S, 91.

[18] A/M, 106; A/S, 92.

those best artists who have "understood this [complex theory] at the first glance."[19] Alberti's meaning here has been discussed by Creighton Gilbert who pointed out that the immediate model for the treatise was Horace's *Ars poetica*.[20] Horace treated three consecutive topics in an order which Alberti introduced in his three separate books. Horace's discussion of poetic content became Alberti's rudiments, or perspective thinly disguised as pertinent for painters. The forms or types of poetry became Alberti's *pictura,* or how to make an *istoria.* Horace's final section discussed the poet who became the *pictor;* here, like Horace, Alberti discussed the content of the artist's product and the rewards of the artist. The *Ars poetica* is an isagogic treatise; the material is arranged in an orderly, deductive fashion and is addressed to a learned amateur who is considering writing a play but who, like Horace, would

play a whetstone's part, which makes steel sharp, but of itself cannot cut. Though I write naught myself, I will teach the poet's office and duty; whence he draws his stores; what nurtures and fashions him; what befits him and what not; whither the right course leads and whither the wrong.[21]

Horace's is a practical treatise in only a very broad sense because it deals with much more than the simple problems of the poet; even in itself it is not a sufficient guide to writing poetry. Alberti, in choosing this form for his treatise, was able to refer implicitly not only to the broad implications of the profession of painting but also to the relationship between poetry and painting which he developed in Books II and III. Alberti's treatise is not a simple guide to practice. His meaning is clear: the theory of painting is a much broader subject than the practice of painting. Although the *istoria* is the painter's highest product, painting is more than producing an *istoria*—or at least the theory of painting is deeper than what is necessary for simple practice—and it is closely related to poetry.[22]

[19] A/M, 74; A/S, 58; also above, n.5.

[20] "Antique Frameworks for Renaissance Art Theory: Alberti and Pino," *Marsyas,* III (1943/45), 87–106. For the divisions of Horace's treatise mentioned by Gilbert see Ernst R. Curtius, *European Literature and the Latin Middle Ages,* trans. W. R. Trask (New York and Evanston, 1963), 439.

[21] A. P., 303–309; trans. by H. Rushton Fairclough (London and New York), 1926.

[22] Simply to state that poetry served as Alberti's model is neither new nor startling. It is the basic historiographical foundation for discussing painting as a liberal art during the Renaissance. See for example Lee, *op. cit., passim;* Spencer, *"Ut rhetorica pictura," op cit., passim;* and Chastel, *op. cit.,* I.2.ii. The claim is of long standing during the Renaissance; poets and painters lumped together by Dante, Boccaccio, Petrarch, *et al.,* need not be repeated here. For Alberti's own related observation that through his paintings the painter appears to be another god (A/M, 77; A/S, 64) see Ernst Kantorowicz, "The Sovereignty of Artists: A Note on Legal Maxims and Renaissance Theories of

Because of his treatment of theory and the analogies he draws to poetry, Alberti has written a treatise which is primarily a contribution to the humanists' discussions of the liberal arts. He dedicated the Latin version to Giovanni Francesco Gonzaga of Mantua; another Latin text was well known in the d'Este court in Ferrara from mid-century on.[23] The liberal arts were an important subject of discussion during the period of Alberti's education and of the treatise's composition; participants included Guarino Guarini, Emanuel Chrysoloras, and Alberti's teacher, Gasparino Barzizza.[24] But Alberti's treatise was written to be read in Florence as well; the isagogic form was first newly referred to by Leonardo Bruni, and perspective was invented by Brunelleschi to whom Alberti dedicated the Italian version.[25] In 1435 Brunelleschi went to jail in a test case aimed at proving that he was a liberal artist.[26] Alberti's treatise was written in that climate; by choosing the model for his treatise carefully to include a broad range of concerns, by organizing the material properly, by drawing the proper analogies, by introducing a theoretical basis for the art of painting, and, finally, by subtly understating the case, Alberti sought to prove that painting is a liberal art.

But Alberti nowhere claims the painter is a liberal artist. There is a continual fissure between what the painter does and what painting is. Only the best painters are truly liberal artists; all the rest are only painters. Alberti's separation of the practitioner from his profession is based on Cicero's *Orator* which was discovered in 1421 and immediately caused a great stir among the humanists.[27] Cicero had said that not all can attain the highest grade but all must aspire to as high an

---

Art," *De Artibus Opuscula XL: Essays in Honor of Erwin Panofsky,* ed. M. Meiss (New York, 1961, 267–79); reprinted in *Selected Studies of Ernst Kantorowicz* (Locust Valley, N.Y., 1965), 352–65, esp. 363.

[23]For observations on the dedication and on the primacy of the Latin text see C. Grayson, "Studi su Leon Battista Alberti," *Rinascimento,* IV (1953), 45–62. For the d'Este court, see Edgerton, *op. cit.,* 375 and other notices there. Alberti's play *Philodoxus* was dedicated to Lionello d'Este in 1436; for Alberti and the Ferrara Court see Girolamo Mancini, *Vita di Leon Battista Alberti* (2d ed., Florence, 1911), 139.

[24]Definite traces of the humanist thought of this circle in Alberti's *della pittura* are pointed out by Baxandall, "Guarino, Pisanello, and Chrysoloras," *op. cit.,* 200–201.

[25]Bruni's treatise was the *Isagogicon moralis disciplinae;* the term, not the form, was used. Gilbert, *op. cit.,* 101, n.17. For the relationship between Brunelleschi and Alberti and the invention of perspective see Krautheimer, *op. cit.,* 229–48. John White, *The Birth and Rebirth of Pictorial Space* (London, 1957), 113–26 attempts to emphasize essential differences between their two systems and to introduce an unnecessary antipathy in their personal and posthumous relationships.

[26]Rudolf and Margot Wittkower, *Born Under Saturn* (London, 1963), 10; see also Cornelius von Fabriczy, *Filippo Brunelleschi* (Stuttgart, 1892), 97.

[27]See the introduction to the Loeb Classical Library edition (Cambridge and London, 1942), by M. H. Hubbell, 299.

achievement as possible: "I will not discourage the studies of many who in the weakness of despair will refuse to try what they have no hope of being able to attain."[28] That Plato had written before him did not discourage Aristotle.

Moreover, not only were outstanding men not deterred from undertaking liberal pursuits, but even craftsmen did not give up their arts because they were unable to equal the beauty of the picture of Ialysus which we saw at Rhodes, or of the Coan Venus. (ii.5.) . . . We must not despair of attaining the best, and in a noble undertaking that which is nearest to the best is great. (ii.6.)

From the ranks of craftsmen a few will attain the status of liberal artist; in dedicating his treatise to Brunelleschi and in citing four other leading Florentine artists, Alberti was perhaps elevating them to that rank, a rank equal to that of the ducal patron who would also receive a dedication of the book. Clearly Brunelleschi was superior; he alone was a genius produced by nature, the first she had produced since antiquity.[29] During a period in which humanists, artists, dukes, and republican governors interacted on the highest level of culture, such an idea would come perfectly naturally to Alberti whose own family had grown old in exile.[30]

In order to prove that the profession of painting was a liberal art Alberti had to do more than cite analogies. He developed a dual proof: painting is supported by a sound theory based on intellectual principles,[31] and the aim, intention, and method of painting is clearly related to that of any other liberal art. These will be treated in turn.

[28]*Orator, ed. cit.,* i.4.

[29]On the status of artists during the fifteenth century see Rudolf and Margot Wittkower, *op. cit.,* 14–16. Only Brunelleschi and Michelangelo came from professional families; all other Renaissance artists, if they rose at all, rose through the professions. Bruni used his talent in liberal arts and his position as chancellor of Florence to found a family acceptable in Florentine society; Lauro Martines, *The Social World of the Florentine Humanists, 1390–1460* (Princeton, 1963). For the ancient topos of geniuses produced by nature see E. H. Gombrich, "A Classical Topos in the Introduction to Alberti's *della pittura," Journal of the Warburg and Courtauld Institutes,* XX (1957), 173.

[30]The rapport between humanists and artists has been stressed by E. Gombrich, "From the Revival of Letters to the Reform of the Arts," *Essays in the History of Art Presented to Rudolf Wittkower* (London, 1967), 71–82, which stresses the first decades of the century, and for the next few decades by Krautheimer, *op. cit.,* "Humanists and Artists," 294–305, and "Ghiberti and Alberti," 315–34. I agree with Gombrich's note 71 which criticizes an approach to Florentine culture at the turn of the century, advanced by Frederick Hartt, "Art and Freedom in Quattrocento Florence," *Essays in Memory of Karl Lehmann,* ed. L. F. Sandler (New York, 1964), 114–31.

[31]Rudolf and Margot Wittkower, *op. cit.,* 16; and P. O. Kristeller, *Renaissance Thought: The Classic, Scholastic, and Humanist Strains* (New York and Evanston, 1961), 118.

A liberal art was a theoretical and systematic method for acquiring and conveying knowledge; God's revelation was the proper source of that knowledge. In producing an *istoria* a painter is not investigating a source of knowledge but is conveying knowledge he has discovered. Alberti therefore emphasized first the investigation and then the production which conveys the discovered truths. The root of knowledge is in nature, Alberti tells us; it is in what we see there through systematic investigation using perspective, which is in its turn a form of intellectual knowledge based on mathematics. But investigation is only a preparation for painting.[32]

In painting, the painter combines mathematics and vision. The visual elements themselves are derived in part from mathematics; these are lines, planes,[33] and lights and shades, including color. In addressing himself to painters in Book II he called these "circumscription, composition, and reception of light."[34] Circumscription defines the planes, composition places them, and depiction of received light molds the planes once they have been placed. These three divisions are taken from nature;[35] in painting, they are placed objectively on the picture plane. Both discovering and placing them are intellectual processes; in order to control the process, Alberti had to separate aspects of objects subject to accident (or the qualities of objects) from essential, permanent quantities. Quantities he defined as geometric, and said that the corresponding visual elements are the configuration of the boundary and the nature of the surface of the plane enclosed by that boundary (flat, concave, convex, or a combination of any two). These quantities are known to vision by the extreme rays and by the "prince of rays," the centric ray. The "prince of rays" is "the last to abandon the thing seen," the ray least subject to intervening humidity in the air, and the combination of all the extreme rays when they have been reduced to a single point by the object's removal to a great distance from the observer. Qualities are permanent to the plane as well,

[32]A/M, 55; A/S, 43. Erwin Panofsky, "Artist, Scientist, Genius: Notes on the 'Renaissance-Dämmerung,'" *The Renaissance: Six Essays*, by W. K. Ferguson, et al. (New York and Evanston, 1962), 121-82; 131; indicates that in this is the significant difference between medieval and Renaissance perspective. The medieval system was "only optics, that is to say, an elaborate theory of vision which attempted to determine the structure of the natural visual image by mathematical means but did not attempt to teach the artist how to reproduce this image in a painting or drawing."

[33]Angles come next, but he says that these are really the relationship of lines and planes and of different directions of planes, that angles and their lines define planes, as we would put it, and are then still the second visual element, planes. A/M, 55-60; A/S, 43-48.

[34]A/M, 82; A/S, 68.

[35]See the elaboration of this instruction to painters in Book II, A/M, 82-83; A/S, 67-68.

but when they are observed they *appear* to change according to changes in place, already defined by reference to the quantities, and in light. These changes are known by color, and color is conveyed by all those rays of the pyramid within the extreme rays (and excepting the centric ray) which Alberti termed the median rays.[36] A systematic discussion of color unrelated to perspective intervenes between these definitions and the next section of Book I, the system of perspective.

These definitions made it possible to handle investigation and representation objectively and intellectually. At the end of Book I Alberti explained how to construct a space on a panel using perspective and how to place planes within the constructed space; in Book II he explained how the *velo sottilissimo* allows the painter to investigate objects with a device based on perspective theory. But he said nothing about how to fill in the perspective space construction on a panel with objects investigated with the veil, although later in the treatise he would offer some hints. Nor did he define the relationship between perspective used for investigation of objects in nature and its use to reproduce those objects on the picture plane. Alberti does not tell the reader how to use perspective to fill in the space. This is a fundamental gap in his principles; in order not to leave this important subject incomplete, he devoted an entire separate treatise to it.

The treatise is called *elementa picturae*.[37] In it he carefully traces the observation of an object systematically through three phases.[38] He defines seven terms *ex mathematicis*. The first four are *punctum, linea, superficies,* and *corpus.* This last, he says, is divisible (*est divisibilis*) into longitude, latitude, and profundity. Thus far, he tells us, he has been speaking like the ancients; now he will cover the ground from our point of view (*Haec igitur dixere veteres. Nos ista subjungemus.*), sentences he especially emphasizes in the text. The *corpus,* he continues, is what we call the object which has the *superficies* whose aspect and light (*aspectum et lumen*) enable us to see it. The *superficies* is not the next or the fifth element; instead, we call the *superficies* the extremes of the body, which is defined now as the *limbus*; this *limbus* is the fifth element. The *limbus,* or that which the *superficies* offers to

[36]These definitions are found in A/M, 56–60; A/S, 44–49.

[37]It is generally considered to follow by not many years the composition of *della pittura* and *della statua.* Alberti apparently originally composed it in Italian and then translated it into Latin; his original Italian version is lost. The Latin version with an anonymous Italian translation has been published by G. Mancini, *Opera inedita et pauca separatim impressa* (Florence, 1890), 47–65; Mancini, *Vita di L.B.A., op. cit.,* 129–30; and Grayson, *op. cit.*

[38]Some of this material is covered in *della pittura,* Book I, at the very beginning, but in an abbreviated way which does not make clear the point to be developed here because Alberti does not go on to discuss the reconstruction on the panel.

our sight, terminates in the sixth, the *discrimen*. This element, the finite part of the *superficies* which constantly changes, is made up of points and terminates in them. The seventh element is again the *punctum* which comes from joining the lines in the *cuspis*.

Next Alberti defines three more terms, shifting the emphasis from the observation of objects to how the painter makes them appear in his work: *Consideravimus ista ut genera, nunc quae ad opus pingendi faciant*. This heading, too, is underlined. The three elements here are *punctum, linea,* and *area*. The point is defined as that which the hand cannot make any smaller; the line is a number of these strung together and which circumscribe the area of the *limbus*; the area "is what we call space in the painting," and makes surfaces appear in their amplitude by imitating their lines and angles.[39]

Alberti has discussed three subjects, that is, the object, its appearance, and its reproduction in a painting. Between the first two subjects and their sets of terms he inserted an odd element, the *corpus*. The *corpus* has the surface which receives the light and reveals by its aspect its place; place and light are seen next as they appear on the *limbus* which in the perspective system is known as the *superficies* and is known mathematically as the *discrimen*. The *limbus,* then, appears in the painting as the mediant between the line (discrimen), or the visual element actually put on the surface by the painter, and the area, that which gives the space, and is the flat form within the line filled in with color by the painter.[40] The artist, in observing nature, shifts his frame of reference from geometry and mathematics to their sister, perspective, with an eye on the object itself. Having then interpreted the object perspectively, he renders it in the painting without further recourse to the object in nature. The object independent of any system or relationship other than the perceptible mathematic and geometric one—i.e., the completely objective, intellectual, and corporeal one—is the means by which nature can be known. Doing the perceiving is man; the intellectual relationship between man and the object is objective.[41] Alberti emphasizes that the *corpus* in the dual role—on the one hand the possessor of that which will be observed by the painter as the *lim-*

[39]"Area apello id spatium in pictura, quo visae superficiei amplitudinem certis lineis et angulis imitemur." *Elementa picturae, ed. cit.,* 51.

[40]Spencer, in his notes to *della pittura, ed. cit.,* 102, missed the point when he misread this and stated that "In *Elementi di pittura* [the title of the anonymous *volgare* translation published by Mancini with the Latin] he is satisfied with lembo (edge or border) and the Latin discrimen (a separation)." Note 11. He interprets Alberti's intention as close to that of Apollodorus' *Physics* transmitted through Diogenes Laertius, whom he quotes, 101, n. 11.

[41]See Mallè's comments in the introduction to his edition of *della pittura, op. cit.,* 17–18.

bus, on the other as the *discrimen* in the perspective system used by the painter in painting—was not known by the ancients. He believed that he was doing more than simply reviving an intellectual system of antiquity. Furthermore, he tells us here exactly where he shifted from the object to the perspective system. Finally, he reveals how it was that he could tell painters that they need not be expert and learned in mathematics and implies that mathematicians will find painters irrelevant. But perspective is relevant for each—as mathematics and as geometry for painters who are theorists, and as the *velo sottilissimo* for the mere craftsman-painter.[42] For the painter of genius, who is the only membei of the guild Alberti is addressing here, the object in its dual role is the hinge between mathematics and perspective, and perspective is the hinge between painting and the source of the object, nature. Since perspective shares in both nature and mathematics and in painting and the intellectual control of painting, it gains tremendously in value as an intellectual discipline. It is on the foundation of this discipline that Alberti raised painting to the level of the liberal arts.

A further observation about perspective does not seem out of order. Perspective allows the painter to enter the world of nature intellectually. As Giulio Carlo Argan said some time ago, for Alberti "geometric forms are pure spatial sites or pure metric relationships which in their own finitude express the whole space" when within the matrix of the perspective system.[43] Geometric forms, metrical relationships, and the natural objects or *corpus* are interchangeable terms. All objects can be approached equally, and the relationship between many objects can be objectively assessed by measuring their height, width, and depth in relation to other objects similarly measured.

The objects of nature open to man through perspective include all of God's creation including man's bodies. Alberti said of them: "Bodies are part of the *istoria,* members are parts of the bodies, planes part of the members. The primary parts of painting, therefore, are the planes. That grace in bodies which we call beauty is born from the composition of the planes."[44] Planes make space; bodies are observed intellectually and objectively and rendered as planes on the flat space. In the *istoria* the proportions of bodies assume no special importance

[42]Panofsky, "Artist, Scientist, Genius," *op. cit.,* 134–40; and Hans Baron, "Towards a More Positive Evaluation of the Fifteenth-Century Renaissance," *J.H.I.* IV (1943), 21–49; 41–45.

[43]Argan, *op. cit.* (n.12 above), 102; necessary for this interpretation of space was a conception of homogeneous space. For the relationship between perspective systems and the space to which they applied see the brief survey in L. Brion-Guerry, *Jean Pèlerin Viator* (Paris, 1962), 18–42, which cites previous literature.

[44]A/M, 87; A/S, 72.

except indirectly; the height of man—only a general, average height—provides the level of the horizon, which in turn defines the sharpness of the diminution, and also provides the approximate length of the *braccio* for division of the baseline of the rectangle within which the spatial layout is established.[45] With the baseline so divided and the diminution of the space measured perspectively back from that scale, as explained at the end of Book I, Alberti would find it quite easy to transpose objects into the space by simply knowing their dimensions.[46] These could be known through measurement, which is apparently the way Brunelleschi worked, or through memory and experience based on use of the *velo*. Figures would be sketched in freehand.[47] Alberti considered the *velo* a supplement to the exact procedure for laying out a space as outlined in Book I. Perhaps he had in mind a device such as Dürer illustrated.[48] It allowed the distance between the placement of the eye and the location of the net to be fixed at a distance which made the eye's height and the distance between the divisions in the net correspond to the scheme laid out in the panel to be painted. Only in the most general way do any of these three procedures make the body of man the *basis* for *proportions* of objects shown in the painting. Alberti introduced man as a standard for the comparison of objects within a composition because "man is among all things the best known," for as Protagoras said, "man was the mode and measure of all things" by which he meant "that one knows of all accidents of things through comparison with the accidents of man."[49] Perspective measures space, space is known through quantities, and quantities measure the permanent order of nature, not the accidents of nature.

[45]A/M, 70-71; A/S, 56. See also Edgerton, *op. cit.,* who discusses the independence of space and the importance of the location of the horizon on the effect the composition will have. See especially his Fig. 6.

[46]Janson, *op. cit.,* 86–87, notes how important a grid system laid out within the space and on the surface could have been when Masaccio was transferring the *Trinity* composition from the cartoon to the wall; he also points out how the full size figures in the foreground (donors; skeleton) establish a scale for the rest of the fresco and allow the observer to locate the other figures relative to their place in the space. Especially crucial is the overlapping of St. John the Baptist with the sarcophagus; this is a more telling relationship between the objects than architectural ones or than the space itself could establish. Alberti himself seems to be speaking of this form of composing the *istoria:* "on panels or on walls, divided into similar parallels [to those of the *velo*], you will be able to put everything in its place." A/M, 84; A/S, 69.

[47]A/M, 89; A/S, 73. See also Robert Oertel, "Perspective and Imagination," *The Renaissance and Mannerism, Acts of the XXth International Congress of the History of Art,* Vol. II, ed. M. Meiss (Princeton, 1963), 146–59.

[48]No. 361 in the handlist in E. Panofsky, *The Life and Art of Albrecht Dürer* (Princeton, 1943), illustrated there, Fig. 310. Panofsky on pp. 252–53 states that this woodcut illustrates Alberti's *velo.*   [49]A/M, 69; A/S, 55.

In *della pittura* Alberti did not discuss proportions either as metric relationships among the three dimensions of objects complete within themselves and divorced from other objects in space or as the metric relationships between objects within space. The basis for such a discussion was there, however, and he did take up the former subject soon after in *della statua* where he outlined the representation of man's body as subject to the control of relationships proportionate to one another. The latter subject he took up in the architectural treatise where he made the proportionate relationships between planes, space, and objects the keystone of his theory by combining the objective, planar space of *della pittura* with the material taken from nature which the sculptor works with. *Della pittura* had only introduced the many and complex applications of perspective, among them the most important being the means to formulate an intellectual assessment of the three dimensions of objects measured objectively.

The second method Alberti used to raise painting to the level of the liberal arts was to have painting emulate the aim, intention, and method of poetry about whose position in the liberal arts there was no question. Poetry attempts to use a distinct method to discover and to convey truth; the method Salutati outlines seems to have served as a model for Alberti when he adapted the theory of poetry to the profession of painting. Poetry was not meter but eloquence; Salutati's theory of poetry differs in no fundamental respect from the general theory of the first third of the *quattrocento*; and it was a part of the general program of liberal studies as these had evolved during Alberti's student years.[50]

Salutati based his theory on what might be called the humanistic trivium;[51] its elements were the familiar ones: dialectic, rhetoric, and grammar. With dialectic the student investigates nature, that is, he weighs and assesses the events of men as conveyed to later ages by the eloquent testimony of past poets. With rhetoric he passes along

---

[50] Bruni's *Life of Dante* (1436) would alter the scheme slightly; Bruni returned to the problem of the two types of poet, the methodical one and the one who uses method to shape divine inspirations he receives from outside the techniques of method. Alberti's *della pittura* says nothing about inspiration but emphasizes method.

[51] The term "humanistic trivium" is chosen out of respect for Salutati's own emphasis and to differentiate it from those he criticized, namely, the sophists who placed rhetoric in first place, and the scholastics who enthroned dialectic. His own sympathies lay with the primacy of grammar. See Berthold L. Ullman, *The Humanism of Coluccio Salutati* (Padua, 1963), 85, for this distinction and for information regarding Salutati's emphasis on grammar. Salutati's method would be the basis for Bruni's, but it would not totally eclipse the scholastics' method emphasizing dialectic. Even in 1485 Giuliano della Rovere, the future Julius II, would show dialectic in a central place in the trivium; see the discussion by L.D. Ettlinger, "Pollaiuolo's Tomb of Pope Sixtus IV," *Journal of the Warburg and Courtauld Institutes*, XVI (1953), 250-55.

this understanding of nature as well as what he has learned through grammar. Grammar is the central term; Salutati calls it "the gateway to all the liberal arts and to all learning, human and divine."[52] Grammar teaches us "how the essential nature of things changes, and how all the sciences work together . . . . All studies in human affairs and in sacred subjects are bound together [by it]."[53] Grammar is the tool for investigating through comparison; it reveals the interrelationships between things (*rerum*) and it is the central contact between nature and the intellect on the one hand and the intellect and rhetoric on the other.

Proof of proficiency in grammar is in poetic eloquence which moves the reader from vice to virtue. B. L. Ullman has shown that Salutati's conception of rhetoric is predicated upon the "Ciceronian (and Horatian) view of rhetorical style [combined] with Aristotle's moral purpose,"[54] but when Salutati presented his views for public consumption he cited Augustine's *On Christian Doctrine*.[55] Alberti cited no authorities for his theories, but he clearly thinks that the *istoria* shares a common didactic end with poetic eloquence.

Painter's perspective had been the principal part of the painter's method, and the tool for knowing, evaluating, and regulating visual events in nature; it showed the interrelationship between things and it served as the theory for the construction (but not for the invention) of the *istoria* which would convey that knowledge. Perspective did for Alberti what grammar did for Salutati; it had to be combined with the other parts of poetry (rhetoric and dialectic) in order to serve the artist, and this it did through combining construction with invention. The poet had ancient eloquence to investigate; the painter unfortunately had few examples of ancient art to investigate, so nature assumed primacy as a source of knowledge. But even with this shift, perspective and grammar are easily seen as supporting the fundamental theory in their respective fields.

The *istoria* acted as poetry in that it conveyed didactic messages effectively as eloquence does. It also acted as rhetoric, in that it depended on invention and on the presentation of discovered material; as grammar, in that it conveyed relationships between things; as history, in that it showed the actions of men affecting history and based its invention on ancient poets; and as strict moral philosophy in that it

---

[52]Salutati, "To His Venerable Father in Christ, Brother John Dominici, O.P.," tr. in E. Emerton, *Humanism and Tyranny* (Cambridge, Mass., 1925); 346 77, 351; and in *Epistolario*, ed. F. Novati, 4 vols. (Rome, 1891 1911); IV.i. (1905), 205 40; 215.

[53]Emerton, *loc. cit.*, and Novati, *loc. cit.*

[54]*Op. cit.*, 62. As an assailant against vice and error, poetry is a liberal art; see p. 59.

[55]Salutati, in Emerton, *op. cit.*, 359; Novati, *op. cit.*, 224.

spoke of vice and virtue and of the goodness of men and of God. These departments of the *studia humanitatis* were never strictly shut off from one another, and all had the same purpose.[56] Painting had the purpose of each individually and of the program collectively. Furthermore, like poetry, painting used parts of the quadrivium (geometry, arithmetic) in its theoretical basis and depended on all three parts of the trivium for the application of that method. Painting, therefore, was quite clearly a liberal art; its intention was to move men from vice to virtue.

If successful in this purpose, the painter was rewarded with praise, admiration, and fame, and these were his only if his *istoria* was successful. It was not enough simply to produce a pretty picture. This, too, is a prominent humanist theme. Humanists felt a deep responsibility to other men as is clear in Alberti's writings at this time. *Della famiglia,* which he wrote shortly before he arrived in Florence and revised and published there in 1444, concentrates on the responsibility of various members of the family to one another and of the family to others. Stressed is the education of youthful members of the family to follow virtuous paths; here Alberti established a background for the theme of the rewards open to the man who is suited to be a painter.

The main speaker in Book II is old Giannozzo who impresses on his young friends that he has learned much from the world. Experience has taught him that there are only three things "which man is able to call his own," the soul (*l'animo*), the body (*corpo*), and a third, "the most precious thing. Not so precious are my hands or even my eyes . . . .You are not able to bequeath it to another, nor to make it diminish; there is no way to make it become yours except by desiring it."

Lionardo: This thing is given to me as it is to others?
Giannozzo: And when you want it, it won't be yours.
    Time, Lionardo my boy, time, my sons.[57]

Waste no time; be actively virtuous and virtuously active. In Book II Lionardo had said that the natural consequence of indolence and sloth is vice. "You will find no means so simple for lowering yourself into dishonor and infamy than sloth."[58] But in what field should one be active? It should be in that for which one is naturally equipped and to

[56] For the *studia humanitatis* and its program see P. O. Kristeller, *Renaissance Thought, op. cit.,* 9–10; and his *Renaissance Thought II: Papers on Humanism and the Arts* (New York, Evanston and London, 1965), 3–4; for the importance of eloquence as the unifying theme of humanist activity, see the important paper by Hanna H. Gray, "Renaissance Humanism: The Pursuit of Eloquence," *J. H. I.* XXIV (1963), 497–514.

[57] Alberti, *I Libri della famiglia,* in *Opere volgari,* ed. C. Grayson (Bari, 1960), I, 169.

[58] *Op. cit.,* 130; also A/M, 53 and 105; A/S, 39 and 91.

which one naturally inclines. It is a gift of nature that allows man to be virtuous; it is man's responsibility to develop that gift.

All mortals are by their nature commissioned to love and to support any sort of the most praiseworthy *virtù*. And *virtù* is nothing other than perfect and well produced nature.[59]

If man exercises his innate and particular *virtù* with vigorous application, he can achieve virtue.[60]

The virtuous man, the man who actively desires virtue, has an advantage because man's natural predisposition is to love God. God made man a unique creature who is able to see and to admire and to appreciate the finest parts of God's creation. Alberti cites authorities who sustain his view and calls attention to the greatness of God's creation:

Man is to render praise to God, to satisfy him with good works for those qualities of *virtù*, the gifts that God gave to the soul of man, the greatest and most valued above all the other earthly animals. Nature, that is, God, made man partly celestial and divine, partly beautiful and noble above every mortal thing.[61]

Although man is filled with base and mortal desires, he is uniquely equipped with the means to overcome them.

This theme touches on man's divinity and would soon be a general topic of humanist thought. Pico della Mirandola's famous formulation of it is generally traced back to Giannozzo Manetti's *de dignitate et excellentia hominis* (1451-52), a work written in response to Innocent III's and B. Fazio's assessments of man.[62] Alberti's treatise on the family already contains important parts of the humanists' position. Man is the mediator and measurer of all of God's creation, capable of moving where he wills; here Pico follows Alberti.[63] But Pico added that man is so constituted that

If happy in the lot of no created thing, he withdraws into the center of his own unity, his spirit, and there remains alone with God, shut out from the world and its activities?[64]

---

[59] *Della famiglia, op. cit.*, p. 63.

[60] A few sentences later Alberti names some areas of activity: "law, the most subtle sciences, elegant and most outstanding letters and doctrines," and, if letters do not appeal, and the man is by nature strong, spirited. and adventurous, military pursuits would also be a proper field in which to follow nature. *Loc. cit.*

[61] *Ibid.,* 131-33.

[62] For this subject see Eugenio Garin, *L'umanesimo italiano* (Bari, 1964), 72-73; P.O. Kristeller, *Renaissance Thought II. op. cit.*, 42; Charles E. Trinkaus, Jr., *Adversity's Noblemen: The Italian Humanists on Happiness* (New York, 1940).

[63] Pico della Mirandola, *Oration on the Dignity of Man.* in E. Cassirer, P.O. Kristeller, and J.H. Randall, Jr., *The Renaissance Philosophy of Man* (Chicago and London, 1948), 223-54; 224-25.   [64] *Ibid.,* 225.

Alberti allowed no such withdrawal. Man must exercise his *virtù;* and he must do it within a social context because

God, you see, established in the soul of man a strong chain to tie together the association of men, justice, equality, liberality, and love with which man is able along with other mortals to merit grace and praise, and with His Creator His piety and mercy.[65]

Man praises God within the bonds of human society because of the very essence of man whom nature, that is, God, created. Alberti acknowledged that he took the words from Plato when he said that men are born for other men, and that part of us must be for our country, part for our family, and part for our friends.[66] Alberti defines virtue as the tireless devotion to exercising in human society the innate gift of the particular *virtù* God gave each individual man. The proper exercising of that *virtù* merits earthly praise, glory, and fame, and celestial virtue.[67]

Della pittura is a manual to guide the man whose *virtù* equips him to be a painter, or, more precisely, it is a manual which reveals the nobility of the profession to the man who has a knowledge of the practice of painting and the *virtù* to achieve the exalted station of the liberal artist. That is one reason the treatise has so much to say about the responsibilities of the artist. Painting itself "is most useful to that piety which joins us to the gods and keeps our souls full of religion."[68] The painter enhances the beauty of God's creation and of things created by Him. And the fame and virtue of the painter are enhanced by the association of painting with the other liberal arts:

... I consider the best indication of a most perfect intellect to be a very great delight in painting, even though it happens that this art is pleasing to the educated as well as to the uneducated.[69]

The fame of ancient painters is known to us through records of their paintings: study their works and lives, but, he adds immediately, it is useful to remember "that avarice has always been the enemy of virtue." Alberti then recites the Petrarchian theme: he who seeks money and fame above virtue loses all three, but he who seeks virtue through the practice of painting will acquire renown, riches, and pleasure.[70]

---

[65] Alberti, *della famiglia. op. cit.,* 133.

[66] It is Alberti's paraphrase of Plato's *Crito. ibid..* 132. See also his *Teogenio.* in *Opere volgari di L.B.A..* ed. Cecil Grayson (Bari, 1966), II, 55-104: 100. The *Teogenio* was dedicated to Lionello d'Este.

[67] The subject had already been sketched out in his *Philodoxus,* written in Bologna c. 1427. See Vittorio Rossi, *Il Quattrocento* (5th ed., Milan, 1953), 137.

[68] A/M, 76; A/S, 63: above, n.12.   [69] A/M, 80; A/S, 66-67.

[70] A/M, 81: A/S, 67.

Works that the painter has painted well are testimonies to his fame, Alberti says at the conclusion of Book III.[71] Petrarch had said: "Our life will be judged by our conversation; when the proof of our actions is gone, only the evidence of our speech will remain."[72] Alberti considered painting to be an activity and the effective painting to be proof of virtuous activity. In exercising his *virtù* the painter acquires praise and fame by striving for virtue through his activity.

The liberal arts in general were the defenders of virtue and in that class Alberti included eloquence or oratory, painting, sculpture, and perspective. He outlined his ideas in a short dialogue in which Virtue complains to Mercury of how she was handled by Fortune. Fortune assaulted her, tore her clothes, and verbally abused her. Fortune insulted her protectors, Plato, whom she called a "blabberer" and a "lackey," and Cicero, who received a mean blow to the face from Fortune's consort, Marc Antony. Virtue's friends fled; "Neither Polyclitus with his brush, nor Phidias with his chisel, nor the others who were similarly armed, could defend themselves against those truculent warriors trained to sack, kill, and wage war."[73]

Although unsuccessful in that encounter, the liberal arts were clearly the protectors of Virtue against Fortune. During the Renaissance, after all, Virtue did not always succeed. But if there was to be success, it would come by practicing the liberal arts and following one's *virtù* actively and conscientiously. Petrarch had sought seclusion and had envisaged Virtue protected by the Christian and theological virtues; an event of Fortune was a lapse of mind, of intellect, or of will. Alberti, however, thought of Fortune as a conflict between man and nature. Nature included historical events, the political fortunes of states and of families, and God's creation or nature pure and simple. In 1434/35 when he began his treatise Florence was a republic in which the activity of each citizen determined the justice of the government. In the northern courts, the liberal artists were among the councillors of the ruling duke, and the duke himself might be a liberal artist. These were the individuals to whom the painter addressed his *istoria,* and the subject of *della pittura* is how to make an effective presenta tion to them. There was little point in discussing the conflict between

[71]A/M, 113; A/S, 98. In Book II in the section cited above Alberti points out in one paragraph that pleasure and praise are gained by the skillful painter and perpetual fame belongs to the master of painting; this clearly establishes a hierarchy of aims.

[72]Petrarch, *The Life of Solitude (de vita solitaria),* trans. by J. Zeitlin, n.p. (University of Illinois Press, 1924), 100.

[73]Alberti, "Virtus," from *Intercoenales,* trans. by Arturo B. Fallico and Herman Shapiro, *Renaissance Philosophy,* Vol. I, *The Italian Philosophers* (New York, 1967), 31–33; published with Italian translation in E. Garin, *Prosatori Latini del quattrocento* (Milan and Naples, 1952), 640–44.

the painter and fortune, especially since Alberti had already treated the subject extensively. *Della famiglia,* "Virtus" and other short works, *Teogenio,* and eventually, *de re aedificatoria,* feature Fortune because each deals with men in nature and society. In the architectural treatise, however, the subject is handled quite differently because the treatise has an additional theme, that of the architect confronting natural elements and events. The office of the painter is much simpler than that of the architect; the painter simply presents to the man on the street an *istoria* which will better equip him to confront Fortune. In this task painting is like poetry and is therefore a liberal art; as in poetry, success in painting brings virtue, and from virtue follows fame.

Finally, not only the purpose and the rewards, but the method itself is taken from the poets. The treatise is on painting in only the broadest sense. Its fundamental thesis—that the sure method of perspective and the sure source of truth in God's creation, nature, can fill the souls of men with religion and piety and can earn for the painter virtue and fame and therefore raise the excellent painter to the level of the liberal artist—was very much a part of humanist thought during the Renaissance.

Amherst College.

VIII

ANCIENTS AND MODERNS IN THE RENAISSANCE: RHETORIC AND HISTORY IN ACCOLTI'S *DIALOGUE ON THE PREEMINENCE OF MEN OF HIS OWN TIME*

By ROBERT BLACK*

The comparison of ancients and moderns, so prominent a theme in western thought until the nineteenth century, was a child of *epideixis* or panegyric, the rhetoric of praise and blame.[1] As in the other branches of rhetoric, there were five stages in composing a pangyric: invention, disposition, diction, memory, and delivery. Of these invention, or thinking of what to say, was the most important,[2] and was based on a series of standard arguments or commonplaces called *loci communes* or *topoi koinoi,* intellectual themes suitable for development or modification according to the circumstances, which could be used on the most diverse occasions.[3] One such *topos* was the contrast between ancients and moderns or between antiquity and modern times. A writer could censure contemporary individuals or institutions by declaring that they were inferior to their predecessors; on the other hand, he could praise them by showing that they were superior to their counterparts in the past.

In Antiquity, for example, Horace censured his contemporaries as impious, factious, and degenerate by contrasting them with the early Romans portrayed as paragons of gravity and severity;[4] similarly,

---

* I am grateful to Professor P. O. Kristeller for his assistance in preparing this article. I should also like to acknowledge the financial support which I have received for this research from the University of Leeds.

[1] The fundamental survey of rhetoric from Antiquity to the Renaissance is P. O. Kristeller, "Philosophy and Rhetoric From Antiquity to the Renaissance," in his *Renaissance Thought and its Sources,* ed. M. Mooney (New York, 1979), 211-59, 312-27. On *epideixis,* cf. *Rhetorica ad Herennium,* III, 10-15; Cicero, *De inventione,* II, 177-78, *De part. orator.* 70-82, *De oratore,* II, 340-49; Quintilian, III, vii; T. C. Burgess, "Epideictic Literature," *Studies in Classical Philology,* 3 (1902), 89-261; M. L. Clarke, *Rhetoric at Rome* (London, 1953), *passim;* E. R. Curtius, *European Literature and the Latin Middle Ages,* tr. W. R. Trask (New York, 1953), 68-69, 154-82; M. Baxandall, *Giotto and the Orators* (Oxford, 1971), 45-46 and *passim;* J. W. O'Malley, *Praise and Blame in Renaissance Rome* (Durham, North Carolina, 1979), 36 ff. Unless indicated otherwise, translations are mine—R. B.

[2] *Rhet. ad Her.* II, i, 1.

[3] On the importance of commonplaces, cf. Curtius, 70-71, 79 ff., and *passim.*

[4] Ode III, 6.

Vergil condemned the corruption of modern Rome by citing the simplicity of old Rome,[5] as did Juvenal, who contrasted old Roman purity with contemporary gluttony, effeminacy, and Greek decadence.[6] This commonplace continued to be found useful in the Middle Ages, for example, by Charlemagne, who, when he wished to point out the shortcomings of his court scholars, is said to have declared, "I wish I had twelve men with the wisdom of Jerome and Augustine."[7] Similarly, Alain of Lille (1114-1203?) wrote of the crudity of modern poetics in contrast to the learning of ancient poets,[8] and a famous medieval example comes from *Carmina Burana:*

> Once learning flourished, but alas!
> 'Tis now become a weariness.
> Once it was good to understand,
> But play has now the upper hand. . . .[9]

The idea of "il buon tempo antico," the golden age of the Italian communes, was a version of this commonplace which became a favorite theme in the literature of the Italian city-states in the thirteenth and fourteenth centuries:[10] Dante referred to the age of his ancestor Cacciaguida to highlight the deficiencies of contemporary Florence,[11] whereas Filippo Villani, writing in the late fourteenth century, saw the time of Dante as a golden age in contrast to the contemporary world.[12] The idea of "il buon tempo antico" may have prepared the ground for Renaissance humanists, who often conjured up a golden age in the past filled with virtues lost to contemporaries. Such, for example, were Petrarch's many condemnations of his own age in contrast to Roman antiquity,[13] Salutati's denunciation of his contemporaries as botchers who patch together the scraps of antiquity without inventing anything new themselves,[14] Niccolò Niccoli's attacks on the modern age in contrast to classical antiquity in Bruni's *Ad Petrum Paulum Histrum Dialogus,*[15] and Bruni's own reference to his

---

[5] Eighth Eclogue, vv. 53 ff.; *Georgics,* II, vv. 458-540.   [6] Satires, II, VI, and XI.

[7] Cf. E. Goessmann, *Antiqui und Moderni im Mittelalter* (Munich, 1974), 52.

[8] Cf. M. -D. Chenu, *Nature, Man, and Society in the Twelfth Century,* ed. and tr. J. Taylor and L. Little (Chicago, 1968), 318-19.   [9] Cf. Curtius, 94-95.

[10] Cf. C. Davis, "Il buon tempo antico," *Florentine Studies,* ed. N. Rubinstein (London, 1968), 45-69.   [11] *Paradiso,* XVI, vv. 34 ff.

[12] *Liber de civitatis Florentiae famosis civibus,* ed. G. C. Galletti (Florence, 1847), 5.

[13] 6th and 7th Eclogues; *Sine nom.* 11 and 17; *Fam.* XIX, 9 and XXII, 14; *Sen.* VII, 1. For an example of the direct influence of Petrarch's views on the superiority of antiquity, cf. N. W. Gilbert, "A Letter of Giovanni Dondi dall'Orologio to Fra' Guglielmo Centueri: A Fourteenth-Century Episode in the Quarrel of the Ancients and the Moderns," *Viator,* **8** (1977), 302, 307-17, 330-38.

[14] Ep. VI, 4, ed. F. Novati (Rome, 1891-1911), II, 145.

[15] E. Garin (ed.), *Prosatori latini del quattrocento* (Milan, n.d.), 52-74.

contemporaries as dwarfs (*homunculi*) in comparison with the stature of the ancients.[16] The commonplace continued to be useful in the later Renaissance, as was shown by Machiavelli, who censured his contemporaries by making a detailed comparison between them and ancient Romans.[17] Similarly, Lazzaro Bonamico, one of the interlocutors in Speroni's *Dialogo delle lingue,* illustrated the deficiencies of contemporary Italian by declaring that compared to the Latin language, which he likened to wine, the vernacular was like the dregs,[18] a view shared by Romolo Amaseo, who argued that Latin was superior to Italian because of its antiquity and universality.[19] Later in the sixteenth century, Trajano Boccalini condemned the contemporary world in which there was no longer any love, even between father and son, contrasting it to a golden age in which money had not yet become man's only concern.[20] Marcantonio Zimara's view was that the contemporary world in contrast to antiquity had fewer great men because human nature had grown weaker,[21] an opinion somewhat more extreme than Doni's view in the *Marmi,* where modern times were censured in comparison to antiquity because "whatever one writes had been said and whatever one imagines has been imagined."[22] This was repeated at the end of the seventeenth century by La Bruyère, who wrote, "All has been said, and it has been seven thousand years since there were men who thought,"[23] which shows that demonstrating the superiority of the ancients over the moderns remained an effective *topos* of epideictic rhetoric after the end of the Renaissance.

Just as important in classical, medieval, and Renaissance thought was the theme that moderns were superior or equal to ancients, a commonplace of panegyric for the present or recent past. Ovid praised the sophistication of contemporary Rome by contrast with the crude manners of early Rome,[24] and Statius said that Lucan was a greater poet than Ennius, Lucretius, and Vergil; this commonplace remained a favorite in late Antiquity, as is shown by many passages from authors such as Ausonius, Claudian, Sidonius Apollinaris, and Fortunatus.[25] It was found particularly useful by Cassiodorus, who

---

[16] *Epistolae,* ed. L. Mehus (Florence, 1741), I, 28. Bruni, *Humanistisch-philosophische Schriften,* ed. H. Baron (Leipzig, 1928), 124-25; P. Bracciolini, *Epistolae,* ed. T. Tonelli (Florence, 1832-61), II, 298-99.

[17] *Discorsi sopra la prima deca di Tito Livio,* esp. preface to Book II.

[18] Cf. G. Margiotta, *Le origini italiane de la querelle des anciens et des modernes* (Rome, 1953), 102-06; A. Buck, *Die "Querelle des anciens et des modernes" im italienischen Selbstverstaendnis der Renaissance und des Barocks* (Wiesbaden, 1973), 15-16.

[19] Margiotta, *Le origini,* 100.   [20] Buck, *Die "Querelle,"* 17.   [21] *Ibid.*

[22] Margiotta, *Le origini,* 131.   [23] Buck, *Die "Querelle,"* 16.

[24] *Ars amandi,* III, 144 ff.

[25] Curtius, 162-65; another version of the *topos* was to ridicule the notion that age confers value: cf. Horace, *Ep.* II, 1, 18 ff.; Curtius, 98, 165-66.

said that some of his contemporaries possessed the morals of the ancients and who praised Boethius as being the equal or superior of ancient authors in logic and mathematics.[26] In the early Middle Ages, Bede said that modern poetry was comparable to Vergil's since both followed the same rules,[27] and at the Carolingian court academy Charlemagne was praised as the new David and Aachen as the new Athens,[28] while Walafrid Strabo, another Carolingian, declared that someone called Probus wrote better poetry than Vergil, Horace, and Ovid.[29] In the eleventh century, Pope Gregory VII praised the modern papacy by maintaining that the pope's jurisdiction was wider than the ancient Roman emperors',[30] and Wido of Amiens said that the battle of Hastings was the greatest since the time of Julius Caesar.[31] In the twelfth century typical examples are Abbot Suger's claim that King Louis VII's triumphs were more distinguished than many in antiquity,[32] John Cotton's statement that "moderns had more subtlety and wisdom in understanding all things,"[33] and Abelard's view that it was his task to reveal and correct the imperfections of Aristotle and Boethius.[34] In the thirteenth century, Aubry of Trois-Fontaines declared that "the ancients devoted themselves to many things which today are held in ridicule,"[35] and the Paduan historian Rolandino scorned the crude works of his father, who in his view had written in the "rude style of the ancients."[36] The appeal of this commonplace did not wane in the early Renaissance: Petrarch said that his law professors at Bologna resembled ancient legislators and praised Cola di Rienzo for his similarity to the two Bruti;[37] Giannozzo Manetti said that Brunelleschi's dome rivalled the pyramids;[38] Poggio said that Alfonso of Aragon was a greater prince than Augustus, Trajan, Marcus Aurelius, or the Antonines;[39] and Flavio Biondo likened the papal domains to the ancient Roman Empire.[40] This theme remained in wide use in the later Renaissance, as is shown by authors such as Bembo, Speroni, Gelli, and Varchi, each of whom justified and de-

---

[26] Cf. Goessmann, *Antiqui und Moderni*, 25-29; H. Silvestre, "'Quanto iuniores, tanto perspicaciores,' Antécédents à la Querelle des Anciens et des Modernes," *Recueil Commémoral Xe anniversaire de la Faculté de la Philosophie et Lettres de l'Université Lovanianum de Kinshasa* (Louvain, 1967), 250.

[27] Goessmann, *Antiqui und Moderni*, 30.   [28] *Ibid.*, 39.

[29] Curtius, *European Literature*, 163.

[30] Goessmann, *Antiqui und Moderni*, 46.   [31] Curtius, *European Literature*, 164.

[32] Goessmann, 38.

[33] Silvestre, "Quanto iuniores," 235. Cf. *New Grove Dictionary of Music and Musicians*, IV, 380.

[34] Goessmann, 67.   [35] Silvestre, 243.   [36] Goessmann, 39.

[37] *Sen.* X, 2; *Var.*48.

[38] Cf. H. Baron, "The *Querelle* of the Ancients and the Moderns as a Problem for Renaissance Scholarship," *Journal of the History of Ideas*, **20** (1959), 18.

[39] *Epistolae*, II, 305-06.

[40] *Scritti inediti e rari di Biondo Flavio*, ed. B. Nogara, in *Studi e testi*, 48 (1927), xci-ci.

fended the vernacular by arguing that as a language it was equal or superior to classical Latin.[41] One of the most important versions of this theme in the Renaissance was praising the moderns by comparing them to the ancients in more general terms; indeed, the idea of the revival of the arts was a variation of this commonplace in which moderns were praised by showing that they had once more equalled or even surpassed the achievements of antiquity.[42] Moderns were praised in these terms by such authors as Filippo Villani,[43] Palmieri,[44] Biondo,[45] Valla,[46] Alamanno Rinuccini,[47] Ficino,[48] Castiglione,[49] Reuchlin, Melanchthon and Le Roy,[50] and in the early seventeenth century by Lancillotti and Tassoni, both of whom wrote extensive works comparing ancients and moderns which were in fact encomia of modern times;[51] Tassoni's *Pensieri diversi*, the last book of which contains his comparison of ancients and moderns, was translated into French and served as the model for Perrault's *Parallel of the Ancients and Moderns*,[52] which too was a version of this traditional commonplace of epideictic rhetoric, as were other works in the well-known *querelle des anciens et modernes* of the seventeenth and eighteenth centuries.[53]

Among the numerous works using the commonplace of ancients and moderns from Antiquity until the eighteenth century, one of the

---

[41] Margiotta, *Le origini*, 101-07, 138.

[42] Cf. H. Weisinger, "Renaissance Accounts of the Revival of Learning," *Studies in Philology*, 45 (1948), 105-18.   [43] Cf. Baxandall, *Giotto*, 70-72.

[44] *Della vita civile*, ed. F. Battaglia (Bologna, 1944), 36 ff.

[45] Weisinger, "Renaissance Accounts," 110.   [46] *Ibid.*

[47] A. Rinuccini, *In libros Philostrati De Vita Apollonii Tyanei . . . prefatio*, ed. V. R. Giustiniani, *Lettere ed orazioni* (Florence, 1963), 104-13.

[48] P. O. Kristeller, *The Philosophy of Marsilio Ficino* (New York, 1943), 22-23.

[49] Margiotta, *Le origini*, 122.

[50] Weisinger, "Renaissance Accounts," 111-12, 116-17.

[51] Cf. Buck, *Die "Querelle,"* 18-23; Margiotta, 151-61.   [52] *Ibid.*, 160-61.

[53] On the quarrel of the ancients and moderns, besides the works already cited, cf. A. Buck, "Aus der Vorgeschichte der 'Querelle des anciens et des modernes' in Mittelalter und Renaissance," *Die humanistische Tradition in der Romania* (Bad Homburg v. d. H., 1968), 75-91; *Antiqui und Moderni: Traditions-bewusstsein und Fortschrittsbewusstsein im spaeten Mittelalter*, ed. A. Zimmermann, *Miscellanea Mediaevalia*, 9 (Berlin, 1974); W. Freund, *Modernus und andere Zeitbegriffe des Mittelalters* (Cologne, 1957); J. Spoerl, "Das Alte und das Neue im Mittelalter," *Historisches Jahrbuch*, 50 (1930), 299-341, 498-524; M. -D. Chenu, "Antiqui, Moderni," *Revue des sciences philosophiques et théologiques*, 17 (1928), 82-94; P. O. Kristeller, "The Modern System of the Arts," *Journal of the History of Ideas*, 12 (1951), 496-527 and 13 (1952), 17-46, who gives further bibliography in note 158 on ancients and moderns in the seventeenth and eighteenth centuries; for more recent bibliography on the quarrel in the seventeenth and eighteenth centuries, cf. Goessmann, *Antiqui und Moderni*, 9-10, notes 1 and 2, and Buck, *Die "Querelle,"* 5-6, notes 3-9.

most notable is the *Dialogue on the preeminence of men of his own time* by Benedetto Accolti, the Aretine lawyer and humanist who served as chancellor of Florence from 1458 until his death in 1464.[54] Both versions of the commonplace are represented in Accolti's dialogue, which takes the form of two long speeches, one made by an unidentified young man and the other by Accolti himself, who takes the side of the moderns, leaving his opponent to defend the ancients. They compare ancient and modern warfare, morals, statesmanship, cities, poetry, rhetoric, philosophy, law, and religion; although the young man offers a comprehensive defence of antiquity and condemnation of modern times, all his arguments are refuted by Accolti, who, by an even more extensive defence of moderns and censure of ancients, emerges victorious in the debate.

Accolti's dialogue is particularly interesting because it was the first long work in western literature expressly devoted to the quarrel of ancients and moderns.[55] Although it was a traditional *topos* of panegyric, the question of ancients and moderns had never been the subject of a full-scale work before Accolti's dialogue. Moreover, Accolti's dialogue contains a far more extensive and detailed treatment of the question than any previous work; in Bruni's *Dialogus ad Petrum Paulum Histrum,* for example, only one aspect of the question was discussed—the superiority of ancient or modern authors, whereas in a series of biographies such as Filippo Villani's *Liber de civitatis Florentiae civibus,* the theme of ancients and moderns was

---

[54] The presentation copy of the dialogue is Codex 54, 8 of the Biblioteca Laurenziana (cf. E. Piccolomini, *Intorno alle condizioni ed alle vicende della Libreria Medicea Privata* [Florence, 1875], 92; A. M. Bandini, *Catalogus Codicum Latinorum Bibliothecae Mediceae Laurentianae* [Florence, 1774-77], II, 640-41), henceforth cited as dialogue. Other manuscripts are: (a) Bibl. Laur. Ashburnham 924 (855), a copy of a manuscript dated 1626 and presented by Leonardo and Pietro Accolti to Cardinal Francesco Barberini; (b) Biblioteca Landau Finaly, 271. When the collection was sold this codex did not become part of the Biblioteca Nazionale in Florence and I have been unable to trace its location. It is described by F. Roediger, *Catalogue des livres manuscrits et imprimés composant la bibliothèque de M. Horace de Landau* (Florence, 1885-90), II, 137, who maintained it was the presentation copy to Cardinal Barberini, (c) Archivio di stato, Florence, Carte Strozziane, ser. iii, 102, fol. 252r, a passage of the dialogue praising a member of the Strozzi family, copied by Carlo Strozzi, from a manuscript deriving from the one dedicated to Barberini. The latter three manuscripts date the dialogue in 1440. The presentation copy is not dated, and there is no evidence in Leonardo Accolti's diary (Biblioteca Comunale, Arezzo, 34) that he owned the autograph or a manuscript deriving from it. Moreover, that date is contradicted by internal evidence (cf. notes 64 and 65 *infra*). The dialogue has most recently been published by G. Galletti, in F. Villani, *Liber de civitatis Florentiae famosis civibus* (Florence, 1847), 105-28, henceforth cited as Galletti. (In the presentation copy the work is called simply "Dialogus": cf. fol. 1r.)

[55] This point is confirmed by Buck, *Die "Querelle,"* 12.

one among many used to praise the author's fellow citizens. Indeed, Accolti's dialogue is unique before the seventeenth century, for there is no subsequent work examining the question in such breadth and detail before the 1620 edition of Tassoni's *Pensieri diversi*.

In its genesis, Accolti's dialogue is surrounded by circumstances which account for its unusual scope. Accolti's dialogue was dedicated to Cosimo de'Medici,[56] who had also received the dedication of another work in which the question of ancient and moderns had a prominent place. Francesco di Mariotto Griffolini, the Greek scholar,[57] translated for Cosimo eighty-eight homilies on the Gospel of St. John by Chrysostom and in the dedicatory letter Griffolini argued that the moderns were equal or superior to the ancients in order to praise Cosimo himself as well as other leading figures of the fifteenth century.[58] Griffolini was a fellow citizen of Accolti's from Arezzo, but they were rivals for Cosimo's attention and there is evidence that Accolti wrote his dialogue in competition with Griffolini in order to demonstrate that he was the better rhetorician and humanist.[59] Indeed, their rivalry seems to have inspired Accolti to outdo Griffolini's version of the ancients and moderns, especially in the number of examples and arguments, and it was apparently Accolti's attempt to surpass Griffolini which led to the unprecedented scale upon which his dialogue was conceived. Accolti was not a Greek scholar and so could not compete with Griffolini as a translator of the Greek classics,

---

[56] Dialogue, fol. 1r; Galletti, 105.

[57] The basic work on Griffolini is G. Mancini, *Francesco Griffolini, cognominato Francesco Aretino* (Florence, 1890), nozze Valentini-Faina, which is very rare; there is a review summarizing its contents in *Archivio storico italiano*, ser. v, 7 (1891), 194-97. Cf. also G. Mancini, "Nuovi documenti e notizie sulla vita e sugli scritti di Leon Battista Alberti," *ibid.*, ser. iv, 19 (1887), 328-34 and *idem*, "Giovanni Tortelli, cooperatore di Niccolò V nel fondare la Biblioteca Vaticana," *ibid.*, 78 (1920), 191-98, 216-17.

[58] The presentation copy is Biblioteca Nazionale, Florence, J. 6. 7, henceforth cited as Griffolini (cf. fol. 1v: Iste liber est conventus sancti Marci de florentia ordinis predicatorum quem donavit dicto conventui vir clar. Cosmas Iohannis de medicis civis nobilis florentinus. There are also numerous autograph corrections by Griffolini in the text: cf. for example fol. 130r, 156r, 188v, 215r-v, etc. For Griffolini's autograph hand, cf. Archivio di stato, Florence, Mediceo avanti del principato, XIV, 47 and CXXXVII, 115). Cf. Mancini, *Francesco Griffolini*, 27-34.

[59] The long-standing enmity between Accolti and Griffolini, hitherto unknown (cf. the erroneous interpretation of Mancini, *ibid.*, 36), cannot be discussed here; lack of space also prevents a discussion of the circumstances leading to the composition of Accolti's dialogue in response to Griffolini's translation of Chrysostom. I shall publish this material in my forthcoming biography of Benedetto Accolti; I also hope to correct the work on Griffolini by Mancini, who did not understand Griffolini's relation with Accolti and his other Aretine compatriots, in a monograph on Griffolini which I am preparing.

but as Florentine chancellor he was a proficient Latinist and rhetorician.[60] Indeed, Accolti made no secret of his concern to display his skill in eloquence, admitting in the preface of the dialogue that he was eager to show how "copiously" and "ornately" he could write and that he would be encouraged to continue as a humanist if the dialogue were a success. Moreover, Accolti clearly hoped the dialogue would gain Cosimo's support for his literary endeavors in the future:

If in your view [he declared to Cosimo] I do not feel myself inadequate, I shall devote myself more boldly to scholarship and letters in the future, confident above all in the support of your name.[61]

In fact, there is internal evidence that Accolti's dialogue was written about the time that Griffolini's translation reached Florence, which was sometime between May and November 1462.[62] A *terminus post quem* is provided by a reference in the past tense to Guarino Veronese, who died on December 4, 1460;[63] a *terminus ante quem* may be inferred from Accolti's mention of Cosimo de'Medici's "sons," indicating that Giovanni, who died in November 1463, was still alive when Accolti was writing.[64] Indeed, Cosimo did not keep his copy of Griffolini's translation as a private possession but personally donated it to the "public library" in San Marco in Florence[65] where Accolti would have been able to gain easy access to it. Further evidence that Accolti composed the dialogue in response to Griffolini's preface to the translation of Chrysostom is the similarity in the encomia of Cosimo de'Medici, which occupy prominent places in both works. Both praise Cosimo for his essential role in making Francesco Sforza Duke of Milan; both celebrate his great wealth, his liberality, his charity, his civic and religious munificence, and his devotion to scholarship; both refer to him as the "first citizen" (*princeps*) of Florence and emphasize his role as one of the arbiters of Italian diplomacy.[66] Similarly, Accolti was particularly concerned to

[60] On the traditions of rhetoric attached to the Florentine chancellorship, cf. esp. R. Witt, *Coluccio Salutati and his Public Letters* (Geneva, 1976), 23-41.

[61] Dialogue, fol. 2v: Nec vereor abs te praesumptionis argui, quasi rem aggressus, quam non omnino ample, nec ornate satis explicare potuerim, in hoc scribendi genere minime versatus . . . pro tua sapientia opinabere, me non ut magistrum sed ut non ignarum discipulum . . . quod si tuo iudicio non ineptum me esse sensero, audacius posthac disciplinis et litteris incumbam, tuo nomine atque auxilio inprimis fretus. Cf. Galetti, 105.   [62] For the date, cf. Mancini, *Francesco Griffolini*, 33-34.

[63] Dialogue, fol. 41r (Galletti, 122); cf. R. Sabbadini, "Guarino Veronese," *Enciclopedia italiana* (Milan, 1933), XI, 27.

[64] Dialogue, fol. 2v, 35v; Galletti, 105, 119.

[65] Cf. note 58 *supra* and B. L. Ullman and P. A. Stadter, *The Public Library of Renaissance Florence* (Padua, 1972), 141.

[66] Dialogue, fol. 32r-36r (Galletti, 118-19); Griffolini, fol. 2v.

display his knowledge of early Christian history and Latin patristic literature in the dialogue, obviously in competition with Griffolini's knowledge of the Greek fathers; praise of the modern church also formed an important part of both texts.[67] Moreover, Accolti's praise of Cosimo as more god than man, which was almost unprecedented among encomia of Cosimo during his lifetime,[68] was probably an attempt to outdo Griffolini's panegyric in which Cosimo was compared to the most distinguished mortals of the Roman republic including Pompey, Cato, Lucullus, Crassus, and Cicero.[69] Similarly, the greater detail and broader scope of Accolti's dialogue would have demonstrated his superiority in eloquence since abundant use of arguments and examples (*copia*) was regarded in the Renaissance as a sign of rhetorical proficiency and literary excellence.[70] If it is correct that Accolti wrote his dialogue in response to Griffolini—and the evidence seems to point in that direction—then the dialogue can be dated sometime between May 1462 and November 1463.

Accolti intended his dialogue as a rhetorical work in which he would have the opportunity to demonstrate how copiously he could illustrate the theme of the ancients and moderns. But at the same time he wrote it as an historical essay, in which he could consider the relationship between two historical periods, antiquity and modern times, examining the changes since the fall of the Roman Empire. Accolti would have seen no contradiction between his intention of displaying his proficiency as a rhetorician and his desire to explore important historical questions in the dialogue; indeed, he regarded history and rhetoric as inseparable because it was eloquence which enabled the historian to perform his essential function of rescuing the deeds of great men from oblivion.[71] Accolti's preoccupation with history is clear from the impressive and even profound passages in the dialogue analyzing the changes which had taken place since the fall of the Roman Empire; one example is his discussion of why histories similar to Livy's and Sallust's ceased to be composed after the fall of the Empire:

I think this happened because, with the Roman Empire in decline and then collapsing, the barbarians who entered Greece and Italy changed the entire

---

[67] Dialogue, fol. 45v-55r (Galletti, 123-27); Griffolini, fol. 2r-2v.

[68] Cf. A. M. Brown, "The Humanist Portrait of Cosimo de' Medici," *Journal of the Warburg and Courtauld Institutes*, **24** (1961), 194.   [69] Griffolini, fol. 2v.

[70] On *copia*, cf. E. A. Palmer, *George Puttenham and Henry Peacham copia and decorum in sixteenth century literature*, unpublished M. Phil. thesis, University of London, 1969. Cf. Cicero, *Orator*, 97; Qunitilian, VIII, iii, 86-87, X, i, 61, X, v, 9.

[71] Cf. R. D. Black, "Benedetto Accolti and the beginnings of humanist historiography," *English Historical Review*, **96** (1981), 36-38, 55-57, for the views of Accolti and other early humanists on the connection of rhetoric and history.

pattern of life; and, because they were hostile to learning, learned men saw that there would be no reward forthcoming and so they preferred to be silent rather than record the deeds of their times for posterity. . . . Nor do I think there was any lack of learned or intelligent men then, for it is manifest that in those days every kind of literature was distinguished by men of accomplishment who, if they had applied their minds to history, would have been able to write with eloquence not inferior to that of previous writers. There was perhaps also another cause, namely, that learned men of the Christian faith wanted to devote their labor to the deeds of the saints and the defence of their religion rather than to this kind of history; and once the tradition of writing history had disappeared and men's intellects had been turned time and again elsewhere, history was rendered almost mute so that the memory of the most eminent men has been obliterated, from the end of barbarian rule up to the present day.[72]

Another example is Accolti's critique of ancient historiography, where he argues that ancient historians were unreliable and exploited their literary skill to exaggerate the merits of their subjects, and that modern men appeared inferior to the ancients only because the moderns lacked competent historians to celebrate their deeds:

According to Sallust the deeds of the ancients were certainly great and magnificent; nevertheless, their writers had such genius that they made mediocre and often even trifling deeds seem great through the force of their eloquence. . . . Among the Greeks especially, innumerable fables are found in their books; the Latins too are not innocent of this offence. According to Livy . . . there was no limit on the falsehoods contained in history, authors including lies in their works according to their whims without regard for truth. . . . Not long ago many Christian princes gathered to recover the city of Jerusalem and Christ's sepulchre from the infidels—how great, how admirable, how similar to those of the ancients would their deeds seem if worthy authors had only celebrated them![73]

---

[72] Dialogue, fol. 16v-17v: idcirco accidisse reor, quoniam nutante iam Romano imperio et in occasum vergente, barbari, Graeciam et Italiam ingressi, omnem vivendi normam mutaverunt, et cum essent litteris infensi, atque ideo illarum periti nullum propositum premium viderent, tacere quam monimentis res sui temporis gestas tradere maluerunt . . . Neque opinor ego tum defuisse ingenia doctissimorum hominum, quoniam liquet per ea tempora multos fuisse claros et in omni literarum genere peritos viros qui, si animum ad hystoriam applicuissent, forsitan non minore quam priores quidam eloquio valuissent scribere. Illa etiam forte suberat causa, quod Christianae religionis homines doctissimi magis in sanctorum rebus gestis et defensione fidei quam in huiusmodi hystoriis laborare voluerunt, et, cum ea scribendi facultas iam obsolevisset, alio iam semel conversis animis, etiam post exactum barbarorum dominatum usque ad haec tempora hystoria pene muta facta est et praestantissimorum hominum memoria obliterata. Cf. Galletti, 111.

[73] Dialogue, fol. 16r-v: iuxta Salustii sententiam, res nempe antiquorum gestas satis amplas ac magnificas fuisse, verum ea vis ingenii apud earundem scriptores fuit

This passage shows that Accolti was contemplating a longer work of history while writing the dialogue, and, indeed, soon after completing that work he began a history of the first crusade, *De bello a christianis contra barbaros gesto*.[74] This work, itself finished shortly before his death in 1464, demonstrated his dedication to the study of history: it was not merely a translation of a medieval chronicle into humanist Latin, but a newly composed history based on three medieval sources, one of which was contemporary with the events narrated. Moreover, in line with his views on the importance of eloquence in history, Accolti went to great lengths to raise his work to the standards of classical historical writing.[75] Accolti's preoccupation with history impressed his fellow Florentine, Vespasiano da Bisticci, who wrote that he "had universal knowledge . . . of histories," and that "he wanted to pursue history up to his own times, part of which he completed, having written the history of Godfrey of Bouillon's expedition to the Holy Land."[76]

It is interesting that Accolti used the rhetorical theme of ancients and moderns as a tool of historical analysis not only in his dialogue but in his history too. To assess the achievement of Godfrey of Bouillon at the end of *De bello,* Accolti compared him to Alexander the Great, who, he argued, was no more than Godfrey's equal. Accolti here developed the theme with an argument he had already used in the dialogue: Alexander appeared more famous than Godfrey only because no author "distinguished in eloquence and learning had celebrated his deeds," whereas the Greeks, who were "extremely erudite, championed Alexander with praise based not only on truth but even on fiction, without regard for the limitations of history."[77] Besides Accolti, other historians had used the contrast of ancients

---

ut mediocres res plerumque etiam parvas pro maximis sua eloquentia fecerint videri . . . apud Grecos maxime innumerabiles fabulae in eorum libris reperiuntur; Latini quoque nec talis culpae insontes extiterunt. Apud Livium . . . sane relatum est . . . nullum in historia mentiendi modum fuisse; id est, auctores pro libito sua litteris mendacia tradidisse non veritati studentes. *Ibid.,* fol. 18r: Convenere iam multi christianorum principes, ut Hierosolymam urbem et Christi sepulchrum ab infidelibus recuperarent . . . Horum res gestas, si qui auctores digni celebrassent, quam magnae, quam admirabiles, quam veteribus illis similes viderentur! Cf. Galletti, 111-12.

[74] On Accolti's history, cf. R. D. Black, "La storia della Prima Crociata di Benedetto Accolti e la diplomazia fiorentina rispetto all'Oriente," *Archivio storico italiano,* 131 (1973), 3-25; *id.* "Benedetto Accolti and the beginnings," 36-58.

[75] *Ibid.,* 39-51.

[76] Vespasiano, *Vite,* ed. A. Greco (Florence, 1970-76), I, 596-97.

[77] Biblioteca Laurenziana, 54, 6, fol. 100v: Quod eius res gestas nemo doctrina et eloquio prestans illustravit; Greci autem, viri eruditissimi, non modo veris laudibus Alexandrum sed etiam fictis extulerunt, modum historie non servantes. Cf. *Recueil des historiens des crosiades. Historiens occidentaux,* V (Paris, 1895), 611.

and moderns as a tool of historical analysis. A famous example is the opening of the *Catiline Conspiracy,* in which Sallust drew a comparison between early Rome and the Rome of Catiline's day, showing how Roman society had degenerated since the end of the Punic Wars.[78] Similarly, Carolingian historians and biographers such as Einhard and Walafrid Strabo observed that Louis the Pious's reign did not measure up to Charlemagne's, which they regarded as a golden age in contrast to their own times.[79] Thietmar of Merseburg (975-1018) used the terms *antiqui* and *moderni* in his discussion of the history of the Ottonian empire, contrasting the shortcomings of modern times, that is, his own age, with the golden age of the ancients, who for him were Emperor Otto I (d. 973) and his contemporaries.[80] The crusading historian William of Tyre described the disintegration of the Latin Kingdom of Jerusalem in the twelfth century, contrasting former times when friendship with Egyptian Moslems had brought prosperity to the kingdom with the present day when hostility with neighbors was leading the Latins to the brink of destruction.[81] A similar use of ancients and moderns to present an interpretation of history was made by Giovanni Villani, who, writing in the early fourteenth century, showed how the Florence of his day, riddled with faction and dissent, had degenerated from the good old days of the 1250s, when there had been a true spirit of the common good.[82] Indeed, Petrarch's analysis of the periods of ancient and modern history is perhaps the most famous example in the Renaissance of how the theme of ancients and moderns offered scope for historical reflection and analysis.[83]

Accolti therefore did not conceive of history as distinct from rhetoric; on the contrary, rhetoric not only provided the historian with eloquence to immortalize the deeds of great men but also gave him the tools of historical interpretation. The influence of rhetoric on his dialogue, therefore, was not confined to form and style, but very much determined the content of his comparison of antiquity and modern times. For example, the critical judgment used by Accolti to evaluate differences between ancients and moderns often derived

---

[78] *Bellum Cat.* v-xiii.

[79] Einhard, *Vita Karoli Magni,* ed. G. H. Pertz, G. Waitz and O. Holder-Egger, in *Scriptores Rerum Germanicarum* (Hannover and Leipzig, 1911), XXVIII-XXIX, 2.

[80] Goessmann, *Antiqui und Moderni,* 36-37.

[81] C. H. Haskins, *The Renaissance of the Twelfth Century* (Cambridge, Mass., 1927), 270.

[82] Davis, "Il buon tempo antico," 45-69 *passim.*

[83] E.g., *Fam.* VI, 2. Cf. T. E. Mommsen, "Petrarch's Conception of the 'Dark Ages,'" *Speculum,* 17 (1942), 226-42, reprinted in his *Medieval and Renaissance Studies* (Ithaca, New York, 1959), 106-29.

from his attempt to compose a panegyric. This can be seen clearly in his discussion of Dante and Petrarch which begins with a conventional comparison between them, as modern poets, with Vergil and Homer as the ancients: "I should think that there were two men namely Dante and Francesco Petrarch, neither of whom was inferior to Vergil or Homer in elegance, suavity, and abundance of wisdom."[84] Comparing modern and ancient authors was a standard technique of panegyric, and Accolti here was working within a well-established tradition.[85] However, rhetoric could also help the humanists to develop a more critical approach. This could occur when they were praising individuals who, like Dante and Petrarch, had received frequent praise before. In the attempt to compose a better encomium, they formed at the same time a more critical judgment. Sometimes they endeavored to concede in advance arguments which might otherwise be held to refute their own—a rhetorical figure, known as *hypophora* or *subiectio*.[86] Thus, Salutati conceded that Petrarch's Latin style (*facultas dicendi*) was inferior to that of the ancients;[87] Bruni admitted that Dante's Latin was poor[88] and that Petrarch's was imperfect;[89] and Manetti said that their Latin was inferior not only to that of the ancients but to the Latin of many of his contemporaries.[90] Accolti too concedes that, although Dante's *Eclogues* and Petrarch's *Africa* are not entirely without merit, they are nevertheless not equal to many ancient works.[91] A further refinement came by way of the observation that Dante and Petrarch were more versatile than the ancients. Thus Salutati, Bruni, Niccoli (in Bruni's dialogue), and Manetti argued that Petrarch was greater than Cicero or Vergil because he excelled in composing both poetry and prose whereas they were proficient in only one or the other genre.[92] This, of course, was a veiled criticism and implied that Petrarch was, as a prose writer, inferior to Cicero and, as a poet, inferior to Vergil. Accolti himself varies this commonplace slightly when he praises Petrarch and Dante for writing in both Latin and Italian, thereby conceding by implication that their Latin was inferior to that of the ancients.[93]

[84] Dialogue, fol. 41v: fuisse imprimis duos, Dantem videlicet et Franciscum Petrarcam, quorum neminem elegantia, suavitate et sententiarum copia Virgilio aut Homero postponendum arbitrarer; cf. Galletti, 122.

[85] Cf. Pliny, Ep. VI, xxi; Curtius, *European Literature*, 163; H. Baron, *The Crisis of the Early Italian Renaissance* (Princeton, 1955), II, 539, 540 (note 38); *Crisis*, 1966 ed. 258, 536 (note 24); Galletti, 15, 78; *Prosatori latini*, ed. Garin, 68.

[86] *Rhet. ad Her.* IV, xxiii, 33; Quintilian, IX, iii, 98.   [87] Baron, *Crisis*, 1966 ed. 258.

[88] Bruni, *Vita di Dante*, in *Schriften*, 61-62.   [89] Bruni, *Vita di Petrarca, ibid.*, 65.

[90] Manetti, *Vitae*, in Galletti, 69.   [91] Dialogue, fol. 42r; Galletti, 122.

[92] Baron, *Crisis*, 1966 ed., 259; *Prosatori latini*, ed. Garin, 92-94; Bruni, *Schriften*, 67; Galletti, 84.

[93] Dialogue, fol. 41v; Galletti, 122.

Certainly the use of commonplaces could lead to unoriginal historical arguments in a work such as Accolti's dialogue; nevertheless, in the Renaissance as well as in the Middle Ages and Antiquity, no stigma was attached to commonplaces, which formed the basis of the rhetorical method. They were essential ingredients of eloquence, and the more of them, the better. According to Quintilian they were the seats of argument (*sedes argumentorum*).[94] For the humanists a knowledge of commonplaces was a sign of erudition; originality was not always a virtue. Nevertheless, sometimes rhetoric could lead an author onto an unusual and even adventurous course. An orator, said Protagoras, can make the weaker cause seem the stronger,[95] and such power was attributed to rhetoric by later writers.[96] In his dialogue, Accolti apparently wished to show that he was capable of defending the indefensible, for he chose to concentrate on a number of weak causes. In this way rhetoric influenced Accolti's choice of topics in his historical comparison of antiquity and modern times, leading him to select subjects in which he could defend an unusual point of view; indeed, Accolti's adherence to the precepts of rhetoric may have stimulated originality in the dialogue.

In the Renaissance it was, of course, unusual to criticize ancient rhetoric, since it had been the admiration of Roman eloquence that had inspired early humanists such as Petrarch to launch their revival of classical learning; nevertheless, Accolti maintains that modern oratory and eloquence compare favorably with the ancient.[97] What is particularly interesting about this section of the dialogue is that, although he was defending an unusual position, Accolti constructed his argument entirely out of commonplaces; in this way he was able to demonstrate his skill as a rhetorician not only through knowledge of commonplaces but also by successfully defending a weak cause. He begins by stating that the ancients' proficiency was the result of fortunate circumstances. Here he uses an argument from Cicero: *"honos alit artes,"* or an art flourishes so long as it is held in esteem;[98] since in antiquity oratory was honored and in constant use, it is no wonder that it flourished. Hence the apology for modern times: since rhetoric is no longer put to practical use, modern orators cannot be expected to equal the ancients. He then goes on to point out the shortcomings of rhetoric in antiquity by showing that the Romans were inferior to the Greeks because orators were less prominent in

[94] V, x, 20.   [95] Plato, *Phaedrus*, 267 A.

[96] Aristotle, *Rhet.* II, 24, 11; Diog. Laertius, IX, 53; Cicero, *Brutus*, 47.

[97] Dialogue, fol. 38r-41r; Galletti, 120-22.

[98] *Disp. Tusc.* I, 4, quoted by Accolti, Dialogue, fol. 38v (Galletti, 120); for this *topos* applied specifically to oratory, cf. Cicero, *Brutus*, 40, 51, 182.

political life in Rome than in Athens.[99] Here Accolti is using two commonplaces of ancient rhetoric: that the Greeks, especially the Athenians, excelled in rhetoric and were ruled by orators,[100] and that in learning the Romans were inferior to the Greeks.[101] Accolti then goes on to say that in Rome rhetoric began to be practised only with Cato the Censor, who was frequently cited in Latin literature as an example of one of the first orators,[102] and that few great Latin orators came after him, also a commonplace in antiquity.[103] Accolti next says that oratory at Rome ceased to flourish under the Empire, for, with all power in the hands of one man, the art of persuasion was neither needed nor valued.[104] Here Accolti makes a specific reference to the elder Seneca,[105] and there were many others who also said that rhetoric was in decline during and after the collapse of the republic.[106] Accolti's argument that the decline was due to political conditions certainly goes back to Antiquity—Cicero says that monarchy is inimical to orator,[107] which generally flourishes among free nations.[108] But the point that the cultural decline of Rome was the result of the rise of the principate played an important role in humanist literature too: it was, for example, Leonardo Bruni's argument for condemning the Empire in his Florentine history.[109] Accolti concludes this section of the dialogue with an encomium of modern rhetoric by pointing to

[99] Dialogue, fol. 38v; Galletti, 120-21.

[100] Cicero, *Brutus*, 26-29, 44 and *De oratore*, I, 13; Quintilian, X, i, 76-80; Cicero, *Opt. Gen. Or.*, 7-13.

[101] Cf. *Disp. Tusc.* I, 1-6, II, 1-9, IV, 1-7. Cf. also Horace, Ep. II, 1, 90-117.

[102] Cicero, *Brutus*, 61; Quintilian, III, i, 19; Cicero, *De oratore*, I, 171 and III, 135 and *Disp. Tusc.* I, 5.   [103] Cicero, *Brutus*, 137-38, 182, 333; *De oratore*, I, 6-18.

[104] Dialogue, fol. 39v-40r; Galletti, 121.

[105] Dialogue, fol. 40r; Galletti, 121. Cf. *Controversiae*, Praef. 7.

[106] Petronius, *Satyricon*, 1-4; Seneca, *Ep.* 114; Pliny, Ep. II, 14; Quintilian, II, x, 3-5; and V, xii, 17-23; Cicero, *Brutus*, 6-9, 22-23 and *Disp. Tusc.* II, 5. Cf. Clarke, *Rhetoric at Rome*, 100-08; H. Caplan, "The Decay of Eloquence at Rome in the First Century," *Studies in Speech and Drama in Honour of Alexander M. Drummond* (Ithaca, New York, 1944), 295-325 (reprinted in H. Caplan, *Of Eloquence: Studies in Ancient and Medieval Rhetoric*, ed. A. King and H. North [Ithaca and London, 1970], 160-95); E. Norden, *Die antike Kunstprosa* (Leipzig, 1898), I, 245-48; R. Syme, *Tacitus* (Oxford, 1958), I, 100-11; C. D. N. Costa, "The *Dialogus*," in *Tacitus*, ed. T. A. Dorey (London, 1969), 19-34.   [107] *Brutus*, 45.

[108] *De oratore*, I, 30. Cf. also *Brutus*, 6-9, 22-23, 46. It is unnecessary to assume that Accolti knew Tacitus's *Dialogus*, which became known in Italy only in 1455 (cf. R. Sabbadini, *Le scoperte dei codici latini e greci ne' secoli XIV e XV* [Florence, 1905-14], II, 254) and in which the same argument is found. Longinus, 44, has the same argument, but it was probably not known until the later fifteenth century: cf. "*Longinus*" *On the Sublime*, ed. D. A. Russell (Oxford, 1964), xliii.

[109] Cf. Bruni, *Historiarum florentini populi libri XII*, in *Rerum italicarum scriptores*, new series, XIX, iii, ed. E. Santini (Città di Castello, 1934), 14-15.

the eloquence of many of his contemporaries.[110] The revival of letters was one of the fundamental aspirations of the Renaissance, other humanists like Accolti finding it a useful way to praise their contemporaries.[111]

Another unpromising cause which Accolti chose to defend in the dialogue was contemporary military practice, and in particular, the mercenary system. Most authorities in Antiquity and the Middle Ages had said that a citizen militia was superior to a mercenary army,[112] and for most humanists contemporary military institutions had become a subject of ridicule.[113] Nevertheless, there were occasions on which it was appropriate for humanists to praise contemporary practice: Stefano Porcari had once had the task of praising the Florentine Signoria for its military policy,[114] while Giannozzo Manetti on one occasion had had to deliver an oration after he had handed over a commission to a condottiere.[115] Accolti's arguments were much the same as those used by other humanists faced with the same task. Different customs, he said, might be equally praiseworthy since the same practice was not suited to all times and places. All pursuits admitted of different types of excellence, not least the art of war; indeed, the ancients themselves used different forms of military organization.[116] Accolti took this argument from Cicero's *De oratore*, where it had been applied to sense perception, painting, sculpture, poetry, and oratory.[117] It was used by other humanists in defence of mercenaries and is found in Manetti's speech, in Campano's life of Braccio, and in Crivelli's life of Muzio Attendolo.[118] Accolti also claims that moderns excel in the subtler military arts of trickery and deceit, a claim based on a statement attributed to Hannibal by Livy that the Romans were unacquainted with the fine points of warfare;[119] like Accolti, Campano regarded his contemporaries' ability to de-

---

[110] Dialogue, fol. 40v-41r; Galletti, 121-22.

[111] Cf. Weisinger, "Renaissance Accounts," 105-18; Palmieri, *Della vita civile,* 37.

[112] C. C. Bayley, *War and Society in Renaissance Florence* (Toronto, 1961), 178-84.

[113] *Ibid.,* 184-231.

[114] Stefano Porcari, "Orazioni" in *Testi di lingua tratti da' codici della Biblioteca Vaticana,* ed. G. Manzi (Rome, 1816), 23-27.

[115] G. Manetti and Bernardo de' Medici, "Orazione . . . quando e' dierono . . . il bastone a Gismondo . . . Malatesta," in *Commentario della vita di G. Manetti, scritto da Vespasiano da Bisticci,* ed. P. Fanfani, in *Collezione di opere inedite o rare,* II (Bologna, 1862), 209.

[116] Dialogue, fol. 23r-24r; Galletti, 114.   [117] III, 25 ff. Cf. Cicero, *Brutus,* 204 and 285.

[118] Manetti and Medici, "Orazione," 204; G. A. Campano, *Braccii Perusini vita et gesta,* ed. R. Valentini, in *Rerum italicarum scriptores,* new series, XIX, iv (Bologna, n.d.), 168; L. Crivelli, *De vita et rebus gestis Sfortiae . . . Historia,* in *Rerum italicarum scriptores,* XIX (Milan, 1731), 635, 639.

[119] XXI, 54, 3, paraphrased by Accolti, Dialogue, fol. 25r (Galletti, 115).

ceive the enemy as a reason for their military superiority over the ancients.[120] Accolti, moveover, cited the support of ancient authority to demonstrate that ancient armies lacked discipline.[121] Campano made the same point,[122] and like Accolti[123] praised contemporary discipline by way of contrast.[124] Finally, Accolti in common with other humanists argued that contemporaries because of the invention of the cannon were superior to the ancients in siege warfare,[125] and that modern cavalry was superior to ancient, especially because of advances in armor.[126]

Scholastic philosophy, usually held by the humanists in high disfavor,[127] was another weak cause that Accolti chose to defend in the

---

[120] Campano, 165-67. [121] He quotes Lucan, X, 407-08, dialogue, fol. 27v (Galletti, 116).

[122] Campano, 166-68. [123] Dialogue, fol. 26v-27v (Galletti, 115-16). [124] Campano, 166-68.

[125] Dialogue, fol. 25r (Galletti, 115); F. Biondo, *Decades* in *De Roma triumphante, etc.* (Basel, 1531), 294; Crivelli, 711; Campano, 167.

[126] Dialogue, fol. 25r-25v (Galletti, 115); Crivelli, 635; Campano, 166, 168. Bayley, *War and Society*, 227-28, and Baron, *Crisis* (1966), 435-37, have assumed that Accolti's defence of mercenaries is connected with declining republicanism in Florence during the later fifteenth century. However, it was a commonplace to praise a citizen militia and criticize mercenaries, and such statements by humanists were not always taken literally as was shown by Roberto Valturio, who dedicated his *De re militari*, which advocated a militia, to the condottiere Sigismondo Malatesta. Nor did all humanists assume that military excellence and republican liberty went together: Biondo, one of the most outspoken critics of mercenaries, declared that the Empire expanded under many of the Emperors (*Decades*, 4). Baron's scheme that the defence of mercenaries signalled the decline of republicanism during the "age of Lorenzo de' Medici" has to make allowance for too many exceptions. Porcari was part of Niccoli's and Bruni's circle (cf. L. Pastor, *Storia dei Papi* [Rome, 1958-64], I, 568-69) and Manetti was, according to Baron, one of the principal continuators of civic humanism after Bruni, but the one in 1427 and the other in 1453 defended the mercenary system; Platina and Patrizi, who according to Baron were connected with Florence, attacked mercenaries as late as 1471 (*Crisis*, 1966 ed. 437-38). Even Bruni argued for and against mercenaries: in the early books of his Florentine history, Bruni consistently praised the militia, whereas in the later books he consistently praised mercenaries (cf. D. J. Wilcox, *The Development of Florentine Humanist Historiography in the Fifteenth Century* [Cambridge, Mass. 1969], 96-98). Bruni here was applying the rhetorical commonplace used by Cicero and then later by Accolti, Campano, Crivelli and Manetti that the same practice is not suited to all times and places. Bruni's point is that in the early period of Florentine history, the militia system was adequate, whereas later, when warfare became more complex, professional mercenaries were needed. Bruni's point of view did not change in response to altering conditions in Florence in the course of writing his history; rather, as a rhetorician writing history, he adapted his ideas to the requirements of his subject, using the rhetorical method of arguing for and against to analyze developments in Florentine history.

[127] P. O. Kristeller, "Humanism and Scholasticism in the Italian Renaissance," repr. with bibliographical additions in *Renaissance Thought and its Sources*, 85-105, 272-87.

dialogue. He points out that *philosophia* means *sapientiae studium* which requires sound arguments, not ornate language. He finds many modern philosophers to praise, while maintaining that in ancient Rome philosophers were for a long time unheard of, and later were accepted only with hostility.[128] Significantly, Accolti fails to mention Cicero among the few Roman philosophers, in contrast to other humanists such as Bruni, who assigned him the highest rank among philosophers.[129] Bruni and other humanists in fact condemned the scholastics for their bad style and maintained that philosophy was inseparable from eloquence.[130] For the source of Accolti's arguments about the merits of scholastic philosophy, one has to consider the influence of Johannes Argyropulos, who began lecturing in Florence in 1457. From the beginning Argyropulos criticized humanists such as Bruni for their ignorance of philosophy, for their insistence that philosophy and eloquence were necessarily linked, and for their disdain of speculative philosophy. Some of Argyropulos's pupils, such as Alamanno Rinuccini, gained from him a respect for the scholastics,[131] which resembles Accolti's views in the dialogue; since the dialogue appears to have been written between 1462 and 1463, the passage on philosophy may show the influence of Argyropulos's early lectures. There is certainly evidence that Accolti was part of Argyropulos's circle in Florence. In the 1450s and 1460s, Accolti's closest friend in Florence was Otto Niccolini, a lawyer and prominent Florentine statesman. The two worked together in the Studio Fiorentino[132] and on private cases,[133] and they came to share intellectual interests. Together with Piero de'Pazzi, they may well have had learned discussions with Argyropulos on such subjects as the relative merits of law and philosophy.[134] Also in Florence at that time was Marsilio Ficino, who as early as 1454 was expressing ideas about philosophy and scholasticism similar to those of Argyropulos.[135] Accolti, Niccolini, and Pazzi befriended Ficino and supported his early career and studies, encouraging his translation of Plato's *Minos*.[136]

[128] Dialogue, fol. 42r-44v; Galletti, 122-23.   [129] *Prosatori latini*, ed. Garin, 54.

[130] Cf. J. E. Seigel, "The Teaching of Argyropulos and the Rhetoric of the First Humanists," in *Action and Conviction in Early Modern Europe. Essays in Memory of E. H. Harbison*, ed. T. K. Rabb and J. E. Seigel (Princeton, 1969), 238-40.

[131] *Ibid.*, 240-56.

[132] *Statuti della Università e Studio Fiorentino*, ed. A. Gherardi (Florence, 1881), 462.

[133] Cf. Biblioteca Nazionale, Florence, Panciatichi, 139, fol. 138v, 139v; *ibid.*, Magliabecchiano, XXIX, 73, fol. 220v, 222r.

[134] Cf. Vespasiano, *Vite*, II, 203; A. Della Torre, *Storia dell'Accademia Platonica di Firenze* (Florence, 1902), 391-92.

[135] P. O. Kristeller, *Studies in Renaissance Thought and Letters* (Rome, 1956).

[136] Cf. P. O. Kristeller, "Marsilio Ficino as a beginning student of Plato," *Scriptorium*, XX (1966), 45; Della Torre, *Storia*, 545 ff; R. Marcel, *Marsile Ficin* (Paris, 1958), 216-17, 258-63, 690-93, 731. J. Seigel, *Rhetoric and Philosophy in Renaissance*

Another difficult cause which Accolti chose to defend in his dialogue was the modern church, which was often compared unfavorably with the ancient or primitive church.[137] The idea of Christian antiquity, implying a division of religious history into an ancient and a modern period, goes back at least to the fifth century when it seems that the writings of the church fathers contain the first references to the primitive church and Christian antiquity. From its first appearances the idea of the early church implied that Christian antiquity was a model for the reform of the modern church and therefore was superior to the modern period in religious history. The primitive church continued to be cited as an ideal for reform throughout the early Middle Ages and provided a justification for the Hildebrandine reform after the middle of the eleventh century. In the writings of twelfth-century moralists such as St. Bernard, the contrast between the ancient and modern churches was drawn even more sharply than before, and in the thirteenth century, with the appearance of the mendicant orders and their call for apostolic poverty, which was supported by heterodox movements such as the Waldensians, Fraticelli, Beguines, and Beghards, the superiority of the ancient church was asserted all the more emphatically. In the fourteenth and fifteenth centuries, the superiority of the ancient church was an assumption so widely accepted that advocates of conciliarism as well as champions of papal supremacy supported their claims by citing the example of Christian antiquity; moreover, the major heresies of the fourteenth and fifteenth centuries, such as Lollardy and the Hussite movement, were based on a call to return to the primitive church.[138]

Humanism (Princeton, 1969), 233-36, 240-41, gives a sociological interpretation of Accolti's defence of scholasticism, maintaining that Accolti's higher social status made him more secure of his position in Florence than Bruni, whose insecurity led him to attack his scholastic rivals. However, this is an oversimplification of both Bruni's and Accolti's social position in Florence and Arezzo, a complex subject which Seigel clearly has not investigated sufficiently. By that argument, Accolti should have been the one to attack scholasticism, for when he wrote the dialogue he admitted that he had had little experience as a humanist.

[137] Dialogue, fol. 45r-57v; Galletti, 123-28.

[138] On the primitive church and Christian antiquity, cf. G. Olsen, "The idea of the *ecclesia primitiva* in the writings of the twelfth-century canonists," *Traditio,* **25** (1969), 61-86; E. McDonnell, *The Beguines and Beghards in Medieval Culture* (New Brunswick, N.J., 1954), *passim;* and his "The *Vita Apostolica:* Diversity or Dissent?," *Church History,* **24** (1955), 15-31; G. Miccoli, *Chiesa Gregoriana: Ricerche sulla Riforma del secolo XI* (Florence, 1966), 75-167 and 225-303; Chenu, *Nature, Man, and Society,* 203-41; H. V. White, "The Gregorian Ideal and St. Bernard of Clairvaux," *Journal of the History of Ideas,* **21** (1960), 321-48; P. De Vooght, "Du *De consideratione* de saint Bernard au *De potestate papae* de Wyclif," *Irenikon,* **25** (1953), 114-32,; E. Kennan, "The 'De consideratione" of St. Bernard of Clairvaux and the Papacy in the Mid-Twelfth Century," *Traditio,* **23** (1967), 73-115; H.

In his panegyric of the modern church, therefore, Accolti could certainly claim to be defending the indefensible; moreover, Accolti was going against the mainstream of humanist thought, in which the superiority of Christian antiquity was a commonplace.[139] Petrarch preached apostolic poverty and condemned the Donation of Constantine as the source of corruption in the modern church;[140] another example is the chapter on poverty in Salutati's treatise, *De seculo et religione*,[141] a widely-read work in the fifteenth century.[142] Salutati argues that although Christians for the first three hundred years were poor, yet by virtue of their sanctity they spread the faith throughout the world; on the other hand, since the Donation of Constantine, although the church has become rich in temporal goods, it is spiritually impoverished, too weak to combat Saracens and schismatic Greeks, and even divided within itself.[143] Another famous instance is Lorenzo Valla's *De Constantini donatione*, in which Pope Sylvester I is cited as an example of Christian simplicity in contrast to Eugenius IV.[144] The theme of Christian antiquity as an ideal for the reform of the modern church has an important place in the thought of the Florentine humanist and Greek scholar, Ambrogio Traversari, who contrasted the almost universal sway of Christianity in the patristic age with shrinking Christendom in his own day; Traversari, general of

---

Kaminsky, *A History of the Hussite Revolution* (Berkeley and Los Angeles, 1967), *passim;* H. Kaminsky *et al.* (eds) *Master Nicholas of Dresden, The Old Color and the New,* in *Transactions of the American Philosophical Society,* new series, 55, part 1 (1965); G. Leff, "The making of the myth of a true church in the later Middle Ages," *The Journal of Medieval and Renaissance Studies,* 1 (1971), 1-15; *idem,* "The Apostolic Ideal in Later Medieval Ecclesiology," *Journal of Theological Studies,* new series, 18 (1967), 58-82; L. B. Pascoe, "Jean Gerson: The 'Ecclesia Primitiva' and Reform," *Traditio,* 30 (1974), 379-409; P. Stockmeir, "Causa Reformationis und Alte Kirche," *Von Konstanz nach Trient,* ed. R. Baeumer (Munich, 1972), 1-13; *idem,* "Die alte Kirche-Leitbild der Erneuerung," *Tuebinger theologische Quartelschrift,* 146 (1966), 385-480; J. S. Preus, "Theological Legitimation for Innovation in the Middle Ages," *Viator,* 3 (1972), 1-26; G. B. Ladner, "Gregory the Great and Gregory VII: A comparison of the Concepts of Renewal," *Viator,* 4 (1973), 1-31; S. H. Hendrix, "In quest of the *Vera Ecclesia,*" *Viator,* 7 (1976), 347-78.

[139] For a general account of ideas on church reform among humanisits, cf. E. Garin, "Desideri di riforma nell'oratoria del Quattrocento," *La cultura filosofica del Rinascimento italiano* (Florence, 1961), 166-82.

[140] *Fam.* VI, 1; VI, 3; XIV, 1. *Sen.* II, 2; XIII, 13.

[141] Ed. B. L. Ullman (Florence, 1957).

[142] Cf. *ibid.,* vi-xvi for a list of many fifteenth-century manuscripts. [143] *Ibid.,* 128-31.

[144] Ed. W. Setz, *Monumenta Germaniae Historica. Quellen zur Geistesgeschichte des Mittelalters,* 10 (Weimar, 1976), 175. Cf. H. Gray, "Valla's *Encomium of St. Thomas Aquinas* and the Humanist Conception of Christian Antiquity," *Essays in History and Literature presented . . . to Stanley Pargellis,* ed. H. Bluhm (Chicago, 1965), 40-42.

the Camaldulensian order, wanted to restore his order to the sanctity of ancient cenobitic life, and in his active role at the Councils of Basel and Florence he upheld the general councils of the primitive church as models by which to judge modern councils.[145] A similar assumption that religion in antiquity was superior to modern Christianity was implicit in the comparisons made by the humanists between the bad style of the scholastics and the eloquence of the church fathers.[146] This view of Christian history was even taken by a member of Accolti's own family, his maternal uncle, Antonio di Rosello Roselli,[147] who wrote an anti-clerical and anti-papal poem, ''Quelli or' veggiam,'' in which he contrasts the purity of the ancient with the corruption of the modern church, distinguishing two periods in Christian history. He maintains that in the modern church appointments go to unworthy candidates to the neglect of better men, argues that the modern clergy misgovern Christendom and lead people to sin, and contrasts the leaders of the modern church, surrounded by luxury, with the ancient saints who suffered martyrdom and persecution.[148]

Accolti's rival, Francesco Griffolini, had undertaken a brief defence of the modern church in his dedicatory letter to Cosimo by praising Pope Pius II, as well as his predecessors, Martin V and Nicholas V:

What shall I say of Martin V, who on his accession to the pontificate found the condition of the church weakened and disturbed by various misfortunes? He settled the long-standing schism and reunited the church into one body, guiding the endangered ship of Peter into the most tranquil harbour out of the greatest disorders and tempests with the skill of a considerable pilot. What was lacking in Nicholas V in comparison with the most distinguished prince? Even though his pontificate was brief, nevertheless in Italy he reestablished the peace of Augustus, and under his auspices and through his leadership the city of Rome and the Roman language were renewed. Even if unwelcome

---

[145] Cf. C. Stinger, *Humanism and the Church Fathers: Ambrogio Traversari (1386-1439) and Christian Antiquity in the Italian Renaissance* (Albany, New York, 1977), 137-38, 167-210, 283-86, 292-93.

[146] Cf. Gray, ''Valla's *Encomium*,'' 37 ff; L. Bruni, *De studiis et literis liber*, in *Schriften*, ed. Baron, 5-19.

[147] On Roselli's life, cf. Biblioteca Comunale, Arezzo, 55, fol. 266r-67v; for examples of his work as an amateur humanist, cf. Biblioteca Ambrosiana, Milan, C 145 inf., fol. 141r-46r, 195r-99v, 291r.

[148] Published in A. Lumini, *Scritti letterari*, ser. 1a (Arezzo, 1884), 159-63. On the possible attribution of the poem to Francesco Accolti, Benedetto's brother, cf. F. Flamini, *La lirica toscana del Rinascimento* (Pisa, 1891), 724-25. For another example of a humanist idealizing the primitive church in contrast to the modern church, cf. Vergerio's *Pro redintegranda unienda que ecclesia ad Romanos Cardinales oratio tempore schismatis in concistorio habita, a. 1406, novembri*, ed. C. A. Combi, *Archivio storico per Trieste, l'Istria e il Trentino*, 1 (1881-82), 360-74.

death had not suddenly removed him in the midst of his work, one could boast that he, no less than Augustus, transformed the city from brick to marble. What is equal to the piety of Pius II? Truly I say pious of a man who has refused no labour with his infirm and weak body in order to care for the church and the Christian religion entrusted to him.[149]

Accolti may have felt that Griffolini had not taken full advantage of the opportunities for rhetorical display offered by a weak cause such as the modern church; certainly a number of arguments in Accolti's defence of modern Christianity show him at work mainly as a rhetorician. For example, Accolti censures ancient pagans who had the opportunity of witnessing many miracles and yet tenaciously clung to their false beliefs; on the other hand, he excuses modern clerics who sin on the grounds that they are only human and argues that in general wicked men would not become members of religious orders in which they would have little opportunity for indulging in sin.[150]

Such arguments have no real historical dimension, but most of Accolti's defence was expressed in historical terms and sometimes based on historical research.[151] Moreover, Accolti brought the critical judgment and wide perspective of an historian to his discussion of church history. He criticizes the allegations, for example, that modern clerics are corrupt, arguing that, however virtuous a man is, he will always find calumniators, and that this is especially true of clerics, whose lives are scrutinized with particular zeal. Denunciations of the modern church must be regarded with caution according to Accolti, for there are many sinners who criticize virtuous clerics in order to draw attention away from their own vices; indeed, not even Christ and the apostles escaped calumny. Moreover, if modern clerics had not been of a high standard, Accolti asks critically, how could the church have survived for so many centuries? In evaluating both the ancient and modern churches, Accolti uses the balanced judgment of

---

[149] Griffolini, fol. 2r-v: Quid nam de Martino quinto dicam qui cum primum ad summum est pontificatum assumptus inbecillum et variis casibus agitatum ecclesiae statum et diuturnum schisma ita sedavit, ita in unum corpus redegit, ut ex maximis perturbationibus et procellis in tranquillissimum portum tanti gubernatoris peritia periclitantem petri naviculam appulerit? Quid ad clarissimum principem Nicolao Qunito defuit? Cuius tempora etsi brevissima quantulacumque, tamen in hac nostra inferiore Italiae Augusti paci contulerim. Cuius ductu et auspicio ut urbs Roma ita et romana lingua renovata est. Quem nisi tam repente invida mors e medio substulisset, non minus quam Augustus urbem e lateritia marmoream reliquisse gloriari potuisset. Quid pio secundo pietate par? Vere inquam pio qui ut commisse sibi ecclesiae et christianae relligioni consuleret invalido et imbecillo corpore nullum recusavit laborem.

[150] Dialogus, fol. 48r-50v; Galletti, 124-25.

[151] Cf. *Dialogus,* fol. 47v-48r; (Galletti, 124), for his research in Augustine, Jerome, Athanasius, Basil, Chrysostom and Eusebius on early Church history.

an historian: in antiquity, there may have been saints, martyrs and scholars, but there were apostates, heretics, and illiterates as well; similarly, in modern times there may be wicked clerics but there are also many saints. Accolti as an historian was able to see the church as a particular historical institution whose character changes in the course of time: poverty may have been appropriate to the primitive church, but riches and luxury are needed by modern clergy in order to maintain the respect of the people; cardinals and popes as princes of the church need magnificence to make their authority effective. Accolti points out that it is not men but historical circumstances which have changed: if there were more martyrs in antiquity, that was because there was more persecution; given the opportunity, men in the modern church would die for their faith. The mendicant orders were founded to revive the customs of the early church, but Accolti with his sense of history realized that they were a novelty of the modern church, different from any religious order of antiquity: from St. Francis and St. Dominic "grew new religious orders the likes of which antiquity never saw." Particularly impressive is Accolti's sense of the historical evolution of civilization under the influence of Christianity. Modern men, he argues, may not be faultless, but the Christian religion has restrained their vicious inclinations; men have gradually abandoned barbarous religious rituals, indiscriminate slaughter in warfare, and cruel pillaging of cities as the influence of Christianity has grown pervasive.[152]

The prevailing opinion during the Middle Ages and particularly the later Middle Ages was that the ancient church was superior to modern Christianity; however, it is clear that the modern church had sometimes been defended during the Middle Ages too. Eleventh- and twelfth-century canonists, for example, often distinguished between ancient and modern ecclesiastical customs without implying that the practices of the primitive church were to be preferred; moreover, canonists occasionally implied that the modern church represented a completion or further development of Christian antiquity and therefore was superior to the primitive church.[153] Similarly, a later medieval theologian such as Gerson looked to Christian antiquity as an ideal for the reform of the modern church, but sometimes he pointed to instances when the modern church had fulfilled the potential of the early church,[154] which implied a sense of historical development similar to Accolti's. Medieval canonists and theologians also demonstrated an acute capacity for historical criticism, as for

---

[152] Dialogus, fol. 45v-55r; Galletti, 123-27.
[153] Olsen, "The Idea of the *Ecclesia Primitiva*," 70-80.
[154] Pascoe, "Jean Gerson," 380-409.

example in Rufinus's discussion of conflicting interpretations of Scripture in which he resolved an apparent disagreement between Augustine and Jerome on the reliability of texts of Scripture by referring to divergent manuscript traditions.[155] Moreover, a fundamental principle in the interpretation of canon law and scripture was that attention had always to be paid to circumstances of place, person, and time,[156] so that a theologian such as Gerson was by no means adopting an unprecedented method of argument when he maintained, like Accolti, that in the ancient church the success of Christianity was achieved through poverty and simplicity, whereas in the modern age of materialism it is more appropriate for the ecclesiastical hierarchy to win respect with magnificence and external splendor.[157]

What distinguishes Accolti's justification of the modern church from that of a theologian such as Gerson is that his arguments are predominantly historical, whereas Gerson mixes history with logic, analogy, and prophecy by arguing, for example, that the whole is greater than the parts, by comparing the modern church to a queen brought in splendor to her king, and by citing the prophecy from Isaiah that "Kings shall be your foster fathers." [158] Accolti's predominantly historical outlook derives from rhetoric, for a fundamental way of praising or blaming an individual was to place him in an historical context. This is actually praise by reference to external circumstances, a basic rhetorical commonplace.[159] The humanists often praised Dante and Petrarch by putting them in historical perspective: "they did very well considering when they lived" or "it must be remembered that they were the first to revive the study of letters." [160] Thus Accolti praises the modern church by reference to external circumstances when he says that miracles are no longer necessary and criticizes the ancient church with the same *topos* by pointing out that in antiquity there were more martyrs because there was more persecution. Similarly, a commonplace of rhetoric was to praise an individual as the sole possessor of a certain accomplishment: hence Accolti's praise of the mendicant orders as a unique characteristic of the modern church. Medieval scriptural exegesis and canonical interpretation were deeply influenced by the classical rhetorical tradition, particularly after the twelfth century when more emphasis began to be placed on the literal or historical significance of the text;[161] this influence of rhetoric is clear for example in Gerson's

---

[155] Olsen, "The Idea of the Ecclesia Primitiva," 77.   [156] *Ibid.,* 73, note 34.

[157] Pascoe, "Jean Gerson," 408-09.   [158] *Ibid.,* 403-04, 407.

[159] Cf. Quintilian, III, vii, 13-14.

[160] For examples by Filippo Villani, Boccaccio, Vergeris, Poggio, and Bruni, cf. Baron, *Crisis,* 1966 ed. 260-68.

[161] Cf. B. Smalley, *The Study of the Bible in the Middle Ages* (Oxford, 1952), esp. 83-195.

historical interpretation of the ancient and modern churches. What is significant is that medieval theologians and canonists did not offer such an exclusively historical analysis of the development of Christianity as did Accolti because they were not primarily rhetoricians and so included philosophical, analogical, and prophetic as well as rhetorical material. As a Renaissance humanist and professional rhetorician, on the other hand, Accolti developed predominantly historical arguments as a matter of course in his discussion of the ancient and modern churches.

Interestingly, it was another humanist who, like Accolti, developed in the fifteenth century an almost exclusively historical defence of the modern church. Lapo da Castiglionchio, in his *Dialogus super excellentia curie Romane*,[162] insisted that, whereas poverty suited the early church, the modern church needs wealth. Christ had to be poor, Lapo argues, in order to convince the world of his own divinity because in that materialistic age a rich man would have gone unnoticed. Moreover, Christ had to confute extremely learned opponents, but since reason and argument were inadequate, he had to resort to miracles, which must have seemed all the more wonderful when invoked by a man of modest social background and position. However, not all periods in history are the same. The church, well established in Lapo's time, needed wealth, for he lived in an age that admired riches and despised poverty. How ridiculous it would be to see the pope riding a donkey![163] Lapo's defence of the modern church does not have the wide range of Accolti's arguments, but it confirms that the germ of Accolti's historical interpretation of the modern church came from rhetoric.

Great significance has generally been attached to the development of the quarrel of the ancients and moderns; it has usually been assumed that in the history of thought a progression occurred in which the first stage was characterized by deference to antiquity, the second by self-confident equality with the ancients, leading to the idea of progress and a sense of ever growing superiority over the ancients. Sometimes the classicism of the Renaissance has been identified as the first stage and the development of modern science in the seventeenth century as the second;[164] recently this has been challenged by the view that Renaissance humanists developed a sense of equality with or superiority to the ancients which prepared the way for the

[162] Ed. R. Scholz, *Quellen und Forschungen aus italienischen Archiven und Bibliotheken*, **15** (1914), 116-53; H. Baron, "Franciscan Poverty and Civic Wealth," *Speculum*, **XIII** (1938), 29-30.

[163] Ed. R. Scholz, 148-50.

[164] For example, R. F. Jones, *Ancients and Moderns* (St. Louis, 1936); J. B. Bury, *The Idea of Progress* (London, 1920).

emergence of the idea of progress in the late sixteenth and seventeenth centuries.[165] Similarly, it has been shown recently that medieval authors had a concept of modern times equal or superior in merit to antiquity, and that some of their writings even contained reference to an idea of progress.[166]

However, all these schemes skirt around the fact that the quarrel of the ancients and moderns was a rhetorical argument for praise and blame, and therefore throughout much of the history of western thought one can find supporters of the moderns and denigrators of the ancients, and *vice-versa;* it is difficult to detect progression or development because both sides of the argument were present from Antiquity until the end of the eighteenth century—in other words, for as long as rhetoric remained a fundamental technique of composition. By attaching particular historical significance to the support of one side or the other, one can overlook the role of rhetoric, which always made both sides of the argument available to an author; when, for example, Griffolini, Accolti, and Rinuccini chose to defend the moderns, they were not so much marching forward in the vanguard of an historical progression which would eventually lead to the overthrow of the authority of the ancients, as choosing the side of the argument which was appropriate to the task with which they were faced as rhetoricians.

Moreover, the attempt to see the history of the quarrel as the gradual triumph of modernity over classicism is bedevilled by the unnerving habit of the leading protagonists to argue on both sides of the question. The case of Leonardo Bruni is now famous,[167] and he is joined by Horace,[168] Einhard,[169] Otto of Freising,[170] Ermenrich,[171] John of Salisbury,[172] Petrarch,[173] Salutati,[174] Alberti,[175] and Machiavelli.[176] Indeed, Accolti himself, the author of the most comprehensive defence of modernity before the seventeenth century, composed a poem on friendship, in which he went beyond his para-

---

[165] Cf. Baron, "The Querelle"; Buck, *Die "Querelle"*; Margiotta, *Le origini.*

[166] Cf. Goessmann, *Antiqui und Moderni.*

[167] Cf. J. Seigel, "'Civic Humanism' or Ciceronian Rhetoric?," *Past and Present,* 34 (1966), 3-48.

[168] Ode, III, 6 and Ep. II, 1.

[169] Cf. preface to *Vita Karoli Magni,* 1-2, where, on the one hand, he criticizes those who find fault with the present and, on the other, sees the age of Charlemagne as a golden age in contrast to developments after his death.

[170] Cf. Goessmann, *Antiqui und Moderni,* 57-58.   [171] *Ibid.,* 84.

[172] Curtius, *European Literature,* 163.   [173] Cf. notes 13 and 37 *supra.*

[174] Cf. Margiotta, *Le origini,* 65-72, and note 14 *supra.*   [175] Cf. Margiotta, *Le origini,* 81-82.

[176] Cf. preface to Book II of the *Discorsi,* where Machiavelli puts both sides of the argument.

phrase of Cicero's *De amicitia* to give his own view of how the moral standards of his century had declined since the days of his ancestors.[177] Such inconsistency, problematic though it may be for some modern scholars, is inherent in the traditions of rhetoric, in which an orator proved his virtuosity by arguing on both sides of a question.

The historical significance of the quarrel therefore is not the overthrow of the authority of antiquity resulting from the final triumph of the moderns over the ancients; rather, what changed in the long history of the quarrel was the definition of antiquity and modern times. Implicit in the quarrel was a concept of historical change, an idea of contrast between two historical periods, and it was what authors meant by these historical labels—antiquity and modern times—that developed in the course of the quarrel. The contrast between *antiquitas* and *modernitas* is one of the most important themes in medieval thought; what is interesting is that medieval authors had no conventional definitions for these concepts. Sometimes the dividing line between antiquity and modern times was placed at the birth of Christ, e.g., in John of Salisbury's distinction between *antiquae* and *modernae historiae*[178] or in the famous contrast in the writings of the scholastics between the old testament as *fides antiquorum* and the new as *fides modernorum*.[179] Another scheme placed the line of demarcation in late antiquity, contrasting church fathers with medieval philosophers and theologians, the decrees of ancient and modern church councils, and ancient authors, including the church fathers, with medieval writers.[180] According to yet another concept the new logic of the twelfth century (*logica nova*) was contrasted with the old logic of Boethius (*ars vetus*);[181] along similar lines was the distinction between teachers of the trivium and quadrivium as *magistri antiqui* and *moderni*,[182] and the famous contrast between realists and nominalists in the *via antiqua* and *via moderna* in the fourteenth and fifteenth centuries.[183] Another historical scheme, expressed in the concepts of *translatio imperii* and *translatio studii*, emphasized the continuity between antiquity and modern times, maintaining that the heritage of the ancients had been handed on to the moderns.[184] According to eschatological theories of history, the most famous of which derived from Joachim of Fiore, the crucial dividing line was not

---

[177] Ed. E. Jacoboni, *Studi di filologia italiana*, 15 (1957), 286, 294; cf. *De amicitia*, IX, 32.

[178] Goessmann, *Antiqui und Moderni*, 70. Cf. *ibid.*, 51 (Augustine), 57 (Hugh of St. Victor), 78 (thirteenth-century scholastics), 100 (Alexander of Villedieu).

[179] *Ibid.*, 102-08, esp. 106-07.

[180] *Ibid.*, 23-24 (Gelasius), 27 (Cassiodorus), 30 (Bede), 36 (Hrabanus Maurus), 38 (Gregory VII), 40 (Vincent of Lerinum), 46 (Humbert), 94-95 (Conrad of Hirsau).

[181] *Ibid.*, 67, 73 [182] *Ibid.*, 64-65. [183] *Ibid.*, 109-16. [184] *Ibid.*, 49-50, 81-82, 101

so much in late antiquity or even at the birth of Christ as in the present or near future.[185] One of the most pervasive concepts of antiquity and modern times in the Middle Ages derived from Antiquity itself. In this scheme, in E. R. Curtius's words, "from century to century, the line of demarcation shifts."[186] As Horace wrote:

A writer who dropped off a hundred years ago, is he to be reckoned among the perfect and ancient, or among the worthless and modern? Let some limit banish disputes. "He is ancient," you say, "and good, who completes a hundred years." "What of one who passed away a month or a year short of that, in what class is he to be reckoned? The ancient poets, or those whom today and tomorrow must treat with scorn?" He surely will find a place of honour among the ancients, who is short by a brief month or even a year. I take what you allow, and like hairs in a horse's tail first one and then another I pluck and pull away little by little. . . .[187]

One of the most famous medieval examples of this shifting antiquity comes from Walter Map, who said, "I call modern times the course of the last hundred years,"[188] and this practice of referring to the recent past as antiquity continued throughout the Middle Ages, for example, in the writings of Einhard, William of Malmsbury, Abbot Suger, Albertus Magnus, Aquinas, Roger Bacon and Rolandino of Padua.[189] This concept of an ever-expanding antiquity continues to be found in the fourteenth century: Dante called the contemporaries of Cacciaguida "*antiqui*" in contrast to "*la cittadinanza, ch'è or mista*,"[190] and Filippo Villani, contrasting the "*saeculi praesentis ignominiam*" with "*antiquorum virtutes*," still meant by the "*antiqui*" the contemporaries of Dante "*nostri Poetae . . . Concives multi*."[191] Complexity characterized historical thought about antiquity and modern times in the Middle Ages; indeed, a number of authors, for example, John of Salisbury and Walter Map, used several different historical schemes in their writings.[192]

Simplicity, on the other hand, was the hallmark of the Renaissance concept of antiquity and modern times; the ancients, once and for all, had become, in Accolti's words, "those who flourished once among the Greeks or Macedonians, or among the Carthaginians and Romans, under the republic or shortly afterwards under the Roman emperors."[193] For Filippo Villani, writing in the medieval tradition,

---

[185] *Ibid.*, 56-62.   [186] *European Literature*, 253.

[187] Ep. II, 1, vv. 34-46, tr. H. R. Fairclough, (London, 1970).

[188] Curtius, *European Literature*, 255.

[189] Cf. Goessmann, 36, 38, 39, 78, 79, 95; Curtius, 251-55.

[190] *Paradiso*, XVI, 49, 91.   [191] Galletti, 5.

[192] Cf. Goessmann, 70, 73, 79, 96.

[193] Dialogus, fol. 3v (Galletti, 106): qui vel apud Graecos et Macedones quondam, vel apud Penos, Romanosque, vigente republica, vel parum postea sub Romanis Principibus floruerunt.

Dante was an *"antiquus,"* [194] but for Accolti, Thomas Aquinas was a man of his own age, a *"neotericus"* or modern in the words of Erasmus. [195] From the great variety of medieval schemes of antiquity and modern times, the humanists took one concept in which antiquity ended sometime between the fourth and sixth centuries A.D., and Accolti's dialogue is the clearest example of how the differing views of antiquity and modernity used during the Middle Ages to represent changes and developments in such fields as philosophy, literature, religion, military practice and political life were simplified by the Renaissance humanists into one comprehensive historical scheme. [196]

Accolti's dialogue does not exemplify all the uses which the quarrel of the ancients and moderns had as a tool of historical interpretation during the Renaissance; Accolti makes no use of the idea of progress, which, although present in medieval authors such as Otto of Freising or Roger Bacon, [197] became one of the major themes of historical speculation during the seventeenth and eighteenth centuries, nor does Accolti discuss the fine arts, the concept of which grew out of developments in the quarrel during the late seventeenth century. [198] In one important respect, however, Accolti's dialogue is a forerunner of the development of the quarrel in the later Renaissance. A number of Accolti's contemporaries, such as Palmieri, Manetti, and Rinuccini, defended the achievements of the moderns in general terms, like Accolti, over a wide range of disciplines; only Accolti, however, included a discussion of the merits of the modern church in a general panegyric of the modern age. The idea of a religious revival accom-

---

[194] Galletti, 5. It is interesting that the letter on ancients and moderns, written by Filippo Villani's contemporary, Giovanni Dondi, still preserves a certain complexity of historical thought reminiscent of medieval writers. In religious history, Dondi places the dividing line at the birth of Christ (Gilbert, "Dondi," 331-32), whereas in secular history he places it in late Antiquity (*ibid.,* 332 ff.). Petrarch had placed the dividing line at the Donation of Constantine for both religious and secular history (cf. *Fam.* VI, 2), and his professional humanist successors such as Salutati (cf. *De seculo et religione,* 128-31) seem to have found it easier to follow his lead than amateur humanists such as Dondi or Filippo Villani, who, as a physician and a lawyer respectively, were on the fringes of the humanist movement.

[195] Curtius, *European Literature,* 251.

[196] For a discussion of the influence of this historical scheme established by the humanists, cf. W. Ferguson, *The Renaissance in Historical Thought* (Cambridge, Mass. 1948), 8 ff. It is interesting that Ulrich von Hutten, in *Epistolae obscurorum virorum,* parodied medieval usage of the terms "ancients" and "moderns" (cf. K. H. Gerschmann, "Antiqui—novi—moderni in den Epistolae obscurorum virorum," *Archiv fuer Begriffsgeschichte,* 11-12 [1967-68]; Goessmann, *Antiqui und Moderni,* 143), showing how conscious the humanists were of the changes that they had made in the historical concepts implicit in the quarrel.

[197] Cf. esp. Silvestre, "'Quanto iuiores, tanto perspicaciores,'" for a collection of ancient and medieval texts implying an idea of progress.

[198] Cf. Kristeller, "The Modern System of the Arts," 525 ff.

panying the rebirth of learning became one of the fundamental ideas of religious reformers such as Erasmus, Melanchthon, Luther, Bèze, Foxe, and Calvin;[199] the view that the renewal of the church accompanied the renaissance of learning was one of the most important links between humanists and reformers during the sixteenth century.[200] The idea that the general revival of culture during the Renaissance embraced religion made it possible for a figure to emerge such as Melanchthon, who was renowned equally as a humanist and reformer, and the first to include religion in a comprehensive historical scheme of antiquity and modern times was Benedetto Accolti.

University of Leeds.

[199] Cf. Ferguson, *The Renaissance in Historical Thought*, 39-57.

[200] The close connection between reformers and humanists has recently been stressed by many scholars; for a survey of current opinion, cf. L. Spitz, "Humanism in the Reformation," *Renaissance Studies in Honor of Hans Baron*, ed. A. Molho and J. A. Tedeschi (Florence, 1971), 641-62, and his "The Course of German Humanism," *Itinerarium Italicum: The Profile of the Italian Renaissance in the Mirror of its European Transformations*, dedicated to P. O. Kristeller, ed. H. A. Oberman with T. A. Brady, Jr. (Leyden, 1975), 371-436.

IX

THE IDEA OF LIBERTY IN MACHIAVELLI*

By Marcia L. Colish

There is a certain class of thinkers who have evoked such perennial interest since their own times that the voluminous literature devoted to them tends to tell us more about the concerns and predispositions of their commentators than it does about the thinkers themselves. Niccolò Machiavelli definitely falls within this class of thinkers. His political writings have frequently been made an arena for the clash of political ideologies that owe their origins to later ages. These debates, carried on over the prostrate bodies of *Il principe* and the *Discorsi*, show no sign of ending. Recently, however, a small number of scholars have called attention to the need for a fresh approach, which seeks to gain an understanding of Machiavelli's ideas through a precise textual and contextual analysis of his use of language.[1] These scholars have stressed, plausibly enough, that the way to avoid a distorted, anachronistic interpretation of Machiavelli is to refrain from applying rigid, preconceived, and technical meanings to his still fluid, pretechnical vocabulary. They point out that such a vocabulary is none the less susceptible of systematic investigation.[2]

The method suggested by this approach has already borne fruit in J. H. Whitfield's study of the idea of *ordini* in Machiavelli's thought[3] and in J. H. Hexter's two articles on Machiavelli's idea of *lo stato* in *Il principe*, articles which destroy the foundations of the *raison d'état*

---

*This paper is dedicated gratefully to the late Ewart Lewis. I would also like to thank J. H. Hexter, Julius Kirshner, John D. Lewis, and J. H. Whitfield for their helpful criticism and suggestions.

[1] Giorgio Cadoni, "Libertà, repubblica e governo misto in Machiavelli," *Rivista internazionale di filosofia del diritto*, XXIX, ser. 3 (1962), 462; Fredi Chiapelli, *Studi sul linguaggio del Machiavelli* (Florence, 1952); J. H. Hexter, "*Il principe* and *lo stato*," *Studies in the Renaissance*, IV(1957), 114, 137; "The Loom of Language and the Fabric of Imperatives: The Case of *Il Principe* and *Utopia*," *American Historical Review*, LXIX (July 1964), 945-58; Daniel Waley, "The Primitivist Element in Machiavelli's Thought," *JHI*, XXXI (Jan. 1970), 91-98; J. H. Whitfield, *Machiavelli* (Oxford, 1947), 67-70, 75-78, 93-105, 131-33; "On Machiavelli's Use of *Ordini*," *Italian Studies*, X (1955), 19.

[2] Cadoni, *loc. cit.*, 462, n. 2; Chiapelli, 39, 111; Hans Freyer, *Machiavelli* (Leipzig, 1938), 78; Hanna H. Gray, "Machiavelli: The Art of Politics and the Paradox of Power," *The Responsibility of Power: Historical Essays in Honor of Hajo Holborn*, ed. Leonard Krieger and Fritz Stern (Garden City, 1967), 34; Hexter, "*Il principe* and *lo stato*," 113-17, 119-25; G. H. R. Parkinson, "Ethics and Politics in Machiavelli," *Philosophical Quarterly*, V (1955), 37; G. Prezzolini, *Machiavelli Anticristo* (Rome, 1954), 3-4.

[3] Whitfield, "On Machiavelli's Use of *Ordini*," *loc. cit.*, 19-39.

school of Machiavellian interpretation in a dazzling syntactical *tour de force*.[4] But despite these important contributions, Eric W. Cochrane's assertion that the linguistic approach to Machiavelli is still in its infancy is as true today as it was in 1961.[5]

Libertà is among the key terms in Machiavelli which both Whitfield and Hexter list as needing close textual study.[6] What I intend to do in this paper is to apply to *libertà* the method already exemplified in the works of these two scholars. This proposal entails four main tasks: (1) the complete works of Machiavelli will be subjected to scrutiny; (2) attention will be paid to the contexts in which the term *libertà* appears, and, where relevant, to the nature of the works in which these references occur; (3) attention will be directed to synonyms of *libertà* and to terms Machiavelli habitually uses in conjunction with it; (4) on the basis of this kind of analysis we will be in a position to consider what *libertà* means in Machiavelli's thought and how it relates to some of his other political ideas.

I. Liberty in the Commonplace Sense. A close reading of Machiavelli's works shows that he has several definitions of liberty, and that the majority of them are quite precise in their content and implications. At the same time, Machiavelli occasionally uses *libertà* and its cognates in a number of contexts where it has no precise meaning or theoretical implications. It may be helpful to dispose of these commonplace uses of liberty in Machiavelli's writings before directing attention to the more important and characteristic meanings of *libertà* in his thought.

The most frequent general use of *libertà* occurs in historical passages where it means freedom from physical captivity.[7] *Libertà* may also mean the freedom of political action enjoyed by a ruler whose country's laws and institutions place him above criticism. The clearest example cited by Machiavelli is the kingdom of France. France, according to Machiavelli, is a "free monarchy" because the *Parlement* serves as a target both for the insolence and ambition of the powerful and for the fear and hatred of the masses, thus neutralizing the impact

[4]Hexter, "*Il principe* and *lo stato*," 113–38; "The Loom of Language," 945–58.

[5]Eric W. Cochrane, "Machiavelli: 1940–1960," *Journal of Modern History*, XXXIII (June 1961), 124.

[6]Hexter, "*Il principe* and *lo stato*," 114; Whitfield, *Machiavelli*, 4.

[7]Machiavelli, *Istorie fiorentine*, I, 24, 25; II, 2, 30; IV, 17; V, 5, 6; VII, 27; VIII, 6, 17, 35, ed. F. Gaeta; *Legazione decima*, a Cesare Borgia in Urbino, 26 June 1502, no. 7, Soderini and Machiavelli to the Signoria; *Legazione ventesima*, seconda presso la Corte di Roma, Cesena, 7 October 1506, no. 50, Machiavelli to the Dieci di Balìa, *Legazioni e commissarie*, I, II, ed. S. Bertelli, *Opere* (8 vols.; Milan, 1960–65), VII, 114, 115, 141, 182, 293, 335, 336, 493, 519, 539, 573; III, 265; IV, 1015. References to the works of Machiavelli will be to this edition.

of political dissent and permitting the king to pursue his policies un-
trammelled by the criticism of either group. It is upon this happy institutional arrangement that the liberty and security of the king depend
(*depende la libertà e sicurtà del re*).[8] Other general political meanings of *libertà* include free surrender, in the sense of unconditional acceptance by the vanquished of the victor's terms[9] and dissociation from
or overthrow of a government held to be objectionable for reasons
not specified.[10]

Finally, *libertà* occurs in Machiavelli's writings a number of times
in a very broad and not necessarily political context. *Libertà* may describe a person's financial position, as in a passage where Machiavelli
ironically contrasts the public and private interests of certain indebted
Florentine nobles who supported the Duke of Athens' *coup d'état* in
1341–42, hoping to free themselves from debt by betraying their city
(*con la servitù della patria dalla servitù de' loro creditori liberarsi*).[11]
Machiavelli defines free men (*uomini liberi*) as those who act on their
own initiative, as opposed to those who act as other people's agents.[12]
"Free from" may be a simple synonym for "lacking in" or "enjoying
(or suffering) the absence of," as when Machiavelli states that the
Florentines have been fortunate in remaining free from many ills
(*liberi di tanti mali*).[13] Freedom is also a mental or psychological
state, as in the case of freedom from fear[14] and freedom from distrac-
tion.[15] Additional examples might be produced to illustrate further
these general usages of *libertà*, but no purpose would be served by
multiplying citations. All that they illustrate, in effect, is that there is a
level in Machiavelli's thought where *libertà* functions as a general
term, without the specific meanings and connotations imposed upon
it by a particular political theory.

II.   *Free Will.* In Machiavelli we find a clear conception of free will
as an attribute of human nature, an idea which he denotes in a number of ways. He uses the term *elezione* to mean freedom of choice in a
general sense.[16] He uses the term *libera occasione* to describe the
freedom of choice which permits the egotistical nature of man to manifest itself.[17] But when most specific, Machiavelli uses the traditional
term *libero arbitrio*; and he uses it in one of the best known passages in
his work, the chapter in *Il principe* where he discusses the relationship between *virtù* and *fortuna*. Although Machiavelli gives express
treatment to the idea of *libero arbitrio* in this one passage alone, its as-

---

[8]*Il principe*, XIX; *Opere*, I, 77.   [9]*Istor. fior.*, VIII, 33; *Opere*, VII, 569.
[10]*Ibid.*, III, 18; *Opere*, VII, 249.   [11]*Ibid.*, II, 33; *Opere*, VII, 190.
[12]*Discorsi sopra la prima deca di Tito Livio*, I, 1; *Opere*, I, 126–27.
[13]*Istor. fior.*, proemio; *Opere*, VII, 69.   [14]*Ibid.*, II, 13, 30; *Opere*, VII, 157, 183.
[15]*Discorsi*, I, 31; *Opere*, I, 203.   [16]*Ibid.*, I, 3; *Opere*, I, 127, 128, 136.
[17]*Ibid.*, 3; *Opere*, I, 135.

sociation with the important question of *virtù* and *fortuna* makes its significance impossible to overlook. For it is on the basis of man's free will that Machiavelli feels compelled to disagree with those who think that Fortune rules all of human existence. It is precisely because he wishes to uphold the dignity of man's free will that he counters with the theory that Fortune rules only half of human life: "Lest our free will be extinguished (*perchè il nostro libero arbitrio non sia spento*), I judge it may be true that Fortune is the ruler of half of our actions, but that she leaves the government of the other half, more or less, to us."[18] He goes on in this passage to elaborate the idea that man expresses his free will in the face of *fortuna* by the exercise of *virtù*.

Although he does not expound his doctrine of free will in detail, Machiavelli thus clearly places himself within the tradition of thinkers who see in man's free will the sign of human independence, the ground of ethically meaningful choices, and the guarantee that man will not be reduced to the status of a plaything at the mercy of capricious and uncaring cosmic forces.[19] At the same time, Machiavelli gives this tradition a characteristically new twist, a point which has been clarified by Francesco Ercole.[20] As Ercole observes, Machiavelli adopts the traditional terminology but he attaches a different meaning to it. He does not see free will as a mental faculty. Nor does he see it as unconditioned arbitrary power. Nor does he see it as the agency through which man acquires virtue by the actualizing of his inner resources, the subjection of his desires to reason, and the exclusion from the realm of moral relevance of events in the world outside the moral subject over which he has no jurisdiction. Machiavelli does not conceive of free will exclusively or primarily in terms of the inner life; he does not analyze it in the light of its effects upon the spiritual condition of the subject vis-à-vis God or the universe. Rather, he applies free will to man as a whole. Machiavelli pits both the mental and the physical endowments of man against a Fortune that is not merely an abstract cosmic force but one which operates in concrete historical circumstances, political settings, and social configurations. To succeed in the contest of *virtù* against *fortuna* is to impose one's directive will upon the realities of the particular historical situation in which one lives.

While this definition of free will as the practical ability to modify or influence external events can be found in the humanists of the *trecento* and *quattrocento*, particularly Leone Battista Alberti,[21] Machiavelli goes beyond his humanist predecessors. Not merely does

[18]*Il principe*, XXV; *Opere*, I, 99.
[19]G. Prezzolini, *Machiavelli* (New York, 1967), 54–55.
[20]F. Ercole, *La politica di Machiavelli* (Rome, 1926), 5–20, 24, 39–40.
[21]*Ibid.*, 11–14.

he de-emphasize the internalizing tendency of classical and Christian
free will theories, he also eliminates their transcendental focus. For
Machiavelli it is always the whole man who acts in the exercise of
libero arbitrio. The subject's aim is not only to form his own mind and
character but, by forming it in the mode of *virtù*, to impose his will on
external events. He is, to be sure, limited, by Fortune, by the *necessità*
entailed by the concatenation of certain sets of circumstances, and by
the generic vices of human nature. These limitations, however, manifest themselves not in the abstract realm of metaphysical and ethical
theory, but in the context of concrete political practice. The goal of
Machiavellian free will is not to avoid being a puppet in the hands of an
omnipotent God or an inexorable universe; it is to avoid being a
puppet in the hands of other men upon the stage of history.

    III. Corporate Libertà. In turning to Machiavelli's specifically
political meanings of the term *libertà* we may begin by noting that he
conceives of liberty on a large number of occasions in the sense of corporate *libertà*. Except for his substitution of the singular *libertà* for
the plural *libertates* or its Italian equivalent, his use of this idea is in
complete conformity with the corporation theory developed in the
Middle Ages on the basis of the Roman legal idea of the corporation.
A free corporation for both the Florentine and his medieval forebears
may be a community as a whole or a sub-corporation within it, but in
either case its freedom consists in its possession of special preroga-
tives and exemptions which release it from obligations that would
otherwise be incumbent upon it. The Church has such privileges for
Machiavelli, no less than for the Middle Ages. In discussing the results
of the Becket affair in England, he observes that King Henry II was
forced to nullify all policies that contravened the liberty of the Church
(*libertà ecclesiastica*).[22] But in dealing with corporate liberty it is
primarily to secular communities and above all to the free city that he
directs his attention.

    Machiavelli defines the nature of the free city in the terms that the
Middle Ages had borrowed from the Romans. Cities are free when
they possess autonomy, when they live under their own laws (*con le
loro leggi*) and not under the jurisdiction of foreigners (*servitù*).[23]
Servitù in this context is Machiavelli's term for rule by foreigners,
regardless of the institutions through which they rule and regardless
of their harshness or leniency.[24] A city which has autonomy is sovereign over herself (*principe di se stessa*),[25] a definition which, as Franco
Gaeta has noted, parallels Bartolus of Sassoferrato's famous formula

[22]*Istor. fior.*, I, 19; *Opere*, VII, 105.
[23]*Ibid.*, I, 25, 39; VIII, 22; *Il principe*, VIII; *Opere*, VII, 114, 134, 550; I, 42.
[24]*Discorsi*, I, 2; II, 2; *Opere*, I, 129, 284.   [25]*Istor. fior.*, II, 26; *Opere*, VII, 177.

for urban sovereignty, *civitas sibi princeps.*[26] Most of Machiavelli's examples of free cities are drawn from Italy. But he does not fail to mention the German free cities (*terre franche, città libere*), which, he observes, also enjoy their liberty (*godersi la sua libertà*).[27] In fact he reserves for the Germans and the Swiss, along with the ancients, the accolade of his vocabulary, the superlative of *libertà*. In ancient times, he states, there were many completely free peoples (*popoli liberissimi*);[28] among the moderns, the Swiss are perfectly free (*liberissimi*); so too the imperial cities of Germany are perfectly free (*liberissime*), obeying the emperor purely at their own discretion.[29]

Since the autonomy of a city-state is what defines it as a political entity vis-à-vis other powers, it is not surprising to find that Machiavelli treats corporate *libertà* in very much the same way that he treats *lo stato* itself. As Hexter has demonstrated, *lo stato*, at least in *Il principe*, is a passive entity, something to be possessed, gained, lost, maintained, or taken away by someone. The fact that Machiavelli regards *lo stato* as an object of political exploitation is signified by the fact that *lo stato* always functions grammatically as the object of an active verb or the subject of a passive verb in the sentence in which it appears.[30] Virtually the same may be said of *libertà* when Machiavelli uses the term to mean corporate freedom. Its syntactical parallels with *lo stato* are not exact, since the idea of liberty is often expressed in terms of the adjectival and verbal cognates of *libertà* as well as in the form of the noun. Also, *libertà* is less likely to be treated as an entity capable of action than *lo stato*, in any era. Where the noun *libertà* is used, however, it invariably functions, as does *lo stato*, as the object of the sentence. Likewise, it is passive; it is something to be possessed or lost, gained or regained, granted or seized, defended, maintained, and preserved. Machiavelli refers to corporate *libertà* dozens of times throughout his writings, including his histories and his minor political works, as well as *Il principe* and the *Discorsi*. Among his works, the *Istorie fiorentine* contains the largest number of references to corporate *libertà*, partly because of its length but largely as a consequence of its subject matter.

The four main headings under which Machiavelli discusses corporate liberty, in order of ascending frequency of occurrence, are the seizing, gaining, regaining, and defense of *libertà*. The seizure of a city's *liberta* is generally achieved by military aggression.[31] A variety

[26]*Ibid.*, n. 5.
[27]*Discorsi*, II, 2, 19; *Opere*, I, 279, 335–36.
[28]*Ibid.*, II, 2; *Opere*, I, 279.
[29]*Il principe*, XIII, X; *Opere*, I, 55, 49.
[30]Hexter, "*Il principe* and *lo stato*," 119–23, 124–25; "The Loom of Language," 953–54.
[31]*Istor. fior.*, II, 19; IV, 18; V, 8; *Opere*, VII, 165, 296, 399.

of circumstances, however, may enable a city to gain its freedom in the first place.[32] The reacquisition of liberty may also be accomplished in various ways. Sometimes Machiavelli is imprecise in describing how this reacquisition of liberty takes place,[33] but in cases where he does specify the means he cites the force of arms more frequently than any other agency.[34] Machiavelli's stress on military means of securing freedom is even more marked in his treatment of the defense, maintenance, and preservation of *libertà*. He does note a few occasions when liberty has been defended by diplomacy.[35] But it is more usually the breakdown of diplomacy into a state of war that cities have to face in defending their liberty.[36] Tenacity in the defense of corporate liberty is wholly laudable; as Machiavelli observes in a well known passage in the *Discorsi*, when the independence of the *patria* is at stake, no considerations, whether of justice or injustice, pity or cruelty, praise or blame, should hinder the saving of her life and the maintenance of her freedom.[37]

Because corporate freedom must be maintained forcibly in the face of omnipresent external threats, Machiavelli places a good deal of stress on the need for a strong military establishment. He states repeatedly that the preservation of liberty depends on good armies, generals, and strategy in the field,[38] all of which are enhanced if the army is composed of citizens,[39] on military preparedness and energetic official leadership at home,[40] and on a high level of public morale.[41] These familiar themes in Machiavelli's writings occur again and again in this connection because he thinks it highly likely that a free city will be called upon to defend herself from outside aggressors, and that con-

---

[32]*Ibid.*, proemio; I, 14, 22, 25, 26; *Opere*, VII, 70, 97, 111, 114, 116.

[33]*Discorsi*, II, 22; *Istor. fior.*, I, 28, 35; II, 30; VI, 13; *Opere*, I, 343; VII, 119, 129, 182, 406.

[34]*Istor. fior.*, II, 26, 36, 38; III, 27; VII, 26; VIII, 8, 23, 34; *Opere*, VII, 178, 198, 200, 204, 266, 492, 521, 552, 571.

[35]*Ibid.*, I, 29; II, 38; V, 9; VIII, 10; *Nature di uomini fiorentini*, ed. F. Gaeta; *Discorso fatto al magistrato dei dieci sopra le cose di Pisa; Opere*, VII, 122, 205, 341, 527; VIII, 217; II, 13.

[36]*Istor. fior.*, III, 11; IV, 11; V, 11, 12; VIII, 19; *Discorsi*, I, 31; II, 1; *Opere*, VII, 234, 296, 343–45, 346, 545; I, 204, 279.

[37]*Discorsi*, III, 41; *Opere*, I, 495.

[38]*Ibid.*, 17, 41; *Arte della guerra*, II; *Istor. fior.*, V, 1; *Opere*, I, 439, 494–95; II, 393–94; VII, 326.

[39]*Il principe*, XII; *Istor. fior.*, VI, 20; *Opere*, I, 55; VII, 418.

[40]*Istor. fior.*, II, 36; IV, 7; VII, 14; *Provvisioni della repubblica di Firenze per istruire il magistrato de' nove ufficiali dell' Ordinanza e Milizia fiorentina. Provvisione prima per le fanterie*, 6 December 1506; *Provvisione seconda per le milizie a cavallo*, 30 March 1512, ed. S. Bertelli; *I Decennali: Decennale primo*, 39, ed. F. Gaeta; *Opere*, VII, 196, 279, 474; II, 111, 116; VIII, 237.

[41]*Discorsi*, II, 21; *Istor. fior.*, II, 29; V, 19; VII, 15; *Opere*, I, 342; VII, 181, 297, 477.

stant vigilance is necessary for the preservation of her corporate *libertà*.

Refracted through the lens of political insecurity, which causes his gaze to focus on the pressing need to defend civic autonomy by the force of arms, Machiavelli's idea of corporate *libertà* is a direct continuation of the medieval idea of corporate *libertates*. His preeminent interest in civic corporations, as contrasted with other kinds of corporations, reflects the urban environment in which he lived and which he wrote about both in his political works and in his histories. Machiavelli's emphasis on military power in connection with the seizure, reconquest, and preservation of *libertà* is likewise a reflection of the events that passed before his eyes. While Machiavelli borrows the idea of a Roman-style citizen army from the civic humanists, he justifies it in the context of corporate *libertà* in practical terms. His reading of history, ancient and modern, leads him to the conclusion that citizen armies are more successful in the field than are mercenaries or troops led by foreign generals. In short, Machiavelli's conception of corporate *libertà* is traditional. It is not a tradition derived primarily from classical antiquity, except in the sense that the idea of the corporation is rooted ultimately in Roman law, but from the Middle Ages. All that Machiavelli adds to this tradition is his own perspective, the treatment of corporate liberty primarily in the context of practical military considerations.

IV. Libertà within the State. While Machiavelli's view of freedom as a commonplace notion, as a moral idea, and as the definition of corporate autonomy is on the whole clear and consistent, his treatment of *libertà* within the state shows a certain lack of univocity and precision. The ambiguity of Machiavelli's ideas on liberty within the state is reflected in the way that his commentators have handled this topic; for it is by far the most controversial aspect of his conception of *libertà*. Most of the scholars who have dealt with this issue have viewed it in the context of the question of whether the "real" Machiavelli is the "republican" Machiavelli of the *Discorsi* or the "despotic" Machiavelli of *Il principe*. It is well known that for centuries there has been a tradition of Machiavellian interpretation promoting the view of Machiavelli as a republican[42] and strenuously opposing the

---

[42]The most recent treatment of the earlier literature on this subject is Mario Rosa, *Dispotismo e libertà nel settecento: Interpretazioni 'repubbliche' di Machiavelli*, Istituto di storia medievale e moderna, saggi, 3 (Bari, 1964). For bibliography on the more recent literature see Hans Baron, "Machiavelli: The Republican Citizen and the Author of 'The Prince'," *English Historical Review*, LXXVI (April 1961), 218–22; Cochrane, "Machiavelli: 1940–1960," *J. of Mod. Hist.*, XXXIII (1961), 132–36; Émile Namer, *Machiavel* (Paris, 1961), 194–225; Luigi Russo, *Machiavelli*, accresciuta, (Bari, 1949³), 210–14.

view, stated most forcefully in recent decades by Friedrich Meinecke, of Machiavelli as a proponent of the *Machtstaat*.[43] Many of the scholars who have studied Machiavelli on liberty have aligned themselves with the republican interpretation and have concluded that, for Machiavelli, liberty within the state can be equated with the constitutional and institutional structures characteristic of republics,[44] or at least characteristic of limited governments.[45] There is even some support in this school for the view that Machiavellian republican *libertà* can be equated with democracy,[46] although several of its members have stressed that Machiavelli's republican *libertà* should not be confused with modern liberalism or social democracy since he is concerned neither with the natural rights of the individual in relation to the state[47] nor with economic and social equality.[48] It is certainly true that, in many passages in his works, Machiavelli identifies liberty within the state with republican institutions based on preliberal and presocialist political assumptions. At the same time, a close scrutiny of the texts shows that Machiavelli's conception of liberty within the state is not always identical with either a purely republican or a purely constitutional definition of the idea of *libertà*.

Libertà within the state is a topic to which Machiavelli adverts with great frequency and interest, although his references to it are confined with only a few exceptions to two works, the *Istorie fiorentine* and the *Discorsi*. There are only two references to this subject in *Il principe*. In one he identifies liberty with aristocracy while enumerat-

[43]F. Meinecke, *Machiavellism: The Doctrine of Raison d'État and Its Place in Modern History*, trans. Douglas Scott (New York, 1965), 1–22, 29–43.

[44]Henry J. Abraham, "Was Machiavelli a 'Machiavellian'?" *Social Science*, XXVIII (1953), 25–29; Rudolf von Albertini, *Das florentinische Staatsbewusstsein im Übergang von der Republik zum Principat* (Bern, 1955), 66; Edward McN. Burns, "The Liberalism of Machiavelli," *Antioch Review*, VIII (1948), 321–30, who, however, associates the idea of liberty in Machiavelli with modern liberalism; Cadoni, "Libertà, repubblica e governo misto," 463–73, 479–82; Eugenio Garin, *Italian Humanism: Philosophy and Civic Life in the Renaissance*, trans. Peter Munz (Oxford, 1965), 79–81.

[45]Augustin Renaudet, *Machiavel: Étude d'histoire des doctrines politiques* (Paris, 1942), 187–93; Gennaro Sasso, *Niccolò Machiavelli: Storia del suo pensiero politico*, Istituto italiano per gli studi storici, 10 (Naples, 1958), 333–34; Antonio Scolari, "Il concetto di libertà in Niccolò Machiavelli," *Atti e memorie della Accademia di agricoltura, scienze e lettere di Verona*, serie V, vol. X, no. 110 (1933), 52–55.

[46]Hans Baron, *The Crisis of the Early Italian Renaissance: Civic Humanism and Republican Liberty in the Age of Classicism and Tyranny* (rev. ed., Princeton, 1966), 428–29.

[47]Prezzolini, *Machiavelli*, 55–57; Renaudet, *loc. cit.*, 187, 188–89, 190–93; Sasso, *loc. cit.*, 333–44.

[48]Renaudet, *loc. cit.*, 190–93.

ing the three forms of government.[49] In the other he observes that peoples ruled by princes are ignorant of free government *(vivere libero).*[50] In the light of the fact that he is perfectly willing in his other works to admit that one-man rule and liberty are compatible, it is noteworthy that he states the case against princes so strongly in *Il principe.* Perhaps this is Machiavelli's way of delivering a backhanded slap either to the civic virtue of the citizens of Florence or to the virtue, wisdom, or potential legislative prudence of Lorenzo de' Medici, the new ruler of Florence to whom the book was ultimately dedicated.

The *Istorie florentine* was also written for a Medici, Giulio, later Pope Clement VII, although it was clearly intended for a wide Florentine audience as well. In this work Machiavelli tries to avoid taking a stand on the Medici, whom he sometimes describes as promoters of liberty and sometimes as its destroyers. He circumvents this issue in the *Istorie* for the most part by expressing opinions on the Medici in the words of other people. He does not use the term *libertà,* its adjuncts, or its antonyms, in describing the Florentine government after the accession of Cosimo de' Medici, relating without comment the constitutional inroads into the republican system made by Cosimo and Lorenzo and their manipulation of civic elections. His restraint breaks down only when he comes to the Pazzi conspiracy, at which point he states that the *coup* failed because the rule of the Medici had so deafened the ears of the Florentines to the cry of liberty that they knew it no longer.[51] The theme of the *Istorie florentine,* stated in the preface,[52] is that ambition, factionalism, and flaccid public spirit have prevented the Florentines from establishing good and stable institutions and from working for the common good. Since he thinks that Florentine history offers few good examples of institutions promoting freedom, the majority of his references to internal liberty in this work are passages identifying good rulers, good laws, the rule of law, and the end of the common weal with liberty.

The largest single source of references to *libertà* within the state is the *Discorsi.* Most of these references are found in Book I, where Machiavelli discusses republics. Considering the fact that the work is a treatise on political theory clothed as a commentary on Livy, it is not surprising to find that it is the source for almost all of his remarks on liberty in ancient history and on the institutional features of free states. It is also understandable that he should tend to generalize and to analyze problems in the abstract more here than in the *Istorie florentine.* At the same time, it is natural for him to devote attention

[49] *il principe,* IX: *Opere,* 1, 45.   [50] *Ibid., V; Opere,* 1, 29.
[51] *Istor. fior.,* VIII, 8; *Opere,* VII, 521. [52] *Ibid.,* proemio: *Opere.* VII, 68-71.

in the *Discorsi* to the principles underlying free governments. It is in this work that we find an important statement in which Machiavelli defines the republic in terms of the common good,[53] as well as his initially perplexing assertion that Florence, despite her free institutions, has not been a republic for two hundred years.[54]

Of less importance is Machiavelli's proposal for a Florentine constitution, the *Discursus florentinarum rerum*, another work written for a Medici patron, Pope Leo X. Here he shows a combined interest in principles and institutions, but stresses the institutions and suggests a list of practical justifications for a republican constitution. Although he calls the constitution he projects in the *Discursus* a republic and asserts that it preserves the traditional liberty of Florence, the polity he outlines is oligarchical in structure and subject in its functions to the princely influence of Leo.[55] The *Arte della guerra*, finally, contributes one of the *loci classici* for Machiavelli's association of a citizen army with civic virtue in a free state, along with its practical justifications.[56]

In the numerous passages where he discusses liberty within the state, Machiavelli uses the noun *libertà* and its verbal and adjectival cognates in much the same way as he does in discussing the corporate liberty of the state from outside control. The Italian city-states, likewise, serve as his chief source of examples. Here too, he often contrasts *libertà* with *servitù*, which, from an intra-state point of view, he equates with tyranny.[57] In the internal, as in the corporate context, *libertà* is passive, not active; it always functions grammatically as the object of a verb or a preposition. Within the state *libertà* may be known,[58] loved,[59] desired,[60] acquired,[61] possessed,[62] established,[63] enjoyed,[64] lost,[65] taken,[66] destroyed,[67] regained,[68] reinstalled,[69] and

[53]*Discorsi*, II, 2; *Opere*, I, 280.   [54]*Ibid.*, I, 49; *Opere*, I, 242.

[55]*Discursus florentinarum rerum post mortem junioris Laurentii Medices*, ed. S. Bertelli; *Opere*, I, 267–69.   [56]*Arte della guerra*, I; *Opere*, II, 348.

[57]*Discorsi*, I, 16; III, 7, 8; *Istor. fior.*, II, 13, 25; III, 25; IV, 1, 19; VIII, 29; *Opere*, I, 174, 412, 416; VII, 157, 176, 263, 271, 299, 562.

[58]*Il principe*, V; *Istor. fior.*, VIII, 8; *Opere*, I, 28–29; VII, 521.

[59]*Discorsi*, I, 52; II, 2; *Istor. fior.*, II, 34; III, 20; V, 6; VI, 13; *Opere*, I, 247, 281; VII, 192, 254, 335–36, 406.   [60]*Istor. fior.*, II, 34; *Opere*, VII, 192.

[61]*Discorsi*, I, 29; *Opere*, I, 199.   [62]*Istor. fior.*, III, 13; *Opere*, VII, 237.

[63]*Discorsi*, I, 17, 29, 40; III, 3; *Istor. fior.*, II, 4; *Opere*, I, 117–78, 199, 224, 386; VII, 144.

[64]*Discorsi*, II, 2; *Istor. fior.*, VI, 13; *Opere*, I, 279; VII, 406.

[65]*Discorsi*, I, 57; *Arte della guerra*, I; *Opere*, I, 260; II, 346.

[66]*Discorsi*, I, 16, 28, 35, 47; II, 2; III, 5, 8; *Istor. fior.*, II, 35, 40; VIII, 22; *Opere*, I, 175, 196, 212, 239, 283, 389, 414; VII, 194, 207, 549.

[67]*Discorsi*, I, 52; *Opere*, I, 247.

[68]*Ibid.*, 16, 17, 46; III, 2, 3; *Opere*, I, 175, 177–78, 235, 385, 386.

[69]*Ibid.*, I, 2, 17; *Istor. fior.*, V, 6; *Opere*, I, 134, 177–78; VII, 335–36.

preserved and maintained.[70] As in the case of the independence of the state as a whole, the preserving and maintaining of its internal *libertà* is discussed by Machiavelli more often than any of the other vicissitudes of freedom.

While Machiavelli's use of *libertà* in connection with internal affairs thus parallels his use of *libertà* with reference to corporate autonomy, in the former context he also has recourse to a number of other terms which he uses interchangeably with *libertà* or in close association with it. Side by side with terms such as *stato libero, comune libero, popolo libero,* and *città libera*[71] we find terms such as *vivere politico, vivere civile,* and *vivere libero;*[72] and Machiavelli often refers to such states as *bene ordinati* or as possessing *buoni ordini* or *buone leggi.*[73] These cognates of *libertà,* as a number of scholars have noted, connote not merely certain institutional forms, but also, and preeminently, civic virtues, such as a respect for law and order and a concern for the common weal.[74] Insofar as Machiavelli identifies liberty with these ideas, his conception of *libertà* is rooted less in a consistent and dogmatic constitutionalism than in the principles and values which institutions may serve in a variety of kinds of states.

While Machiavelli refers to *libertà* within the state on a few rare occasions in an unspecified sense[75] and on two occasions as an attribute of a class or group within a given community—in particular, as the power of the lower classes[76] and the *Parte Guelfa*[77] to influence or control events in Florence—he usually applies the term to communi-

---

[70]*Discorsi,* I, 4, 5, 7, 16, 17, 18, 23, 29, 40, 49; II, 2; III, 2, 3, 49; *Istor. fior.,* II, 6, 21; VI, 23, 24; *Opere,* I, 137, 138, 139–40, 146, 173–76, 177–78, 179–80, 188–89, 199, 229, 235, 241–42, 283, 385, 386, 504; VII, 146, 168, 423, 425–26.

[71]*Discorsi,* I, 4, 7, 8, 16, 17, 18, 25, 29; III, 3, 12; *De rebus pistoriensibus,* ed. S. Bertelli; *Istor. fior.,* I, 8; II, 13, 35; III, 5; VII, 19; *Nature di uomini fiorentini; Opere,* I, 138, 146, 150, 174, 177, 179–80, 192, 200, 387, 426; II, 30; VII, 88, 157, 194, 219, 482; VIII, 220.

[72]*Il principe,* V; *Discorsi,* I, 2, 6, 16, 17, 23, 24, 25, 29, 49, 55; II, 2, 4, 19, 21, 30; III, 7, 8; *Parole da dirle sopra la provisione del danaio, fatto un poco di proemio e di scusa,* ed. S. Bertelli; *Istor. fior.,* II, 4, 18, 34; III, 5; V, 6; VI, 13; *Opere,* I, 28–29, 134, 141, 173, 177, 188–89, 191, 192–93, 199, 241, 255, 279–83, 288, 336, 341, 370, 412, 416; II, 62; VII, 144, 164, 192, 220–23, 335, 406.

[73]*Il principe,* XIX; *Discorsi,* I, 2, 4, 10, 17, 18, 37, 40, 49; II, 2; *Arte della guerra,* I; *Istor. fior.,* IV, 1; *Opere,* I, 77, 129–30, 133, 134, 137, 157–59, 177–78, 179–80, 218, 224, 241–42, 283; II, 339; VII, 271.

[74]This notion has been analyzed most fully by Whitfield, *Machiavelli,* 131–47; "On Machiavelli's Use of *Ordini,*" 22–39; Albertini, *loc. cit.,* 53, 60–61, 62–63; Federico Chabod, *Machiavelli and the Renaissance,* trans. David Moore (London, 1960), 97; Hexter, "*Il principe* and *lo stato,*" 133–34; Prezzolini, *Machiavelli,* 56; Sasso, *loc. cit.,* 333–34; Scolari, *loc. cit.,* 52–53. A similar point with respect to the idea of power has recently been made by Gray, "Machiavelli," *The Responsibility of Power,* 39.

[75]*Discorsi,* I, 23, 49; *Istor. fior.,* III, 1; *Opere,* I, 188–89, 241–42; VII, 213.

[76]*Istor. fior.,* III, 13; *Opere,* VII, 237.   [77]*Ibid.,* IV, 19; *Opere,* VII. 299.

ties as a whole, and especially to those possessing definite characteristics. There is a great deal of evidence pointing to an identification
of free communities with republics in Machiavelli's thought. Sometimes he achieves this identification in negative terms, contrasting
libertà with tyranny, monarchy, aristocracy, license, and factionalism by defining liberty simply as the absence of these conditions. At
other times he refers positively to certain institutional features of republics in describing *libertà*.

Tyranny is clearly antithetical to liberty for Machiavelli. He regards the institutions of the city of Genoa, which combine *libertà* and
tirannide, as distinctly anomalous.[78] He describes a group of disgrun-
tled Florentine citizens who urged Veri de' Medici in 1395 to effect a
coup d'état and to free them from the tyrannical rule of the current
government *(prendere lo stato e liberargli dalla tirannide).*[79] He notes
that Athens returned to *libertà* after the overthrow of the heirs of the
tyrant Pisistratus.[80] In these and many other passages he defines liberty as the absence or elimination of tyranny.[81]

Machiavelli also defines *libertà* as the absence of princely or monarchical rule, treating them on many occasions as clear antitheses.
Thus, he notes, when the Blacks of Florence asked the Pope in 1300
to send a man of royal blood to come and rule the city, the Whites
denounced the ploy as a conspiracy against freedom *(una congiura
contra al vivere libero).*[82] After the death of the last Visconti, when
the citizens of Milan set up a new government, some wanted a prince;
but the lovers of liberty *(quelli che arnavano la libertà)* wanted to live
in freedom *(vivere libero).*[83] Sometimes Machiavelli simply contrasts
liberta with princely rule without indicating approval or disapproval
of one arrangement or the other. Thus, he sets forth advice to the ruler of a newly conquered state, whether he governs by freedom or by
a principality *(per via di libertà o per via di principato).*[84] If it is hard
to preserve *uno stato libero,* he observes, it is also hard to preserve *uno
regno.*[85] It was more difficult for Florence to conquer the towns in
Tuscany, he considers, than for Venice to conquer the towns in the
Venetian *contado,* since the Venetian towns were unfree *(non libere),*
accustomed to living under princes, while Florence's neighbors were
all free cities *(tutte città libere).*[86]

More usually, Machiavelli is not content to contrast liberty with

[78] *Ibid*. VIII. 29; *Opere.* VII. 562.   [79] *Ibid.,* 111, 25; *Opere.* VII. 262.
[80] *Discorsi.* I, 2.28; II, 2: *Opere.* I. 134. 196 97. 279.
[81] *Ibid.,* 1. 2, 25, 28, 35; II, 2; III. 5.7, 8: *Istor. fior.,* III. 17, 20; IV, 1, 19.27. 28:
Opere. I. 132. 192 93, 195-96. 212. 279-83, 389. 412. 416; VII, 248, 254, 271,299, 312.
313.
[82] *Istor. fior.,* II, 18: *Opere.* VII, 164.
[83] *Ibid.,* VI. 13, 24; *Opere.* VII. 406. 425-26.   [84] *Discorsi,* I. 16; *Opere,* 1, 175.
[85] *Ibid.* III. 3; *Opere,* 1. 387.   [86] *Ibid.,* 12; *Opere.* I. 426.

monarchy, but rather makes a point of stressing that they are basically incompatible. People who are ruled by princes, he states, simply do not know how to live freely (*vivere libero non sanno*).[87] A people ruled by a prince, he argues, loses the habit of liberty, and, if it becomes emancipated, finds it difficult to preserve its newly gained freedom (*Uno popolo uso a vivere sotto uno principe, se per qualche accidente diventa libero, con difficultà mantiene la libertà*).[88] Thus, when Rome became free after overthrowing her kings, she lacked many establishments necessary for freedom (*che era necessario ordinare in favore della libertà*).[89] As in the case of Tuscany in ancient times, the more that a free people has enjoyed its liberty, the more it has hated the name of prince (*e tanto si godeva della sua libertà, e tanto odiava il nome di principe*).[90] The reason Machiavelli usually gives for the view that liberty cannot exist in a monarchy is that the rule of one man tends to be despotic and tyrannical. Thus, he observes, the lovers of Florence's liberty assumed automatically that the rule of the Duke of Athens would lead to an absolute government, a fear to which the Duke showed his sensitivity by stressing in his propaganda that he was not taking away the liberty of Florence but strengthening it.[91] Elsewhere he makes the same point by referring to princes and tyrants in one breath as if there were no difference between them.[92]

Machiavelli also expresses the idea that the rule of one man, even if he is not a prince or king, is incompatible with liberty. He chooses his examples from members of the Medici family and states his case both in the words of persons whose speeches he reports and in his own words. Thus, he notes, Piero Soderini, who had gained a reputation as a lover of liberty, refused to support Medici rule in Florence because he felt it would destroy that liberty; and, in even stronger terms, Giovan Francesco Strozzi described the rule of Piero de' Medici as tyranny.[93] Earlier, Rinaldo degli Albizzi had urged his fellow citizens to free the city (*liberare la patria*) from the threat of Cosimo de' Medici, who, he argued, would reduce Florence to slavery (*servitù*).[94] And Machiavelli himself states that the Pazzi conspiracy of 1478 failed to free Florence from Medici rule because Lorenzo's regime had deafened her ears to the cry of freedom, and it was no longer known there (*la libertà . . . in Firenze non era cognosciuta*).[95]

But Machiavelli is by no means consistent on this point. In discussing the problem of reforming an outmoded government in a free

---

[87] *Il principe*, V; *Opere*, I, 29.
[88] *Ibid.*, 2; *Opere*, I, 134.
[89] *Istor. fior.*, II, 34, 35; *Opere*, VII, 192–93, 194.
[90] *Ibid.*, I, 52; *Istor. fior.*, VII, 19; *Opere*, I, 247; VII, 482.
[94] *Istor. fior.*, IV, 28; *Opere*, VII, 313.

[88] *Discorsi*, I, 16; *Opere*, I, 173.
[90] *Ibid.*, II, 2; *Opere*, I, 279.
[92] *Discorsi*, II, 2; *Opere*, I, 280.
[95] *Ibid.*, VIII, 8; *Opere*, VII, 521.

city, he advises those who want to set up a new and free polity (*uno vivere nuovo e libero*), whether it be a republic or a monarchy (*o per via di republica o di regno*), to preserve some of its ancient customs, in contrast to those who want to set up a despotism (*potestà assoluta*), whom he advises to wipe the slate clean and start afresh.[96] Here he clearly distinguishes between monarchy and absolutism and includes monarchies, along with republics, among those states capable of internal freedom. Likewise, he asserts, Rome enjoyed liberty under monarchical rule, at least until Tarquinius Superbus despoiled her of all the liberty she had possessed under the other kings (*spogliò Roma di tutta quella libertà ch'ella aveva sotto gli altri re mantenuta*).[97] Kings promote liberty primarily by their legislation, according to Machiavelli. Thus, while Rome did not have the advantage of starting out with a Lycurgus whose establishments would guarantee her a long and free life (*che la potesse vivere lungo tempo libera*), Romulus and her other kings still issued ordinances conformable to a free government (*conformi ancora al vivere libero*);[98] and the ancestors of King Tullus and King Metius attempted to organize the city in such a way as to enable her to live freely for a long time and to make her citizens the defenders of their liberty (*per farla vivere lungamente libera e per fare i suoi cittadini difensori dalla loro libertà*).[99] Also, he notes, since most people want freedom in order to live securely (*desiderando la libertà per vivere sicuri*), a prince can satisfy their desires by ruling according to laws that guarantee security.[100]

At the same time, the rule of one man, even if he is not a king, and even if he is a Medici, is by no means necessarily tyrannical. A single ruler may, indeed, foster liberty. He does this in precisely the same way that kings do, by sage and prudent legislation. As Machiavelli notes, "It is true that when . . . by good fortune there arises in the city a wise, good, and powerful citizen who ordains laws whereby the animosities of the nobles and the people are calmed or whereby they are restrained from evil-doing, that city may be called free and that government may be judged stable and firm."[101]

Even when the role of a single ruler as a legislator and peacemaker is not specified, he may act as the liberator of his city from a government seen as tyrannical or oppressive. Thus, in a passage previously cited, Veri de' Medici was urged by a group of Florentine citizens in 1395 to seize the government and free them from tyranny.[102] Also, the Lombard towns substituted dukes for kings between the sixth and

---

[96] *Discorsi*, I, 25; *Opere*, I, 92–93.
[98] *Ibid.*, I, 2; *Opere*, I, 134.
[100] *Ibid.*, 16; *Opere*, I, 175.
[102] *Ibid.*, III, 25; *Opere*, VII, 262.

[97] *Ibid.*, III, 5; *Opere*, I, 389.
[99] *Ibid.*, 23; *Opere*, I, 188–89.
[101] *Istor. fior.*, IV, 1; *Opere*, VII, 271.

eighth centuries in order to be free states (*per essere stati liberi*),[103] although it is not at all clear that the regimes of Veri de' Medici or the Lombard dukes would be any less inclined to despotism than the governments they were designed to replace.

For Machiavelli, then, the antithesis between *libertà* and monarchies, principalities, and governments characterized by the rule of one man is not as clear cut as the antithesis between *libertà* and tyranny. He frequently describes monarchical government as inconsistent with liberty, and often defines liberty in contrast or opposition to it, on the grounds that monarchy tends to degenerate into arbitrary and absolute rule. On the other hand, he sometimes describes states ruled by one man, be he a citizen, a noble, or a king, as free governments, either because the ruler apparently has popular support or because he establishes wise and good laws that promote the internal harmony, general welfare, and longevity of his state.

Machiavelli also defines *libertà* negatively as the absence or elimination of aristocracy, although here, as in the case of principalities or states ruled by one man, he is extremely ambiguous, for he associates liberty with aristocracy almost as often as he opposes them to each other.[104] At times he criticizes the nobility severely as a menace to freedom. He describes nobles in general as promoters of slavery (*ministri ... della servitù*),[105] and notes that in ancient Corcyra they took away the people's liberty (*togliessono la libertà al popolo*).[106] He praises Giano della Bella, whose Ordinances of Justice in 1293 prevented the Florentine nobles from serving on the *Signoria*, as having freed the city from aristocratic tyranny (*dalla servitù de' potenti*).[107] Not only do the nobles have despotic inclinations themselves, they may also sin against liberty by cooperating with despotic princes. Thus, the aristocracy of ancient Heraclea urged Clearchus to return from exile and seize the people's *libertà*.[108]

On the other hand, Machiavelli sometimes identifies aristocracy with liberty. In a well known passage in the *Discorsi*, he restates the Aristotelian definition of the three major forms of government: the principality which degenerates into tyranny, the aristocracy which degenerates into oligarchy, and the popular government which degenerates into licentiousness.[109] In a less frequently cited passage in *Il*

---

[103]*Ibid.*, I, 8; *Opere*, VII, 88.

[104]A good recent study of Machiavelli's view of aristocracy is by Alfredo Bonadeo, "The Role of the 'Grandi' in the Political World of Machiavelli," *Studies in the Renaissance*, XVI (1969), 12–30.

[105]*Istor. fior.*, IV, 1; *Opere*, VII, 271. [106]*Discorsi*, II, 2; *Opere*, I, 283.

[107]*Istor. fior.*, II, 13; *Opere*, VII, 157. [108]*Discorsi*, I, 16; *Opere*, I, 174.

[109]*Ibid.*, I, 2; *Opere*, I, 130–31. The schema of principality, aristocracy, and popular government is also in *Parole da dirle*. *Opere*, II, 57.

principe, he defines the three major forms of government as princely rule, liberty, and licence (*o principato o libertà o licenzia*),[110] thus appearing to assimilate aristocracy to freedom. Further, if nobles, as noted above, are willing to betray the liberty of the people to a despot, they are also capable of acting as the people's liberators (*suoi liberatori*) from tyranny.[111] Thus, while the nobles sometimes try to increase their power at the expense of the people, they can also serve the people's interests, and can act as a mean between the extremes of autocracy and mob rule.

The people themselves have an ambivalent relationship to liberty. Machiavelli asserts that the desires of a free people are seldom injurious to liberty (*I desiderii de' popoli liberi rade volte sono perniziosi alla libertà*).[112] After raising the question of whether the people or the nobles are better guardians of liberty he concludes that the people are; since they wish not to dominate others but merely to be left alone, they have a stronger motivation toward freedom (*maggiore voluntà di vivere liberi*).[113] On the other hand, he observes that the people revere freedom in name only, wishing in reality to submit neither to the rule of law nor to the rule of men (*della libertà solamente il nome ... è celebrato, desiderando ... non essere nè alle leggi nè agli uomini sottoposto*).[114] Thus, for Machiavelli, it is not surprising that when the constitutional crisis in Milan brought on by the ending of the Visconti regime led to a *coup d'état* by the masses (*licenza*), the city failed to preserve her liberty, and its seizure by a despot was a foregone conclusion.[115]

Finally, Machiavelli defines *libertà* negatively in opposition to factions. But, in this case also, he points to circumstances in which factions may promote liberty as well as to circumstances in which they impede or destroy it. Freedom and factionalism are incisively contrasted in a speech Machiavelli reports as given in 1372 by a Florentine citizen who charges that the Italian cities of the day have organized themselves not as free but as divided into factions (*non come libere ma come divise in sètte*). The speaker asserts that factionalism is inimical to liberty, since the parties do not seek laws and policies directed to the common good but only the gratification of their own ambitions. He therefore urges the suppression of factions and their replacement by means of laws suited to a free and law abiding community (*vivere libero*).[116] Machiavelli notes that the conflicts between the popular and senatorial parties in Rome led to the destruction of her

---

[110] *Il principe*, IX; *Opere*, I, 45.
[112] *Ibid.*, 4; *Opere*, I, 138.
[114] *Istor. fior.*, IV, 1; *Opere*, VII, 271.
[116] *Istor. fior.*, III, 5; *Opere*, VII, 219, 220-23.

[111] *Discorsi*, I, 2; *Opere*, I, 132.
[113] *Ibid.*, 5; *Opere*, I, 138, 139-40.
[115] *Ibid.*, VI, 24; *Opere*, VII, 425-26.

freedom (*furono cagione della rovina del vivere libero*) at the time of the Gracchi.[117] He observes that a newly freed state is particularly liable to partisanship inimical to its liberty, a point he illustrates with several examples.[118] The main reason why factions undermine liberty, according to Machiavelli, is that they breed internal weakness and corruption in the body politic, which render the community too vitiated to maintain the liberty it already possesses or to enter into a free life if it is enfranchised.[119]

At the same time, Machiavelli asserts, in states that are healthy and uncorrupted, factional conflicts not only are harmless, but are positively beneficial to the freedom and vitality of the community. In Rome, for example, dissension between the Senate and the people produced laws favoring liberty,[120] as a consequence of which the freedom of the state was established more firmly (*per le quali si stabilisse più la libertà di quello stato*).[121] Thus, when the Roman people recovered their freedom after the fall of the Decemvirs, many different parties arose to defend liberty (*difendere la libertà*).[122] While maintaining that the factional rivalries between the patricians and the plebeians were one of the reasons why Rome remained free for so long (*cause del tenere libera Roma*), Machiavelli admits that such rivalries do create a certain amount of tumult. Nonetheless, he states categorically that in Rome all the laws made in favor of liberty arose from this disunity (*tutte le leggi che si fanno in favore della libertà, nascano dalla disunione loro*). He defends this view in the following terms:

Neither can one rightly call a republic disordered in any way where there are so many examples of virtue. For good examples arise from good education, good education arises from good laws, and good laws arise from these tumults, which many uncritically condemn. For he who examines their outcome well will not find that they led to any exile or violence disadvantageous to the common good, but to laws and ordinances beneficial to public freedom.[123]

Machiavelli's distinction between the negative and positive effects of factionalism on liberty seems to rest on the question of whether the state in which factions operate is corrupt or uncorrupted. In an uncorrupted state, factional conflict is productive of freedom and civic virtue, but elsewhere it leads to corruption which in turn leads to the erosion of civic virtue and the loss of liberty. While providing a rationale for the fact that factions may have different effects in differ-

---

[117]*Discorsi*, I, 6; *Opere*, I, 141.
[118]*Ibid.*, 16; *Opere*, I, 173–76.   [119]*Ibid.*, 17; *Opere*, I, 177–78.
[120]*Ibid.*, 37; *Opere*, I, 218.   [121]*Ibid.*, 40; *Opere*, I, 224.   [122]*Ibid.*, 46; *Opere*, I, 235.
[123]*Ibid.*, 4; *Opere*, I, 136–37.

ent historical circumstances, Machiavelli's reasoning on this point still fails to explain how an uncorrupted state, like Rome, could grow corrupt enough so that factionalism, which had earlier been a sign and cause of her political health and freedom, could become the cause of the collapse of her liberty in the era of the Gracchi.

In addition to Machiavelli's various negative definitions of liberty he has a strong tendency to identify it positively with republics. This tendency can be seen in his repeated references to Brutus as the father of liberty and as the liberator of his people.[124] Machiavelli connects *libertà* with specific characteristics of republican constitutions. In particular, he notes, freedom in republics is associated with the ability of the people to make their own laws and to consent to government policy.[125] It is also associated with officials and magistrates who are elected, not appointed,[126] and whose power is delegated by the people through unmanaged elections. Genoa, he observes, when she was free (*quando la vive nella sua libertà*), elected her Doge by free elections (*per suffragi liberi*). A republic cannot be considered free without such means for the expression of the public will.[127] Free republics also need legal mechanisms for enforcing the laws, for penalizing citizens who attempt to contravene the public order and the general good, for calling the rulers to account, and for redressing the grievances of the ruled. Commenting on the popular institutions of Pistoia, Machiavelli observes that if it did not have legal channels for penalizing graft the commune would not be free at all (*il comune ne sia al tutto libero*).[128] He approves of the proscription of immoral officials in Rome by the Censors, and praises this office as one of the provisions which helped keep Rome free (*che aiutarono tenere Roma libera*).[129] He goes into some detail on the need for legally instituted guardians of liberty, concluding, as noted above, that this responsibility is best vested in the people,[130] and he defines the functions of the guardians as the prosecution of any citizen, official, or group that sins in any way against free government (*quando peccassono in alcuna cosa allo stato libero*).[131]

Another institution essential to the maintenance of republican

---

[124]*Ibid.*, III, 1, 2, 3, 6; *Opere*, I, 384, 385, 386, 389. For other general identifications of liberty and republics: *ibid.*, II, 4, 21; *Istor. fior.*, VI, 13; *Opere*, I, 288, 341; VII, 406.

[125]*Il principe*, V; *Discursus florentinarum rerum*; *Opere*, I, 28–29; II, 261–63.

[126]*Discorsi*, I, 40, 46, 49; *Discursus florentinarum rerum*; *Istor. fior.*, VI, 23, 24; *Opere*, I, 229, 235, 242; II, 263, 267; VII, 423, 425–26.

[127]*Istor. fior.*, V, 6; *Opere*, VII, 335–36. On *suffragi liberi*: *Discorsi*, I, 20, 49; *Opere*, I, 185, 242.   [128]*De rebus pistoriensibus*; *Opere*, II, 30.

[129]*Discorsi*, I, 49; *Opere*, I, 241–42.   [130]*Ibid.*, 4–5; *Opere*, I, 138–40.

[131]*Ibid.*, 7; *Opere*, I, 146.

liberty is a strong citizen army. In this context, Machiavelli defends a citizen army not merely because he thinks it is more effective in the field than mercenaries but also because he thinks it reflects and reinforces civic virtue, and is hence appropriate to a free government.[132] A citizen army conscripted of amateurs, which should characterize a free republic, has more valor and self-respect, according to Machiavelli, than a professional standing army. Thus, he notes, while the Romans sometimes bought off their enemies under the empire, they never pursued this cowardly policy while they lived in freedom (*vissono liberi*).[133] In contrast to foreign mercenaries, who fight languidly and are easily suborned because they have no concern for the well-being of the city, citizen armies fight enthusiastically and have a patriotic *esprit de corps*. They manifest and strengthen civic virtue. Cities keep themselves uncorrupted (*immaculate*) much longer with citizen armies than without them.[134] While, as noted above, Machiavelli's case for a citizen army in the defense of corporate liberty is purely practical, his argument in the context of liberty within the state is based as much on moral as on practical grounds.

In analyzing the characteristics of free republics, Machiavelli does not merely fasten on a few assorted institutions. He also provides two systematic descriptions of free republican constitutions as a whole. Both of them pertain to Florence, one being drawn from her past history and the other being a reform proposal written by Machiavelli himself. In the thirteenth century, he notes, the Florentines united and agreed to form a free state (*pigliare forma di vivere libero*). The constitution they set up provided for an executive and legislative council of twelve citizens, representing equally six electoral districts and holding office for one year. Two non-Florentine judges were appointed, a *Capitano di Popolo* and a *Podestà*, to deal with civil and criminal cases respectively. Military ordinances were established subdividing the state into ninety-six districts for the conscription of a citizen army. The military leaders were changed annually. On this civil and military government, says Machiavelli, the Florentines founded their liberty.[135] Outside of the fact that the council and the army were composed of citizens, it is not too clear why he thinks that this constitution was free, for he does not indicate how the council was elected, by whom the judges were appointed, or whether the populace retained the right to scrutinize the activities and policies of the officials.

Machiavelli is much more detailed and specific in the tentative constitution for Florence which he wrote at the request of Pope Leo

---

[132]*Parole da dirle*; *Opere*, II, 62.

[133]*Discorsi*, II, 30; *Opere*, I, 370.   [134]*Arte della guerra*, I; *Opere*, II, 348.

[135]*Istor. fior.*, II, 4, 5; *Opere*, VII, 144, 145–46. This point has been noted by Baron, *Crisis*, 386.

X in about 1520. Machiavelli outlines a republic, giving a purely practical justification for it—the argument that it would be easier to establish than a principality, that it would preserve and increase Leo's
control over the city, and that it would enable him to secure and honor
his friends and to satisfy the people.[136] This argument is possibly attributable to the fact that Leo might plausibly have been expected to
support a return to the Medici system. In any event, Machiavelli pro-
poses the elimination of the current institutions in Florence and their
replacement by a hierarchy of three councils, a *Signoria*, a Council
of Two Hundred, and a Great Council of one thousand, or at least six
hundred. The main links among these councils are to be the offices of
Gonfalonieri and Provosts, who may veto decisions of the *Signoria*
and appeal them to the Two Hundred and who in turn may veto decisions of the Two Hundred and appeal them to the Great Council.[137]

Machiavelli offers two justifications in support of this polity, a polity which, he says, lacks nothing necessary to a republic.[138] In the
first place, he observes that there are three kinds of citizens, the important, the middle, and the lowest—distinctions, he stresses, which do
not prescind from the political egalitarianism characteristic of Florence but which refer to differences in the political ambitions of these
three groups. The three councils in his system are designed to accommodate these differences in ambition.[139] He also points out that
his provisions for veto and appeal enable the three groups to scrutinize
each other's actions, thus preventing the abuse of power by all
branches of the government.[140]

Machiavelli's constitution, however, is neither egalitarian nor
truly balanced. All governmental power is concentrated in the *Signoria* and the other two councils enjoy only residual functions or those
that the *Signoria* chooses to delegate to them. The membership of the
two upper councils is dominated by the wealthy upper guilds, and is to
be appointed by Leo for life. The membership of the Great Council
is also to be controlled by Leo, either by appointment or by electoral
management. The electoral procedures outlined for the *Gonfalonieri*
and Provosts by no means rule out the possibility of management in
these cases as well.[141] An economic and social oligarchy hence commands most of the power, tempered by the princely initiative of the
patron, with only a few symbolic gestures in the direction of participatory government and electoral franchise.

The fact that Machiavelli at some points connects the idea of freedom with a republic marked by broad participation in government and

---

[136]*Discursus florentinarum rerum*; *Opere*, II, 268–69.
     [137]*Ibid.*, 268–75.   [138]*Ibid.*, 274.
     [139]*Ibid.*, 267–69. Cf. *Parole da dirle*; *Opere*, II, 57, on Florence as an egalitarian
polity.   [140]*Discursus florentinarum rerum*; *Opere*, II, 268–75.   [141]*Ibid.*

at other points, as in the case of Florentine constitutions both actual
and hypothetical, with a narrow oligarchy of the rich[142] is somewhat
confusing. To a certain extent this confusion may be dispelled by a
closer look at the meaning of *republica* in his thought. Here Machiavelli diverges noticeably from his Florentine predecessors of the
trecento and *quattrocento*. A tradition of republican thinking existed
in Florence throughout the period, its emphasis shifting in response
to internal and external events and cultural interests. Thus, in the
trecento the republican principle could be advocated in terms of
Guelfism; in the early *quattrocento* Leonardo Bruni could justify it in
terms of Aristotelian ethics and on the grounds that it stimulated art
and literature; and at the end of the *quattrocento* Savonarola could
assimilate it to Christian moral reform. Notwithstanding these shifts,
the proponents of republicanism tended to conceive of the Florentine
republic in constitutional terms, identifying it with participatory
government. In some cases they even identified it with political equality and, like Machiavelli, did not hestitate to apply this description to
the Florentine government of their day without worrying too much
about the disparity between description and political fact.[143] While

[142]Machiavelli's oligarchical proclivities have been noted by Cadoni, *loc. cit.*,
466–72; Renaudet, *loc. cit.*, 189.

[143]Generalizations may be foolhardy considering the fact that scholarship on
this controversial subject is currently in a state of flux and revision. Debate centers on
the origins, constituents, and causes of Florentine republican theory in the *trecento*
and *quattrocento* as well as on the types of evidence apposite to these questions. Many
of the primary sources still remain unedited. A detailed consideration of the literature
would require an excursus not entirely germane to this paper. For further discussion:
Albertini, *loc. cit.*, 21–31, 37–45, 53–74; Baron, *Crisis, passim*, which includes references to Baron's other writings; Marvin B. Becker, "Florentine 'Libertas': Political
Independents and 'Novi Cives,' 1372–1378," *Traditio*, XVIII (1962), 393–407; "The
Republican City State in Florence: An Inquiry into Its Origin and Survival (1280–
1434)," *Speculum*, XXXV (Jan. 1960), 48–49; and more recently *Florence in Transi-
tion* (Princeton, 1967–68), I, *passim*; II, 18–22, 60–61, 93–149, 200, 204, 221, 223, 226–29;
Garin, *Italian Humanism*, 37–81; Felix Gilbert, *Machiavelli and Guicciardini:
Politics and History in Sixteenth-Century Florence* (Princeton, 1965), including
references to Gilbert's other writings; Peter Partner, "Florence and the Papacy in the
Earlier Fifteenth Century," *Florentine Studies: Politics and Society in Renaissance
Florence*, ed. Nicolai Rubinstein (London, 1968), 383; N. Rubinstein, "Florence and
the Despots: Some Aspects of Florentine Diplomacy in the Fourteenth Century,"
Transactions of the Royal Historical Society, 5th series, II (1952), 21–45; "Florentine Constitutionalism and Medici Ascendancy in the Fifteenth Century," *Florentine
Studies*, 445–60; "Political Ideas in Sienese Art: The Frescoes by Ambrogio Lorenzetti
and Taddeo di Bartolo in the Palazzo Pubblico," *Journal of the Warburg and Courtauld Institutes*, XXI (1958), 184–85; J. E. Siegel, " 'Civic Humanism' or Ciceronian
Rhetoric?" *Past and Present*, XXXIV (1966), 19–23; Donald Weinstein, "The Myth
of Florence," *Florentine Studies*, 24–44. For the Roman background: C. Wirszubski,
Libertas as a Political Idea at Rome during the Late Republic and Early Principate,
Cambridge Classical Studies (Cambridge, 1950), *passim* and esp. 3–4, 7–17, 27–30,
78–87, 95–127.

he is undoubtedly aware of the ideas of his Florentine predecessors, Machiavelli also uses *republica* in the sense derived by the Romans from its generic Latin meaning of *respublica*, the commonwealth or the common weal. Thus, Machiavelli feels free to apply the term *republica* to any kind of commonwealth regardless of its constitutional form. After defining the three major forms of government, he says that the founder of a state (*republica*) may choose from among the three.[144] He does not hesitate to call a monarchy, that of ancient Rome, a *republica*.[145] While any kind of polity can hence be a republic, the best kind of republic, he asserts, is a mixed government. Rome, for example, in developing from a monarchy to a popular government, retained some elements of monarchy and aristocracy, and thus, remaining mixed, formed a perfect republic (*rimanendo mista, fece una republica perfetta*).[146] On the other hand, Florence, which Machiavelli describes as having had mixed government under the Medici,[147] has not been a republic for two hundred years.[148]

Machiavelli provides an explanation for this startling and contradictory judgment. *Republica* is a norm, not merely a description. A republic is defined by its concern for the common weal: "It is not private interest but the common good that makes cities great. And without doubt this common good is observed only in republics, for they carry out everything that advances it."[149] A constitution, even if it embodies the best form of government, cannot make its people desire the common good. Lacking this overriding concern for the common weal, a state, even with all the institutional advantages, would be no republic at all.[150]

Machiavelli's somewhat ambiguous treatment of republics can be resolved to some extent by admitting the principle that the meaning of *republica* transcends specific institutional forms. The ambiguity in his handling of the relationship between *libertà* within the state and various institutional arrangements can be dealt with in the same way. As we noted above, there are circumstances under which Machiavelli thinks that virtually any kind of political arrangement, from tyranny to principality to aristocracy to popular rule to factions, can be detrimental to liberty. At the same time, there are circumstances under which all of these arrangements, with the exception of tyranny, are conducive to liberty. Free governments, thus, may take a variety of forms. Their parity lies not in their constitutional similarity, but in their objectives, their animating principles, their procedures, and the advantages they hold out to their citizens.

To illustrate this idea, Machiavelli often connects *libertà* with cer-

---

[144]*Discorsi*, I, 2; *Opere*, I, 130–31.   [145]*Ibid.*, 23; *Opere*, I, 188–89.
[146]*Ibid.*, 2; *Opere*, I, 133, 135.   [147]*Discursus florentinarum rerum*; *Opere*, II, 261–63.
[148]*Discorsi*, I, 49; *Opere*, I, 242.   [149]*Ibid.*, II, 2; *Opere*, I, 280.
[150]*Discursus florentinarum rerum*; *Opere*, II, 263–64.

tain personal rights and community benefits that characterize free states regardless of their constitutions. He clearly identifies freedom with the protection of private rights. One has a right to one's good name, and in free cities (*nelle città libere*) there is legal recourse against slander.[151] One also has the right to the freedom and security of one's person and one's property and to those of one's family: "The common advantage provided by a free polity . . . is to be able to enjoy freely one's own possessions without suspicion, not to worry about the honor of one's women and children, and not to fear for oneself."[152] Another common advantage enjoyed by free communities is the increase of power and wealth, which, according to Machiavelli, occurs only in free states (*Si vede per esperienza che le cittadi non avere mai ampiato nè di dominio nè di richezza se non mentre sono state in libertà*). Free states tend toward growth and prosperity, he says, because their people are secure. Thus, they have many children, confident that they will be able to make careers for themselves on the basis of ability, and they work hard, confident that they will be able to enjoy the fruits of their labor.[153]

This sense of security and confidence is a reflection of the civic virtue animating free communities. A state cannot long be free if it is corrupt;[154] and, if uncorrupted, it will be able to benefit even from factionalism, which otherwise would be a grave menace to liberty.[155] As noted above, Machiavelli holds that the high level of civic virtue attained in ancient Rome enabled her to endure for a long time as a free state; in the present he praises the imperial cities of Germany for the honesty, goodness, and friendliness of their people, which virtues explain, he says, why so many of them live freely.[156] A free state enhances its civic virtue and preserves itself from corruption from within as well as conquest from without by instituting a citizen army,[157] by giving appropriate rewards and punishments to its citizens,[158] and above all by subordinating private interests to the well-being of the whole.[159]

[151]*Discorsi*, I, 8; *Opere*, I, 150.

[152]*Ibid.*, 16; *Opere*, I, 173-74. This point has also been noted by Abraham, *loc. cit.*, 29; Cadoni, *loc. cit.*, 479-80, although he sees this security as available only in a republic; Prezzolini, *Machiavelli*, 56; Renaudet, *loc. cit.*, 186, 188-90; Russo, *loc. cit.*, 217-18, although he interprets this security in terms of hedonism; Scolari, *loc. cit.*, 49, 53.

[153]*Discorsi*, II, 2; *Opere*, I, 279-83.   [154]*Ibid.*, I, 16, 29; *Opere*, I, 173, 199-200.

[155]*Ibid.*, 17; *Discursus florentinarum rerum*; *Opere*, I, 178; II, 263-64.

[156]*Discorsi*, I, 55; II, 19; *Opere*, I, 255, 336.

[157]*Ibid.*, II, 30; *Arte della guerra*, I; *Opere*, I, 370; II, 348.

[158]*Discorsi*, I, 16, 24, 29; III, 28; *Opere*, I, 173, 191, 199-200, 463.

[159]*Ibid.*, I, 4, 18; *Istor. fior.*, III, 5, 25; *Opere*, I, 137, 179-80; VII, 220-23, 262. This point has been noted by Albertini, *loc. cit.*, 62-63; Chabod, *loc. cit.*, 97; Hexter, "*Il principe* and *lo stato*," 133-34; Whitfield, "On Machiavelli's Use of *Ordini*," 34-35.

In fact the promotion of the common good can be called the norm of *libertà* within the state just as it is the norm of the *republica*. Free states are characterized by good rulers who promote liberty by ordaining just and wise legislation which conduces to the welfare of the community at large.[160] The common weal and the liberty of the community are served not merely by prudent policy. Like the private rights of the individual, they are guaranteed by the law. The law is the means of instituting *libertà*; it is also the bastion of the citizens against arbitrary government, narrow partisan interests, violent breaches of the peace, and internecine strife. Hence the crucial importance for Machiavelli of *buoni ordini* and of the well ordered state, which he so often associates with *libertà*, and which can manifest itself in a wide number of governmental forms.[161] Hence also the importance of the rule of law, the guarantee that known and legally instituted procedures will be followed, that criticism and dissent will respect the needs of public order and the powers of duly constituted authorities, and that the laws will be binding and enforceable on all without distinction.[162] The rule of law may likewise characterize states with a wide variety of constitutional forms, ranging from that of the Roman Empire to the Italian city-state republic. But in all cases it is the security of the individual and the uncorrupted health, growth, and well-being of the whole community, as instituted by good laws lawfully administered by good men, that Machiavelli sees as the principles underlying *liberta* within the state in the broadest sense.

Conclusion. In summarizing Machiavelli's idea of *libertà* it is evident that some aspects of Machiavellian liberty are rather simple and straightforward while one aspect, the question of *libertà* within the state, is quite complex. Machiavelli's nontechnical uses of *libertà* are commonplace and need not detain us. When he deals with *libertà* in connection with free will, however, he adopts a position that is in some respects conventional and in other respects distinctively his own. Along with other commentators on the traditional *topos* of *libero arbitrio* versus determinism, Machiavelli places a high valuation on free will as a manifestation of human independence and as a condition necessary for meaningful moral choices. At the same time, the kinds of choices made possible by *libero arbitrio* are not, for Machiavelli, directed primarily to the perfection of the intellect and the spirit, and are not oriented to transcendent moral goals. Rather, they involve the

---

[160]*Discorsi*, I, 10; *Istor. fior.*, IV, 1; *Opere*, I, 157–59; VII, 271.

[161]*Il principe*, XIX; *Discorsi*, I, 2, 16, 17, 37, 40; II, 2; *Arte della guerra*, I; *Istor. fior.*, IV, 1; *Opere*, I, 77, 129–30, 133, 134, 175, 177, 218, 224, 280; II, 339; VII, 271. This point has been noted by Whitfield, "On Machiavelli's Use of *Ordini*," *loc. cit.*, 30, 31, 33–35, 38–39.

[162]*Discorsi*, I, 7, 10, 29; *De rebus pistoriensibus*; *Istor. fior.*, II, 21, 40; III, 5; IV, 1; *Opere*, I, 146, 157–59, 200; II, 30; VII, 168, 207, 220–23, 271.

development of all the capacities possessed by the individual and are oriented to the imposition of his will on the course of history.

On the other hand, Machiavelli's ideas of corporate *libertà* are fully traditional. They are completely consistent with the medieval and *trecento* conception of corporate *libertates* derived ultimately from Roman corporation theory. For Machiavelli, as for his medieval predecessors, the desirability of corporate liberty as a value in itself is a foregone conclusion and does not require any justification. The only noticeable difference between the two is the fact that Machiavelli concentrates almost exclusively on city-state corporations, and emphasizes the numerous threats to their autonomy which, he feels, must be counteracted by strong military institutions. In this connection he stresses the need for citizen armies, a classical and humanistic theme, but he bases this preference here on the purely practical argument that they are more successful in the field than are other kinds of troops.

When he discusses *libertà* within the state, however, Machiavelli shows little dependence on medieval ideas of liberty, but instead reveals a close dependence on the Roman past as well as on his immediate forebears in the Italian *trecento* and *quattrocento*. Machiavelli sometimes defines liberty within the state in institutional terms, both positively in association with republican institutions and negatively in opposition to tyranny, principality, aristocracy, popular rule, and factions. At other times he indicates that all of these political structures, except tyranny, are capable of fostering liberty. To the extent that this inconsistency can be resolved, and there is no point in assuming that Machiavelli is or needs to be completely consistent, it can be done by referring both republics and free states in general to the legal principles and moral ideals which promote internal and external security, order, prosperity, and civic virtue. Thus, Machiavelli lays heavy emphasis on the protection of private legal rights and the promotion of the common weal, which is as close as he gets to proposing an inclusive norm for judging a polity free.

Machiavelli treats liberty within the state principally in his *Discorsi* and *Istorie fiorentine,* and to a lesser extent in *Il principe,* the *Arte della guerra,* and his *Discursus fiorentinarum rerum.* The character and intention of the works in which passages on liberty within the state occur take on a significance which they do not have in his discussions of free will or corporate liberty, and his handling of the theme of liberty within the state serves in a number of cases as an implicit commentary on the audiences for whom these works were written.

Wherever found in his works, Machiavelli's references to liberty within the state indicate that he regards *libertà* as a positive value and as the norm of the good state, whether defined in institutional or moral

terms. Following in the footsteps of the Romans and the civic humanists, he does not view liberty as an end in itself, as an abstract idea, or
as a natural right. His justifications for liberty, like theirs, are fairly
concrete; in all cases liberty is valued because of its beneficial effects
on the individual and the community. Although Machiavelli stands
closer to the *trecento* and *quattrocento* than to ancient Rome in point
of time, his ideas on liberty within the state are much more a
thoroughgoing revival of the Roman point of view than a simple
perpetuation of the views of his immediate predecessors.[163]

Machiavelli restores the Roman focus on liberty as the enjoyment
of private legal rights, a notion present in both the republican and imperial eras of Roman history.[164] With the Romans, he defines liberty
as the security of the individual and the protection of hearth and home,
and enshrines the law as the greatest guarantee of liberty, a point not
emphasized by previous Florentine political writers. Machiavelli is
also much more flexible than the *quattrocento* humanists in his use of
the term *republica*, although both are capable of stretching the concept of participatory government to accommodate more or less
oligarchical Florentine constitutions both actual and hypothetical.
Fully at home in the recent Italian past, Machiavelli uses Roman history quite freely to support his theories. He shares with his Florentine predecessors the Renaissance taste for a selective and *ad hoc* use
of classical precedents; having, as they do, a civic cause to argue, he
seeks not to exhume Caesar but to blame him. He is well aware, however, of the humanists' reduction of *libertà* to a propaganda slogan,
and reflects this awareness with ironic wit by putting *libertà* into the
mouths of rebels, aggressors, and defenders of the *status quo* regardless of the nature of the regimes they propose to install or perpetuate.[165]
Machiavelli's approach to republican liberty is much broader than
that of the *quattrocento* theorists. While they define the republic in
exclusively institutional terms, Machiavelli, like the Romans, views it
sometimes in institutional terms, in which context he sees it as the
bastion against tyranny, and sometimes, like his *trecento* predecessors, in literal terms as the common weal, in which context he associates it with good rulers, good laws, and lawful procedures, which can
be found in any well ordered state regardless of its constitutional form.

While Machiavelli's wholesale restoration of Roman justifications for liberty shows a distinct broadening of his approach in com-

---

[163]Cf., on the other hand, Albertini, *loc. cit.*, 53–74; Baron, *Crisis, passim*; Gilbert,
Machiavelli and Guicciardini, 28–200; Renaudet, *loc. cit.*, 188–89.

[164]Fritz Schulz, *Principles of Roman Law* (Oxford, 1936), 140–63, provides a useful summary of this question and a helpful introduction to the literature.

[165]E.g., *Istor. fior.*, II, 35; III, 25, 27; VII, 19, 26; VIII, 34; *Opere*, VII, 194, 262,
266, 482, 492, 571.

parison with that of the *trecento* and *quattrocento* writers, in other respects his point of view is narrower if less doctrinaire than theirs. Although he retains the Aristotelian definition of the forms of government and the Aristotelian norm of the common weal, he omits the Aristotelian moral rationale for the republic adopted by some *quattrocento* humanists. For Machiavelli the moral corollaries of liberty rest in the civic virtue of the whole community expressed in its concern for the common good, not in the moral perfection of the individual achieved through his participation in politics. He retains in this connection only the idea that participation in a citizen army increases the civic virtue of the individual and of the community, but even here offers practical reasons for a citizen army as well. Machiavelli also limits the cultural justification for free government advocated by Leonardo Bruni and his followers. Culture has only the most tenuous connection with liberty for Machiavelli, and only in the limited sense in which a civic religion and an educational system that indoctrinate civic virtue may be called culture. He certainly adduces no artists or men of letters to demonstrate the advantages of republics.

In place of the perfection of the spirit and the immortality of art, Machiavelli offers two more original justifications for free government, which distinguish his idea of liberty from both that of his Florentine predecessors and that of the Romans. One is the idea that a free state is more dynamic economically and politically than an unfree state. The other is the idea that a free, well ordered state where individual ambitions and partisan rivalries are subordinated to the common good is better able to preserve its autonomy in the face of foreign aggression than its opposite. Since it is stable and harmonious within, it will be able to maintain a united front to the world outside. These two justifications he could have found in *trecento* political theory,[166] but he bases them on purely practical and empirical grounds, claiming to have inferred them from experience.[167] But, while the practical, "realistic" Machiavelli is often regarded as having abandoned the idealism of the *quattrocento* and of having submerged the individual in the group, by restoring a fuller appreciation of the Roman idea of liberty he also resurrects the centrality of the legal rights of the individual and reemphasizes the supremacy of the common good as the norms of *libertà* within the state.

Oberlin College.*

[166]Rubinstein, "Political Ideas in Sienese Art," 184.   [167]Sasso, *loc. cit.*, 334–44.

*This paper was delivered at the Sixth Conference on Medieval Studies, The Medieval Institute, Western Michigan University, Kalamazoo, Michigan, 18 May 1971.

X

TRUST AND DECEIT IN MACHIAVELLI'S COMEDIES

By Martin Fleisher

In a letter to his friend Soderini, Machiavelli makes the following general obesrvation: "When Fortune becomes weary, ruin follows. A family, a city, the fortune of each is based on its way of proceeding, and when it tires, it must be revived with a different method." [1] But, he adds, to be on fortune's side all the time is to be able to change with every change in fortune. Machiavelli implies this may not be possible. It would, for example, require one and the same person to perform such psychological gymnastics as to be, in quick and arbitrary succession, cruel and merciful, pious and impious. Later, in this same letter, he flatly states that it is impossible for men always to change to fit the requirements of new situations. "But as times and events are always changing, both as a whole and in detail, and men cannot change their attitudes or unlearn their ways, it happens that they sometimes have good fortune, and sometimes bad." [2]

Thus constancy, the ancient and classical virtue of steadfastness in the face of changing fortune, no longer appears to be held in high esteem by Machiavelli. The pity is not that men alter with the changing times, but that they cannot do so. The truly wise man, in diametric contrast to the Stoic sage, would understand the times and events and accommodate his ways to them. In consequence, he would always experience good fortune.[3] To Machiavelli, wisdom appears to be the ability to understand the particular situation in which one finds oneself without being misled by wishes (*fantasie*) and to change one's way (*modo del procedere*) in order to exploit the situation in one's interest.[4]

These reflections on men and events had a specific and personal bearing on the condition and prospects of the correspondents. At the time Machiavelli wrote to Soderini the fortunes of both had dramatically declined. Soderini had been Gonfaloniere of Florence when Machiavelli was Florentine secretary in charge of the second Chancery of the republic. He was now in exile, driven there by the Medici, who had reestablished their control of Florence. And his ally, Machia-

---

[1] J. R. Hale, trans. and ed., *The Literary Works of Machiavelli* (Oxford, 1961), 128. Hereafter cited as *Hale*. The letter is lost; what has come down to us is a draft copy. The Italian: "Come la fortuna si stracca, così si rovina. La famiglia, la citta, ognuno ha la fortuna sua fondata sul modo del procedere suo, e ciascuna di loro si stracca, e quando la e stracca, bisogna racquistarla con un altro modo." G. Mazzoni e M. Casella, ed., *Tutte le Opere di Niccolò Machiavelli* (Firenze, 1929), 879. Hereafter cited as *Opere*. It will be noted that Hale omits a phrase, viz., "and the fortune of each does tire," in his translation.   [2] *Hale*, 129.

[3] *Opere*, 880.   [4] *Ibid.*, 879.

velli, held in suspicion by the Medici, had been turned out of office. In these circumstances is there not some consolation for Soderini and for Machiavelli in the latter's insistence that no man can change with every change in fortune and, therefore, cannot be successful on every occasion? If all that can be asked of a person in such crises is that "each man must do what his spirit prompts" and do it "with audacity," [5] both Soderini and Machiavelli can take some comfort in their conduct under fire. But Machiavelli refuses to convert this into a philosophy of consolation. Almost in the same breath in which he makes this observation he implies that the responsibility for fortune is one's own and is not to be foisted "on the heavens and the hand of fate." [6] There are no compensations for failures and losses in this world, in a hereafter, in internal peace of mind, or in a private world of pleasure. In other words, the losses that we suffer are as real as the gains we enjoy; both are the very stuff of life, as are the feelings associated with them. The psyche, therefore, cannot be inured to or purged of these disturbances by a philosophical or religious discipline. It is of little avail to try to ignore or to try to rise above these misfortunes; the only course open to the loser is to endeavor to recoup his fortune.

It would appear, as Machiavelli intimates when he talks of fortune growing weary, that it is in the nature of things for one's fortune to be sapped. This idea of fortune becoming weary is linked to Machiavelli's notion that both desires and circumstances change. From one perspective the wearying *of* one's fortune is merely the obverse of the weariness *with* one's fortune. Incapable of permanent satisfaction, men always grow weary with their fortune. This is one possible starting point of the decline of fortune leading to ultimate ruin. Since fortune is grounded in a way of doing things, to regain one's fortune, or to halt its further decline, involves the adoption of different ways.

These, in brief, are some of Machiavelli's thoughts on fortune and on the wishes and ways of men. Now, one of the most interesting features of the letter to Soderini is Machiavelli's application of his general observations to the family as well as to the city. He would seem to be saying that with respect to these observations there is no difference between the public life of the city and the private life of the family. I propose to follow up the hint in this letter and to analyze Machiavelli's writings for his idea of the nature of the private life of the family, as the first step in a systematic exploration of the problem of the moral and political realms in Machiavelli. Before beginning the analysis it will be useful to review some traditional interpretations of this problem.

[5] *Hale*, 127. With slight change. The Italian is "Che ognuno faccia quello che gli detta l'animo, e con audacia." *Opere*, 879.   [6] Hale, 128.

A commonplace in the vast literature devoted to the interpretation of Machiavelli is that he *does* separate the public and private, or
the political and moral realms. Sabine, in his standard text, talks of
"Machiavelli's separation of political expediency from morality." [7]
But Sabine dissociates himself from the tradition which roots this
separation in Machiavelli's immoralism. "For the most part he is
not so much immoral as non-moral. He simply abstracts politics from
other considerations and writes of it as if it were an end in itself." [8]
Allen finds ambiguity in the cliché that Machiavelli separates ethics
and politics and also in Machiavelli's own position. However, he is
willing to suggest a way of getting beyond these ambiguities. "It
would be more accurate to say that he separated political ethics from
the ethics of social life, by applying the same principle to both." [9]
This principle is that goodness consists in promoting welfare, where
welfare consists in "security for person and property." [10] This very
principle, Allen indicates, entails different rules of conduct for the
individual and for the government: "The morality of politics cannot
be that of private life." [11]

Beginning with Ranke, XIXth-century German historical literature locates Machiavelli's particular contribution to western thought
in the idea of the independence of the realm of the state and of its
guiding principles. Coming at the end of this tradition, and no longer
as sanguine as some of his fellow countrymen about the mission of
the state, Meinecke's history of the doctrine of *raison d'état* represents one conclusion of this tradition. He identifies the idea of reason
of state in Machiavelli's writings with the justification of the use of
state power for purposes of political "regeneration." This idea of the
"curative" use of power Meinecke sees linked to an "idealist" concept of the state. However, Meinecke contends, in addition to this
idealist element, Machiavelli's notion of reason of state also contains
the conflicting notion of power unrestrained by any ethical considerations. The breach between the political and the moral spheres which
was to manifest itself in the phenomenon of Machiavellianism,
Meinecke insists, was already latent in Machiavelli's own writings.[12]

Although Cassirer works in a Kantian tradition alien to Meinecke's historicism, he comes to a closely related conclusion on the
import of Machiavelli's thought. "The political world has lost its
connection not only with religion or metaphysics but also with all
the other forms of man's ethical and cultural life." [13]

[7] G. H. Sabine, *A History of Political Theory* (New York, 1937), 340. [8] *Ib.*, 339.
[9] J. W. Allen, *A History of Political Thought in the Sixteenth Century* (London,
1951), 472.
[10] *Ibid.*, 471.   [11] *Ibid.*, 472.
[12] F. Meinecke, *Machiavellism: The Doctrine of Raison d'Etat and its Place in
Modern History*, trans. D. Scott (London, 1957), Ch. I.
[13] E. Cassirer, *The Myth of the State* (New Haven, 1961), 140 .

Obviously, the resolution of the problem of the nature, status, and relation of the public and private worlds, and of the political and moral domains, is central to an understanding of Machiavelli. It is now time to turn to the one facet of this problem which will concern us: Machiavelli's idea of private life as found in his notion of the family. And since Machiavelli himself proclaims the function of comedy to be to hold up a mirror to private life,[14] it is quite natural to turn to his comedies for the material for this study.

All three of Machiavelli's plays are comedies. Of these, two are linked to the Greek new comedy by way of Roman intermediaries. *Andria* is Machiavelli's faithful translation of Terence's *The Woman of Andros* [15] which, in turn, adheres closely to a comedy by Menander. In *Clizia*, while basing himself on Plautus' *Casina*, itself an adaptation of a Greek comedy by Diphilus, Machiavelli freely introduces elements of his own invention. The *Mandragola*, on the other hand, is the single original comedy by Machiavelli. Chance has thus presented us with an unusual opportunity to control the identification and analysis of Machiavelli's ideas as discovered in his comedies. *Clizia* is crucial in this respect. The very fact that it is an adaptation enhances its usefulness by permitting us to note the changes between Plautus' text and Machiavelli's version and to assess the significance of these changes. The *Mandragola* affords another occasion to enter and examine the domestic world of Machiavelli. It may also serve as an independent check on the findings suggested by *Clizia*. Finally, *Andria* lends itself to a use similar to that assigned to Plautus; a reference point by which to discern and measure Machiavelli's own innovations.

Let us turn to *Clizia*. The prologue makes the first claim to our attention. It is used by Machiavelli as an occasion to emphasize his own views of what the play is about and to alert the audience to his favorite themes. Its opening sentence is pure Machiavelli. "If men could return to the world in the way that events repeat themselves, not a century would pass without our finding ourselves together again doing just what we are doing now." [16] This observation is offered as a justification for shifting the scene of the play from ancient Athens to contemporary Florence. The repetition of events, not to be confused with notions of historical cycles, is a favorite theme with Machiavelli.[17] It provides the fundamental rationale for the study and use of the past and, presumably, it is also the basis for the utility of comedy. Machiavelli feels that the audience, recognizing

---

[14] *Opere,* 777. "Il fine d'una commedia sia proporre uno specchio d'una vita privata. . . ."

[15] A line by line comparison of *The Woman of Andros* and *Andria* reveals that Machiavelli does not deviate from the Latin text.   [16] *Hale,* 67.

[17] It underlies the structure as well as the content of Machiavelli's *Discourses.*

the truth of this observation, will have little difficulty in believing
that the same set of events which had occurred in ancient Athens
could have been witnessed a short while ago in Florence.

Now following Plautus' lead, Machiavelli addresses himself directly to the audience, presenting them with an outline of the plot.
The play concerns a family whose peace and order is disrupted by a
series of conflicts over Clizia, a young girl. Having said this Machiavelli departs from Plautus to make the generalization that it is
desires and passions which are the stuff of conflict. If plotting and deception constitute the form of comedies, desires comprise their content. "Comedies are written to please and delight the spectators"
and we take pleasure, Machiavelli notes, in observing "an old man's
cupidity, a lover's frenzy, the tricks of a servant, the greed of a
sponger, the misery of a poor man, the ambition of a rich one, the
wiles of a harlot." [18]

Comedies please by making people laugh. This determines the
characters and language at the disposal of the writer. Quite simply,
to give pleasure you must make people laugh; people are moved to
laughter not by sober and serious talk but by dialogue which is
foolish, malicious, or amorous; therefore, to produce laughter it is
necessary to present characters who are foolish, given to malice, or
in love.[19] Machiavelli closes the prologue with the announcement that
he will take lovers as his comic characters since, while wishing to
make people laugh, he does not want to be malicious or deal with
fools. Anyone acquainted with Machiavelli's comedies knows this is
not strictly the case. While the principal characters are people in love,
part of the comic effect depends upon foolish or malicious characters
and dialogue; yet foolishness and maliciousness are not the central
elements of the comedies.

Machiavelli's idea that the comic or the risible has its source in
the incongruous and the inappropriate is of ancient lineage; it is the
obverse of the classical idea of the wise man, the sage who knows
what is right and fitting in every situation. Possessing the sense of the
proper time and place of things the wise man acts with perfect propriety and justice. The existence of the sage, and the distinction between wise man and fool, presumes a cosmos in which everything
does have its proper place, its fixed limits and determinations. The
fool does not know this; he is a fool precisely because he has no sense
of the proper limit to, and of the appropriate context of, things, words,
and acts. He is, therefore, out of harmony with the nature of things.
Unlimited or falsely delimited, he is never "right" but always "left."
Himself an aberration or abnormality, he moves others to laughter

---

[18] *Hale*, 68. In his *Discorso o Dialogo Intorno alla nostra Lingua* Machiavelli
repeats and enlarges on what he says about comedy in his prologue to *Clizia*.
The list of passions and characters in the *Discorso* is very similar to the one in
Clizia. Cf. *Opere*, 777.   [19] *Hale*, 68–69.

(in itself a piece of foolishness) by the spectacle of an aberration. All this foolishness is rooted, ultimately, in the domination of the passions. The lover is possessed by a passion which seems to know no bounds. The *persone malèdiche*, literally, are persons who cannot refrain from talking wrongly or ill. Men and women driven by desires are incapacitated by these very desires from perceiving their situation in its proper dimensions. Using tricks and deceits or being subject to them, they pursue the objects of their desires. This is the stuff of comedy, and, it can be added, of tragedy. The difference between the two, as Machiavelli may have understood it, can be inferred from his remark that comedy must avoid dignified characters (*persone gravi*) [20] and serious dialogue (*parlare grave e severo*).[21] Gravity, the prototypical Roman aristocratic virtue, is the death of comedy. Levity is sustained by lightweight characters involved in ludicrous situations.

However, although comedy must give pleasure through laughter, pleasure is only its means, a necessary means, but not its goal. The desire for pleasure draws people to a comedy, and laughter puts them in a receptive frame, but the end of comedy is to be found in the moral which it draws. Comedy, then, is didactic. Machiavelli repeats what in his own day had become a Ciceronian commonplace: comedy seeks to teach lessons useful to life (*l'esemplo utile*) by holding up a mirror to domestic life.[22]

The moral message of *Clizia*, however, as Machiavelli states in the prologue, is quite un-Ciceronian. By observing the various characters in their passions and plots, everyone, and especially the young, will be taught "what little trust can be put in anyone." [23] Needless to say, no such moral is to be found in Plautus. Taken in its context, Machiavelli's statement can be construed as his judgment regarding the real lesson of all comedies.[24] It would appear from the prologue that desires and intrigues, and not *bona fides*, bind and loosen people in their relation to each other in both private and public spheres of life.

Turning now from the prologue to the play itself, *Clizia* confronts the audience with the spectacle of a family in a state of high disorder. A young girl of unknown parentage, taken in and raised by a very proper and respected Florentine family, has become the cause of a series of conflicts which engulf the entire family. Father and son lust after her and the former has lost no time in devising a scheme to possess and enjoy her. He will marry off the young girl, Clizia, to his servant who has agreed, as his part of the bargain, to share her with his master. Aware of the plan of his father Nicomaco, the son and rival desperately casts about for a way to thwart him. Sofronia, Nicomaco's wife, desiring to make as good a marriage as she can for Clizia,

<hr>

[20] *Opere*, 777.   [21] *Ibid.*, 662.   [22] *Ibid.*, 777.   [23] *Hale*, 68.
[24] See the context, *Opere*, 662.

while taking into account her uncertain social position, actively opposes her husband's arrangement. She is also deeply suspicious of Nicomaco's motive in rushing Clizia into marriage with his servant. She would also oppose her son's designs on Clizia if she were aware of them. Anything short of her son's marriage to Clizia she would not tolerate, and she would be too prudent to sanction his marriage to a girl who lacked social position and a dowry.

Family disorder, then, is the product of three sets of conflicting desires, those of husband and wife, father and son, and mother and son. Machiavelli chooses to emphasize these elements of human conflict with greater vigor and in more ways than are to be found in Plautus. The very words he employs call attention to the fact that the audience is witnessing a domestic battle. The use of metaphors drawn from the politico-military field was not unusual in the Roman comedies of Terence and Plautus. But a comparison of *Casina* and *Clizia* shows that Machiavelli not only employs them more frequently, but in ways that are quite foreign to Plautus. Thus, lover and soldier are alike, in that both have need of *l'animo*.[25] Pursuing a woman is termed laying siege to her.[26] And finally, in a direct application of a military term to love, nowhere to be found in *Casina*, lovemaking is assimilated to an act of war.[27] In general, where the choice of language in *Clizia* departs from *Casina* it is in the direction of stressing the element of conflict. To cite one more example: Cleandro, the son, bitterly complains of his fate, having combatted the *amore* of his father, he must also battle the *ambizione* of his mother.[28]

Love, ambition, jealousy, fear—these are the various desires and passions which breed conflict. The dynamics of Machiavelli's world are such that as passion qualifies passion new passions are spawned. Cleandro describes one phase of the dynamics of human relations in a passage which has no counterpart in Plautus: "As soon as my father fell in love with her [Clizia] . . . he wanted to get his way: he was half crazy with wanting her and thought that there was no way out but to marry her to someone he could share her with afterwards. . . . But Sofronia, my mother, had already suspected that he was infatuated and discovered the plot and now she is doing all she can to spoil it, with jealousy and hatred to drive her on." [29] In *Clizia* the passions have spread to encompass the entire household from master and mistress to bailiff and servants.

The plot, sub-plots, and complications of *Clizia* adhere closely to their Plautian model. But, as we have seen, Machiavelli introduces revealing changes in dialogue and shifts in emphasis and ideas. Many of these are brought together in the longest speech of the play, a soliloquy by Sofronia, which is not to be found in Plautus. In her

---

[25] *Opere*, 666.   [26] *Ibid.*, 668.   [27] *Ibid.*, 683.   [28] *Ibid.*, 691.
[29] Hale, 75. *Opere*, 665.

speech, Sofronia compares the state of the family today and its condition a year ago. The household was then headed by a man whose ordered life set an example worthy of imitation by all men. Under his leadership the family enjoyed a welcome prosperity and peace. Suddenly the family fortunes have been altered, now that Clizia has captured Nicomaco's fancy (*fantasia*). The change (*la gran mutazione*) is amazing. The sober and responsible head of the family has given way to the laughingstock of the neighborhood. In his newly found desire for Clizia he flies in the face of the desires of other members of the family. He neglects family affairs and his behavior undermines the family's reputation. In short, as a result of a series of changes consequent upon Nicomaco's transformation, the family is threatened with ruin.[30]

The focus on the problem of family order, the reference to the earlier condition of the family, the contrast between present disorder and previous order, the notion of change, and the idea of the ruin of the family are all Machiavellian innovations. They comprise Machiavelli's commentary, so to speak, on the affairs Plautus recounts. In one perspective, then, *Clizia* concerns itself with order and disorder. The audience is informed that the family disorder they now witness has infected a once well-ordered household. But what constitutes the nature of family order and what now constitutes the essence of family disorder? First, the idea of order must not be taken to imply that no desires are present, or that desires are controlled or suppressed by reason. No such classical idea of desire or passion as antithetical to order is discoverable in *Clizia*. Rather, family order is constituted by a dynamic set of relations which, more or less, satisfies the desires of its members. Now, what caused the change from order to disorder is a change in the objects of desire, first on the part of Nicomaco and Cleandro, then, as they react, on the part of Sofronia and the others. But even this does not quite accurately describe the situation. It is not the mere change in the object of Nicomaco's desires that produces disorder in the family. Had Sofronia and Cleandro been willing to accommodate their desires to Nicomaco there would be no disorder and consequent danger of ruin. It is the incompatibility of the objects of desire, or the conflict among the members of the family over the objects of desire which produces the disorder, or better, is the disorder. This disorder if not halted will spell the utter ruin of the family. The pattern should be familiar to readers of the *Discourses,* as also should the special nature of the disorder.

Machiavelli, then, conceives of order as well as disorder as having elements of conflict in it. What is crucial is not the existence of conflict but its outcome. Disorder is that state of affairs where conflict *does* threaten ruin. It follows that conflicts are to be judged in the light of their consequences.

[30] *Hale,* 84–85; *Opere,* 671.

In domestic conflict, as in all other struggles, the one aim of the parties is to win, that is, to reorder things so that their *fantasia* is fulfilled and the objects of their desire are secured. All parties husband their resources for the struggle and for all combatants the means are the same, force and fraud. If the good wife, Sofronia, is represented as a sober and pious woman, she is also portrayed as a woman who harbors no illusions and is ruthlessly effective. Her faith in God does not prevent her from using every trick and plot at her disposal to aid God in his work. Her trust in mankind does not diminish, in any way, either her suspicion of men's aims or her ability to analyze their motives and her skill in detecting their schemes and plots. She sees through every one of her husband's deceptions. Machiavelli, indeed, makes it clear beyond a doubt that without deception (*inganno*) she would have been hopelessly outmatched. Faith would not have staved off her defeat, and with it the ruin of the family. The "poca fede di tutti li uomini" of the prologue is echoed at several critical points in the play. This theme, not to be found in *Casina*, is brought to its culmination in a passage in which Machiavelli explicitly questions good faith (*bona fides*) itself: "there would be no deceit if there were no trust." [31] Faith stands indicted as the mother of deceit. In a world which is not constituted in faith and trust, suspicion becomes a necessity. A man would be a fool to allow his life to depend upon his trust in another person. What better lesson can a comedy teach the young than not to be fools?

The good Sofronia confesses to her errant husband, at the close of the comedy, that she has been behind all the deceptions played upon him.[32] She then proceeds to justify the use of deceit as necessary to shame him into his senses.[33] But we may observe that if Nicomaco's sense of shame is activated, it is only after he has suffered defeat in his attempt to win the object of his desire. It is his defeat and not his moral sense which has forced him to abandon hope for the object.

Machiavelli makes it clear that Nicomaco's defeat is Sofronia's victory. Resolution of conflicts, as often as not, involves real defeats and victories and not the reconciliation of differences. Sofronia now assumes the rulership of the family. Her triumph illustrates several of Machiavelli's favorite theses. First, that ability generally outweighs chance in human affairs. Sofronia gains her victory in spite of, not because of, *fortuna*. When the conflict between her and Nicomaco comes to a head, he suggests it be resolved by submitting it to *fortuna*:[34] let lots be drawn. All agree to abide by the outcome, but

---

[31] *Opere*, 679. My translation of "che non è ingannato se non chi si fida." Hale renders it "trust encourages deception," 97.   [32] *Opere*, 690.

[33] *Ibid*. Machiavelli has Sofronia refer to shame three times in this one speech.

[34] *Ibid.*, 678.

both Sofronia and Nicomaco indicate, in asides to third parties, that if *fortuna* or God go against them, they will have recourse to other remedies.[35] *Fortuna* sides with Nicomaco, but Sofronia devises a plan to snatch victory from defeat. Her *bello inganno* overcomes adverse fortune.[36] It would seem that ultimately one's fortunes in this world, be they public or private, are controlled to a large degree by one's own abilities. Sofronia had prayed to God to perform a miracle and make Nicomaco abandon the hope of attaining Clizia. The miracle has been wrought, not by God, but by Sofronia's superior abilities.

Nicomaco, in addition to being favored by the luck of the draw, had superior force on his side. This underlines a second Machiavellian thesis: as influencing the outcome of human affairs, wit or fraud counts for more than force. Virtuosity must not be underestimated. Sofronia's skill delivers family rule into her hands. Her prescription for reversing the fortunes of the family and halting the decline into ruin echoes a remedy to which Machiavelli shows partiality in his *Discourses*. Ruin is to be halted and order reinstituted in the family by the return to its original principles. Nicomaco should make a new start, become once again the person he was a year ago, and with him the entire family will agree to return to its beginnings.[37] It must be emphasized, however, that it is a return to the original principles and not to the original state of things. A year ago Nicomaco ruled, now he has been replaced by Sofronia. Her suggestion to return to the principles upon which the fortunes of the family had been based is a command to which the defeated Nicomaco submits. "Do whatever you want," he says, and Sofronia begins her rule.[38]

Order, however, is not fully restored. Cleandro is also in love with Clizia. His father had opposed him in the name of his own desires; he is no longer a problem. But Sofronia remains. She too opposes Cleandro's marriage to Clizia, arguing that Clizia is no fit match for her son, since nothing is known of her background. Cleandro bemoans his fate: "first I was fighting my father's infatuation, now I am up against my mother's ambition."[39] The conflict of passions has not been completely resolved. The play having already been played out, this last conflict is quickly settled by means of the old Greek and Roman device of a recognition scene. It is abruptly discovered that Clizia is of worthy parentage and therefore is a proper match for Cleandro. This satisfies the *ambizione* of Sofronia and removes her opposition to the marriage.

[35] *Ibid.*, 678-679. Machiavelli puts the same word, *remedio*, in the mouth of both husband and wife.   [36] *Ibid.*, 685.

[37] *Ibid.*, 690. The Italian is "ritornare al segno." Needless to say nothing of this is to be found in Plautus' *Casina*.

[38] *Hale*, 117. "Governala come tu vuoi," *Opere*, 690.

[39] *Hale*, 118. "Io combattevo prima con l'amore di mio padre; ora combatto con l'ambizione di mia madre." *Opere*, 691.

This last resolution differs from the earlier one in that neither side is defeated. The desires of both mother and son are satisfied. Total defeat of one side by the other is not always the only possible way of settling a conflict. Occasionally, it will happen that both parties can realize their objectives. This was not the case in the instance of the major conflicts in the play, the conflicts between husband and wife, father and son. Here the reconstitution of order meant the utter defeat of one person by the other.

To see if we may discern the operation of some independent moral norm in the private sphere, let us again review the nature of the outcome. First, wit and wish gained the victory over wit and wish, and not reason over desire. On this level there is nothing to distinguish or choose from between the combatants. Both sides were moved by their desires and both employed all the force and deception at their disposal in the ensuing struggle. Neither side could boast of moral superiority in the origin or nature of motives or in the choice of tactics. But, as noted above, the consequences would have been different with a different victor. Had Nicomaco won and the family order thus been altered to accommodate to his desires, it would have spelt ruin for the family, and not merely moral ruin. Let us recall what Machiavelli had written to Soderini: "When Fortune becomes weary, ruin follows." [40] Fortune grows weary, among other reasons, because men's wishes change, circumstances change, etc. The fortune of a family or a city, its ability to satisfy its desires and to exist and persist, is grounded in its own way of doing things. When fortune begins to decline and ruin threatens, the only way to avert disaster and recoup one's fortunes is by changing one's ways.[41] The fortune of the family had been based on Nicomaco's earlier desires and the ways of doing things which succeeded in achieving their objectives. Nicomaco's new desire did not of itself signal the wearying of the fortunes of the family. It was the consequence of the clash of his desires with those of the other members of the family which threatened the ruin of the family: the decline in its wealth, reputation, power, and internal cohesion. Sofronia's triumph, the defeat of the ruinous passion and the institution of a new mode of ordering desire, assured the securing and maintaining of the family fortunes. Herein lies the significance for Machiavelli of the outcome of the struggle.

In *Clizia* the threat to the order of the family is an internal one, originating in the passions of its members. Machiavelli's *La Mandragola* also deals with a family situation; this time the threat to its fortunes is, in part, foreign in origin. In *La Mandragola*, Callimaco, a young Florentine who has taken up permanent residence in Paris, where life seems more secure, suddenly decides to return to Italy.

[40] *Hale*, 128.   [41] *Opere*, 879.

Ironically, it is not the plight of his homeland, subject to invasion by those barbarians, the transalpine Europeans, that brings him back to Florence after all these years. Someone in Paris has described to him the incomparable charms of a Florentine beauty and Callimaco wildly desires her. But there are complications. Unfortunately she is married. Worse, she appears to be happily married. In assessing the situation and estimating his chances of success Callimaco notes that Lucrezia is virtuous and the desires of love (*amore*) are alien to her. In brief, the lady's nature provides a major obstacle to his desires.[42] Her relation to her husband also offers little hope to Callimaco. She governs him firmly and prudently, and he is more than satisfied with the arrangement. The family is well ordered and there would seem to be no place for corruption (*corruzione*) to enter.[43] Callimaco reasonably concludes that there is almost no chance of success.

But Callimaco cannot listen to this judgment, even if it is his own, since it says no to his passion. Hope does not spring from reason but from desire.[44] Even if the hope is illusory the will and desire (*la voglia e il desiderio*) to succeed blinds him, as it blinds most men, to the great odds against it. Desire gives rise to hope and hope seeks nourishment in plans, no matter how hopeless, to sustain it.

It would appear that no family or city is so well ordered and incorruptible as to be totally immune to dangers of change and decay. It is clear, in this case, that the risks are grave and the odds are heavily against Callimaco. But the power of desire is so great as to overwhelm the cautions of prudence. Desire allows Callimaco no peace. It rules the soul and demands satisfaction. Apparently even the thought of death cannot bring it to reason and check or limit it.[45] It is better to die trying to achieve desire's object than to die of the desire itself. At this point Callimaco talks of being brought back to life by mounting hopes.[46] Hope is born of desperation, and life is born of such hope. Only thoughts of plans and schemes to capture Lucrezia make the desire bearable. Thought and reason function as the servants and instruments of the passions and the buttress of hope.[47] Callimaco's hope feeds on the simple-minded and foolish nature of the husband.[48] This, when linked to the desire which both parents have for a child and heir, affords some room for maneuvering, for the use of deception

---

[42] "Mi fa la guerra la natura di lei," *ibid.*, 696.   [43] *Ibid.*

[44] The idea that hope comes from desire and has little relation to reality also occurs in several places in *Clizia. Ibid.*, 678–79.

[45] *Ibid.*, 698.   [46] *Ibid.*, 699.

[47] In some of the plays of the New Comedy, particularly those of Plautus, the relation between reason and passion is personified in the relation between master and slave or servant. The clever slave using deception makes it possible for his master to win the object of his desires. Here reason is literally the slave of passion.

[48] "El piu semplice e el piu sciocco omo di Firenze," *ibid.*, 696.

(*inganno*) and the manipulation of the desires of others as a means to attaining one's own.

The analysis of how and why Callimaco succeeds despite Lucrezia's virtue helps to reveal both the structure of the play and the nature of Machiavelli's world. The plot or *inganno* of our hero and his advisors begins to take shape around the calculation of the nature and extent of the barriers to his desires. This assessment focuses on factors —desires and wants, cunning and deception, spirit—which are crucial to Machiavelli's understanding of human affairs. Nicia and Lucrezia, husband and wife, long for a child and heir. In Nicia's case the desire for a child is so great that he is ready to do anything to realize it.[49] To use the desires of another to achieve one's objective calls for the employment of *inganno* rather than force. In this regard Callimaco has a decided advantage over Nicia, who is described as a simple fellow "of little sense and less courage." [50] But the overriding power of desire equally drives both of them. Callimaco will risk reputation, fortune and life to satisfy it. Nicia, a prosperous burgher and a happily married man, will, in his own words, allow himself to be cuckolded and his wife whored to get the child he desires and does not have. It would seem that man is never satisfied with his condition.

If desire disturbs the existing order of things in *La Mandragola* it must again be recognized that the order in the life of Callimaco and the family of Nicia, which is disturbed, is itself a dynamic interplay involving a system of desires and their modes of satisfaction. It is disturbed, as in *Clizia*, by the rise of desires for new things, and such desires always do arise. Hence no order is permanent; if a new order is to emerge it will involve a new relation of desires and their satisfaction.

Desire, then, binds and loosens men. The human being relates to another person as the instrument and object of his desires. Thus the "other person" is constituted in a simple and straightforward way by Machiavelli as the means or object of one's desires. This is true of all the social relations in *La Mandragola;* it characterizes the relation between husband and wife, servant and master, priest and flock, lovers. In this respect they do not differ in kind from the social relations as described by Machiavelli in his political writings— in essence, they are exploitative relations. Machiavelli's treatment of the theme of the faithful servant is a case in point. Callimaco can count on the help of his trusted servant Ligurio because Ligurio is tied to him by bonds of need and desire. In truth, trust does not and cannot provide an adequate basis for conducting one's life. In *La Mandragola*, as in *Clizia*, Machiavelli is explicit on this matter. Only a foòl would have

[49] "Per fare ogni cosa," *Ibid.*, 698.
[50] My translation of "di poca prudenza, di meno animo," *ibid.*

fede in another person and govern himself accordingly.[51] Callimaco and Ligurio can "trust" each other and act in concert because each needs the other as a means to the fulfillment of his own desires.

Recognition of desire as central to the affairs of life is linked to the recognition that people can be led as others will.[52] Where there is a will there is a way; the want of another offers the means to the realization of one's own desire. And this is precisely the content of the plot within a plot. Employing *inganno* on behalf of his master, Ligurio succeeds in accomplishing what seemed to be impossible: to get Nicia to force his wife to sleep with Callimaco. Thus through fraud Callimaco gets Nicia to use his force as master of the family, to accomplish Callimaco's ends. Under duress, the wife agrees, against her *natura*, after her mother, husband, and priest persuade her it is the right and moral thing to do. And in this way the moral and intellectual orders are accommodated to the changes in the order to wants and desires. All this is accomplished by *inganno*.

The resolution of conflict in *Clizia* was primarily the product of *inganno* but to some degree also of fortune. The recognition scene was the means of overcoming the mother's opposition to her son's wishes. Such recognition scenes had been the principal device for the resolution of the complications in Terence's *Andria*. They were highly favored by the playwrights of the new comedy. Machiavelli banishes them from *La Mandragola:* there is no rôle for chance. Indeed, at one point Machiavelli waxes poetic over *inganno*. He bursts into song at the end of Act Three in a hymn in praise of it. "How sweet is the deceit which leads to the dear imaged goal." [53] The poem goes on to praise *inganno* as the rarest and best remedy for life's troubles.[54] Its strength is great,

> Whose mighty power and sacred love
> Rocks, spells, and poisons yield before.[55]

Quite fitting this last: it was *inganno* and not the mandrake root which wrought the cures in *La Mandragola*. In the opening scene of *Clizia*, Cleandro laments the fact that *la fortuna* has landed him in a situation for which there are few remedies.[56] By the end of the play the audience is well aware of the remedial power of *inganno*. Is this the moral of the two plays? With respect to *Clizia* Machiavelli says so in the prologue, and the theme of the superiority of *inganno* or *fraude* to *fortuna* and to *forza* runs through both plays.

The old family order of *La Mandragola* had been undermined. It

---

[51] *Ibid.*, 702 and also 705.   [52] *Ibid.*, 703.

[53] My own translation of the sense, if not of the poetry, of "Si suave e l'inganno/Al fin condotto imaginato e caro," *Ibid.*, 713.

[54] Both Nicomaco and Sofronia had recourse to this remedy.   [55] *Hale*, 40.

[56] *Opere*, 663. The Italian is "pochi remedii."

had not fully satisfied the desires of the husband, nor did it permit Callimaco to fulfill his wishes. *Inganno* has accomplished both these ends, and produced a new order based on the satisfaction of these desires. Callimaco has satisfied his desires and, more important, secured their satisfaction in the future. Lucrezia, persuaded against her will to spend the night with Callimaco, experiences a rebirth (*rinascessi*).[57] She now has new tastes; her nature has changed. Now willingly and knowingly she will seek to satisfy her new wants with Callimaco. Meanwhile Nicia is happy in the knowledge that he will get his wish for an heir. In the slightly disguised form of a *ménage à trois* a new family order replaces the old.

But to interpret this as a happy ending in the sense that "they lived happily ever after" would be to misinterpret both the play and Machiavelli's view of life. There may be happiness but it is not permanent. There is no final end, peace or harmony. At the play's end, Callimaco is united with the object of his desires. In this moment of supreme joy Callimaco comments on his own fortunate state. "I am the happiest and most contented man that ever lived, and if neither death nor time destroy my happiness—the saints themselves shall call me blessed." [58] But this is equivalent to saying that happiness and contentment are temporary conditions, since, in Machiavelli's world there is no constancy in circumstances or in objects of desire. As the introductory song of *La Mandragola* reminds us, eternal happiness is enjoyed only by nymphs and shepherds in their never-never world of pastoral bliss.[59]

Is there any doubt that Callimaco or some other character will experience a change of *fantasia?* Machiavelli gives us every reason to believe that this will be the case since there is no unchanging essence at the core of man, nothing that is fixed and remains constant over time, a measure and a guide to which man may refer and return. In Machiavelli's private world of the family, as in his public world of politics, we can find none of the old reference points—Stoic conscience, Epicurean pleasure principle, Christian faith—which serve to guide us to the right rules and limits of human conduct. Absent, too, from Machiavelli's world is the operation of a natural social sympathy or benevolence to account for the existence and preservation of family or city. In all these indicated meanings there is no private morality to be found in Machiavelli's portrayal of family life which distinguishes it from his portrayal of city life.

In public and private life, Machiavelli discovers the goods of life in the goods of fortune. Gone are the distinctions and ranking of goods of the soul and goods of the body, and gone also are the goods of the various divisions of the soul (as contrasted with the external goods of

---

[57] *Ibid.*, 725.   [58] *Hale*, 58–59.   [59] *Opere*, 693.

fortune) characteristic of the Aristotelian ethic, and the other distinctions and ordering of goods associated with stoic, epicurean, or sceptic ethics. In a fundamental sense, for Machiavelli, all goods are goods of fortune. The satisfaction of wishes and desires requires power over external objects and other people. As we have seen in Machiavelli's plays, there is no question of controlling or suppressing wishes and desires. Felicity, the good or end of action—contentment in this sense —is not to be confused with peace or tranquillity of soul, with the absence, that is, of psychic tensions and perturbations. Here, in a letter to a friend, is Machiavelli's description of the delicious tensions of his own enchainment by love.

I can think of no way to free myself, and even if chance or any turn of human affairs would open up some unexpected avenue of escape, I would not want to take it: sometimes the chains seem so soft and light, and sometimes so heavy, alternating [more accurately "mixing"] in such a manner that now *I doubt whether I could exist happily in a different way of life.*[60]

It is the conflicting pleasure-pain, bitter-sweet mixture, and not the harmony of the parts of the soul, which is the source of felicity.

The analysis of Machiavelli's plays has failed to disclose a principle for separating the moral from the political spheres, or the public from the private domains, which conforms to the suggestion of Meinecke or Cassirer, Sabine or Allen. It will be recalled that they all agreed, in one sense or another, with Allen's statement that for Machiavelli "the morality of politics cannot be that of private life." [61] Yet we have been unable to find an independent moral norm in the private world of Machiavelli's comedies. Instead, that world is characterized by the rule of will and desire (*la voglia e il desiderio*) using force (*forza*) and fraud (*fraude*) as their means of acquiring the ever-changing objects of desire. It is a world in continuous flux: men change, situations change. But since trust is prudent only where one can count on constancy in desire and circumstance, *fede* cannot provide an adequate basis for human relations and social order in this world. This, above all, Machiavelli explicitly takes pains to inform us, is the lesson of his comedies.

Brooklyn College, City University of New York.

[60] *Hale*, 154. My emphasis. Another description of what it is to be in the grip of the desire for a woman is given in Callimaco's soliloquy which opens the fourth act of *La Mandragola*. Callimaco speaks but it is unmistakably Machiavelli's voice. Still a third instance is the song to love which comes at the end of the first act of *Clizia:* "Who loves not cannot feel/The mingled pain and bliss. . . . How fear and hope by turns/Can freeze and burn the heart." *Hale*, 78 .

[61] Allen, *Op. cit.*, 472.

XI

COMPOSING MODERNITY IN MACHIAVELLI'S *PRINCE*

By Robert Hariman

Machiavelli's status as the progenitor of modern political thought has long been uncontested and is reaffirmed frequently.[1] Likewise, *The Prince* remains his most representative text, the sure embodiment of his innovative intelligence. The specific character of his innovation, however, has been the subject of an astonishingly diverse and dense history of interpretation that belies the apparent simplicity of his text.[2] This essay offers another attempt to identify Machiavelli's genius. I argue that by setting *The Prince* in opposition to the rhetorical sensibility of his genre Machiavelli invented the peculiar assumption informing modern political consciousness that power is autonomous, material force. Thus, Machiavelli marks the transition from politics understood as a text to the modern understanding of a political text as something awaiting realization in the material world.

It is somewhat odd that Machiavelli has been less prominent in analyses of modernity per se. In Hans Blumenberg's *The Legitimacy of the Modern Age*, for example, he is mentioned only once as a minor illustration of how other historians have overextended the secularization thesis,[3] despite the fact that a discussion of political theory occupies an

---

[1] The testimonies are legion. According to Lord Acton, he was "the earliest conscious and articulate exponent of certain living forces in the present world" ("Introduction" to L.A. Burd, *Il Principe* [Oxford, 1891], xl). Max Lerner: "It is a truism to point out that Machiavelli is the father of power politics . . . [I]t is still true"("Introduction" to *The Prince and the Discourses* [New York, 1950], xlii). Felix Raab: "As far as the modern world is concerned, Machiavelli invented politics" (*The English Face of Machiavelli: A Changing Interpretation, 1500-1700* [London, 1964], 1). Even those maintaining their scholarly circumspection admit to "the beginning of a new stage—one might say, of the modern stage—in the development of political thought" (Felix Gilbert, *Machiavelli and Guicciardini: Politics and History in Sixteenth Century Florence* [Princeton, 1965], 153).

[2] The contrast between the simplicity of the text and the welter of interpretations animates reviews at least since Burd (*Il Principe*, 12). For the most eloquent marking of the problem, see John H. Geerken's presentation of Machiavelli "the radical enigma" in "Machiavelli Studies Since 1969," *JHI*, 37 (1976), 351. For other review articles, see Eric W. Cochrane, "Machiavelli: 1940-1960," *Journal of Modern History*, 33 (1961); Felix Gilbert, "Machiavelli in Modern Historical Scholarship," *Italian Quarterly*, 14 (1970); Richard C. Clark, "Machiavelli: Bibliographical Spectrum," *Review of National Literatures*, I (1970). Isaiah Berlin addresses the hermeneutical question most directly in "The Originality of Machiavelli," in Myron P. Gilmore (ed.), *Studies on Machiavelli* (Florence, 1972).

[3] Hans Blumenberg, *The Legitimacy of the Modern Age*, tr. Robert W. Wallace (Cambridge, 1983), 14. Previously published as *Die Legitimität der Neuzeit* (Frankfurt, 1966), and as a revised and enlarged edition in three volumes (Frankfurt, 1973, 1975, 1976).

important place in the unfolding of Blumenberg's argument. This oversight is consistent with Blumenberg's aversion to the Renaissance, which is seen as a brief and almost reactionary period of mystification,[4] but it should not distract others from the larger issue of how the political literature written at the beginning of the modern epoch incorporates the tensions within modernity. I present modernity as an act of writing and Machiavelli as one of its model writers. By confronting Blumenberg's important discussion of modernity with this account of Machiavelli as the author of a modern discourse, we can contribute to our understanding of modern political thought as well as to the search for an authentic rationale for the epoch. In particular this reading of *The Prince* strengthens Blumenberg's break with secularization theory and his emphasis upon self-assertion being the genesis of modernity, and contests his argument that modern absolutism (in any conceptual realm) stems from "reoccupation" of prior cultural positions rather than from any tendency in modern thought itself.

Although Blumenberg provides a theoretical context for this interpretation of Machiavelli, my method comes from another tradition of analysis currently being revived as a means for understanding modern thought. The tradition of rhetoric provides the contemporary reader of *The Prince* with both intellectual continuity and a means of self-understanding, for it served as a culture of erudition active within Machiavelli's world and operates today as a perspective upon the history of ideas.[5]

The particular sense of rhetorical inquiry at work here employs the following precepts. First, texts are composed not simply as records but as acts—they are addressed toward a particular end and comprehensible in the last analysis in terms of their effects. We read *The Prince* less as a description of political reality as the author observed it and more as an attempt to construct a political world arrayed according to the author's understanding and for his advantage. Second, the meaning of a text arises from the relationship between its content and its form. If we claim that *The Prince* says something, we have to show how that saying is reinforced within the text, which we discern by comparison with others in its genre. Third, as texts are composed for advantage, the authority of a text comes

---

[4] The intensity of Blumenberg's attitude animates his last sentence: "History knows no repetitions of the same; 'renaissances' are its contradiction" (596).

[5] For a good review of Renaissance rhetoric, see Nancy Struever, *The Language of History in the Renaissance: Rhetoric and Historical Consciousness in Florentine Humanism* (Princeton, 1970); also James J. Murphy (ed.), *Renaissance Eloquence* (Berkeley, 1983); Brian Vickers, "On the Practicalities of Renaissance Rhetoric," in Brian Vickers (ed.), *Rhetoric Revalued* (Binghamton, 1982); Hanna Gray, "Renaissance Humanism: The Pursuit of Eloquence," *JHI*, 24 (1963), 497-514; Jerrold Seigel, *Rhetoric and Philosophy in Renaissance Humanism* (Princeton, 1968), and the debate between Seigel and Hans Baron in *Past and Present*, nos. 34 and 36. For the most recent presentation of rhetoric as a tradition of analysis, see Brian Vickers, *In Defence of Rhetoric* (Oxford, 1988).

in part from establishing that its other, related discourses are less authoritative, deserving of less *status*.[6] There are two methodological implications here: one is that we can discern a text's persuasive design by
looking for those moments in the text when other discourses are subordinated. Thus, in order to discover Machiavelli's rhetorical stance, I have
examined those points in his text when he writes against other discourses. The second implication is that when a text does appear enigmatic we
might be able to discern why it has this effect by considering how it
might so effectively tear down related texts that it weakens its own foundation. Thus, Machiavelli is recognizable as a modern thinker to the extent his *incompleteness* becomes a characteristic design in his text.

Incompleteness is a relational term, marking a difference between a
text and its genre (or, more properly, the reader's expectations regarding
such a text), and a genre criticism supplies the best mix of the traditional
and contemporary strains of rhetorical analysis.[7] The following reading
of *The Prince* draws upon prior scholarship regarding Machiavelli's relationship with his genre in order to identify how he crafts the "endemic
assumption" in modern thought that political power is an automous material force. This perspective does not displace the prior arguments that
Machiavelli was writing against his genre, that he was an original thinker, or that he challenged ethical sensibilities, but I do question whether
these accounts have been presented in the' best terms for understanding
how his simple text has articulated modern consciousness.[8] The following pages will review the current understanding of Machiavelli's break
with the genre, offer an alternative account by looking at several celebrated passages typically used to define Machiavelli's sensibility, aug-
ment the case by analyzing Machiavelli's most significant omission of
the genre's conventions, and close with a discussion of the problematic
of modernity.

The genre of the *speculum principis*, or mirror-of-the-prince, comprises
those texts bearing such names as *De regimine principum, De institutio*

---

[6] Robert Hariman, "Status, Marginality, and Rhetorical Theory," *Quarterly Journal of
Speech*, 72 (1986), 38-54. For another synopsis of this trope's operation within the tradition of rhetoric, see Roger Moss, "The Case *for* Sophistry," in Vickers, *Rhetoric Revalued*,
207-24.

[7] For a defense of genre criticism, see Quentin Skinner, "Some Problems in the Analysis of Political Thought and Action," *Political Theory*, 2 (1974), 277-303. Skinner illustrates his approach in "Sir Thomas More's *Utopia* and the Language of Renaissance
Humanism," in Anthony Pagden (ed.), *The Languages of Political Theory in Early Modern Europe* (Cambridge, 1987), 123-58.

[8] Nor am I challenging the consensus today that the *Prince* and the *Discourses* are
"interdependent aspects of an organically unified outlook" (Geerken, 357). Each does
have its strengths, however, and though the *Discourses* may give us the more sophisticated
account of Machiavelli's political philosophy, it is the *Prince*, with its unique combination
of radical content and radical form, that gives us the new philosopher.

principis, and *De officio regis,* all of which were directed to educate the prince toward the end of governing well. The distinguishing conventions of the genre proved remarkably stable, for the thousands of texts all followed the same topics as they developed the same themes: e.g., each would discuss the relation of king to counselors, caution against flattery, and observe that prudence comes from reading good books such as the one before the reader. As Lester Born observed, "we conclude at once that originality is not one of the prime essentials of a good treatise on the education of a prince."[9] This lack of originality probably issues from the corresponding high degree of intertextuality among the works. Born suggested as much when he again remarked that "There is little originality displayed; the main argument is nearly always supported by wholesale quotations."[10] The texts represented a tradition of political commentary, and they relied upon the authority of tradition to accomplish their object of persuading the prince to behave decently.

The first two systematic accounts of *The Prince*'s relationship to this genre appeared simultaneously in 1938-39. Allan Gilbert provided a comprehensive comparison of the text in respect to many similar works that appeared before and after 1513. He conceived of the genre as relatively uniform across historical time, attempted to establish only a probable context for reading rather than to demonstrate direct influence upon Machiavelli's composition, and argued that *The Prince* so essentially conforms to the genre that it remains the "best representative" of the type.[11] By contrast, Felix Gilbert's analysis emphasized the changes occurring within the literature during the Renaissance to demonstrate both that the humanists had direct influence upon Machiavelli and that he consciously repudiated the fundamental tenet of both medieval and Renaissance writers that the virtues were necessary for political success.[12] Both writers agreed upon the manner in which we can determine the nature of the genre, noting the ubiquity and locales of the manuals, their allusions and direct references to prior texts, and the many instances of direct parallelism. They also followed similar approaches to placing Machiavelli within the genre, noting primarily the similarity of the dedication to Isocrates' letter *To Nicocles,* which was regarded at the time (and

[9] Lester K. Born, "Introduction" to Desiderius Erasmus, *The Education of a Christian Prince,* ed. Lester K. Born (New York, 1936), 45.

[10] Born, "Introduction," 125. M. L. W. Laistner's description of the genre carries the same implication: "They contrast the good and the bad ruler; in enumerating the virtues that make up the good ruler and the duties that devolve upon him, if he is to remain a just king, they reproduce examples from the Bible and citations from earlier writers of authority" (*Thought and Letters in Western Europe: A.D. 500 to 900* [Ithaca, N.Y., 1957], 317).

[11] Allan H. Gilbert, *Machiavelli's Prince and its Forerunners: The Prince as a Typical Book de Regimine Principum* (Durham, N.C., 1938), 232.

[12] Felix Gilbert, "The Humanist Concept of the Prince and *The Prince* of Machiavelli," *Journal of Modern History,* 11 (1939), 449-83.

today) as the origin of the genre, the Latinate chapter headings (despite the text being in the vernacular), adherence to such conventions as the catalog of virtues, and Machiavelli's two oblique references to other political writers, which occur in the dedication and at the beginning of his review of the virtues.

These readings set the agenda for understanding Machiavelli's text as a literary composition. They represented a creative attempt to reconcile Machiavelli with the subsequent history of interpretation by providing a counterweight made from its antecedent tradition, and they contained many sound answers to important questions of interpretation. They advanced previous work establishing the character and influence of the genre as a major form within which political inquiry was conducted in the centuries preceding the modern era, and they demonstrated that understanding *The Prince* required articulating its relationship with that genre. Yet their inconsistencies also revealed that there was more to be said about the extent to which Machiavelli's innovation arises from his use of the genre.

Quentin Skinner provided the next major attempt to read Machiavelli in this manner, and his approach amplified the common tendencies of the previous essays. Skinner also gave additional emphasis to Felix Gilbert's identification of Machiavelli with the Renaissance writers' ideas of civic humanism. Skinner specifies, first, early *quattrocento* ideas of the ideal of the *vir virtutis* living for glory found in honor, while struggling against *fortuna*, by means of his *virtù*, which is developed via the right education,[13] and then refines this placement to emphasize the innovations of the later *quattrocento* writers, including the ideas that security is the primary purpose of government and that the leader's virtue will of necessity be different and more heroic than the ordinary citizen's.[14] He also articulates Machiavelli's innovation as a break with the genre, specifically through the two references to other texts, which make Machiavelli the exponent of "the significance of sheer power in political life"[15] and the debunker of the idea that the conventional virtues were the effective means to political rule.[16]

The question following Skinner is not whether a break occurred between *The Prince* and its genre but whether the break has been presented in the most revealing terms. Here Allan Gilbert becomes useful again, for he not only shows us explicitly (as does Skinner) that the text was the less evil for being more akin to its genre than had been recognized, but also implies that the genre was the less utopian as it was closer to

---

[13] Quentin Skinner, *The Foundations of Modern Political Thought* (2 vols; Cambridge, 1978), I, 118-22.

[14] *Ibid.,* 123-28.

[15] *Ibid.,* 129.

[16] *Ibid.,* 131-38.

the text. Yet all subsequent commentary, including Felix Gilbert and Skinner, has followed Machiavelli's own account of his relationship to his genre, which is that he is realistic where others are idealistic. Skinner's assumption that Machiavelli agrees with his contemporaries about the goals of politics reinforces this point,[17] for they then must disagree over means, and the better assessment of means must come from objectivity, calculation, and realism, rather than from wishfulness, moralizing, and idealism. But here Skinner is tripped up by his method: he is so keen on giving Machiavelli a sound historicist reading that he is too quick to take him at face value on this point. Instead, we should ask whether any writer provides the best account of his or her relationship to other writers, particularly when writing for advantage against them.

This consideration points toward a more radical implication of the general claim that *The Prince* accomplishes a break with the genre. I argue that Machiavelli's innovation in political thought did come through a break with his genre of the *speculum principis*, although not in the terms with which he announced that break. The realism he opposed to the genre's idealism is itself a sign of the more fundamental difference, which is that he suppressed the received relationship between textual consciousness and political thought in order to free political innovators from the restraints consciously imposed by that relationship. We have to see him not as someone who was realistically describing new political formations being built in the clear air of Northern Italy but as someone who was crafting a characteristically modern political sensibility by opposing politics to its texts.

A brief look at Machiavelli's celebrated announcement of his innovation can suggest how his own account of his work can distort our understanding of his relationship with the genre. Chapter 15 begins the portion of *The Prince* that most directly addresses the *specula*: here Machiavelli directly follows the conventional catalog of virtues, including the standard disputations regarding their application (such as whether it is better to be feared or loved); he speaks primarily in response to other (though unnamed) commentators rather than in his typical mode of address to the prince; and he begins by directly opposing himself to the other writers. "And because I know that many have written about this, I fear that, when I too write about it, I shall be thought conceited, since in discussing this material I depart very far from the methods of the others."[18] Now if this had been the extent of his description, we

---

[17] *Ibid.*, 134.
[18] Allan Gilbert, *Machiavelli: The Chief Works and Others* (Durham, N.C., 1965), 67. "E perché io so che molti di questo hanno scritto, dubito, scrivendone ancora io, non essere tenuto prosuntuoso, partendomi, massime nel disputare questa materia, dalli ordini deli altri" (*Tutte le Opere*, ed. Francesco Flora and Carlo Cordie [Rome, 1949], 48; subsequent quotations use these works).

would still conclude that he was attempting to break with the genre but the break would be judged solely in respect to its originality.

But this theme becomes eclipsed by the following claim, which is original and more: "But since my purpose is to write something useful to him who comprehends it, I have decided that I must concern myself with the truth of the matter as facts show it rather than with any fanciful notion. Yet many have fancied for themselves republics and principalities that have never been seen or known to exist in reality. For there is such a difference between how men live and how they ought to live that he who abandons what is done for what ought to be done learns his destruction rather than his preservation."[19] Three ideas are stated here regarding the other commentaries: they are imaginary rather than realistic, normative rather than descriptive, and they weaken rather than strengthen the prince. The key to this passage is not the truthfuiness of the several claims themselves so much as it is in their implicit association. In Machiavelli's world political success—i.e., dominion—[20] comes from seeing what is the case, and saying what ought to be leads to political failure. Any other equation is itself one of the fantasies leading to failure. Therefore, if one is speaking of what ought to be, the advice cannot be realistic; if one is speaking of what is the case, the advice must be effective; etc.

If we are to be realistic about the design at work in the text, then we should see that Machiavelli is twice masked. First, the opposition between realism and idealism disguises the motive of writing for advantage. Whereas the more conventional writers competed for a reader's attention by their artistic evocations of artistically perfected government, Machiavelli suggests that his epistemological standard is the only legitimate means for measuring advice; the quest for advantage has been separated from writing and moved to the realm of the prince's actions. The prince reads to gain advantage over his opponents, but writers write (properly) only to record the real. Second, it should be obvious that the declaration that he will choose to record the real is no less idealistic than the portrait of the ideal prince; in fact, it may be less responsibly so, for whereas the *speculum* metaphor carried a profound understanding of the process by which we negotiate between the real, the apparent, and the

---

[19] *The Prince* (hereafter, "P"), 57-58. "Ma sendo l'intento mio scrivere cosa utile a chi la intende, mi è parso più conveniente andare drieto alla verità effetuale della cosa che alia imaginazione di essa. E molti si sono imaginati republiche e principati che non si sono max visti né conosciuti essere in veto. Perché egli è tanto discosto da come si vive a come si doverrebbe vivere, che colui che lascia quello che si fa per quello che si doverrebbe fare, impara più tosto la ruina che la perservazione sua" (48-49).

[20] J.H. Hexter, *"Il Principe* and *Lo Stato, "Studies in the Renaissance,* 4 (1957), 113-38. "Persistently and dominantly he had in mind political command over men" (126). Revised essay printed in J.H. Hexter, The *Vision of Politics on the Eve of the Reformation: More, Machiavelli, Seyssel* (New York, 1973), 150-78.

ideal,[21] the Machiavellian narrator feigns the ease of his cognitive skills and emotional control. By claiming to see the world as it is (while looking to one's own advantage as advisor) the narrator applies the courtier's technique of suggesting mastery by ease. As Castiglione advises: "So this quality which is the opposite of affectation, and which we are now calling nonchalance ... brings with it another advantage; for ... it not only reveals the skill of the person doing it but also very often causes it to be considered far greater than it really is.... Our courtier, therefore, will be judged to be perfect and will show grace in everything, and especially in his speech, if he shuns affectation."[22]

Recall now Machiavelli's other allusion to the genre, found in his dedication. "This work of mine I have not adorned or loaded down with swelling phrases or with bombastic and magnificent words or any kind of meretricious charm or extrinsic ornament, with which many writers dress up their products, because I desire either that nothing shall beautify it, or that merely its unusual matter and the weight of its subject shall make it pleasing."[23] Here the writer of *The Prince* is announcing himself. Yet his own terms are false, for he is not the individual set against the others who are in turn known by their artifice and their conventionality. He is equally conventional: he follows the convention of implying virtue through nonchalance and lack of affectation. He is equally artificial: he crafts the illusion that his writing is only a transparent medium between the reader and "the weight of its subject." The other writers are described in terms of their textuality and he is correspondingly aligned with the natural world. Their texts are made of the stuff of words alone and are extrinsic to their subject; his text is indigenous to reality itself.

This attack upon textuality, hiding under the guise of a disposition to realism, is continued in his following metaphor. "No one, I hope, will think that a man of low and humble station is overconfident when he dares to discuss and direct the conduct of princes, because, just as those who draw maps of countries put themselves low down on the plain to observe the nature of mountains and of places high above, and to observe

---

[21] Marianne Shapiro, "Mirror and Portrait: the Structure of *Il libro del Cortegiano*," *Journal of Medieval and Renaissance Studies*, 5 (1975), 41-44.

[22] *The Book of the Courtier*, tr. George Bull (Harmondsworth, 1976), 69-70. "Questa virtù adunque contraria alla affettazione, la qual noi per ora chiamiamo sprezzatura, ... porta ancor seco un altro ornamento, ... non solamente sùbito scopre il saper di chi la fa, ma spesso lo fa estimar molto maggior di quello che è in effetto.... Sara adunque il nostro cortegiano stimato eccellente ed in ogni cosa averà grazia, massimamente nel parlare, se fuggirà l'affettazione" (*Il libro del Cortegiano*, ed. Ettore Bonora [Milan, 1981], 64-65).

[23] P, 10. "La quale opera io non ho ornata né ripiena di clausule ample o di parole ampullose e magnifiche, o di qualunque altro lenocinio o ornamento estrinesco con li quali molti sogliono le lore cose descrivere e ornare; perché io ho voluto, o che veruna cosa la onori o che solamente la varietà della materia e la gravità del subietto la facci grata"(3).

that of low places put themselves high up on mountain tops, so likewise, in order to discern clearly the people's nature, the observer must be a prince, and to discern clearly that of princes, he must be one of the populace."[24] Here Machiavelli is addressing the classical problem of decorum, itself fundamental to the rhetorical tradition. How does one speak to one of higher station without breaching the social code under-lying speech itself? No wonder that he is concerned about the problem for he has just refused to use the words conventionally used in addressing a prince. This refusal could stand for a turn from the idea of decorum itself, and given its architectonic function in classical rhetoric his words then overrule the entire classical tradition of stylistics.[25] Machiavelli rec-ognizes that this act requires explanation. His answer shows us that he is indeed displacing textuality and willing to rely upon the appeal of its substitute. As only the subject matter (rather than the situation of the communicator) should determine one's diction, so textuality is overruled with the topographical metaphor: prince and political subject, in their common object of knowing their world, are each best known from the vantage of the other. This trope is nothing less than a paradigm shift, substituting observer for writer, vision for language, the subject for its mode of expression, observation for invention, knowledge for convention, and objectivity (with its corollary common sense) for decorum.

This shift from textuality to topography constitutes the radical strat-egy of the text: it is the means by which the text asserts its authority and becomes the standard by which all political texts are judged. We are brought to see the other writers as idealistic because they are subjects of their discourse; Machiavelli becomes realistic because he has shunned artifice. For an indication of the power of this trope, imagine a political scientist today claiming that he would rather be known as a writer accomplished in the artistically pleasing invention of phrases according to conventions of usage in order to appropriately address a ruler, rather than an observer capable to objective knowledge of the subject matter of politics. But before the full significance of this shift can be articulated we need to consider the counterargument that Machiavelli was a devout disciple of the literary culture of the Renaissance.

Most commentators find the essence of Machiavelli's relationship with his milieu in his letter of 10 December 1513 to Francesco Vettori, and within that letter in the passage where he turns from the empty pastimes

---

[24] P, 10-11: "Né voglio sia reputata presunzione se uno uomo di basso e infimo stato ardisce discorrere e regolare e governi de'principi; perché, così come coloro che disegnano e paesi si pongono bassi nel piano a considerare la natura de' monti e de'luoghi alti, e per considerare quella de'bassi si pongono alti sopra e monti, similmente, a conoscere bene la natura de' populi bisogna essere principe, e a conoscere bene quella de' principi bisogna essere populare" (3).

[25] Robert Kaster, "Decorum," American Philological Association National Meeting, Philadelphia, 29 December 1982. Cf. Struever, *op. cit.*, 67-68.

of daily life to his solitary evenings in his study.[26] This passage also is taken too quickly at face value, for what is read as a testament to the life of the mind also operates as the artifice of the Machiavellian writer. To discover the cunning here we need only examine how the letter, from start to finish, turns on the subordination of other discourses to the medium of the writer's mind. Note, for example, how Machiavelli sets himself among but against the multitude known by their incessant wordiness: here known by the vulgarity of playing at the tavern games that "bring on a thousand disputes and countless insults with offensive words, and usually we are fighting over a penny, and nevertheless we are heard shouting as far as San Casciano."[27] Machiavelli, playing the realist, admits not only to his participation but to his enjoyment, even need, for such things; but Machiavelli the strategist has again made language extrinsic to reality, and so capable only of the exaggerated expression of desire. Not surprisingly, the entire letter is a record of false or idle speaking: He kills time with the woodcutters, "who have always some bad-luck story ready,"[28] loses in business because of the bad promises of his customers, to whom he then responds in kind, and speaks idly with others to learn of the "different fancies of men."[29] There are only two instances prior to the evening scene in which language seemingly has intrinsic value: He values Signor Vettori's letters as a sure sign of his good will, and he reads poetry to learn of tender loves and "enjoy myself a while in that sort of dreaming."[30] So we can discern that writing is superior to speech—and that rhetoric, now known part for whole by the act of speaking, is again discounted. Furthermore, writing becomes the more realistic as it is the sign of Machiavelli's relationship with his patron, and otherwise it remains explicitly the medium of desire. The realist hides the strategist, for language's capacity for fact is unquestioned within the relationship of patronage, denied otherwise, and the actual basis for the distinction is never admitted. Again, after the evening scene we return to a world where those capable of helping Machiavelli speak clearly, while others are represented by the potential plagiarist Ardinghelli.

We do not come innocently to this scene, then, nor leave it unfollowed. And what is within? "On the coming of evening, I return to my house and enter my study; and at the door I take off the day's clothing, covered with mud and dust, and put on garments regal and courtly; and reclothed

[26] For a recent example see Eugenio Garin, "Retorica e 'Studia Humanitatis' nella Cultura del Quattrocento," in Vickers, *Rhetoric Revalued*, 226.

[27] Allan Gilbert, *The Letters of Machiavelli* (hereafter, "L"), (New York, 1961), 142. "... et poi dove nascono mille contese et infiniti dispetti di parole iniuriose, et il piú delle volte si combatte un quattrino et siamo sentiti non di manco gridare da San Casciano" *(Lettere,* ed. Franco Gaeta [Milan, 1961], 303; subsequent quotations use these works).

[28] L, 140: "che hanno sempre qualche sciagura alle mane o fra loro o co'vicini" (302).

[29] L, 141: "diverse fantasie d'huomini" (303).

[30] L, 141: "godomi un pezzo in questo pensiero" (303).

appropriately, I enter the ancient courts of ancient men, where I am received by them with affection, I feed on that food which is mine alone
and which I was born for, where I am not ashamed to speak with them
and to ask them the reason for their actions; and they in their kindness
answer me;. and for four hours of time I do not feel boredom, I forget every trouble, I do not dread poverty, I am not frightened by death; entirely
I give myself over to them."[31]

We begin by leaving the world, a passage emphasized by a series of
passages—from day into night, public realm into house and there into the
study, a pause at the threshold of the inner sanctum to shed the day's
clothing, known by the mud and dust symbolizing the world and its temporal finitude, which is echoed at the close of the paragraph by his fear
of death. Then, to become fit to enter, he dons clothing "regal and courtly," the appropriate garb for one entering the ancient courts. Here Machiavelli assumes all the conventions of speech repudiated in *The Prince*.
He speaks grandiloquently while observing the principle of decorum and
even celebrating its sensibility. He ornaments himself without shame in
order that he may speak as a peer among those at court. Faced with the
same problem he acknowledged at the beginning of *The Prince*, that of
speaking appropriately with one of higher status, he here calls upon the
resources for resolving that problem that he rejects there for the better alternative of plain speech.

Yet the letter remains at one with *The Prince*, for in both texts speech
and action are opposing worlds. Fundamental to his time with the ancients is that it is a time of reverie, more a time of psychological recovery
than of theoretical curiosity, and it is wholly separate from the world.
When within the world of texts he behaves accordingly—speaking in a
grand style for a grand place, happy to be clothed and ornamented with
words, savoring good conversation far more than the naked truth. But it
is a separate world. The world of texts is not the world of princes. There
is a continuity between text and world for Machiavelli as well, but it is a
strange one. "I feed on that food which only is mine and which I was born
for." Language again becomes the medium of desire. The continuity between text and world is the same as between this letter and *The Prince:*
the gigantic personality of Machiavelli. Here is the lion lurking behind
the stratagems of the fox, the individual who devours the tradition that so
easily absorbs the works of the other writers.

---

[31] L, 142: "Venuta la sera, mi ritorno in casa, et entro nel mio scrittoio; et in su l'uscio
mi spoglio quella veste cotidiana, piena di fango et di loto, et mi metto panni reali et curi-
ali; et rivestito condecentemente entro nelle antique corti degli antiqui huomini, dove, da
loro ricenuto amorevolmente, mi pasco di quel cibo, che *solurn* è mio, et che io nacqui per
lui; dove io non mi vergogno parlare con loro, et domandarli della ragione delle loro
actioni; et quelli per loro humanità mi rispondono; et non sento per quattro hore di tempo
alcuna noia, sdimenticho ogni affanno, non temo la povertà, non mi sbigottiscie la morte:
tucto mi transferisco in loro" (304).

The letter, then, articulates signs of classical textuality, and so illuminates the conception of the rhetorical values Machiavelli was rejecting when he attacked the generic writers. It can still be read as a mark of Machiavelli's education, yet it simultaneously reveals that Machiavelli's rejection of the traditional texts on princely rule was part of a consistently held repudiation of the Medieval textual consciousness. *He* might speak with the ancients, but the prince could only fall who would turn his eyes from the world.

We have come a long way from Isocrates' letter *To Nicocles*, the supposed model for the dedication.[32] What is not observed is that although the parallel is obvious the resemblance is both superficial and misleading. Most of Isocrates' appeals are ignored, and Machiavelli's most important appeals are additions. Consider this difference: where Isocrates' opening scheme to gain the king's attention aims to establish the superior value of words when compared to the conventional gifts of material wealth, Machiavelli makes no use of this topic but instead argues for the prince's attention by debunking other writers. Each has the same rhetorical problem—the intellectual's competition for the ruler's attention—and each follows the obvious strategy of finding an advantageous basis for comparison with one's competitors, but there is an enormous difference between them. Isocrates could have set himself against other advisors— that is, against oral advice—just as Machiavelli could have opposed those attempting to purchase the prince's favors. But each is writing as a metaphysician as well. Isocrates opposes those bearing material gifts not because he alone of all the Greeks attempts to gain favor by advising but because he is writing the spirit of his age by writing a textual politics. We can confirm this idea by looking to Isocrates' second letter for Nicocles. Here Isocrates produces one of his more brilliant passages when anticipating the very argument Machiavelli advances: that eloquence contains nothing useful to a King. Isocrates, an able realist in his own right, nonetheless lives in a textual world: "There is no institution devised by man which the power of speech has not helped us establish."[33] The key implication here is that what is made by language can only be known fully through language; although words have the power to distort, they alone have the capability for the reflexive consciousness required for understanding anything made of words.

Machiavelli follows a different strategy to a different end. He places himself over the other writers not because he alone of all the Florentines attempts to provide realistic advice but because he is writing the spirit

of his age by writing to liberate himself from a textual consciousness.[34]
He does so from inside, of course—in contemporary terms, he writes a
deconstructive text—by drawing upon the proven technique of artfully
professing the artlessness of his text as the means of hiding his artistry.
As Aristotle advised, "a writer must disguise his art and give the impression of speaking naturally and not artificially. Naturalness is persuasive,
artificiality is the contrary."[35] Machiavelli has turned rhetoric against
itself; his kin are Socrates before him and Descartes after, but not Isocrates.[36] Machiavelli would have us believe the *specula* distort their subject
in the attempt to persuade, while he lets the subject itself speak in its
native discourse. His full implication is that the essence of his subject is
something that is correctly communicated only through artlessness; he
abjures explicit textuality because his subject of power is not itself textual.
As rhetoric is extrinsic to the subject, so power becomes objectified,
something existing outside of the subjective realm of language, texts, and
textual authority. The many commentators who have read Machiavelli
for his epistemology were accurate enough, but erred if they failed to see
to corresponding ontology carried in the same passages as well.[37] Felix

[34] For a recently published essay on the same theme, see Thomas M. Greene, "The
End of Discourse in Machiavelli's 'Prince'," *Yale French Studies*, 67 (1984), reprinted
in Patricia Parker and David Quint (eds.), *Literary Theory/Renaissance Texts* (Baltimore,
1984): "The dedicatory epistle repudiates rhetoric; the clipped opening chapter repudiates
the graces of humanist elegance; from the beginning, the book refuses to be literature, . . .
The Prince signals its willed estrangement from the cultural processes it claims to analyze. . . . Machiavelli's authorial stance as his book opens seems to reject that *textual*
conclusiveness and to promise only whatever *analytic* conclusiveness can be wrung from
the perennially continuous" (64).

[35] Aristotle, *Rhetoric* 1404b.18, tr. W. Rhys Roberts (New York, 1954): "Διὸ δεῖ
λανθάνειν ποιοῦντασ, καὶ μὴ δοκεῖν λέγειν πεπλασμένωσ 'αλλὰ πεφυκότωσ:
τοῦτο γὰρ πιθανόν, ἐκεῖνο δὲ τοὐναντίον."

[36] For other studies of the strategy see, Chaim Perelman and L. Olbrechts-Tyteca,
The New Rhetoric: A Treatise on Argumentation, John Wilkinson and Purcell Weaver
(Notre Dame, 1969), 450-59; Gerald L. Bruns, "A Grammarian's Guide to the *Discourse
on Method*," in his *Inventions: Writing, Textuality, and Understanding in Literary History*
(New Haven, 1982). For a succinct comparison of Machiavelli and Descartes as authors
of modernity, see Eugene Garver, *Machiavelli and the History of Prudence* (Madison,
1987), 3-5.

[37] Gilbert argues that the basic continuity between Machiavelli and the humanist
writers in the genre was that they all were grappling with the new problems thrust upon
them by reality, but that only Machiavelli succeeded in establishing "realism" as the
basis of political thought (457). Moreover, Gilbert's explanation as to why the others
had "no manifestation of a thoroughgoing realism, no appreciation of the power-factor
and the egoistic purposes which dominate the political life" (468) is itself an example
of the pattern of thinking Machiavelli authored: First, the other writers continued to be
misled by their literary sensibilities—"As soon as an author had literary ambitions, he
felt it necessary to set an ideal standard and write of an imaginary political world"
(469)—and second, reality itself had not intervened, in for the form of an act of force
known as the French invasion, to correct the writers (470). Reinforcing this pattern is
a strict association of tradition with illusion and innovation with realism (e.g., 457).

Gilbert and Skinner are additionally correct in identifying Machiavelli's discovery of the significance of "sheer power" residing in "force,"[38] but they fail to show how Machiavelli created the very means for the compliment: the modern terms "power" and "force" are ontological terms, and that ontology exists because Machiavelli so artfully defined them as something wholly separated from textuality.

The basic similarity between Isocrates and Machiavelli is that as each used the dedication to craft an argument for securing the ruler's attention he simultaneously was creating a metaphysics of power. The crucial difference is that Isocrates created a textual metaphysics, where power is an articulation of speech and rulers can only rule effectively if they, like speakers, adapt themselves to the restraints imposed by their audiences, whereas Machiavelli developed the modern metaphysics of power by writing in a manner that subverted the authority of the textual mind.

This shift in consciousness required subverting the genre of the *speculum principis* because the genre was the symbolic container of the textual metaphysics. The basic implication of the formal elements of the genre was that power is the consequence of authority, and so a social relation expected to conform to the culture's authorities, including not least of all its authors. Power was intelligible at all because it moved through the appropriate channels, was conducted largely by persuasion (and the norms of persuasion such as decorum), and was at bottom a form of speech. So for example, the idea of love served as the master metaphor for both persuasion (as in Plato's *Phaedrus*) and for power (as in Castiglione's *Book of the Courtier*). And Isocrates observes sternly that the ruler must train his soul more than any athlete trains his body, and the "discourse which is true and lawful and just is the outward image of a good and faithful soul."[39] (Or recall Plato's testament in *Phaedo* [115e] that to speak incorrectly not only is a fault in itself but corrupts the soul.) The writer of the *specula* inherited this metaphysic and reproduced it by writing conventionally. The basic orientation of the genre was persuasive—as Isocrates claimed that the first letter for Nicocles was "pleading the cause of his subjects"—[40] and the conventions stressed the authority of past writers, the value in restating commonly held ideals, and the necessity of clothing the king in the appropriate speech: "I, myself, welcome all forms of discourse which are capable of benefiting us even in a small degree; however, I regard those as the best

---

[38] Gilbert: "The dominating idea . . . is an appeal to recognize the crucial importance of force in politics" (*Machiavelli and Guicciardini*, 154). Skinner: Machiavelli denounces the other writers "for failing to emphasise the significance of sheer power in political life" (*Foundations*, I, 129).

[39] *Nicocles* 7: "καὶ λόγοσ 'αληθὴσ καὶ νόμιμοσ καὶ δίκαιοσ ψυχῆσ αγαθῆσ καὶ πιστῆσ εἴδωλόν εστιν."

[40] Isocrates, *Antidosis* 70, tr. George Norlin, *Isocrates II* (Cambridge, 1929): "'αλλὰ τοῖσ 'αρχομένοισ ἐπαμύνων.'"

and most worthy of a king, and most appropriate to me, which give directions on good morals and good government."[41] This idea operated in both the Isocratean school and in the Renaissance not as an opinion but as a program of study and political invention. Hence, "eloquence was the distinctive concern of the Humanists,"[42] and the premier example of how any political instrument was by its very nature—i.e., its textual nature—continuous with ethics.[43]

The extent of Machiavelli's break from this set of ideas is visible in the structure of *The Prince*. Although highlighting Machiavelli's break with the genre does not entail that the text should be read *sui generis*—in fact, it is the imitations that set up the moments of innovation—there are several deviations in form that each reinforce his redefinition of political power away from an association with textual authority toward an association with force.[44] First, the text gives unusual attention to military matters, and particularly to the place of instruction in military attitudes, strategies, and tactics in the education of the prince. Neal Wood has shown how this topic suffuses the text, and we can observe its special prominence in chapters 3, 7, 10, 12, 13, 14, 19, 20, and 24, as well as its odd intrusion in the final chapter's peroration.[45] Second, Machiavelli gives less than usual emphasis to the literary education of the prince. Whereas the other writers were laboring to create a Renaissance Man, Machiavelli "only glancingly mentions the question of the ruler's 'intellectual training.'"[46] The reason for this difference is simple: why study what will mislead you? Machiavelli fills the gap here by recommending hunting, which was suggested in the conventional texts as a form of physical exercise but is given additional significance in *The Prince* because it provides training in topography (chapter 14). Finally, the structure of Machiavelli's text reinforces his break with his genre by substituting instruction in propaganda for the standard discussion of eloquence. What

---

[41] *Nicoles* 10: "ἐγὼ δ' ἀποδέχομαι μὲν ἅπαντασ τοὺσ λόγουσ τοὺσ καὶ κατὰ μικρὸν ἡμᾶσ ὠφελεῖν δυναμένουσ, οὐ μὴν 'αλλὰ καλλίστουσ 'ηγοῦμαι καὶ βασιλικωτάτουσ καὶ μάλιστα πρέποντασ 'εμοί τοὺσ περὶ τῶν ἐπιτηδευμάτων καὶ τῶν πολιτειῶν παραινοῦντασ."

[42] Struever, *The Language of History*, 63.

[43] Delio Cantimori, "Rhetoric and Politics in Italian Humanism," *Journal of the Warburg and Courtauld Institutes*, 1 (1937-38), 97 ff.

[44] "Both Felix Gilbert and Skinner stressed the extent and importance of recognizing Machiavelli's continuity with the genre: "The Humanist Concept," 451-52; *Foundations*, I, 129. Gilbert's subsequent analysis of how Machiavelli's point of view "left its mark on the structure of *The prince*" (477) established the now-standard reading of chapters 15-19 as refutative.

[45] Neal Wood, "Machiavelli's Concept of *Virtù* Reconsidered," *Political Studies, 15* (1967), 159-72. I. Hannaford provides a critical rejoinder, "Machiavelli's Concept of *Virtù* in *The Prince* and *The Discourses* Reconsidered," *Political Studies*, 20 (1972), 185-89.

[46] Skinner, *Foundations*, I, 122.

were lessons in conventional pedagogy and composition become a treatise on the use of verbal deception, that is, a redefinition of the art of rhetoric consistent with his metaphysic. Chapters 18, 19, and 21 detail the prince's manipulation of discourse, while chapters 22 and 23 offer guidance against those capable of persuading the prince. Taken as a whole, then, where *The Prince* most obviously follows the format of its genre (in the dedication and chapter 15) it denounces the genre's entanglement with language, and it then deviates obviously from the conventional topics of the genre by omitting attention to literary study while articulating ideas of force and verbal deception.

Machiavelli's break with his genre is evident in another manner as well. The gist of his innovation is that he repudiated the genre's most basic assumption—its belief that politics is circumscribed by words. Thus, an interesting sign of the break is his omission of the one element of the genre that most signified the metaphysic of textuality: the frequent citation of prior writers. The citation of sources was a common characteristic of the genre, allowing the writer to incorporate political commentary into a reflective field of sacred and secular literatures. This habit seems trivial today, as Allan Gilbert observed: "The scholasticism and classicism of the majority of these authors, taken together, has hidden their import from the modern world, even from professed students of politics. Our forgetfulness of the relation of ethics and politics, . . . our assumption that citations from classical authors are merely pedantry, . . . such things have allowed us to suppose that the books of advice to rulers that casually come to our notice were always as lifeless as they now appear."[47]

This hint is a good one, for those citations gave life to the texts by giving them both persuasive power and meaning. The citation operated as a rhetorical technique (the appeal to authority), as an epistemology (where knowledge was lifted above the confusions of *fortuna* by being based in texts), and as a sign of the nature of power being created and restrained by the *logos* known through both sacred and secular texts. But not in *The Prince*: despite some allusion in the work,[48] and widespread

---

[47] A. Gilbert, *Machiavelli's Prince*, 5.

[48] Machiavelli quotes Tacitus (in chapter 13) and Livy (in chapter 26) without naming them, and, as Burd, Allan Gilbert, and others have documented, the work reflects the allusiveness characteristic of its educated author and his milieu. But of course other writers were allusive as well, and some *specula* were written without frequent citation of authorities. There are two key determinations guiding this analysis of Machiavelli's text. First, the use of another author's name usually is meaningful semiotically and rhetorically: the name operates as a sign of authority that in turn constitutes at once a higher appeal to argumentative authority and a more limiting definition of the text's relationship to other texts and to the world. Second, the presence or absence of such signs can be determined to be significant only in respect to specific considerations of situation and strategy pertinent to that text. Rather than applying a universal linguistic rule, we need to determine in specific cases how the presence or absence of these signs functions, along with other textual dynamics, to create characteristic forms of consciousness. In this

appropriation in his other works,[49] *The Prince* refers to only two authors by name—Virgil in chapter 17 and Petrarch in chapter 26. Interestingly, these do the conventional work of shoring up his argument when it is most controversial. For the most part, however, *The Prince* is presented as a sheer text, directly communicating unencumbered experience. In short, I am suggesting that Machiavelli's omission of this convention operates as one of the changes by which he altered his form of expression to articulate a new political consciousness. Although this break with convention cannot demonstrate entirely his subordination of textuality, it can perhaps serve as an apt illustration of the difference in sensibilities that I am attempting to chart.

The following texts can illustrate the importance of Machiavelli's omission of citations: a major contemporary text, Erasmus's *Institutio; a* subsequent translation, Edward Dacres's text with "animadversions"; and most interestingly, a Renaissance plagiarism of *The Prince*. The first comparison shows us a masterful presentation of the conventional form, while the other texts demonstrate attempts by lesser writers to "correct" Machiavelli's text by restoring the missing conventions.

The contemporary text that stands as the model of the genre in Desiderius Erasmus's *Education of a Christian Prince*, which was printed in 1516, ran through eighteen editions and several translations during his lifetime, and continued to be widely read and quoted through the seventeenth century, after which the record grows hazy.[50] Erasmus stands at every corner as Machiavelli's opposite: the scholar, writing in Latin, for a hereditary ruler, to engender Christian government. The difference in literary consciousness can be marked easily, however, by observing Erasmus's "constant references to classical antiquity in true humanistic fashion."[51] The dedicatory epistle can suffice for this comparison, for it refers directly to Aristotle, Xenophon, Proverbs, Plato, Homer, Plutarch (who in turn is quoting Alexander the Great on Diogenes the Cynic), and Isocrates, as well as alluding to two Biblical stories and to scholasticism. As an interesting complement, when he does refer to the present circumstances of the Prince he compares him (favorably) to Alexander, to his ancestors surrounding him on every side, and to his deceased father. The unbroken impression, then, is that the Prince is inextricably enmeshed in a society of prior authorities, some of whom are the authors of texts while others serve as texts themselves. The dead have become *exempla*, rhetorical figures having as much presence as the living and

---

manner we can determine both patterns of usage, as with the genre, and moments of radical change, as with The *Prince*.

[49] "Great parts of the *Discourses* are simply straight comments on succeeding chapters of Livy. In his other works he pursued traditional patterns still more slavishly" (F. Gilbert, *Machiavelli and Guicciardini*, 164).

[50] Born, "Introduction," 29.

[51] *Ibid.*, 30.

more authority, and any distinction between ancient author, prior ruler, and current prince is, well, something not quite determined. Power has been denominated as *personae* themselves defined simultaneously by their words and their affinities for each other. The political world is textual and texts social, and so the personality of the prince can only be found in the common association of these prior authors and authorities. Erasmus is well aware of the abuse of power—witness his discussions of tyrants— but he sees them from within a textual universe where the difference between forms of power is determined by the influence of persuaders upon the prince's soul. So it is that Erasmus can fret about the very order of the young prince's reading.[52]

The conflict between textual and non-textual metaphysics is exemplified further in the subsequent history of Machiavelli's text. An interesting case here is the English translation "with some marginal animadversions noting and taxing his errors" by Edward Dacres in 1640.[53] Dacres's edition provides a graphic depiction of the conflict between these two modes. On the one hand we have Machiavelli's text, and set against it we have Dacres's commentary, which is designed both to establish that *The Prince* does merit reading despite its reputation as being "pernicious to all Christian states and hurtful to all humane societies,"[54] and to repair the damage done by some of Machiavelli's advice. Dacres is no fool— witness the realism in his deft comment that Machiavelli is "much practiced by those that condemn him"[55]—but his arguments are quite different than Machiavelli's use of experience.

Dacres writes a dedication to his prince (James, Duke of Lenox), an epistle to the reader, and five animadversions. The appeals rest largely upon analogy or citation of authority, or both: for example, the dedication argues that Machiavelli should be read because poisons have medical uses, because the lamprey becomes a choice dish once the venom is removed, because, as Epictetus says, everything has two handles like a fire brand and because sin is like fire though worse. The basic manner of thinking here is textual: you either cite a text, or allude to one (principally Scripture), or connect separate elements of the world by making texts such as analogies which are patently artificial.

The rest of his text elaborates this pattern. The reader is cautioned against severe application of Christian values, for the bee and the spider use the same flower. Dacres objects to the use of Cesare Borgia as the exemplary leader by invoking the analogy of the body politic and Daniel 4.17. He objects to the discussion of virtue and vice by analogy to stories

---

[52] Born, *Education of a Christian Prince*, 200.

[53] Edward Dacres, *Machiavel's Discourses upon the First Decade of T. Livius, translated out of the Italian. To which is added his Prince: with some Animadversions noting and taxing his errors*, the second edition much corrected and amended (London, 1674).

[54] Dacres, *Prince*, 513.

[55] *Ibid.*

about David from I Samuel 26, 25, 26. He challenges the claim that it is better to be feared than loved by protesting that it is "contrary to which all stories show us,"[56] referring to two figures from Roman history, and citing Psalm 15, a quotation in Latin by Charles V, and Gulielmus Xenocarus. He endorses, for rather transparent motives, Machiavelli's emphasis upon good councilors, and cites Proverbs 20, 25, 28, Isocrates (*To Nicocles*), and Plutarch. Finally, he opposes Machiavelli's account of fortune in chapter 25, for it "can't satisfy a Christian about causes of things,"[57] by making the world like a game at tables and citing Ecclesiastes 9, Proverbs 16, and Genesis 39. Note also how the analogy of gambling is hardly an application of Christian doctrine, suggesting that Christianity is less at issue than is the manner of thinking. If we apply the maxim that thinking is the development of available symbolic material, then we can conclude that Machiavelli's elision of the textual authorities subverted one way of thinking, including its characteristic ideas, and that Dacres's attempt to maintain those ideas consisted primarily of recovering the elided material.

The extreme example of this response to *The Prince* is provided by one of Machiavelli's contemporaries. Agostino Nifo was an academic whose works include fourteen volumes of commentaries upon the works of Aristotle and a defense of the doctrine of the immortality of the soul. He also produced a plagiarism of *The Prince* under the title *De regnandi peritia* at Naples in 1523.[58] This plagiarism demonstrates perfectly how a conventional reader of Machiavelli's time would understand his genre. Nifo has impressive credentials as a conventional thinker, and his many changes are direct reactions to *The Prince*'s deviations from the genre's sensibility. For example, the work is written in Latin, the language of the medieval cultural hegemony, and the title is changed to subordinate the concept of the new ruler to the concept of government understood as a process of administration. (Nifo naturally would assume that "Most of the works *de regimine principum* are based on settled hereditary rule.")[59] Most importantly, he supplied the missing citations, including Aristotle (repeatedly, with reference to his *Rhetoric* more than any other work), Cicero, Plato and Socrates, Herodotus, Hesiod, Varro, Plutarch, Ovid, Demosthenes, Strabo, and others. It is reasonable to read these changes as the chief signs of the difference between Nifo's mind and Machiavelli's—that is, between the genre as Machiavelli found it and as he changed it. Moreover, the greater the deviation from the original argument the more Nifo relies upon his authorities: so the typology of

[56] *Ibid.*, 596.

[57] *Ibid.*, 634.

[58] Augustino Nipho, *De regnandi perita*, 1523.

[59] A. Gilbert, *Machiavelli's Prince*, 23. The old debate about the two names for Machiavelli's work—*Il Principe* and *De principatibus*—covers the same ground Nifo is plowing. See, e.g., A. Gilbert, *Machiavelli's Prince*, 8f., Burd, *Il Principe*, 175-76.

the forms of government beginning the work is a relatively plain text, while the last book's argument for moral government follows a litany of authorities to the last paragraph's reference to Isocrates—the letter *To Nicocles*. Nifo has worked his way backwards through the turn Machiavelli constructed: where *The Prince* began with Isocrates in order to repudiate him, so Nifo has begun with Machiavelli in order to return to Isocrates.

In order to clarify further this agon between Machiavelli and the other writers, two counter-arguments should be discussed briefly. The first contention is that Machiavelli's omissions were more a mark of medieval textuality than of modernity. Despite feeling the need to argue the point, Burd states emphatically that "it is quite natural that Machiavelli should not acknowledge his authorities; a literary conscience was only developed when the spread of printing made it likely that plagiarism would be detected."[60] Burd errs in both the specific counterpoint and his general suggestion that the omission is remarkable yet uninteresting. It is a truism that Machiavelli was free of the contemporary fetish with citations, but we know from the letter of 10 December 1513 that his literary conscience was developed enough to fret about the plagiarism of his own work. The general excuse ignores the fact that Machiavelli's other works are much more directly derivative than is *The Prince*.[61] The other works appropriated traditional forms without strain, yet he wrote *The Prince* both in antagonistic reference to his genre and without use of one of its conventions; why then should we conclude that the literary sensibility is unchanged?

The second claim, which underlies all attempts to chronicle Machiavelli's allusions, is that Machiavelli, like any learned writer addressing an erudite audience, was steeped in and so influenced by his (classical) learning. Marcia Colish recently gave this claim special significance when she argued that *The Prince* relied upon no less a precursor than *De officiis*.[62] This argument does introduce a helpful corrective into my analysis, for we should not assume that Machiavelli's attack upon textuality worked in the manner of inducing either absolute affirmation or absolute repudiation of prior authors, or that his designs would be effective only if his artistry was never recognized by his readers. The argument that influence upon the writer is demonstrated by allusion for the reader faces a deeper problem, however. It is one thing to observe Machiavelli's appropriation of Cicero and many other classical authors,

---

[60] Burd, *Il Principe*, 173.

[61] Gilbert, *Machiavelli and Guicciardini*, 164.

[62] Marcia L. Colish, "Cicero's *De Officiis* and Machiavelli's *Prince*," *Sixteenth Century Journal*, 9 (1978), 81-93. For a reassertion of the argument that Machiavelli used the allusions to Cicero—and especially the strong allusion to *De officiis* in Chapter 18—to subvert conventional ethics, see Mark Hulliung, *Citizen Machiavelli* (Princeton, 1983), 212-13.

but quite another to square this fact with his reputation as an innovator. Put simply, Machiavelli is not Machiavelli because he read Cicero, Aristotle, or anyone else. Once we weigh both his allusiveness and his reputation, we have to accept that the appropriation of prior writers cannot be determinative of the basic action of his text upon other texts and so upon the political consciousness of the reader. We do have to account for how Machiavelli managed this tension within his text, however, and this is why the letter of 10 December 1513 figures so prominently on all sides. What Colish and others miss here is that Machiavelli not only is defining his relationship with his precursors but is also renegotiating the relationship between the reader and those texts. He not only reads the classical authors, he secrets himself with them. We then become disposed to see the texts as hermetic, valuable to the world only via the interpreter. They are guides, but tricky, and so a basic trade-off is offered: they are removed from the world, in the sense of no longer providing a check upon princely power, and are replaced by the office of the princely advisor, who now reads for the prince and so receives an oblique transfer of the power previously residing in the texts.[63] Despite the role of the advisor being held quite self-consciously in *De officiis* and in the generic texts written for princes, we find there nothing like Machiavelli's rhetorical stance, which we know too well today as the stance of the expert.

Thus, the more plausible case is that *The Prince* has acquired its status as a premier object of modern political commentary precisely because it did accomplish a change in sensibility. Why else would its reputation be so untouched by the common perceptions that it ignores key dimensions of modern political experience and that it is too often flat wrong, especially when these are the author's professed standards for evaluation? Yet, the full significance of Machiavelli's invention of modernity in *The Prince* lies beyond the claim that his political thought is another example of modern thought. Here Blumenberg can help us, for by entering into his argument against the secularization thesis on behalf of a reconsideration of the rationale for modernity, we are brought to consider more fully the implications of Machiavelli's innovation. For example, how can Machiavelli's invention of the modern metaphysics of power contribute to an understanding of the modern age as a culture whose ideas come neither from an act of radical self-creation *ex nihilo* nor from the awkward continuation in the modern habitat of the deeply compelling ideas of the past? Furthermore, has his reputation as the inspiration of so many modern experiments and modern evils been due to his successful understanding of modern self-assertion or due to the extension of his precepts beyond the limits of a rationality he himself imposed? I shall close by discussing how rhetor Machiavelli alternately confirms and challenges Blumenberg's argument.

[63] Cf. Colish, *op. cit.*, 93.

Blumenberg has developed his impressive case against the conventional wisdom that modern thought is the secularization of key concepts in medieval theology and on behalf of a careful reaffirmation of the modern age's capability for the production of a more humane world. He argues that the secularization thesis fails to meet basic standards of explanation, requires a muddled view of language, confuses or overlooks other forms of historical change, and, generally, counters one myth of modernity (the myth of an epoch created *ex nihilo*) only by smuggling in propositions "that cannot be credited to or expected of the understanding of reality that is itself characterized as 'worldly.' "[64] In short, the secularization thesis is itself an example of the thought it labels inauthentic. Blumenberg's reconsideration of the legitimacy of modern thought relies upon an alternative model of the historical process. Those ideas of our time that appear most abusive, susceptible to critique, and illustrative of secularization—ideas such as "progress" and "the state"— are actually authentic and melioristic innovations that have become monstrous by their "reoccupation" of the vacated positions in the prior epoch's cultural system. By discriminating between the modest and imperial versions of modern ideas, we can discover the legitimacy of the modern age. Genuine modernity lies in the modest versions of such ideas as self-assertion and theoretical curiosity, and the role of the modern thinker is essentially the Kantian project of discerning the internal limits of any form of rationality in order to reverse the objectification of culture.

Just as Skinner and J. G. A. Pocock have done for modern political thought, Blumenberg has raised the stakes for the study of all early modern thought. Machiavelli lies in a blind spot of his epochal perspective, however; consequently, the following comments are offered as an attempt both to extend Blumenberg's account to clarify our understanding of Machiavelli as a composer of modern thought, and to use this emphasis upon rhetor Machiavelli as a means of contributing to Blumenberg's discussion of modernity.

The most obvious connection here is Machiavelli's doctrine of self-assertion: it is no news to observe that he is encouraging princes to behave as individuals striving to dominate others in a hostile world. This is only half the story, however, for a full consideration of this stance requires analysis of how the form of his text reinforces its content—that is, how the text itself is a form of self-assertion. *The Prince* not only provides a representation of a natural world in which the individual has to be self-assertive in order to survive his predators,[65] but it also is a text in which

---

[64] Blumenberg, *Legitimacy*, 5.

[65] This representation, which suffuses the text, also challenges Blumenberg's argument that self-assertion and self-preservation are, respectively, the modest and imperial versions of modern thought. Machiavelli discovers self-assertion, but in a world where self-preservation rules.

self-assertion is the essential speech act. The truly sovereign individual in the work is the author's persona, which is created explicitly as the assertion of an individual against the medieval community maintained through the rules of generic composition and the common sense of decorum. Furthermore, this individual then becomes the sole means for holding together what has been broken by his arrival: the personality of Machiavelli alone is the means for overcoming the contradiction between the language of texts and the world of actuality. Once discourse (especially known by its sensibility of decorum) has been discarded as a means of completing a scene, and so incapacitated as a source of political motives, the individual becomes the principle of cohesion by default, whether within a text or a polity. Thus, in the modern conception, the state is defined not as a collectivity but as a supreme individual. Not surprisingly, "international law" then assumes all the properties Machiavelli attributed to conventional political texts: it neither confers nor restrains the sovereignty states hold by force.

In other words, although the book does celebrate self-assertion by discussing the means for achieving legitimacy, presenting arguments on behalf of innovation, presenting portraits of successful and unsuccessful innovators, etc., it also illustrates the technique for creating a discourse of power suited to the self-conception of the modern age. Machiavelli himself eschews the conventional means for assuming textual authority— he does not identify himself with the signs of legitimate discourses, but instead subverts them by portraying them *as discourses* and so alienated in a material world. This "logic" of self-assertion has since been reproduced endlessly, from the doctrine of raison d'état,[66] to Hegel's definition of the German state against the German constitutions, to our mass media's incessant debunking of political speech. In every case, understanding the modern age requires reading Machiavelli not only as the proponent of self-assertion for the few fortunate enough to have *lo stato* within their reach, but also as the modern writer schooling all of us to attain self-assertion by overruling our texts.

This successful composition of modernity in turn shapes its counterpoints, for which two examples may suffice. First, among those who do continue to take political texts seriously, the stakes are raised, for now meaning has to have an identity similar to individuality and a presence similar to materiality. Hence, the insistence, for some, upon identifying textual meaning with authorial intention—that is, with the original act of self-assertion—and the difficulty experienced by others who wish to locate meaning in something more communal, such as "discourse." Second, reliance upon the individual as the principle of meaning in a material

---

[66] Here I am following the argument of Friedrich Meinecke, *Die Idee der Staatsräson in der neueren Geschichte* (Berlin, 1924); tr. Douglas Scott as *Machiavellianism: The Doctrine of Raison d'Etat and Its Place in Modern History* (New Haven, 1957).

world results in the trauma that occurs whenever the idea of the individual is weakened (as when, in Kenneth Burke's comic words, Freud made the self a "parliment"), or whenever a collectivity asserts itself independently of state representation (as when any "people" announces itself).

This reconsideration of self-assertion requires in turn a reappraisal of Machiavelli's "realism," for the two ideas are mutually supportive in his text, particularly in respect to questions of legitimacy. Put bluntly, the strongest form of self-assertion appears most legitimate in respect to the harshest realism, and as our ability to define reality becomes qualified self-assertion becomes more suspect. Here Blumenberg's critique of secularization theory can be instructive. Following Hannah Arendt, he distinguishes two models of modernity: on the one hand, we can conceive of the shift from a transcendent system to a realistic perception of the world; on the other hand, we can conceive of leaving a transcendent system for another "unworldly world." Clearly, Machiavelli's break with his genre conforms exactly to the first model of modernity. In Blumenberg's language, his break with the transcendent system represented by the genre still occurred under "the influence of the theological system of categories,"[67] and it is this hidden logic that allows him to meld classical and contemporary events into a common world of experience, and that impels both Machiavelli and his successors to equate artifice with an imaginary world.[68] By contrast, the second model brings us to emphasize Machiavelli the writer, striving perhaps for a realistic style but never comprehensible entirely in respect to the accuracy of his propositions. More to the point, it is the "unworldliness" of *The Prince* that should interest us, for if the text contains an internal check upon any tendency toward an imperial form of self-assertion, it must lie there. Conversely, if the sole check is taken to be the intractability of reality itself, then the legitimacy of his self-assertion diminishes as that reality is revealed to be a construct created through the language of self-assertion.

This discussion in turn leads to Blumenberg's accounts of secularization and reoccupation. The easy observation here is that Machiavelli was a maker of modern thought in a milieu and by a means that belie secularization.[69] Furthermore, both his stance of hostile engagement with his genre and his role as a model of discourse are elements in a historical process that can be misconstrued easily as secularization. The more interesting consideration here, however, is determining the shape of the

---

[67] Blumenberg, *Legitimacy*, 9.

[68] Cf. Blumenberg, "An Anthropological Approach to the Contemporary Significance of Rhetoric," in Kenneth Baynes, James Bohman, and Thomas McCarthy (eds.), *After Philosophy: End or Transformation?* (Cambridge, Mass., 1987), 454, offering an aside on Hobbes that has him authoring modernity in the same manner as Machiavelli.

[69] The argument that Machiavelli wrote to restore pagan thought addresses many of the points involved here. For the most extended presentation of this perspective, see Hulliung, *Citizen Machiavelli*.

historical process that rhetor Machiavelli exemplifies. Only a suggestion can be made here: modernity emerges less as a doctrine of assertion (of the right to know, the will to power, etc.) and more as an act of disassociation. Modernity begins not as new ideas but as new strategies of writing, which, furthermore, work more by indirection than frontal assault. Modernity then is less a process of empirical discovery and more a process of invention, in the rhetorical sense of the term—the generation of the means for persuasion. Here we can challenge the self-conception of the modern age as an epoch of increasingly clear vision, plain speech, and efficiency. Modern discourses are crafted to create such an effect,[70] and in succeeding they demonstrate that characteristic of our time that we least admit to: subtlety.

Although this emphasis upon the composition of thought can enhance the case against secularization theory by encouraging "non-theological" accounts of modernity, it also challenges Blumenberg's construct of reoccupation. We can always distinguish humble and imperial versions of Machiavelli—he can stand for the humble idea of mastering skill to exercise political command in a world of contingency, or for the imperial idea of controlling all choice in all spheres of life by use of force and deceit—and the latter idea can be explained as an example of reoccupation, and the former idea can be used to criticize the latter. But the reoccupation model requires overlooking the origination of ideas in discourse. (Here is the cost of Blumenberg's working without having made a linguistic turn, which admittedly contributes to the freshness of some of his assertions.)[71] Machiavelli's composition of modernity provides no discrimination at the level of discourse between the new ideas of his time. Both are created by removing textual restraints on power and appraising the legitimacy of each requires recognizing how they master, or fail to master, a paradoxical condition of their own making. Furthermore, the shift from textuality to topography creates a tendency to move from the lesser to the larger idea, and without benefit of any prior system's gravitational pull. When power is understood in terms of speech it is checked, relational, circumscribed by the exigencies of being heard by an audience or understood by a reader, and always awaiting a reply. When power is understood in terms of vision it is unchecked, expansive, requiring only the movement of the person seeing to acquire the means for complete control of the environment. Machiavelli is comprehensible as the exponent

---

[70] See John S. Nelson, Allan Megill, and Donald N. McCloskey (eds.), *The Rhetoric of the Human Sciences: Language and Argument in Scholarship and Public Affairs* (Madison, 1987).

[71] See William Bouwsma's review of *Legitimacy* in *Journal of Modern History*, 56 (1984), 701; also Hans Blumenberg, *Work on Myth*, tr. Robert M. Wallace (Cambridge, Mass., 1985), and the review by Bouwsma in *JHI*, 48 (1987), 347-54; "A Bibliography of Blumenberg's Work and Responses to It" appears in *Annals of Scholarship*, 5 (1987), 97-108, an issue devoted to a symposium on Blumenberg.

of the modern state not because he described the state but because he composed a discourse capable of articulating the expansive potential in state power. Moreover, his strategy of defining power against discourse proves to be the perfect antidote to the great body of legal literature comprising the constitution of the state as an incarnation of law rather than power. Thus, at the level of discourse, the basic division of ideas essential to Blumenberg's case seems to break down. If we accept that Machiavelli figures prominently in the composition of modernity, then we perhaps should hope that the legitimacy of the modern age lies less in holding to weaker forms of now long-amplified tendencies to excess, and more in recognizing possibilities for recovering, by reinterpretation, the terms of our own making.

This essay has been one attempt to begin such reinterpretation. Machiavelli looms ever larger in contemporary political thought because his use of the speech act of the individual speaking against the received text generates both the metaphysics of modern political understanding and the paradoxical condition of political commentary becoming aggressively deconstructive. The classical rhetoricians had advised making one's discourse the more persuasive by making it appear natural; Machiavelli was a rhetorician with a vengeance, for he did the same with the world that was made of discourse. Politics was made to appear natural, which made political discourse its shadow and prior commentary the futile attempt to discern the light in the shadows.

Thus, his strategies for aggrandizing his own text ultimately work against him. He does set his discourse over the other writers, but only by setting in motion an attack upon all political discourse that has to destroy his own position. *The Prince* is not enigmatic, strictly speaking, but the experience of reading it is paradoxical. Machiavelli's reader loses through the act of reading itself the resources for integrating this political treatise into the political world. This is the sense in which *The Prince* is a truncated text: it articulates a metaphysie requiring its own incompleteness. The world of political powers—of "great powers" and "superpowers," of states and reasons of state—is set over the world of texts; politics is ubiquitous, suffusing all our affairs, all our texts, but power is autonomous, subject to no textual restraints, a sovereign mode of reality known only by its hard natural laws which can never be fully known within any medium clouded by desire.

Therefore, interpretation has to be endless, never capable of being surely validated, always somehow compensating for its own weakness before the force of events. Yet interpreters will always feel a need to complete the truncated text, for it at once stimulates and offends the textual intelligence, simultaneously promising and denying its own integrity. We now live in a world where power is a material force that manipulates discourses but never originates in them, yet any text still contains within it the reactionary turn to textual values, and so can goad us to imagine an "unworldly" world where political, ethical, religious, aesthetic, philosophical, economic, and other discourses are unified in an eloquence at once representing and consummating the community of interpreters.[72] This reaction is completed in the idea, perhaps not a modern idea, that textual values are the source of political community.[73] Maybe he is the realist—the rhetorician's dream that *una est eloquentia*[74] certainly is idealistic—but Machiavelli's demotion of textual values is at once a sharper perception of force and fragmentation and a limitation upon the motives for political renewal.

Drake University.

---

[72] For contemporary affirmations of this ideal, see the essays on Renaissance rhetoric by Vickers and by Garin in Vickers, *Rhetoric Revalued*.

[73] This perspective is championed today by, e.g., Alasdair MacIntyre, *After Virtue* (Notre Dame, 1984) and *Whose Justice? Which Rationality?* (Notre Dame, 1988).

[74] "Una est enim . . . eloquentia, quascumque in oras disputationis regionesve delata est" (Cicero, *De oratore* 3.23).

I am indebted to University House and the Rhetoric of Inquiry seminar at the University of Iowa for their support, and especially to Allan Megill.

XII

THE DISENCHANTED WITNESS: PARTICIPATION AND ALIENATION IN FLORENTINE HISTORIOGRAPHY

By Mark Phillips*

In modern practice history has become an investigation of the deep past for the enlightenment of the present, and we are only too aware that with each new present a new past will take shape. Earlier historians, on the contrary, troubled by the limits of living memory, wrote to preserve a record of the shallow past for the benefit of the future. Accordingly, for medieval and Renaissance writers of history the authority of the eyewitness carried more weight than written documents, the touchstone of modern research.[1] Intimacy with events, not objective distance from them, was the historian's best qualification.

In the small world of a late medieval commune like Florence many active citizens possessed just such a deep intimacy with public life, and scores of them expressed it in notebooks, diaries, and chronicles that often mixed 'indiscriminately,' as we would say, the record of private and public affairs. (The semi-official historiography of the humanist chancellors, Bruni and Poggio, was the exception, not the rule.) Even the growing rigidity of the Medici regime, though restricting the circle of the politically privileged, did not undo this fundamental identification of the citizen with his commonwealth as long as the communal ideal remained alive.

This intimacy of the citizen with his commonwealth, of the historian with his history, also implied a burdensome sense of responsibility. When the historian had to confront failure and frustration, which as will be seen was often the case, he could not easily dismiss the question of his own culpability. Thus the writing of history could also serve as an examination of conscience, individual and communal. Though the preservation of the collective record necessarily remained history's chief purpose, more particular memories might also urge the historian on, begging their place in the final accounting.

In this essay I examine a series of five such moments of personal participation as depicted by Florentine historians from the early 14th

* I am grateful for the support of the Humanities and Social Sciences Research Council of Canada and the Research Fund of the Arts Faculty, Carleton University. I also wish to thank Professors Felix Gilbert and Blair Neatby for their comments and criticism.

[1] A. Momigliano, "Historiography on Written Tradition and Historiography on Oral Tradition," *Studies in Historiography* (London, 1969), 211-20; D. Hay, *Annalists and Historians, Western Historiography from the VIII to the XVII Century* (London, 1977); and M.T. Clanchy, *From Memory to Written Record, England 1066-1307* (London, 1979).

to the mid-16th centuries. The choice of texts is, of course, selective, not exhaustive;[2] each of the narratives, however, has some importance in its own right, and taken together they reveal a common and compelling theme in Florentine historical writing. In each case the author identifies himself with the proper order of society, with what he would call the common good; and in each the unfolding of events leaves him bitter or alienated as he sees the common good betrayed for private interests. Naturally, Florentine society did not remain static over this lengthy period. Perceptions of the common good changed considerably, as did the nature of the forces that were thought to threaten it. To these changes as well as to the underlying continuities the following scenes of participation and alienation are a useful index.

Dino Compagni (ca. 1260-1324)

Compagni's *Chronicle* is the first full-scale work of the Florentine historiographical tradition, and none of its successors surpasses it in dramatic intensity. Unlike his more famous successor, Giovanni Villani, Compagni did not attempt a universal chronicle. Instead, he concentrated on the events of his own lifetime and told the story of the bitter rivalry between the White and Black Guelfs in Florence that lead to the triumph of the Blacks. As a prominent member of the defeated party, Compagni had followed the factional struggle closely. In his view, however, this involvement made him a privileged witness, not a biased one. In his opening pages, he proclaims his intention of telling "the truth concerning those things of which I was certain through having seen and heard them. . . which in their beginnings no one saw so clearly as I."[3] Thus he has no doubt that his authority as a witness is strengthened where he is most involved. Any reading of the *Chronicle* will reveal, however, the frustration and anguished intensity of a man who was once at the center of events and now spends his hours hopelessly reviewing their fatal outcome.

---

[2] My intention is not to deny the existence of other motifs in Florentine historical writing, but simply to point to the existence of the one under discussion here. Not every Florentine history was written by a disappointed politician, nor did every disappointed politician write a history. The *Commentarii* of Capponi (whether composed by the father or the son) are a tribute to a successful leader, while Rinaldo degli Albizzi could well have chosen to turn his *Commissioni* into history, but did not.

[3] "Quando io incominciai propuosi di scrivere il vero delle cose certe che io vidi e udi', però che furon cose notevoli, le quali ne' loro principi nullo lo vide certamente come io." *La Crónica di Dino Compagni*, ed. I. del Lungo, *Rerum Italicarum Scriptores*, vol. IX, pt. 2 (Città di Castello, 1913), 5-6. The English translation is taken from E.C.M. Benecke, *The Chronicle of Dino Compagni* (London, 1906), 5-6. On Compagni, see I. del Lungo, *Dino Compagni e la sua Cronica* (Firenze, 1879-1887). See also the useful introduction by Gino Luzzatto to *La Crónica di Dino Compagni* (Milan, 1906); rpt. Turin, 1968.

Compagni presents himself as being in the center in another sense, too. As Florence tore itself into opposing factions, Compagni was a Prior exercising his office in the name of the whole community and of peace. At a crucial moment in his *Chronicle* Compagni describes his effort to play this mediating role.[4] Charles of Anjou, the French prince who was regarded by the Black Guelfs as their leader and protector and by the Whites as a tyrant, was approaching the city. Things being in this state, says the historian, a holy and sincere (*santo e onesto*) thought came to me. This lord will come and find the citizens divided and great harm (*scandalo*) will follow. Because of the office he held and the good will he felt in his companions, he decided to bring together the many good citizens in the Church of San Giovanni, Florence's Baptistry. With all the officials present he spoke:

Dear and worthy citizens, who have all in common received Holy Baptism from this font, reason compels and urges you to love one another as dear brethren; and the more so because ye possess the noblest city in the world. Some ill will has arisen amongst you through rivalry for the offices of the State; but, as ye know, my colleagues and I have promised you with an oath to allow both parties to share them. This Prince is coming, and it behoves us to do him honour. Put away, then, your ill-will and make peace amongst yourselves, so that he find you not divided; put away all the offences and the wicked desires which have hitherto been amongst you; let them be pardoned and remitted for the love and the good of your city. And on this hallowed font, whence ye drew Holy Baptism, swear good and perfect peace betwixt one another, to the end that the Prince who is coming may find the citizens all united.[5]

Compagni's appeal was a powerful one using the most potent sanctions of the moral community. For his audience as for himself unity was an assumed good and division an inherent evil. Moreover, the dangers presented by the arrival of a powerful foreigner in a time of disorder were obvious and could be expected to impress even those who hoped to profit from Angevin power. Apparently the speech, and perhaps even more its setting, was too powerful for anyone openly to resist. And so, Compagni tells us, the citizens took the oath to keep

[4] The episode is contained in Bk. II, Chap. 8; *Cronica*, 98-101.

[5] Compagni, *Chronicle*, 92-93. "Cari e valenti cittadini, i quali comunemente tutti prendesti il sacro baptesmo di questo fonte, la ragione vi sforza e strigne ad amarvi come cari frategli; e ancora perchè possedete la più nobile città del mondo. Tra voi è nato alcuno sdegno, per gara d'ufici, li quali, come voi sappete, i miei compagni e io con saramento v'abiamo promesso d'accomunarli. Questo signore viene, e conviensi onorare. Levate via i vostri sdegni e fate pace tra voi, acciò che non vi trovi divisi: levate tutte l'offese e ree volontà state tra voi di qui adietro; siano perdonate e dimesse, per amore e bene della vostra città. E sopra questo sacrato fonte, onde traesti il santo battesimo, giurate tra voi buona e perfetta pace, acciò che il signore che viene truovi i cittadini tutti uniti." *Crónica*, 99-100.

the peace and preserve the honor and jurisdiction of the city by touching "the book"; and then they departed.

Unfortunately for Compagni and his fellow priors the concord that they had gained proved only to be a cover for political maneuver, and the powerful sanctions of the moral community were violated. Those citizens, Compagni laments, who had given the greatest show of assent, crying and kissing the Gospels, were chiefly responsible for the destruction of the city. Though for *onestà* he will not list their names, he cannot resist pinning the guilt on the first of these evil citizens, whose example caused the others to follow suit. This man, Rosso dello Stroza, "fierce in aspect and in deeds", shortly would pay the price of his false oath.

Compagni had done what he could to impose a moral order on the community, and the failure of the community to respond appropriately is seen unequivocally as moral failure, as hypocrisy and bad faith. But these accusations could cut both ways, and the historian records that the opponents of the peace said that the *caritevole pace* had itself been a deception. Writing decades after the events he chronicles, Compagni raises a personal voice of protest against this accusation and swears to the truthfulness of his account, not as a historian but as a participant: "If there was any fraud in the words spoken, I ought to suffer the penalty; although a good intention ought not to receive an ill reward."[6] In his own mind there is no question of the rightness of his course, and he concludes the chapter by recalling the many tears he had shed over this episode of the oath, "thinking of how many souls are damned for it through their wickedness."

Compagni's sense of pathos and injured merit gives this passage a personal appeal and directness that is usually the mark of a memoir rather than history. But Compagni resisted the temptation to fall into mere self-justification, perhaps because his own role in the events was in the end secondary. Nonetheless, the extraordinary appeal of his history must owe a great deal to this moment of personal participation and his sense of righteousness in confronting a city that had profaned its oath.

The Chronicle of Alamanno Acciaioli, 1378

Compagni's chronicle long remained hidden and thus exerted little influence on subsequent historical writing in Florence. On the other hand, the situation he described was to recur frequently. The Ciompi revolt of 1378 was Florence's most dangerous political crisis, the one time when factional strife broadened and deepened into a full social

---

[6] Compagni, *Chronicle*, 93. "Se nelle parole ebbe alcuna fraude, io ne debbo patire le pene, benchè di buona intenzione ingiurioso merito non si debba ricevere." *Crónica*, 101.

revolt. Among a series of relatively brief chronicles recording that
event, there is one that bears resemblance to Compagni's account:
this chronicle is presumed to be the work of one of the Priors,
Alamanno Acciaioli, and it too stands as a memorial to the frustrations
of a peacemaker in a bitterly torn city.[7]

Acciaioli and his colleagues inherited the political crisis. A virtual
coup and mob violence had destroyed the conservative Guelf faction.
But the new Priors, Acciaioli tells us, brought the city hope of peace
because they were seen to be pacific men. They put these hopes into
action by settling the commune's disruptive three-year war with the
States of the Church and, in the best traditions of medieval government, they sought the counsel of the citizens. Despite a lull, however,
the citizens failed to disarm and return to their workshops. Stirred up
by leading citizens, popular agitation resumed.[8] Acciaioli's chronicle
soon becomes a graphic description of the progressive deterioration of
the Priors' position and their abandonment by the other elements in
the communal government. The Eight of War, the powerful commission responsible for military matters, was clearly working against
them. When the Priors requested protection, they were told that no
soldiers were available, but the Priors soon discovered that they were
being used to protect the houses of the Eight. Nor did the traditional
communal militia respond. They, too, gave their first thoughts to
protecting their own houses. Neither commands nor prayers were of
any use, wrote Acciaioli.[9]

Still the depths of the Priors' personal crisis had not yet been
reached. Having been abandoned by all others, now they abandoned
each other.[10] One of their number made an excuse to leave his place
at the side of his colleagues and slipped out of the Palazzo to go home.
This defection was noticed by the crowds gathered outside, and
shortly the cry went up for all the others to follow. Here Acciaioli,
from the core of his own personal stake in the events, gives us a
brilliant evocation of the Priors' sense of themselves as lost and aim-
less men. "Each looked at the others, wondering what to do." Typically, they decided to consult with their colleagues in the other magistracies. Their fellow magistrates in the Colleges cried, he writes, some
wringing their hands, some striking their faces. All, dumfounded, did

---

[7] The Acciaioli chronicle is printed in *el tumulto dei Ciompi, Crónache e Memorie*,
ed. G. Scaramella, *R.I.S.* vol. 18, pt. 3 (Città di Castello, 1917-34) pp. 13-34. On the
Ciompi revolt and its interpretation, see G. Brucker, "The Ciompi Revolution" in
N. Rubinstein (ed.), *Florentine Studies* (London, 1968), 314-56; N. Rodolico, *I
Ciompi* (Florence, 1945); and V. Rutenburg, *Popolo e movimenti popolari nell' Italia
del '300 e '400*. trans. G. Borghini (Bologna, 1971), esp. Chap. V.

[8] Acciaioli, "Crónaca," 16-20.   [9] *Ibid.*, 25-27.
[10] For what follows, the climax of Acciaioli's account, see *ibid.*, 30-32.

not know what side to take. The Eight seemed sad and pained. The Priors were distracted, bewildered (*smemorati*). Finally, they were advised to submit to the ever increasing threats against their persons and their families. The *gonfaloniere*, leader of the Priors and chief magistrate of the city, "cried like a coward for his sons and his wife."

"Never were magistrates so abandoned as these Priors, since no one came forward or offered comfort." (*Mai si vide signori abbandonati, come furono questi priori, che non era nessuno che li confortasse e che si proferisse.*) Their desertion was complete. Even the staff and servants had hidden themselves, and no soldier was to be seen in the hall. The Priors themselves seemed lost men, wandering the Palace aimlessly, "some here, some there, some up, some down, and they did not know what to do." (*I priori, in quella, chi andava in qua, e chi in la, chi giu, chi su, e non sapevano che si fare.*)[11]

The first to escape was the chief magistrate of the city, the Standard Bearer of Justice, "cowardly and wicked," who sneaked away from his colleagues. The others followed. Only two priors wanted to remain, Acciaioli among them, but when they descended from their rooms to the audience hall, they found none of their companions. Thinking themselves as good as dead, they too went down, leaving the keys as they departed. "And thus," writes Acciaioli, "one can say that the happiness, calm, and well-being of the city was lost."

Acciaioli had no doubt of the lesson of the Ciompi revolt. The most conservative of the memorialists of 1378, he held to the Guelf vision of history, most impressively exemplified by Giovanni Villani a generation earlier. To Acciaioli it was perfectly clear that Florence had offended God by its conflict with the Church (1375-78) and that its present troubles were a well-merited punishment.[12] But Acciaioli's

---

[11] Consciously or unconsciously, Acciaioli's description echoes Dante's description of lost souls of lovers who because of their carnal desires forget reason for passion. They are like starlings whirling endlessly on the wind:

> E come li stornei ne portan l'ali
> nel freddo tempo a chiera larga e piena,
> cosi quel fiato li spiriti mali.
> Di qua, di la, di giu, di su li mena;
> nulla speranza li conforta mai,
> non che di posa, ma di minor pena.

(As in the cold season their wings bear the starlings along in a broad, dense flock, so does that blast the wicked spirits. Hither, thither, downward, upward, it drives them; no hope ever comforts them, not to say of rest, but of less pain.) Canto V, *Inferno*, trans. J. D. Sinclair (New York, 1939), 75.

[12] Acciaioli, "Crónaca," 18: "Per lo peccato commesso contro la santa chiesa d'Iddio, perché non rimanesse impunito . . . promise Iddio di dare questa disciplina a questa nostra città, come in questa scritta si racconta."

moralism was not joined to the sort of prophetic passion that inspired Compagni's denunciation of the crimes of the Blacks. Though his chronicle is briefer and more centered on the events of his own priorate than Compagni's, Acciaioli is less concerned with a personal betrayal or a personal vindication. His judgments are softened by a sense of frailty. Fear, irresolution, impatience, or petty ambition, not sheer wickedness, carry the current of men's actions. Many he emphasizes, who were neither good nor bad (*altri non rei uomini, ne buoni*) followed the artisans out of fear rather than love, and often private vendettas were accomplished in the midst of public turmoil.[13]

The uncertainties that frustrated and darkened Acciaioli's time in office remained with him as he reviewed the mistakes and lost opportunities of those days. Would matters have worked out better if the Priors had accepted the resignation of the Eight? Should they have treated the chief instigator of the riots, Salvestro de' Medici with such mercy? "They later regretted it deeply," he comments with regard to Salvestro, "but perhaps it was for the best not to deal with him as he deserved."[14]

In the end there are no traitors, as in Compagni, only cowards. Though Acciaioli insists that "stupidity and cowardice do not excuse them," he must spread his displeasure almost equally over all the leading magistracies of Florence: the Eight who manoeuvred rashly for power; the militia who failed to defend order; the Priors who through "cowardice and bewilderment" abandoned the Palace. It was a collective failure, and behind it stood the judgment of God on a city that had abandoned her Church, her traditions, and those few men who attempted to maintain peace and justice, Acciaioli among them.

Giovanni Cavalcanti (ca. 1381-1451)

It was traditional in medieval Europe that governments or rulers take counsel with the leading men of the realm and the obligation to give counsel, as well as to receive it, was taken seriously. In Florence this giving and taking of opinion took place in the *pratiche* consultative sessions which allowed the regime to sound the opinion of those not currently in the highest magistracies. The records of these sessions have provided recent historians with their most direct view of the working political language of the time. But no *pratica* session has given us a more palpable feeling for the realities of 15th-century Florentine political life than that attended by Giovanni Cavalcanti, as

---

[13] Acciaioli, *ibid.*, 25.

[14] On the offer of the Eight to resign, see *ibid.*, 20; on Salvestro, see 23: "I priori misericordiosi, come che àlcuni parlassero altrimenti, non di meno onestamente il ripresero e perdonarongli. Di che poi ne furono molto ripentiti. E forse fu per lo meglio di non fargli quello che ed e' meritava."

recounted at the beginning of the second book of his *Florentine History,* written in the 1430s.[15]

Cavalcanti was an impoverished member of an old and noble family. He belonged, therefore, to a class long discriminated against politically, and his poverty further restricted his political role. In fact, he composed his history while suffering a lengthy term of imprisonment for debt. He opens the second book of his sometimes eccentric narrative with language that takes us back a century to the chronicle of Villani. The city, he pronounces, was then at the height of its "worldly power" and the citizens, their "sails blown up" with aggrandizement, were ungrateful to Him from whom all gifts come. Caring nothing for anyone living or immortal, they took all credit to themselves for their own success. But, says Cavalcanti in language newer than Villani's, Fortune would have her rights recognized.

Against the background of this warning, Cavalcanti tells the story of a consultative council that he had attended. He found himself in assembly with the Priors along with many other citizens and with all the principal officials. Letters were read out by the Priors concerning reports of current military dangers. This done, those who had been asked to this audience were requested to give their counsel for the salvation of the Republic and to remedy the dangers of "our Commune."

Thus the opening moralisms are quickly passed over, and as we listen, Cavalcanti spreads before us a perfect tableau of the Commune in full participatory glory:

Do not seek, said the Lord Priors, why we ask counsel, since we do not ask it for our own concerns and interests. Indeed, we ask it as men who speak

---

[15] Giovanni Cavalcanti, *Istorie fiorentine* ed. F. Polidori (Firenze, 1838-39), 27-30. On Cavalcanti, see Marcella T. Grendler, *The "Trattato politico morale" of Giovanni Cavalcanti (1381-1451)* (Geneva, 1973); Claudio Varese, *Storia e politica nella prosa del Quattrocento* (Turin, 1961); Gian Mario Anselmi, "Contese politiche e sociali nelle 'Prime Storie' del Cavalcanti: il ruolo di Giovanni de' Medici," *Archivio Storico Italiano,* 134 (1976), 119-36; and esp., the recent and perceptive essay by Dale Kent, "The Importance of Being Eccentric: Giovanni Cavalcanti's View of Cosimo de' Medici's Florence," *Journal of Medieval and Renaissance Studies,* 9 (1979), 101-32. Dr. Kent's essay appeared after this paper was completed, but her sympathetic and enthusiastic reading of Cavalcanti confirms and amplifies my own. She argues strongly for Cavalcanti's importance as a historian and emphasizes his commitment to Florentine politics: "It is thus a sense of substantial identification with, not alienation from, the ruling class which informs his critique of it in the *Istorie*" (108). Similarly, also commenting on this same scene, she writes: "His own experience of that world gave him sufficient opportunity to gratify his passion for politics and to observe its operations, but he retained the critical detachment of a partial outsider towards its accepted norms and assumptions" (106). My own argument, of course, is that the "partial outsider"—a figure combining commitment and detachment— was a common type in Florentine historiography.

in the name of your Commune since, although today we are in this place, tomorrow you will be here . . . and we will have left this lordly office.[16]

These and other suitable words having been uttered, many citizens made their way to the rostrum to give counsel. "Diverse citizens gave their views," says Cavalcanti, "and their views were diverse." Meanwhile the historian himself, unused to public councils, listened attentively, and he waited especially for the counsels of one leading citizen, Niccolò da Uzzano.

And because I was not experienced in seeing how the affairs of the Republic were administered, I set my mind entirely to give myself some rule to govern me. And as the surest way, I chose the rule and skill of the famous citizen, Niccolò da Uzzano, the most esteemed and expert master.[17]

This was indeed a model occasion and its auditor a model citizen. The Priors self-consciously speak with the voice of the community, denying any private or particular interest in what they do. They are only temporary magistrates and the next bi-monthly rotation of office will put the audience itself in their place. Thus, it is only appropriate that those in attendance give their counsel, too, and give it in the same spirit of the common good. The diversity of the speakers and their views seems to fulfill this requirement and guarantee that the whole community will be heard. The historian himself, as one unused to government, prudently elects to follow the counsel of a leading citizen, whose experience and fame seem to guarantee his probity. It is interesting, too, that Cavalcanti here adopts language more suggestive of the classroom than of the political arena. He chooses to follow the rule and skill (*la regola e l'arte*) of Niccolò, while describing this famous citizen as the most esteemed and most learned master (*maestro più reputato a più dotto*).

But Cavalcanti's lesson in civics soon takes an ironic turn. While the letters were being read, while the proposition was being put, while the crowd (*la turba*) gave counsel, "the noble citizen slept soundly, and nothing of these matters did he hear, let alone understand." Finally, after much discussion, Niccolò awoke and, still "very sleepy,

---

[16] "Non guardate, dissono i Signori, perché noi addimandiamo consiglio; conciossia cosa che noi non lo chieggiamo per le nostre proprietadi, né per le nostre ispezialitadi: anzi il chieggiamo come uomini che favelliamo in nome del vostro Comune; conciossia cosa che, se oggi noi siamo in questo luogo, domani ci sarete voi . . . e noi ne saremo fuori del signorile magistrato." *Istorie*, 28.

[17] "E perché io non ero pratico a vedere come si amministravano i fatti della Repubblica, disposi l'animo mio al tutto a portarne alcuna regola di governo con meco; e per meno fallibile, elessi la regola e l'arte del preclaro cittadino Niccolo da Uzzano, maestro più reputato e più dotto." *Storie*, 28.

ascended the rostrum. Niccolò said: I am of this opinion... And Niccolò having given his opinion all the counsellors agreed with it." [18]

The lesson was not lost on Cavalcanti. It was clear that Niccolò and other powerful citizens had already reached an agreement over these letters in some private and secret place (nel luogo privato e segreto, accordato e conchiuso). The disillusioned "innocent" turned to some companions and they confirmed his opinion that the Commune was being governed at dinners and in studies and not in the communal Palace.[19] "While many were elected to office," they concluded, "few governed."[20]

Cavalcanti, often a rambling writer, here dramatizes with great literary skill a sense of the sharp division of public and private which is the common starting point of all Florentine historians. For Cavalcanti the substitution of private interest for the public good is the unmistakable sign of political wrongdoing. When the Priors exhort the citizens to give counsel in the light of common needs and deny any private interest of their own, they are manipulating the hallowed language of chroniclers of the communal period. But their selfconscious exploitation of the communal myth does not anger Cavalcanti in quite the same way as it would have angered Compagni or Villani. Niccolò and his following have demonstrated publicly a callous disregard for the constitution of the republic, and from this gross flaunting *(abbominevole audacia)* of political propriety, great evils would follow. Thus, for Cavalcanti the essential issue is the violation of constitutional form. The effect, he charges, is the subverting of republicanism by tyranny *(tirannesco e non politico vivere)*.

Alamanno Rinuccini (1426-1499)

Now we advance a half century to the time of outright Medici domination as witnessed by Alammano Rinuccini, a cultivated humanist as well as a chronicler. Though a far more cultured man, Rinuccini lacks Cavalcanti's skill in evoking the travesty of communal institutions. Instead, Rinuccini's *Ricordi storici* has a humbler purpose. It is not a narrative in the classical mode, but a simple *priorista*,

[18] "Mentre le preallegate lettere si leggevano, e la proposta si faceva, e la turba consigliava, il nobile cittadino fortemente dormiva, e niente di quelle cose udiva, non che le intendesse.... (Niccolò) tutto sonnolento saìl alla ringhiera. Disse Niccolò: Io sono di questo parere... Detto che ebbe Niccolò questo così fatto parere, tutti i consigliatori si accordorono al suo detto." *Istorie* pp. 28-29.

[19] At the beginning of the next century Guicciardini, in his *Florentine History.*, employs the same image but to very different effect: contrasting an earlier age of rationality before 1494 with the violent period that followed he writes: "And finally, states were maintained, mined, given, and taken away not by plans drawn up in a study, as used to be the case, but in the field, by force of arms."

[20] "... e che il Comune era più governato alle cene e negli scrittoi, che nel palagio: e che molti erano eleletti agli uffici, e pochi al governo. La qual cosa mi parve assai chiara che così fosse, e che ne seguisse grandissimi mali nella Repubblica di sì abbominevole audacia." *Istorie*, 30.

a chronological list of office-holders with marginal commentary. Rinuccini's main concern is to record the debates and decisions of the Florentine government, which as a ranking member of the Florentine oligarchy he was able to do so with great precision.[21] His *priorista* is distinguished from other records of this kind, however, by the strained and angry tone in which constitutional changes are reported. The reason is not hard to find in his report of the *Balìa* of 1480:

These priors, on the 8th day of April, without the ringing of bells or other public sign created, one can say, a parliament, for a *balìa* or truly a great council was created, in this way. On the said day, they convinced the Council of 100, and proposed and carried a provision in this form, and the same petition was carried in the Council of the People and The Council of The Commune on the 9th and 10th. The effect of this was that the Priors alone by the 6 beans would have the authority to elect 30 citizens, who would have authority to elect 210 other citizens, who, along with the above named 30 and the Priors and the Colleges then in office should be understood to be a council, or truly a *balìa*. And then the above mentioned 30 men in the month of November next should, together with the Priors who will then be in office, elect another 48 citizens, and thus all together with those named above should carry out a scrutiny of the magistracies, internal and external. From which one understands, or one is able to understand, that all liberty was taken away from the people, and they are entirely reduced to servitude of the above mentioned 30, as one reads happened before in Athens, from which followed the ruin of that city and the loss of liberty. And this I say truly, although I, Alamanno Rinuccini was made one of the number of that *balìa*.[22]

---

[21] Alamanno's chronicle or *priorista* is the continuation of his father's: *Ricordi storici di Francesco di Cino Rinuccini,* ed. Aiazzi (Florence, 1840). See also A. Rinuccini, *Lettere ed orazioni,* ed. V. Giustiniani (Florence, 1953); V. Giustiniani, *Alamanno Rinuccini, 1426-1499* (Cologne, 1965); and F. Adorno, "La crisi dell'umanesimo civile fiorentino da Alamanno Rinuccini al Machiavelli," *Rivista critica di storia della filosofia,* VII (1952) pp. 19-40.

[22] "Questi signori, a dì 8 di Aprile, sanza suono di campana o altra dimostrazione feciono, si può dire, uno parlamento; conciosiacosache' creassino una balìa ovvero consiglio maggiore in questo modo: Che detto dì ragunorono il consiglio del Cento, e proposono e vinsono una provisione in questa forma, e quella medesima petizione poi a dì 9 e 10 vinsono ne' consigli del popolo e comune, lo effetto della quale fu questo: che i signori soli per le 6 fave avessino autorità di eleggere trenta cittadini, i quali avessino autorità di eleggere uno numero di altri cittadini 210, i quali insieme con i soppradetti 30 e signori e collegi che allora erano in uficio, s'intendessino essere uno consiglio ovvero balìa, la quale durasse per tutto il mese di Giugno prossimo avvenire, ed avesse tutta la autorità che aveano i consigli del popolo, del comune e del Cento, e oltre a questo potessino dare qualunche autorità *et alia* a minore numero di cittadini, come a loro paresse; e che poi i sopradetti uomini 30 del mese di Novembre prossimo avvenire dovessino insieme con i signori, che al tempo fussino, eleggere altri 48 cittadini, e così tutti insieme con quelli nominati di sopra avessino a fare lo squittino degli ufici drento e di fuori; donde s'intese o si potè intendere esser levata ogni libertà al popolo, e in tutto esser ridotto in servitute de' sopradetti 30, come si legge esser già avvenuto ad Atene, di che seguì la rovina di quella cittade e la perdita della libertate; e questo parlo per il vero, benchè io Alamanno Rinuccini fossi creato uno del numero di quelli della balìa." *Ricordi storici,* CXXXI-CXXXII.

Two impulses are working here at the same time: a fascination with constitutional machinery and a conviction that the constitution was a cover for tyranny. The violation of communal practice is manifest from the start, with the creation of a *balìa* unsanctified by the symbols of the commune. The description of the complex electoral machinery that set up the *balìa* is full and detailed, and twice our attention is directed to the ambiguous constitutional status of the council of 30. Is it a *balìa*, a special commission with limited terms, or is it a council with overtones of permanence? But there is no doubt whatever as to the significance of this maneuvering, and the numerical correspondence with the thirty tyrants of Athens is given the fullest play. Both the loss of liberty and the destruction of the city will ensue, as happened in Athens. Thus an historical dimension is added to the political. These events signify the inevitable decline of the city when the energies of free citizens are suppressed.

Even for a man of Rinuccini's classical education, however, the classical parallel, though telling, is not the trump card. For Rinuccini, as for the simplest chronicler, the testimony of the eyewitness sets the final seal on the trustworthiness of his reconstruction of events: *e questo parlo per il vero, benché io Alamanno Rinuccini fossi creato uno del numero di quelli della balìa.* Yet there remains something ambivalent and troublesome in this final assertion, hinging as it does on the crucial conjunction "although" (benché). A simpler chronicler would have written that he knew these things to be true *because* (perché) he had been present. Rinuccini asserts, however, that *although* he recognized the tyrannical nature of the manipulations, he became a member of the Thirty. He remains, then, an eyewitness, but a troubled one, a participant, but a reluctant one. For Rinuccini, in short, unlike his predecessors, to be a witness meant some complicity, and his claim to truthfulness was asserted at some cost to his claim to righteousness.

Rinuccini saw himself as a defender of traditional Florentine republicanism against Medici usurpation. In his dialogue "On liberty" (written at the same time as this part of the chronicle), he presents himself as a philosophic exile from the corruptions of Medici rule, a man who has fled the city for the dignity and freedom of the countryside. His posture well suited to the traditions of classical dialogue; in chronicles, however, the eyewitness always possesses a certain authority, and Rinuccini is drawn into revealing a troublesome closeness to the sordidness he decried. With his understanding of constitutional intricacies, he cannot claim, like Cavalcanti, to have attended the councils as an innocent; nor will he offer to swear, like Compagni, to the sincerity of his actions. For once the inherent potential for tension between the two roles of participant and observer has been acknowledged, if only fleetingly. But, short of the dignified withdrawal

Rinuccini envisioned in his dialogue, the tension must remain. History is not written in complete detachment.

Francesco Guicciardini (1484-1540)

The last of our five scenes presents new variations on a familiar theme. The author and protagonist this time is Francesco Guicciardini, who of all the historians we have examined had the fullest and most successful political career.[23] The occasion is an abortive coup in Florence attempted by a group of young nobles, an event which came just before the sack of Rome of 1527 and hinted at the weakness of the Medici regime in Florence. The young insurgents managed to occupy the Palazzo, but they failed to raise the city to arms as they had hoped. This was the time of the second Medici Pope, Clement VII, and Florence was ruled from Rome. The Cardinal of Cortona, who acted as governor of Florence, prepared to defeat the rebellion with the aid of French soldiers in camp nearby. But, says Guicciardini, Cortona gave no thought to what an armed clash might cost the vulnerable city:

Thus preparations were being made for the dangerous contest, for the palace could not be captured without the death of almost all the nobility within it, and also there was the peril that once having set hand to arms and killing, the victorious soldiers would sack the city. Thus the Florentines prepared for many bitter and unhappy days. However, the Lieutenant Governor swiftly cut this most difficult knot. . . .[24]

The Lieutenant Governor is Guicciardini himself, though he does not say so here. Having noticed another papal official, Federigo da Bozzole, come out of the Palazzo after fruitless negotiations with the rebels, the Lieutenant Governor intercepted Federigo before he could tell the Cardinal of the weakness of the rebels' position. This information, which would have provoked an immediate attack by the soldiers, was suppressed, and going to the Palazzo himself, the Lieutenant Governor persuaded the youths to give up their revolt.

[23] On Guicciardini as a historian, see F. Gilbert, *Machiavelli and Guicciardini; Politics and History in 16th century Florence* (Princeton, 1965); and my own *Francesco Guicciardini: The Historian's craft* (Toronto and Manchester, 1977), where the same incident is discussed in a somewhat different context (117-19). The standard edition is *Storia d'Italia*, ed. C. Panigada (Bari, 1929), and the most extensive recent translation is *The History of Italy*, trans. S. Alexander (New York, 1969), which I have used here.

[24] *History of Italy*, 377. "Donde preparandosi pericolosa contesa, perché lo espugnare il palazzo non poteva succedere senza la morte di quasi tutta la nobiltá che vi era dentro, e anche era pericolo che, cominciandosi a mettere mano all'armi e all'uccisioni, i soldati vincitori non saccheggiassino tutto il resto della cittá, si preparava dí molto acerbo e infelice per i fiorentini; se il luogotenente con presentissimo consiglio non avesse espedito questo nodo molto difficile. . ." *Storia*, V, 132.

Looking back on these events ten years later with the perspective of the historian of Italy, Guicciardini still had no doubt that his quick action had saved Florence. But he had no cause to feel complacent about the part he had played. Though the Lieutenant Governor was greatly commended at the time, he writes, his actions earned him the enmity of both sides:

> The Cardinal of Cortona complained a little later that he was more concerned about the safety of the citizens than the grandeur of the Medici, and that this had been the reason why Medici rule had not been established permanently on that day by arms and the blood of citizens. And the multitude also blamed him afterwards, because when he went to the palace presenting the dangers to be greater than they were, he had induced them unnecessarily to give up for the benefit of the Medici.[25]

Thus, as we have seen so often before, the efforts of the peacemaker were attacked from both sides and the common good disregarded for the sake of factional interests. And although Guicciardini's intervention may seem to have been more successful than the others we have examined, this was only temporary. Shortly afterwards, Rome was sacked and Florence took the opportunity to overthrow the Medici. But within three years, this new republic also fell and the Medici tyranny was established permanently in Florence. For him personally the conclusion had to be that "ingratitude and calumny are more present than remuneration and praise for good works."

On a less personal level, it is clear that between Rinuccini and Guicciardini the axes of political discussion have shifted markedly. For Rinuccini the abuse of constitutional structures spelled loss of liberty, a perception of power which reflects the informal basis of Medici rule in the 15th century. But in the 16th century Medici hegemony was exercised more openly, without the cloak of constitutionalism and republicanism. What Guicciardini depicts in this episode is the preparatory clash of prince and people now clearly separate and opposed. But for Guicciardini neither choice was desirable. Subsequent pages reveal his dislike of the democratic republic; here it is clear that he recoils from founding a princely state on the blood of the citizens. For Guicciardini, in fact, the issue is no longer liberty or tyranny—these words are notably absent—but stability and good government. Cortona's carelessness of the lives of the citizens is a sign of the decay of civil government under the Medici. But, as subse-

---

[25] *History of Italy,* 378. ". . . nondimeno e il cardinale di Cortona si lamentò, poco poi, che egli, amando piú la salute de' cittadini che la grandezza de' Medici, procedendo artificiosamente, fusse stato cagione che in quel dí non si fusse stabilito in perpetuo, con l'armi e col sangue de' cittadini, lo stato alla famiglia de' Medici; e la moltitudine poi lo calunniò che, dimostrando, quando andò in palagio, i pericoli maggiori che non erano, gli avesse indotti, per beneficio de' Medici, a cedere senza necessitá." *Storia*, V, 133-34.

quent events proved, the attempt to overthrow this government by force would be equally destructive. Political violence would only lead to further political violence; the pendulum of power would swing further to the left and then further to the right. In the process the possibility of stable government by moderate men would be all but eliminated.

Conclusion

Early in the 14th century Compagni justified his actions by writing that "good intentions should not be rewarded by injury." And seven generations later Guicciardini echoed him in saying that "ingratitude and calumny are more present than remuneration and praise for good works." This sense of injured merit, disillusionment, and alienation runs through all of our accounts. Each one of these historians has seen himself as the supporter of a truer community than the one which events proved to be dominant; each one presents himself as a witness to the betrayal or destruction of this true community by men who were self-interested, cowardly, manipulative, or evil. We must conclude that in some sense each of them wrote to be such a witness. At the same time the differences between them remain as interesting as their common motives.

For Compagni, as we have seen, the community was both political and moral. Florence had been disrupted by the competition for office—that is, by factionalism and self-interest—and its political health could be restored by a redistribution of participation in government. At the same time the city was also a moral community whose peace and unity were guaranteed by sacred sanctions. The violators, therefore, were inescapably perjurers and traitors. For Acciaioli, a half century later, much of this remained true, though in a reduced and less confident form. For him too peace was the prime purpose of government. Similarly, Florence remained a moral community, though primarily in its obligation to protect the Church. Nonetheless, in his chronicle, though divine judgment operates over the city as a whole, specific moral sanctions are absent, and individuals are condemned more often for their fear and cowardice than for their sinfulness. Another half century later, in Cavalcanti's history, the sense of the sacred is gone and is partially replaced by a sense of the sanctity of republican forms and traditions. These forms remain rather broadly conceived, but in Rinuccini a far more strict and technical sense of the constitution appears. Thus, in retrospect, the somnolence of a leading citizen at the consultative council seems a violation of the spirit of the republic, while the electoral manipulations of the Medici constitute deliberate tyranny. Finally, in Guicciardini the dialectic between tyranny and liberty is set aside, or rather this clash of forces is itself held to be destructive. In the wake of a long line of crises and upheavals good government is identified with stability, order, and the protection of the citizens. Once again, as in Compagni's time, peace is the chief need of the community and the prime object of government.

Each of these histories, too, is an account of failure and, at the same time, a record of an individual historian's attempt to distance himself from the general calamity. The intimacy of a small-scale society made this a necessary and difficult task, at least for those born into the political class. Thus, of all of our authors only Cavalcanti, descendant of a disenfranchised nobility and a prison inmate, could afford in some ways to stand aside. Even so, his profession of naivety contains within it an aspect of self-accusation. Compagni, the first of the series, found it necessary to attest to his own sincerity with an oath in order to fend off the implication that, like his enemies, he too might have acted to protect factional interest rather than the common good. Acciaioli, for his part, found himself musing over past errors, only to shake off the thought by dwelling on the divine punishment the Florentines had merited by attacking the Church. For both of these early chroniclers, then, the sacred offered a kind of absolution, but their secularized successors, Rinuccini and Guicciardini, were more vulnerable to self-accusation. The boundaries of the politically responsible class were shrinking, and both Rinuccini and Guicciardini saw themselves as defending the traditional position of the patriciate and the political moderation it represented. As intimates of the Medici, however, they were implicated in the advance to princely rule. The irony was inescapable. In a time when forthright opposition was impossible, only the inner circles possessed either knowledge or influence. Under such circumstances to be a witness to failure was necessarily to be a party to it.

Carleton University, Canada.

XIII

Girolamo Cardano and the Art of Medical Narrative

Nancy G. Siraisi

The story Girolamo Cardano (1501-76) told most frequently was his own. He was not only the author of one of the most striking of Renaissance autobiographies but also recounted fragments of his own history throughout his voluminous writings.[1] In several bibliographies of his own works, in sample horoscopes in astrological treatises, in case histories in medical works, in examples in a treatise on dreams, as inspiration in moralistic treatises, he told and retold of his wretched childhood, his rejection by medical colleagues, his successes as a medical practitioner, mathematician and astrologer, his prolific career as an author, his impotence and other physical afflictions, the portents, dreams, and visions that came to him, and the tragedy of his elder son's execution for wife-murder. Here, for example, is Cardano on his own impotence in a treatise on *The Usefulness that Can Be Drawn From Adversity*:

This incredible evil happened to me in my twenty-first year. Then ... I first began habitually to lie with a girl, and was already as it seemed to me sufficiently strong and ready for sex. But the thing ended otherwise. For being obliged to return home [*in patriam*] from that time until my thirty-first year was completed, that is for a whole decade, it was never permitted to me to lie with a woman. For even though I took many to bed with me, especially in the year in which I was lecturing at the University of Padua, when I was carefree, at the most flourishing age, and had strong forces for everything else—in the case of foods, I used abstinence and enjoyment with equal industry—yet I left them all dry. So that as since I often did the same thing with tedium, shame, and despair I decided totally to desist from this experience. For indeed sometimes I had little women with me for three whole nights and I could not do anything. Frankly, I think this one thing was to me the worst of ills. Not servitude to my father, not poverty, not illnesses, not enmities, quarrels, injuries from citizens, rejection by the medical profession, false calumnies, and that infinite heap of troubles could drive me to

[1] I am grateful to Anthony Grafton, Michael R. McVaugh, Vivian Nutton, and Noel M. Swerdlow for helpful comments on various stages of this paper.

despair, hatred of life, contempt of pleasures and perpetual sadness; this one thing
certainly could.[2]

This particular adversity suddenly left Cardano at the age of thirty-one
after a bout of illness; his subsequent fertile marriage brought its own
troubles. Despite the intensity of feeling revealed in the passage quoted,
he succeeded in finding a usefulness in impotence, as the title of his treatise
promised: it guaranteed freedom from syphilis and prevented one from
wasting money and time on women.

Cardano was no doubt a compulsive autobiographer. But his interest
in recounting his own experiences can also be seen as part of a broader
concern, evident in many of his works, with the narration of experience
as a tool for understanding both human society in its physical environment
and the health and fortunes of individuals. In medicine Cardano attached
special and explicit importance to what he termed *historia* or *historiae*.
He declared emphatically that "in ancient times the medical art held
historiae in the greatest esteem" and that one of the leading merits of his
own commentaries on the revered Hippocratic books was that they "give
delight by *historia*."[3] His association of the use of *historia* in medicine
with *antiqua tempora* and with Hippocrates constituted an encomium,
since Cardano was among those Renaissance learned physicians who
proclaimed the superiority of Hippocratic medicine. This paper is an
inquiry into what precisely Cardano meant by *historia* in a medical context
and how his concept and usage related to traditional forms of medical
narrative. Such an inquiry will, I hope, tell us something about Renaissance scientific method; but it cannot be separated either from the uses
Cardano made of *historia* in his other works in a variety of fields or from
the broader topics of the meanings attached to the term *historia* in the
Renaissance and of Renaissance narrative in general.

Sixteenth-century writers of Latin commonly used *historia* in two

---

[2] Girolamo Cardano, *De utilitate ex adversis capienda*, Book 2, Chapter 10, in his
Opera omnia: The 1662 Lugduni Edition, intro. August Buck (facsimile, New York, 1967;
original title page bears the date 1663), II, 76-77. For convenience of reference all citations
are to this edition; passages quoted or discussed have been checked in sixteenth-century
editions where available, and differences noted. Separate editions of those of Cardano's
works published before 1600 are catalogued in the *Index aureliensis: Catalogus librorum
sedecimo saecolo impressorum* (Part 1), VI (Orleans, 1976), 511-23, hereafter abbreviated
IA. In the first edition of *De utilitate ex adversis capienda* (Basel, 1561; *IA* *132.082),
280-81, the wording of the first two sentences of the passage quoted is slightly different,
but the sense is the same. For general biobibliographical references relating to Cardano,
see Alfonso Ingegno, *Saggio sulla filosofia di Cardano* (Florence, 1980), 21-31. The relation
between Cardano's autobiography and autobiographical elements in his other writings is
discussed in Carlo Gregori, "Rappresentazione e difesa: Osservazioni sul *De vita propria*
di Gerolamo Cardano," *Quaderni Storici*, 73 (1990), 225-34.

[3] Cardano, *De methodo medendi sectiones tres, Opera*, VII, 199; *De libris propriis, Opera*
I, 107, and similarly in the earlier *De libris propriis, Opera*, I, 70.

senses, both of which preserved the ancient connotation of a narrative presenting the results of an inquiry exemplified respectively in the *Histories* of Herodotus and the *History of Animals* of Aristotle: the record of human experience and the description of nature. And the term might also be applied, as it had been by Galen and was by Cardano, to specific experiences or cases encountered in medical practice—a usage that addressed both human experience and natural phenomena.[4]

Cardano was engaged by *historia* in all these meanings. He was the author of several short works on ancient history, the most noteworthy of which is an *Encomium of Nero*. In this he pointed out the prejudices and moral failings of Tacitus and Suetonius, the main sources for Nero's life, and observed that alienating the powerful, as Nero had done, was likely to result in lasting ill-repute; he further alleged that Nero's recorded behavior was no worse than that of other less notorious rulers, drew attention to his various meritorious or constructive activities, and attributed any remaining failings to youthful exuberance and inexperience or the seductions of his mother Agrippina.[5]

The encomium is doubtless ironic, but also seems to have aspects that qualify it to be considered a pioneering exercise in historical revisionism; it may show signs of the influence of Machiavelli in its love of paradox and occasional attempts to use ancient history to teach modern political lessons. In fact, the parallel drawn by Machiavelli between the value of the collection and use of ancient *experimenta* in medicine and in political history[6] could well serve as a justification of the historical interests of Cardano the physician. In the *Encomium of Nero*, moreover, Cardano clearly showed an interest in analyzing how and on what basis historical judgments are arrived at. Indeed, the *Encomium (Nero* simultaneously exemplifies two characteristics of historical writing in the Renaissance: the persistence of the ancient and medieval tradition that regarded history as a branch of rhetoric and the emergence of more analytic concepts.[7] Yet

---

[4] See, for example, *De optima secta ad Thrasybulum*, ch. 14, in Galen, *Opera omnia*, ed. C.G. Kühn, (Leipzig, 1821), I, 142-49, where the misuse of *historia* by the Empiric sect is criticized. The celebrated "case histories" collected in the Hippocratic *Epidemics* are not so termed in the text; see Josef-Hans Kuhn and Ulrich Fleischer, *Index Hippocraticus*, fasc. 2 (Gottingen, 1987), 400. As will become apparent, sixteenth-century usage of the term *historia* in a medical context does not necessarily translate as "case history."

[5] Cardano, *Encomium Neronis* (also entitled *Neronis encomium), Opera*, I, 179-220 (with his *Somniorum synesiorum* [Basel, 1562; 1.4 *132.083]). The *Encomium* is discussed in Ingegno, *Saggio*, 184-208; on Cardano's views on Roman history, see also Alexander Demandt, *Der Fall Roms* (Munich, 1984), 100-101.

[6] *Discorsi*, preface to Book 1. I owe this reference to Anthony Grafton. On Cardano and irony and the ancient example of Lucian, see Dilwyn Knox, *Ironia: Medieval and Renaissance Ideas on Irony*. (New York, 1989), 49-50, 93-94.

[7] See Arno Seifert, *Cognitio historica* (Berlin, 1976); also, regarding Renaissance readings of ancient historians, George H. Nadel, "Philosophy of History Before Historicism," *History and Theory*, 3 (1964), 291-315.

another view of human history, the product of his commitment to and training in astrology and medicine, presents itself in Cardano's astrological works. In them he tried to develop a causal account, in which historical examples illustrated how the stars shaped human events.

Thus, many of the horoscopes in his *One Hundred Examples of Genitures* belong to major figures of recent history, among them Pope Julius II, Luther, Francesco Sforza, and Cosimo de' Medici.[8] Cardano's horoscopes of historical personages filled a function similar to that he attributed to autopsy of deceased patients (see below): they supposedly yielded manifest evidence, certain confirmation, and underlying reasons for conclusions that had previously been arrived at in a more impressionistic way. An idea of his method can be gathered from his treatment of the question "Will spouses love one another?" in a work *On [astrological] Interrogations*. He chose as an example the marriage of Henri II of France and Catherine de' Medici. Cardano rated this as an instance of marital harmony because of Henri's alleged refusal to divorce Catherine when she failed to have children for several years and her consequent good fortune: not of noble or royal blood, married to a second son, at one time apparently barren and threatened with divorce, she ended up a queen and the mother of kings. He evidently either did not know about or regarded as insignificant Henri's notorious devotion to Diane de Poitiers throughout most of his marriage to Catherine. And he also attributed indirect political consequences of this marriage to the stars: the marriage and hence the stars contributed to the continuing enmity between Francis I and Charles V.[9]

The use of horoscopes as a tool of historical analysis at least had the merit of avoiding the perils of prediction. Cardano's misfortune in foretelling a long and prosperous reign for Edward VI of England shortly before the latter died at the age of fifteen is well known. Like his entire approach to astrological history, Cardano's subsequent essay in self-criticism and self-exculpation for a failed prediction overtaken by events combines laborious astrological computation with political and historical judgments arrived at on other grounds.[10]

---

[8] *Liber de exemplis centum geniturarum, Opera*, V, 458-502 (Nuremberg, 1547); *IA* *132.054. On Cardano's astrological writings and ideas, see Germanna Ernst, *Religione, ragione e natura: Ricerche su Tommaso Campanella e il tardo Rinascimento* (Milan, 1991), 191-219. On astrology and history in the Renaissance in general, see Paola Zambelli, "Introduction: Astrologers' Theory of History," *"Astrologi hallucinati": Stars and the End of the World in Luther's Time* (New York, 1986), 1-28; and Eugenio Garin, *Lo zodiaco della vita* (Bari, 1976).

[9] Cardano, *De interrogationibus, Quaesitum* 17, *Opera*, V, 557-58.

[10] Both the original horoscope and Cardano's subsequent reflections are printed in his *In Cl[audii] Ptolemaei Pelusiensis IIII de astrorum iudiciis . . . libros* [= *Tetrabiblos*] *commentaria. . . . Eiusdem Hier[onymi] Cardani Geniturarum XII . . . liber* (Basel, 1554; *IA* *132.063), 403-13. The version in *Liber duodecim geniturarum, Opera*, V, 503-8, contains Cardano's apologia together with a version of the horoscope from which some of the specifics about Edward's future have been omitted.

Cardano's endeavor to construct a history that was simultaneously human and natural and mathematical applied concepts found in two works to which he attached particular significance: Ptolemy's astrological *Tetrabiblos* and the Hippocratic treatise about geographic and climatic influences on human society entitled *Airs Waters Places*. Both books asserted with examples that the physical environment—celestial in the case of the *Tetrabiblos*, climatic and geographic in that of *Airs Waters Places*—shaped the characteristics of peoples. In one form or another these theories of environmental influence were, of course, a standard part of cosmological theory in western Europe from the twelfth to the seventeenth century. They received a notable Renaissance reworking at the hands of Jean Bodin, who applied them to the European societies of his day.[11]

But few or none of Cardano's contemporaries could equal the attention he devoted to the *Tetrabiblos* and *Airs Waters Places* as texts. Cardano seems to have been alone in writing full-scale commentaries on both. He alleged that the *Tetrabiblos* was "as useful for knowing the present and the past as the future."[12] He assigned *Airs Waters Places* first place in the entire Hippocratic corpus in terms of both authenticity and importance of content—a judgment that meant he considered it one of the most important works in the entire literature of medicine—and prided himself on introducing it into medical education.[13]

In the example of the story of Henri II and Catherine de' Medici and elsewhere, Cardano used *historia* in connection with human affairs to mean not an extended sequential narrative, but a brief story about a set of closely related events or a single individual or occurrence. Only a few sixteenth-century writers on human history—notably Guicciardini in practice and Bodin in theory—conceived of development over time as an essential component of the subject. More generally, human history appeared as a series of episodes, whether these were treated as subjects for analysis, data from which rules could be constructed, or *exempla* on which to base rhetorical moralizing. Seen in this way, natural and human history were indeed closely associated. Natural histories (for example, Pliny's *Naturalis historia*, Aristotle's *Historia animalium*, and such contemporary contributions to the genre as Fuchs's *De historia stirpium* [1542]) were made up precisely of a multitude of separate short descriptions of different organisms, objects, or phenomena. Moreover, in Cardano's lifetime the

---

[11] See Bodin's *Methodus ad facilem historiarum cognitionem* (1566), ch. 5, and the *Six livres de la République* (1576), Book 5, ch. 1. For discussion, see Marian J. Tooley, "Bodin and the Medieval Theory of Climate," *Speculum*, 28 (1953), 64-83; and Clarence J. Glacken, *Traces on the Rhodian Shore: Nature and Culture in Western Thought From Ancient Times to the End of the Eighteenth Century* (Berkeley, 1967), 434-47.

[12] Cardano, comm. *De astrorum iudiciis, Opera*, V, 93; (for the first edition, see note 10, above). For Cardano's commentary on *Airs Waters Places*, see note 31, below.

[13] Cardano, *Ars curandi parva quae est absolutissima medendi methodus, Opera*, VII, 193. (Basel, 1564; *IA* *132.094).

descriptive approach to nature was attracting notable individuals—one thinks of Vesalius, Gesner, Rondelet, Aldrovandi, and so on.

In whatever other ways human and natural history might be linked, both rested on description. But in the mid-sixteenth century the epistemological status of the knowledge that could be obtained from descriptions of particulars was far from clear. Aristotelian tradition maintained that certain knowledge—*scientia*—was obtainable only by disciplines proceeding by means of syllogistic demonstrations to universal truths, a formulation that certainly did not fit the assembling of particulars about plants, animals, minerals, human cadavers, or historical anecdotes (I do not address here the issue of, or modern literature on, Aristotle's own view of the relation between his philosophical and biological works). In his use of historical examples in astrological treatises, Cardano seems to have been in search of a theoretical basis on which to build a science of nature and man that was both mathematically exact and genuinely descriptive, and in which particulars could somehow lead to certain knowledge.

But Cardano was also always intensely aware of the random and apparently inexplicable nature of many occurrences, of the uncertainty of medical and astrological prognostication,[14] and the difficulty of distinguishing between the natural and the anomalous.[15] Hence throughout his works, which covered an encyclopedic diversity of subjects, he often seems to have turned to narrative when he wished to ponder a topic that engaged him in a number of different fields: the relation and relative preponderance of predictability and randomness,[16] the normal and the anomalous in human experience.

All of the intellectual concerns outlined above can be traced in Cardano's use, and manipulation, of medical narrative. But his medical *historiae* were also shaped by medical tradition and the needs of his own professional career. As an epistemological issue, the relation of the particulars of experience to theoretical knowledge of nature had a long history within medicine, starting with the empirical and rationalist medical sects of antiquity. Between the thirteenth and the sixteenth century the topic was repeatedly discussed by learned physicians, initially probably because of the ambiguous status of their own discipline in the world of the universities. Medicine was both a branch of academic learning for at least some aspects of which *scientia* and an association with scholastic natural philosophy could be claimed and an *ars* supposedly transmitted according to ordered rules and principles; but it was also a practical activity, involving

---

[14] Cardano, comm. *De astrorum iudiciis*, proem, *Opera*, V, 93.

[15] On this aspect of Cardano's thought see Jean Céard, *La Nature et les prodiges: L'insolité au XVIe siècle en France* (Geneva, 1977), 229-51.

[16] His best known contribution to the subject, *De ludo aleae* (*Opera*, I, 262-76), is translated into English and discussed in Oystein Ore, *Cardano, the Gambling Scholar* (Princeton, 1953).

technical skills best learned by experience and ad hoc responses to particular situations.

Moreover, traditions and models of medical narrative existed in a diversity of medieval and early Renaissance contexts. Medical writers provided descriptive accounts of the nature and course of diseases, parts of the body, the spread of epidemics, and the cases of individual patients. Patients and other people who were not medical practitioners also produced accounts of illness—the author's or another's, individual or epidemic. Such "lay" narratives of illness occur in many different types of medieval and Renaissance writing: collections of miracles assembled at shrines or in the course of canonization processes, saints' lives, letters, chronicles or other historical works, and literary texts (of which the best known is presumably the prologue to the *Decameron*).

For present purposes, I shall confine "medical narrative" to accounts by medical practitioners of individual cases or patients. But it cannot be assumed that medical practitioners were unaware of or uninfluenced by non-professional forms of medical narrative. Patients told or tried to tell their stories to doctors, who reorganized and reinterpreted them according to the canons of medical knowledge; Taddeo Alderotti (d. 1295) was doubtless only one of many practitioners who worried over the extent to which patients' accounts of their own symptoms should be relied on.[17] Medical practitioners were as likely as anyone else to be familiar with accounts of miraculous healing and as little likely to reject them. Moreover, all forms of medical narrative were stories that were put together, organized, and doubtless often improved upon for a purpose.[18] This is obviously likely to be the case in accounts of the illness and treatment of individual patients, which could easily be made to serve social, professional, or even religious purposes. But the same is true of medieval and Renaissance medical or physiological narratives where the authors had no discernible motivation other than to order data coherently and in accordance with accepted scientific principles. Accounts of disease tried to make sense of the relation of symptoms to processes going on inside the body that could not be directly investigated, to explain how medical theory (for example, of humors and complexions) related to perceived changes in bodily condition, or to hypothesize ways in which epidemics spread. The most rigorously descriptive anatomy that the medical Renaissance of the sixteenth century afforded—Vesalius on the bones—involved narratives about the function of internal parts in the living body intended

[17] Taddeo Alderotti, *Expositiones in arduum aphorismorum Ipocratis volumen, In divinum pronosticorum Ipocratis librum, In preclarum regiminis acutorum Ipocratis opus, In subtilissimum Joannitii Isagogarum libellum* (Venice, 1527), fols. 247v-50v; for discussion, Nancy G. Siraisi, *Taddeo Alderotti and His Pupils* (Princeton, 1981), 124-25.

[18] Interesting comparisons are suggested by the analysis of narratives of personal history for a purpose in Natalie Z. Davis, *Fiction in the Archives: Pardon Tales and Their Tellers in Sixteenth-Century France* (Stanford, 1987).

to accommodate Galenic physiological theory to new anatomical observations on the cadaver.[19]

The two chief genres of medical narrative about individual patients and their diseases employed by medieval and Renaissance medical practitioners were anecdotes embedded in general medical or surgical treatises and *consilia*, or letters of advice for individuals. Both emerged in the thirteenth century, apparently to a large extent independently of ancient antecedents. Some of the most important ancient examples of medical narrative about individuals were unknown or ignored in the medieval West. In the thirteenth to fifteenth centuries all that was known of the seven books of the Hippocratic *Epidemics*, which contain numerous individual case histories, was a commentary including lemmata on the disjointed *Epidemics* Book 6, in which the case histories are extremely brief and undeveloped.[20] Galen's *On Prognosis* is largely given over to accounts of cases he had attended, but it was not translated into Latin until the fourteenth century and attracted little attention before the second half of the fifteenth.[21] Some case histories were included in two major Galenic works, the *Method of Healing*, Galen's principal book on therapeutics, and *On the Affected Places*, on internal diseases, that were available in Latin from the twelfth century. Unquestionably, these books were esteemed and used by thirteenth- to fifteenth-century medical and surgical practitioners. But in the case of *The Method of Healing*, its great length and the variety of topics covered ensured that the work was not always read, or copied, in its entirety. The case histories are few in number, a single one being deployed by Galen as the starting point for discussion in each of several of the later books. However important in Galen's own design of his book, the narratives about individual patients may not have stood out for medieval readers as a major element in the work.[22]

[19] See for example Vesalius, *De humani corporis fabrica*, 7.11 (Basel, 1543), 640-42, translated with anatomical annotation in Charles Singer, *Vesalius on the Human Brain* (New York, 1952), 51-56.

[20] According to Hippocrates, *Epidemie libro sesto,* ed. and tr. Daniela Manetti and Amneris Roselli (Florence, 1982), lxii-lxiii, lxx, the medieval Latin manuscripts probably all contain either a Latin translation of a commentary by Johannes Alexandrinus or a compilation of the lemmata therefrom.

[21] The translator of *On Prognosis* was perhaps Niccolo da Reggio (fl. 1308-45); of the five Latin manuscripts, only two antedate the mid-fifteenth century. See Galen, *On Prognosis*, ed. and tr. Vivian Nutton, *Corpus medicorum graecorum*, V, 8, 1 (Berlin, 1979), 26-34.

[22] *Methodus medendi* occupies the whole of Galen, *Opera omnia*, ed. C. G. Kühn, X (Leipzig, 1825). There were three medieval translations, of which, according to Pearl Kibre and R. J. Durling, "A List of Latin Manuscripts Containing Medieval Versions of the *Methodus medendi*," in *Galen's Method of Healing*, ed. Fridolf Kudlien and Richard J. Durling (Leiden, 1991), 117-22, there are collectively over one hundred manuscripts. *De locis affectis* was known in an Arabo-Latin version under the title *De interioribus*. Galen's use of case histories in *Methodus medendi* is discussed in Vivian Nutton, "Style and Context in the *Method of Healing*," *ibid.*, 9-11.

Medieval medical narratives in the form of accounts of individual cases embedded in treatises are relatively rare and only a minor feature of the works in which they occur. Authors sometimes claimed that their purpose in including stories from their own practice was exemplary or pedagogical. But it often seems evident that self-advertisement and the denigration of rivals were also motivations. Characteristically, the stories emphasize the skill and success of the author's cures, concluding triumphantly with the complete recovery of recipients of apparently fatal wounds, previously given up for dead by bystanders, family members, or rival practitioners.[23] Such anecdotes are indeed much more often found in books by surgical rather than by medical writers. In the course of the fifteenth century, however, physicians seem to have become somewhat readier than before to introduce anecdotes from their own practice into treatises and commentaries.[24]

By that time consilia certainly constituted a recognized and reputable genre of medical writing appropriate for learned physicians. The earliest date from thirteenth-century Bologna but the popularity of the genre greatly increased in the fifteenth century, when some physicians wrote them in large numbers.[25] They continued to be produced through the sixteenth century, and older ones were printed in sixteenth-century editions. *Consilia* were not designed to provide complete histories of episodes of disease in individuals. They are essentially records of consultations for which physicians received a fee; one of Cardano's notes a payment of four Hungarian gold coins. Requests for advice came, often by letter, from patients, their local physicians, or their family. All *consilia* provide recommendations for treatment; most identify the illness, although often very briefly. Some, but by no means all, tell the story of an illness, describing the patient, his or her symptoms and the course of the disease up to the point when advice was sought. In the fifteenth century, some collections of *consilia* (often assembled and edited by admiring pupils of the author) became highly formal and scholastic, being replete with references to learned authorities and, in some instances, organized to follow the se-

[23] For example, Lanfranco of Milan (fl. 1296), *Cyrurgia*, in *Cyrurgia Guidonis de Cauliaco. Et Cyrurgia Bruni Theodorici Rogerii Rolandi Bertapalie Lanfranci* (Venice, 1498), fols. 177 (176), 187 (186); Guglielmo da Saliceto (fl. 1276), *Cyrurgia*, printed with his *Summa conservationis et curationis* (Venice, 1489), Book 2, Chapter 15, sig. X4v; Rolando da Parma (fl. early thirteenth century), *Libellus de cyrurgia*, in *Cyrurgia Guidonis de Cauliaco*, etc., Book 3, Chapter 25, fol. 157(156)r.

[24] Danielle Jacquart, "Theory, Everyday Practice, and Three Fifteenth-Century Physicians," *Osiris*, 6 (1990), 140-60, especially 160.

[25] For example, there are 304 in a collection by Bartolomeo da Montagnana (d. before 1452), printed in eleven editions between 1472 and 1673, often together with over 150 by Antonio Cermisone (d. 1441). Manuscripts and editions are listed in Tiziana Pesenti, *Professori e promotori di medicina nello Studio di Padova dal 1405 al 1509: Repertorio biobibliografico* (Trieste-Padua, 1984), 76-89, 143-54.

quence of contents in learned works.[26] The structure of *consilia* that do
describe illnesses suggests that the description was likely to be arrived at
by asking a standard set of questions, a practice that must have made it
difficult for the patient freely to tell the story of his or her own illness, or
for the physician to make observations outside established categories.
Hence, although the story of an individual's illness doubtless lies behind
most *consilia*, it is not necessarily fully reflected in the written result.[27]

Consilia*, like surgeon's stories, if in less blatant ways, provided opportunities for a medical practitioner to paint a professional self-portrait in
colors of his own choice. In his *consilia* a physician could display his
learning by including references to medical literature in support of the
treatments prescribed. He could identify by name any specially rich, noble,
or otherwise distinguished patients. And since a *consilium* was essentially
a record of a consultation, he was under no obligation to mention outcome.

The appearance of all seven books of the *Epidemics* in both Greek
editions and Latin translations in the early sixteenth century introduced
numerous examples of an entirely different type of medical narrative.[28] A
salient feature of the *Epidemics* is the inclusion of individual case histories
that stand in strong contrast to the genres just described. Typically, histories in the *Epidemics* carefully follow the patient's progress over time,
noting variations in his or her symptoms and general condition through
days, sometimes months, of illness; they are minimally interventionist, in
some instances mentioning no treatment of any kind; and they bleakly
record frequent deaths. Whatever the motivation for noting down the
information may have been, it was clearly neither self-advertisement on
the part of the practitioner nor a request on the part of the patient. To
take the example of the first case history in *Epidemics* 1, Philiscus who

---

[26] For example *Consilia Jo[hannis] Ma[tthaei] de Gradi . . . secundam viam Avicen[nae]*
(Venice, 1521).

[27] See further, Jole Agrimi and Chiara Crisciani, *Consilia*, forthcoming in the series
Typologie des sources du Moyen Age occidental, general editor L. Genicot, and Siraisi,
Taddeo, ch. 9.

[28] A Latin translation of the complete *Epidemics* was included in *Hippocratis Octoginta
volumina . . . nunc tandem per M. Fabium Calvum Latinitate donata. . . .* (Rome, 1525).
The Greek text was first printed in the Aldine Hippocrates, Ἅπαντα τὰ τοῦ
Ἱπποκράτους. *Omnia opera Hippocratis* (Venice, 1526). A translation by Manente
Leontini, made between 1513 and 1521, was never printed. Six other complete or partial
Latin translations followed before the end of the century. See Innocenzo Mazzini, "Ma-
nente Leontini, Übersetzer der hippokratischen Epidemien (cod. Laurent. 73, 12): Bemer-
kungen zu seiner Übersetzung von Epidemien Buch 6," in *Die hippokratischen Epidemien:
Theorie—Praxis—Tradition*, ed. Gerhard Baader and Rolf Winau, *Sudhoffs Archiv*,
Beiheft 27 (Stuttgart, 1989), 312-15. The *Epidemics* was likely to be read in conjunction
with Galen's commentaries on Books 1, 3, and 6 (also recently made available); editions
are listed in Richard J. Durling, "A Chronological Census of Renaissance Editions and
Translations of Galen," *Journal of the Warburg and Courtauld Institutes*, 24 (1961),
294-95.

lived by the wall was ill with fever and upset bowels for six days; his active treatment consisted of the administration of a single suppository, the content of which is not mentioned; on the sixth day he died.

Cardano was among the earliest Latin commentators on sections of the *Epidemics*.[29] Moreover, these commentaries are only one manifestation of an interest in Hippocrates that began early in his career and continued almost to the end of his life. He planned to produce an edition of the entire corpus with complete commentary on each treatise.[30] Although this grandiose project was never finished, he published lengthy commentaries on four Hippocratic treatises as well as a shorter exposition of a fifth, and left partial expositions of several more books. In their final form, most of these commentaries appear to be based on his teaching at the University of Bologna in the 1560s. As well as the standard *Aphorisms* and *Prognostic*, he expounded a highly unusual selection of other treatises, including not only the *Epidemics* and *Airs Waters Places*, but also *On the Seven Month Child, On the Eight Month Child*, and *Aliment*.[31]

Cardano perceived in Hippocrates a practitioner who late in life recorded those particulars of his own experience from which good rules of practice could be constructed.[32] Such a view accorded well with his own self-presentation; as he or his editor proclaimed on the title page of the 1568 edition of his commentary on *Prognostic*, "these men, Hippocrates and Cardano, besides excellent doctrine should be admired for long and happy use and experience in the works of the art, since both of them wrote

---

[29] Cardano's commentaries on *Epidemics* 1 and 2 (*Opera*, X, 193-387) and his *Examen XXII aegrorum Hippocratis* (*Opera*, IX, 36-46) (also on cases from the *Epidemics*) were not published during his lifetime. In their final form the commentaries probably date from 1563-64. The brief *Examen* "edidit annum agens LXXIII." Commentaries published in Latin before 1563, in addition to those of Galen, were by Leonhart Fuchs on Book 6 (The Hague, 1532), Pedro Jaime Esteve, on Book 2 (Valencia, 1551), and Gianbattista Da Monte on part of Book 1 (Venice, 1554).

[30] *De libris propriis, Opera*, I, 106-7.

[31] *In septem Aphorismorum Hippocratis particulas commentaria* (Basel, 1564; *IA* *132.093); *Opera*, VIII, 213-580; *In Hippocratis Coi prognostica, opus divinum. . . . Atque etiam in Galeni prognosticorum expositionem, commentarii absolutissimi. Item in libros Hippocratis de septimestri et octomestri partu, et simul in eorum Galeni commentaria, Cardani commentarii* (Basel, 1568; *IA* *132.102); *Opera*, VIII, 581-806; IX, 1-35; *Commentarii in Hippocratis de aere, aquis, et locis opus* (Basel, 1570; *IA* *132.107); *Opera*, VIII, 1-212; *In librum Hippocratis de alimento commentaria* (Rome, 1574; *IA* *132.109); *Opera* VII, 356-515; *Opera* IX, 36-47; *Commentaria in libros Hippocratis de victis acutis, Opera*, X, 168-92. The extensive use of Hippocrates in Cardano's *Contradicentia medicorum* (*Opera*, VI, 295-923) is pointed out in a series of lengthy notes in Ingegno, *Saggio sulla filosofia di Cardano*, 209-71. On Cardano's Hippocratism, see also Jackie Pigeaud, "L'Hippocratisme de Cardan: Etude sur le Commentaire d'AEL par Cardan," *Respublica litterarum*, 8 (1975), 219-29.

[32] On sixteenth-century ideas about the value of the Hippocratic books and the merits of Hippocrates, see Vivian Nutton, "Hippocrates in the Renaissance," *Die hippokratischen Epidemien*, 433-39.

these things at over seventy years of age." He advanced narratives of his successes in practice with an assertiveness that indicates he viewed them as evidence authenticating not only his skill, but also his medical learning and his suitability to teach medical theory in an academic context—a suitability challenged at different points in his career by professional, civic, and religious authorities.[33] The best professor, Cardano maintained, was one who began to teach after long experience of practice as he himself had done.[34]

But the implied claim that his own practice and teaching was comparable to that of Hippocrates involved him in a contradiction. His understanding of Hippocrates certainly included the author of the epidemics as a model narrator of medical histories. Yet the norms of medical practice led Cardano to write some wholly conventional *consilia*. Although Cardano described his collected *consilia* as "examples of... new remedies and of [new] diseases," there seems little to distinguish them from the productions of his thirteenth- to fifteenth-century predecessors, except for the occasional case of *morbus gallicus* and perhaps somewhat more attention to the factor of development of disease over time.[35]

In other works, moreover, Cardano's confessional urge and professional difficulties impelled him to recount many *historiae* about his own practice that—in strong contrast to the histories in the *Epidemics*—were rich in autobiographical detail and strongly emphasized success. Here his model is likely to have been Galen, who also wrote autobiography, provided a bibliography of his own books, and included in his treatises accounts of cases illustrating his own therapeutic successes.[36] If one may judge by the number of translations, sixteenth-century interest in Galen's *On Prognosis*, which consists almost entirely of accounts of his own successful cases, was no less than in the Hippocratic *Epidemics*. Fresh interest in the *Method of Healing* stimulated by Renaissance concern with method may also have engendered greater appreciation of Galen's use there of case history as the starting point for detailed analysis of diagnosis and treatment.[37]

It was presumably in imitation of Galen that Cardano published a collection of his own "remarkable" (*admiranda*) cures and prognostica-

---

[33] In addition to inserting anecdotes in his treatises and commentaries and compiling the collections of his cases and *consilia* to be mentioned below, Cardano devoted Chapter 40 of his autobiography to his "Felicitas in eurando" *(De vita propria, Opera,* I, 31-34).

[34] Cardano, corem. *Prognost, Opera,* VIII, 708.

[35] Cardano, *Consilia, Opera,* IX, 245.

[36] See Vivian Nutton, "Galen and Medical Autobiography," in his *From Democedes to Harvey.' Studies in the History of Medicine* (London, 1988).

[37] Six new Latin translations of *On prognosis* were made between the 1520s and 1560s (Galen, *On prognosis,* ed. Nutton, 34-42). Nutton, "Style and Context," 9-11, and Jerome J. Bylebyl, "Teaching *Methodus medendi* in the Renaissance," *Galen's Method of Healing,* 157-89.

tions as part of a short work that he had the temerity to entitle *Methodus medendi*.[38] Unlike *consilia*, the "remarkable cures" give few details of treatment. But they are remarkably free with revealing details about the role of social contacts, patronage, and luck in fostering or hindering a medical career. Across accounts of several cures Cardano told the story of his relations with the pharmacist Donato Lanza. He chanced to become acquainted with Lanza, an upright man, through a common interest in music. Later, Lanza confided that he was running a fever, spitting blood, and had been losing weight. Cardano agreed to treat him, and "ordered him to foretell to everyone that he would be healthy; however, the spitting of blood did not altogether cease." Subsequently Cardano treated another member of Lanza's family. Perhaps Cardano and Lanza entered into an arrangement then common among physicians and pharmacists whereby the pharmacist recommended the physician's services and the physician prescribed the pharmacist's remedies. In any event, "on account both of his own benefit and [my] treatment of his relative and others, Donato Lanza worked hard to ensure that my name would be known to everyone and that I might shine in the city [Milan]." Then Lanza left his pharmacy and entered the service of Francesco Sfondrato, a distinguished leading citizen. When his employer's small son fell ill Lanza saw to it that Cardano was summoned. Two other more famous physicians were at a loss. Cardano saw the child's neck contorted backwards, demonstrated that it could not be straightened, and pronounced his diagnosis: "opisthotonos" (tetanic spasm). Only the most distinguished of the other physicians even knew what the word meant. "Impelled by divine inspiration" he handsomely acknowledged Cardano's skill in diagnosis. "Therefore," Cardano concluded, "in this part I had propitious fortune and I cured the boy, and fairly quickly. . . . Therefore from that hour so much glory accrued to me that if Sfondrato had remained in Milan for an entire year all the citizens would have flowed to me, and so in a short time I would have obtained first place among all the *medici* of our city." But, alas, Sfondrato left Milan,[39] and Cardano's booster Donato Lanza while fleeing the police [*praetoris familia*] (his probity having presumably temporarily deserted him) jumped out of a window and hid for a long time in a water tank; this adventure taxed his already weakened constitution and he died four years after Cardano first treated him.[40]

In the *Remarkable Cures* the narrative about chance, luck, professional rivalries, and social climbing coincides with some very realistic

---

[38] Cardano, *De methodo medendi libri tres, Opera*, VII, 199-264 (*De methodo medendi sectiones quatuor* [Paris, 1565; *IA* *132.098]). *Sectio tertia, De admirandis curationibus et praedictionibus morborum*, 253–64.

[39] In 1555. A widower, he subsequently became a cardinal. For his horoscope by Cardano, see *Liber XII genitarum, Opera*, V, 515-16.

[40] *Ibid.*, cures 5, p. 254; 14, p. 256; 15, pp. 256-57.

evaluations of disease and of the powers of medicine. Cardano knew of only one person who had ever been cured of *phthoe*, but sufferers from it often lived for a number of years and then died of something else (he named Lanza as an example). But at the same time, Cardano claimed some cures that were indeed remarkable. There is of course no way of knowing what the patients—including the child with "opisthotonos," whom Cardano cured by means of "linen cloths soaked in oil of camomile and lilies kept continually on the neck"—were actually suffering from. The language of the following example seems especially worth considering:

But what happened concerning Gaspare Roulla . . . an innkeeper who ran three music establishments [*tibicina*] in the region surrounding our Milan seemed very like a miracle to everyone, so that many ran to see it. For he seemed to be incurable by any human agency before he was cured by us. But it is agreeable to narrate the history. He was already lying contracted in bed for a whole year, but in the last five months of that year wholly immobile, he could not move foot, nor head, nor arm, nor anything whatever. For besides great pain, the limbs lay hard and rigid like stone. And it was the middle of winter. Therefore it was agreed by me that this would be fully healed within 40 days, not to the wonder but to the stupefaction of those who saw him. For some were saying he was starstruck [*sideratus*], others smitten by divine wrath, others paralyzed [*resolutus*], others possessed by the devil [*daemone correptum*], so that prayers and execrations were not lacking. We therefore cured this in the following manner. We abstained from all unctions, the use of which, if the body is not correctly purged beforehand, contributes to such great magnitude of disease. We let blood three times, although with great difficulty because the arms were contracted, nor could they be extended. For as I said the whole neck, thighs, back and arms were hard like stone or wood. But while I was curing him, he rather often despaired of his health and therefore wanted me to stop the cure. For in the first twenty-five days he was not alleviated, or very little.

Bleeding was necessary "not only on account of the magnitude of the disease, but also because by consideration of his life and the disease itself I conjectured that the whole mass of blood was corrupted. Nor did the judgment made about this thing fail me in any part. Indeed all the blood that went out was putrid." In the end Roulla was completely cured, except for a twisted neck, and returned to his trade of innkeeper.[41]

Despite Cardano's explanation of the rational grounds for his choice of treatment, the language in which this cure is presented reads very like that of a miracle story. The paralytic disease, the emphatic description of symptoms, the assertion of the impossibility of cure by any human means, the expectations of the crowd, the allusions to the power of God and the devil, to prayers and curses all create an atmosphere more reminiscent of shrine healings or accounts of possession and exorcism than of the clinic.

---

[41] *Ibid.*, cure 18, p. 258.

Even the numbers—forty days treatment and three bleedings—might be thought to have religious or magical overtones. The story of the cure of Gaspare Roulla has a very different thrust from the self-congratulatory anecdotes recorded by medieval surgeons. Those stories, however exaggerated and conventional, are straightforward advertisements of the author's skill and knowledge. Their atmosphere is pragmatic and technical, rather than marvelous.

Cardano, too, evidently wished to record his own skill and knowledge. The heightened drama and rich social context of some of his accounts may have been inspired by Galen's descriptions of his own cures in *On Prognosis*;[42] indeed, Cardano indirectly acknowledged the influence of that work on the *Remarkable Cures* with an unblushing claim to have cured more patients of desperate diseases than Galen himself. Nevertheless, his insistence on the way in which some of his cures seemed miraculous to others also suggests that he himself recognized the role of luck, fortune, or special gift in some of his own successes. Such an awareness would be fully compatible with his interest in chance and anomaly and his belief in his own peculiar receptivity to dreams and omens. Thus, his concluding comment on his "remarkable cures" was that "I was always exceptionally happy in the works of the art, to the extent that just as some might refer it to chance, so might others to the devil. But just as no one was happier with perpetual success in curing, so no one was safer from errors and adverse chances than me."[43]

Cardano's expressions of awareness of the role of special gift and fortune in his success undercut his other claim that success in practice was the result of Hippocratic wisdom and knowledge gained through experience of many cases. These *historiae* of Cardano's remarkable cures also tell stories of a different kind about his awareness of randomness, incomprehensibility, and the difficulty of securely linking causes and effects in disease and its treatment.

Yet on a few occasions Cardano made explicit and thoughtful endeavors to evaluate the worth of accounts of individual cases as a source of medical knowledge. And these endeavors were closely connected with his interest in the *Epidemics*. As he explained, the usefulness of the *Epidemics* was above all for learning prognosis, and this usefulness was of two kinds. Firstly, the physician could go through the case histories looking for common elements: thus he could, for example, collect and categorize examples of abnormal varieties of urine and see with what diseases or symptoms they were associated.

The second utility is something I used to practice in my youth, trying for myself, and it was that I would read whatever had happened to a sick man without the

---

[42] I owe this suggestion to Vivian Nutton.

[43] Cardano, *De admirandis curationibus*, cure 30, 261.

outcome [*exitu*], and judge whether he would die, or not, and when; and if a man follows this in a few cases, how much glory he will hope for in medical practice, and if in many it is better, and if in all and fully then he will know he is already perfect.[44]

Elsewhere, Cardano explained that in 1526 he had made a collection of his own cases on the lines of the case histories in the *Epidemics*, although it did not bear comparison with the books of Hippocrates.[45] This was the same year in which the Aldine Hippocrates appeared, and just one year after the publication of the first Latin collected *Opera* of Hippocrates translated by Fabio Calvo. Another translation of the whole of the *Epidemics* into Latin, completed between 1513 and 1521, remained unpublished.[46] Cardano's casebook, which unfortunately does not appear to survive, thus stands at the very beginning of Renaissance Hippocratism. It predated by some fifty years the personal notes and casebook loosely modelled on the *Epidemics* kept by Guillaume de Baillou at Paris in the 1570s, to which attention has been drawn as a pioneering effort. Baillou's work, like Cardano's commentaries on the Hippocratic *Epidemics*, was not published until the seventeenth century, a delay that appears to confirm Vivian Nutton's conclusion that Hippocrates was decidedly a minority interest during the sixteenth-century flowering of Renaissance Galenism.[47] Even though his approach to Hippocrates was, inevitably, mediated by Galenism, genuine innovation was involved in Cardano's occasional endeavors to apply a methodology derived from the *Epidemics* in his practice.

Despite the lack of Cardano's casebook inspired by the *Epidemics*, the way in which these Hippocratic books influenced his ideas about the uses of descriptive accounts of individual cases can be gathered both from his commentaries on them and from a few accounts of cases that he used as illustrative material in other commentaries or treatises. In Cardano's commentaries on *Epidemics* 1 and 2, Galen is never far away. Cardano's idea that the reasoned analysis of Hippocratic case histories would yield rules of prognosis in medicine has obvious parallels with his interest as an astrologer in analyzing the horoscopes of historical personages; yet the concept is also fundamentally Galenic. His exposition of Book 1 included

[44] Cardano, *Commentaria in libros Epidemiorum Hippocratis, Opera*, X, 195.

[45] Cardano, *De libris propriis, Opera*, I, 97.

[46] See note 28, above.

[47] Iain M. Lonie, "The Paris Hippocratics" in *The Medical Renaissance of the Sixteenth Century*, ed. A. Wear, R. French, and I. M. Lonie (Cambridge, 1985), 169-74; Nutton, "Hippocrates in the Renaissance." According to Vivian Nutton, "Pieter van Foreest and the plagues of Europe: some observations on the Observationes," *Pieter Van Foreest: Een Hollands medicus in de zestiende eeuw*, ed. H. L. Houtzager (Amsterdam, 1989), 25-39, Van Foreest's *Observationes et curationes medicinales* (1588), also makes use of the model of the *Epidemics* and contains observations of cases probably made many years before the work was published.

discussion of Galen's commentary; for Book 2, the Galenic commentary being largely unavailable, he frequently turned to other works of Galen for help (for example, by referring to Galen's discussion of simulated illness to explain an obscure Hippocratic allusion to fear[48]). But Cardano was also highly critical of Galen as an interpreter of the *Epidemics*, claiming that Galen's failure to explain the causes of the symptoms described therein showed that he had forgotten his own maxim that medical precepts ought to be useful for reaching health. And the specifics of Galen's explanations of the Hippocratic cases were, according to Cardano, quite likely to be wrong: "Galen saw few *experimenta* of internal diseases and made fewer observations about them"; "Galen indeed does not attain to any of the difficult things"; "Galen was ignorant of what this was"; and "on account of his [Galen's] excessive erudition and study in those things [grammar], he exercized himself less in serious and more useful things."[49]

Moreover, Cardano was evidently attracted by very unGalenic aspects of these Hippocratic books: their non-interventionism and the unembarrassed detachment with which the author(s) recorded the death of patients. He held that the *Epidemics* should be classified as works on medical theory rather than practice, because in them "only the essence of the thing is narrated, nor is it taught what to do."[50] Part of the attraction Hippocrates held for Cardano—as we shall see some of his own case histories show—was surely that here was a great, famous, and universally acclaimed physician who did not always cure his patients and had no hesitation about saying so.

The influence of Cardano's reading of the *Epidemics* is as one might expect particularly strong in his exposition of the Hippocratic *Prognostic*. There examples drawn from the case histories in the *Epidemics* occur side by side with examples drawn from Cardano's own practice. Occasionally, indeed, Cardano criticized Hippocrates on the basis of his own experience:

---

[48] Cardano, comm. *Epidemics*, Book 2, *Opera*, X, 366-67. Cardano here showed considerable perspicuity. He knew Galen's discussion in the form of a short work that circulated under the title of *Quomodo simulantes sint deprehendi*, or some variant thereof. In the twentieth century, *Quomodo simulantes* was identified as a fragment of Galen's commentary on *Epidemics* 2; see Galen, *In Hippocratis Epidemiarum libros I et II*, ed. Ernst Wenkebach and Franz Pfaff, *Corpus Medicorum Graecorum*, V, 10, 1 (Berlin, 1934), 206-10, and Karl Deichgräber and Fridolf Kudlien, *Die als sogenannante simulantenschrift griechisch überlieferten Stücke des 2. Kommentare zu den Epidemien II*, in *Galens Kommentare zu den Epidemien des Hippokrates, Corpus Medicorum Graecorum*, V, 10, 2, 4 (Berlin, 1960), 107-16. It is in fact Galen's commentary on the passage to which Cardano applied it. On Renaissance knowledge of Galen's commentary on *Epidemics* 2, see *Galeni in Hippocratis Epidemiarum Librum VI Comm. I-VI*, ed. E. Wenkebach, *Corpus medicorum Graecorum*, V, 10, 2, 2 (Berlin, 1956), xi.

[49] Cardano, *Examen, Opera*, IX, 36, 39, 40, 45, 44, and elsewhere similarly.

[50] Cardano, comm. *Epidemics, Opera*, X, 197.

I knew a man from Brescia (he was a friend of mine) by the name of Ortensio who had been chained for 18 years in a galley among the [North] Africans, who indeed got married. When he closed his eyes and did not move any part of his body he could not be said to differ in anything from a dead man. Pallor, emacia-tion, stretched skin, pinched nostrils, leaden and purplish color with a certain swelling near the eyes made him resemble a dead man. But it is obvious that someone who was like this was not healthy. Yet Hippocrates calls a man healthy who may perform the functions of the healthy.[51]

More often he accepted Hippocratic narratives without comment; he endorsed a story from *Epidemics* 5 about a youth who accidentally swal-lowed a snake while sleeping open-mouthed by the addition of directions for luring the snake to leave in such cases and an anatomical discussion based on Galen and Vesalius of the muscles that open and close the mouth.[52]

Finally, a few examples show what Cardano meant by, and how he applied, the method he claimed to have learned from the *Epidemics* and undertaken at the beginning of his career. Occasional narratives of cases scattered through his surviving works record the entire course of a pa-tient's illness over time together with the outcome—up to and including death—and incorporate the kind of analysis that Cardano claimed could be learned from considering the case histories in the *Epidemics*. Yet even these cases do not, in reality, read very like the *Epidemics*. The use of description as a jumping-off point for explicit causal analysis of the illness and explanation of the reasons for the preferred method of treatment is much more reminiscent of Galen in *Methodus medendi* than of Hippocra-tes. Moreover, the physician-narrator's presence and intervention are much more assertive than in the *Epidemics*. Professional colleagues and competitors also often enter the story. The patient dies, but not before Cardano has reported his own repeated interventions and his reflections during the course of treatment. And although failure in therapy is admit-ted, success in diagnosis and prognosis is invariably claimed. Such is his description of the illness and death of

Vicenzo Cospo of Bologna, a senator and a friend of mine. . . . On 21 October 1569, he was seized by a double tertian fever; but there was rigor on Friday, and with it vomiting and dark feces, he was not sweating: the fever was finishing. Having been called in during the fifth day, around the evening, I knew of no other symptoms. In the morning he seemed to be more or less all right: but he had already taken food, bread cooked with liquid, however he also drank water for the accession [of fever] was threatening. In the evening when I came back, I noticed his pulse was weak. He was cheerful, lying on his left side so that he could receive (I believe) visitors. Where I kept on trying to feel the pulse, I did not find it, and I was wondering if this happened because of me, that is on account

[51] Cardano, comm. *Prognost., Opera*, VIII, 595.
[52] *Ibid.*, 613-14.

of my stupidity. I undertook to touch him again, I noticed I had not been deceived, for indeed I found the pulse, but it was very languid, small, not very fast but rather frequent. Certain therefore about his status, I admonished the other physician that he should be given a little bit of diluted wine for supper, along with a dish of egg yolk. The following morning we gave him theriac and fomented his belly with absinth and even anointed the heart. There succeeded fever without vomiting or defecation. A sufficiently robust pulse, and as usual, large, rapid, and frequent. Copious sweating followed, since he had also sweated the previous night. When the seventh day had gone past we were fearing the circuit [of critical days]; the remedies of the previous day were applied. When I came about the sixteenth hour (indeed he had already taken food), I found him feverish, since the accession had not yet supervened (but it was exacerbated on even days and took place later). When the accession [of fever] and a little rigor came, his forces collapsed but he defecated a little, as on the sixth day, and he vomited nothing. Before sunset, he died.[53]

On the basis of exhaustive consideration of every symptom and its timing, Cardano's analysis of this narrative eliminated diagnoses of poisoning (the corpse did not swell up or putrefy immediately), an internal abscess (the fever was not acute and continuous), and plague (there was no plague in the city) and settled on double tertian fever, even though the symptoms were, in his view, abnormal for that complaint. Careful observation in conjunction with an endeavor to explain the phenomena in terms of established disease theory yielded only a second *historia* put together by Cardano, that of the internal bodily processes; and this second story could only be linked to the original narrative of illness in What seems—given the range of diseases considered—a highly arbitrary manner.

And indeed, Cardano himself seems to have perceived results of this kind as ambiguous at best. Certainly, he had great faith in autopsy as a superior technique for confirming previous diagnosis.[54] Appearances in autopsy could, of course, only be interpreted in terms of current disease theory, so that the idea was probably more prescient than useful. However, it led him to append a description and interpretation of postmortem appearances to his account of the case of Giovan Battista Pellegrini.[55] This one last example of Girolamo Cardano's medical narratives brings together in a single *historia* the characteristics that have emerged from the separate examples discussed above. It combines autobiography and case history, self-advertisement—as a diagnostician and anatomist if not as a therapist—with a carefully observed and vividly recounted story of

[53] Cardano, *Paralipomena*, Book 3, *Opera*, X, 501.

[54] Cardano, comm. *Prognost*, *Opera*, VIII, 705-6.

[55] *Ibid.*, 649-50; on Pellegrini, see Andrea Cristiani, "Docenti di medicina e 'Disputa delle arti' a Bologna fra Quattrocento e Cinquecento," *Sapere e/è potere: Discipline. Dispute e Professioni nell'Università Medievale e Moderna. Il caso bolognese a confronto.* Atti del 40 convegno, Bologna, 13-15 aprile 1989 (II: *Verso un nuovo sistema del sapere*, ed. Andrea Cristiani, 140-48).

the fatal illness of a patient; and, for once, this physician's story also incorporates recognizable echoes of the patient's own account of his sensations.

But I will tell an outstanding example which happened so that I might see it today, while I am writing these things, that is on September 7, 1566. . . . Giovan Battista Pellegrini of Bologna, professor of arts and medicine was already ill for some months. He was a most studious and very upright man of 48, of completely melancholy habit, timid, slow, dark, emaciated, a small eater and moderate in drink, having the somewhat younger wife whom his temperament and cares needed, with five children. He had a scanty domestic establishment and many difficulties. Therefore from the beginning his belly swelled, he called a celebrated medicus who having judged it to be dropsy, as it was, applied many hot fomentations externally. . . . In the end almost spontaneously after months, almost exactly a year ago, that is on September 6, 1565 (for he died yesterday) he began to excrete crude humors and much water in his feces for many days and so the swollen belly went down; he got up and through the winter was walking about, but with a cane and only in his house, there seemed to be a hard tumor in the right hypochondrium and he could not straighten himself, he was dragged down as if by a chain within, and he breathed with difficulty. But really both his breathing got worse and the tension of the place increased; he used to feel while he turned over as if a weight in the parts around the heart was transferred from the right to the left, and the fever intensified, and again he was compelled to go to bed and to resort to those hot remedies and softening unguents, and so through the whole summer he was treated while declining from bad to worse. [Another physician arrives, carries on with the prior treatment and accomplishes nothing.] When I chanced to carry some commentaries to him [Pellegrini], in order that I might seek [some in] exchange, I found him burning with continuous fever, with a very rapid and frequent pulse, now hard, now sufficiently soft; the fever attacked him about midday sometimes—that is on alternate days—with coldness, at other times it was very much exacerbated, with almost no sleep, constant appetite for food, great difficulty in breathing, the parts about the heart were palpitating and the right [side] was sufficiently tense. That other physician was treating him as for hectic fever. . . . I said . . . I did not believe it to be hectic fever, but after 40 days, and it was about the middle of August (for he lived about 20 days from this opinion) I said openly that it was not in any way a hard tumor in the liver, nor in any of the digestive or reproductive organs, but the whole disease was almost principally in the lungs: and was oedema and it was going to suffocate him. Therefore I undertook treatment, but achieved nothing, but a little while afterwards he choked to death [*strangulatus*].
I therefore asked if I might dissect the cadaver, and I undertook it with an outstanding German anatomist who was skilled in the art named Folcherio and we dissected him.[56] No hard tumor was found in the muscle of the right part,

---

[56] Volcher Coiter (1534-76) received his doctorate in medicine at Bologna (1562), and lectured on surgery and published tables on human anatomy there. He left Italy in 1566 or 1567. See Dorothy M. Schullian, "Coiter, Volcher," *Dictionary of Scientific Biography*, 3 (New York, 1971), 342-43, and Robert Herrlinger, *Volcher Coiter* (Nuremberg, 1952), 18-25.

nor in the liver, nor in any of the inferior viscera, nor anything hard, only we saw the liver was of rather languid and pale color, that is tending toward white, but it was not attached to the diaphragm by the usual transverse adhesions as in the rest of men, but it was almost wholly connected to it by other adhesions, so that that whole part was joined to it; similarly his stomach was also connected by ligaments of an unnatural kind to the diaphragm. Again the whole lung in the bottom part was everywhere joined in the same way by adhesions to the diaphragm, and the membranes surrounding the ribs in front at the back and on the sides, which indeed Folcherio said he had observed in many others who died especially from phthisis. Besides the lung was very large so that it occupied almost the whole chest, and joined to the pericardium. But it was all full with hard tumors and blisters full of water.

Despite the vividness and particularity of some of his descriptions, Cardano's accounts of his own cases, like those of any single practitioner, provide only a limited point of entry into the history of the case history. No general picture of the Renaissance prehistory of the early modern case history based on clinical and pathological observation—to the development of which Sydenham (1624-89) and Morgagni (1682-1771), respectively, were leading contributors—can yet be drawn. In particular, we have still to reach a satisfactory general assessment of the relative importance of, and the interaction between, the growing readiness of fifteenth-century practitioners to record details about their own cases within traditional medieval genres of medical writing and the sixteenth-century study and imitation of newly edited, translated, or printed ancient examples and interpretations of case histories.[57]

But Cardano's *historiae* are highly informative about his own concepts of scientific method and good medicine, and how these worked out in his actual practice as astrologer, historian, and physician. His medical narratives show all the inconsistencies and contradictions characteristic not only of the man but more generally of Renaissance reworkings of ancient scientific authorities and traditional epistemologies. His desire for a natural and human history based on the record of particular experiences and guaranteed by the exactitude of mathematical astrology or autopsy; his awareness of the role of chance and social factors in building medical reputations, including his own; his keen sense of randomness, uncertainty, and lack of control of results in medical treatment; his understanding of the gulf separating Hippocratic case histories from the forms of medical narrative most common in his own day—none of this was in fact sufficient to cause him to abandon the traditional ways in which physicians described their experiences in treating patients. Instead, he added new methodologies—mostly derived from ancient sources—to traditional ones. The

[57] Suggestive connections between G. B. da Monte's (d. 1551) interest in the *Epidemics* and innovative descriptions included *among* his *consilia* noted in Bylebyl, "Teaching 'Methodus Medendi,' " 183-85, merit further exploration.

capacity for innovation of even such a profoundly idiosyncratic and non-conformist individual as Cardano was bounded on the one hand by ancient texts and on the other by his professional needs. Nor could even the most detailed of medical *historiae* yet offer much in the way of better understanding of disease. But Cardano's *historiae* surely contributed a lively appreciation of the importance of particular experiences and descriptive detail in a picture of the world and some grasp of the actual limitations of medical knowledge.

Hunter College and the
Graduate School of the City University of New York.

XIV

RENAISSANCE MUSIC AND EXPERIMENTAL SCIENCE

By Stillman Drake

The influence of early modern science on musical theory and practice has not gone unnoticed by historians of music. Professor Claude Palisca has called particular attention to the impact of scientific thought on the music of the late sixteenth and early seventeenth centuries. His "Scientific Empiricism and Musical Thought" concludes with this summary: "It would be wrong to conclude from this exposition that the sensualism and freedom of early Baroque music can be ascribed mainly to the liberalizing force of scientific investigation. . . . Scientific thought did reveal, however, the falsity of some of the premises on which existing rationalizations of artistic procedures had rested. . . . By creating a favorable climate for experiment and the acceptance of new ideas, the scientific revolution greatly encouraged and accelerated a direction that musical art had already taken. Finally, the new acoustics replaced that elaborate conglomeration of myth, scholastic dogma, mysticism and numerology that had been the foundation of the older musical theory, giving it a less monumental but more permanent base."[1]

The reciprocal influence of musical theory and practice upon early modern science, however, has been neglected by historians of science. This is somewhat surprising when we consider that music in medieval education held an equal place in the quadrivium with arithmetic, geometry, and astronomy as the recognized mathematical disciplines. For that reason alone, music might be expected to have remained rather closely associated with mathematics and science, and to have shared in their sudden transformations during the late Renaissance. I am convinced that that was indeed the case, and that the origins of the experimental aspect of modern science are to be sought in sixteenth-century music, just as its mathematical origins have been traced to the ancient Greek astronomers and to Archimedes.

In saying this, I have in mind the emergence of physics as a distinct separate study, no longer an integral part of philosophy, after the work of Galileo. The new physics, in which mathematics and experiment replaced logic and authority, was so successful as to become a sort of model for other sciences, at least so far as method was concerned. It is, of course, possible to trace the lineage of physics as far back as one wishes. Any form of intellectual activity that exists in one

[1] C. Palisca's article in *Seventeenth Century Science and the Arts*, ed. H. H. Rhys (Princeton, 1961), 91-137.

generation can be found to have some counterpart in the preceding generation, and it is instructive to detect and study these. On the other hand, it is no less instructive to recognize the occurrence from time to time of fundamental changes in patterns of intellectual activity. One way to do this is to select some pattern in modern times, and to move back until an essential element in the pattern disappears, or at least becomes of negligible importance in the writings of men who pursued the activity under study.

It is easy to trace modern physical science back in an unbroken line to Sir Isaac Newton, who unquestionably linked experimental evidence in his work with mathematical laws, in a way that is highly characteristic of science today. Many historians of science feel that it is proper to trace this same unbroken line further back, to Galileo. Others, who would pursue it yet further, are soon confronted with definite evidence of discontinuities, to say the least. The most influential historians of science (e.g. Pierre Duhem, Alexandre Koyré) contend that the work of Galileo was merely a continuation of lines of thought laid down in the Middle Ages by men whose work subsequently fell into obscurity until very recent times. In that way a link with classical antiquity is found, through commentators on Euclid and Aristotle who flourished in the Middle Ages. But if Galileo's work was a continuation of medieval thought, there seems to have been some interruption, for it is hard to find any sixteenth-century writers on mechanics whose conception of the relation of mathematics to experimental evidence even resembles that of Galileo. Hence, if we want to go farther back than Galileo in an unbroken line, we have to proceed with caution.

Obviously the unbroken line reaching back from the present will end wherever we discover the disappearance from physics of either mathematics or experiment. Now, the sixteenth century marked a notable increase of emphasis on and development of mathematics, ushered in by the publication and translation of ancient Greek works such as those of Euclid, Archimedes, and Pappus of Alexandria. And since mathematics pervades all typically sixteenth-century writings on mechanics, our quest turns automatically into a search for the origins of experiment. But here we shall need some kind of definition of experiment in its characteristically scientific sense.

For such a definition we can eliminate at once the concept of experiment that is associated with the name of Sir Francis Bacon; that is, the idea that we can arrive at the true explanation of things by the systematic and patient accumulation of observed facts, without any preconceived theory. In Bacon's view, the explanation would ultimately force itself upon us as a result of this procedure. That may be true, though in many matters it is open to doubt; but whether it is true or not, it has really nothing to do with science. The mere accumulation of data, useful though its results may be, does not constitute scientific knowledge as such. I shall cite a single example in illustration of this. One of Galileo's "Two New Sciences," published in 1638, was the science of strength of materials. There had been an impressive accumulation of information on that subject by earlier builders and engineers. But it was not such knowledge that gave rise to that science, or ever would have given rise to it, though that knowledge can be seen to fit into Galileo's new science. The new science was mathematical in character, and it developed not out of engineering, but out of the theoretical science of mechanics, and it was derived by Galileo from the Archimedean law of the lever. So in eliminating the Baconian definition of experiment, I am not denying the existence from time immemorial of accumulated observational data. Still less am I denying the usefulness of such activities. I mean only that it is not the Baconian type of experimentation that did, or could, account for the rise of modern science.

The kind of experimentation which interests historians of physics is the deliberate manipulation of physical objects for the purpose of corroborating by their behavior a definitely preconceived mathematical rule, or for the purpose of discovering a mathematical rule applicable to their behavior. Some physical objects are not amenable to manipulation—e.g., the heavenly bodies—so in their case deliberate selections of precise observations are made, and comparisons of them serve in place of manipulation. Thus some kind of tinkering with external measurements, directly or indirectly, is involved. Such an investigation, with an exact rule in question, for the purpose of seeing whether that rule is obeyed, or of discovering some exact rule, constitutes scientific experimentation. In physics and astronomy, "exact rule" means some mathematical expression; in other sciences, a rule may be considered precise without its being mathematically expressed. But it is always the testing of exact rules by some kind of external activity that distinguishes experimental method in science from various other possible approaches to knowledge and truth.

It is therefore natural for historians of science to be interested in discovering when, and under what circumstances, this approach began its uninterrupted prosecution down to the present time. It is equally natural for them to suppose that, so far as physics is concerned, experiment in the sense of manipulations to confirm or establish a law began in mechanics.

Proceeding thus, it is tempting to suppose that the first physical experiments were concerned with relatively simple measurements of equilibrium and of motion; for example, with the balancing of weights and the measuring of speeds by comparing distances and times. Suppositions of that kind are so easily made, and so intrinsically plausible that they tend to go unquestioned. It is thus that people reconstruct the invention of the wheel by supposing that it must have evolved from the use of logs or rollers in the moving of heavy objects. Fortunately for those who enjoy that kind of speculation, the invention of the wheel goes so far back that they need not fear contradiction, though they cannot adduce the slightest positive evidence in favor of their unanimous conjecture. A historian who may try to discover the origin of scientific experimentation, however, is less fortunate. In unbroken succession, this really does not go very far back in time; not even as far back as the invention of printing, let alone of writing. Hence he may expect to see any assumption or conjecture he makes about the origin of scientific experimentation challenged, and he is obliged to look for something that can be supported by some kind of recorded evidence.

With these things in mind, let us take a new look at the idea that scientific experimentation began in mechanics. A very simple and fundamental law in mechanics is the law of the lever. Of course, that law may have been discovered by a Baconian accumulation of observations, but then again it may not. The law is a mathematical statement, and it is perfectly possible that nobody ever knew it in that form before Archimedes. Levers may have been used long and widely without their exact law having been known, and that law may have been deduced by someone who never used a lever, or at least never experimented with it. Certainly Archimedes made no use of experimental induction in his proof of the law of the lever, nor do his postulates suggest an experimental origin. I say this not to suggest that there was no scientific experimentation in antiquity, but to show that the most natural conjectures about its role in the origin of mechanics may be quite misleading. In any event, the law relating distances and weights for the lever was both discovered and mathematically formulated so long ago that it would have been simply silly to perform any experiments to verify it as late as the sixteenth century. Not only that, but the law of the lever is so simple and so far-reaching, once it is known, that there was also little point in performing actual experiments to determine the laws of any of the other simple machines. They could be much more effectively discovered and demonstrated mathematically from the law of the lever. And that, I am quite certain, is exactly the attitude that was taken by writers on mechanics in the sixteenth century.

Reliance on mathematical reasoning had by then driven out of physics any feeling of need for experimentation that may once have existed. We shall see presently what the analogous situation was in music. The reason I am quite certain of the situation in mechanics is the following.

Pappus of Alexandria, writing in the fourth century of our era, had derived mathematically a law for the force required to drive or draw a heavy body up an inclined plane. His law was quite mistaken, because he had employed a false assumption, but the mathematical derivation was very ingenious and complicated, and it had the lovely aura of remote antiquity to recommend it to sixteenth-century mechanicians. From the theorem of Pappus, there easily followed a law for the equilibrium of bodies suspended on different inclined planes, also false, of course. Now, it happened that the correct law of equilibrium on inclined planes had been stated in the thirteenth century by Jordanus Nemorarius, who did not know the work of Pappus. In 1546, Niccolò Tartaglia published the medieval theorem, with some improvements in its purported proof. So all later writers were confronted with two different laws, each of which was accompanied by an attempted mathematical demonstration. If ever there was an occasion for experimental test, this was it; moreover, the deciding experiment would have been very easy to perform. But that is not what happened. In 1570, Girolamo Cardano, who was certainly familiar with the correct medieval theorem and who in all probability also knew the work of Pappus, ignored them both and published a brand-new law for inclined planes, which had to be in error, since the medieval theorem was correct. Seven years later Guido Ubaldo del Monte published the first comprehensive work on mechanics. An astute critic of his predecessors, he certainly knew the correct theorem of Jordanus, and probably also knew the erroneous theorem of Cardano; yet he adopted in his own book the false (but ancient and elegant) theorem of Pappus. These events are hardly explicable if the idea of experimentation in mechanics, to test a preconceived mathematical rule or to discover a new one, is assumed to have been prevalent in the sixteenth century.

I might add that even in the later work of Galileo we find evidence of the use of experiment only to confirm a preconceived mathematical law, and not of its systematic use to discover new laws. That step came after his time, as a logical extension of his work. But we are interested in tracing the probable origin of Galileo's application of experiment (in the scientific sense) to mechanics, which means that it is time to turn to the history of music.

In the sixteenth century, music and mechanics were more obviously closely related sciences than they are today. Tartaglia wrote in his revised preface to the first vernacular translation of Euclid ever published: "We know that all the other sciences, arts and disciplines need mathematics; not only the liberal arts, but all the mechanical arts as well. . . . And it is also certain that these mathematical sciences or disciplines are the nurses and mothers of the musical sciences, since it is with numbers and their properties, ratios, and proportions that we know the octave, or double ratio, to be made up of the ratios

4:3 and 3:2, and it is similarly that we know the former [that is, the interval of the fourth] to be composed of two tones and a [minor] semitone, and the latter [that is, the perfect fifth] to be composed of three tones and a minor semitone. And thus the octave (or double) is composed of five tones and two minor semitones; that is, a comma less than six tones; and likewise we know a tone to be more than 8 commas and less than 9. Also, by virtue of those [mathematical] disciplines, we know it to be impossible to divide the tone, or any other superparticular ratio, into two equal [rational] parts [in geometric proportion], which our Euclid demonstrates in the eighth proposition of Book VIII."[2]

But if, about the year 1550, the sciences of music and mechanics were alike in their purely mathematical character, the relations of those two sciences to the practical arts that bore the same names were totally different. Musical theorists were in possession of mathematical rules of harmony that they believed must be very strictly followed in practice. It would be unthinkable for musicians to depart from those rules, lest the very basis of music be destroyed. Musical theorists, moreover, received a good deal of respectful attention from musical practitioners and even had a certain authority over them. This was certainly not the case with theorists in mechanics. Musicians quite frequently studied under musical theorists, but engineers did not study under mechanical theoreticians. And if there were any theorists of mechanics who believed that their rules must be strictly followed in practice, this would have been in the sense that failure to observe the rules would result in wasteful use of materials or in the collapse of buildings, not in the ruin of architecture.

There was a further difference between the arts of music and mechanics in the sixteenth century, a difference that probably has a bearing on the events which (in my opinion) led to the origin of experimental physics. This was the fact that commencing about 1450, and quite markedly after 1550, musical practice underwent fundamental changes, while mechanical practice did not. Those changes in musical practice brought about a real need to expand or alter musical theory, and with it a need for critical examination of its basis and its claims to correctness. No such need was felt by engineers. It was just as easy to test the mathematical rules of music in practice as it would have been to test those of mechanics; the difference in applying or neglecting such a test lay only in the feeling of need. Furthermore, the tests could be carried out in music with a great deal more accuracy, for no sixteenth-century mechanical measurement came even close to the precision of the trained ear of a musician. I believe that

---

[2]*Euclide . . . diligentemente rasettato . . . per . . . Nicolò Tartalea* (Venice, 1543), has a shorter and incorrect reference to musical proportions.

that may very well still be true today, if we restrict ourselves to mechanical measurement and do not bring in electronic devices.

Finally, one might go so far as to say that the only possible means of detecting errors in, and ultimately of overthrowing, incorrect musical theories, was the appearance of experimental evidence against them. This was perhaps not equally true of errors in theoretical mechanics, which were in fact corrected by the detection and elimination of certain false assumptions, rather than by the revision of the whole theoretical structure of the science. But a discussion of that would lead us too far afield.

The heart of ancient musical doctrine was an arithmetical theory of proportion credited to the Pythagoreans. The very existence of musical consonances and dissonances was ascribed in it to certain numbers, related as ratios. That is, the cause of consonance itself was thought to be the so-called sonorous numbers. According to the Pythagorean rule, the musical intervals of the octave, fifth, and fourth were governed by the ratios 2:1, 3:2, and 4:3. Music owed the possibility of its existence to these ratios, which are made up of the smallest integers. Here we have a marvellous example of the use and abuse of mathematics and experiment. It is said that Pythagoras discovered these ratios as a result of his having noted, in good Baconian fashion, the different tones given out by hammers of different weight when striking an anvil. The story is certainly apocryphal, but observations of string-lengths would have led to the ratios. Having obtained their simple numbers in this or some other empirical way, ancient theorists put them in the place of any further experimentation, and derived from them an elaborate theory of musical intonation. In time, the arithmetical theory was seen as transcending in authority its original source in pleasant sensation. The consequences were not serious for a very long time, but by the late sixteenth century it was no longer possible to maintain the ancient idea of simple numerical ratios as the cause of harmony. We must pause to see how that came about.

Ancient Greek music, though it bore the name "harmony," was largely innocent of harmony in its present musical sense. Singing was chiefly homophonic, and when it was accompanied by instruments, they were played in unison with the voice, or, at most, in the octave. The fitting-together that was implied by the word "harmony" was not a fitting-together of different melodies or of parts sung simultaneously, as with us, but a fitting-together of succeeding notes so as to preserve consonance within the recognized *tonoi*, ancestral to the medieval modes, which differed in an essential way from our keys. These facts, coupled with the limited range of the human voice, and the practice of remaining within the selected mode during a given song, made it possible to decide on the intervals that were to divide the octave without imposing limitations on the composition of music.

By the thirteenth century, however, the simultaneous singing of two or three airs had long been in vogue, and thereafter much ingenuity was exercised in the composition and arrangement of motets in such a way that separate voices might interweave without clashing. The use of perfect fourths and fifths exclusively as chief accents, or points of repose, fitted in very nicely with this purpose, and the momentary appearance of imperfect consonances, as thirds and sixths had come to be regarded, did not disturb the ear so long as they were not carried to excess.

In time, however, deliberate violation of the ancient rules began to be attractive; the ears of singers and of listeners came to recognize a sort of general harmonic flow, though the form of composition remained polyphonic. Along with this came the development and multiplication of instruments, used at first to accompany voices, but later coming to be played together with or without voices. Instruments introduced a new element, because unlike voices, most instruments are incapable of producing whatever note the player desires with the exactitude of the human voice. Lutes, recorders, and viols, for example, unlike trombones and the later violins, are limited to definite sets of notes by fretting or by the positions of wind-holes. Organ pipes emit specific notes that cannot be varied in pitch by the organist, just as the harp and most of the keyboard instruments are governed by fixed string-lengths. Inevitably, problems arose over the proper tuning of instruments, particularly when different kinds of instruments began to be played together, which brings us to the sixteenth century.

The fretting of early stringed instruments had led quickly and naturally to tempered scales for them. Octaves simply must be in tune; even the untrained ear cannot tolerate much variation for the octave, which is heard instinctively much the same as unison. Intervals of the fourth and fifth together must also make up the octave, and while it is nearly as easy to tune perfect fourths or fifths as it is perfect octaves, you cannot make several strings agree over a range of two or three octaves by tuning them in perfect fourths or fifths. There is that plaguey "comma" that Tartaglia mentioned, and it has to be divided up in some way. For lutes and viols, this is accomplished by tempering, usually by making each successive fret interval 17/18ths the length of the preceding lower fret, a rule advocated by Vincenzo Galilei late in the sixteenth century. Organs, however, seem to have been tuned by the mean-tone system from an early period, certainly by the fifteenth century. Recorders, on the other hand, were generally tuned in C or F, depending on size, in just intonation. But temperament, mean-tone tuning, and just intonation do not make use of precisely the same intervals.

The nature of the difficulty that gave rise to those various intervals is purely mathematical in a sense; the numbers 1, 2, 3 . . . are very useful for counting, but they do not form a continuum. Musical sounds do form a continuum, and hence the whole numbers, even when they are formed into fractions, have a limited application to musical sounds. The set of fractions that will divide a given octave into seven different tones will obviously divide a different octave into seven analogous tones; but if we give them names in the ordinary way, those which bear the same names will not all be in unison or separated by exact octaves. As Tartaglia remarked, and as the ancients knew, the ratio 2:1 for the octave and the ratio 3:2 for the fifth implied the ratio 9:8 for the whole tone between the fifth and the fourth. This in turn implied too small a value for the exact semitone. As Simon Stevin, the Flemish counterpart of Galileo, wrote, "The natural notes are not correctly hit off by such a division. And although the ancients perceived this fact, nevertheless they took this division to be correct and perfect, and preferred to think that the defect was in our singing—[which is] as if one should say the sun may be wrong, but not the clock. They even considered the sweet and lovely sounds of the minor and major third and sixth, which sounded unpleasantly in their misdivided melodic line, to be wrong, the more so because a dislike for inappropriate numbers moved them to do so. But when Ptolemy afterwards wanted to amend this imperfection, he divided the syntonic diatonic in a different way, making a distinction between a major whole tone in the ratio 9:8 and a minor whole tone in the ratio 10:9, a difference that does not exist in nature, for it is obvious that all whole tones are sung as equal."[3] By "sung," Stevin meant "sounded" in general, and his final remark is rather an exaggeration.

Regarding the musical string as a continuum, Stevin announced flatly that rational proportions had nothing whatever to do with music, and declared that the proper division of the octave into equal semitones was as the twelfth root of two. It is in this way that we tune pianos today; it enables us to play in all keys without seriously disturbing the ear in any. His conclusion was, however, not experimental but purely mathematical; one might say that it is only accidental that it opened the door to modern harmony. I shall say no more about it here except to mention that Stevin, in a characteristic aside, considered the whole problem to have arisen from an inadequacy of the Greek language: ". . . the Greeks were of the most intelligent that Nature produces, but they lacked a good tool, that is, the Dutch language, without which in the most profound matters one can accomplish as little as a skilled carpenter without good tempered tools can carry on his trade."[4] For Galileo, the book of Nature was written in mathematics; for Stevin, the book of mathematics was written in Dutch.

[3] *The Principal Works of Simon Stevin*, 5, *Music*, ed. A. D. Fokker (Amsterdam, 1966), 431–33.
[4] *Ibid.*, 433.

And so, finally, we come to the sixteenth-century controversy over musical tuning that created modern music, with experimental physics as a by-product. In one corner stood the mathematical theory of antiquity, which took sonorous number as the cause of concord and asserted that number must *govern* string-length, or the placement of wind-holes, or the like. In the other was the human ear, with that curious taste for pleasant sounds that goes along with—or at least once went along with—the composition and performance of music. They were in conflict, as Stevin observed, and with or without the Dutch language, that conflict had to be resolved. The question was, which was to be master, numbers or sounds? The conduct of the debate is instructive, because it is symbolic in many ways of the debates that created the modern world, and of many that are still going on in it. For it was at once a battle of authority versus freedom; of theory versus practice; of purity versus beauty, and so on. Curiously enough, the issue was partly decided by antiquity; that is, by the recovery of an ancient treatise that was largely neglected by theorists before the sixteenth century. Nothing helped a good cause in that century like the discovery that some ancient writer had already thought of it. Copernicus was careful to mention some ancient writers, e.g., some Pythagoreans, who were said to have subscribed to the motion of the earth. It was of great help to musicians in their struggle for emancipation from the syntonic diatonic tuning of Ptolemy to be able to cite the view of Aristoxenus that when all was said and done, the ear of the musician must prevail.

I should like to remark at this point that in a paradoxical way, the struggle to free and broaden music in our own time is a mirror image of the struggle that freed and broadened it in the seventeenth century. Electronic computer music has much in common with the program of the late Renaissance conservatives who fought to preserve the mathematical beauty of sonorous number and superparticular ratios against the mere pleasure of the human ear. The argument of Gioseffo Zarlino, roughly paraphrased for its philosophical content, was that there could be only one correct tuning, established by the mystic properties of numbers, and if that put limitations on instrumental music, then so much the worse for instruments. The voice must govern instruments, and must in turn be governed by divine proportions of numbers. It is amusing that the argument for the divine right of theory, used at one time to impose narrow bounds on music, is now used to support the abandonment of all bounds, and with them all mere sensory criteria for music. Theory before pleasure, once conservative, is now avant-garde.

On purely theoretical grounds, Zarlino advocated the extension of the Pythagorean ratios up to the number 6, from the ancient 4. This would allow as consonances, in addition to the fourth and fifth, the major sixth as 5:3, the major third as 5:4, and the minor third as 6:5. He was also willing to allow the minor sixth as 8:5, but that finished the list; no other consonances were admissible. The number 6 was, after all, the first perfect number—that is, the lowest number that was equal to the sum of its factors—so the sonorous numbers could safely be extended that far, but no further. Zarlino's *Harmonic Institutions*, published in 1558, did away with all rivals of the syntonic diatonic tuning, such as temperament and the mean-tone system, as theoretically unjustifiable. His treatise on composition thus limited music to polyphony as before, though this was given a somewhat larger range. Method had been perfected. Mathematics was saved by the *senario*, as Zarlino called his six-based ratio system, but harmony was stillborn if his system prevailed.

About five years later, Zarlino's scheme was subjected to criticism, both mathematical and experimental, by G. B. Benedetti. Benedetti has long been recognized among historians of science as the most important by far of the Italian precursors of Galileo in mechanics, but only recently Professor Palisca has called attention to his achievements in the physics of music. These are contained in two letters written to Cipriano da Rore at Venice, probably in 1563, and published in 1585 together with Benedetti's more famous contributions to mathematics and physics. First, he showed by means of examples that a strict adherence by singers to Zarlino's ratios for consonances could result in a considerable change of pitch within a few bars. Benedetti argued from this that singers must in fact make use of some kind of tempered scale in order to preserve even the most elemental musical orthodoxy with regard to pitch of opening and closing notes.

Next, Benedetti proceeded to examine the problem from the standpoint of physics. Instead of relating pitch and consonance directly to numbers, that is to string-lengths and special ratios, he related them to rates of vibration of the source of sound. Consonance, he asserted, was heard when air waves produced by different notes concurred or recurred frequently in agreement; dissonance, when they recurred infrequently or broke in on one another. Thus strings vibrating in the ratio 2:1 would concur on every other vibration; in the ratio 3:2, on every sixth vibration, and so on. The direct cause of consonance was thus related to a physical phenomenon, which in turn bore a relation to certain numbers; but the numbers as such were not regarded by Benedetti as the cause of the phenomenon of consonance. Pursuing this reasoning, he suggested an index of consonance, formed by multiplying together the terms of the ratio. The smaller this product, the greater the consonance. Viewed in this light, consonance and dissonance were not two separate and contradictory qualities of sounds, but rather they were terms in a continuous series without sharp divisions. A similar view was soon to emerge for heat and cold, speed and slowness, and other ancient physical concepts. Also, by Benedetti's index, it followed that the traditionally abhorred subminor fifth, with the ratio 7:5, was in fact a better consonance than the minor sixth, with the ratio 8:5, which Zarlino himself had allowed even though it lay outside his *senario*. Obviously this was not just a further modification of the old theory, but a fundamental attack on the very basis of that theory.

In framing these ideas, Benedetti had had recourse to experiment; that is, to the deliberate manipulation of physical equipment in order to test a preexisting mathematical theory. The physical equipment consisted of a monochord, on which a movable bridge permitted the division of a single stretched string into any desired ratio, and allowed the measurement of the ratio to a fair degree of accuracy by measurement of the lengths of the two sections, which could then be sounded simultaneously by plucking in order to determine the tonal effect. Benedetti's basis for asserting that string-lengths were proportional to frequencies of vibration is not stated; it may or may not have been experimental. But the appeal to physical results over the authority of a mathematical theory that had been developed over many centuries was in any case a novel event. Experiments similar to Benedetti's, though probably not directly inspired by him because he did not publish them, will presently be shown to have been intimately connected with Galileo's work in mechanics. First, though, I want to comment on the step-by-step nature of the process, for Benedetti's results were in an important sense only a small start toward the modern physical science of musical acoustics.

Benedetti's brief writings on music did not remove mathematics from musical theory; they merely changed its role. For his contemporaries, as for the ancients, numbers were the cause of harmonious sound in a totally different way from that in which Benedetti saw them as related to that cause. Others regarded numbers as ruling the nature of sound; Benedetti formulated a physical theory of sound that was capable of explaining the association of certain numbers or ratios with certain tonal effects. But Benedetti himself was not a composer, and therefore did not concern himself with the possibility or desirability of expanding the range of acceptable tonal effects. He seems not even to have noticed the phenomenon of partial vibrations. These things were soon to come. What Benedetti contributed was in the nature of a new explanation of known effects, rather than a basis for the exploration of new ground. Thus to the question, "Why is the fifth more harmonious than the major third?" the classical answer was of this form:

"Because the ratio 3:2 contains two sonorous numbers, and the ratio 5:4 does not." Zarlino's reply might have been: "The ancients were mistaken; both are equally harmonious, for all numbers within the *senario* are sonorous numbers. But since sonorous numbers are the cause of harmony, the slightest departure from the ratios named must be avoided, or dissonance will result." Benedetti's reply would have been, "Because harmony proceeds from agreement of vibrations, which occurs every sixth time for the fifth, and only every twentieth time for the major third." But to the question, "What can we do to widen the scope of harmonious music?" no one gave an answer. To Benedetti's opponents, the question was unthinkable; and to Benedetti, the first man who would have been able to answer, the question never occurred; he was a scientist and not a musician.

It is virtually certain that Zarlino, who opposed any tempering of the vocal scales, never heard of Benedetti's demonstration that such tempering was necessary in practice and theoretically justifiable. But Zarlino was opposed in print by a former pupil of his, Vincenzo Galilei, father of Galileo. In 1578 Galilei sent to Zarlino a discourse in which the departures of practicing musicians from the tuning recommended by Zarlino were stated and defended; there was no escape from a tempered scale in the music of the late sixteenth century. Zarlino paid no attention to this attempt of Galilei's to refute his theory; indeed, he appears to have attempted to suppress the printing of his former pupil's book, which nevertheless appeared much expanded, in 1581. Galilei, who had long followed Zarlino's teaching, began to question it only after he had learned from Girolamo Mei, the best informed man in Italy on the music of the ancients, that among the ancients themselves there had been musicians who questioned the absolute authority of mathematical theory over sense. It was Mei who invited Galilei to put to actual test certain doctrines of the old theory. The result was Galilei's abandonment of Zarlino's teaching and his publication of the contrary view in favor of tempered scales.

Zarlino, far from accepting these criticisms, counterattacked in 1588 with his final book on music theory, the *Supplementi musicali.* Though he did not mention Galilei by name, he quoted from his book and identified him as a former pupil. Galilei lost no time in replying; in 1589 he published a little volume which he dedicated, with obvious sarcasm, to Zarlino. The first part of this book is merely polemical and personal, but the balance of it is of the greatest interest with respect to the beginnings of experimental physics. Galilei was, first of all, outspokenly against the acceptance of authority in matters that can be investigated directly. He did not even accept the idea that some musical intervals were natural, or that any were consonant by reason of their being capable of representation by simple proportions. Any sound was as natural as any other. Whether it pleased the ear was quite another matter, and the way to determine this was to use the ear, not the number system. Zarlino had extolled the human voice as the greatest musical instrument, being the natural one, and concluded that musical instruments, as artificial devices, were bound by the laws of the natural instrument. Galilei replied that instruments had nothing to do with the voice, and made no attempt to imitate it; they were devised for certain purposes, and their excellence could be determined only by the degree to which they successfully carried out those purposes. Mathematics had no power over the senses, which in turn were the final criterion of excellence in colors, tastes, smells, and sounds.

For a tuning system, Galilei advocated an approximate equal temperament as determined by the trained ear. Here we should recall that Stevin, about the same time, went still further: he boldly declared that ratios and proportions had nothing to do with music and that the proper and ideal intervals were those given by the twelfth root of two. Stevin, like Benedetti, failed to publish his discussion of music, but it is likely that he was influential in his own country.

It is in Galilei's final refutation of Zarlino that we find for the first time the specific experimental rejection of sonorous number as the cause of consonance. Referring to the celebrated opinion of Pythagoras that the small-number fractions are always associated with agreeable tones, Galilei stated first that he had long believed this, and then said that he had determined its error by means of experiment. The ratios 2:1, 3:2, 4:3 will give octaves, fifths, and fourths for strings of like material and equal tension but of lengths in these ratios, or for columns of air of similar lengths. But if the lengths are equal and the tensions are varied, then the weights required to produce the tensions are as the squares of these numbers. In a later, unpublished manuscript, he added that the cubes would have to be calculated where volumes determined the sounds. Thus, he said, the ratio 9:4 was just as closely associated with the fifth as the ratio 3:2; and by implication, so was the ratio 27:8— ratios which were simple abominations to the Pythagorean and Ptolemaic numerologists who believed in sonorous number as a cause.

In addition, Galilei experimented with strings of different materials and weights, discovering that unison cannot be consistently obtained between two strings if they differ in any respect whatever. Stringing a lute with strings of steel and gut, he found that if these were brought into agreement as open strings, they would not be in perfect agreement when stopped at the frets.

The removal of number magic from musical theory performed a doubly significant service. First, it deprived number of causal properties; second, and perhaps more important, it called attention to the real significance of number as it referred to a specific dimension, such as length, surface, and volume. The trouble with the older musical theory was not only that it failed to provide anything fruitful for expanding musical practice, but also that by purporting to give an explanation in mystical numerical terms, it tended to prevent the direct study of the actual application of number to the material instruments of music. A similar double error pervaded most of physics; not only did the erroneous physical principles of Aristotle fail to agree with observation, for example with regard to falling bodies, but their very existence discouraged the search for correct principles.[5]

The experiments of Vincenzo Galilei, like those of Benedetti, were true scientific experiments in the sense in which we have defined that term: the manipulation of physical objects for the purpose of verifying a mathematical rule preconceived as applicable to their behavior, or for the purpose of discovering a rule involved in that behavior. Whether music inspired the first such experiments in an unbroken line to the present remains to be seen. If others preceded them, it would seem that they must have been independent of them, for it is hard to see how Benedetti and Galilei might have attacked musical theory experimentally under the influence of some earlier experimental attack on some other mathematical theory. And to establish the probable continuity of their work with the application of experiment to mechanics, which has had such profound consequences for all science, we may now turn briefly to Galileo himself.

Galileo was enrolled at the University of Pisa in 1581, his father having selected for him a medical career. Two years later he became deeply interested in mathematics under the guidance of a family friend, Ostilio Ricci. The chair of mathematics at the University appears to have been vacant when Galileo was there. His new interest distracted him from the study of medicine, and in 1585 he left the University without a degree. During the next five years he lived mainly in Florence, giving some private instruction in mathematics and commencing on researches that obtained for him the chair of mathematics at Pisa in 1589. Now it was precisely during those years, and particularly in 1588-89, that Vincenzo Galilei is most likely to have carried out many of the experiments in refutation of Pythagorean music theory that he never published, but that survive in manuscripts among Galileo's papers. It seems to me extremely likely that Galileo was himself involved in his father's experiments, some of which he appropriated and published many years later in his *Two New Sciences*. Galileo was an accomplished amateur musician, instructed by his father, and as a young mathematician he could hardly have remained indifferent to

[5]C. Palisca, 130; cf. V. Galilei, *Discorso intorno alle opere di Gioseffo Zarlino* (Venice, 1589; facs. repr. Milan, 1933), 127-28.

what his father was doing in the measurement of tuned strings and the examination of Pythagorean musical numerology. Thus the conception of experimental verification of mathematical laws in physics, which is often illustrated in Galileo's books, may very well have been inspired by his father's work during the years in which he had just left the university and was developing his own mathematical skills. It was precisely at this time that Galileo applied experiment to an ancient theory; he devised a hydrostatic balance and reconstructed the reasoning of Archimedes in the famed detection of the goldsmith's fraud in making the crown of Hiero of Syracuse.

If we consider the nature of Vincenzo Galilei's experiments, we gain also a possible clue to Galileo's early interest in the pendulum, a device with which his future work in physics was to be intimately connected. One of the most interesting of his father's experiments concerned the determination of the numbers associated with particular musical intervals under different conditions of the production of tones. You will recall that the celebrated ratios 3/2 for the fifth, 4/3 for the fourth, and 2/1 for the octave were related to string lengths, given strings of the same material and diameter. It was Vincenzo Galilei who remarked for the first time, in his final diatribe against Zarlino, that the same ratios did not hold at all for the weights that must be used to stretch a given string to the equivalent pitches; here, the inverse squares of the ratios would hold, and to raise the pitch an octave, where half the length would suffice, quadruple the weight was required. The experiment is not particularly difficult, but however it is carried out, an observer can hardly escape the phenomena of the pendulum. This is obvious if one thinks of suspending two strings of equal length and size, and weighting one with four times the weight attached to the other. In order to set up the experiment, let alone to elicit a tone, say by plucking, the strings and their weights are bound to be set in at least a slight swinging motion. If Vincenzo Galilei used instead the apparatus commonly illustrated for the false Pythagorean rule, the pendulum effect would also occur; here, parallel strings are stretched over a flat bed, weights being applied to the ends handing down from a terminal bridge. The application of different weights to these relatively short vertical strings would set them swinging and would invite attention to the lengths and periods of oscillation.

Galileo's observations of the pendulum were already reflected in his earliest contribution to the analysis of motion and of the law of falling bodies. About 1590 he composed a treatise on motion, which was never published. In this treatise he attempted to analyze the motions of bodies on inclined planes, and this was done in a manner that treated inclined planes as tangents to a circle. By 1602, we find him discussing the motions of bodies along arcs and chords of circles, and it is quite evident that he and his patron, the Marquis Guido Ubaldo del Monte, were doing some experimental observations of those motions. Galileo's decision not to publish his first treatise on motion seems to be related to his discovery, by experimental test, that the rules he had deduced for speeds on inclined planes were incorrect. By 1609, after various false starts that can be traced in his letters and notes, he had got to a point where he planned to publish a systematic treatise on motion, having ironed out the earlier false assumptions by means of a combination of mathematical reasoning and simple experimental tests. But in 1609 his attention was diverted to the newly invented telescope, and as a result his science of motion was not published until many years later, in 1638.

As one would expect, Galileo's first use of experiment in physics was limited to rough and simple tests to see whether the rules he had worked out mathematically were actually followed. As time went on, he took a greater interest in devising experiments to corroborate or illustrate his science of motion. The extent to which he actually conducted experiments such as those he described late in life is a matter of debate, but there is no question that they served as models to his pupils and his readers.

Such I believe to have been the origin of experimental method in physics in the sense of the unbroken thread leading from the late sixteenth century to the present. The first conscious experiments to test a preexisting mathematical theory were probably the musical experiments of Benedetti and Vincenzo Galilei. They were extended into mechanics by Galileo, whose pupils Castelli and Torricelli carried them on over into hydraulics and phenomena of air pressure; refined by Pascal and Boyle experiment led to the gas law. Boyle's law is said to have been the first scientific law to be experimentally discovered. Yet Vincenzo Galilei's discovery that the weights required for producing tensions corresponding to given pitches are as the inverse squares of lengths must have been empirical. In any event, the manipulation of physical equipment set up to test a mathematical law had come much earlier than Newton, even earlier than Galileo; and it came because of the conflict between numerology and physics in the field of music.

The desire for ever-increasing precision in experiment, a necessary counterpart of the new method in science that sought certainty in the reconciliation of sense experience and mathematics, was strikingly evidenced by Marin Mersenne, the friend of Descartes and the spokesman of Galileo in France. Mersenne is best known for his *Harmonie Universelle* of 1636–37, a monumental work on the theory and practice of music in which the role of the science of mechanics is much emphasized. It was Mersenne who carried out with great care the experiments on falling bodies and on bodies descending along inclined planes which Galileo mentioned but only roughly described in his books.[6] The intimate linkage of music to mechanics, mathematics, and experiment that is made in Mersenne's work tends to increase the probability of my general thesis concerning the origin of experimental physics.

I should like to conclude with a remark about a totally different relationship between Renaissance music and modern science, in an area where experiment in the sense of deliberate physical manipulation is not possible; that is, in astronomy. This second musical approach to science found expression in the work of Johannes Kepler, an almost exact contemporary of Galileo. Kepler was deeply motivated by precisely the kind of faith in the domination of the universe by numerical harmonies in astronomy that Galileo's father fought to destroy in music. Little interested in mechanics, Kepler devoted his life to the discovery of that Pythagorean music of the spheres that ought to be produced by the celestial motions. His goal turned out to be as illusory as that of the rule of musical harmony by exclusively small-number fractions. In the course of his work, however, Kepler discovered the mathematical laws that do describe the planetary motions. Those laws destroyed the heavenly spheres themselves, replacing circles with ellipses and uniform motions with varying speeds, much as physical laws destroyed the Pythagorean musical ratios. With varying distances from the sun, the planets were freed from monotony; but they could only grind out, on Kepler's most favorable calculations, a dreary succession of uninteresting scale-passages. Nevertheless, in his unending quest for better results and his devotion to precision of measurement, Kepler established a new physics of the heavens as firmly in mathematics and observation as Galileo founded a new terrestrial physics in the same solid base.

The fountainhead of Renaissance music was thus at least partly responsible for the emergence not of experimental science alone, but of a whole new approach to theoretical science that we now know as mathematical physics. It is well known that Sir Isaac Newton accomplished the synthesis of Kepler's astronomical laws and Galileo's science of motion, setting the pattern of modern physics that unifies terrestrial with cosmic events. In retrospect, it seems not to have mattered greatly which side the scientist took, provided only that he was deeply interested in the musical controversies of the Renaissance. What did matter was that the older mathematical theories of music were capable of exact test by experiment and precise observation. That was a key which, in the hands of Galileo and of Kepler, opened the door to modern science.

University of Toronto.

---

[6]Mersenne, *Harmonie Universelle* (Paris, 1636–37), I, 112; *Les nouvelles pensées de Galilée* (Paris, 1639), 188.

XV

HISTORIA INTEGRA: FRANÇOIS BAUDOUIN AND HIS CONCEPTION OF HISTORY

By Donald R. Kelley

Since the XVth century the prestige of historical studies has reached extraordinary heights. From handmaid of the liberal arts history has been promoted to *scientia scientiarum;* indeed, in the minds of many post-Hegelian philosophers, it has become the distinguishing characteristic of man himself. Croce, for example, has identified history with philosophy, while Ortega y Gasset, under a similar debt to German idealism, has suggested that man has not a nature but only a history. These notions are derived, no doubt, from the romantic view of man. Yet neither was a specifically XIXth-century invention. Each was embedded deep in the western tradition: each was first and most self-consciously formulated not in that historical revival called Romanticism but in that earlier historical revival called—by the Romantics themselves—the Renaissance. We might go still further and argue a classical origin for these two ideas except that in this case, for once, Renaissance humanism transcended its antique heritage. While antiquity had defined history as "philosophy teaching by example," it remained for a XVIth-century humanist, Andrea Alciato, to term it *certissima philosophia;* [1] and while the ancients had taught that self-knowledge was the key to wisdom, it remained for another humanist, François Baudouin, to point to history as the true path to this *sapientia.* [2] As one of his successors wrote,

Among the aphorisms of the ancients . . . , the most remarkable was that of Clio, one of the seven sages . . . : γνῶθι σεαυτόν. Know thyself. Now this knowledge depends upon history, sacred as well as profane, universal as well as particular. . . . [3]

This statement contains, of course, the oldest of commonplaces, but it also offers the basis for a more profound conception of man as a creature living and learning in time, as *homo historicus.*

[1] *Le Lettere,* ed. G. L. Barni (Florence, 1953), 222 ("Encomium historiae," first published 1518); cf. Dionysius of Halicarnassus, *Ars rhetorica,* XI, 2.

[2] *De Institutione historiae universae et eius cum Jurisprudentia conjunctione,* in Johann Wolf, ed., *Artis historiae penus octodecim scriptores* (Basel, 1579), I, 609.

[3] Pierre Droit de Gaillard, *Methode qu'on doit tenir en la lecture de l'histoire* (Paris, 1579), 1, and also "De Utilitate et ordine historiarum praefatio," in *Bap. Fulgosii Factorum dictorumque memorabilem libri IX* (Paris, 1578), a ii r.

Thus, although the links between the humanist scholarship of the Renaissance and our science-mongering XXth century are few and fast-diminishing, we have from that source at least one bequest whose value has increased with age—the awareness of the indelibly historical nature of civilization, if not of man himself. This sense of history represented not only a deepening of the range of experience but a real psychological transformation, a Copernican revolution in man's attitude toward his culture. It is with good reason that our history-mindedness is traced back to the new "philological" attitudes which Italian humanists of the XIVth and XVth centuries adopted toward classical antiquity.[4] These scholars were responsible not only for the revival of historiography but, more important, for the creation of those basic techniques of historical criticism which they gradually went on to apply to other branches of learning, especially to the study of Roman law and of the Bible. Italian humanism was not, however, the only force which has shaped modern historical thought. The early generations of humanists did not fully understand the new complex of ideas they had begun to assemble; they failed even to reach a conception of historical knowledge broad enough to combine the "auxiliary sciences" of history with historical writing. In fact it was not in Italy but in France that such a systematic view was attained, that— to adapt a formula of Guillaume Budé, the arch-humanist of France —*philosophia* superseded *philologia*.

How can we account for this? First of all, while the Italians, in their *artes historicae*, were concerned with the praise of history and with its literary and moral value, the French, by the second half of the XVIth century, had begun to compose "methods" of history.[5] Their purpose was, among other things, to improve the pedagogical value of history and to investigate its political and legal possibilities. Since they viewed history as a social science rather than as a branch of literature, it was the French, in practice as well as in theory, who did most to establish history as an independent discipline. In the conventional Italianate scheme history was regarded as an art related to if not identical with rhetoric and on a par, at most, with poetry. The French, on the other hand, accorded it a much higher dignity: Jean Bodin, for example, placed history "above all sciences," while for his disciple Gaillard it transcended the medieval hierarchy of learning altogether, since it was "the origin of all disciplines." [6] Finally, it was

---

[4] Most recently, A. Buck, *Das Geschichtsdenken der Renaissance* (Krefeld, 1957).

[5] See J. L. Brown, *The Methodus . . . of Jean Bodin* (Washington, 1939), ch. 3. From Gaillard's "De Utilitate . . . ," which was "deprompta ex suis institutionibus historicis," i.e. his *Methode*, it appears that "method" is an acceptable translation of "institutio." [Accents are often omitted in XVIth-century French texts.]

the French who first and most effectively began to consider history itself from a historical point of view. All of this was accomplished by a series of historical "methods" composed by Baudouin (1561), Bodin (1566), Gaillard (1579), and by La Popelinière's *History of Histories* and *Idea of History* (1599). These works are rhetorical rather than "methodological" in nature and concerned more with pedagogy than with philosophy, but for this very reason they are important reflections of the XVIth-century idea of history. Indeed they represent, in my opinion, the highest point of historical consciousness before the continental Enlightenment.

Of all these pioneering books, perhaps the most interesting and significant is François Baudouin's *Institution of Universal History and its Conjunction with Jurisprudence,* written five years before Bodin's more famous *Method* and more directly concerned with the technical problems of historical scholarship.[7] The work is certainly more relevant to historical thought than the Italianate *artes,* partly because of Baudouin's polemical interests, partly because he was not simply a humanist, a "grammarian," but a practicing historian and a devotee of the XVIth-century "historical school of law." It is also more relevant than the more ambitious treatise of Bodin, who according to his most perceptive commentator wanted to extract a science from history, not to make a science out of history; Baudouin was a legal antiquarian, not a philosopher of law.[8] In Baudouin's book we can see how, in a number of ways, history was entering into alliances with other fields of knowledge, not only with Roman law but also with political thought, ecclesiology, geography, and chronology. We can see too, both explicitly and implicitly, the convergence of many traditions of XVIth-century historical thought. Of these, the dominant one was the humanist conception of history, derived from Greek and Roman antiquity. Related to this was the historical and philological method of studying Roman law, called by contemporaries the *mos gallicus,* established in France by Budé and by his chosen successor Alciato, and adopted by Baudouin even earlier than by its most illustrious practitioner, Jacques Cujas, who was his exact contempo-

[6] Bodin, *Methodus ad facilem historiarum cognitionem,* in Mesnard, ed., *Oeuvres philosophiques* (Paris, 1951), 113; Gaillard, *Methode,* 552.

[7] See J. Franklin, *Jean Bodin and the Sixteenth-Century Revolution in the Methodology of Law and History* (New York, 1963), ch. VIII, and E. Fournol, "Sur quelques traités de droit public du XVIe siècle," *Nouvelle revue historique de droit français et étranger,* XXI (1897), 298–325, making comparisons with Bodin's *Methodus* and François Hotman's *Anti-Tribonian.*

[8] J. Moreau-Reibel, *Jean Bodin et le droit public comparé* (Paris, 1933), 69, noting the use Bodin made of Baudouin's book.

rary. A third tradition was ancient political philosophy, which Baudouin found most illuminatingly expressed in Polybius' "pragmatic history." Finally the idea of "universal history," which again had a Polybian precedent but which was most directly descended from the Christian world-chronicles, recently revitalized by German historians.[9] For in this as in other matters Baudouin did not, unlike the most fastidious Italian humanists, find it expedient to reject the medieval theory and practice of history. Such is the eclectic—perhaps we should say syncretistic—"method" of history which introduced the *ars historica* into France, which placed the "historical school of law" on a solid theoretical basis, which described and assessed the development of western historiography, and which in general was perhaps the most remarkable synthesis of historical ideas of the XVIth century. Such is the book on which this analysis of the Renaissance conception of history is principally centered.

The *ars historica,* of which Baudouin's *Institution of Universal History* was the first example in France, was a rhetorical tradition which has still not been fully investigated.[10] Classically *ars historica* meant simply historiography, but in the XVIth century, especially after the publication of Johann Wolf's collection in 1576, the term came to denote didactic essays—on the analogy of the *artes poetica* and *rhetorica*—on the reading as well as the writing of history. These essays included both the rhetorical *laus historiae* as well as the more technical *ratio scribendi historiae*. Both types had classical precedents, the first as a topos in historical or rhetorical works (such as those of Polybius or Isocrates), the second in Lucian's *How to Write History* and Dionysius of Halicarnassus' *Criticism of Thucydides' History*.[11] Both had also—and this is often overlooked—medieval examples, as in Isidore of Seville's chapters on history and in certain educational treatises such as Cassiodorus' *Divine and Human Readings*.[12] Finally both were, in modern times, Italian revivals, for exam-

---

[9] See A. Klempt, *Die Säkularisierung der universalhistorischen Auffassung* (Göttingen, 1960), which, however, neglects Baudouin.

[10] Besides Brown, *op. cit.,* see E. Maffei, *I Tratatti dell'arte storica* (Naples, 1897), and B. Reynolds, "Shifting Currents of Historical Criticism," *Journal of the History of Ideas*, XIV (1953), 471–92, all of which are limited to the *artes* in Wolf's collection.

[11] The last two appearing in Wolf.

[12] Isidore, *Etymologiarum libri XX*, Migne, *Patrologia* (Patres . . . ecclesiae latinae), LXXXII, 122 sqq.: c. xlii, "De primis auctoribus historiarum"; c. xliii, "De utilitate historiae"; and c. xliv, "De generibus historiae." Cassiodorus, *An Introduction to Divine and Human Readings*, trans. L. W. Jones (New York, 1946), XVII, "On Christian Historians."

ple, the *encomia* of Lorenzo Valla, Giovanni Pontano, Bartolommeo della Fonte, and Andrea Alciato (to mention some of the earliest), and Francisco Robortello's *How to Write History*.[13] The separation between the reading and writing was not, however, inviolable; for the most frequently cited formula of each—the *prima lex historiae* and the *historia magistra vitae*—were both taken from Cicero and may often be found together, especially in Baudouin's and La Popelinière's works. The "praise of history," in particular, was discussed in every sort of work—in orations, letters, prefaces to historical works or translations, the mirrors-of-princes, as well as more encyclopedic sources like Polydore Vergil's *Inventors of Things* and Barthélemy de Chasseneuz' *Catalogue of the Glories of the World* and, again, educational treatises, such as Juan Vives' *Teaching of the Disciplines*.[14] Consequently, from a historical point of view, it makes more sense to treat the *ars historica* as a complex of rhetorical topoi than as a literary genre. Baudouin's eclectic contribution to this tradition further complicated the question of its nature, but his "methodizing" approach also gave further impetus to the rising prestige of historical studies.

In spite of humanist hyperbole, however, the official, that is, the institutional, *dignitas* of history in the XVIth century remained quite humble. There were certainly no professional historians in the sense that there were professional lawyers, nor a place in the schools for such a person had he existed. It may have been true, as Daniel Heinsius said in the early XVIIth century, that "if history have no professorship, if all universities be closed, she will always have an honorable reception in palaces and in the innermost chambers of kings and princes." [15] But from a philosophical standpoint, advising statesmen was menial work; a courtier's life inspired any self-respecting humanist with at least a conventional horror. Even the subsidization of history through official historiographers was not really effective since the office was a polemical, not a scholarly one. The only real sign of status, that is, a fixed abode in the medieval curriculum, history lacked. Inside and outside the arts faculty history had at best

[13] Valla's *encomium* prefaces his *Historiarum Ferdinandi Regis Aragoniae libri tres* (Paris, 1521); Alciato's cited in note 1; on Fonte, Charles Trinkaus, "A Humanist's Image of Humanism," *Studies in the Renaissance*, VII (1960), 99–105. For other examples, see Klempt, *op. cit.*, and B. Weinberg, *A History of Literary Criticism in the Italian Renaissance* (Chicago, 1961), I, 13 sqq.

[14] Vergil, *De Rerum inventoribus* (Basel, 1536), 46–49, "Qui primis historiam condiderunt"; Chasseneuz, *Catalogus gloriae mundi* (Geneva, 1617), 394–95, "Laus historicorum"; Vives, *De Tradendis disciplinis*, in *Opera omnia* (Valencia, 1785), 388 sqq.

[15] *The Value of History*, trans. G. W. Robinson (Cambridge, Mass., 1943), 14.

an ancillary position, furnishing literary models or vicarious experience, moral *exempla* or legal precedents. Although it might be placed in the service of one of the "practical" sciences (especially politics or ethics), it could hardly be regarded as *scientia* because it lacked a sufficiently methodical arrangement; and although it might be subsumed under grammar or rhetoric, it did not qualify as a liberal art either. On the other hand, in terms both of style and purpose, history had long maintained a relationship with rhetoric so close as practically to be identified with it: above all other forms of discourse, as Baudouin recalled, history was *munus oratoris*.[16] History was also closely allied with grammar, not only because the *grammaticus* was obliged to concern himself with the whole classical encyclopedia but because his philological method, especially as exemplified in the *mos gallicus*, was fundamentally historical, that is, literal as distinguished from allegorical or tropological signification. So it was largely through the *studia humanitatis* that history began to gain a foothold in the universities and, in the company of these disciplines, to achieve independence of the professional faculties—even some control over them, to the extent that they were invaded by humanists in the name of philology. Indeed, through Alciato and his disciples, the *grammatici* had actually captured the law faculty of the University of Bourges, where Baudouin began his teaching career. In Protestant Germany history made even more substantial gains. As a result especially of Melanchthon's educational reforms, some universities began to provide for *professores historiarum*, so that history achieved parity not only with poetry but even, according to some pedagogical schemes, with law and theology. This happened in particular at Strassburg and Heidelberg, where Baudouin taught during those years when his conception of universal history was formed.[17] Indeed the Protestant promotion of historical studies may be considered another, and in some ways the most pervasive, element in Baudouin's historical thinking.

The circumstances of Baudouin's personal life intensified both his religious and his scientific—both his ideological and his methodological—attachments to history. From the beginning Baudouin was in sympathy with religious reform; from the beginning, too, his schol-

---

[16] *De Institutione*, 640; cf. 689.

[17] In fact, a professor of poetry and history was instituted at Heidelberg in 1557, the very year Baudouin arrived. On this general subject see the well documented work of E. Scherer, *Geschichte und Kirchengeschichte an den deutschen Universitäten* (Freiburg, 1927). According to Chytraeus, whose *De Lectione historiarum* was also printed in Wolf, the four higher *genera artium*, placed above the trivium, were theology, ethics (including law), physics (including medicine), and history: Detloff Klatt, *Davis Chytraeus als Geschichtslehrer und Geschichtschreiber* (Rostok, 1908), 35.

arly interests were historical. In his native Arras Baudouin was brought into early contact with the Erasmian tradition, and he received a good humanist education at Louvain. By 1540 he was living in Paris, acting as secretary to the great jurist Charles Dumoulin, perhaps assisting in his famous commentary on feudal law.[18] Baudouin was deeply impressed not only by Dumoulin's historical attitude but by his Gallican politics and by his religious radicalism. Like Dumoulin, Baudouin became an early adherent of Calvin and like him was led from legal to historical studies, ultimately to religious polemic.[19] Baudouin's historical method is shown in his first work, published when he was twenty, a study of Justinian's agricultural legislation (1542), and in his more famous contribution to legal humanism, the *Justinian* of 1546; more formally, it appears in the prolegomenon to his commentary on the *Institutes* (1545), which amounted to a brief history of Roman law down to the XVIth century.[20] By this time Baudouin was already beginning to be torn between law and theology—or rather, began to attempt to combine the two. During his years at Bourges (1548–1555) he remained a nominal, if hardly a model, discipline of Calvin; in 1556 he rejected "calvinolatry" and became, at least in his "father's" eyes, a quasi-Lutheran turncoat; finally in 1563 he returned to orthodoxy.[21] But in spite of this apparent religious "versatility," Baudouin was following his own line all along; the trouble was that nobody else could follow it. In fact he never abandoned his Erasmian program for religious reconciliation (based on Melanchthon's theology) and a return to *prisca pietas*. In pursuit of this irenic ideal Baudouin—who belongs to the patristic rather than the Biblical school of irenists—made good use of his historical point of view.[22] His intellectual development followed very closely the classic pattern of Newman, a gradual surrender to Romanism as a result of studies in early Christian history. He associated history, in short, with *catholica traditio*.[23] His apostasy (as

---

[18] The best biography is still Julius Heveling, *De Francisco Balduino jurisconsult* (Arras, 1871), to which A. Wicquot, *François Balduin d'Arras* (Arras, 1890), adds little. Better but more specialized is J. Duquesne, "François Bauduin et la réforme," *Bulletin de l'Académie delphinal*, 5e sér., IX (1917), 55–108. See also J. Brodeau, *La Vie de Maistre Charles Du Molin* (Paris, 1654), 32.

[19] Baudouin was banned from Arras for heresy in 1545; his correspondence with Calvin, published in the *Corpus Reformatorum*, lasted from 1546 to 1556.

[20] Baudouin's legal works are collected in J. G. Heineccius, *Jurisprudentia romana et antiqua*, I (Leiden, 1737).

[21] "Charte relative à François Baudouin 1563," ed. R. Dareste, *Bulletin de la Société de l'histoire du protestantisme français*, I (1863), 147.

[22] See Pontien Polman, *L'Elément historique dans la controverse religieuse du XVIe siècle* (Gembloux, 1932), 367 sqq., and P. Fraenkel, *Testimonia Patrum* (Geneva, 1961).

Calvin viewed it) began with his part in the controversy over the state of the early church in 1556; even his *Constantine the Great* of that year was concerned with the Emperor's moderate ecclesiastical policy, which Baudouin considered exemplary.[24] The result was that Baudouin was forced to leave Bourges, then even Strassburg, and so he ended up in 1557 at the University of Heidelberg, where, through his friendship with Melanchthon and his correspondence with the Magdeburg Centuriators, he came into contact with German historical scholarship. Even after the irenic issue was dead (with the failure of the Colloquy of Poissy in the fall of 1561) and after his notorious controversy with Calvin in the following year, Baudouin's historical interests in the question did not cease. In succeeding years, inspired by the obvious parallel with the Huguenots, he published editions of Optatus' *Donatist Schism* and documents of the subsequent "Carthaginian collation." [25] By then Baudouin had returned not only to orthodoxy but to royal favor, and his last historical labors, including an unpublished Angevin history, were written on behalf of Henry of Anjou.[26] He died in 1573, a year after the massacre of Saint Bartholomew demolished what was left of his irenic dream.

Now let us return to Baudouin's *Institution of Universal History*. Based on lectures delivered at Heidelberg in 1561, Baudouin's masterpiece was published in the summer of that year and dedicated to the newly appointed Chancellor Michel de l'Hôpital. The book shows more than an attachment to encyclopedic humanism, whose purpose was to restore the integrity of classical and Christian culture; it reflects also Baudouin's involvement in the irenic movement, whose purpose was to repair the crumbling foundations of the *respublica*

[23] George Cassander, *De Officio pii viri*, in *Opera omnia* (Paris, 1616), 782. This work of Cassander, Baudouin's friend and the real leader of the irenic movement, was mistakenly attributed to Baudouin by Calvin and started a violent quarrel in 1562. In his *Responsio altera ad Joan. Calvinum* (Paris, 1562), 111–14, Baudouin also cited the views of Melanchthon against Calvin's "inhuman decrees."

[24] Baudouin's *Responsio Christianorum jurisconsultorum* of 1556 included an attack on François Le Douaren's *De Sacris ecclesiae ministeriis* (Paris, 1551); see the article "Duaren" in Bayle's *Dictionnaire*. Even after his death Baudouin's apostasy was still being attacked, and so Beza, for example, criticized La Popelinière for his praise of Baudouin's learning: Letter of 29 March 1581, in Bibliothèque Nationale, Manuscrits, Fonds Dupuy, DCCXLIV, 237 r.

[25] *Historia Carthaginiensis collationis* (Paris, 1566) and *Delibatio Africanae historiae ecclesiasticae sive de Optate Milevitani libri VII ad Parmeniam de schismate Donatistarum* (Paris, 1563).

[26] Apparently only the fourth part of Baudouin's Angevin history has survived, a historiographical critique of earlier writers on the subject, including Paolo Emilio and Panvinio: "Proposition d'erreurs sur les memoires d'Anjou," Bibliothèque Nationale, Manuscrits, Fonds français, vol. 5409, 5 r–40 v.

christiana. The basis of this movement was an Erasmian plan to reconcile Catholics and Huguenots in France and incidentally to forestall the recalling of the Council of Trent. Baudouin's contribution was to offer himself as intermediary between certain interested German princes, especially the Elector-Palatine Frederick the Pious, and the *moderatores* in France, including L'Hôpital and the Cardinal of Lorraine, and to publicize their cause.[27] The "collation of opinions" mentioned in Baudouin's book was to be achieved after the example of primitive Christianity, especially the moderate policy of Constantine and the conciliatory ideas of St. Augustine, towards the Donatists anyway. The theme of the "integrity" of history reflected Baudouin's commitment to the integrity of Christendom. It was such ideological concerns that led Baudouin to emphasize the importance and the inseparability of legal and ecclesiastical studies and to condemn the idea of schism on any level, institutional or intellectual. Such a syncretic spirit—such, we may almost say, a compulsive monism—appears on several levels in the *Institution of Universal History*. Underlying his demand for a "universal," not a particular or narrowly national point of view, was a nostalgic feeling for a united Christianity; underlying his distaste for chauvinists, including humanist *philopatrides*, was a desire for religious brotherhood and tolerance; and underlying his conception of the indivisibility of history was an idea of European culture, continuous in its traditions, unified in its institutions and ideals. It is in the light of Baudouin's irenic utopia that his idea of "integral history" must be examined.

In spite of endless philosophic distinctions and justifications, the concept of history had not, by the XVIth century, lived down—or even outgrown—its commonplace origin. The "sister" of history may have been political science, but its "mother" was "the oratorical art."[28] History's pedigree, in short, was not philosophical but rhetorical, and so historical thought was quite literally "commonplace." The historian and the orator each had, for example, to present his discourse *probabiliter, dilucide,* and *breviter;* each had to cultivate a "continuous" style, *ratione oratoris* as Baudouin put it; each placed particular emphasis on the faculty of *memoria.*[29] It is only natural, then, that

[27] See H. O. Evennett, *The Cardinal of Lorraine and the Council of Trent* (Cambridge, 1930), 235 sqq.

[28] Isaac Casaubon, *Polybii . . . Historiarum libri* (Paris, 1609), 6 v., and Valla, preface to *Historiarum Ferdinandi.*

[29] Most of these formulas are derived from Cicero's *De Oratore,* I and II; on their later use see M. Schulz, *Die Lehre von der historischen Methode bei den Geschichtschreibern des Mittelalters* (Berlin, 1909), ch. 4.

the normal definition of history should have been the series of topoi taken from Cicero's *Orator*. According to this famous passage history was "the witness of time, the light of truth, the life of memory, the mistress of life, and the messenger of antiquity." [30] If any of the *artes* fail to mention this text, the reason is forbearance and not neglect: for humanists in general it had become a sort of semantic reflex. Not that these phrases had been exhausted of all meaning; on the contrary, each concealed a host of interesting implications, often a full-fledged topic of debate. And since literary topoi, which were defined classically as *sedes argumentorum*, were more vital to the thinking of humanists than the old Aristotelian categories, an analysis of these "places" should provide an ideal introduction to Renaissance historical thought in general, and to that of François Baudouin in particular.

To its mission as "the messenger of antiquity" history owed some of its most impressive credentials. For Baudouin, as for Budé, this slogan involved the whole "encyclopedia" of classical culture, though with perhaps more emphasis on the doctrine than on the eloquence of the ancients—the *res non verba* topos becoming an axiom of historical writing.[31] Being a legal scholar, however, Baudouin concentrated his energies on the monuments of Roman law, which in his opinion constituted the most valuable of all historical sources. "What is all history," Petrarch had asked, "but the praise of Rome?" [32] And Baudouin extended this query: "To explain the history of the Empire and the Republic, what are more appropriate than the laws of Justinian?" [33] The restoration of these "images of antiquity," as Budé called them, was clearly not a job for lawyers or for those *doctores scholastici*, notoriously ignorant of history and literature; [34] it was an encyclopedic task suitable only for a trained philologist, since "it was by means of literature and its sources that Roman law began to be revived and, out of the shadows of earlier times cast by barbarism, to recover some of its pristine splendor." [35] Baudouin, however, transcending the narrowness of conventional Romanism, insisted on the importance also of feudal law and of archival sources, especially the

[30] *De Oratore*, II, ix, 36; cited by Baudouin, *De Institutione*, 609; La Popelinière, *Idée de l'histoire accomplie* (Paris, 1599), 22; Gaillard, *Methode*, ch. 2–4, consists of an extensive gloss on this passage.

[31] *De Institutione*, 621; cf. Vergil, *De Rerum inventoribus*, 49.

[32] Cited by T. E. Mommsen, *Medieval and Renaissance Studies*, ed. E. Rice (Ithaca, 1959), 122.   [33] *De Institutione*, 682.

[34] Budé, *Annotationes . . . in XXIIII pandectarum libros* (Lyon, 1546), 19, 21; Petrarch, *Epistolae de rebus familiaribus*, ed. Fracassetti (Florence, 1863), III, 18.

records of the church. He deplored the policy of secrecy adopted by the curia, and he contrasted this with the candor of the ancient church, whose "actuaries . . . by public authority diligently and faithfully kept its monuments uncorrupted in the archives, yet which were open to all." [36] National pride led him to suggest "that the noblest and fullest material of this sort would be the . . . records of the kingdom of France and the court of the parlement of Paris," although these too, as La Popelinière complained, were closed to the public.[37] Since "the later and more recent account of ancient things is usually the least reliable," [38] both lawyers and historians regarded as the best arguments those derived from antiquity, "the authority of which even the boldest adversaries respect." [39] Indeed, in this veneration for age, humanists, reformers, canonists, and civilians could all agree. "For out of the monuments of antiquity," as Baudouin said, "the integral memory of things may be recaptured." [40]

Distance lends enchantment and age brings honor, and it was the task of history to preserve both of these qualities by acting as "the life of memory." In many ways memory, "the treasury of the understanding," the most fundamental requirement of the historian (as well as of the orator and the lawyer), was identified with history, which itself, according to another Ciceronian phrase recalled by Baudouin, was *memoria rerum gestarum*.[41] It was partly through memory, moreover, that law and history made their "conjunction" in the XVIth century. Both, for example, were to be read in the same sequence, "from the earlier to the later, so that by a proper arrangement the latter issue from the former." [42] Both too, as parallel forms of public memory, followed a similar pattern of development: just as history passed from fable and folklore to written history so law passed from unwritten *consuetudo* to *ius scriptum*.[43] For written records belong to a more reflective, if a more litigious age. As everyone realized, "to

---

[35] "Praefata de jure civile" (the "Prolegomenon" of 1545), in Heineccius, *op. cit.*, 13–14. [36] *De Institutione*, 653.

[37] La Popelinière, *Idée de l'histoire*, 256. On La Popelinière, see G. W. Sypher, "La Popelinière's *Histoire de France*," this *Journal*, XXIV (1963), 41–54.

[38] *De Institutione*, 653. [39] *Historia Carthaginiensis collationis*, "Lectori."

[40] *Justinianus sive de jure novo* (Halle, 1728), "Lectori."

[41] *De Institutione*, 615; cf. Amyot's preface to his Diodorus Siculus, in B. Weinberg, *Critical Prefaces of the French Renaissance* (Evanston, 1950), 165: "Just as memory is the treasury of man's understanding . . . so it can be said that history is truly the treasury of human life. . . ."

[42] *De Institutione*, 713.

[43] They pass from the level *de facto* to that *de jure*: Ad Leges de jure civile, in Heineccius, *op. cit.*, 174.

be ignorant of history is forever to be a child," [44] and it was the destiny of humanists to reconstruct those most neglected ages of cultural infancy, as Baudouin claimed to be doing, for instance, in his *Chronicle of Artois.*[45] He had no patience with those classicizing snobs—those "fonder of antiquity than of reason," said La Popelinière [46]—who avoided medieval studies. "If we are French, English, German, Spanish, or Italian," he argued, "we must not, in speaking of ourselves, be ignorant of the history of the Franks, Angles, Saxons, Goths, Lombards. . . ." [47] In particular this meant investigating feudal law and the work of barbarian poets, who like Homer should be regarded not only as makers of myth but as keepers of tradition. History had no doubt to be "purged of fable." [48] but this required a critical not a pyrrhonistic attitude. It was, in short, through a "cooperation of archeology and mythology" that the historian could revive the life of memory.[49]

The chief beneficiary of this laboriously acquired legacy was, of course, Posterity, which was not only a kind of hypostasized final judge but a pupil for whom, in the words of the French humanist Louis Le Roy, "it is necessary to do . . . what antiquity has done for us." [50] One function of historians had always been to preserve fame, "the names of good men and the renown of distinguished actions," [51] in order, according to Polydore Vergil, "partly that no one should be unjustly praised, partly that those who wish to follow examples should know whom to imitate." [52] For humanists didactic motives began to supersede commemorative duties, and so the notion of history as "the mistress of life" became perhaps the most popular of all the Ciceronian themes. "The memory and knowledge of the past," said Le Roy, "is the instruction for the present and a warning for the future." [53] It was another commonplace that the guiding principle of history, as distinguished from poetry, was profit and not pleasure

[44] Chasseneuz, *Catalogus gloriae mundi*, 395; cf. Melanchthon's version, cited by H. Brettschneider, *Melanchthon als Historiker* (Insterburg, 1880), 20, that "human life without the knowledge of history is nothing but perpetual childhood, perpetual obscurity or blindness"; cf. Baudouin, *De Institutione*, 624.

[45] *Chronique d'Arthois* (Arras, 1856), 2-3. This work was an outgrowth of his study of the Artesian *coutume.*

[46] *Idée de l'histoire*, 1.   [47] *De Institutione*, 623.

[48] *Constantinus magnus*, in Heineccius, *op. cit.*, 569.   [49] *De Institutione*, 626.

[50] *De la Vicissitude ou variété des choses en l'univers* (Paris, 1584), 255 r. On Le Roy, see W. Gundersheimer, "Louis Le Roy's Humanistic Optimism," this *Journal*, XXIII (1962), 324-339.

[51] La Popelinière, *L'Histoire des histoires* (Paris, 1599), 26.

[52] *De Rerum inventoribus*, "Praefatio."   [53] *Vicissitude*, 247 r.

(*utilitas non voluptas*).[54] Baudouin's originality consisted in being more concerned with the public than with the private utility of history. His whole irenic program rested, as we have seen, on a historical foundation; and as for legal value, he found it hard to decide "whether history received more illumination from the books of law or law from the monuments of history." [55] Above all Baudouin saw in history the key to political philosophy, a means of discovering a causal pattern, "the successions and concatenations of actions." [56] This concern was reinforced by humanist historiography, whose "continuous style" stemmed as much from a desire to relate cause and effect as from a regard for the rules of rhetorical argument.[57] For Baudouin the model for this philosophic or "pragmatic history" was Polybius. "The ancients called that history 'pragmatic,' " said Baudouin, "which narrates, explains and usefully accounts not only for the events but their causes and which describes the actions as well as the policies." [58] And as La Popelinière wrote, "Not to be aware of the causes, progress, and good or bad results is unpardonable ignorance." [59]

Of all the Ciceronian motifs the most disputed was probably "the light of truth." One reason for this was the humanist scorn for the credulity of medieval chroniclers and for the triviality of theologians; another was the need to answer charges by skeptics like Henry Cornelius Agrippa that humanist historians, such as Vergil and Paolo Emilio, were mere hired flatterers.[60] Consequently, humanists made much of Cicero's *leges historiae,* which insisted on the priority of truth.[61] The endorsement of this rule had important formal, if not practical, consequences, namely, the promotion of history's independence in terms both of literary form and of subject matter. When Baudouin called for "true history not fabulous rhetoric or scholastic declamation" and when he demanded that history be "purged of fable," he implied several things. First, he was denying that history

---

[54] *De Institutione,* 620.   [55] *Ibid.,* 668–69.   [56] *Ibid.,* 617.

[57] Poliziano, for example, had distinguished between annals and history on the grounds that the latter dealt with causes and so required a continuous style, "stylus fusus et continuus non periodicus": *Opera omnia* (Basel, 1553), 471.

[58] *De Institutione,* 618.   [59] *Histoire des histoires,* 416.

[60] *De Incertitudine et vanitate scientiarum declamatio invectus* ([Cologne], 1537), ch. 5. Cf. Charles de la Ruelle, *Succincts adversaires . . . contre l'histoire* (Poitiers, 1574).

[61] *De Institutione,* 640, citing Cicero, *De Oratore,* II, xi, 62: "For who does not know history's first law to be that an author must not dare to tell anything but the truth? And its second that he must make bold to tell the whole truth?" Cf. *De Legibus,* I, i, 5.

[62] *De Institutione,* 636.

was bound to any of the liberal arts, for, especially with regard to
Roman law, "history was more necessary than either dialectic or rhetoric." [63] Second, he was recommending a return to historical concreteness, on the basis of the Aristotelian distinction between particular
and general truth, since history meant above all the observation of
particular events.[64] Third, he was requiring that history be kept separate from poetry, whose practitioners, he recalled, Plato had expelled
from his republic; admittedly, the *carmines* contained a measure of
historical truth, but it was the historian's job to isolate it, as Ronsard acknowledged in his *Franciade*.[65] Finally, Baudouin was de-
manding an end to the classical practice of inventing speeches, for
history was not dramatic, it was pragmatic. "The testimony of the
ancients," he said, "should be read without any interpolation, nor
should any new orations be added nor any of my own words be substituted for theirs . . . lest I seem not so much to adorn history as to
make it faulty and mendacious." [66] "The surest procedure for a historian," remarked La Popelinière, who also despised harangues, "is to
leave the praise and blame of men to the testimony of their actions,
which he must describe faithfully." [67] Here is how Baudouin summarized his position:

Quintilian understood more clearly [than Plato] that there are three types
of narrative. The first is false and is called *fabula*, such as poetry, which is
remote not only from truth but from plausibility. The second is verisimilar,
which however is fictitious and is called *argumentum*, customarily employed
in comic drama. The third is true and should be called *historia*.[68]

So again it could be argued that history had its own literary pedigree,
that it might be considered an independent discipline.

If history had shed light on the past, it had also born the marks
of age; if it was "the light of truth," it was also "the witness of
time." The theme of devouring time was of course the commonest of
commonplace. Regarding a mangled copy of Quintilian, Petrarch
had observed, "I recognize therein the hand of time—the destroyer
of all things," [69] while the mutilated state of the *Digest* inspired Budé
with a desire to restore the text through the resources of philology.[70]

---

[63] *Ad Leges de jure civile*, in Heineccius, *op cit.*, 174.

[64] Isidore, *Etymologiarum*, 122, giving this standard view.

[65] *De Institutione*, 627; Ronsard's preface in Weinberg, *Critical Prefaces*, 219–
20. On this subject see B. Hathaway, *The Age of Criticism* (Ithaca, 1962).

[66] *De Institutione*, 638.   [67] *Idée de l'histoire*, 324.

[68] *De Institutione*, 627; Isidore, *Etymologiarum*, 124, cites the same distinction
without mentioning Quintilian; the passage is his *De Oratore*, II, iv, 2.

[69] *Petrarch's Letters to Classical Authors*, trans. M. Cosenza (Chicago, 1910),
84.   [70] *Annotationes*, 40.

Much the same feeling came over Baudouin when he saw the *lacera membra* of civil law, the Justinianean corpus, which in the anti-Tribonian tradition he disparagingly called "new law." "I can never read without great sadness the old jurists," he lamented, "so miserably assessed by Tribonian and so mutilated that today we see merely a copy. . . . But so much the more do I want to assemble these scattered pieces and to preserve the holy relics from which we may learn how great and majestic was the splendor of ancient jurisprudence." [71] With great enthusiasm, therefore, Baudouin joined in the humanist hunt for interpolations in order to make amends for "Tribonian's crime." [72] "Our job," said Baudouin, "is to know what is whole and what is fragmentary, what is old and what new and added. Often what in a particular title is attributed to Ulpian . . . belongs not to Ulpian but to Justinian or to Tribonian." [73] Like Cujas, Baudouin contributed substantially to the restoration of classical Roman law, as in his work on Scaevola, and later carried this concern for original sources over into history.[74] Like Cujas too, he had a particular fondness for the infantile science of chronology. For this there were both legal reasons—"since later law abrogates or derogates from earlier law, it is obviously necessary to observe the sequence of laws and for that purpose to use *fasti, annales, diaria. . . .*" [75]—and historical reasons, that is, to avoid the "ridiculous errors" due to an ignorance of chronology.[76] Thus, through the philological techniques of the *mos gallicus*, Roman law was to be replaced in its proper perspective. Through an analogous but wider-ranging kind of criticism, the *integra narratio* of history itself was to be established.

There was one significant difference between Baudouin's conception of history and Cicero's. While Baudouin continued to employ the topoi of Greek and Roman rhetoric, he did not view historical writing

[71] *Scaevola*, in Heineccius, *op. cit.*, 437–38.

[72] "Oratio de instituenda in repub. juventute ad senatum populumque tolosatem" (1559), in Bodin, *op. cit.*, 9.

[73] *Justinianus*, 3. See the excellent work of L. Palazzini-Finetti, *Storia della ricerca della interpolazioni nel corpus juris giustinianeo* (Milan, 1953), 178 sqq.

[74] Especially his edition of Optatus in which he claimed to have made 600 emendations: "Praefationes Fr. Balduini ad primam editionem Optati," Migne, *Patrologiae*, XI, 1105. In this Baudouin made use of a manuscript of Jean du Tillet, as did Cujas in some of his early works. Baudouin's own legal scholarship has still not lost all of its usefulness, according to G. La Pointe, *Quintus Mucius Scaevola* (Paris, 1926), 4.

[75] *Justinianus*, 4. See P. Mesnard, "'La Place de Cujus dans la querelle de l'humanisme juridique," *Revue historique de droit français et étranger*, 4ᵉ sér., XXVIII (1950), 521–37.

[76] *De Institutione*, 663, giving some amusing examples of anachronisms.

as a static literary genre but rather as a developing attitude toward the past; he viewed history itself, in other words, from a historical point of view. This "temporalizing" of history was most perfectly realized in La Popelinière's *History of Histories,* but long before this there was at least a primitive awareness of historiographical progress, arising from the humanist attitude toward culture in general. Bartolommeo della Fonte, for example, in his "Oration in praise of History" (1485), included a historical sketch of historical writing from the Greeks down to his own times, as, a generation later, did Juan Vives.[77] So, more systematically than either, did Baudouin. In a general fashion he saw a succession from Judaic and prophetic to Christian, apostolic and ecclesiastical history—or, alternatively, from *historia ethnica* to *historica ecclesiastica.*[78] This, of course, was mainly an adaptation of the Augustinian idea of spiritual progress, although for Baudouin it represented not so much a movement toward the heavenly city as an approach to historical certainty. More technically, Baudouin saw the development of historical writing in terms of a progression of literary genres: first from "mythistory," or epic poetry, to prose; then, within the sphere of history proper, from simple chronicles to narrative history. In particular he pointed out a progression from the chroniclers, those "somewhat unpolished writers . . . without pretense of formal learning but faithful to the testimony of truth," to those "learned and lettered men who adorn what the former describe"—such as Flavio Biondo, Polydore Vergil, and Paolo Emilio.[79]

This scheme very much resembles La Popelinière's account of the progress of historiography from the epic to the antiquarian stage. For Baudouin it was through the *carmines* that all barbarians "first preserved the memory of their public actions"; for La Popelinière likewise, "it is evident that the poets are the first historians." [80] Making use of the age-old distinction between chronicles (and/or annals)

---

[77] Charles Trinkaus, *op. cit.,* 99, and Vives, *op. cit.,* 393 sqq. ("Quis ordo in historiae studio servandus . . ."). The works cited of Isidore, Chasseneuz, and Vergil all have chapters on the first historiographers, each beginning with Moses, whom Baudouin also recognized as the first historian (*De Institutio,* 649); and even Cicero (*De Oratore,* II, xii) discussed previous Greek and Roman historical writing.

[78] *De Institutione,* 671; cf. Melanchthon's preface to the *Chronicon Carionis* (Wittemberg, 1880), and Chytraeus, *De Lectione historiarum,* Wolf, II, 998. See also A. Klempt, *op. cit.,* 22 sqq.

[79] *De Institutione,* 662.

[80] Baudouin, *De Institutione,* 648; La Popelinière, *Histoire des histoires,* 137; cf. Quintilian, *De Oratore,* X, i, 31.

and history, La Popelinière divided the growth of history into four
"seasons." First a period of "natural history," or oral tradition; second a period of fabulous history when truth was not yet a necessary
ingredient; third a period of annals, which were simply lists of un-
connected events; fourth a period of "continuous history," in which,
ideally at least, eloquence and philosophy were joined to the chronological narration of facts.[81] So history like law in the XVIth century
underwent a process of "historicization." Neither Baudouin nor La
Popelinière, however, believed that this improvement of history was
complete, and each set down in some detail his own idea of "perfect history."[82]

The central themes of Baudouin's historical thought, indeed of
his whole life, converged in the idea of integrity, whether expressed as
unity, universality, or continuity. By "perfect," "integral," "universal," or "perpetual" history, Baudouin did not mean an aggregation
of national histories fitted into an Augustinian world-plan; he meant
the synthesized—and synchronized—view of history which could only
be achieved by a philosophic scholar trained in the techniques of encyclopedic humanism. And this historical unity was more than pedagogical, it was virtually biological since history was, according to
another Polybian metaphor, "a body composed of many inter-related
parts."[83] No doubt this coherence was to be attributed ultimately to
God's great lesson plan, but its concrete, human manifestation had
little to do either with teleology or with theology. The unity of
Baudouin's history bore a remarkable resemblance to the unity of
Aristotelian drama; each was three-fold according to time, place, and
action. "History is universal," said Baudouin, "in terms of the times,
the places, and actions."[84] The major difference was that, in this
great "amphitheater" of the world, man was both an actor and a spec-
tator. More than that he was a judge; for, far from being an epistemological liability, his two-fold function as performer and observer
gave him the most comprehensive view of this human drama.[85] The
various aspects of history's unity are perhaps best summed up in

[81] *Histoire des histoires*, 68, 33, 45, 158, 416.

[82] Baudouin speaks of "historia perfecta" (*De Institutione*, 604), Bodin of "historia consummata" (*Methodus*, 254), La Popelinière of "histoire accomplie." Not,
of course, that these ideals are to be identified: La Popelinière accepts many of
Bodin's ideas, though not without reservations, and is sharply critical of Baudouin's
"long and excessive discourses, . . . the commonplace and unprofitable rhapsodies"
(*Idée de l'histoire*, 31).   [83] *De Institutione*, 614; cf. Polybius I, 3, 4.

[84] *Ibid.*, 613.   [85] *Ibid.*, 599, 742.

Baudouin's often repeated term *historia integra*.[86] Our survey of Baudouin's historical ideas will be complete when we understand the manifold meanings of the *integritas* of history.

It was on chronology above all else that the *individuitas*, the indivisibility, of history depended. Repeating another well worn Ciceronian formula, Baudouin asserted the necessity of arranging history *ordine temporum*.[87] This meant, first of all, that history, because of its quasi-biological unity and according to the old Eusebian tradition, had to be understood *ab ovo*. Since it concerned the whole human race, it had to be written *ab orbe* not merely *ab urbe condita*.[88] Nor, in view of the historical value of poetry and the extraordinary continuity of ancient and medieval historiography, was it beyond the bounds of possibility to construct an "integral narrative" of universal history. But there were philosophic as well as literary reasons for arranging history in chronological rather than in "natural," that is, topical, order. One, as we have seen, was to permit the demonstration of cause and effect. Another and more subtle reason was to permit the analysis and even the measurement of historical change. "According to the times," and or "according to the diversity of the times," expressed not only a concern for chronology and perhaps a sense of decadence, but also—especially for the grammarians, who had developed an intense sensitivity to style—an awareness of anachronism. In the opinion of Etienne Pasquier, who was among Baudouin's very first auditors, all writers had to be understood "selon la portée de leurs siècles"; and regarding the civil law in particular he remarked that "it would be impossible to say how many visages the laws of Rome have taken according to the diversity of the times." [89] Justice itself, said Baudouin's patron L'Hôpital, varied "according to the places, the countries, the times, the individuals, the events. . . ." [90] Through philology, however, this sense of mutability could be transformed into a kind of historical relativism; historical change could practically be calibrated *ratione temporum*. In fact, the method of the legal humanists was based on the identification of historical

[86] *Ibid.*, 604 *et passim; Delibatio Africanae historiae*, b i v. Alciato, *Lettere*, 326, also used this term.

[87] *De Institutione*, 684; Vergil, *De Rerum inventoribus*, 49; cf. Cicero, *De Oratore*, II, xv, 63. On "ordo temporum" and "ordo naturalis," see Schulz, *Die Lehre von der historischen Methode*, 98 sqq.   [88] *De Institutione*, 617.

[89] Pasquier, *Les Lettres* (Paris, 1619), I, 83 (to Cujas, c. 1560), and *Interpretation des Institutes de Justinian*, ed., Pasquier (Paris, 1847), I, 481.

[90] *Traité de la réformation de la justice*, ed. P. Duféy (Paris, 1825), I, 60.

"styles"—the *genus scribendi* of different periods.[91] And as Pasquier's work shows, the transition from the notion of literary style to a more general cultural style, as illustrated for example by architecture,[92] was quite natural. In this way a rhetorical commonplace gained the status of a fundamental historical technique: Petrarch's "pursuit of the historical Rome" passed from the level of sentiment to that of science.

History was universal in geographic as well as in temporal terms and was not limited to *nostra Europa*. "Diodorus Siculus . . .," said Baudouin, "attacked the ancient historians who wrote the history only of a single nation because they were writing not history but only a certain disconnected piece of history." [93] The history of Polybius, on the other hand, was "catholic," or "oecumenical," because it was imperial, *Romanitas* being practically synonymous with civilization, while more significantly, the history of Eusebius, who "ransacked whole libraries," was "catholic" because it concerned all of creation.[94] For history was, in Melanchthon's phrase, *pictura generis humani*.[95] In modern times, moreover, this meant including "those distant parts of the earth which were once hidden and are now known." [96] (So history benefited from one of the arguments demonstrating the superiority of the "moderns" to the "ancients.") [97] This meant also an alliance between history and geography, that is, understanding events not only *ratione temporum* but *ratione regionum*, supplementing historical with geographical relativism. Baudouin realized that "sprinkling a little geography on history is far from making geography an auxiliary of perpetual history": [98] what he wanted was a scientific union of the two fields such as Strabo had tried to establish, or, according to Le Roy's conception of political science, the formulation of "the variety of things in terms of the diversity of places." [99] Of course Baudouin did not follow this geohistorical plan with the ingenuity and rashness of Le Roy or of Bodin, but at least he showed himself aware of those "new horizons" of the Renaissance—and of the old astrological formulas of antiquity—which helped to discredit

[91] See E. Albertario, "I Tribonianismi avvertiti dal Cujacio," *Zeitschrift der Savigny-Stiftung für Rechtsgeschichte*, Röm. Abt., XLIV (1910), 158–75.

[92] *Lettres*, I, 445.　　　　　　　　　　　　[93] *De Institutione*, 614.

[94] *Ibid.*, 608, 614; cf. *Scaevola*, 437–38.

[95] Cited by Brettschneider, *op. cit.*, 20.　　　　[96] *De Institutione*, 615.

[97] La Popelinière, *Idée de l'histoire*, 13–14; Le Roy, *Vicissitude*, 215 sqq.

[98] *De Institutione*, 665.

[99] *De l'Origine . . . de l'art politique* (Paris, 1567), 5 v.

the parochialism of medieval historiography.[100]

Baudouin's encyclopedic interests tended to open up new horizons in still another sense—or was it it rather that he was returning to the more traditional orientation of the medieval world-chronicles? In any case, as early as 1546 he was urging that history ought to encompass ecclesiastical as well as political and military matters.[101] Like Melanchthon and the Magdeburg Centuriators, Baudouin had a pragmatic, that is, a polemical interest in church history. Not that he considered his Erasmian program and his involvement in ecclesiastical matters obstacles to scholarship; they marked his conversion to a *vita activa*. But on any level, to be universal, history had to be divine as well as human. "We are only making progress," Baudouin wrote, "if we pursue sacred as well as civil history, not confusedly but joined together." [102] In fact one of the reasons the Greeks had failed to achieve "integral history" was their neglect of this subject, whereas Christian writers, such as Optatus, who realized that the church was the soul of the body politic, fulfilled at least this part of Baudouin's program. "I say that if we are rightly and wisely to examine the history of the world," he concluded,

we should observe the condition and state of the church and of religion. For we should not forget the necessity of understanding that principle of human society, lest we neglect not only the head but the heart and soul of history. Thus when I speak of history I mean integral and perfect history. So the history of our pontiffs, emperors and kings should be joined as if practically one.[103]

This principle of the inseparability of church and state affairs reflects Baudouin's politics as well as his historical ideals: "integral Gallicanism," in a sense, reinforced "integral history."

The most promising partnership within the *universitas* of history was clearly that between history and law, which was the subject of the second part of Baudouin's book. "I have become aware," he said, "that law books are the product of history and that historical monuments evolve into the books of law." [104] The XVIth century had seen, in the work of Alciato and Paolo Giovio, the highest achievements in these two fields, but as yet the communication between them was imperfect. Ignorance of law marred the judgment, for example, of even

---

[100] G. Atkinson, *Les nouveaux Horizons de la renaissance française* (Paris, 1935), ix.

[101] *Justinianus*, "Lectori."   [102] *De Institutione*, 618.
[103] *Loc. cit.*

[104] *Ibid.*, 669. Cf. Gaillard, *Methode*, 550: "Jurisprudence has emerged from history, as is testified by those excellent jurists Caius and Pomponius, discussing its origin."

so erudite a historian as Flavio Biondo.[105] Consequently, Baudouin took it upon himself to unite these two disparate realms of fact and abstraction, to recall the formulas of law to the realities of history, to combine (in a sense) the *ars historica* with the *mos gallicus*. Historians had long made use of legal materials, of course, and some jurists were famed for their knowledge of history. But Baudouin, who has not without reason been called a predecessor of Mommsen,[106] had more ambitious plans. Not only did he want to enrich legal education through the study of history (this was an aim of all the legal humanists), he wanted historians to be trained in the law. The real subject matter of history, he thought, ought to be laws and institutions. The *casus foederis* of this alliance of law and history had several aspects. One, as we have seen, was the common relationship to rhetoric,[107] in which each field had taken refuge during the middle ages, law asserting its professional independence from the XIIth century, history, as we have suggested, from the XVIth century. Another point of contact was the common philosophic basis, both law and history being divided into natural, human, and divine categories. But the most important consequence of the overlapping of the two fields was the importation of legal habits, sources, and standards of proof into history. Lawyers and historians alike had a perhaps exaggerated respect for tradition and precedent and were afflicted with a fascination for the problem of "origins"; and not infrequently legal formulas, such as the *translatio imperii* or the notion of "authenticity," were adopted by historians. Like the lawyer, the historian was well advised to go back to the *primi auctores*. Like the lawyer too, the historian had to seek out reliable witnesses and to examine their "good faith." "I prefer those witnesses who describe what they have taken part in . . . , while those who give hearsay evidence are only indirect witnesses, but they are always rejected by the jurists." [108] In this way Baudouin transformed the commonplace judgment that (in Montaigne's words) "the only good histories are those written by men who themselves have conducted affairs . . ." [109] into a rule about what we should call "primary sources." "Certainly in the matter of validity and reliability of documents," Baudouin continued, "jurists are not satisfied with copies but require

---

[105] "Proposition d'erreurs," 34 r.

[106] F. von Bezold, *Aus Mittelalter und Renaissance* (Munich, 1918), 367.

[107] Beside the formulas of Cicero and Quintilian associating rhetoric and history, we may place the famous definition of Cassiodorus (*Divine and Human Readings*, 148): "The art of rhetoric . . . is expertness in discourse on civil questions."

[108] *De Institutione*, 635.

[109] *Les Essais*, ed. Strowski and Gebelin (Bordeaux, 1919), II, 116.

authentica, or originals." The alliance of law and history involved also
what the latest historian of legal humanism has called the "historicization of law"—analogous to the temporalization of history itself—
especially as outlined by Pomponius' sketch in the Digest title "De
Origine juris" and as exemplified by Baudouin's "Prolegomenon" of
1545.[110] From several points of view, then, "Historical studies were to
be placed on a solid foundation of law, and jurisprudence was to be
joined to history." [111]

The final and perhaps most striking point of resemblance between
law and history was their common philosophic goal. According to one
of the Digest's definitions often cited by Baudouin, law was the
knowledge (*notitia* or *scientia*) of things divine and human, that is to
say, wisdom (*sapientia*).[112] So, we may recall, was history. History
and law both had, in other words, not only universality but a kind of
philosophic unity based on the attempt to achieve a systematic understanding of society. The chief difference was that history had to take
into account the factor of time. Baudouin summarized his many-sided
conception of history in this way:

I have said that the course of universal history ought to be described, and
that its universality ought to be presented according to the times, places,
and events, the events being of three sorts, the state of religious, foreign
and domestic affairs, that is, of ecclesiastical, political and military history.[113]

As usual, this is not too far removed from La Popelinière's formulation of his own *histoire accomplie:*

A proper history will be a general narrative, eloquent and judicious, of the
most notable actions of men and other occurrences, represented according to
the times, places, their causes, progress, and results.[114]

La Popelinière would go beyond Baudouin, however, in his definition
of the *ratio rerum,* the actions of men, since he would include "the
origin, progress and transformation of the arts and sciences." [115] Here
we can see a tendency—illustrated by such diverse contemporary
works as Pasquier's *Researches of France* and Le Roy's *Vicissitude of
Things*—toward a broad conception of cultural history. If memory
was "the mother of muses," history became "the inventor and pre-

[110] See D. Maffei, *Gli Inizi dell'umanesimo giuridico* (Milan, 1956), 22.

[111] *De Institutione,* 668.

[112] *Ibid.,* 609, 668; *Delibatio Africanae historiae,* a ii v; *Scaevola,* in Heineccius,
op. cit., 437–38; and *Ad Edicta veterum principum Rom. de Christianis* (Basel,
n.d.), 6. See also E. Rice, *The Renaissance Idea of Wisdom* (Cambridge, Mass.,
1958).   [113] *De Institutione,* 626.   [114] *Histoire des histoires,* 36.

server of all the arts." [116] Not only jurisprudence, said Gaillard, but "all disciplines take their origin . . . from history as from an overflowing fountain." [117] Moreover, the humanist encyclopedia, in Budé's view, had the same kind of structure as Baudouin's universal history; for just as the *orbis doctrinae* that constituted philology was useless when it was not assembled into one functioning body,[118] so "catholic history," which was the source of that "true and integral knowledge of human and divine things offered by jurisprudence," formed "a body whose members may not be severed." [119] Thus the unity of knowledge, as established by humanism, reinforced the unity of human history, and potentially at least, integral history provided a new framework for "integral humanism."

"Human eyes perceive things," remarked Montaigne, "only through the forms of their understanding." [120] History is one form of understanding that was still being shaped in Montaigne's time—that owed its existence, in fact, to that same encyclopedic humanism which inspired Montaigne's own search for wisdom. For it was through the good offices of humanists like Baudouin and La Popelinière that history was given a logical—even a "methodological"—structure. This happened not only in the realm of theory, by laying down rules for institutional and cultural history, but also in practice, although primarily in specialized areas which would hardly touch the main stream of historiography for another two centuries. Finally, the encyclopedia of the humanists, from which their historical method had been drawn, became itself the material on which this historical "form of understanding" was imposed. So, after having long been considered a valuable but somewhat untidy store of human experience, history was transformed into a new principle for the organization of human knowledge, the point of departure for a new world view.

Queens College, New York City.

[115] *Idée de l'histoire*, 269. [116] *Methodus*, 112. [117] *Methode*, 552.
[118] *De Asse et partibus ejus* (Paris, 1528), CLXXXVIII r.
[119] *Scaevola*, in Heineccius, *op. cit.*, 437–438. In general, see A. Klempt, *op. cit.*, 69 sqq., "Das Program universalhistorischer Betrachtung der Bildungs- und Geistesgeschichte."
[120] *Les Essais*, II, 272.

XVI

MONTAIGNE AND THE RISE OF SKEPTICISM IN EARLY MODERN EUROPE: A REAPPRAISAL

BY ZACHARY S. SCHIFFMAN*

The rise of skepticism in Early Modern Europe has been attributed primarily to the revival of Greek Pyrrhonism, which fueled the fires of doubt ignited by the Reformation. An analysis of the evolution of Montaigne's thought will reveal a more fundamental cause, the failure of the humanist program of education. Humanist education united a normative view of the world with a skeptical mode of thinking, balancing one against the other. This balance was upset by a growing appreciation of the diversity and complexity of the world. Montaigne was one of the first thinkers to cultivate this appreciation, which consequently intensified the skeptical mode of thinking imparted by his education. Montaigne's skepticism in particular, and the rise of skepticism in general, owes much to the collapse of an intellectual system no longer suited to the world in which it flourished.

The traditional interpretation of the rise of skepticism was formulated by Richard Popkin in his *History of Scepticism from Erasmus to Spinoza*.[1] According to Popkin, the successful challenge to the doctrinal authority of the Church during the Reformation undermined the possibility of establishing with certainty any religious truth, Protestant or Catholic. Popkin argued that the problem of certainty in religious knowledge spread to all branches of knowledge with the revival of Greek skepticism in the sixteenth century, particularly through the works of Sextus Empiricus.

The Greek physician Sextus, who lived around 200 A.D., compiled the only extant account of Pyrrhonism, a branch of skepticism distinct from that of the New Academy. Whereas the latter school asserted that man could not attain truth or certainty, the former doubted even this assertion. By contradicting all assertions, the Pyrrhonists fostered a suspension of judgment which ultimately induced a state of philosophical tranquillity. Until 1562, when Henri Estienne published a Latin translation of the *Outlines of Pyrrhonism*, Sextus had attracted little attention.

* I am grateful to Profs. Kathleen Mullen and Richard Maxwell, of Valparaiso University, who read drafts of this paper and offered valuable criticisms.

[1] Richard H. Popkin, *The History of Scepticism from Erasmus to Spinoza* (Berkeley, 1979). This work is a revised and expanded edition of *The History of Scepticism from Erasmus to Descartes* (Van Gorcum, 1960; rev. ed., Humanities Press, 1964; Harper Torchbook, 1968).

Virtually everyone identified skepticism solely with the Academy, whose doctrines were known primarily through Cicero's *Academica.*[2]

Montaigne popularized Sextus in the "Apology for Raymond Sebond," the central chapter of his *Essais.* According to Popkin, Montaigne experienced a *crise pyrrhonienne* after reading Sextus which led him to formulate a so-called "Catholic Pyrrhonism." This doctrine supposedly combated religious innovation by demonstrating human ignorance, thereby confirming Catholics in their accustomed faith and recalling reformers to the fold. Popkin also argued that Montaigne extended his skepticism beyond the Reformation debate to encompass all human knowledge, thus administering "the *coup de grâce* to an entire intellectual world."[3]

Popkin's interpretation of Montaigne's skepticism hinges on his contention that Montaigne experienced a personal *crise pyrrhonienne* upon reading Sextus.[4] I will show that the roots of Montaigne's skepticism lie not in his reading of Sextus but rather in the breakdown of the intellectual system inculcated by his education. The first chapter of the *Essais* reveals how the normative component of this intellectual system failed to counterbalance the skeptical component.[5]

The title of this chapter, "By diverse means we arrive at the same end," is a commonplace. In the Renaissance, commonplaces were known interchangeably as either *loci* or *loci communes;* but in antiquity, these two terms had different meanings. *Loci* were universal categories of argumentation by means of which all statements could be analyzed, mental "places" where one searched for knowledge. *Loci communes* were those words and ideas acceptable to all listeners, "commonplaces" embodying the traditional wisdom of society. By the early sixteenth century, though, the meanings of these two terms had become fused, signifying a system of commonplace thought in which all knowledge was classified in mental places embodying the traditional wisdom of society. Thus, Montaigne's commonplace title represents both a category or heading

---

[2] On the *Academica,* see Charles B. Schmitt, *Cicero Scepticus: A Study of the Influence of the Academica in the Renaissance* (The Hague, 1972).

[3] Popkin, *History of Scepticism,* 42-54.

[4] Popkin has taken into account Donald Frame's argument, in *Montaigne's Discovery of Man* (New York, 1955), that Montaigne's skepticism developed not as a sudden "crisis" caused by his reading of Sextus but as a gradual "revolt" against the principles of "Stoical humanism." Note that even in Frame's interpretation, Montaigne's reading of Sextus culminated in his so-called "skeptical revolt."

[5] Although this is the first chapter of the *Essais,* it is not first in chronological order of composition (this point will be explained later). It is significant that Montaigne chose to place this chapter first, for it highlights the central problem of the first edition of the *Essais,* the breakdown of commonplace thought. See Pierre Villey, *Les Sources et l'évolution des Essais de Montaigne,* 2 vols., 2nd rev. ed. (Paris, 1933) for the most likely order of composition of the *Essais.*

classifying the contents of the chapter and a maxim or proverb serving as a guide to conduct.[6]

In the first two sentences of the chapter, Montaigne stated the problem which, theoretically, would be explicated by the commonplace: popular opinion holds that the vanquished can save himself by submitting to the victor and begging for mercy; however, defiance in the face of defeat sometimes achieves the same end.[7] Citing diverse examples, Montaigne recounted how some victorious princes ruthlessly ignored pleas for mercy but responded favorably to displays of bold and courageous defiance. He concluded that pleas for mercy moved weak hearts—like those of women, children, and the *vulgaire*—whereas acts of bravery moved strong hearts. By this point in the chapter, Montaigne had fulfilled the promise of the commonplace title, for he had demonstrated that by diverse means we arrive at the same end. Whoever found himself at the mercy of an enemy could judge the quality of that man's heart and act accordingly.

But no sooner had he established this conclusion than he overturned it, citing the example of a vulgar Theban mob comprised of weak-hearted men who, disdaining Pelopidas's pleas for mercy, admired Epaminondas's defiant courage. This example heralded Montaigne's real conclusion: "Truly man is a marvelously vain, diverse, and undulating object. It is hard to found any constant and uniform judgment on him." Then he added, almost as an afterthought, that Pompey had once spared an entire city out of admiration for the courage of one man; whereas Sulla, after witnessing a similar display of virtue, had spared neither the individual nor the city. Montaigne had demonstrated ironically that by the same

---

[6] The following works have contributed most to my understanding of *loci, loci communes,* and commonplace thought: Quirinus Breen, "The Terms *loci communes* and *loci* in Melanchthon," in his *Christianity and Humanism,* 93-105 (Grand Rapids, Mich., 1968); August Buck, "Die studia humanitatis und ihre Methode," in his *Die humanistiche Tradition in der Romania,* 133-50 (Berlin, 1968); Wilbur S. Howell, *Logic and Rhetoric in England, 1500-1700* (Princeton, 1956); Lisa Jardine, *Francis Bacon: Discovery and the Art of Discourse* (London, 1974), Chap. 1; Paul Joachimsen, "Loci communes: eine Untersuchung zur Geistesgeschichte des Humanismus und der Reformation," *Luther-Jahrbuch* 8 (1926): 27-97; George Kennedy, *The Art of Persuasion in Greece* (Princeton: Princeton University Press, 1963), especially pp. 87-103; Sister Joan Marie Lechner, O.S.U., *Renaissance Concepts of the Commonplaces* (Westport, Conn., 1974); Alain Michel, *Rhétorique et philosophie chez Cicéron* (Paris, 1960), esp. pt. 2, Chap. 4; Walter J. Ong, "Commonplace Rapsody: Ravisius Textor, Zwinger, and Shakespeare," in *Classical Influences on European Culture, A.D. 1500-1700,* ed. R. R. Bolgar (Cambridge, U.K., 1976), 91-126.

[7] After the publication of the first edition in 1580, Montaigne continued to revise and expand the *Essais* until his death in 1592. My analysis of the first chapter is based on its original 1580 version. All references to the *Essais* are from *Oeuvres complètes de Montaigne,* eds. Albert Thibaudet and Maurice Rat, Bibliothèque de la Pléiade (Paris, 1962). Translations from the *Oeuvres complètes* are adapted from *The Complete Works of Montaigne,* trans. Donald M. Frame (Stanford, 1958). Quotations from the *Essais* will conform as closely as possible to their original state in the first edition.

means we can arrive at diverse ends, thus overturning the commonplace title.

In this chapter, Montaigne subverted commonplace thought by means of a specific mode of arguing. He confronted the popular opinion that submission ensured mercy with the opposite opinion: that defiance, too, ensured mercy. Likewise, he confuted the conclusion that only the strong-hearted admired courage by citing the example of a weak-hearted mob which also admired courage. And finally, he juxtaposed the example of the strong-hearted Pompey who favored a virtuous act with that of the strong-hearted Sulla who disregarded a similar act. In short, he argued *in utramque partem*, from both sides.

Aristotle had originated the technique of arguing *in utramque partem* in order to establish verisimilitude in matters where truth could not be ascertained, reasoning that the probability of a proposition increased in proportion to the improbability of its opposite. This technique was later adopted by the Academic skeptics, the most influential of whom was Cicero. Unlike Aristotle, Cicero denied that one could ever attain truth or certainty, thus limiting all human knowledge to probability or verisimilitude revealed by discoursing *in utramque partem*. This Ciceronian attitude, eclipsed during the Middle Ages, was subsequently revived in the Renaissance. Yet Montaigne used the discourse *in utramque partem* to demonstrate that one could not even establish verisimilitude in human affairs; for any given question, the diversity of human reality provided too many contradictory answers. In other words, Montaigne transformed the instrument of Academic skepticism into that of an even more radical skepticism.[8]

This transformation resulted from the gradual breakdown of commonplace thought. In school Montaigne had been trained to anchor the discourse *in utramque partem* with commonplace norms which enabled him to arbitrate between contrasting positions and derive the more reasonable solution. This mode of thinking began to fail him years after his formal schooling, when he undertook a philosophical quest of great personal importance. Frustration at his inability to find what he was seeking led him to begin writing the *Essais* in 1572. Even at this early date, a skeptical crisis is apparent in Montaigne's thought, as commonplaces began to lose their normative value, detaching the discourse *in utramque partem* from its anchor in "truth" and unleashing a more

[8] For Academic skepticism and the mode of arguing *in utramque partem*, I have relied primarily on Michel, *Cicéron*, 158-73; Lisa Jardine, "Lorenzo Valla and the Intellectual Origins of Humanist Dialectic," *Journal of the History of Philosophy*, 15 (1977), 149-53; Jerrold E. Seigel, *Rhetoric and Philosophy in the Renaissance* (Princeton, 1968), 16-18; Sextus Empiricus, *Outlines of Pyrrhonism*, trans. R. G. Bury, Loeb Classical Library (Cambridge, Mass., 1933), xxxii-xxxiii. Also of interest is Joel B. Altman, *The Tudor Play of Mind* (Berkeley, 1978), which traces the role of the argument *in utramque partem* in Elizabethan drama.

radical form of skepticism. The crisis intensified until 1576, when his reading of Sextus finally resolved it, enabling him to transcend the limitations of his education. The evolution of Montaigne's thought will reveal how the failure of the humanist program of education contributed to the rise of skepticism in Early Modern Europe.

Montaigne received his formal education at the College de Guyenne, which he entered in 1539 at the age of six.[9] Only five years earlier the noted humanist educator Andre Gouvéa had reorganized the school's curriculum. In typical humanist fashion, he dedicated the Collège to the task of teaching Latin: *Latino sermoni cognoscendo haec schola in primis destinata est.*[10] Latin was the medium of eloquence, and eloquence was the means of applying wisdom to human affairs. Indeed, true eloquence was wisdom.[11] Gouvéa intended to teach his students proper Latin by having them emulate the best classical authors, requiring that they not only imitate the style but also assimilate the spirit of the ancients.[12]

Early humanists had emulated ancient literature by constantly re-reading their few, cherished manuscripts. Petrarch, for example, reread his Cicero countless times and thus internalized the Ciceronian style and spirit. With the spread of printing, however, virtually the whole corpus of ancient literature became available in reliable, inexpensive editions. This larger body of literature came to be assimilated through the use of notebooks, known as commonplace books.[13]

Petrarch, among others, had anticipated the technique of note taking.

---

[9] Montaigne is presumed to have also studied law at the University of Toulouse, although this is a conjecture based on circumstantial evidence. In his *La Jeunesse de Montaigne* (Paris, 1972), Roger Trinquet has argued persuasively that Montaigne remained at the College de Guyenne for two years of advanced study after his graduation in 1546. Trinquet has also argued, less persuasively, that Montaigne then went to Paris to study Greek with Turnebus. For the educational program at the College de Guyenne, I have relied primarily on Elie Vinet, *Schola Aquitanica: programme des études du Collège de Guyenne au XVIe siècle*, ed. and trans. Louis Massebieau (Paris, 1886). Although Vinet wrote his booklet in 1583, he intended it as a record of the educational reforms instituted by Andre Gouvea around the time that Montaigne was a student at the Collège. For other accounts of the Collège and its educational program, see Ernest Gaullieur, *Histoire du Collège de Guyenne* (Paris, 1878); William H. Woodward, *Studies in Education during the Age of the Renaissance* (Cambridge, U.K. 1906; reprint ed., New York, 1965); Paul Porteau, *Montaigne et la vie pédagogique de son temps* (Paris, 1935); Trinquet, *Jeunesse de Montaigne, op. cit.*

[10] Vinet *Schola Aquitanica*, 6.

[11] Hanna H. Gray, "Renaissance Humanism: The Pursuit of Eloquence," in *Renaissance Essay*, eds. P.O. Kristeller and P.P. Wiener (New York, 1968), 200-01.

[12] Buck, "Studia humanitatis," 139-41; R.R. Bolgar, The *Classical Heritage and Its Beneficiaries* (Cambridge, U.K., 1954), 265.

[13] Buck, "Studia humanitatis," 141-49; Bolgar, *Classical Heritage*, 265-75; William H. Woodward, *Desiderius Erasmus Concerning the Aim and Method of Education* (New York, 1964), xv-xvi.

He recommended annotating and cross-referencing one's readings in order to provide a stock of words, idioms, and ideas for use in one's own compositions. Leonardo Bruni first suggested keeping these references in notebooks; and Guarino da Verona later proposed using two kinds of notebooks—the *methodice* (containing rhetorical forms and idioms) and the *historice* (containing general information). Because the latter could easily become disorganized, Rudolf Agricola recommended classifying its contents under headings *(loci)* paired with their opposites for easy recall—like virtue and vice, love and hate, life and death, and so on—in the manner of medieval sermon books. The *historice*, later known as a *liber locorum rerum*, was the largest and most important of the commonplace books.[14]

In *De copia*, Erasmus popularized Agricola's plan for a *liber locorum rerum*.[15] He described a notebook divided into pairs of *loci* representing virtues and vices, like piety and impiety, which were in turn divided into subheadings, like piety (or impiety) toward God, the fatherland, the family, and so on. By means of this arrangement, Erasmus encouraged students to view the world in moral terms. They were to extract content for their *loci* from even the most unlikely sources, such as mathematics, physics, and geometry:

[No] learning is so far removed from rhetoric that you may not enrich your classifications from it. . . . For example, a wise man, happy in his wealth, not dependent on anyone else, constant and unmoved in his own virtue whatever way the winds of fortune blow, is compared with a sphere everywhere similar to itself. . . .[16]

Thus, even the physical world reflected the moral norms underlying human experience.

Whereas Erasmus simply implied that *loci* underlay human reality, Melanchthon actually asserted it. In his textbook, *De rhetorica libri tres*, Melanchthon referred to Erasmus's system of note taking and concluded that such *loci* were not mere arbitrary categories but rather represented the essential forms of all things—*formae sunt seu regulae omnium rerum*.

[14] Buck, "Studia humanitatis," 141-42; Bolgar, *Classical Heritage*, 268-72.

[15] Desiderius Erasmus, *De duplici copia verborum ac rerum*, in *Opera omnia*, 10 vols. (Leyden, 1703-06), vol. 1, cols. 100-105. A slightly abridged version of this work has been translated as *On Copia of Words and Ideas*, trans. D. B. King and H. D. Rix (Milwaukee, 1963), see esp. 87-97. For an analysis of *De copia*, see J. K. Sowards, "Erasmus and the Apologetic Textbook: A Study of the *De duplici copia verborum ac rerum*," in *Essays on the Northern Renaissance*, ed. Kenneth A. Strand (Ann Arbor, 1968), 92-106. Erasmus also emphasized the importance of note taking in his blueprint for secondary education, *De ratione studii*, in *Opera omnia*, vol. 1, cols. 522A-B, 523A-B. Erasmus's role in the development of commonplace thought is analyzed in Joachimsen, "Loci communes," 54-61.

[16] Erasmus, *De copia*, col. 101E; the translation is from *On Copia*, 90; also, see Joachimsen, "Loci communes," 57-58.

For Melanchthon, *loci* actually represented objective truths.[17] The influence of Erasmus and Melanchthon on the theory and practice of education was enormous. Erasmus's *De copia* was one of the most popular textbooks in history; over a hundred editions were published in the sixteenth century alone. Melanchthon's *De rhetorica libri tres* went through only about eight editions, but its remarks on note taking were frequently excerpted and published separately, together with Erasmus's and Agricola's systems. After mid-century, virtually every progressive educational treatise included a discussion of note taking and recommendations for structuring a *liber locorum rerum*. Humanist schools inculcated commonplace thought by exposing pupils to this notebook technique and the normative view of reality which underlay it.

Montaigne probably compiled commonplace books during his tenure at the Collège de Guyenne, as we can infer from the *Schola Aquitanica*, which describes Gouvéa's educational program. Students worked from notebooks which served as the bases for commonplace collections. They read a passage from a classical text at home and copied it into a notebook, leaving extra space between each line. They carried this notebook to school in lieu of the text itself. In class, the teacher analyzed the passage word by word, identifying parts of speech, indicating striking phrases and idioms, and elucidating commonplaces, along with examples in the passage illustrating each commonplace. As the teacher analyzed the passage, his students glossed it in their notebooks, using the extra space left for this purpose.[18] When they returned home, they probably copied their notes into three separate commonplace books, a *liber styli* which served as a reference grammar, a *liber sermonis* which served to provide eloquent expressions for their compositions, and a *liber locorum rerum* which served as a storehouse of moral examples.[19]

[17] Philip Melanchthon, *De rhetorica libri tres* (Paris, 1529), 32v. This text is not published in the *Corpus Reformatorum*, although an excerpt from it entitled *De locis communibus ratio* and containing the above quoted phrase is included—see Philip Melanchthon, *Opera quae supersunt omnia*, 28 vols., in *Corpus Reformatorum*, vols. 1-28, eds. C. G. Bretschneider and H. E. Bindseil (Brunswick, 1834-60), 19: cols. 693-98.

[18] The widespread use of such notebooks at the Collège eventually led Simon Millanges, the foremost printer in Bordeaux, to publish student editions of classical texts with extra space between each line; see Vinet, *Schola Aquitanica*, 19, n. 39.

[19] Paul Porteau, *Montaigne et la vie pédagogique*, 178-89. Trinquet (*Jeunesse de Montaigne*, 445-48) disputes Porteau's conclusion that Montaigne used commonplace books at the Collège; he argues that the *Schola Aquitanica* made no mention of this practice. However, the compilation of commonplace books was not, strictly speaking, part of a humanist school's curriculum; rather, students were expected to undertake this task at home. Also, the *Schola Aquitanica* does describe the use of notebooks which probably served as the bases for commonplace collections. Finally, even Trinquet affirms the widely held opinion that Montaigne composed the *Essais* using his own commonplace notebooks. When would he have learned this technique of note taking if not during his tenure at the Collège de Guyenne?

Throughout the Collège de Guyenne, students worked from notebooks rather than from classical texts themselves, which were usually left at home. This practice indicates that reading was not emphasized at the Collège. Rather, students were drilled in the grammar and rhetoric requisite for effective speaking and writing. Indeed, throughout the entire ten year course of instruction, students hardly read more than some Cicero, Terence, Ovid, and Horace. In class these texts were minutely analyzed for their grammatical and rhetorical content, in which students were drilled relentlessly. This regimen illuminates Montaigne's complaint that the Collège instilled a hatred of books.[20] Students were not encouraged to search for knowledge but to present it effectively. This emphasis is characteristic of commonplace thought, for the task of presenting knowledge stored in *loci* required more skill than that of finding it.[21]

Students at the Collège used the material in their commonplace books to formulate discourses *in utramque partem*. They were trained in this technique through exercises in disputation, which were facilitated by the arrangement of benches in each classroom. The best students sat on the first bench, the second best on the next bench, and so forth. During class, students on the first bench drilled those on the second, while those on the third tested their opposites on the fourth, and so on. A student's position in the classroom advanced or regressed according to his daily performance; he could even challenge someone ahead of him and win his seat. The physical layout of each classroom fostered the spirit of rivalry necessary for vigorous disputation.

The school day consisted of three periods of instruction, each concluding with a half hour of disputation. During these exercises, students questioned each other on the previous lesson. In elementary classes, they tested each other on grammatical points; in more advanced classes, they disputed *in utramque partem*. The teacher would assign one group of students the task of defending a proposition and another group that of attacking it. After the completion of this assignment, the teacher often had the students switch sides. Thus, students became skilled in the presentation of knowledge; they learned to think and speak *in utramque partem*.

---

[20] *Essais,* 175.

[21] Howell's analysis of the relationship between judgment and invention in Thomas Wilson's treatise on dialectic is analogous to my conclusion here: "Wilson justifies himself for placing judgment before invention by saying that you have to know how to order an argument before you seek for it, and that anyway 'a reason is easier found than fashioned.' This attitude is a significant phenomenon in intellectual history. It really is a way of saying that subject matter presents fewer difficulties than organization, so far as composition is concerned. A society which takes such an attitude must be by implication a society that is satisfied with its traditional wisdom and knows where to find it. It must be a society that does not stress the virtues of an exhaustive examination of nature so much as the virtues of clarity in form." (*Logic and Rhetoric in England,* 23.)

Daily disputations within each class were supplemented by weekly ones between classes. These disputations were aptly termed *certamina*, contests or combats; they instilled an intense spirit of rivalry between classes. This spirit, fostered both within and between classes, honed each student's competitive edge. Students learned to be quick-witted and facile with their knowledge, eager and able to defend or attack any proposition from a variety of perspectives. This goal reflects the skeptical attitude toward truth characteristic of the Ciceronian orator, who was prepared to argue *in utramque partem* on any given question.

In this extremely competitive atmosphere, Montaigne acquired the propensity for arguing *in utramque partem* and the skeptical habit of mind which underlay it. Seven years of schooling—during which classes met six days a week, eleven months a year—nourished these tendencies. By the time he reached the first form, not even his Sundays were free. This intense experience imparted what he would later portray as his "scar" of irresolution:

... I do not want to forget this further scar, very unfit to produce in public: irresolution.... I do not know which side to take in doubtful enterprises.... I can easily maintain an opinion, but not choose one.

Because in human matters, whatever side we lean to, we find many probabilities to confirm us in it ... so in whatever direction I turn, I can always provide myself with enough causes and probabilities to keep me that way.[22]

When Montaigne wrote these lines around 1578, about thirty years after graduating from the Collège, he recognized that the skeptical habit of reasoning *in utramque partem* was an ingrained part of his personality, just like another famous "scar," bad memory. It is significant, however, that he perceived this characteristic as a defect, for he had not always done so.

At least eighteen years after his graduation from the Collège, Montaigne still had not questioned the value of his education, as we can see from an annotation in his copy of Nicole Gilles's *Annales et chroniques de France*, which he read around 1564. In this book he encountered a passage relating how a father had commanded his son to attack a man with whom the son had previously sworn a truce. Montaigne noted that this story could serve as the basis for a discourse on whether a paternal command could supersede a son's other obligations:

It would be possible to draw from here the foundation of such a discourse: if the authority of paternal commandment could release the son from his promise. Our history furnishes us with enough examples of popes, kings, and magistrates who do it; but fathers are subordinate to them. Which leads me to that perfect

---

[22] *Essais*, 637; Porteau, *Montaigne et la vie pédagogique*, pp. 192-98; also, see Philip P. Hallie, *The Scar of Montaigne* (Middletown, Conn., 1966).

virtue of the ancient Romans and Greeks—indeed I know I will find that the magistrate would never undertake it, quite to the contrary.[23]

Although Montaigne's argument here is only a sketch, it reveals his complete acceptance of commonplace thought and the mode of reasoning *in utramque partem*. Montaigne started with a general question concerning the nature of paternal authority, which he explored with reference to particular examples, like those found in a *liber locorum rerum*. His argument clearly proceeds *in utramque partem*. On the one hand, modern magistrates (taken as father figures) claim the ultimate allegiance of their citizens; on the other, fathers do not have the authority of magistrates in modern society. And again, whereas modern magistrates hardly scruple to compromise their citizens' personal obligations, ancient magistrates— in their "perfect virtue"—would never have assumed such authority. The entire argument devolves upon this observation about the "perfect virtue" of the ancients. Thus, Montaigne anchored his argument *in utramque partem* with an accepted cultural norm which enabled him to arbitrate between contrasting positions.

Montaigne probably noted this passage in Gilles because he sensed an underlying commonplace. Doubtless, the story recalled his love and respect for his own father, to whom Montaigne was especially devoted. Yet he did not sketch a discourse on whether *he* should respect his father's wishes regardless of his own obligations. Rather, he outlined it in terms of paternal authority in general, as if the whole range of examples from ancient and modern history could be distilled into a single moral statement—a commonplace which could serve as a universal rule of conduct.

By the time Montaigne began writing the *Essais* in 1572, he had difficulty finding such commonplaces due to problems in his plan of retirement. He had retired in 1571 to live the life of the sage, an ideal exemplified by his late friend, Estienne de La Boétie. In the solitude of his library Montaigne expected his mind, "weightier and riper with time," to "stay and settle in itself," thus inducing sagelike tranquillity.[24] But sitting alone in that library—dedicated to La Boétie's memory and housing his books—Montaigne could not but be reminded of his loss. Although La Boétie had been dead for nine years, "a wise man sees his dying friend hardly less vividly after twenty-five years than after the first

---

[23] "Il se pourroët tirer d'ici le foundemant d'un tel discours: si l'authorite du commandemant paternel pouuoët desobliger le fis de sa promesse. Nostre histoëre nous fournist d'asses d'examples que les papes, les roës, et les magistras le font; mais les peres sount au dessous. Qui me ramenra a ste vertu parfaite des anciens romeins et grecs, ie scai bien que ie trouuerrai que le magistrat ne l'antreprenoët jameis, eins au rebours." R. Dezeimeris, "Annotations inédites de Michel de Montaigne sur les *Annales et chroniques de France* de Nicole Gilles," *Revue d'histoire littéraire de la France*, 16 (1909), 218-22.

[24] *Essais*, 34.

year." [25] A soul pained by sorrow cannot "stay and settle in itself";
Montaigne was forced to meditate on the means of inuring himself against
his grief in order to attain the tranquillity characteristic of true wisdom.

His meditations formed the basis for the chapter "Of sadness," probably the first chapter of the *Essais* to be composed. [26] Here he recalled
the example of Psammenitus, the king of Egypt captured by Cambyses,
who watched impassively the enslavement of his daughter and the execution of his son but later wept for the fate of a friend. Likewise, Montaigne recalled how his contemporary, Charles of Guise, had borne
steadfastly the deaths of two brothers in quick succession, only to mourn
the loss of a servant soon thereafter. Montaigne surmised that Guise was
so "brimful of sadness" that the slightest surcharge caused him to over-
flow. Perhaps one could deepen the soul by means of reason and discipline
so as to contain even the greatest shocks. But the example of Psammenitus
belied such hopes, for this man was so stunned by the fate of his family
that he could not even register emotion; whereas, he was less moved by
the fate of his friend and thus could express his grief with tears. This
example led Montaigne to conclude, "In truth, the impact of grief, to be
extreme, must stun the whole soul and impede its freedom of action."
How could any sage hope to free himself from the grip of such emotions?

In the profoundly moralistic system of commonplace thought, the
ideal of the sage represented the supreme norm for Montaigne, yet his
grief for La Boétie hindered his attainment of this ideal. Instead of
questioning the ideal, and the commonplace mentality which underlay
it, Montaigne simply redoubled his efforts to pursue it. Since he could
not attain it naturally in the solitude of his library, he began searching
for rules of conduct to guide him in his retirement. In this search, he
automatically employed the intellectual techniques provided by his education, examining any given question from both sides in order to determine a rule of conduct.

The results of this search are recorded in the earliest chapters of the
Essais, where Montaigne consistently failed to find norms underlying the
diversity of human reality. For example, in "Whether the governor of a
besieged place should go out to parley," Montaigne sought to establish
a rule of military conduct, for the wisdom of the sage should be apparent
in action as well as contemplation. He began by asserting that the ancient
practice of waging war fairly and honorably could not be emulated in

---

[25] *Ibid.,* 814; also, see Montaigne's *Journal de voyage en Italie,* in *Oeuvres complètes,*
1270.

[26] Villey described this chapter as one of Montaigne's earliest; furthermore, it is the
first chapter in a large block of early chapters, all written around 1572. Villey has
concluded that Montaigne usually published the chapters of such blocks in their order
of composition. Thus, although "Of sadness" is only the second chapter of the *Essais,* it
is probably the first chapter Montaigne wrote (Chapter One having been composed around
1578). See Villey, *Sources et évolution des Essais,* 1:349, 395.

the modern world where everyone relied on treachery. On the one hand, he cited recent events confirming the popular opinion that a besieged commander should not negotiate with the enemy in person for fear of betrayal. On the other hand, he mentioned the example of a commander who negotiated successfully at a place where he had military superiority. And he concluded with the story of a commander who entrusted himself to his enemies, negotiated with them in their own camp, and thereby saved himself and his men from annihilation. Each successive example in this chapter contradicts rather than confirms its predecessor, thus preventing the establishment of a rule of conduct and fostering the suspension of judgment characteristic of radical skepticism.

Because the mode of reasoning *in utramque partem* served not to discover new norms but to apply accepted ones to particular problems, Montaigne's search for rules of conduct was inevitably thwarted. In his annotation to Gilles, Montaigne had used this mode of arguing to highlight the "perfect virtue" of the ancients, which enabled him to arbitrate between contrasting examples. In "Whether the governor . . . should go out to parley," however, he rejected the norm of ancient probity in war and set out to find a new one by arguing *in utramque partem.* In other words, he transformed an instrument used to exploit truths into one used to search for them. But this attempt to establish new norms emphasized the diversity of examples rather than their similarity. Instead of building commonplaces, Montaigne unwittingly found himself demolishing them.

This unexpected development was genuinely frustrating for a man imbued with the idea that reality could be systematized in terms of commonplaces. He disparaged his meditations as "chimeras and fantastic monsters" which he put into writing in order to make his mind "ashamed of itself."[27] In short, he wanted to regain his accustomed manner of thought. But these attempts to discipline his mind by writing only exacerbated its unruliness.

In response to this impasse, Montaigne invoked the ideal of the sage in his so-called "Stoical" chapters. With this ideal, which was not specifically Stoic but more broadly ancient, he could transcend the diversity of human reality to attain the higher reality of truth and wisdom. He would no longer need to find rules of conduct by discoursing from both sides; rather, he could once again anchor his skeptical habit of mind with a normative idea of wisdom. The titles of these chapters, like "That to philosophize is to learn to die," are commonplaces reinforced by the contents of the chapters. Instead of searching for truths, Montaigne now propounded them.

After Montaigne had clearly enunciated the ideal of the sage, he began to realize that it was almost too lofty: "In all antiquity it is hard

[27] *Essais,* 34.

to pick out a dozen men who set their lives to a certain and constant course, which is the principal goal of wisdom."[28] But rather than reject this ideal entirely and fall back into the skeptical confusion of his earlier thinking, Montaigne now tried to humanize it: "For all his wisdom, the sage is still a man—what is there more vulnerable, more wretched, and more null."[29] In order to redefine this ideal, Montaigne naturally relied on his habit of discoursing *in utramque partem*. Unlike the earliest chapters of the *Essais,* however, the subject of this discourse was the very ideal which Montaigne had previously taken for granted. As Montaigne redefined this ideal, he undermined its normative value, thus loosening the anchor which held his skeptical habit of mind in check.

For example, he explored the nature of vice in the chapter "Of drunkenness," written around 1573-74. Although the Stoics believed that all vices were equal (because the slightest vice betrayed an inconstant soul), Montaigne could not equate the theft of a cabbage with the desecration of a temple. If he permitted a gradation of vice, however, he had to determine when behavior transgressed acceptability. He examined drunkenness in this context, beginning with the general statement that drunkenness was a "gross and brutish vice" because it overturned the mind. He then examined this statement from both sides. On the one hand, Josephus plied an enemy ambassador with wine, loosened his tongue, and learned all his secrets. On the other hand, both Augustus and Tiberius had confidants who were heavy drinkers, and neither emperor had reason to regret this. And furthermore, German mercenaries, besotted with wine, always remembered their quarters, watch words, and rank. Not content with this simple exposition, Montaigne continued to pile example on example, demonstrating the difficulty of determining whether drunkenness was truly a vice. The ancients did not decry it too strongly; some philosophers even recommended it to relax the soul. Cato, "the true image of Stoic virtue," enjoyed his drink all too well.[30] The ability to hold one's liquor was a prized attribute in some of the most noteworthy states. Montaigne had even heard a famous doctor recommend drunkenness as an aid to digestion. And there was no better remedy for the discomforts of old age. Thus, this apparent vice had many useful attributes. Indeed, the very notion of vice itself—along with the ideal of the sage—began to crumble under the weight of human diversity.

In "Of drunkenness," Montaigne experienced the same suspension of judgment as in his earliest chapters, but he now began to accept the radical skepticism which he had previously rejected. By 1574, he no longer believed that to philosophize was "to learn to die" but "to doubt":

[28] *Ibid.,* 316.

[29] *Ibid.,* 328.

[30] *Ibid.,* 327. In the first edition, Montaigne confused Cato the Younger with Cato the Censor; in later editions, he corrected this error.

"If to philosophize is to doubt . . . then to play the fool and follow my fancies as I do, is all the more to doubt."[31] Montaigne's "fancies" were generated by the habit of thinking *in utramque partem,* which was now undermining the system of commonplace thought it had traditionally upheld.

In following his fancies, however, Montaigne claimed "to play the fool," an admission signifying more than mere false modesty, for the doubts of a fool need to be taken seriously. Even if the ideal of the sage was difficult to attain in practice, it remained a theoretical possibility for Montaigne. He believed that the soul, though vulnerable to external accidents, could still regulate itself if left undisturbed: ". . . when straightness and composure are combined with constancy, then the soul attains its ultimate perfection; that is, when nothing jars it, which a thousand accidents can do."[32] In other words, Montaigne was a reluctant skeptic still yearning for an ideal by which to orient himself rather than accepting the consequences of his doubts, which could cast him adrift without any norms for guidance.

Montaigne was reluctant to accept his radical skepticism not only because it threatened his traditional orientation but also because it lacked philosophical justification. He was familiar with the limited skepticism of the Academy, which employed the mode of arguing *in utramque partem* to establish verisimilitude; but, he was not yet familiar with the radical skepticism of the Pyrrhonists, which challenged the possibility of attaining verisimilitude. By 1574, he may have read Diogenes Laertius's "Life of Pyrrho" which, along with the works of Sextus, provided the principal account of Pyrrhonism; but even if he had, he probably did not equate Pyrrhonism with his own suspension of judgment, for Diogenes did not provide a very forceful or detailed account of Pyrrhonism.[33] Without the justification of a philosophical precedent, Montaigne tended to dismiss his difficulty in reasoning *in utramque partem* as a personal idiosyncrasy.

He did not fully accept his own radical skepticism until reading Sextus's *Outlines of Pyrrhonism,* probably around 1576, when he composed the Pyrrhonistic core of the "Apology." Sextus provided Montaigne with a detailed, forceful account of Pyrrhonism and its challenge to Academic skepticism. After reading this text, Montaigne realized that his own inconclusiveness resembled Pyrrhonism: "Their expressions are: 'I establish nothing; it is no more thus than thus, or than neither way; I do not understand it; the appearances are equal on all sides; it is equally legitimate to speak for and against.' "[34] Pyrrhonism provided philosoph-

---

[31] *Ibid.,* 330.

[32] *Ibid.,* 328.

[33] Villey suggested that Montaigne did not pay much attention to the "Life of Pyrrho" until after reading Sextus around 1576 (*Sources et évolution des Essais,* 1:126-27).

[34] *Essais,* 485.

ical legitimacy to a mode of arguing *in utramque partem* which was no longer anchored by normative truth. Thus, Montaigne's reading of Sextus did not induce a skeptical crisis; rather, it resolved one born of the breakdown of commonplace thought.

After reading Sextus, Montaigne found not only a philosophical justification for his radical skepticism but also a new orientation to supplant the traditional one of commonplace thought. His Pyrrhonistic arguments in the "Apology," even his devastating critique of the senses, led him to one certainty—that he was only a man, a simple, vain, ignorant creature: ". . . I would hardly dare tell of the vanity and weakness that I find in myself. My footing is so unsteady and so insecure, I find it so vacillating and ready to slip, and my sight is so unreliable, that on an empty stomach I feel myself another man than after a meal."[35] Montaigne's appreciation of his creatural nature soon provided the basis for his self-portrait, as he surmised that he was the only man among his contemporaries to know that he was only a man. In the first chapter devoted to self-portrayal, Montaigne wrote with self-conscious modesty, "The only thing which makes me think something of myself is the thing in which no man ever thought himself deficient . . . for who ever thought that he lacked sense."[36] As Montaigne explored this paradox, he began to supplant the objective view of the world fostered by commonplace thought with the subjective one characteristic of his "essays." For Montaigne, an essay was basically an argument *in utramque partem* undertaken for its own sake, not to establish rules of conduct but to portray the workings of a unique mind. In this activity, the more diverse the examples he considered the more varied was the image reflected by his mind. Thus, Montaigne's skeptical habit of mind now served as a many faceted mirror which he held before himself, and the self he beheld served as his point of orientation in a complex world.

This brief survey of the evolution of Montaigne's thought, from his education at the Collège de Guyenne to the publication of the first edition of the *Essais* in 1580, reveals how commonplace thought broke down for him. In school he had been trained to argue from both sides of a question using an accepted cultural norm to arbitrate between contrasting positions. In this way, he would derive a commonplace conclusion serving as a universal rule of conduct. Years later, when his persistent sorrow for La Boétie spurred him to seek rules of conduct to guide his quest for wisdom, Montaigne naturally employed the mode of reasoning inculcated by his education. But the discourse *in utramque partem* was now detached from its normative anchor; it served in the search for new norms rather than in the application of accepted ones. Consequently,

[35] *Ibid.*, 548.
[36] *Ibid.*, 640.

Montaigne found himself arguing on the first hand, the second . . . the third, the fourth, and so on, with no means of arriving at a conclusion. The attempts to discipline his mind, first by recording its "chimeras" and later by invoking the ideal of the sage, inevitably failed as Montaigne's new mode of reasoning progressively undermined accepted cultural norms. This erosion of commonplace thought led to a suspension of judgment in the midst of perpetual doubt, a condition which Montaigne finally accepted as philosophically legitimate after reading Sextus Empiricus. In short, Montaigne's "Pyrrhonism" was really Academic skepticism gone awry.

The reappraisal of Montaigne's skepticism necessitates a revision of Popkin's thesis about the rise of skepticism. Montaigne occupies a pivotal position in this thesis, marking the transition from the intellectual crisis of the Reformation to the skeptical crisis of the seventeenth century. According to Popkin, Montaigne married "the Cross of Christ and the doubts of Pyrrho," supposedly in order to create an ideology for the Counter-Reformation, "Catholic Pyrrhonism."[37] Popkin then showed how Montaigne's disciples, the *nouveaux Pyrrhoniens,* communicated his so-called "Catholic Pyrrhonism" to the *libertins érudits* of the early seventeenth century who, in turn, applied it to the whole spectrum of human knowledge. This intensification of skepticism then led to a series of "counter-attacks," culminating in Cartesian rationalism.

Despite the persuasiveness of Popkin's thesis as a whole, I am not convinced that Montaigne was an agent of the Counter-Reformation. He was, of course, a fideist, claiming that religious truth could only be revealed by God; and he was, as Popkin has shown, fully aware of the conservative value of this fideism.[38] Yet in the "Apology," Montaigne's chief aim was not to keep Christians loyal to the Church but rather to make them see themselves for what they really were, mere creatures incapable of knowing God's will. This message informs his fideism in the closing lines of the "Apology":

But to make the handful bigger than the hand, the armful bigger than the arm, and to hope to straddle more than the reach of our legs, is impossible and unnatural. Nor can man raise himself above himself and humanity; for he can see only with his own eyes, and seize only with his own grasp. He will rise, if God lends him his hand; he will rise by abandoning and renouncing his own means, and letting himself be raised and uplifted by divine grace; but not otherwise.

Montaigne's humility here has the intensity of religious feeling; yet, it derived not from his awe of God the Creator but from his understanding

---

[37] Popkin, *History of Scepticism,* 47.
[38] *Ibid.*

of man the creature. This understanding ultimately enabled Montaigne to reorient himself in a complex world devoid of apparent norms.

Although Montaigne was not a "Catholic Pyrrhonist," Popkin has shown that the *nouveaux Pyrrhoniens* viewed him as such and used his skepticism to promote fideism. Pierre Charron, Montaigne's foremost disciple, was one of the most popular authors of the seventeenth century; his fideistic arguments imparted Pyrrhonism to the *libertins érudits*. The spread of Pyrrhonism, however, was a necessary but not sufficient cause of the skeptical crisis of the seventeenth century. For example, Charron adopted Montaigne's skepticism without questioning commonplace thought; his *La Sagesse* resembles a commonplace book in which Montaigne's ramblings have been arranged topically. Despite popularizing Pyrrhonism, Charron reinforced the traditional normative view of the world which would have been challenged by any thoroughgoing skepticism.

Montaigne's disciples failed to understand their master because he was, quite simply, far ahead of his time. He was one of the earliest products of institutionalized humanist education and the first to recognize its deficiencies. Contemporaries like Charron never thought of questioning this progressive educational system. After it had become well established, by the early seventeenth century, its defects became more apparent. Only at this point did the spread of Pyrrhonism, acting in conjunction with the breakdown of commonplace thought, generate a skeptical crisis.

The ultimate response to this crisis was the rejection of the humanist program of education. Descartes opened his counter-attack against skepticism by criticizing his humanistic education at the Jesuit Collège of La Flèche. In his *Discours de la Méthode* (1637), he complained that his education had failed to provide him with clear and certain knowledge by which to guide his life. Like Montaigne before him, Descartes was reacting to the breakdown of commonplace thought, which was no longer capable of providing moral guidance in a diverse and complex world. But unlike Montaigne, who delighted in this new found complexity, Descartes despaired of it and cleansed his mind of all but clear and distinct ideas, on which he attempted to restructure human knowledge. The humanist curriculum was excluded from this new intellectual edifice.

Humanist educators taught their curriculum by means of commonplace notebooks which served not only to aid literary composition but also to systematize human knowledge. The need for system was due to a growing awareness of the diversity and complexity of the world. The revival of antiquity had heightened the contrast between the pagan and Christian worlds; the reform movement in the Church had divided the Christian world into competing denominations; overseas explorations had revealed the existence of a strange New World; and the advent of printing had not only accelerated the effects of all these changes but had also created an information explosion. Commonplaces provided a means of ordering and digesting this complexity, as long as one did not question established norms too closely. By the seventeenth century, however, commonplace thought had succumbed to the very diversity it had been meant to control. And with the breakdown of commonplaces, the skeptical mode of thinking they had previously held in check was freed from its former constraints, engendering a *crise pyrrhonienne.*

Clarkson University, New York

XVII

ON THE REARMING OF HEAVEN: THE MACHIAVELLISM
OF TOMMASO CAMPANELLA

BY JOHN M. HEADLEY

Johann Henricus Boeclerus in Tacite annales lib. 3.57: "Larvis ille
Thomas Campanella, novae religionis ut jactitat repertor, revera autem ... homo callidus & ad fraudem acutus, sine ulla religione ac fide,
publicis judiciis voluit imponere. Cum enim vidisset Macchiavellum
(sic), ob vafra & improba ejusmodi consilia, apud plerosque vapulare,
ipse velut mangonio quodam adornata, quae Macchiavellus nuda
protulerat, ita denuo in theatrum induxit, ut & reprehenderet Macchiavellum, & Macchiavelli tamen placita sedulo sub diversis nominibus
teneret." At non novae religionis, sed novae philosophiae repertorem
tantum se jactitavit Campanella. (Ern. Sal. Cyprian, *Vita Th. Carn-
panellae* [Utrecht, 1741], 167-68.)

After Aristotle the greatest single intellectual antagonist of Campanella was Niccolò Machiavelli. Although Campanella was born forty
years after the author of *The Prince* had died, he experienced a dramatic
encounter with some of the immortal remains of his future archenemy.
Campanella reports of his going to Florence in October 1592 in the hope
of some university appointment: the Grand Duke Ferdinand I had given
him permission to be escorted by the librarian Baccio Valori through the
Laurentian, one of the first libraries of Europe, and, to the young Dominican, a treasury of learning that surpassed the much vaunted library

*The author wishes to thank Professor Marcia Colish of Oberlin College and his col-
league Professor Peter Kaufman (UNC/CH) for their valuable criticism of this paper at its
inception and, at a later stage, Professors Lloyd Kramer (UNC/CH) and James Michael
Weiss of Boston College. The following abbreviations have been used for works of Campanella that are frequently cited. **Af. Pol.**: *Aforismi Politici con sommari*, ed. Luigi Firpo.
(Turin, 1941); **AP**: *Articuli prophetales*, ed.Germana Ernst, (Florence, 1977); **AT**: *Atheis-
mus Triumphatus seu Reductio ad religionem per scientiarum veritates ... contra Anti-
christianismum Achitophellisticum* (Rome, Zannetti, 1631); **AV**: *Antiveneti*, ed. Firpo
(Florence, 1945); *De genL: De Gentilisrno non retinendo* (Paris, 1693); **DPI**: *Discorsi ai
principi d'Italia*, ed. Firpo (Turin, 1945); **DUGE**: *Discorsi universali del governo eccle-
siastico per far una gregge e un pastor* in *Scritti Scelti di Giordano Bruno e di Tommaso
Campanella*, ed. Firpo (Turin, 1968); **Lett.**: *Tommaso Campanella: Lettere*, ed. Vincenzo
Spampanato (Bari, 1927); **Meta.**: *Metafisica*, ed. Giovanni di Napoli, vol. III (Bologna,
1967); **MN**: "Le monarchie delle nationi ..." in L. Amabile, *Fra T. Campanella ne Castelli*
(Naples, 1887), II, 299-347; **MS**: *De monarchia hispanica* (Amsterdam. L. Elzevir, 1653);
PO: *Poetica*, ed. Firpo (Rome, 1944); **PR[3]**: "Quaestiones super tertia parte suae philos-
ophiae realis, quae est De politicis" in *Disputationum in quatuor partes suae Philosophiae
realis libri quatuor* (Paris, Denis Houssaye, 1637); **RC**: "Risposte alle censure dell
'Ateismo Triunfato" in *Opusculi inediti di Tommaso Campanella*, ed. Firpo (Florence.
1951).

of the Ptolemies at Alexandria. In the course of the tour Valori at one point took the intent visitor back to a secluded treasure chamber where the most precious codices and manuscripts were kept. There Campanella tells of being shown the books of Machiavelli written in his own hand, and as the librarian proceeded to regale him with an inaccurate biography of their writer, the already hunted friar stared down upon the manuscript books of the *Florentine History*.[1] During his long life our aspiring world reformer would have cause to reflect upon this encounter.[2]

Whatever the profound differences and opposition distinguishing the relationship between Tommaso Campanella and Niccolò Machiavelli, their strong affinities and even identity of interests most impressed contemporaries. Despite all his own disclaimers Campanella only managed further to convince his readers regarding this identity. In his immediately subsequent surviving letter, again to the Grand Duke Ferdinand, written two months later, Campanella recommended himself to the prince as a political expert and one whose special knowledge could enhance the Tuscan potentate's esteem and power.[3] And in his most expressly anti-Machiavellian work, the notorious *Atheism Conquered*, which announced his antipathy in its original title, Campanella only confirmed the belief of many in his own and subsequent generations that he was himself both Machiavellian and atheist[4]—in fact a "Second Machiavel" to his second English editor.[5] Yet this very curious relationship to the cunning Florentine seemed to be a disease of the age. Two decades earlier Christopher Marlowe in the *Jew of Malta* had allowed his Machiavel to say: "Admir'd I am of those that hate me most." And Gabriel Naudé, Campanella's own friend and advocate, remarked that Machiavelli's doctrines were practiced by those who forbade them to be spread; to distrust all and dissimulate with each as he advises, would become the prescription for effective conduct in this Tacitean age.[6] In short the relationship between the two apostles of guile was nothing if not ambiguous and complex.

It seems almost superfluous to rehearse here a subject that has been so beautifully treated by Friedrich Meinecke in one of the more memorable chapters of his classic *Machiavellism*. And yet for all its virtues Meinecke's effort to resolve the apparent enigma of Campanella's lifelong struggle with the idea of *ragione di stato* fails to get to the nub of the

---

[1] RC, 53-54.

[2] Cf. Lett., 4-5; 388-89.

[3] Lett., 7.

[4] Andrzej Nowicki, "Gli incontri tra Vanini e Campanella," in *Tommaso Campanella (1568-1639). Miscellanea di studi nel 4° centenario della sua nascita* (Naples, 1969), 473-85.

[5] Luigi Firpo, *Bibliografia degli scritti di Tommaso Campanella* (Turin, 1940), 65-66.

[6] See Roman Schnur, *Individualismus und Absolutismus. Zur politischen Theorie vor Thomas Hobbes, 1600-1640* (Berlin, 1963), 53, 77.

matter. Only at one point does his inquiry engage the question of religion as understood by the two combatants, but without pursuing it to a possible resolution.[7] And it is upon the issue of religion that we need to focus our attention. In fairness to Meinecke it should be noted that our inquiry is concerned less with the rival uses of *ragione di stato* by the two political thinkers than with the relationship of religion and politics for each.

Italian scholarship on the subject of our present controversy seems nearer the mark when it observes that for Campanella, Machiavelli represented not simply a political doctrine but a general conception of the world which has its distant roots in pagan philosophy, currently designated as gentilism, and its more recent associations with Renaissance Averroism and libertinism. For when Campanella claims that Machiavelli derives from Aristotlelianism, he means far more than what had become a virtual commonplace by 1600; namely, that Machiavelli had modelled his prince upon the tyrant of Aristotle appearing in the *Politics*, Book V. Rather, to Campanella Machiavellism meant an all too broad intellectual current, a cultural phenomenon which indeed was taking its toll upon Campanella himself. Machiavelli's beckoning of his generation to the *verità effettuale della cosa* had by the end of the sixteenth century broadened in its implications to involve a sharpened appreciation of the concrete, a tireless scrutiny of political and social phenomena, a *sapientia humana*, all contributing to the new autonomy of politics. Indeed the terrible, haunting vision of "an orphaned world" continued to obtrude itself, never completely to be suppressed or thrust aside. The *Atheism Conquered* can be seen as directed against its own author and as assuming the nature of an interior colloquy, thus implicitly making something of Machiavelli integral to Campanella.[8] While incongruities abound, similarities, even correspondences, glare.

Any effort to achieve a more precise understanding of Campanella's relationship to Machiavelli as well as his very indebtedness to the Florentine must penetrate beyond both the obvious, pronounced points of opposition and also the express points of correspondence and appropri-

---

[7] Friedrich Meinecke, *Machiavellism. The Doctrine of Raison d'Etat and its Place in Modern History* (New Haven, 1957), 98; and cf. Rodolfo De Mattei, *La politica di Campanella* (Rome, 1928), 148-66, and Mario D'Addio, *Il pensiero politico di Gaspare Scioppio e il Machiavellismo del seicento* (Milan, 1962), 358-80.

[8] See Giuliano Procacci, *Studi sulla fortuna del Machiavelli* (Rome, 1965), 45-77, 97-98, 106; Giorgio Spini, *Ricerca dei libertini* (Florence, 1950, 1980) has survived the attack of Vittorio De Caprariis, "Libertinage e libertinismo," *Letteratura moderne*, 2 (1951), 241-61, whose effort to deny the existence of an Italian libertine movement at this time is rejected by Sergio Bertelli, introduction to *Il libertinismo in Europa* (Milan/Naples, 1980), 11; see also Tullio Gregory et al. *Ricerche su letteratura libertina e letteratura clandestina nel Seicento* (Florence, 1981), and *Theophrastus redivivus. Erudizione e ateismo nel Seicento* (Naples, 1979); P. O. Kristeller, "The Myth of Renaissance Atheism and the French Tradition of Free Thought," *Journal of the History of Philosophy*, 6 (1968) 233-43.

ation to the basic assumptions and different frames of reference which motivate the thought of each. Standing in contrast to the crisp, refreshing clarity of Machiavelli's analysis, the ambiguities, obscurities, and tensions characteristic of any Baroque thinker suffer an abnormal accentuation in the tortuous existence of the Calabrian prophetic reformer, magus, and prisoner. If his social and political thought seems "to pull apart in opposite directions," if it undergoes an undeniable torquing,[9] there remains nevertheless throughout his work more than sufficient consistency, impelled by his consuming world vision, to warrant an examination of the present problem and its peculiar relevance to the period of the early seventeenth century—this *machiavellisticum saeculum*.[10]

Campanella's acquaintance with Machiavelli's works may well have extended beyond the *Prince* and the *Discourses*, but these alone are discernible in his own writings. Of course a dispassionate, impartial reading of *The Prince* was no more possible of Campanella's period than that of a comparably explosive work would be for our own. Campanella's controversy was as much with a Counter-Reformation image of Machiavelli as it was with the political thinker himself. According to this image successful politics required freedom from traditional moral and religious principles. To the sixteenth century Machiavelli was the teacher of evil, a vital commodity, for being evil was more useful than being good.[11] The positive aspect of Machiavelli, his desire to promote civic virtue and public spirit, was quite lost on Campanella. The latter's formal effort to contend with the threat presented by *ragione di stato* to religion came in his *Atheism Conquered*, wherein Machiavelli emerges as the symbol of skepticism and cunning, and the Machiavellians as libertines undermining the profoundly natural and supernatural reality of all religion. Composed in the dreadful dungeon of San Elmo between April and July 1605 and written in Italian under the more revealing title of *The Philosophical Recognition of the True, Universal Religion against Antichristianism and Machiavellism*, this work first appeared in Rome in 1631 and then only to be suppressed by the censors.[12] By his melding of Machiavelli with an Averroistic Aristotelianism, which he represented as being diametrically

---

[9] Joan Kelly-Gadol, "Tommaso Campanella: The Agony of Political Theory in the Counter Reformation," in ed. Edward P. Mahoney, *Philosophy and Humanism: Renaissance Essays in Honor of Paul Oskar Kristeller* (New York, 1976), 164-65.

[10] AP, 89. cf. Cecilia Dentice di Accadia, "Tomismo e Machiavellismo," *Giornale critico della filosofia italiana*, 6 (1925), 1-16.

[11] Felix Gilbert, "Machiavellism," in *History: Choice and Commitment* (Cambridge, Mass., 1977), 158; cf. AV, 128: "La ragion di stato del Machiavello e dei politici consiste in due cose: una, amar solo se stesso e nullo altro al mondo, se non quanto è utile al nostro stato, ed uccidere senza riguardo ad ogni santo ed amico nostro, mentre non va a volontà nostra. L'altra è solo sapere l'istorie de' passati principi, o buoni, o rei, ed acquistar con l'esempio loro, a dritto o a torto, quel che potemo, con simulazioni ingannando gli amici e li nemici."

[12] Firpo, *Bibliografia*, 101-2.

opposed to his own rationalized, naturalistic Christianity, Campanella saw the Florentine to be more than a political menace: indeed he assumed the proportions of a total and most hostile view of reality. In his desperate efforts to get the book approved and republished by meeting the individual censures, Campanella comes forth with some of his most extreme and exaggerated statements against Machiavelli.

These responses to censured passages conduct us beyond Machiavellism and allow us to approach Campanella's Machiavelli. All the evils of the present age in political and religious matters, he argues, derive from Machiavelli's *ragione di stato*, which perceives all faith to be just so many conspiracies and arts of *statisti*.[13] Against the seventh censure Campanella has to explain his statement concerning the Duke of Valentinois; he says that he is writing against the Machiavelli who makes religion a craft of state and urges the prince to disregard veracity, oaths, and justice. On the contrary Campanella wishes to prove that this is not the true art of State because all who have followed such a doctrine have lost *lo stato* and their lives as well. He then proceeds to prove this point with all the historical examples that Machiavelli used, including Valentinois, Caesar Borgia himself, as an example of a prince who lost both the State and his life.[14] Campanella would appear to be arguing, in the same vein as the current anti-Machiavellian moralists, that crime does not pay and that for the statesman honesty is the best policy and advantageous to the state.[15] He now becomes still more vituperative: it is well known how much evil Machiavelli has done to *Cristianità*, legitimating and even prescribing to all princes injustice, treachery, perjury, the killing of parents and of any who are suspected by the *stato politico*, all for purposes of personal self-aggrandizement and not in the interest of the community. Machiavelli makes a trifle of religion and claims that Christ, the prophets, and Campanella's fellow Dominican Savonarola preached only to acquire *lo stato* for themselves, as do all tyrants, but that through their ignorance of politics, not knowing how to arm themselves, these unarmed prophets were killed. To which Campanella retorts that the unarmed prophets obtain an empire over the minds of men through their deaths, while the armed prophets, like John of Leyden at Münster, only manage to get themselves and their states destroyed. To the censors the recently freed prisoner explains that he seeks to remove the esteem in which Machiavelli is held by the *politici* and *heretici*—as well as by the unknown author of the *Three Impostors*, earlier ascribed to Campanella himself. Campanella desires to explode the claim that

[13] RC, 9.

[14] RC, 35.

[15] On the utility of moral virtue and religion for political success and state building see the forthcoming study by Robert Bireley, S.J. and his "Antimachiavellism, the Baroque and Maximilian of Bavaria," *Archivum Historicum Societatis Iesu*, 53 (1984), 139-40.

Machiavelli was learned in the sciences and to reveal him as knowledgeable only in human histories and in the practice of perverted politics. On the very same grounds which Machiavelli would be most appreciated by the modern age, namely his sense of the concrete, the historical, the experiential, and his basing of politics upon human history and experience, Campanella now takes violent issue, for here human cunning becomes *jus politiae.*[16]

In conveying a further, somewhat more specifically political measurement of his enemy, Campanella addresses the issue of the Machiavellian ethos of power as it relates to political performance in his own day and what we have come to associate with the practices of the emerging absolute State. Struck by the increasing omnipresence of the political dimension, Campanella avers: "All the actions of men are directed to the state [*regnum*], as there is nothing that man does not do for its sake, since every prince transgresses religion and virtue, as they say for *ragion di stato*, because domination compensates one for all evils." To Machiavelli's praise of the wickedness of Caesar Borgia and Agathocles, Campanella objects that virtues are in conformity with nature and vices counter to it, and princes who violate religion and nature are ultimately the most unfortunate and condemned before God. Drawing closer to the political events of his own day, Campanella observes that religion, which should direct men to God, is abused for purposes of ruling and that princes change religion in accordance with the greater political utility, as is frequently evinced these days in Germany. Campanella entertains the ideas that the Spaniards occupy the kingdoms of the new hemisphere for political gain, although under the pretext of religion, while a king of France for similar reasons will abjure his sectarian beliefs. To the statesmen and Machiavellists of his day Campanella says that unless at the outset they believe God to exist, to exercise his providence and to recompense us, by no means are we able to dispute with them. For who will dispute with the insane? Thus religion, however much embattled, is inescapably fundamental to the politics and the political consciousness of Campanella's thought.[17]

At this time the term "religion" was undergoing a number of significant transformations in its meaning. Traditionally associated with the life of the monastic orders, the term less prominently referred to a worshipful attitude, a genuine fear or a love of God, a personal engagement with God first defined by Augustine and most recently expressed by some

---

[16] RC, 38-39; 51-52; on Campanella's perception of the specifically historical in Machiavelli's impact see AT, 85, 162-63.

[17] These passages from Campanella's not readily available *Quaestiones super secunda parte suae Philosophiae realis Quae est ethicorum* (Paris, 1637), 1-2, 11-13, have been incorporated into the footnotes of D'Addio, *Scioppio*, 376-80. For bibliographical information see Firpo, *Bibl.*, 73-97, esp. 86-87, 94-95.

of the Protestant reformers.[18] With the Reformation, however, had come a confessionalism, a bitter hostility between two religions which by the middle of the sixteenth century had made explicit what had long been threatening: religion becomes pluralized and reified; "a religion" begins to signify an assemblage of practices and beliefs, expressing a complex external reality distinct from its previous definitions. By the early seventeenth century a polemical work has for its title *Calvinismus bestiarum religio*: from a polemical context the age of the *-isms* had emerged.[19] Yet within Italy itself such an important transformation in the understanding of the notion did not have to wait for the Reformation. Since the thirteenth century a primitive sociology of religions had been nursed at the University of Padua. There a heterodox form of Aristotelianism understood religion as *lex*, ushered in by an astral cycle, established by a *legifer*, and supported by a suitable allotment of miracles. Indeed Paduan Averroism had come to look upon religions as social and even naturalistic phenomena subject to growth, efflorescence, and decay. Crudely expressed, religion at its best served as necessary social-political cement. From the early fourteenth century with Pietro d'Abano to Pietro Pomponazzi in the early sixteenth century, Padua harbored a distinct tradition that makes more understandable Machiavelli's own ability to consider religion as an object of thought and a human phenomenon.[20] Indeed in his political conception of religion Machiavelli represented only an aspect of a much larger development that had been in preparation for over two centuries and would continue to flow from its north Italian headwaters long after he had departed.[21]

Campanella stands among a growing number in the early seventeenth century seeking to redefine religion as something rooted in the rational capacity of all men and therefore natural. Religion is the natural *virtus*

---

[18] Wilfred Cantwell Smith, *The Meaning and End of Religion* (New York, 1962), 28-44.

[19] Michel Despland, *La Religion en Occident: Evolution des idées et du vécu* (Montreal, 1979), 227-30; 178, 292. However, Peter Biller, "Medieval Notions of Religion," *Journal of Ecclesiastical History*, 36 (1985), 351-69, in criticizing John Bossy, "Some Elementary Forms of Durkheim," *Past and Present*, 95 (1982), 3-18, and indirectly Smith and Despland, suggests that the thirteenth century may have had the notion, if not the word, for the diversity of religions and their "reification" as external systems. Of the Paduans only Marsilius, in connection with *lex* and *secta*, is mentioned.

[20] On Averroism in general see the article by M. M. Gorce in *Dict. d'hist. et de géog.*, V, 1032-92, and on Pietro d'Abano, Lynn Thorndike, *A History of Magic and Experimental Science* (New York, 1923), II, 882-99, and "Franciscus Florentinus, or Paduanus," in *Mélanges Mandonnet* (Paris, 1930), II, 353-69. More recent studies, focussing on method, are of course those of John Herman Randall, Jr., *The School of Padua and the Emergence of Modern Science* (Padua, 1961); "Paduan Aristotelianism Reconsidered" in Edward P. Mahoney (ed.), *Philosophy and Humanism: Renaissance Essays in Honor of Paul Oskar Kristeller*, 275-82.

[21] Spini, *Ricerca*, 23-32.

with which we are all endowed by God: it is the natural return to God and thus can never be an *arte di stato*.[22] Drawing on Stoic, Platonic, and Hermetic sources, he recognizes a universal rationality in mankind that serves as a preparation and basis for the overgrafting of Christ, who is seen in turn as the primal reason.[23] Campanella readily admits the multiplicity of religions, all of which are established by the decree of nature; but in his view only Christianity is established by supernature, thereby making that religion uniquely true.[24] In the current reshaping of science Campanella perceived a force which, by reinforcing and informing the Catholic religion, might decisively increase its possibilities for becoming not the religion of a special people but the religion of all.[25] The world has one natural law in all peoples which no diversity can obliterate. Yet Thomist that he is, Campanella can claim that this natural law is fulfilled and elevated by the supernatural law evident in Christ.[26] In Christianity alone, he concludes, can the perfect rationality be found.

The problem turns upon a controversy over the nature and purpose of religion. According to Campanella, Machiavelli transforms religion into a political art for retaining the people in hope of paradise and fear of hell.[27] It becomes a means of political manipulation, the cunning of friars and clergy being applied to the rulers' domination of the people.[28] Referring to Melchior Cano's *Loci* X, Campanella claims that the Florentine learned from Aristotle and more specifically from the Paduan Averroists that religion is instrumental in the art of ruling.[29] Apparently horrified by Machiavelli's total subjection of religion to the principle of utility, the Calabrian prophet, gazing northwards, sees that in those kingdoms the *politici* have made religion a suit or hat that can be changed at will. Yet while rejecting this Machiavellian view of politicized religion, Campanella himself affirms religion's political utility, although on a different basis. He insists that no community can last a day without religion;[30] in fact the social necessity of religion is axiomatic for Campanella.[31] As the very soul of the political, religion exercises a natural magic in

---

[22] Lett. 103; 192.

[23] Af. Pol, 34.

[24] AT, 163.

[25] Nicola Badaloni, *Tommaso Campanella* (Milan, 1965), 269.

[26] AT, 72-75; AP, 135.

[27] Lett. 66-69.

[28] Lett. 102.

[29] *De gent.*, 32; Lett. 66. The original 1636 edition of *De gentilismo* has not been available to me but the second and final version of this work, published under a different title one year before Campanella's death, includes the same passage, which is common enough in the friar's works. See "Disputatio in prologum instauratarum scientiarum ad scholas Christianas," in *Philosophiae realis libri quatuor* (Paris, 1637), sig. ciii.

[30] AT, 167.

[31] AT, 26; Badaloni, *Campanella*, 260-65.

uniting members of a community.[32] In the *Monarchia di Spagna* we learn that religion, whether true or false (*ò vera ò falsa*), possesses sovereign virtue commanding bodies, swords, and tongues, which are the instruments of empire.[33] No ruler, he observes, is able to establish and retain *imperium* unless he is truly sent and authorized by God or at least is *believed* to be. Religion thus provides the necessary glue binding men to God and subjects to their rulers *in causa imperandi*.[34] With Campanella the political uses of religion seem at times to strain perilously beyond whatever claims religion has to ultimate truth.

On points of detail and tactics he can also agree with Machiavelli:[35] never at a loss for effective resort to cunning acts of political advantage to the state, he can advocate the prompt annihilation of opposition—a measure that would have received the approval of Caesar Borgia.[36] Other Machiavellian moments recur, expressive of political cunning: the lettered, the intelligentsia, should be kept occupied in the studying of nature, thereby diverted from such politically troubling matters as the study of theology and of philology—a point that would be echoed two generations later by the founders of the Royal Society;[37] or again, so important is it for the Papacy to have a well stocked treasury that the church would be well-advised to raise money *sotto pretesto* of war against the Turk.[38]

Does Campanella expressly tap those rich springs of political deception deriving from Plato, Averroes, and Padua, wherein the idea of the Noble Lie and deception as a necessary ingredient of political stability and order had received such important consideration and loving care? In the course of a lengthy treatment of religion that appears in Book XVI of the *Metaphysics* Campanella takes up the problem of deceivers as it pertains to a religion. After detailing ten criteria (*notae*) whereby the validity of one claiming to bear a *religio* and *lex* from God might be determined[39]—all reasonable enough tests and for the most part applicable today—he addressed the problem of the deceived as well as the deceiving legislator, sent by demons or devils with God's permission for the sake of a greater good. Among such are Muhammad, the Talmudists, and the gods of the pagans, contrary to nature and to the express prescriptions of God. As one sent by nature while being motivated by reason

---

[32] AV, 74, 109.

[33] MS, 27. References will also be given to the most authoritative manuscript for the *Monarchia di Spagna* (Paris, Bibliothèque Sainte Geneviève, MS 3343, fols. 47-47ᵛ); cf. Machiavelli, *Discourses*, I, 12.

[34] Af. Pol. (Part Ii) IX, 1; MS, 97, 162.

[35] Af. Pol., 99-100; cf. also Dentice, 6-10.

[36] Af. Pol. (Part II) XIII, 27.

[37] MS, 64-65; St. Geneviève MS 3343, fol. 55ᵛ.

[38] DUGE, 508-9; cf. Dentice, 10.

[39] Meta., III, 266-68 (*Metaphysica* XVI, cap. 7, art. 4); cf. R. Amerio (ed.), *Theologia* (Milan, 1936), I, 1.3, where these are later less succinctly set forth.

and love, Lycurgus bore holy laws regarding morals; nevertheless, deceived by the authority of the old religion, he established perverse laws on religious rites and doctrines.

Among the deceivers are also some who are not themselves deceived, for while a pernicious deception is something to be fled, it is rather something to be esteemed when promotive of service and utility (*non autem officiosam et utilem*). Thus Pythagoras imagined himself for two years to have conversed with the gods and Numa meditated laws in a forest and then gave them to the Romans as if received from God. Varro praises this deception and reckons Romulus to have been killed and concealed by the fathers so that it might be believed that he had been taken up by God with the consequence that his laws would be observed as divine; thus Minos is believed to have done, imagining himself in a grotto speaking with Jove, unless deceived by the devil as was Muhammad from the very beginning. . . . But those who possess all the said marks are immune from suspicion of deception, passive or active. Indeed if God deceives them in having them bear a false religion and false dogmas, hellish and heavenly, so that men may be held to their duties thereby, nothing further must be disputed. For where God wants us to be deceived, we ought to obey. But because this dogma is perverse, that God might be a liar, I judge that religion ought to be embraced which is conferred by God with the ten marks until that religion should come forth having the same signs of God, which have departed from the earlier one. For from this we know the Mosaic law to cease at the disposition of God because the prophets, miracles, martyrdom and the spiritualization of the believers ceased therein and they passed to Christianity, and the Jews have been given over to a reprobate understanding; they honor Talmudic impieties contrary to Moses, to God and to nature. But because with Muhammad these gifts of God have not passed from Christianity to Islam, therefore man has known by natural reason that Muhammad has not been sent by God against Christianity but rather by an impure demon which has not been able to give to him those charisms nor to deprive the Christians of theirs. Among the latter I daily see the saints accomplishing the same miracles, which in their time the apostles accomplished, and are refulgent with the same sanctity of life. If Porphyry might have considered this fact, he would not have preferred paganism to Christianity.[40]

Campanella here appears to go well beyond Machiavelli in the *Discourses*, I, 11-12, in accepting the details of Paduan Averroism regarding the political utility and historical course of religions. While recognizing the social need for religious belief and savoring the utility of possible deception in this respect, he dissociates himself from affirming that God might inflict upon man an enduring deception merely for purposes of political order.

Nevertheless, on one significant issue the two clearly agree. In the vast heap of Campanella's writings and particularly in the work entitled *Philosophia realis*, it is easy to ignore the *Quaestiones . . . de politicis*,

---

[40] Meta. III, 270-72 (Meta. XVI. 7.4.); cf. Po., 264-66.

confusedly paginated, which had undergone several redactions since 1609 before appearing for the first time in Paris, 1637. The four questions constitute a criticism of Aristotle's *Politics* and most specifically his concept of the citizen as narrowed to the warriors and governors. In Campenella's repeated efforts to extend the concept to include artisans, peasants, and in fact all the people, we begin to expect from him an idealization of *il popolo* reminiscent of the heresiarch himself, Machiavelli. In fact that is precisely what we encounter:

Truly workers constitute a great part of the State. We are not able to do without them. For that reason they must not be excluded from the body of citizens. . . . For if the peasants and workers are not so learned in Aristotle's logic, they nevertheless share a common nature and religion. Each artisan is king in his own craft as far as partaking in wisdom, as Solomon said. Justice and temperance however are more to be found in the common people (*plebe*) than in the nobility, for they believe in the law that is preached daily in the temple and what they hear from their mothers and fathers as well as in daily intercourse, and reverently they obey. The educated, in contrast, reliant on doctrine and agitated by conflicting syllogisms, are not as stalwart in justice, temperance and fortitude. Even Machiavelli acknowledged this when he noted the people to be more just and trustworthy than princes.[41]

Elsewhere in the same *Quaestio* Campanella can specifically attack Aristotle's portrait of the tyrant that culminates in *Politics* v, 11;[42] he can also linger over a Thomistic understanding of deception that is neither hypocritical nor malign for the good of this same people "because we are still in the world and not yet in paradise."[43] However, here he

---

[41] PR³, 92: "Opifices vero sunt magna Reipubl. pars: sine qua esse non possumus. idcirco ex ciuium numero non sunt excludendi, neque enim quia non est oculus idcirco pes non sit de corpore. Argumentum Apostoli validissimum, fundatum in natura: erubescat Arist. Nam & si docti non sunt rustici, & opifices in sua Logica, sunt tamen in naturali & Religione communi. Omnis etiam artifex est Rex in sua arte, quatenus particeps sapientiae, vt dicebat Salomon. Iustitia autem, & temperantia magis inuenitur in plebe, quam in nobilitate: credunt enim legi, quae praedicatur quotidie in templo & a patribus, & matribus audiunt, & a commercio: & reuerenter obtemperant: literati vero confisi in doctrina, & syllogismis contrariis agitati, non sunt sic firmi in iustitia, & temperantia, & fortitudine. Hoc etiam Macchiauellus agnouit, vbi iustiorem esse populum, & in faederibus observantiorem, quam principes, notauit." Cf. Machiavelli, Disc. II, 58; Pr. IX & XX. Campanella's attack here upon Aristotle's *Politics* and especially the whole argument regarding an expanded concept of citizenship and the citizenry seem to have been ignored by scholars and deserve separate attention. Surprisingly, in her admirable Marxist interpretation of Campanella's career and thought, Gisela Bock, *Thomas Campanella: Politisches Interesse und philosophische Spekulation* (Tübingen, 1974), never gives "Quaestio II," or for that matter the entire work constituting *Tertia Pars*, the centrality and force that it would provide for her argument; cf. Bock, 165, 209, 269.

[42] PR³, 87-92.

[43] Pr³, 94: "Quoniam sumus in Mundo adhuc, nondum in Paradiso."

consciously and admittedly stands on common ground with Machiavelli in idealizing the populace.

If the two political thinkers are so apparently similar, how then does one account for the revulsion that Campanella experiences in confronting the Florentine? If to be Machiavellian means to be capable of resorting occasionally to the amoral, cunning act for purposes of maintaining political community, then Campanella is a Machiavellian. It was in this broad, shallow sense that his age understood Machiavelli and in this same sense that William Prynne, that provocative Puritan bigot, would refer to its author as a "Second Machiavel" in the second English edition of Campanella's *Monarchia di Spagna* (London, 1660).[44] Yet this is hardly a very satisfactory understanding of Machiavelli, and in particular it fails to explain what Meinecke dramatically referred to as a sword, thrust into the flank of the body politic of Western humanity, from which it has been reeling ever since.[45] The nature of that sword thrust has been perceptively defined by Isaiah Berlin in his observation that nothing is so offensive to one brought up in a monistic, religious system than a breach in it. To be confronted by a valid, even necessary, alternative to a hitherto total universal order can only prove devastating to an adherent of that order. For anyone "to attack and inflict lasting damage on a central assumption of an entire civilization is an achievement of the first order."[46] By endowing politics with its own autonomous existence, its own moral and social order, Machiavelli opened the door to another world, another dimension of reality: he shattered the circle, the encyclopedia, the idealized unity of traditional medieval culture, and beckoned to the other provinces of life to follow.[47]

Campanella saw this, although not with the precision that later hindsight may afford us. Rather he sensed himself struggling with something darkly monstrous, and what he lacked in clarity of perception he made up for in passion of conviction. For him the issues are what we would call pluralism and atheism. At the end of his *Atheism Conquered* he charges Machiavelli with not knowing that encyclopedia wherein all science is for the common use and edification; ethics, politics, the economy of the household are here one cake. When Machiavelli says that probity is good for saving souls but not states, he speaks not only against piety but also, according to the Calabrian, against nature, which through virtue, not through vice, saves all.[48] Having continually referred to Machiavelli

[44] Firpo, *Bibliografia*, 65-66.

[45] Meinecke, *Machiavellism*, 49.

[46] Isaiah Berlin, "The Originality of Machiavelli," in *Against the Current* (New York, 1982), 76-77.

[47] On the principle of autonomy as a determinant of the Renaissance in general and Machiavelli in particular, see Federico Chabod, *Machiavelli and the Renaissance* (London, 1958), 174-91.

[48] AT, 174-76.

as an atheist, for he grants nothing to God but Aristotle's formal initial motion, Campanella will add to the *Atheism Conquered,* composed around 1605, a preface in 1630 asserting that it is necessary to begin not with "I believe in the Holy Church" but "I believe in God," compelling him, Campanella, to demonstrate that God is, that He is one, that man is endowed with an immortal soul and that God is to be worshipped not fictitiously but by the true religion.[49] For all its confusions the *Atheism Conquered* is a powerful document—confessional, apologetic, an inner dialogue. Here the great strands of heterodox Aristotelianism and Neoplatonic syncretism that constitute in large part the complex cultural formation of Campanella's youth compete for ascendancy, only to be resolved by the triumph of the latter. But Paduan Averroism as a somewhat heterodox form of Aristotelianism is never so displaced as not to be able to reassert itself at critical moments.[50]

At this stage in our investigation a closer contrast can prove revealing. Campanella and Machiavelli, each driven by his political demon, differ both with respect to the right interpretation and use of a political Christianity as well as with respect to the context and frame of reference in which each finds himself. It would be wrong to assume that the autonomy won by Machiavelli for the expression of his political demon is devoid of all religion. On the contrary, religious bonds and habits of mind inhere to the new political enterprise as envisaged by the Florentine; they are for the rulers, however, divorced from any transcendental or metaphysical reference and to be exploited at will. Religion becomes entirely human, a civil matter, and like everything else is mortal. The notorious passage in which Machiavelli clearly prefers pagan religion to Christianity because of the former's greater capacity to generate public spirit will also include the haunting notion that there is no necessary reason for heaven now to be disarmed; and at present, political Christianity suffers to a significant extent from not having the proper leadership and from a false interpretation prompted by indolence.[51] Indeed Machiavelli would appear to have

---

[49] AT, "Praefatio" (2). On the possible influence of Campanella on Lord Herbert of Chefbury see D.P. Walker, The *Ancient Theology* (Ithaca, 1972), 168-89.

[50] Cf. Spini, *Ricerca,* 99-104.

[51] Machiavelli, *Discourses* II, 2. Mark Hulliung's *Citizen Machiavelli* (Princeton, 1983), an extended meditation on the text of the *Discourses* II.2, curiously fails to treat that passage which suggests the possibility of an appropriately militant rendering of Christianity: "E benchè paia che si sia effeminato il mondo e disarmato il Cielo, nasce più sanza dubbio dalla viltà degli uomini, che hanno interpretato la nostra religione secondo l'ozio e non secondo la virtù. Perché se considerassono come la ci permette la esaltazione e la difesa della patria, vedrebbono come la vuole che noi l'amiamo ed onoriamo, e prepariamoci a essere tali ehe noi la possiamo difendere. Fanno adunque queste educazioni e si false interpretazioni..." *(Opere,* ed. Maria Bonfantini [Milan, 1963], 227-28). On some of the Spanish-Italian reactions to Machiavelli's accusation that Christianity has disarmed heaven, see Adriano Prosperi, "La religione, il potere, le élites incontri italo spagnoli della Controriforma," *Annuario dell'Istituto Storico Italiano per*

room for the warrior saints and armed prophets as well as for St. Francis and St. Dominic—those popular leaders of a former age whose austerity, poverty, and sacrifice could move the first beginnings of urban masses in the Western world.[52] Meanwhile, he scorns the canon lawyers, the curial administrators, and ecclesiastical lords of his own day. Yet whatever scattered evidence may lurk in the interstices of Machiavelli's writings for his espousal of a militant, crusading Christianity,[53] the weight of his argument falls upon a church and clergy that need to attend to their properly pastoral function and upon a papacy which he viiities for its excessive involvement in worldly power.[54] Idealist and more specifically in this respect Marsilian, Machiavelli would reduce the church to its pastoral role and denounce what his friend Guicciardini referred to as those "wicked priests."[55]

With his far-ranging imagination and aspirations, Campanella on the other hand understands the potentialities of the church for world rule and thus not only can make his peace with the fact of the Ecclesiastical State astride the peninsula but can also see it as the nucleus for a larger state, including the better part of Italy and thereby serving as an effective base for the exercise of a universal theocracy.[56] More profoundly and astonishingly, early in his career he made the striking observation that Machiavelli, for all his cunning, while admiring papal stability, had failed to see it as a common ground for unity or unified action.[57] Ten years later and almost a full century after the composition of the *Prince,* Campanella, living in the transformed Italy of the high Counter Reformation and the apparently imposing restored papacy, could turn with new eyes to Chapter XI, "On Ecclesiastical Principalities": there Machiavelli showed himself to be impressed by Alexander VI's demonstration of how a pope might prevail by recourse to money and to force. In the *Antiveneti* Campanella expressly takes issue with the claim made by the master of *ragione di stato* in the next chapter that the pope was the ruin of Italy; Machiavelli's observation pertaining to the Renaissance

---

l'età moderna e contemporanea, 29-30 (1977-78), 499-529. For a comprehensive analysis of Machiavelli's religion see Alberto Tenenti, "La religione di Machiavelli," in his *Credenze, ideologie, libertinismi tra Medioevo ed Età moderna* (Bologna, 1978), 175-219, esp. 185, 206, and 219.

[52] See the concluding sentences of *Disc.* I. 12. On the Mendicant Orders cf. *Disc.* III. 1.

[53] Cf. Timothy J. Lukes, "To Bamboozle with Goodness: The Political Advantages of Christianity in the Thought of Machiavelli," *Renaissance and Reformation,* 8 (1984) 266-77, esp. 273-75.

[54] Gilbert, "Machiavellism", 156-57.

[55] Francesco Guicciardini, *Ricordi,* B14.

[56] DUGE, 476-80, 506-7; DPI, 151-54.

[57] DUGE, 505-6: "Questo [the political capability of the Papacy working among Christian princes and states] non conobbe l'astutissimo Machiavello *[sic],* che si ammira della stabilità del papato.... Quando il Papa sarà signore d'Italia, sara anche del mondo; però deve procurar ogni via di arrivar a questo."

Papacy prior to the *Sacco* seemed to a shrewd observer of the early
seventeenth century to be ignorant and unfounded.[58]

Frankly espousing the vigorous exercise of a political Christianity,
Campanella counters Machiavelli by preferring the political-administra-
tive responsibilities of prelates to their pastoral function; in contradis-
tinction to a papal pronouncement of 18 March 1624, Campanella
recommends that if compelled to make the choice, cardinals who are
bishops should remain in Rome to serve in the curia rather than pursue
in their dioceses those pastoral functions prescribed by the Council of
Trent.[59] Linking *potestas* to *charitas* in the cleansing of the church itself,
Campanella, despite his motley, magical heterodoxy, speaks with an
authority and force which neither Guicciardini nor Machiavelli could
muster: from the depths of his cell and from his inhuman physical
suffering he can invoke not some assortment of armed prophets for
purposes of clerical reform but rather God Himself, calling upon Christ
to come, but to come armed!

> My life, my sufferings bear Thy stamp and sign,
> If Thou return to earth, come armed; for lo,
> Thy foes prepare fresh crosses for thee, Lord!
> Not Turks, not Jews, but they who call them Thine.[60]

In what might be taken as an express reply to the implicit challenge
presented by Machiavelli in the *Discourses* II.2, Campanella avers that
Christian laws, if not providing marvelous heroes like Caesar and Alexander, will produce a Moses, Peter, and Paul whose surpassing heroism
is adored and resounds throughout the world.[61] Yet Campanella's efforts
go beyond trying to give more bite and greater snap to the athletes of
the faith. Ever desirous of uniting faith with power, love with force, he
occasionally alludes to the Moslem example of an armed high priest.

---

[58] AV, 89-90; cf. *Disc.* I, 12.

[59] DUGE, 515-17. By claiming that Campanella had written a now lost work on this
matter "per compiacere qualche porporato mal disposto ad allontanarsi da Roma," Luigi
Firpo suggests, without any apparent evidence, that Campanella was not in earnest. In
1940 Firpo dated this work early 1631, following Amabile (Bibl., 194-95), then in both
the 1949 and the 1968 edition of DUGE he backdated it to around 1624, when Urban
VIII had made a comparable demand, arguing that it would be unlikely for Campanella
to have directly contravened a papal bull in the later period because his own status at
the curia then hung in the balance. In either instance of papal legislation, 1624 or 1631,
Campanella, according to Firpo, was seeking to please some high placed official, whether
pope or cardinal. Given, however, Campanella's commitment to papal theocracy and the
apparatus of power, one may not have to devise extraneous motives.

[60] "A Cristo, Nostro Signore," Sonnet 18 in "Scelta di poesie filosofiche," Luigi Firpo
(ed.), *Tutte le opere di Tommaso Campanella*, (n.p., 1954), 33. The translation is that
of John Addington Symonds, *The Sonnets of Michel Angelo Buonarroti and Tommaso
Campanella* (London, 1878), 135.

[61] Amabile, *Castelli*, II, 140.

Furthermore he will remain consistent throughout his life in advocating that the supreme pontiff should be armed: indeed the very wealth, magnificence, and power of the Papacy secure its position over all other princes.[62]

Nevertheless it is in distinguishing the respective contexts of the two that we discover the decisive difference. Machiavelli's vision of politics is a product of long exposure to the rampant individuality and political illegitimacy of the Italian Renaissance brought to a pitch by the unhinging event of the French invasion of 1494. Fragmentation and permanent improvisation characterize this world:

> And as the observance of divine institutions is the cause of the greatness of republics, so the disregard of them produces their ruin; for where the fear of God is wanting, there the country will come to ruin, unless it be sustained by the fear of the prince, *which may temporarily supply the want of religion.*[63]

And from this observation Machiavelli will go on to argue the greater value of good laws to a mortal prince, while admitting the improbability of ever attaining to the relatively solid ground provided by such good laws. If the Florentine knows neither the State nor *Raison d'Etat* as we today know, or think we know it, he grasps the essential temporality, the harsh necessities, the continuing improvisations that mark the life of that entity which we call the State, both product and attestation of a persisting emergency. On the other hand Campanella, venturing globally amongst vast imperial conglomerates that dwarf the restricted, intense view of his predecessor, never loses his holistic perspective, uniting religion with power, and remains thoroughly within a single universal order which he aspires to drive to an even greater, more effective realization.

There is yet another perspective in which we can better appreciate the controversy between these two political giants over the issue of religion and its relation to *ragione di stato*. Running through the *Discourses* and the *Prince* is a kind of nostalgia for an earlier age when a basic religious fervor infused civil society with greater fear, reverence, and natural discipline, so badly lacking in the Italy that Machiavelli experienced. In the cataclysm marked by the French invasion of Italy, partly explicable by the disappearance of religious customs,[64] the astute Florentine reacted with a sense of loss to an age wherein religious fervor was generally at

---

[62] DUGE, 471-72, 476, 507 (1593/95); AV, 87-88 (1606); DPI, 151-54 (1607); MN, 301 (1635)

[63] *Disc.* I, 11, tr. Christian E. Detmold (my italics), "Perché dove manca il timore di Dio, conviene o che quel regno rovini o che sia sostenuto dal timore d'uno principe che sopperisca a' defetti della religione" (ed. Bonfantini, 124).

[64] Cf. Chabod, *Machiavelli*, 46-61, where in treating the phenomenon of the Prince as the final expression of Renaissance life, Chabod incisively analyzes the more general malaise.

a low ebb.[65] A century later, however, Campanella stands at the height of the Catholic Church's revival in the Counter Reformation; thus he belongs to a time that could address more moralistically the problem of the wound in Europe's side. Machiavelli stood at the threshold of a new dimension divorced from religion as an ontological reality but eager to exploit its political utility. Campanella lived in the revival, no matter how inadequate, of Catholicism; and in his own political theory he would incorporate not only religion as a reinforced and expanded catholicity but the state itself into his church.

Yet whatever Campanella's moralistic ministrations to the wound in Christendom's side, his opposition to Machiavelli differed drastically from that of the contemporary anti-Machiavellians. The gulf separating the Calabrian prophet both from his own age and specifically from all the other self-proclaimed opponents of Machiavelli can best be appreciated under the category of time. With respect to time conceived as the potentiality for expectation or hope, for liberation or redemption, Campanella, despite all his magical, astrological, and naturalistic vagrancies, stood closer to the intrinsically Christian perspective on the future than did his contemporaries. For "an age without apocalypse" had from the beginning of the century come to settle upon Italy and gradually extend itself to the rest of Europe: by 1660 England seemed the last to succumb, following the death of the more florid Puritan dreams. It can well be urged that Europe certainly needed to cool off after the excess of apocalypses experienced during the long sixteenth century. The new age, however, placed worse than a low premium on such a destabilizing factor as eschatology or any tension toward the future. Implicitly the absolutist conception of time sought an obliteration of any challenging comparison or basis for criticism and amounted to a recrudescence of the harsh, mythic cycles of pagan naturalism, creating its own *aevum*: "in philosophy supporters and negators of Aristotelianism remain substantially enclosed in the iron circle of natural reality without opportunity for escape or final redemption; in politics Machiavellism, Tacitism, and *ragione di stato* likewise constitute expressions of a radical distrust in the possibility of subverting the empirical data of historic actuality; the religion, ecclesiology, and piety of the late Counter Reformation lack any suggestion of eschatological tension or criticism of the existent. *Il Seicento italiano* is in large part prisoner of man of the present."[66] On the other hand both Machiavellians and anti-Machiavellians played the game within the constituted, recognized order. Little wonder that *il secolo senza apocalisse* would find it necessary to keep the exceptional, the radically prophetic, securely confined in the bottom of successive Neapolitan prisons for over a quarter of a century.

---

[65] *Prince*, Chap. 11; *Disc.* I, 11
[66] Spini, *Ricerca*, 42-44.

In concluding let us once more confront the question: in what sense can Campanella be understood to be a Machiavellian? For good reason did Campanella's English readers refer to him as a "second Machiavel" or as "that most politick friar."[67] The actual indebtedness of Campanella to Machiavelli was more than peripheral, exceeding simply the incidental resort to cunning tactics. By profoundly appropriating the idea of religion's social and political utility, originally a product of Paduan Averroism, Campanella joined many political theorists of the Counter Reformation in judging religion by its effects, its utility, while nevertheless maintaining for himself its claims to truth.[68] Similarly preoccupied with power and its effective exercise in this world, Machiavelli formulated and imparted to Campanella what became the central problem of his life: the empowerment of Christianity. The friar attempted to resolve for his own age the question which the secretary had hesitated to address in his own time; in his quest to achieve the predominance of a viable ecclesiastical state in Italy as well as papal theocracy throughout the world, Campanella in effect took up Machiavelli's challenge to realize a politically militant Christianity. That other interpretation of Christianity, to which Machiavelli occasionally alluded, Campanella would spend a lifetime pursuing in order that heaven might truly be rearmed.

Yet in the end Machiavelli and Campanella are worlds apart: the Florentine is willing to divorce himself from the traditional system in order to construct a new dimension of reality and to use religion for whatever it can provide: in contrast the Calabrian remains within the old system, using some of the new materials of the age not only to shore up but also to universalize the traditional, monistic order.

University of North Carolina at Chapel Hill.

---

[67] Henry Stubbe, *Campanella Revived or an Enquiry into the History of the Royal Society* (London, 1670), 3.

[68] Cf. Prosperi, "La religione," 528, n. 53.